MW00681213

PERSPECTIVES ON HEADQUARTERS-SUBSIDIARY RELATIONSHIPS IN THE CONTEMPORARY MNC

RESEARCH IN GLOBAL STRATEGIC MANAGEMENT

Series Editor: William Newburry

Recent Volumes:

RESEARCH IN GLOBAL STRATEGIC MANAGEMENT
VOLUME 17

PERSPECTIVES ON HEADQUARTERS-SUBSIDIARY RELATIONSHIPS IN THE CONTEMPORARY MNC

EDITED BY

TINA C. AMBOS
University of Geneva, Geneva, Switzerland

BJÖRN AMBOS
University of St Gallen, St Gallen, Switzerland

JULIAN BIRKINSHAW
London Business School, London, UK

United Kingdom – North America – Japan
India – Malaysia – China

Emerald Group Publishing Limited
Howard House, Wagon Lane, Bingley BD16 1WA, UK

First edition 2016

British Library Cataloguing in Publication Data
A catalogue record for this book is available from the British Library

ISBN: 978-1-78635-370-2
ISSN: 1064-4857 (Series)

Printed and bound by CPI Group (UK) Ltd, Croydon, CR0 4YY

ISOQAR certified
Management System,
awarded to Emerald
for adherence to
Environmental
standard
ISO 14001:2004.

ISOQAR
REGISTERED
Certificate Number 1985
ISO 14001

INVESTOR IN PEOPLE

CONTENTS

PART IV
ADDITIONAL CONTRIBUTIONS BY AIB FELLOWS
(EDITED BY JEAN BODDEWYN)

LIST OF CONTRIBUTORS

Björn Ambos	University of St Gallen, St Gallen, Switzerland
Tina C. Ambos	Geneva School of Economics and Management (GSEM), University of Geneva, Switzerland
Ulf Andersson	Mälardalen University, Västerås, Sweden; BI Norwegian Business School, Oslo, Norway
Tomomine Aoki	Kowa Company, Ltd., Tokyo, Japan
Kazuhiro Asakawa	Keio University, Yokohama, Japan
Suma Athreye	Brunel Business School, Brunel University London, Uxbridge, UK
Georgios Batsakis	Brunel Business School, Brunel University London, Uxbridge, UK
Gabriel R. G. Benito	BI Norwegian Business School, Oslo, Norway
Julian Birkinshaw	London Business School, London, UK
Jean Boddewyn	Baruch College, City University of New York, NY, USA
Wendy Chapple	Nottingham University Business School, Nottingham, UK
Àngels Dasí	University of Valencia, Valencia, Spain
Benoit Decreton	Vienna University of Economics and Business, Vienna, Austria
Frank Elter	Telenor Research, Fornebu, Norway
Jörg Freiling	University of Bremen, Bremen, Germany

Jens Gammelgaard	Copenhagen Business School, Frederiksberg, Denmark
Stefan Gold	Nottingham University Business School, Nottingham, UK
Paul N. Gooderham	NHH Norwegian School of Economics, Bergen, Norway
Gabriela Gutierrez Huerter O	King's College London, London, UK
Perttu Kähäri	Aalto University, Helsinki, Finland
Mitchell P. Koza	Rutgers Business School, Newark and New Brunswick, NJ, USA
Rajesh Kumar	Menlo College, Atherton, CA, USA
Sven Kunisch	University of St Gallen, St Gallen, Switzerland
Randi Lunnan	BI Norwegian Business School, Oslo, Norway
Jeremy Moon	Copenhagen Business School, Frederiksberg, Denmark
Phillip C. Nell	Vienna University of Economics and Business, Vienna, Austria; Copenhagen Business School, Frederiksberg, Denmark
Kiyohiro Oki	The University of Tokyo, Tokyo, Japan
Torben Pedersen	Bocconi University, Milan, Italy
Rebecca Piekkari	Aalto University, Helsinki, Finland
Marty Reilly	Dublin City University, Dublin, Ireland
Karl P. Sauvant	Columbia Center on Sustainable Development, Columbia Law School and The Earth Institute of Columbia University, New York, NY, USA
Fabian Schmutz	University of Bremen, Bremen, Germany

Adrian *Schulte Steinberg*	The Boston Consulting Group (BCG), Munich, Germany
Pamela Sharkey Scott	National University of Ireland Maynooth, Maynooth, Ireland
Stephen Tallman	Robins School of Business, University of Richmond, Richmond, VA, USA
Sverre Tomassen	BI Norwegian Business School, Oslo, Norway
Svein Ulset	NHH Norwegian School of Economics, Bergen, Norway

To Alan Rugman for his many years of exemplary service to Research in Global Strategy Management and the broader global strategy academic community.

EDITOR'S LETTER

Dear Reader

Welcome to the seventeenth volume of *Research in Global Strategic Management* and the first under my series editorship. Going into this volume, we first wish to recognize the outstanding efforts of long-time series editor Dr. Alan Rugman, who is fondly remembered for his contributions to this book series, amongst many others in the field of global strategy. Without Dr. Rugman's efforts over the years, this book series would most likely not exist. While it will be difficult to fill his shoes, we aim to continue his strong tradition of publishing innovative and thought provoking research in the area of global strategic management.

For this volume, Tina C. Ambos, Björn Ambos, and Julian Birkinshaw have graciously agreed to assume the roles of volume editors under the title, *Perspectives on Headquarters-Subsidiary Relationships in the Contemporary MNC*. As a basic component of foreign direct investment, understanding the relationship between MNC headquarters and their overseas subsidiaries is crucial for successful global strategic management. As such, the volume provides an important complement to prior volumes in the *Research in Global Strategic Management* book series. The volume editors have done a truly excellent job in crafting a volume of thought provoking chapters on this important topic. The volume includes contributions from some of the most well-established scholars in the field, in combination with a number of younger scholars showing great promise as future scholarly leaders. The edited chapters are organized under three broad and important themes related to *management mechanisms of the MNC, tensions and conflicts in HQ-subsidiary relationships*, and *knowledge transfer in the MNC network*. We'll avoid going into more specific detail on these themes here since Tina, Björn, and Julian overview the chapters in their introductory piece to this volume. Nonetheless, these are three critical areas in the headquarters-subsidiary management literature and the volume editors are to be congratulated for their efforts in producing a coherent set of chapters that will prove an asset to researchers on the topic of headquarters-subsidiary relationships, along with the three important subthemes, for years to come.

In addition to the work under the main theme of the volume, we are also pleased to present three chapters authored by Fellows of the Academy of International Business (AIB) and edited by Jean Boddewyn. The first chapter, *History of the AIB Fellows: The Deanship of Alan Rugman (2011–2014)*, complements a prior chapter on the history of the AIB Fellows that appeared in volume 14 of this series. The chapter simultaneously serves as a tribute to one of the many roles assumed by Alan Rugman during his illustrious academic career. Dr. Rugman's contributions to the international business and global strategy communities were numerous, and his election as Dean of the AIB Fellows demonstrates the regard he held amongst the Fellows. This chapter will help serve as a reminder of this important component of his overall legacy.

The second chapter in this volume section, *How Does the Context of Language Use Affect the Perception of Language Barriers?* is by Àngels Dasí and Torben Pedersen. Within this chapter, the authors recognize that language has multiple dimensions, each of which may vary in importance depending upon the specific context of its usage. Language is a central component within the practical implementation of global strategy, but has received relatively little academic attention in this field. As such, this chapter makes an important contribution that has both academic and practical implications. Using a unique dataset of 390 multinational corporations headquartered in Finland, South Korea, New Zealand, and Sweden, the authors examine perceptions of language barriers in these four country settings, with a particular focus on the moderating effects of language incidence and distance on these perceptions. The results are insightful and will hopefully serve as a catalyst for additional future work on the context of language usage.

The final chapter in the volume, *The Next Step in Governance: The Need for Global Micro-regulatory Frameworks in the Context of Expanding International Production*, is authored by Karl P. Sauvant. In this chapter, Dr. Sauvant calls for an attention shift from focusing on international rules addressing macro issues related to international economic transactions at the nation level to a focus on more micro-level rules governing the principal actors in international transactions, particularly firms. Given the significant reduction in explicit barriers to international trade and investment in recent decades, Dr. Sauvant argues that attention of global organizations would be better spent developing complementary international rules to provide better global governance of global production and trade. Overall, the chapter provides an insightful view of current global governance practices and highlights an important area where extension of these practices is needed.

Once again, I wish to thank all the contributors to this latest volume in the *Research in Global Strategic Management* series, including the authors, volume editors Tina C. Ambos, Björn Ambos, and Julian Birkinshaw, AIB Fellows Section Editor Jean Boddewyn, and Martyn Lawrence and his team at Emerald. We hope that this volume spurs academic thought in the important volume topic area of headquarters-subsidiary relationships, along with the broader global strategic management field in general.

Best regards,
William Newburry
Series Editor
Research in Global Strategic Management

INTRODUCTION TO VOLUME THEME

Within the broad stream of research on the interplay between strategy and structure and on conceptual models for managing multinational corporations (MNCs), the debate on how to configure the MNC so that it is resilient, ambidextrous, and adaptive continues to grow. In the center of this debate is the relationship between organizational units in the corporation. This not only includes the classic headquarters-subsidiary relationship but also relationships between sister subsidiaries, corporate and regional HQs, and physical and virtual units.

Since the introduction of such concepts as the Heterarchy (Hedlund, 1986), the Transnational (Bartlett & Ghoshal, 1989), and the Metanational (Doz, Santos, & Williamson, 2001), a large stream of subsidiary-level research has emerged in the international business literature. This has recently been complemented by a new focus on the role and value-added of MNC headquarters. For example, over the last few years three special issues on the topic have appeared, in *Management International Review* (Ambos & Mahnke, 2010), *the Journal of International Management* (Kotabe & Sokol, 2013), and most recently *the Journal of Management Studies* (2016), with also a special conference on the new role of headquarters (Strategic Management Society, 2015).

The emerging view on headquarters has contributed significantly to our understanding of modern multinational firms, in particular to the question of "corporate parenting," but has not helped significantly in explaining the dynamic relationships between headquarters and their subsidiaries. As MNCs in practice move toward more hybrid structures (e.g., Cisco with multiple HQs or Tata Communications with virtual instead of physical centers), we need to know more about the operating challenges of these new phenomena. New forms of organizing have challenged headquarters-subsidiary relationships, raising a number of questions such as: How much autonomy do modern business units need, and are they getting it? How much autonomy should modern headquarters grant? How are we dealing with power imbalances? Which control instruments do headquarters apply for managing their SBUs? How do headquarters direct attention as a scarce resource and set direction? Which role do cognitions on both levels play? Is there a surge in regional headquarters? What is their function?

This volume of *Research in Global Strategic Management* aims to provide new perspectives on headquarters-subsidiary relationships in the context of the contemporary MNC. The authors in this volume take different angles, some focus on knowledge and R&D, others on services, structure, or autonomy. A common denominator, however, is the predominant focus on the role and the management of subsidiaries. Thus, this volume provides a complement to recent research on headquarters in multinational firms. The contributions included in this volume can be grouped into three categories: the management mechanisms of the MNC, tensions and conflicts in HQ-subsidiary relationships, and knowledge transfer in the MNC network. In the following, we provide a brief outline of each section and its chapters that will guide you through the volume. We hope to send you on an insightful journey through the diverse field of headquarters-subsidiary relationships and provide you with the most recent research insights.

PERSPECTIVES ON THE MANAGEMENT MECHANISMS OF THE MNC

These chapters address the need for new concepts and mechanisms to understand the challenges of the modern MNC. They take very different angles looking at bottom-of-the-pyramid business model innovation (Gooderham et al.), at regional management structures (Freiling et al.), at new concepts such as "strategic animation" (Tallman & Koza), or the application of agency theory to multi-nodal structures (Schulte Steinberg & Kunisch). What they have in common is the view that our understanding of the MNC needs to incorporate the specificities of the globalized world, such as emerging economies or global service firms, and the need of MNC units to interact.

Beyond Local Responsiveness — Multi-domestic Multinationals at the Bottom-of-the-Pyramid by Paul N. Gooderham, Svein Ulset, and Frank Elter

Tapping into the increasingly important topic of bottom-of-the-pyramid (BOP) markets, the first chapter analyzes obstacles that MNCs face when operating in such a market. Based on a case study, it is shown that BOP markets are not best served by adapting top-of-the-pyramid products to the local requirements, thereby only reaching a fraction of the population, but rather by developing radically new ideas with only the BOP customers in mind. Contrary to past and popular approaches by MNCs, this path poses challenges to the MNC, especially with respect to centrally managing and integrating capabilities.

Regional Management in Multinational Service Operations: Do Services Drive Regional Management Structures? by Jörg Freiling, Perttu Kähäri, Rebecca Piekkari, and Fabian Schmutz

Staying within the regional context and acknowledging the ever increasing importance of services in today's MNCs (the so-called "servitization" process), the next chapter explores the role of regional management as well as the structural implications with respect to managing multinational service operations. Based on case studies, it is stated that challenges of servitization lie in the increased importance of local presence due to higher urgency in service requests, in the related need for closer control of both quality and efficiency, in the even higher need for knowledge integration and sharing across borders and in the pure nature of services, namely the customer as the ultimate driver of any business. In this respect, regional headquarters are prone to serve as a valuable node between headquarters and subsidiaries. By taking on these challenges, MNCs are well served to understand the unique organizational requirements imposed by servitization and offer the right "thickness" of regional management to its subsidiaries.

Strategic Animation and Emergent Processes: Managing for Efficiency and Innovation in Globally Networked Organizations by Stephen Tallman and Mitchell P. Koza

This chapter addresses the topic of managing global operations. It is postulated that the globally networked organization (GNO) is the most suitable archetype for today's geographically distributed, globally integrated, and organizationally networked information-age MNE. New insights on the network(s) related to an organization, organizational principles to best manage both efficiency and innovation within a GNO, and an approach to providing a strategic direction to GNOs are put forward. In this respect, strategic animation serves as the central concept. It entails a set of mechanisms to motivate and guide the intentionally loose combination of internal and external networks that a GNO comprises and hence offers the vision of a new type of strategic direction for a new type of firm in the setting of the global information economy.

The Agency Perspective for Studying Headquarters-Subsidiary Relations: An Assessment and Considerations for Future Research by Adrian Schulte Steinberg and Sven Kunisch

In the field of management research, the agency perspective enjoys prominent use. There is, however, considerable debate connected to its value for studying headquarters-subsidiary relations in the MNC. This chapter seeks to contribute to resolving this debate in two ways. First, previous studies using agency theory are evaluated regarding their underlying assumptions, and it is argued that these assumptions are too strict and overly simplified. Second, the research presents contemplations aiming for a more effective use of the agency perspective, and specifically for an approach to agency theory that reflects the multi-dimensional character of headquarters-subsidiary relations in the MNC.

PERSPECTIVES ON TENSIONS AND CONFLICTS IN HQ-SUBSIDIARY RELATIONSHIPS

A large number of articles submitted to this volume addressed the inherent tensions and conflicts that intra-organizational relationships entail. We selected the most insightful and thought provoking pieces of research: Kumar and Gammelgaard investigate the micro-social dimension of conflict resolution in headquarters-subsidiary relationships, while the tension between subsidiary alignment and adaptation at the organizational level is discussed in terms of ambidexterity (Reilley & Sharkey Scott), initiatives and organizing costs (Lunnan et al.), and subsidiary control and autonomy (Asakawa; Oki).

Conflict Resolution in Headquarters-Subsidiary Relationships: The Roles of Regulatory Fit and Moral Emotions by Rajesh Kumar and Jens Gammelgaard

Given the obstacles that different institutional environments impose on MNCs, it seems apparent that conflict resolution is essential in achieving the optimum alignment of both headquarters and subsidiaries in all business aspects. This chapter builds on this central aspect of the headquarters-subsidiary relationship and elucidates the topic of conflict resolution by taking on a micro-behavioral perspective with boundary spanners (top-level-decision makers) at the unit of analysis. Boundary spanners are proven to play a central role in conflict resolution both on the headquarters as well as on the subsidiary side. While headquarters boundary spanners can ultimately take the dominating position, outcomes are also influenced by the cognitive orientations of both parties. This chapter hence improves our understanding of the role of decision makers in the headquarters-subsidiary relationship.

The Ambidextrous Subsidiary: Strategies for Alignment, Adaption and Managing Allegiances by Marty Reilly and Pamela Sharkey Scott

Taking an ambidexterity perspective, this chapter sheds light on the apparent conflict that subsidiaries in MNCs face in being aligned with the parent's strategy while remaining adaptive to local opportunities and developing new capabilities. It is argued that contextual ambidexterity is valuable for a subsidiary and seen as a critical means of survival. Findings of a multiple case study research support this proposition and bring new insights on the parent strategy alignment and local adaptation mechanisms employed by subsidiaries. Essentially, alignment and adaptation should not be perceived as mutually exclusive or requiring sequential alternating, but rather as complementary.

Exploring Subsidiaries' Perceptions of Corporate Headquarters: Subsidiary Initiatives and Organizing Costs by Randi Lunnan, Sverre Tomassen and Gabriel R.G. Benito

Keeping the subsidiary perspective, the following chapter focuses on subsidiary initiatives and organizing costs faced by subsidiaries when interacting with headquarters. It is shown that organizing costs do exist, but vary across subsidiaries and with distance, coordination mechanisms, and business atmosphere (behavioral and motivational assets in relationships). It is further shown that subsidiary initiatives are influenced by organizing costs in that they negatively influence radical initiatives and positively influence emergent initiatives, potentially due to the different levels of autonomy granted to subsidiaries by headquarters.

Informed Headquarters, Legitimized Subsidiary, and Reduced Level of Subsidiary Control in International R&D Management by Kazuhiro Asakawa and Tomomine Aoki

Being more context-specific, the next chapter analyzes the headquarter-subsidiary relationship in an R&D setting by examining the impact of subsidiary legitimacy and headquarters' knowledge about subsidiaries on the level of control over the subsidiaries. Building on the control and R&D literature, it is argued that the level of control over overseas R&D subsidiaries depends on subsidiary legitimacy as well as on the level of knowledge that headquarters possess about their subsidiaries. Findings indicate that headquarters' subsidiary knowledge is negatively correlated to the level of control exercised by the headquarters and hence positively related to subsidiary autonomy. Furthermore, subsidiary legitimacy is positively influenced by higher levels of headquarters' subsidiary knowledge, however, without subsidiary legitimacy itself being negatively related to the level of control. This chapter hence significantly helps in comprehending the interplay between knowledge and the level of headquarters' control.

Subsidiary Autonomy and Factory Performance in Japanese Manufacturing Subsidiaries in Thailand by Kiyohiro Oki

Based on a similar context, the next chapter analyzes Japanese manufacturing subsidiaries in Thailand. It provides more detailed insights on the topic of subsidiary autonomy and its relation to the performance of the subsidiaries' factories (in comparison to Japanese factories). Subsidiary autonomy is found to be related to factory performance when compared to Japanese factories (but not when compared to other foreign factories), thereby indicating that the level of control exercised by Japanese headquarters depends on the factories' performance compared to the home country factories. Contrary to the original hypotheses, evidence of a negative relationship between subsidiary autonomy and factory performance is found. This relationship is supported by the argument that high performing factories lead to a higher strategic importance and more headquarters support, thereby to less subsidiary autonomy. A key insights from this chapter is the very different behavior of Japanese headquarters toward subsidiaries in Thailand, compared to the equivalent subsidiary function in the home country.

PERSPECTIVES ON KNOWLEDGE TRANSFER IN THE MNC NETWORK

Knowledge transfer is probably one of the most researched topics in the context of headquarters-subsidiary relationships since the late 1990, but important questions still remain. The view on knowledge transfer in these chapters is certainly more differentiated and also provides a nice representation on issues that are much debated in the current literature. One contribution focuses on the issue of reciprocity and complementarity in the MNC (R&D) networks (Andersson et al.). Another sheds light on the much debated, but still unresolved, question of how distance affects knowledge flows (Nell et al.). It is also interesting to note that the subjects of knowledge flows are changing: from R&D and other forms of functional know-how to include emerging topics such as environmental and social practices (Gutierrez Huerter O et al.) that may also require different transfer mechanisms.

Complementarity and Substitution in the Knowledge Networks of R&D Subsidiaries by Ulf Andersson, Suma Athreye and Georgios Batsakis

This chapter provides new insights on three diverse networks accessible to R&D subsidiaries (external home country network, external host country network, and internal (MNE) knowledge network). By taking into account costs and benefits associated with obtaining knowledge from these different sources of knowledge, new insights with respect to potential substitutabilities and complementarities of these sources are found. Internal and home-external sourcing are shown to have a substitutive effect due to coordination costs and inefficiencies, implying that R&D subsidiaries opt to substitute one source of knowledge with another if these costs reach a certain threshold and limited new information can be gained. In contrast, internal and host-external as well as home-external and host-external sourcing are found to be complementary and hence the combination of these sources are valuable for the MNC.

How does Geographic Distance Impact the Relevance of HQ Knowledge?
The Mediating Role of Shared Context by Phillip C. Nell, Benoit Decreton
and Björn Ambos

Staying within the field of knowledge, but leaving the R&D context, this chapter explores the role of shared context, proposing that it can serve as a "catalyst" for successful knowledge transfer. It addresses the shortcomings of previous studies that have often investigated knowledge flows abstracted from their context. Focusing on the relevance of headquarters' knowledge within the context of knowledge transfer, it is shown that shared context (both normative and operational aspects) has a positive effect. Shared context is, however, negatively influenced by geographic distance.

Transfer of Social and Environmental Accounting and Reporting Knowledge:
Subsidiary Absorptive Capacity and Organisational Mechanisms by Gabriela
Gutierrez Huerter O, Stefan Gold, Jeremy Moon and Wendy Chapple

Further examining the phenomenon of knowledge transfer, the last chapter in this volume concentrates on the transfer of SEAR (social and environmental accounting and reporting) knowledge, which is seen as an essential element of competitive advantage. Within the context of intra-MNC transfer of SEAR knowledge between headquarters and subsidiaries, the role of the antecedents of subsidiaries' absorptive capacity (ACAP) is examined. It is demonstrated that prior knowledge, considered as an antecedent to ACAP, does not serve as the only explanation for its development. In addition, organizational (control and social) mechanisms can also be regarded as ACAP-triggers.

THE WAY FORWARD

The numerous submissions to this volume and the selected contributions show that the topic of headquarters-subsidiary relationship is still very much under debate. The three sections of the volume point to three specific areas of ongoing research. The chapters presented us with some new perspectives, and they also suggest what we are leaving behind.

While we see the pendulum swinging between an emphasis on subsidiaries to headquarters (Ambos & Mahnke, 2010) and back again, we can also identify a shift toward a more pronounced focus on the context factors in the MNC and on the importance of tensions and dynamic interactions. What we seem to leave behind are broad and abstract frameworks and typologies that framed the discussion on models of the MNC, subsidiary mandates, or types of headquarters. Instead, we see more work on the management mechanisms and their theoretical foundations (e.g. Tallman & Koza; Schulte Steinberg & Kunisch). This can also be interpreted as a shift from structural to process-based and relational issues (see also Piaskowska, Tippmann, Ambos, & Sharkey Scott, 2015).

What is high on the research agenda is the question how subsidiaries or other units perform in these nested organizations, build legitimacy, form self-identities, or handle ambidextrous situations for their benefit. The inherent tensions within MNCs are most visible in discussions about the adaptation of business models (Gooderham et al.), CSR practices (Gutierrez Huerter O et al.), or specific subsidiary initiatives (Lunnan et al.). These perspectives acknowledge that modern organizations are often built around stretch goals, and that managers and operating units find it challenging to navigate these different demands. As shown in the contributions of this volume, conflicts and tensions arise on the micro-social (Kumar and Gammelgaard) as well as on the organizational level (e.g., Lunnan et al.) and our theorizing needs to include these different methodological levels in order to address these questions.

Related to this, some chapters also address the costs of organizing and of resolving conflicts that were often ignored in previous research. This is a very important topic that needs to be addressed more thoroughly by future research in order to understand that benefits and drawbacks of complex organizations, for example, those with multiple headquarters or virtual models (e.g., Ambos & Muller-Stewens, forthcoming) and of the efforts to in-source or out-source key activities.

In terms of the context of research, the management of global R&D networks, that spurred the discussion on subsidiary mandates and centers of excellence in the 1990s (Birkinshaw & Nobel, 1998; Håkanson & Nobel, 2001; Holm, Birkinshaw, Thilenius, & Arvidsson, 2000), still remains high on scholars' agenda. Also the question how to optimize knowledge flows remains an important topic. However, unlike "older" contribution in this field, questions of contextual factors and of complementarity (see also Ambos, Nell, & Pedersen, 2013) are much more pronounced than in earlier research.

Despite the progress the selected chapters make, like any research, individual or collective, the volume at hand leaves a number of questions

unanswered: For example question of intra-MNC competition vs cooperation, or research on power relationships and dysfunctional games. We also
feel that we still need to learn more on how firms deal with multiple agency,
that is, the differing interests of multiple parents as well as the fact that
subsidiaries are not always faced with a benign or benevolent parent, that
itself may engage in dysfunctional behavior and empire building. As organizations evolve, subsidiaries are often terminated or change ownership
from one firm to the other. However, research has treated this role devolu-
tion only very sparingly (Ambos, Schlegelmilch, Ambos, & Brenner, 2009).
Furthermore we know little about identity formation within those sub-units
that change ownership.

Tina C. Ambos
Björn Ambos
Julian Birkinshaw
Editors

REFERENCES

Ambos, B., & Mahnke, V. (2010). How do MNC headquarters add value? *Management International Review, 50*(4), 403–412.
Ambos, T. C., & Mueller-Stewens, G. (forthcoming). Rethinking the role of the centre in the multidivisional firm: A retrospective special issue long range planning.
Ambos, T., Nell, P., & Pedersen, T. (2013). Combining stocks and flows of knowledge: The effects of intra-functional and cross-functional complementarity. *Global Strategy Journal, 3*(4), 283–299.
Ambos, T., Schlegelmilch, B., Ambos, B., & Brenner, B. (2009). Evolution of organisational structure and capabilities in internationalising banks: The CEE operations of UniCredit's Vienna office. *Long Range Planning, 42*(5–6), 633–653.
Bartlett, C., & Ghoshal, S. (1989). *Managing across borders: The transnational solution.* Boston, MA: Harvard Business School Press.
Birkinshaw, J., & Nobel, R. (1998). Innovation in multinational corporations: Control and communication patterns in international R&D operations. *Strategic Management Journal, 19*(5), 479–496.
Doz, Y., Santos, J., & Williamson, P. (2001). *From global to metanational.* Boston, MA: Harvard Business School Press.
Håkanson, L., & Nobel, R. (2001). Organizational characteristics and reverse technology transfer. *MIR: Management International Review, 41*(4), 395–420.
Hedlund, G. (1986). The hypermodern MNC—A heterarchy? *Human Resource Management, 25*(1), 9–35. doi:10.1002/hrm.3930250103

Holm, U., Birkinshaw, J., Thilenius, P., & Arvidsson, N. (2000). Consequences of perception gaps in the headquarters–subsidiary relationship. *International Business Review*, 9(3), 321–344.

Kotabe, M., & Sokol, S. (Eds.). (2013). The role of headquarters in the contemporary MNC. *Journal Of International Management*, 18(3), 213–301.

Nell, P. C., Kappen, P., & Laamanen, T. (forthcoming). Divide and rule? The emergence and implications of increasingly disaggregated and dispersed headquarters activities in contemporary firms. *Journal of Management Studies*.

Piaskowska, D., Tippmann, E., Ambos, T., & Sharkey Scott, P. (2015). Progressing the relational perspective on MNCs: Beyond headquarters-subsidiary relationships. In R. Van Tulder, A. Verbeke, & R. Drogendijk (Eds.), *The future of global organizing* (1st ed., Vol. 10, pp. 79–95). Progress in International Business Research. Bingley, UK: Emerald Group Publishing Limited.

Strategic Management Society. (2015). *Rethinking corporate headquarters: Innovative approaches for managing the multi-divisional firm*. Strategic Management Society (SMS) Special Conference, St. Gallen, May, 2015.

PART I
PERSPECTIVES ON THE
MANAGEMENT MECHANISMS
OF THE MNC

BEYOND LOCAL RESPONSIVENESS – MULTI-DOMESTIC MULTINATIONALS AT THE BOTTOM-OF-THE-PYRAMID

Paul N. Gooderham, Svein Ulset and Frank Elter

ABSTRACT

The purpose of this chapter is twofold. First, to investigate how multi-domestic, multinational corporations (MNCs) can develop business models that are appropriate to "Bottom-of-the-Pyramid" (BOP) settings. Second, to address how they can apply elements of BOP business models across their operations. We use the case of the entry of the Norwegian mobile telecom MNC Telenor into India as the empirical context. Prior to India, Telenor had operated successfully in Asian emerging economies by adapting its business model to local conditions. However, it had only operated in the upper income tiers of these countries. In India, its late entry meant that for the first time in its history it had to move beyond these upper income tiers and develop a business model suited to BOP. We apply an economic model terminology as a means to gauging the degree of business model innovation Telenor undertook. Telenor succeeded in its development of a BOP business model by

Perspectives on Headquarters-Subsidiary Relationships in the Contemporary MNC
Research in Global Strategic Management, Volume 17, 3–26
ISSN: 1064-4857/doi:10.1108/S1064-485720160000017001

working in close partnership with local firms. Although Telenor in India was operating at BOP, a number of the resultant innovations were deemed by Telenor to be transferable to top-of-the-pyramid operations across Telenor. In order to succeed in developing BOP business models MNCs must go beyond local responsiveness and engage closely with local partners. However, transference of elements of BOP business models to other parts of the MNC is contingent on there being a centralized integrating capability.

Keywords: Multi-domestic MNCs; bottom-of-the-pyramid; business model innovation

INTRODUCTION

Since 1995 annual flows of foreign direct investment (FDI) into emerging economies have increased from about $100 billion to nearly $800 billion (UNCTAD, 2014, p. 2). While a major part of these inflows is accounted for by "offshoring," that is, manufacturing for export, increasingly multinational corporations (MNCs) have turned to emerging economies such as India, Indonesia, Brazil, China, and Mexico, as a growth market (London & Hart, 2004). The potential of this market is such that, "Established global firms ignore this market at their own peril" (Prahalad, 2012, p. 6). However, Prahalad and Lieberthal (2003) observe that MNCs have tended to bring their existing products and marketing strategies to emerging markets and generally fail to consider consumers beyond the wealthy elite at the top of the economic pyramid. A common assumption has been that emerging markets are at an earlier stage of the same developmental path followed by developed economies and that it is sufficient to operate with locally adapted versions of the products and business models used in the developed world (Arnold & Quelch, 1998). The outcome has been a failure by MNCs to tap into the potential in tiers of consumers beneath the elites at the very top of the pyramid (Hart & Christensen, 2002).

By way of reaction to this, a "bottom-of-the pyramid" (BOP) approach has emerged whereby "poor people are identified as potential customers who can be served if companies learn to fundamentally rethink their existing strategies and business models. This involves acquiring and building new resources and capabilities and forging a multitude of local partnerships" (Seelos & Mair, 2007, p. 49). An important implication of the BOP approach is that there is a need to develop business models anew for BOP markets, thus limiting the ability to leverage existing models.

Plainly, radical business model innovation in BOP settings will sit uncomfortably with "global" MNCs, that is, MNCs that pursue global standardization supported by a centralized hub organization. However, we will argue that BOP business model innovation is also a testing challenge for the other main generic MNC, the "multi-domestic." Even though multi-domestic MNCS are decentralized federation organizations characterized by considerable local autonomy that compete by customizing products to the local market (Bartlett & Ghoshal, 1989; Roth, 1992; Yip, 1989), London and Hart (2004) argue that the idea of adapting pre-existing solutions to BOP conditions is wholly inadequate. Furthermore, they argue, the local responsiveness heritage of multi-domestics may be a liability in confronting the need to engage with BOP business model innovation.

Our focus in this chapter is on multi-domestic MNCs — characterized by devolved decision-making and local responsiveness — and the specific challenges they confront in BOP settings. Taking as our starting point London and Hart's (2004) BOP thesis that BOP operations must cut loose from corporate top-of-the-pyramid operations in developing BOP business models that go beyond local responsiveness and that capabilities from these can be of value for top-of-the-pyramid operations, we address two gaps in their approach. The first is that they do not develop a business model schema that represents the economic implications of developing a BOP business model. The second is that they do not address the mechanisms that would be required for any transfer of capabilities from BOP operations to other parts of the MNC.

In the next sections, we first outline London and Hart's (2004) view that local responsiveness is inadequate for developing successful business models in BOP markets. We then present our view on how to conceptualize business models in economic terms. Thereafter we present the case of the Telenor in India, a multi-domestic mobile telecom MNC, which failed in its initial strategy to serve the upper income tiers and which subsequently sought to deliver its services to BOP. Our analysis indicates that it was only by abandoning its "replicator" approach to internationalization (Winter & Szulanski, 2001) — that is, taking its business model into each market it enters and then adapting it to local conditions — that Telenor was able to succeed at the base of the Indian pyramid. In addition, the second part of our analysis suggests that it is possible to leverage the practices developed at the BOP across the MNC. However, that depends on the MNC having developed some form of centralized best practice transfer mechanism. Such mechanisms are not a feature of multi-domestic MNCs, which are characteristically decentralized. Our analysis indicates that their emergence at Telenor, while coincidental to Telenor's BOP entry, was highly effective for transferring practices from BOP to other Telenor operations.

LOCAL RESPONSIVENESS AND THE BOP CHALLENGE

In broad terms, London and Hart (2004) propose that the successful pursuit of low-income markets in emerging economies requires MNCs in general to rethink their business models in fundamental ways. One aspect of their critique is particularly relevant for multi-domestic MNCs: London and Hart (2004) argue that in pursuing low-income markets in developing countries, MNCs must go far beyond the traditional idea of local responsiveness. Thus, when entering BOP pyramid markets, the specific reliance by multi-domestic MNCs on their traditional capability of local responsiveness is wholly inadequate. Indeed, it might actually inhibit effectiveness to such an extent that performance is critically undermined.

Given that multi-domestic MNCs must engage in business model development that involves significantly more than local adaptation of centrally developed solutions, what then? London and Hart (2004) accentuate one factor in particular that they view as critical for achieving success in BOP markets, the identification of local partners who can actively contribute to venture conceptualization by adding local content to the product design. Properly identified local partners who understand what set of functionalities are most important to BOP customers can contribute to the co-design of the product from the "bottom up." In addition, local partners can provide the necessary insight into the marketing and delivery of the final product or service.

Thus, London and Hart (2004) argue that rather than adapting solutions created elsewhere to local conditions, successful pursuit of BOP markets requires MNCs to build, consolidate, and leverage learning from the "bottom up." Employing a case-based approach, London and Hart (2004) propose that what characterizes successful MNCs in BOP markets is the capability to value and facilitate bottom-up co-invention of locally appropriate solutions by a diversity of partners. These solutions involve investing resources to develop capacity beyond the defensive boundaries of the firm.

They refer to this capability as "social embeddedness" and define it as "the ability to create competitive advantage based on a deep understanding of and integration with the local environment. This capability involves the ability to create a web of trusted connections with a diversity of organizations and institutions, generate bottom-up development, and understand, leverage, and build on the existing social infrastructure" (London & Hart, 2004, p. 364).

In addition to proposing that BOP success depends on abandoning imported, locally adapted business models and developing fresh business models in partnership with local entrepreneurs, London and Hart (2004) suggest this could create benefits for those parts of the MNC that operate in top-of-the-pyramid markets. While capabilities developed for and in top-of-the-pyramid markets do not appear to travel well to BOP business environments, they argue that the opposite may not be true: "Hence, capabilities and strategies developed at the base of the pyramid may provide the missing means by which firms can catalyze internal creative destruction" (London & Hart, 2004, p. 367). New routines from BOP operations can potentially generate the capability to break old routines and in so doing MNCs reinvent themselves.

However, London and Hart (2004) do not specify how this transfer could occur and nor do they consider what types of new BOP-generated routines could be of value in an MNC's top-of-the-pyramid operations. Further, London and Hart (2004) do not consider the possibility of transferring a business model generated in one BOP context to another BOP context. We will address both of these issues in our analysis of Telenor's operation in India.

Like many others, London and Hart (2004) employ the concept of the business model but do not provide any operationalization of it. Without a precise operationalization of the concept, it is problematic to judge whether an MNC is abandoning its business model for a fresh, innovative model or whether it is merely engaging in some degree of local adaptation. Thus, before exploring London and Hart's (2004) propositions in the context of Telenor in India, using economic terms, we operationalize the main components of the business model.

BUSINESS MODEL COMPONENTS

At its simplest, a business model is "a statement of how a firm will make money and sustain its profit stream over time" (Stewart & Zhao, 2000,

p. 290). However, Zott, Amit, and Massa (2011) argue there is a lack of clarity among scholars as to how to define the concept of the business model in precise terms. The business model literature variously uses three output components: value creation, delivery, and capture (Leih, Linden, & Teece, 2015; Teece, 2010). In addition, it is common to use the concept of the value proposition as the core transaction content concept (Foss & Saebi, 2015). We argue that it is expedient to relate these four key components of the business model concept to the economic value they are supposed to represent. The left-hand part of Fig. 1 articulates Peteraf and Barney's (2003, p. 214) view that the total surplus created by an enterprise in the course of providing a good or service, "is the difference between the perceived benefits gained by the purchasers of the good (B) and the economic cost to the enterprise (C)." We refer to this part of the figure as "the economic model" of total surplus.

To exemplify the economic model of total surplus, let us suppose that a consumer has paid $80 (P) for a product he/she perceives as having a benefit equivalent to $100 (B): this equals a consumer surplus (B – P) of $20. The economic cost of production (C) is $60 meaning that the producer surplus (P – C) is $20. The total surplus is B – C = $40. To further exemplify; while keeping perceived benefit (B) and price (P) constant, if the economic cost of production (C) increases to $100, the producer surplus is –$20 making the total surplus (B – C), $0.

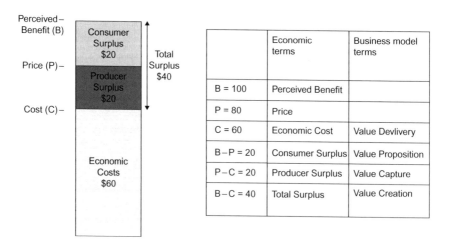

Fig. 1. Business Model Components.

When moving into BOP markets price (P) becomes a critical issue. If that has to be radically reduced for there to be any possibility of there being any perceived benefit (B) to the consumer, then economic costs (C) will have to be at least equally radically reduced. The new capabilities and routines required to achieve this is at the core of "the immense difficulty" Teece (2010, p. 181) argues is endemic to business model innovation by established businesses.

Moving to the right-hand part of Fig. 1, we divide the economic model into six main components or terms. Next to it, in the right-hand column, we list the four standardly employed business model terms next to their corresponding economic terms. That is, to the business model terms of value delivery, value proposition, value capture, and value creation we specify their economic model equivalents, that is, economic costs, consumer surplus, producer surplus, and total surplus, respectively. There are two economic terms that cannot be converted into business model terms, price and perceived benefit.

While the issue of price or pricing (P) does feature in the business model literature (e.g., Kindström & Kowalkowski, 2015), and can be readily estimated, the concept of customer "perceived benefit" (B) does not. Further, it is problematic to calculate. However, if the concept of the business model is to achieve any expression in economic terms there is a need to incorporate it. Without it we submit that the concepts of "value proposition" $(B - P)$ and value creation $(B - C)$, both partially a function of perceived benefit, are effectively worthless. Immediately after the next section in which we present the case of Telenor, we propose operationalizations of these concepts that are sufficient for this particular case.

THE CASE OF TELENOR

In order to explore how moving into BOP settings affects multi-domestic MNCs and their business models we focus on Telenor's Indian subsidiary, Uninor. With 172 million subscribers in 13 markets and with 2010 revenue of NOK 95 billion, Telenor ranks seventh among the world's mobile operators. Telenor has its corporate headquarters in Oslo and significant operations in Scandinavia, Central and Eastern Europe and in Asia. Although a decentralized MNC with considerable local autonomy at the business unit level, each region has had an overall chief to provide a measure of regional coordination.

When Telenor entered India in 2009, it was far from a newcomer in Asian emerging economies. However, its India entry was different in important ways. In the case of Telenor's operation in Bangladesh, its entry in 1999 was that of a first-mover – there was little competition – and was undertaken as part of a joint venture with the high-profile Grameen Bank of Bangladesh. The joint venture, GrameenPhone, enabled Telenor to serve "the wealthier people and the business community (profitably)" (Seelos & Mair, 2007, p. 56). As an addition to this top-of-the pyramid operation, GrameenPhone in close alliance with Grameen Bank undertook the organization of GrameenPhone's less commercial activities in rural, BOP, areas. In Pakistan, which Telenor entered in 2005, it was also an early entrant and similarly able to target and serve the local "top-of-the pyramid." Similar conditions applied to its entries into Thailand (DTAC) and Malaysia (DiGi).

Thus, prior to its India entry, Telenor had had a 10-year history as a successful top-of-the pyramid operator in Asia: with the exception of Malaysia, where it occupied number 3 position in the market, Telenor had always been either number 1 or 2 in its Asian markets. Not only had it enjoyed substantial first-mover advantages but tariff regimes had been stable. These conditions enabled Telenor to pursue its standard strategy of adaptive business model replication. In India, none of this applied. Telenor was a late entrant that faced strong incumbents at the top-of-the-pyramid and a tariff regime in flux. In 2010, failing revenue streams meant that Uninor either had to accept complete defeat and withdraw from India, or abandon its top-of-the pyramid strategy and develop a business model appropriate to the BOP market. It chose the latter.

For the first part of the case, our primary source of data is a series of loosely structured interviews with mangers on site at Uninor conducted in January 2012. We undertook several interviews with Uninor's second management team including COO, Yogesh Malik, and MD, Sigve Brekke. Prior to becoming MD, Brekke had been Telenor Asia chief and therefore had an overview of the workings of Telenor's various Asia operations. In late 2013, Brekke gave up his position as Uninor MD in order to concentrate on his duties as Telenor Asia chief.

In addition, we conducted interviews with the Uninor Head of HR and two senior engineers at Uninor headquarters in Gurgaon. We also visited one of Uninor's regional offices at Aggra where we first conducted a group interview with its four most senior managers followed by a field visit to a local distributor of Uninor SIM-cards. In November 2012, we interviewed Uninor's first MD at Telenor corporate headquarters in Oslo.

For the second part of the case in which we explore the role of Telenor headquarters in enabling Telenor to globally integrate functions developed by Uninor, we interviewed three senior managers. We conducted the first of these loosely structured interviews in November 2014 and the two others in August 2015.

As well as interviews, we have employed internal company documents, internal news on the Telenor intranet portal, press announcements, and documents shared on Telenor capital market days. These, as well as informal conversations conducted by one of the research team who was employed as a senior researcher at Telenor headquarters meant that the research team were in a position to follow the development of the Uninor BOP business model and its impact on the rest of Telenor.

MEASUREMENT ISSUES

Our discussion of Fig. 1 points to a number of difficulties in assessing the degree of change in the various components of the business model concept. Not least, the lack of method for calculating perceived benefit (B) is a particular challenge that means it is problematic to calculate changes to the value proposition $(B - P)$ and value creation $(B - C)$. There are no ready solutions to this. As a result, in our analysis of changes at Uninor we employ proxy indicators for value proposition and value creation. Value capture $(P - C)$ is also challenging to estimate.

Arguably, an indicator of a positive "value proposition" $(B - P)$ is an incremental expansion of customer market share. This shows that an increasing proportion of potential customers perceive benefit as exceeding price.

"Value capture" $(P - C)$ is problematic in that estimating it depends on the company being able to provide precise information on "value delivery" (C). As it was not possible for Uninor to supply this measure, we have settled on growing earnings before interest, taxes, depreciation, and amortization (i.e., EBITDA) as a reasonably adequate indicator of increasing value capture.

Given the difficulties involved in calculating both perceived benefit (B) and value delivery (C), "value creation" $(B - C)$ is yet even more challenging to calculate. Positive value creation depends on perceived benefit being higher than the costs associated with value delivery. In line with the practice of many mobile telecom operators, we employ average revenue per user (ARPU) (Tardy & Fahlander, 2002) as an estimate.

CASE PART 1: THE FAILURE AND THE TURNAROUND OF UNINOR

India is the second largest economy in the world with 50% of its population under 25 years of age. Since 2001, the Indian mobile market has been the fastest growing in the world: between 2001 and 2011, it expanded from 3–4 million to almost 900 million "SIM" subscribers. However, lack of brand loyalty and, from 2009, a relatively large number of operators means that it is also a highly competitive market: particularly below the top-of-the-pyramid, many subscribers have two or more SIM cards that they use according to whichever company at any one time is providing the best deal.

Despite this competitiveness and despite the presence of strong local incumbents, in late October 2008, after several years of probing the potential of the Indian market, Telenor formally announced its plans to enter the Indian mobile market. A window of opportunity had opened when in early 2008 the Indian telecom ministry decided to increase the number of licensed operators from seven to fifteen. Defying industry analysts who stressed the ultra-competitiveness of the Indian telecom market, Telenor entered India by paying $1.1billion (INR 61.35 billion) for a 60% stake in one of the new licensees, Unitech Wireless. Together they launched the Uninor brand.

To lead the local operation, Telenor Corporate CEO Jon Fredrik Baksaas selected one of Telenor's most successful Norwegian subsidiary managing directors (MDs). Corporate headquarters held him in particular regard for his highly effective turnaround of one of Telenor's central European operations. Rapidly installed at Uninor he had to confront the size and diversity of the Indian telecom market – consisting of 1.2 billion people, 29 languages, 2,000 ethnicities, huge distances, social inequalities, many rival companies, and uncertain regulations. Pre-entry, Telenor had had neither the time nor the resources to develop comprehensive business cases covering each of the "circles" (i.e., regions) it planned to enter. Instead, Telenor relied on the experience of its Norwegian MD and his European team to adjust the company's well-established business model to yet another setting. Delegating this responsibility to the Uninor MD for getting the Telenor business model into place and making any necessary local adaptations was standard practice at Telenor.

The notion was that Uninor was to focus on the top-of-the-pyramid and was to do so based on Telenor's "premium service" business model: that is, a high level of customer service; choice of plans; comprehensive presence; and high-end value-added services (but not streaming). The Uninor MD set about constructing the Uninor brand around the ambition to target "aspirational" India, using "emotional messages" to stimulate growing consumption of premium services. In terms of Fig. 2, Uninor positioned its business model in the top left quadrant alongside the long established Indian national champion, Bharti Airtel.

In this positioning, Uninor was aligning its operations with the recommendations it had received from the consultancy McKinsey hired by Telenor to assist in Uninor's implementation phase. Two factors in particular underpinned the recommendations. First, there was an assumption that the high ARPU that Telenor required from Uninor was most readily achievable in the premium services, higher-income segment of the market. Second, although incumbent operators already occupied most of the premium service market, the assumption was that there was a sufficiently high level of churn to provide an opportunity to capture a viable share of the top-of-the pyramid market.

To achieve the aggressive target of launching services in the Indian market within nine months after the entry decision, Uninor allied itself with Ericsson as its equipment supplier and Indian Wipro as its IT partner. Further, Uninor decided that the pressure to launch its services and the availability of a local call-center industry meant that unlike any other Telenor business unit it would *outsource its customer service*. In order to avoid lock-in, it chose four competing firms to deliver customer service.

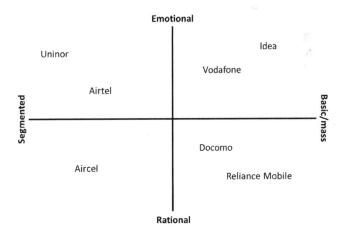

Fig. 2. Uninor's Initial Market Positioning. *Note*: Within the quadrants with more than one company, there is minimal difference in the positioning of the companies.

Not only was this expedient for getting the launch under way, but Uninor calculated that it led to a much lower cost and greater flexibility than if it had had the opportunity to develop customer service in-house.

Following its launch in December 2009 in eight of India's 22 telecom circles, Uninor made a strong start. The company racked up 1.3 million subscribers in its first month of operation. As it launched services in five additional circles giving it coverage of over 75% of India's population, Uninor was capturing a higher share of new subscribers than the other newcomers. However, almost as soon as it started launching its services, it registered that most higher-income potential subscribers seemed more reluctant than had been assumed to move from incumbent operators to an unfamiliar late entrant. With a limited subscriber base, the giant incumbents like Bharti and Vodafone with subscriber bases of 75–100 million each and unrivaled network coverage across all of India's 22 telecom circles dwarfed Uninor. By early 2010, Uninor's distribution channels began to lose confidence in Uninor's services and retailers demanded additional commission to accommodate them. With a premium service offering and a business model that did not differ significantly from the established top-of-the pyramid incumbents, the Uninor campaign rapidly lost momentum. As 2010 progressed, Uninor's results quickly deteriorated. Further, in a highly congested market, a price war broke out causing rapidly shrinking margins. When Telenor took its decision to enter India the average tariff for mobile phone call was two-and-a-half US cents a minute. By 2010, it was less than one US cent per minute (Financial Times, 2010).

By the end of June 2010, 7 of the 15 operators accounted for 96% of India's 636 million mobile subscribers, "leaving the newcomers (such as Uninor) to battle it out for the scraps" (Total Telecom, 2010). Panic broke out at Telenor corporate headquarters.

The Uninor MD considered declining growth to be more of a normal downtime event following a massive service launching, and decided to stick with the Telenor business model. However, the Telenor Asia chief Sigve Brekke was of another opinion. As the more Asia-experienced of the two, Brekke read the signals from leading media, distributors, retailers, subscribers, and competitors entirely differently. Following a series of unsuccessful attempts at revamping the Uninor launch, Telenor Corporate CEO Jon Fredrik Baksaas finally decided to intervene. After just 18 months in India, Uninor's first MD and his entire team returned to Norway. Telenor announced the installment of an entirely new management team headed by Brekke.

One of Brekke's new management team was the Indian-born, Canadian-educated COO, Yogesh Malik who arrived at Uninor in November 2010. Malik had worked for Telenor at its corporate head-quarters as well as having had roles in its operations in Ukraine and Bangladesh. Brekke and Malik were both committed to a radical turn-around initiative that would involve moving down the pyramid signifi-cantly beyond the 15% of the population with incomes above $10 a day (Open Magazine, 2011).

In terms of Fig. 2, Uninor aimed to move from the top left quadrant to the bottom right. Serving BOP customers with their limited spending power meant taking their needs explicitly into account and then developing an entirely new business model that addresses these (Demil, Lecocq, Ricart, & Zott, 2015). In the view of Brekke and Malik, the only serviceable part of the Uninor operation was the outsourcing of customer service. Every other aspect of the operation needed to be drastically changed. To analyze the changes Uninor undertook to its business model, we employ the four busi-ness model terms in Fig. 1. However, we start our analysis with changes to perceived benefit and price.

Perceived Benefit and Price

A feature of Uninor's top-of-the pyramid business model was the seg-mented marketing of premium services with an overtly emotional, aspira-tional appeal. Uninor definitively abandoned this approach. It replaced it with mass marketing of basic local services with a purely utilitarian appeal: the essence of the message it repeatedly communicated was "Uninor provides you with the best basic local services at the lowest price." This new "value for money" position was underscored by adver-tisements that were intended to be "simple, clear and light-hearted" and where plain but functional product benefits would be readily evident to prospective BOP customers.

A critical part of the offering to highly price-sensitive BOP customers was a significant reduction in Uninor's tariffs particularly at "excess capa-city" times of the day. Uninor was the first mobile operator in India to introduce "Dynamic Pricing," a concept that gave consumers substantial discounts based on current network traffic at an individual site. For BOP customers, the reward for placing their calls at times and places where there was excess network capacity was "super-low" call charges.

Value Delivery

In Fig. 1, we have indicated that a business model's value proposition is a function of price subtracted from perceived benefit. Before directly analyzing the outcome of changes to Uninor's value proposition, it is important to consider value delivery. As Fig. 1 indicates, value delivery is essentially about economic cost. Without addressing this aspect to its business model, Uninor would have been unable to deliver a price suited to the BOP market. Failing to meet that condition would have meant no perceived benefit could emerge. Our analysis of Uninor indicates two significant changes to value delivery. The first of these involved cost cutting and the second the development of an innovative distribution system.

One very palpable aspect to basic cost cutting at Uninor involved making 600 of its total 2,600 employees redundant. For those who remained they had to adapt to being involved in a very different operation to the one they had joined. Gone was any perception that they were working for a company serving aspirational India and in its place was the notion that from now on all activities aimed at delivering ultra-low-cost basic services. Uninor had already outsourced its customer service and this was to be further developed. However, Uninor's new, acute focus on getting rid of all unnecessary costs led to fundamental changes in its network operations, its mode of partnering with its IT vendor, and its sales distribution.

To enhance utilization of its networks, Uninor developed a *cluster-based operating model*. The first step was to concentrate base stations to high traffic areas. Thereafter, Uninor's local Indian engineers developed a network utilization method that meant squeezing more network capacity out of its base stations than any of its competitors. Uninor then grouped neighboring base stations to form clusters headed by managers whose task was to enable local dynamic pricing as a means to achieving the highest possible revenue streams.

Another novel initiative aimed at cost reduction concerned aligning its IT vendor, Wipro, with Uninor's goals. Uninor had already outsourced application development and management to Wipro. It now persuaded Wipro in lieu of direct payment to accept *"gain sharing."* As a result, the Uninor-Wipro relationship became so close that Wipro engineers literally moved into Uninor's headquarters in Gurgaon on a permanent basis. Incentivized and integrated, Wipro IT engineers focused on significantly reducing the number of IT service personnel it employed at Uninor and in simplifying the IT architecture.

Both of these cost-cutting efforts represented significant contributions to enhancing value delivery suitable to a BOP market. However, equally important was developing *a cost-effective distribution system* geared to and embedded in the BOP market. One aspect to the new distribution system involved Uninor replacing its top-of-the-pyramid points-of-sale with an extensive network of "C" and "D" level retailers. These "Mom & Pop stores" sold a vast array of products (combs, candy, comics, "you-name-it-we've got-it") aimed at the BOP market. Part of this extensive assortment of merchandise included the competing offerings of other mobile operators. Any one Mom & Pop store would be displaying the logos of four or five of Uninor's competitors meaning that Uninor had to address how to confer some advantage on its particular offerings.

A second aspect to Uninor's overhaul of its distribution system involved abandoning distributors who offered competing products and services. Instead, it set about developing a network of Uninor exclusive, but independent, distributors, thereby avoiding divided loyalties. Most of these distributors were local entrepreneurs who had proved themselves in other, unrelated businesses. Attached to each distributor was a comprehensive network of field sales agents, known as "Retail Sales Executives" (RSEs). While the distributors supervised the RSEs, they did not employ them. Instead, RSEs were employees of employment agencies but trained and incentivized by Uninor to in turn coach and incentivize storeowners to voice the benefits of the Uninor offerings to customers. The outcome was that the Mom & Pop stores were supplied with Uninor products and services (SIM cards, subscriptions, recharges, special offers, etc.) by a dedicated sales arm that Uninor did not actually own. By the end of 2011, Uninor had 400,000 bottom-of-the pyramid points-of-sale served by 7,000 RSEs attached to 1,700 distributors across 13 circles, serving 36 million subscribers.

One particular aspect of creating a cost-effective distribution system involved the status and the motivation of the RSEs. As employees of employment agencies such as Manpower and Adecco, they were guaranteed medical insurance and a certificate of employment, both of which are highly valued by BOP personnel. Although employed by agencies, Uninor not only selected all RSEs, it also provided them with training and an undertaking that success would lead to direct employment and a career within Uninor. In contrast, in other mobile operators, RSE equivalents were employees of the distributor who, in Uninor's view, generally engaged in recruiting sub-standard employees, avoided training them properly, frequently under-paid them, and denied them medical insurance. That type of human resource policy could be sufficient for incumbents with well-regarded brands and sales performance driven by market pull, but Uninor saw it as entirely unsuitable for them as a newcomer. Uninor's very different approach to their RSEs reflected their belief that only by developing a push model could it achieve cost-efficient sales in the context of a BOP market.

Value Proposition

At the close of 2011, Uninor's combination of "no-frills" services and mass market "sabse sasta" or "lowest-in-the-market" tariffs had resulted in significant increases to its customer market share relative to other operators. In perceiving benefit as exceeding price, BOP customers were responding to a value proposition that resonated with them. In the next years, an ever-increasing number of BOP customers bought in to the Uninor combination of basic services and "lowest-in-the-market" tariffs. In May 2014, Uninor reported that in the first quarter of 2014 it had achieved a 20% share of incremental customer market share in its circles of operation (Uninor, 2014). In simple terms, every fifth new mobile subscription in these circles went to Uninor. Compared to the same quarter in 2013, it had expanded its customer base by 25%. In other words, Uninor's value proposition was succeeding in the BOP market.

Value Capture and Value Creation

In terms of value capture, which we operationalize as EBITDA, for the first time since it entered India Uninor achieved break-even in December 2013. Concerning value creation, Uninor reported a year on improvement of gross revenue by 44% and 13% on its ARPU (Uninor, 2014).

Summary

At the core of Uninor's BOP business model is considerable attention to value delivery. Without reducing costs significantly, no BOP value proposition could have emerged. Likewise value capture and value creation would have failed. London and Hart (2004) argued that success in developing business models appropriate to BOP markets depends on bottom-up co-invention with local partners. We see this clearly illustrated at Uninor. Some of its most radical changes to value delivery were a product of engaging with external partners who crossed the protective boundaries of the firm. Its early outsourcing of customer service was deemed successful. However, under Brekke it went much further, achieving substantial cost savings through a win-win contract with Wipro for IT services. Again, in line with London and Hart's (2004) BOP success thesis, Uninor's new cost-effective distribution system was a product of close collaboration with local businesses including local entrepreneurs, employment agencies, and Mom & Pop stores. Even its internally developed cluster-based operating model was locally embedded in that its innovators were indigenous Indian engineers. The issue we now turn to is the second of London and Hart's (2004) proposals, that BOP business models can have relevance for the rest of the MNC located at the top-of-the pyramid.

CASE PART 2: GLOBAL REPLICATION OF BOP INNOVATIONS

In 2011, Uninor's difficulties in India were not the only source of concern at Telenor corporate headquarters. Another concern was the lack of coordination across Telenor.

We have observed that Telenor had developed as an essentially multi-domestic MNC, that is, a decentralized MNC with each business unit having extensive local autonomy to adapt services to the local market. In 2004, Telenor developed a Knowledge Management Information System (KMIS) that generated systematic overviews of local best practices (Gooderham & Ulset, 2007). Further, corporatewide teams drawing on a range of local senior executives employed the KMIS to select best practices for replication across business units. However, as a multi-domestic MNC, Telenor business units retained a veto and would regularly reject any best practice initiative that they viewed as maladapted to their specific local needs. Thus, while Telenor corporate headquarters were not ignorant of developments at its various business units, local autonomy meant that it lacked the capabilities to convert its knowledge of local best practices to global best practices.

In 2011, Telenor concluded that this degree of local autonomy was preventing effective implementation of global best practices. While building on previous experiences, it decided to create a new central unit, "Group

Industrial Development" (GID), that was given responsibility for cross-unit learning, replication of best practices within marketing and technology, and the governance of selected functions such as shared services and procurement (Elter, Gooderham, & Ulset, 2014).

GID

In 2012, GID decided that procurement or sourcing was an obvious function with which to start: globally coordinated sourcing of equipment would reap scale advantages that would benefit all business units. GID established a souring organization that had as its aim to realize savings of 3 billion NOK by the end of 2015. Already by the end of 2013, there was broad recognition of GID's success in delivering substantial savings across Telenor's business units.

GID's achievements with global sourcing were at least in part a political feat. Although it had a mandate from a CEO Baksaas, GID nevertheless had to develop its operations in the context of a multi-domestic MNC with relatively autonomous business unit MDs who have a focus on their own respective results. The governance outcome was certainly not a centralized autocracy but nor was it the voluntarism that had characterized Telenor until 2012. One aspect to GID was that from the outset it recognized that developing centralized solutions and delivering these as "manuals" to the BUs would not work by themselves. Instead, GID recruited among managers who had had operational roles in the various BUs and who could therefore enter into a dialogue based on a mutual understanding of local BU needs with erstwhile BU colleagues about what "blue-prints" could work. Thus, while GID had a clear mandate to centralize and coordinate sourcing it did so based on robust dialogue. Olav Sande, who was a manager in Uninor from 2009 to 2011 prior to joining GID, commented that he could only recall one occasion when dialogue did not work and when differences escalated into a head-on collision with a BU that was resolved top-down. Otherwise, instead of the use of fiat, GID would allow recalcitrant BUs to opt out of corporate purchasing solutions on the condition that they accepted full-transparency and full-accountability to verify that their local solutions had delivered superior results. However, these were exceptions and as GID delivered substantial, rigorously quantified and thoroughly communicated savings based on "robust dialogue" and an understanding that it needed to prove its worth through demonstrable value delivery, its standing increased and BU exceptionalism decreased.

GID and Transfer from BOP

In 2014, GID had become so well established that it could move beyond sourcing. Its decision to assess what could be replicated from Uninor's rein-vented business model across other Telenor business units was partly a function of the recognition of Uninor's success but also partly because GID contained a number of former Uninor managers who had inside knowledge of how it had achieved a successful turnaround. GID identified four particular practices as fundamental to the Uninor BOP business model: the outsourcing of customer service; the cluster-based operating model; gain sharing with IT vendors; and the cost-effective distribution sys-tem geared to and embedded in the BOP context. One conclusion GID drew with Sigve Brekke, who by 2014 had relinquished his MD role at Uninor to concentrate on his role as Telenor Asia chief, was that all of these practices — indeed the whole of the Uninor model — were transfer-able to Telenor's new BOP operation in Myanmar.

Another conclusion drawn by GID and Brekke was that the outsourcing of customer service, the cluster-based operating model and gain sharing with IT vendors were all transferable to Telenor's other Asian business units. However, GID and Brekke viewed the Uninor distribution system inappropriate to the significantly more top-of-the pyramid operations of these business units. There was simply no need to employ a combination of local entrepreneurs, Mom & Pop stores, and an army of RSEs in these settings.

Finally, GID concluded that the Uninor distribution system was also equally unsuitable for Telenor's Scandinavian and European business units that operate in almost exclusively postpaid markets as opposed to Uninor's prepaid market. Based on the learning from Uninor, gain sharing with IT vendors began to be used particularly in the original market, Norway. Additionally GID viewed the outsourcing of customer service as a practice with significant potential for all markets, including Scandinavian and European markets, where there is a functional call-center industry. The prospect of outsourcing customer service was subject to a great deal of discussion. There were skeptics who regarded customer service as a core competence in their customer-centric top-of-the-pyramid positioning. However, GID recruited the head of this function at Uninor and gave him the opportunity to create a business case adapted to the specific require-ments of the Scandinavian and European business units. In this, he and his team were effective and GID began to replicate modified versions of custo-mer service outsourcing across all Scandinavian and European business units. The cluster-based operating model was viewed as having significant potential in all Asian markets.

Summary

London and Hart (2004) suggest that BOP business models can have relevance for top-of-the pyramid business units. The evidence is that because of the formation of GID, which not only had a mandate to identify and

Table 1.   Transfer of Practices from BOP in India to Other Business Units in Telenor.

Practice Developed in Uninor	Transferred to Other Asian Markets	Transferred to European Top of the Pyramid Markets
Outsourcing of customer service Outsourcing practice established in Uninor. Generic blue-prints developed by GID based on Uninor experiences and some early outsourcing attempts in other markets.	Blue-prints deployed in two additional BUs.	Blue-prints deployed in five business units in Europe. Local adaptations influences by maturity of local call-center industry.
Cluster-Based Operating Model (CBOM)	All Asian BUs	Modified versions in all European BUs
Gain sharing with IT vendor New partner model for IT services co-developed with Wipro (IT development and maintenance).	Agreement between Uninor and Wipro was extended to most other Asia operations.	Gain sharing model with vendor applied in Scandinavia, but with other vendors.
Cost-effective distribution systems Systems developed in Uninor together with Wipro (distribution, intelligence, commission management toward retailers).	Modified version in all Asia BUs.	
Replication of the whole Uninor operating model	When establishing a new operation in Myanmar the whole operating model used in Uninor was replicated with some adaptations to Myanmar, a pure BOP market.	

transfer best practices across Telenor, but by 2014 also a high standing across Telenor, certain core practices developed by Uninor crossed into top-of-the-pyramid business units not least in Asia but also in Scandinavia and Europe. However, we also observe that the replication of the entire Uninor business model was confined to Myanmar, another BOP market. We summarize our findings in Table 1.

DISCUSSION

London and Hart's (2004) BOP thesis suggests that in the context of BOP business model development, the BOP operation has to go further than local responsiveness. This involves achieving a significant degree of local strategic latitude and a significant break with top-of-the pyramid operations and corporate headquarters. They also suggest that practices developed in BOP settings can be highly relevant for top-of-the-pyramid operations. We have advanced this thesis by applying an economic model terminology that communicates the scale of business model innovation required for a BOP setting. We have further developed this thesis by detailing the mechanisms involved in ensuring a transfer of practices from the BOP operation to other parts of the MNC.

In broad terms, our context is that of multi-domestic MNCs characterized by substantial local responsiveness. More specifically, we have employed the case of Telenor to explore the effects on the relationship between corporate headquarters on strategy making at its BOP operation in India, Uninor. As with any single case, it has its idiosyncratic features. The BOP business model innovation that occurred in Uninor was originally unintended. It was not Telenor's initial aim to pursue business model innovation (Teece, 2010). Indeed, it was the product of a breakdown of its locally adaptive business model approach in the face of a significant miscalculation of the challenges in entering a particularly demanding, disparate and in price-terms, volatile emerging market, coupled to the need to avoid complete failure after its first failed attempt to enter the market. However, in line with London and Hart (2004), success was a consequence of abandoning an approach that worked at the top-of-the-pyramid in favor of an approach embedded in the BOP setting. An important feature of the new approach to designing the Uninor business model suited to BOP was to have a pronounced focus on value delivery (C). One critical aspect of this was extensive bottom-up co-invention with local partners.

Arguably, London and Hart (2004) do not detail the resources required to engage in business development at BOP. Our analysis indicates at least two resources, a "deep pocket" and managerial capabilities. Thus, the turnaround at Uninor was partly dependent on Telenor having the resources or "slack" to allow Uninor to survive its initial failure (Berrone, Fosfuri, Gelabert, & Gomez-Mejía, 2013). In addition, Telenor could draw on managers with well-developed BOP insight (Berrone et al., 2013). Headed by Sigve Brekke, Uninor's second management team brought to bear an entirely different repertoire of skills and insights that enabled them to innovate rather than to continue with local adaptation. The economic terms in our business model schema provides an indication of the innovation challenge.

The question as to why Telenor did not draw on these managers prior to the launch of Uninor would appear to be a product of an assumption that Uninor would be operating, as usual, at the top-of-the pyramid and a degree of "overconfidence" that competition could be overcome (Cain, Moore, & Haran, 2015). Thus, its initial choice fell on managers who had been successful and, because they were in geographically proximate areas to Telenor corporate headquarters, were relatively frequent visitors to corporate headquarters. Eventually necessity triggered the need for Telenor to look for managerial resources outside its immediate circle. Sigve Brekke, who for many years had been located in Asia but who had been preoccupied with fine-tuning these operations during the Uninor launch, was persuaded to double up as Telenor Asia chief and MD of Uninor for an interim period and to recruit managers that were locally adapted.

In line with London and Hart (2004), we observe that practices developed at the BOP are relevant not just for other BOP business units, but also for Telenor's top-of-the pyramid business units. In other words in this phase the corporate headquarters-BOP operation relationship had to be reconstructed. However, as we have observed, London and Hart's (2004) BOP thesis does not address how this development is actually triggered. In the context of Telenor, our analysis indicates that the transfer of BOP practices was only possible because GID had achieved a standing across Telenor that gave it the credibility to engage in the facilitation and coordination of their transfer. Part of this standing derived from its ability to deliver substantial savings from sourcing that benefitted the BUs. However, a second part derived from its style of interacting with BUs. Instead of top-down, centralized autocracy, because GID contained many managers with extensive BU experience, GID was able to develop a relationship with the BUs based on "robust dialogue." Finally, GID's understanding of its authority was based on having to "prove its worth" to the BUs rather than being able to deploy sanctions.

We would go beyond arguing that transfer of GID practices was contingent on the existence of GID and raise two other possibilities. Had the BUs perceived GID as too domineering, there may have been resistance to transfer from BOP. Equally, had a domineering GID existed at the point in time at which Uninor engaged in business model reinvention, this could have blocked BOP innovation. After all, one critical advantage of Telenor's multi-domestic heritage was that Brekke and his team had considerable autonomy to engage with the turnaround at Uninor and thus significant latitude to innovate. A more globally integrated MNC would likely have insisted that corporate blueprints be given yet another opportunity. It appears that in the context of multi-domestic MNCs that the second part of London and Hart's (2004) BOP thesis — that capabilities developed in BOP business environments can travel up the pyramid — is conditional on the emergence of a global integrative function regarded by BUs as credible, capable, and non-threatening (Bartlett & Ghoshal, 1995).

REFERENCES

Arnold, D. J., & Quelch, J. A. (1998). New strategies in emerging markets. *Sloan Management Review, 40*(1), 7–20.

Bartlett, C. A., & Ghoshal, S. (1989). *Managing across borders: The transnational solution.* Boston, MA: Harvard Business School Press.

Bartlett, C. A., & Ghoshal, S. (1995). *Transnational management. Text, cases and readings in cross-border management* (2nd ed.). Chicago, IL: Irwin.

Berrone, P., Fosfuri, A., Gelabert, L., & Gomez-Mejia, L. (2013). Necessity as the mother of green inventions: Institutional pressures and environmental innovations. *Strategic Management Journal, 34*(8), 891–909.

Cain, D. M., Moore, D. A., & Haran, U. (2015). Making sense of overconfidence in market entry. *Strategic Management Journal, 36*(1), 1–18.

Demil, B., Lecocq, X., Ricart, J. E., & Zott, C. (2015). Introduction to the SEJ special issue on business models: Business models within the domain of strategic entrepreneurship. *Strategic Entrepreneurship Journal, 9*(1), 1–11.

Elter, F., Gooderham, P. N., & Ulset, S. (2014). Functional-level transformation in multi-domestic MNCs: Transforming local purchasing into globally integrated purchasing. In T. Pedersen, L. Tihanyi, T. M. Devinney, & M. Venzin (Eds.), *Orchestration of the global network organization: Advances in international management* (pp. 99–120). Bingley, UK: Emerald Group Publishing Limited.

Financial Times. (2010). Telecommunications: A tough call. *Financial Times*, May 24.

Foss, N. J., & Saebi, T. (2015). Business models and business model innovation. In N. J. Foss & T. Saebi (Eds.), *Business model innovation: The organizational dimension* (pp. 1–23). Oxford: Oxford University Press.

Gooderham, P. N., & Ulset, S. (2007). Telenor's "third way". *EBF – European Business Forum, 31*, 46–49.

Hart, S. L., & Christensen, C. M. (2002). The great leap. Driving innovation from the base of the pyramid. *Sloan Management Review, Fall, 44*(1), 51–56.

Kindström, D., & Kowalkowski, C. (2015). Service-driven business model innovation: Organizing the shift from a product-based to a service-centric business model. In N. J. Foss & T. Saebi (Eds.), *Business model innovation: The organizational dimension* (pp. 191–216). Oxford: Oxford University Press.

Leih, S., Linden, G., & Teece, D. J. (2015). In N. J. Foss & T. Saebi (Eds.), *Business model innovation and organizational design: A dynamic capabilities perspective* (pp. 24–42). Oxford: Oxford University Press.

London, T., & Hart, S. L. (2004). Reinventing strategies for emerging markets: Beyond the transnational model. *Journal of International Business Studies, 35*(5), 350–370.

Open Magazine. (2011). *The wealth report.* Retrieved from http://www.openthemagazine.com/article/business/the-wealth-report. Accessed on March 12, 2011.

Peteraf, M. A., & Barney, J. B. (2003). Unraveling the resources-based tangle. *Managerial and Decision Economics, 24*(4), 309–323.

Prahalad, C. K. (2012). Bottom of the pyramid as a source of breakthrough innovations. *Journal of Product Innovation Management, 29*(1), 6–12.

Prahalad, C. K., & Lieberthal, K. (2003). The end of corporate imperialism. *Harvard Business Review, 81*(8), 109–117.

Roth, K. (1992). Implementing international strategy at the subsidiary level: The role of managerial decision-making characteristics. *Journal of Management, 18*(4), 769–789.

Seelos, C., & Mair, J. (2007). Profitable business models and market creation in the context of deep poverty: A strategic view. *The Academy of Management Perspectives, 21*(4), 49–63.

Stewart, D. W., & Zhao, Q. (2000). Internet marketing, business models, and public policy. *Journal of Public Policy, 19*(Fall), 287–296.

Tardy, O., & Fahlander, A. (2002). *Creating value in mobile telecom: Beyond ARPU.* bcg perspectives. Boston Consulting Group. Retrieved from http://www.bcg.com/documents/file13853.pdf. Accessed on May 12, 2012.

Teece, D. J. (2010). Business model, business strategy and innovation. *Long Range Planning, 43*, 172–194.

Total Telecom. (2010). Mobile services in India: Too many cooks. Total Telecom Plus, business analysis for telecom professionals. Retrieved from http://www.totaltele.com/plus.aspx?ID=8. Accessed on September, 2010.

UNCTAD. (2014). *World investment report, 2014. Investing in the SDGs: An action plan.* New York, NY: UNCTAD.

Uninor. (2014). Retrieved from https://www.uninor.in/about-uninor/news-and-media/Pages/Uninor-reports-strong-business-growth-in-India.aspx

Winter, S. G., & Szulanski, G. (2001). Replication as strategy. *Organization Science, 12*(6), 730–743.

Yip, G. (1989). Global strategy – In a world of nations? *MIT Sloan Management Review, 31*(1), 29–41.

Zott, C., Amit, R., & Massa, L. (2011). The business model: Recent developments and future research. *Journal of Management, 37*(4), 1019–1042.

REGIONAL MANAGEMENT IN MULTINATIONAL SERVICE OPERATIONS: DO SERVICES DRIVE REGIONAL MANAGEMENT STRUCTURES?

Jörg Freiling, Perttu Kähäri, Rebecca Piekkari and Fabian Schmutz

ABSTRACT

This study sheds light on the uncharted phenomenon of regional management in coordinating services across borders. Based on a multiple case study of four German industrial manufacturing firms with servitization strategies we seek to better understand what kind of organizational challenges servitization poses for the MNC and whether these challenges can be met through regional management models. This chapter initiates a conversation on the available design options for running service operations regionally.

Keywords: Regional management; multinational service operations; management structure

Perspectives on Headquarters-Subsidiary Relationships in the Contemporary MNC
Research in Global Strategic Management, Volume 17, 27–57
ISSN: 1064-4857/doi:10.1108/S1064-485720160000017002

INTRODUCTION

A growing trend in the contemporary multinational corporation (MNC) is the increasing importance of service components in product offerings (Baines, Lightfoot, Benedettini, & Kay, 2009; Wandermerwe & Rada, 1988). Many manufacturing firms develop 'hybrid products' as inseparable blends of tangible and intangible components of a solution adding value to the customer (Davies, Brady, & Hobday, 2007; Freiling & Dressel, 2015; Gebauer, Edvardsson, & Bjurko, 2010). In this context, 'servitization' is a term that describes the shift of suppliers – in our case the MNCs – from a logic of 'making and selling' products to the principle of 'sensing and responding' (Vargo & Lusch, 2004). The principle of sensing the customer's needs and responding through well-tailored solutions is the centrepiece of the well-established concept of 'service-dominant logic', put forth by Vargo and Lusch (2004). Although serving the customer is a process, services can be regarded as the intangible output of a solution that may consist of both tangible and intangible components, as is typical in business-to-business settings.

International business research has traditionally paid limited attention to services and service operations. For a long time the MNC was almost equated with the manufacturing company that orchestrated the global supply chains. Not surprisingly, international business researchers have focused on how to best configure the production and distribution of goods over distances. More recently, however, research on regional strategies has shown that compared to manufacturing firms, service firms tend to select regional rather than global structures to carry out their strategies. Almost half of the top 25 home-region-based companies that Rugman (2005) and Rugman and Verbeke (2009) studied represented various service industries. 'Servitized' solutions and hybrid products raise particular challenges for the MNC because they often imply physical proximity and access to the customer's location, and may thus require different organizational structures than manufacturing operations. The customer perspective needs to be integrated into the MNC's value-adding process through close interaction between the two parties (Freiling, 2012; Ramírez, 1999). To date, the research tradition in international business has led to an oversight – perhaps unintendedly – of service-based solutions in MNCs.

This chapter explores the role of regional management in the way MNCs organize multinational service operations and solution providing. Research on regional organizations – including regional headquarters (RHQ) and regional management mandates – has made important advances in recent years (Alfoldi, Clegg, & McGaughey, 2012; Ambos &

Schlegelmilch, 2010; Piekkari, Nell, & Ghauri, 2010). The field has developed from its phenomenological origins (Daniels, 1986; Enright, 2005; Lasserre, 1996; Schütte, 1997) to theorizing about the underlying causes and consequences of organizing regionally (Kähäri, 2014; Laudien & Freiling, 2011; Li, Yu, & Seetoo, 2010; Lunnan & Zhao, 2014). So far, however, this growing stream of research has hardly considered the specificities of services (for exceptions, see Enright, 2005; Ho, 1998; Poon & Thompson, 2003). This chapter intends to initiate such a conversation.

The management of customer service is typically delegated to local subsidiary organizations, on the grounds that it is an operative activity. Birkinshaw, Toulan, and Arnold (2001, p. 206) invite us to rethink this view. Their study, which underscores the strategic value of customer management, 'suggests that it is in the organizational implementation ... that future research should be directed'. In this chapter we respond to this call by focusing on the organizational aspects of servitization and pose the following two research questions in the context of four German case companies: Firstly, how do MNCs organize their multinational service operations? Secondly, what role do regional headquarters (RHQ) and other regional management units play in supporting service coordination? Our focus is on industrial services since the phenomenon of servitization is particularly relevant in this type of business. Germany is known for its internationally strong industrial firms, which are undergoing an evolution from being pure manufacturing firms to being providers of services and hybrid solutions (Freiling & Dressel, 2014). The organizational structures of MNCs are often very complex and context-specific, which supports the use of a case study approach as a research strategy (Piekkari & Welch, 2011).

This study makes the following contributions to the existing body of research on organization design and headquarters-subsidiary relationships in MNCs. Firstly, it sheds light on the uncharted phenomenon of regional management in coordinating services across borders. It examines the servitization strategies of the four MNCs we studied and what the available design options were. Secondly, this study seeks to better understand what kind of organizational challenges servitization poses for the MNC and whether these challenges can be met through regional management designs. Thirdly, it contributes to the growing stream of research on regional management, which to date has largely focused on the internal dynamics of the MNC rather than the customer interface and the boundary spanning role of the RHQ.

The chapter is structured as follows. Two key streams of literature, one on regional management and another on servitization are first introduced. Thereafter, we detail our study of four German case companies, the data collection and analysis process. In the findings section, we contrast and compare the use of regional management models for service provision across the four companies. In order to initiate a conversation on this topic, we offer conceptual ideas and theoretical models that integrate the previously disconnected streams of literature and invite future research on regional management in multinational service operations.

LITERATURE REVIEW

As mentioned above, the research streams on regional management and servitization have largely remained disconnected, perhaps due to their disciplinary backgrounds in international business and strategic management, and marketing, respectively. Our research questions integrate the two fields with each other.

Regional Management and Regional Headquarters

Service operations typically require a local presence, and MNCs face the challenge of organizing and structuring them globally, regionally and locally. A regional approach implies having a regional strategy in place, potentially supported by a regional structure or regional headquarters (RHQ).

The mainstream view of regional management associates regional management with RHQ. Regional headquarters can be defined as intermediate organizational units with a mandated role, geographic scope and location (Kähäri, 2014). RHQ are concerned with, and involved in, the control, coordination or integration of activities of one or more subsidiaries in their mandated region (Schütte, 1997). RHQ may also add value through entrepreneurial activities (Lasserre, 1996). Structurally, RHQ are organized as independent units, fully dedicated to their regional roles and functions. Alternatively, existing local subsidiaries are given regional responsibilities alongside their local business obligations. The latter units have also been called 'regional management mandates' (Alfoldi et al., 2012).

Two comprehensive and empirically verified models have been introduced to conceptualize the roles and functions of RHQ, by Ambos and Schlegelmilch (2010) and Alfoldi et al. (2012), both models detail the integrative and entrepreneurial activities of RHQ. According to Alfoldi et al.

(2012), the entrepreneurial role includes the functions of strategic leadership, planning and direction; resource development, acquisition and deployment; seeking and exploiting new opportunities; driving organizational adaptation; and attention and signalling, while the integrative role covers such functions as monitoring, control and governance; resource and knowledge management; representation and mediation; coordination and harmonization; and integration and facilitation of inter-unit linkages.

Previous research has also identified other forms of regional management than RHQ. Ghemawat (2005) argues that RHQ may be a necessary means to put a regional strategy into practice although not a sufficient one. Lasserre (1996) points out that there are alternatives to RHQ, such as 'a corporate-based regional office, a local subsidiary mandate, and regional networking' (p. 34). Li et al. (2010) also mention subsidiary cooperation through 'a friendly regional culture' (p. 8). In this context, Alfoldi et al. (2012) suggest 'regional management mandates' are a cost-effective alternative compared to the dedicated RHQ.

In their comprehensive volume on regional management, Ambos and Schlegelmilch (2010) introduce four ways to organize regionally: a single country market approach, where the RHQ acts as a 'central hub'; a subregional approach, with subordinate country clusters; a mix of these two approaches; and a virtual network, where the responsibilities are shared (pp. 73−74). They also note that RHQ can reside in the corporate headquarters (CHQ) and be an RHQ *for the region*, in comparison to the more typical situation of an RHQ *in the region*. Pla-Barber and Camps (2012) have identified an RHQ residing in Spain with a geographic mandate for Latin American markets and consequently introduced a concept of 'extra-regional headquarters'.

While prior research has charted the benefits of regional management and RHQ to the MNC (e.g. Asakawa & Lehrer, 2003; Daniels, 1986; Enright, 2005; Lasserre, 1996; Schütte, 1997), the number of analytical and theoretically grounded approaches to understanding the value added remains low. One exception is the study by Ambos and Schlegelmilch (2010) that builds on Chandler's (1962, 1991) original idea and further work by Campbell, Goold, and Alexander (1995) and Foss (1997) on parenting advantage. They suggest that RHQ offer three types of advantages to MNCs, namely parenting, knowledge and organizational advantage, which together form a regional advantage. Ambos and Schlegelmilch note that the parenting advantage requires RHQ to know their local environments and to be able to support the local units, by, for example, pooling resources. The knowledge advantage requires RHQ to assume a role that

combines knowledge of global operations with information from local markets (see also Lunnan & Zhao, 2014). RHQ can also transfer knowledge
directly between local subsidiaries. The organizational advantage in turn
allows RHQ to act as 'an organizational pressure valve' in managing the
tension between global integration and local responsiveness (p. 63). The
conceptualization by Ambos and Schlegelmilch (2010) functions as a sensi-
tizing framework for our case analysis.

Servitization and Multinational Solution Providing

The other stream of research that we draw on is the research on servitization, which is a growing area particularly in marketing. Industrial services
are core elements of customized offerings that respond to specific customer
problems. This 'solution providing' (Davies et al., 2007; Gebauer et al.,
2010) includes a sound analysis and evaluation of the needs of a particular
customer – independent of the physical location.

Servitization (Desmet, van Dierdonck, & van Looy, 2003; Wandermerwe &
Rada, 1988) refers to an evolutionary process that illuminates the growing
significance of services, primarily in manufacturing-based businesses. The
definition of servitization (Baines et al., 2009; Oliva & Kallenberg, 2003;
Wandermerwe & Rada, 1988) implies, firstly, a fundamental shift in the
operational *set-up and running of value-added processes*. Secondly, it covers
the *basic logic of designing and governing value-creating systems* in modern
economies and societies (Vargo & Lusch, 2004). Let us start with the latter.

Servitization relates to the basic design and governance of value-creating
systems. Vargo and Lusch (2004) introduce the concept of the 'service-
dominant logic', in contrast to the 'goods-dominant logic', to illustrate two
fundamentally different ways of thinking. Whereas a goods-dominant logic
follows the principle of 'making and selling' finished products via market
governance mechanisms with separated players, the service-dominant logic
emphasizes the process of serving the customer at every step of a collaborative process during which the customer and the supplier, that is the MNC,
form a temporary unit. The principle of sensing the customer's needs and
responding to them (Freiling & Dressel, 2014; Vargo & Lusch, 2004) priori-
tizes the customer's problems and brings rigour to the customization process by making the customer an active part of the value-added process – at
the customer's, the MNC's, or a 'neutral' site. Insofar, solution-orientation,
which is at the heart of servitization, rather than product-orientation
requires more intensive modes of collaboration between the MNC and its

customers, and hence the MNC needs to find ways to be close to its local customers (Baines et al., 2009; Vargo & Lusch, 2004). Troubleshooting services are an example of the type of coordination challenges where MNCs require instant access to the customer. In order to be able to provide customers with relevant experts – be they internal or external – MNCs can rely on organizational models such as expert databases, remote services and access to competent local service partners. Overall, the servitization process forces the MNC to consider its options for resourcing and organizing its service activities alongside its manufacturing operation (Salonen & Jaakkola, 2015).

As a concept, the servitization of value-added processes can be better understood with the help of three interconnected dimensions, namely input, throughput (process) and output (e.g. Freiling, 2012). Originally, services were defined in output terms (e.g. intangibility, cf. Bruhn & Georgi, 2006; Desmet et al., 2003; Lovelock & Wirtz, 2007). Later on, the throughput dimension was added (e.g. customer integration, cf. Lovelock & Wirtz, 2007). More recently, all three dimensions have been used (Freiling & Dressel, 2015). In the following we will discuss servitization starting from the output dimension.

In *output* terms, servitization implies adding service elements to solutions (e.g. full service contracts for machines) or extending the range of products and solutions with customized services (e.g. 24/7 troubleshooting worldwide by means of remote services; Davies et al., 2007; Gebauer et al., 2010; Lovelock & Yip, 1996). As these elements are to a large extent intangible and provided on demand, customers can neither perceive the quality of the entire solution prior to purchase nor comprehensively thereafter. To reduce uncertainty, MNCs have to demonstrate their skills and service-mindedness regardless of whether they represent corporate, regional or local units.

As for the *throughput (process)*, servitization implies customer integration in the MNC's value-added process by providing specific information as well as transaction-specific objects and personnel. This takes place when the MNC's personnel assist the customer by providing training, troubleshooting or upgrading (Freiling & Dressel, 2015). Accordingly, customer-supplier interaction, on-site visits and physical closeness to the customer in international transactions are inherent elements of servitization. Although current ICT provides many opportunities to manage the interaction virtually, physical interaction still remains as an important component of the service process and thus creates a coordination challenge.

Besides output and throughput, servitization also plays a role at the *input* level of service transactions. Alchian and Woodward (1988) classify transactions into exchanges (of finished products) and contracts (as a promise of future performance). For a credible promise, the bilateral adaptations of assets (e.g. ICT systems) and resource commitments (e.g. access to MNC's experts) are useful in order to reduce the customer's uncertainty. This underlines the need for alignment and proximity in service provision and servitization, posing challenges for coordination internationally.

In the present study, we ask the following research questions that integrate the two previously disconnected streams of research: regional management and servitization. Firstly, how do MNCs organize their multinational service operations? Secondly, what role do regional headquarters or other regional management units play in supporting service coordination?

A MULTIPLE CASE STUDY

We undertook a qualitative multiple case study because of several reasons (Graebner, Martin, & Roundy, 2012). Firstly, the prior research on the topic of multinational service provision and regional management is too limited to allow theory testing through large-scale quantitative surveys. We therefore bridged two previously unconnected streams of research on servitization and regional management to shed light on the phenomenon at hand. Our study can be positioned as an 'inductive theory building' case study (Welch, Piekkari, Plakoyiannaki, & Paavilainen-Mäntymäki, 2011). Secondly, organizational architecture and structural design are rarely available in company documents. Even when they are available, these configurations are often employed in a very context-specific manner. Therefore, gaining an understanding of complex organizational models and designs tends to require detailed fieldwork and questions that are specifically tailored to each case company and informant. Thirdly, our purpose was to contextualize the research phenomenon and reflect our informants' understandings of their world.

Case Selection

To address our research questions of how MNCs organize their multinational service operations and what role regional headquarters or other regional management units play in supporting service coordination, we selected four German manufacturing firms. They offer hybrid products to industrial customers in the fields of gear motors, medical equipment, moulding machines and laser technology including related tools and systems. These four firms are producers of capital goods and operate in the business-to-business segment. For reasons of anonymity, we have named these firms as Gear [GmbH], Medical [AG], Moulding [KG] and Laser [KG]. They could also be categorized as small and medium-sized enterprises or family businesses, which have received far less attention than large MNCs in previous work on regional management. These four firms were selected from more than 100 German firms on the grounds that they showed a high degree of servitization in their product offerings and that they had internationalized early and set up international service networks (see the appendix). The firms were identified by searching on the Internet and by consulting industrial, business and trade associations. Eisenhardt (1989) recommends 4–10 cases as an ideal number in order to handle the complexity and volume of data. In the data collection stage, it became clear that we in fact had two paired cases (Buck, 2011; Piekkari, Welch, & Paavilainen, 2009): two case firms that relied on regional coordination in providing services internationally, and two that did not. However, this became obvious only during the course of the study, that is it was not an a priori selection criterion at the outset (Fletcher & Plakoyiannaki, 2011).

Data Collection

The case companies were approached by first contacting the person responsible for the global service organization. Suitable interviewees were identified from corporate and divisional headquarters, local branches, as well as regional headquarters in case they existed. The data were collected during April to July 2014 and the four-month period allowed us to adjust the interview questions during the course of the fieldwork when necessary. Table 1 shows the distribution of the interviewees across headquarters, units and local branches.

We conducted 13 semi-structured interviews at the different case companies. As all the interviewees were German by nationality, the interview questions were developed in German, based on prior research as well as on the experience of the pilot case (see also Welch & Piekkari, 2006). The interviews, as the main data source, were complemented with information from secondary sources, such as the Internet, and company documents such as brochures. These data sources provided detailed information

Table 1.   Overview of Interviewees.

Case Firm	Job Title	Unit
Medical AG	Head of marketing services	CHQ
(4 informants)	Vice president sales	CHQ
	Vice president global key account management	CHQ
	Vice president region Asia Pacific	DHQ
Moulding KG	Director service	CHQ
(2 informants)	Team manager service	Local branch
Gear GmbH	Vice president global sales	CHQ
(4 informants)	Director sales Europe	CHQ
	Director key account management	RHQ
	Global service manager	CHQ
Laser KG (3 informants)	Head of sales spare parts	CHQ (formerly branch)
	Head of global sales services	CHQ
	Head of global service center	CHQ (formerly branch)

on the products and history of the different case companies. A key characteristic of the case study is the use of multiple data sources (Piekkari et al., 2009).

Data Analysis

The two research questions guided the data analysis, which can be divided into two steps: within-case analysis and across-case analysis. The electronically recorded interviews were fully and immediately transcribed. Also field notes were taken during interviews. Data analysis was undertaken in German because it was the native language of the interviewees and two members of the research team (see also, Marschan-Piekkari & Reis, 2004). One member of the research team then translated the selected interview quotations.

The analysis was supported by the software called MAXQDA 11. The interviews were coded and categorized based on how the interviewees described the structure and the organization of the service network. Attention was paid to the responsibilities of the various units (CHQ, DHQ, RHQ and local branch) as well as the linkages and interaction between them. After various rounds of coding, patterns of relationships between the categories and the conceptual framework were developed and compared across the four case companies.

As part of the analysis process, the results were discussed within the research team as well as with industry experts. The emerging findings were also returned to the companies for factual verification and additional data collection. Finally, we used member checking as a validity procedure by taking our account back to one of the research participants for comments and review (Creswell & Miller, 2000). His feedback suggested that our interpretation of the findings accurately reflected the role that regional management played in the global service provision of his firm.

FINDINGS

The four case companies differed in terms of the type and overall use of regional management units, the explicitness and formal authority of these units, and the entity in charge of local service transactions (regional, local or external partner). It is noteworthy that none of the case companies operated completely without (formal or informal) regional structures, thus exhibiting some level of regional advantage. In what follows, we outline how each case company coordinated its global service network.

Medical AG

Medical sells medical equipment to hospitals and national health services across the world. Medical has experienced many of the opportunities and pitfalls of having regional units and currently has RHQ in the United States, Malaysia and Dubai. The company faced a strong need to decentralize governance structures and thus establish RHQ partially between the CHQ and local units '*With regional headquarters, deeper and more frequent regional communication is possible. Furthermore, regional headquarters have a better understanding of the regional conditions than the headquarters which is located far away*' (Vice President Region Asia Pacific of Medical AG). Moreover, external partners are involved in providing services to Medical's customers globally. CHQ acknowledges its limitations in liaising with various countries and customers and thus subordinate units such as RHQ are empowered. Central coordination by CHQ is restricted to an indispensable core, which includes 'strategic services' like consulting, process optimization of customers' activities, as well as basic support services. Whenever coordination becomes too complex and the regions can step in, RHQ structures are relied on. However, this only holds for a selected number of regions; for the other regions CHQ directly collaborates with the local units. '*In some regions, the various branches are supervised directly by the central headquarters, other branches are supervised by regional headquarters. The decision which way we choose depends on the complexity of coordination, homogeneity of regions, importance of regions and related issues*' (Head of Marketing Services, Medical AG).

When RHQ play a role in coordination, they provide 'strategic services'. To some extent they are something like an extended arm of CHQ. RHQ also monitor the activities of local units and external partners. Due to the frequent interaction with local units, external partners and customers, RHQ are in a sound position to absorb knowledge and behave as internal knowledge brokers. Local units provide primarily technical services like repairs, maintenance and spare parts logistics, and they also control external partners in operational matters.

Within Medical, the vertical communication is much stronger than the horizontal, as intended by the CHQ. Nevertheless, some exchanges of information and experience take place horizontally, but this is mostly on an informal and ad-hoc basis. Although RHQ have an identifiable role in Medical, in many instances they are not necessary from the viewpoint of CHQ.

Moulding KG

Moulding produces moulding machines, which are used in their customers' production process. Moulding believes in the power of hierarchical coordination by CHQ. Moulding's policy is to maintain global service coordination without a regional structure: '*We don't need any expensive intermediate units*' (Team Manager Service, Moulding KG). The reason for this is their perceived inefficiency, due to the additional costs and the added complexity to the command structures. However, CHQ is aware of its own limitations in terms of local and customer-related knowledge and their pivotal role in providing industrial services. Thus, CHQ grants considerable discretion to local units and acknowledges explicitly their local expertise.

While officially regional structures are not wanted, unofficially they do exist. Under the current structure, the local units seem to miss out on support for the training of employees and external service partners, the selection of new external service companies that operate internationally rather than nationally, and complex troubleshooting. What has emerged informally within Moulding, as a response, can be called 'regional experts', that is persons or – more frequently – groups of experts who coordinate service activities nationally beyond local units. This is illustrated well by one interviewee: '[...] *it is not unusual, that a Czech service technician calls his specialized colleague in Germany directly – without any interference of the HQ*' (Director Service, Moulding KG).

Regional experts serve several local units and act as boundary spanners between them. In contrast to an RHQ or similar formal structures, they emerge out of daily coordination needs that are poorly handled. Local units remain solely responsible for integrating external partners into service transactions and for providing technical services (e.g. spare parts, repair and maintenance, revamping).

Moulding's current structure is hierarchical and communication between the local units is rare. Since horizontal communication tends to improve business routines, local units regard regional experts as useful. This regional management design seems to work informally and, as such, rather effectively.

Gear GmbH

Gear manufactures gear motors, which are typically sold to industrial companies, other manufacturers and retailers in over 50 countries. Gear is a company that prefers central coordination but not in a very hierarchical sense. Gear put in place RHQ rather early in running an international service network and accumulated substantial experience over time. '*We learned that regional headquarters help to make the service network more efficient and flexible. They bring the headquarters' expertise directly into the region*' (Global Service Manager, Gear GmbH). The basic principle is that the CHQ is able to manage and coordinate the entire service value chain. However, the CHQ explicitly acknowledges the expertise of local partners and regional units, and practices a more participative style of managing the service chain. The RHQ work closely with the CHQ and the regional personnel spend most of their time in Gear's CHQ.

As external service companies that closely collaborate with Gear carry out the service operations in most countries, the RHQ are of utmost importance. The RHQ are responsible for a thorough selection process of

external partners; Gear is particularly interested in collaborating with certified partners. Moreover, the RHQ coordinate with the available partners to
ensure quick and comprehensive service to customers. The integration of
external partners rests to a large extent on their prequalification, their
expertise in all aspects of the service business and, not the least, on trust.
Trust is required as these partners have, due to the absence of local units,
considerable discretion in what they do.

Gear's RHQ enjoy a privileged position within the entire service network due to their expertise. They are regarded as 'expert hubs' in the region
they are responsible for. Coordination is rather formalized in order to provide stability in the network. *'Formalized coordination helps to ensure that
no information will be lost'* (Vice President Global Sales, Gear GmbH).
Even troubleshooting is well planned and organized so that RHQ are
prepared in case of urgency. Communication is vertically oriented and
supports the coordination processes. Horizontal knowledge sharing is not
encouraged because Gear fears that critical know-how leaks to rivals via
external partners. Members from different RHQ meet every once in a while
but with limited interest in sharing knowledge and ideas.

Laser KG

Laser produces equipment applying laser technology and sells them
through over 20 of their own subsidiaries across the world. Laser believes
in the power of hierarchical coordination, where CHQ sets the frame for
the entire coordination process. However, Laser has tried out the RHQ
model, but, from the CHQ's point of view, the results were disappointing
in terms of the costs and benefits. *'The regional coordination was not efficient and although we invested a lot of money it did not get better'* (Head of
Global Sales Services, Laser KG). Therefore, Laser decided to discontinue
the RHQ structure completely.

However, the CHQ was aware of regional coordination needs beyond
the local units. This is why regional mandates were initially introduced.
Local units with pivotal positions or outstanding expertise in the region
were chosen to respond to the regional management challenges. These
regional mandates were given to a small number of existing local subsidiaries located in key markets. Although no formal decision-making authority was granted to them, these units were not powerless. Their real
influence largely depended on their skills and expertise: *'When a local*

problem comes up and the appropriate service technician does not find any solution he seeks for help at the Regional Service Center' (Head of Global Service Center, Laser KG). While the communication in the entire Laser service network was vertically oriented, the only significant exception to the rule was the horizontal knowledge sharing by regional mandates.

CHQ has given leeway to local units and their expertise, as these units predominantly coordinated service transactions. For example, the local units decided when external partners needed to be involved in service provision and could make autonomous decisions instantly. *'The local units know best how the customers can be helped ... and they need the opportunity to be able to act accordingly'* (Head of Global Service Center, Laser KG).

Multiple Ways of Managing Regionally

As Fig. 1 demonstrates, we found two key structural designs that the case companies applied in organizing their multinational service operations. The first exhibits a preference for direct reporting and a limited role of regional management. Two of the firms in our study — Laser and Moulding — applied this model to their global service networks. They practiced regional management without introducing formal RHQ and argued that this approach reduced complexity in the international coordination of network activities, providing clearer and shorter communication

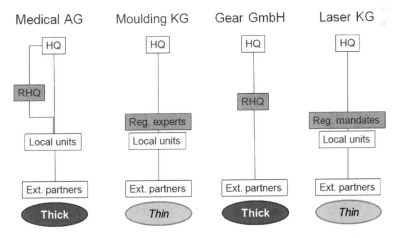

Fig. 1. Service Operations Structures of the Four Case Companies.

channels. A manager in Laser explained this with an industry metaphor: '*Complexity in administration increases the more "cutting surfaces" you have*'.

The other two firms in our study opted for an alternative approach that puts more emphasis on regional management, in terms of regional support and coordination. Medical and Gear used RHQ as an intermediate hierarchy level between CHQ and the local service subsidiaries and external service partners. RHQ were given various tasks in managing regional service operations, as Vice President Global Sales, Gear GmbH put it: '*They are a real added value for our corporation, a distinguishing feature, as well as a part of our value proposition*'.

In order to better understand why the different case companies, with somewhat homogenous backgrounds, selected so different regional management models, we draw on the conceptualization of regional advantage developed by Ambos and Schlegelmilch (2010). They argue that RHQ may potentially have three types of advantages, namely a parenting advantage, a knowledge advantage, and an organizational advantage, which together make up the regional advantage. Two of the companies we studied benefitted from a regional advantage to the extent that they established RHQ. With respect to the other two, the regional advantages remained so low that RHQ were not considered an efficient structural design. The concept

Table 2.   Factors Underlying the Selected Regional Management Model.

	Thin Regional Model (Laser KG and Moulding KG) Benefits of Centralization	Thick Regional Model (Gear GmbH and Medical AG) Benefits of Decentralization
Parenting factors	• Short communication lines • CHQ grants considerable discretion to local units and acknowledges explicitly the local expertise • Previous experiments with formal regional coordination proved inefficient and costly	• Proximity improves coordination • Deeper and more frequent communication possible • Monitoring activities of both local units and external partners
Knowledge factors	• Emergence of informal regional experts due to lack of formal regional structure	• Better understanding of regional conditions and formation of 'experts hubs' • Provide assistance to solve language and culture issues
Organizational factors	• Reduce organizational complexity	• RQH as an 'extended arm' • Helps to make global service networks more efficient and flexible

of regional advantage can be used to explain why and how the companies in our study selected the models they did for coordinating their multinational service operations (see Table 2).

Parenting Factors

Ambos and Schlegelmilch (2010) point out that the parenting advantage requires RHQ to know their local environments in order to be able to support the local units, for example by pooling resources. Interestingly, these factors mattered for both models. Within both Moulding and Laser, the CHQ coordinated the service networks that formally operated on two levels of hierarchy, namely the local service subsidiaries and CHQ. The interviewees at Moulding and Laser argued that this provided the CHQ with clear and short communication channels. Under this regional model the local units gained autonomy, as CHQ granted them considerable discretion and explicitly acknowledged their expertise. On the other hand, it required CHQ to coordinate, monitor and frame local activities to keep them on track.

However, these two cases also show that this is not a perfect model for coordination. The companies further fine-tuned their structures with quasi-intermediate levels — either formally, through regional mandates, as in case of Laser, or informally, as in the case of Moulding, through emerging regional experts.

The parenting factors were relevant also for Medical and Gear when deciding on their regional structures. They considered RHQ beneficial, as they were closer to local subsidiaries than CHQ. This made coordination easier, as the Vice President Region Asia Pacific of Medical confirmed: '*There is the clear advantage of geographical proximity*'. The proximity improved coordination and made deeper and more frequent communication possible. In Medical and Gear, RHQ were used as regional coordination hubs and helpdesks. They assumed such roles as service delivery, knowledge transfer, monitoring activities and looking for regional synergistic effects. All these tasks were fundamentally the headquarters' tasks, which meant that in these instances the RHQ provided a parenting advantage over the CHQ.

Knowledge Factors

The knowledge advantage materializes when RHQ assume a role in combining knowledge from global operations with information from local markets. The RHQ can also transfer knowledge between the subsidiaries. Knowledge factors were present in all the four cases. The RHQ enabled the exploitation of regional synergies, the promotion of networkwide knowledge transfer, and the formation of a cultural and linguistic bridge between CHQ and the local service units. As the Vice President Sales of Medical suggested: '*Yes, it [RHQ] is necessary, because you have language and cultural problems*'. Besides this, RHQ were important hubs in the strategic coordination of services and in selecting reliable external partners. They accumulated service-related know-how that was different from the knowledge gathered by local units and thus vital for the smooth running of global service activities.

Our case study suggests that regional management structures may also foster knowledge transfer horizontally, that is between regions or between local units. Interestingly, this was the case at Moulding and Laser, where regional experts played an important role. Thus, a knowledge advantage may emerge that to some extent undermines the existing formal organizational structure while promoting a complementary regional design.

Organizational Factors

Organizational factors refer to those underlying characteristics that will (or will not) give RHQ an organizational advantage to manage other units. According to Ambos and Schlegelmilch (2010) organizational advantage allows RHQ to act as 'an organizational pressure valve' in managing tension between global integration and local responsiveness (p. 63). Whether this advantage exists depends thus both on the relevance of such tension for the MNC and the capability of any organizational unit to relieve such tensions.

A manager at Gear provided evidence of such an advantage: '*But if it´s possible to solve the problem with a regional headquarters it is good and we will do it with a regional headquarters*' (Global Service Manager, Gear GmbH). Furthermore, RHQ were needed at Gear for network coordination to relieve the resources of CHQ: '*We need RHQ to reduce coordination work for the headquarters, because only in Germany we have 30 or 40 service partners*' (Director Key Account Management, Gear GmbH). Medical went even further as its RHQ had been delegated some of the functions of CHQ: '*The regional function is more or less the extended arm of the central function [...]*' (Vice President Asia Pacific, Medical AG).

On the other hand, Moulding and Laser managed their service networks directly from the CHQ. In both companies, external service partners played an important role in the service networks, and the number of local players (internal units and external partners) brought about a significant amount of complexity. The two companies perceived that their 'thin' model, without RHQ, reduced managerial and organizational complexity. Therefore, in their view, no organizational advantage existed at the regional level.

DISCUSSION

Having analysed the organizational architecture of our case companies, let us now explore whether and how services and customized solutions drive the design of regional management structures. We will start by discussing what kind of organizational challenges servitization may introduce, and thereafter look into how these challenges favour one regional organization model – thin or thick – over the other.

How Will Servitization Challenge Organizational Architecture and Design?

For a manufacturing firm, servitization means introducing a new type of business to an existing organization, which brings about challenges. We identify three groups of challenges that stem from customer requirements.

Urgency of Demand Requires Local Presence
Customers often depend on the high availability of equipment, and therefore request short response times to address urgent needs such as avoiding downtimes. This requires local availability of skilful experts. It is often difficult to find the right experts within the relatively small local units. Instead, it can be easier to identify the right persons for a certain service problem on a regional scale.

Local Presence Requires Closer Control for Quality and Efficiency
Due to the nature of the services being comprised of not only output, but also input and throughput (process) components, there is a need to control the quality at different instances and locations. Since services are intangible and (partly) perishable by nature and produced in dispersed locations – often at the customer's site – they are difficult to control from a distance. Also, service

provision is often labour-intensive, particularly in case complex solutions are needed, which sets new requirements for controlling the efficiency of the operation, through, for example, benchmarking across the service network.

Responding to Customer Needs Requires Pooling and Exchanging Knowledge across Borders
In industrial services, it is necessary to gather and use expertise from a variety of firm functions and locations to address the customer's needs. Different options are available for doing this, such as calling in experts from the CHQ, the regions or the local units, using (local) external partners or running problem-oriented communities. Applying these options requires knowledge regarding both the expertise available across the organization and regarding the specific local needs; and thus, this introduces a need for additional coordination (Almeida, Song, & Grant, 2002; Ardichvili, Maurer, Li, Wentling, & Stuedemann, 2006; Birkinshaw & Hood, 1998; Dhanaraj, Lyles, Steensma, & Tihanyi, 2004; Foss & Pedersen, 2002, 2004; Gupta & Govindarajan, 2000; Hansen, 2002). The same holds for learning from troubleshooting. As every service transaction is a learning opportunity, a key task is to store this knowledge within the organization and make it available for future customer needs.

Applying the Regional Model: Thin or Thick?

In our case analysis, we identified two types of approaches to regional management, which we have labelled 'thin' and 'thick'. The thin approach was

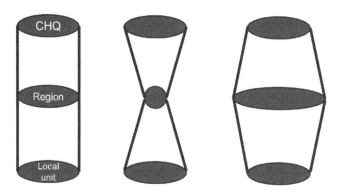

Fig. 2.   Regular, Thin and Thick Model of Regional Management.

identified in Moulding and Laser, and had a lighter regional structure, while the 'thick' approach was present in Medical and Gear. These two firms preferred more regional support and coordination. The two approaches are illustrated in Fig. 2.

In Fig. 2, the wider circle refers to a broader, 'thick' regional role, while the smaller circle means a narrower 'thin' role. As discussed earlier, RHQ roles have been studied extensively and two comprehensive categorizations have been provided by Ambos and Schlegelmilch (2010) and Alfoldi et al. (2012). Both of these categorizations apply a distinction between entrepreneurial and integrative roles. At its narrowest, there will be no regional management role at all when the CHQ manages the local units directly. Ultimately, the MNC management will decide on an organizational model and structure that they find optimal for each situation. This model may be standardized across the organization or it may vary between regions or other organizational dimensions.

The organizational challenges raised by servitization – local presence, closer control for quality and efficiency, and pooling and exchanging knowledge across borders – resonate well with regional management designs. Our case analysis gives some indications why servitized MNCs may apply a thick regional model, but also why two of the case companies in our study preferred a thin regional model despite the growing challenges.

The first challenge posed by increased local presence may affect the MNC in two ways. Firstly, it may translate into a higher number of and larger local units as more customers are in direct contact with these. Secondly, this challenge may also expose the MNC to new languages and cultural environments. It is evident that with the increasing size of the organization, a thick model may relieve the CHQ from some of the pressure involved in managing many units with different local needs. Certain host countries in the region may also need more guidance than others, which calls for a thick model. For example, the local markets may be unknown to the MNC, distant from the CHQ or changing rapidly. The Swedish telecom vendor Ericsson is a case in point. In 2000, Ericsson introduced a regional management model in Africa, Sub-Saharan Africa and North Africa, to strengthen the ties and improve the services for local customers and operators (Holmstedt, 2015). There may also be a need for regional embeddedness (Hoenen, Nell, & Ambos, 2014) due to, for example, regional legislation or trade agreements, as in the European Union. In such cases, a thick model may prove particularly appropriate.

The second organizational challenge – the need for closer control over quality and efficiency – can also be well served through RHQ, thus leading to a thick model. However, in this respect the case companies in our study differed: some considered RHQ to improve information flows while others felt the communication was simpler without an additional layer. Although our case analysis does not offer any definitive answers, it suggests that these differences are due to their different regional strategies and varying information needs.

Pooling and exchanging knowledge across borders − the third organizational challenge introduced by servitization − is at the heart of the benefits that regional structures may provide. Regional units are, thanks to their accumulated knowledge, in a privileged position to identify available expertise residing in subsidiaries and within external partners. Their knowledge allows them to locate the relevant expertise to a given problem across the global network. Moreover, smooth collaboration between regional and local units is decisive in better understanding the customers' needs, wishes and problems, and in providing sound solutions. In this regard, servitization calls for going beyond individual service transactions to improving the entire management process of the customer interface. The companies in our study responded to the challenges associated with knowledge sharing and information processing by adopting either thin or thick regional management models.

Our case study also suggests that the decision of whether to introduce a regional model or not and what kind of a unit is established may be highly context-specific and path dependent (Sydow, Schreyögg, & Koch, 2009). The existing organizational architecture is often difficult to change, as historical events shape internal dynamics and accumulate capabilities to certain (local) units. For example, a regional structure may be introduced as a consequence of a merger or an acquisition. Also, cost considerations affect design options. Kähäri (2014) argues that an MNC will implement RHQ only if the combined agency costs are lower in comparison to a direct relationship between the CHQ and the local unit.

To conclude, we argue that servitization prompted the four case firms in our study to apply thicker regional models than what they had previously used. The increasing need for customer information was difficult to satisfy from the CHQ directly. Also, the need to understand the local circumstances (e.g. legislation, standards, culture) was emphasized by the companies in our study. While it is too costly to build all these capabilities in each local unit, a regional support organization provides a cost-effective compromise to attend customer relationships in a continuous and intensive manner (Alfoldi et al., 2012; Kähäri, 2014). Thus, servitization and the accompanying customer needs posed novel organizational challenges that the companies in our study resolved through regional means.

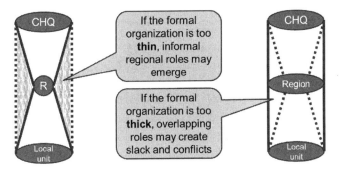

Fig. 3.   The Dynamic Effects of Regional Management Model Selection.

Adjusting the Thickness

The new requirements set forth by servitization trigger a kind of 'ideal' thickness of the regional organization. In practice, however, the realized model rarely corresponds with this idealized form due to situational, historical and other contextual constraints. Therefore, the implemented regional model is often out of sync with the ideal regional model as illustrated in Fig. 3.

We argue that this mismatch may cause organizational friction and require structural adjustments. If the formal regional organization is too thin, that is if local units are lacking regional support, an informal organization may emerge. For example, in the case of Moulding local units informally contacted regional experts who provided the necessary support. Over time, such an informal organization may also be formalized. On the other hand, if the formal organization is too thick, there is slack, overlapping tasks and conflicts between organizational units. Lunnan and Zhao (2014) provide supporting evidence of this from China.

CONCLUSION

In this chapter, we have explored servitization and its effects on regional management models. We contribute to the existing body of research on organization design and headquarters-subsidiary relationships in MNCs by integrating these two steams of literature and by investigating four German firms providing industrial services across their global networks.

We analysed the companies in our study with the help of the framework developed by Ambos and Schlegelmilch (2010) on the parenting advantage, knowledge advantage and organizational advantage. This framework allowed us to better understand the underlying factors that drove these four companies to select particular regional structures. We argued that servitization prompted new organizational challenges that can be well satisfied with various regional management designs. Depending on the environmental circumstances, the MNC regional strategy and the perceived advantages attached to the structural design, a thin or thick regional management model is applied. Over time this model is likely to be adjusted in order to better meet the increasing customer needs that shape service provision.

Our study places the customer in a central position when analysing regional management designs. In servitization, the customer is the ultimate driver, and a key dimension of any organizational structure, because service networks exist for the sole purpose of serving customers and satisfying their needs. In fully servitized MNCs, the organizational structure may be designed in such a way that it reflects the number of customers, their location, the languages the customers want to be served in, and the ways these customers want their solutions to be delivered (e.g. in terms of urgency and local support).

Going beyond the case study, it seems that the thick regional management model resonates particularly well with the needs of industrial service customers. While global customers may call for a global structure, a large number of local customers with differentiated service needs may go well with a thick regional management model. This is because customer interaction and customer integration call for proximity and knowledge management that favour thicker regional management models. Holmstedt's (2015) study of Ericsson in Africa shows that the close collaborative relationship between Ericsson and local telecom operators was decisive for locating the regional organization in Cairo and Johannesburg. Ericsson provided extensive training programmes to these local customers in how to manage and develop telecom networks. Moreover, the regional organization offered local employees ample career opportunities and rendered Ericsson a more attractive employer than before the regional management model had been implemented (Holmstedt, 2015).

We believe that combining the stream of literature on servitization with the stream on regional management has been a useful exercise, which has helped us understand more holistically the factors that influence the adoption of regional management units. The increasing complexity of servitized businesses require structures that have a higher capacity to deal with both internal and external demands. Birkinshaw et al. (2001) note that the organizational architecture shapes the capacity of the firm to transfer, share and process information. It provides the basis for linking, grouping and connecting units and individuals with each other. As such, RHQ facilitate knowledge flows into the region, within the region and outside the region (Lunnan & Zhao, 2014). In this regard, they are like spiders in the web that 'hear' the customer's voice and echo it in the broader organization if motivated to do so. While our research focused on regional management in the global service networks, we did not explore other organizational forms of service provision. These could include, for example cross-border service centres (see, e.g. Enright, 2005), or MNCs organized according to customer segments instead of geographies. One may speculate that over time the regional structures will give way to customer-based structures as the firms continue to move along the servitization path.

Related to this, our cross-sectional analysis offers only a glimpse of the organizational challenges stemming from servitization. A limitation of our study is that we did not trace the transition process that the manufacturing case companies in our study underwent when becoming more service- and solution-oriented. We acknowledge that regional management designs are highly sensitive to time. For example, one of the case companies, Laser, had tried out an RHQ structure but abandoned it due to lack of efficiency. Recently, longitudinal approaches have started to emerge in regional management research, but they remain a minority pursuit (see, Kähäri, 2014; Kähäri & Piekkari, 2015; Piekkari et al., 2010; for exceptions).

One of the current megatrends is digitalization, supported by the evolution of the Internet-of-Things, which will have profound effects on the way industrial services are organized and delivered. Digitalization will remove or at least reduce the effect of geographical distance and transform the way multinational service operations are managed. This might be a fruitful avenue for future research as it has clear organizational implications.

ACKNOWLEDGEMENTS

We are grateful to the anonymous reviewers and participants in the conferences and seminars where we had an opportunity to present earlier versions of our paper, for their comments and ideas, including EIBA 2014 Conference in Uppsala, SMS 2015 Special Conference in St. Gallen, Vaasa 2015 IB Conference, and ICSB 2015 World Conference in Dubai.

We would also like to thank Anna Salonen for her insightful comments and suggestions on the final draft. Finally, we owe a debt of gratitude for the interviewees at the four German case companies in our study.

REFERENCES

Alchian, A. A., & Woodward, S. (1988). The firm is dead; long live the firm. A review of Oliver E. Williamson's the economic institutions of capitalism. *Journal of Economic Literature*, *26*, 65–79.

Alfoldi, E. A., Clegg, L. J., & McGaughey, S. L. (2012). Coordination at the edge of the empire: The delegation of headquarters functions through regional management mandates. *Journal of International Management*, *18*, 276–292.

Almeida, P., Song, J., & Grant, R. M. (2002). Are firms superior to alliances and markets? An empirical test of cross-border knowledge building. *Organization Science*, *13*, 147–161.

Ambos, B., & Schlegelmilch, B. B. (2010). *The new role of regional management*. Houndmills: Palgrave Macmillan.

Ardichvili, A., Maurer, M., Li, W., Wentling, T., & Stuedemann, R. (2006). Cultural influences on knowledge sharing through online communities of practice. *Journal of Knowledge Management*, *10*, 94–107.

Asakawa, K., & Lehrer, M. (2003). Managing local knowledge assets globally: The role of regional innovation relays. *Journal of World Business*, *38*, 31–42.

Baines, T. S., Lightfoot, H. W., Benedettini, O., & Kay, J. M. (2009). The servitization of manufacturing. A review of literature and reflection on future challenges. *Journal of Manufacturing Technology Management*, *20*, 547–567.

Birkinshaw, J., & Hood, N. (1998). Multinational subsidiary evolution. *Academy of Management Review*, *23*, 773–795.

Birkinshaw, J., Toulan, O., & Arnold, D. (2001). Global account management in multinational corporations: Theory and evidence. *Journal of International Business Studies*, *32*, 231–248.

Bruhn, M., & Georgi, D. (2006). *Services marketing. Managing the service value chain*. Harlow: Prentice Hall.

Buck, T. (2011). Case selection informed by theory. In R. Piekkari & C. Welch (Eds.), *Rethinking the case study in international business and management research* (pp. 192–209). Cheltenham: Edward Elgar.

Campbell, A., Goold, M., & Alexander, M. (1995). The value of the parent company. *California Management Review*, *38*, 79–97.

Chandler, A. D. (1962). *Strategy and structure: Chapters in the history of the industrial enterprise*. Cambridge, MA: MIT Press.

Chandler, A. D. (1991). The functions of the HQ unit in the multibusiness firm. *Strategic Management Journal*, *12*, 31–50.

Creswell, J. W., & Miller, D. L. (2000). Determining validity in qualitative inquiry. *Theory into Practice*, *39*, 124–130.

Daniels, J. D. (1986). Approaches to European regional management by large U.S. multinational firms. *Management International Review*, *26*, 27–42.

Davies, A., Brady, T., & Hobday, M. (2007). Organizing solutions – Systems seller vs. systems integrator. *Industrial Marketing Management, 36*, 183–193.

Desmet, S., van Dierdonck, R., & van Looy, B. (2003). Servitization: Or why services management is relevant for manufacturing environments. In B. van Looy, P. Gemmel, & R. van Dierdonck (Eds.), *Services management: An integrated approach* (pp. 40–51). Harlow: Pearson Education.

Dhanaraj, C., Lyles, M. A., Steensma, H. K., & Tihanyi, L. (2004). Managing tacit and explicit knowledge transfer in IJVs: The role of relational embeddedness and the impact on performance. *Journal of International Business Studies, 35*, 428–442.

Eisenhardt, K. M. (1989). Building theories from case study research. *Academy of Management Review, 14*, 532–550.

Enright, M. J. (2005). Regional management centres in the Asia-Pacific. *Management International Review, 45*, 59–82.

Fletcher, M., & Plakoyiannaki, E. (2011). Case study selection: Key issues and challenges for international business researchers. In R. Marschan-Piekkari & C. Welch (Eds.), *Rethinking the case study in international business and management research* (pp. 171–191). Cheltenham: Edward Elgar.

Foss, N., & Pedersen, T. (2002). Transferring knowledge in MNCs: The role of sources of subsidiary knowledge and organizational context. *Journal of International Management, 8*, 49–67.

Foss, N., & Pedersen, T. (2004). Organizing knowledge processes in the multinational corporation: An introduction. *Journal of International Business Studies, 35*, 340–349.

Foss, N. J. (1997). On the rationales of corporate headquarters. *Industrial and Corporate Change, 6*, 313–338.

Freiling, J. (2012). New service ventures: Struggling for survival. In T. Burger-Helmchen (Ed.), *Entrepreneurship: Creativity and innovative business models* (pp. 99–114). Rijeka: InTech.

Freiling, J., & Dressel, K. (2014). Innovative service business models and international market resistance: Insights from service-dominant logic. *International Journal of Business and Information, 9*, 389–410.

Freiling, J., & Dressel, K. (2015). Exploring constrained rates of adoption of 'Total cost of ownership' models: A service dominant logic analysis. *International Small Business Journal, 33*, 774–793.

Gebauer, H., Edvardsson, B., & Bjurko, M. (2010). The impact of service orientation in corporate culture on business performance in manufacturing companies. *Journal of Service Management, 21*, 237–259.

Ghemawat, P. (2005). Regional strategies for global leadership. *Harvard Business Review, 83*, 98–108.

Graebner, M. E., Martin, J. A., & Roundy, P. T. (2012). Qualitative data: Cooking without a recipe. *Strategic Organization, 10*, 276–284.

Gupta, A., & Govindarajan, V. (2000). Knowledge flows within multinational corporations. *Strategic Management Journal, 21*, 473–496.

Hansen, M. (2002). Knowledge networks: Explaining effective knowledge sharing in multi-unit companies. *Organization Science, 13*, 232–248.

Ho, K. C. (1998). Corporate regional functions in Asia Pacific. *Asia Pacific Viewpoint, 39*, 179–191.

Hoenen, A. K., Nell, P. C., & Ambos, B. (2014). MNE entrepreneurial capabilities at intermediate levels: The roles of external embeddedness and heterogeneous environments. *Long Range Planning*, *47*, 76–86.

Holmstedt, M. (2015). *L.M. Ericsson' internationalization in Africa from 1892 to 2012: A study of key factors, critical events, and core mechanisms.* Ph.D. thesis, Uppsala University, Uppsala.

Kähäri, P. (2014). *Why do regional headquarters live and die?* Ph.D. thesis. Aalto University School of Business, Helsinki.

Kähäri, P., & Piekkari, R. (2015). The evolution of a regional headquarters population: An ecological analysis. In S. Lundan (Ed.), *Transnational corporations and transnational governance* (pp. 271–296). Houndmills: Palgrave Macmillan.

Lasserre, P. (1996). Regional headquarters: The spearhead for Asia pacific markets. *Long Range Planning*, *29*, 30–37.

Laudien, S. M., & Freiling, J. (2011). Overcoming liabilities of foreignness by modes of structural coordination: Regional headquarters and their role in TNCs. *Advances in International Management*, *24*, 107–125.

Li, G.-H., Yu, C.-M., & Seetoo, D. H. (2010). Toward a theory of regional organization. *Management International Review*, *50*, 5–33.

Lovelock, C. H., & Wirtz, J. (2007). *Services marketing: People, technology, strategy* (6th ed.). Harlow: Prentice Hall.

Lovelock, C. H., & Yip, G. S. (1996). Developing global strategies for service businesses. *California Management Review*, *38*, 64–86.

Lunnan, R., & Zhao, Y. (2014). Regional headquarters in China: Role in MNE knowledge transfer. *Asia Pacific Journal of Management*, *31*, 397–422.

Marschan-Piekkari, R., & Reis, C. (2004). Language and languages in cross-cultural interviewing. In R. Marschan-Piekkari & C. Welch (Eds.), *Handbook of qualitative research methods for international business* (pp. 224–263). Cheltenham: Edward Elgar.

Oliva, R., & Kallenberg, R. (2003). Managing the transition from products to services. *International Journal of Service Industry Management*, *14*, 1–10.

Piekkari, R., Nell, P., & Ghauri, P. N. (2010). Regional management as a system: A longitudinal case study. *Management International Review*, *50*, 513–532.

Piekkari, R., & Welch, C. (Eds.). (2011). *Rethinking the case study in international business and management research.* Cheltenham: Edward Elgar.

Piekkari, R., Welch, C., & Paavilainen, E. (2009). The case study as disciplinary convention: Evidence from international business journals. *Organizational Research Methods*, *12*, 567–589.

Pla-Barber, J., & Camps, J. (2012). Springboarding: A new geographical landscape for European foreign investment in Latin America. *Journal of Economic Geography*, *12*, 519–538.

Poon, J. P. H., & Thompson, E. R. (2003). Developmental and quiescent subsidiaries in the Asia Pacific: Evidence from Hong Kong, Singapore, Shanghai, and Sydney. *Economic Geography*, *79*, 195–214.

Ramírez, R. (1999). Value co-production: Intellectual origins and implications for practice and research. *Strategic Management Journal*, *20*, 49–65.

Rugman, A. M. (2005). *The regional multinationals.* Cambridge: Cambridge University Press.

Rugman, A. M., & Verbeke, A. (2009). Location, competitiveness, and the multinational enterprise. In A. Rugman (Ed.), *The Oxford handbook of international business* (pp. 146–180). Oxford: Oxford University Press.

Salonen, A., & Jaakkola, E. (2015). Firm boundary decisions in solution business: Examining internal vs. external resource integration. *Industrial Marketing Management, 51*, 171–183. doi:10.1016/j.indmarman.2015.05.002

Schütte, H. (1997). Strategy and organisation: Challenges for European MNCs in Asia. *European Management Journal, 15*, 436–445.

Sydow, J., Schreyögg, G., & Koch, J. (2009). Organizational path dependence: Opening the black box. *Academy of Management Review, 34*, 689–709.

Vargo, S. L., & Lusch, R. F. (2004). Evolving to a new dominant logic for marketing. *Journal of Marketing, 68*, 1–17.

Wandermerwe, S., & Rada, J. (1988). Servitization of business: Adding value by adding services. *European Management Journal, 6*, 314–324.

Welch, C., & Piekkari, R. (2006). Crossing language boundaries: Qualitative interviewing in international business. *Management International Review, 46*, 417–437.

Welch, C., Piekkari, R., Plakoyiannaki, E., & Paavilainen-Mäntymäki, E. (2011). Theorising from case studies: Towards a pluralist future for international business research. *Journal of International Business Studies, 42*, 740–762.

APPENDIX

Table A1. Key Information on the Case Companies.

	Medical AG	Moulding KG	Gear GmbH	Laser KG
Personnel	approx. 10,000 (2014)	approx. 2,500 (2014)	approx. 700 (2014)	approx. 11,000 (2014)
Share of revenues abroad	80%	60%	>50%	>75%
Number of regional units	3	Only subsidiaries (but regional experts all over the service network)	7	Only subsidiaries (and regional mandates)
Location of regional units	Dubai, Malaysia, USA	No regional units	USA, UK, Finland, China, Russia, Italy, Belgium	Regional mandates in USA, China, Malaysia, Brazil
Main role of regional units	Technical support, monitoring, initiation of regional projects	No regional units	Qualification and auditing of external partners, technical support and monitoring of external service partners	Technical support
Number of own subsidiaries	60	24	7	25
Location of own subsidiaries	Every important market	Europe: 10 America: 5 Asia: 6 Africa: 2 Australia: 1	See above (location of regional units)	Europe: 11 America: 4 Asia: 8 Africa: 1 Australia: 1
Number of external service partners	30	35	125, located in 57 different countries	30

Who are the external service partners?	Ordinary companies which only carry out simple tasks	Specialized companies doing similar work as own subsidiaries, not working for other purchasers than Moulding	Specialized companies doing sales and complete ordinary after-sales services for Gear, also working for other purchasers	Specialized companies doing similar work as own subsidiaries, not working for other purchasers than Laser
Degree of servitization	Very high	High	High	Very high

STRATEGIC ANIMATION AND EMERGENT PROCESSES: MANAGING FOR EFFICIENCY AND INNOVATION IN GLOBALLY NETWORKED ORGANIZATIONS

Stephen Tallman and Mitchell P. Koza

ABSTRACT

The Globally Networked Organization (GNO) is an archetype of the geographically distributed, globally integrated, and organizationally networked information-age multinational enterprise. While its organizational form has been widely discussed, methods for providing strategic direction to all or part of a GNO have been largely overlooked. We propose the concept of strategic animation as an innovative leadership approach to strategic management in the GNO and offer a set of guiding principles for installing such a system in organizations. Strategic animation employs sophisticated incentives to motivate voluntary buy-in, utilizing principles of self-organization to replace the command and control of the unitary firm and the uncertainty and transactional costs of real markets. This makes possible virtual integration of the multiple highly

Perspectives on Headquarters-Subsidiary Relationships in the Contemporary MNC
Research in Global Strategic Management, Volume 17, 59–85
Copyright © 2016 by Emerald Group Publishing Limited
ISSN: 1064-4857/doi:10.1108/S1064-485720160000017003

separable businesses that comprise the value-added proposition of the firm and encourages the development of emergent processes for both exploitation and renewal of assets. From a scholarly perspective, this model suggests a new framework for studying the strategic direction of GNOs. For practice, it offers an organizational solution to conditions where process control is preferred, but command of resources is limited. Strategic animation, set in motion through multiple managerial actions, facilitates the timely and flexible responses to chaotic environments that are the sine qua non *of today's global businesses.*

Keywords: Global network firm; strategic animation; multinational; network firm; motivation

INTRODUCTION

The advent of an information-based world economy in recent years has expanded the possibilities for the organization and management of multinational enterprises (MNEs) dramatically. As new models for the organization of the MNE have developed over the years since Hymer (1976) introduced the concept of the modern multinational firm, we observe that each emerging model has taken on a less bureaucratic, less hierarchical organizational form (Bartlett & Ghoshal, 1989; Buckley & Casson, 1976; Ghoshal & Bartlett, 1990; Hedlund, 1986; Narula & Dunning, 2010; Tallman & Koza, 2010). In parallel, strategic management models have evolved from centrally controlled, rigidly hierarchical approaches toward more flexible behavioral models, reflecting a general trend toward mixed or hybrid models of organizational governance. As network forms of governance have developed in the organizational literature (Powell, 1990), so concepts of the multinational firm as an organizational network (Ghoshal & Bartlett, 1990) or as the locus of multiple local networks surrounding the firm's many subsidiaries (Andersson, Forsgren, & Holm, 2007) have become increasingly popular. The most recent approaches to the organization of the MNE as a decentralized international network (Cantwell, 2013) recognize that the most forward looking MNEs work with both intra-firm and inter-firm networks and network governance. However, the networks of wholly owned subsidiaries and those of suppliers, allies, contractors, and other loosely affiliated units continue to be differentiated by ownership status.

Moreover, a historical focus on "what the firm is," that is, the organizational form of the MNE, rather than on "what the does" (its strategy) or "how the firm does what it does" (its managerial mechanisms and motivations) has persisted in the discussion of multinational organizations. Strategic management within multinational enterprises generally has been seen as an issue of command and control, possibly an artifact of the international business definition of the MNE as a hierarchical solution to the failure of markets for goods (exports) and technology (licensing), rather than the consequence of pursuing strategic objectives. However, the latest generation in organizational models for multinational enterprises considers these firms as differentiated interorganizational networks (Ghoshal & Bartlett, 1990), radically decentralized heterarchies (Hedlund, 1986), global network organizations (Ghoshal & Nohria, 1989), metanationals with balanced ties between center and subsidiaries (Doz, Santos, & Williamson, 2001), or nearly virtual global multi-business firms (Tallman & Koza, 2010). Key to these models is a small corporate headquarters element that orchestrates but does not (or, in practice, cannot) apply command and control to the global value chain (GVC) of the firm (McDermott, Mudambi, & Parente, 2013). It is fairly apparent that an ownership-based, centrally controlled global bureaucracy is neither efficient nor capable of maintaining the decentralized character of a network. On the other hand, neither market nor relationship-based clan (Ouchi, 1980), network (Powell, 1990), or cultural (Bartlett & Ghoshal, 1989) models of finding common purpose seem to offer the level of effective strategic purpose needed to compete in modern global industry. The key research question for us becomes, "How can a complex, decentralized global network organization be given common strategic direction to offer innovative products and processes and to pursue organizational efficiency?"

In providing a solution to this question, we begin with two new insights on the concept of the globally networked organization (GNO). First, we find that the most forward looking MNEs are bringing the external network directly into the network of primary suppliers reporting to the international headquarters (Tallman & Koza, 2010). This contrasts with the model of an internally networked firm of headquarters and owned subsidiaries tied to multiple external networks through the linking effects of the subsidiaries that are embedded in their host country networks (Andersson et al., 2007; Cantwell, 2013; Cantwell & Mudambi, 2005; Ghoshal & Bartlett, 1990). We find that the development of modular strategies (McDermott et al., 2013), modern contracting (Grandori, 2006), and modern IT have combined to make the incorporation of external networks directly into the primary network structure of the MNE both feasible and increasingly necessary.

Second, we focus on presenting formally a set of principles that address how a globally networked firm can provide common strategic direction, pursuing objectives of both efficient organization and strategic innovation, to an intensively decentralized GNO. This is a complex question deserving of increased attention as information intensity makes such organizations more possible. We introduce considerations from the strategic management literature to offer an innovative framework describing how market and hierarchical mechanisms can be blended to guide and motivate subsidiary and affiliated firms within combined inter- and intra-firm networks (Zenger & Hesterly, 1997). These concepts allow us to propose a comprehensive and integrated framework of actions that allow GNOs to be managed for both efficiency and innovation − the bookends of a successful modern global strategy.

We propose that the concept of strategic animation (Tallman & Koza, 2010) is a possible solution to the issue of providing strategic direction to the radically decentralized GNO. Strategic animation proposes that after GNO management assembles the parts of the network, they must then create an organizational system in which the elements or units of the network are influenced to follow the strategic direction of the overall organization without central control or common culture. Subordinate units must be allowed autonomy, but within a system that rewards desired behavior with outsized benefits while punishing, or at least minimizing, the returns to behavior that destroys integration. Strategic animation proposes to extend the incentive for innovation to all network elements that will seize it, while offering strong-form market incentives to managers of units ranging from wholly owned subsidiaries to contractual alliances to maintain operational efficiencies. At its essence, strategic animation is an innovative leadership approach to strategic management in the GNO, which functions through coordination and communication to provide (1) common purpose to the far-flung and differentially governed parts of the network firm, (2) autonomy in relevant product-market activities, (3) incentives to all elements of the network to create new capabilities and resources while also pursuing individual operational efficiency, and (4) collective benefits to local subsidiary and affiliate units to encourage and support joint competence creation, diffusion, and exploitation worldwide.

We begin by reviewing key concepts addressing the MNE's development from international bureaucracy to global network organization. Then, we define strategic animation, creating a framework to describe its unique value in exploring and developing the role of the competence-creating subsidiary. We conclude with a discussion of the challenge of maintaining stability and adaptability in the new global firm, and the ways that strategic animation may contribute both in practice and in the research literature.

EVOLUTION OF THE CONCEPT OF THE INTERNATIONAL FIRM

The concept of a globally networked organization (GNO) was described by Ghoshal and Bartlett (1990). It comes from the sense that the most advanced global business firms, while they may be actively selling products in only a portion of the world's markets (Rugman, 2005), have value-adding activities in many more widely spread countries, and have certainly considered organizing their operations with the possibility of global innovation, production, and sales in mind – they take a global perspective on their entire value-adding proposition. At the same time, more and more firms are moving activities, from IT to business processes to manufacturing and marketing and even to critical activities such as product development and R&D, outside the legal boundaries of the firm. Offshore outsourcing of vital operations has become characteristic of information-age international businesses.

We consider that the GNO, as a form of international business organization, has co-evolved in concert with a fundamentally changing global business environment, with innovations in corporate strategies, and with new technological and administrative capabilities among organizations. The focus of international strategies began as the need to adapt products to differences in demand across the geographic, institutional, and cultural gaps between nations, resulting in local production rather than exports from home country sources (Buckley & Casson, 1976; Prahalad & Doz, 1987; Rugman, 1981). Globally homogeneous strategies existed, but typically were only in primary and intermediate product markets where customer needs were likewise homogeneous. The key strategic demands on most early multinational firms were related to growth and diversification of markets, often in an incremental and regionally focused (Johansson & Vahlne, 1977; Rugman, 2005) fashion, demonstrating slow mastery of the complexities of international markets and of managing multinational companies – and, we note, with slow and limited communication links between elements of the MNE. Governance options were essentially those of a price structure in the international markets for exports and licensing or of the command and control of hierarchical direction when multinationals brought international transactions inside the firm by taking ownership of them when price mechanisms failed (Buckley & Casson, 1976; Teece, 1985). National subsidiaries were generally expected to focus on local-market focused innovation while new competences originated from the parent company. Value-adding processes tended to be focused in the home country when unique technology or large economies of scale were involved or in the host market when local adaptation was required or when transportation costs and other barriers to the shipment of intermediate goods were high.

More recently, Bartlett and Ghoshal (1989) proposed the concept of the Transnational firm, which shifted the focus of global strategy away from choosing between local-market portfolios or simple scale-based economies and toward satisfying both of these demands while also leveraging knowledge assets internationally. As a result of these innovative ideas, concepts of MNE management shifted away from command and control through foreign direct investment toward a more open approach based on corporate culture and coordinated relationships between subordinate units and between subsidiaries and the headquarters (Ghoshal & Nohria, 1989). The transnational solution recognized that subsidiaries held differentiated roles, and that key Strategic Leader subsidiaries could become sources of innovation for the worldwide organization. However, this model retained a focus on wholly owned subsidiaries overseen by the headquarters. The transnational also recognized some aspects of multinational firms as network organizations (Ghoshal & Bartlett, 1990). The strict hierarchical relationships of earlier models are augmented by informal network ties among subsidiaries, such that the headquarters is not necessarily involved in every internal transaction, and subsidiaries struggle with the headquarters for a balance of internal power. The model also provided a model of governance means corresponding to their three archetypical organizational forms − centralization, formalization, and enculturation − all tied to the idea of the unitary, wholly owned if more loosely governed, firm.

Similar concepts such as the global heterarchy (Hedlund, 1986) saw headquarters' functions migrating to subordinate units, whether regionally or product-focused, greatly increasing the leadership roles of key subsidiaries and distributing responsibilities for competence creation across the organization, but only to particularly designated units. Narula and Dunning (2010) describe the multinational enterprise as no longer in thrall to foreign direct investment or full ownership, but as a production network with many direct and indirect ties between units to include the parent firm. Other studies (Andersson et al., 2007; Birkinshaw, Hood, & Jonsson, 1998) discuss subsidiary initiative and influence in multinationals, but present these as part of an internal power struggle in the networked or federated multinational firm. Cantwell (2013, p. 21) summarizes this emerging model of the networked MNE, as being "… conceptualized as integrated global networks, with multiple geographically distributed higher value creating centers." Further, he argues that "… advantages can be argued to derive from a continuous process of innovation throughout an international network …." At the same time, he proposes that growing use of open networks "… may create a new potential for tensions or conflicts with the MNC, or between subsidiaries and their local external partners" (p. 22).

This last point reflects again the two issues that are particularly relevant to our model. First, external networks are envisioned as networks of local firms tied to individual subsidiaries, which neglects the rise of external or outsourced activities within the primary value-adding network of many MNEs. Second, the idea that decentralizing authority and innovation to subsidiaries may generate resistance to strategic direction and increase managerial inefficiencies emphasizes the importance of creating a govern-ance system that can both instill incentives to align the interests of increas-ingly loosely tied network members with the strategic direction of the core MNE and maintain the level of innovation required by global competition.

ORGANIZING AND MOTIVATING THE GNO

Our model of the GNO, as an evolutionary development of earlier models, offers a vision of the modern international business organization as a net-work of geographically dispersed, value-adding processes, both owned and outsourced, that provides the flexibility and insight necessary to adapt to a dynamic global business environment in a co-evolutionary process (Tallman & Koza, 2010).[1] The GNO is consistent with Westney and Zaheer's (2009) fairly standard description of the modern MNE as an orga-nization that maintains multiple units in multiple environments. The GNO concept presented here also is consistent with Zenger and Hesterly's (1997) view of the information-age networked corporation and with the modular production model of the MNE presented by McDermott et al. (2013). It provides for widely distributed, increasingly autonomous units each pursu-ing specific value-adding activities, all with integrated access to worldwide markets and global innovation provided by the parent MNE under the gui-dance of a core headquarters function. In this way, the GNO offers the operating efficiencies that come from optimally located and controlled individual activities combined with global scope and scale provided through the integrated worldwide system. It also retains strong incentives for the sort of locally based, often outsourced, innovation that can be leveraged into new products with worldwide market potential as well as the ability to rapidly disseminate innovation to and from the center or the network.

Zenger and Hesterly (1997, p. 209) argue that the form of value production of goods and services has changed fundamentally in the face of innovations in IT, organization design and measurement systems. They provide evidence that large firms are disaggregating into smaller units with increased strategic autonomy and with mixed ownership ties. Controls of both internal and external units are converging on a mix of reward-based output controls and incentives for coordination and joint value production. This model is remarkably similar to, if stated in different fashion from, the modular organizational design of MNEs described by McDermott et al. (2013, p. 2). They describe "functional partitioning" of activities into "isolated, self-contained functional elements" with "well-defined modular interfaces" based on "technology transparency and industry standards." They point out that such modularity "greatly increases the ease and reduces the cost of using market transactions to acquire component inputs" with which a coordinating orchestrator can manage processes of outsourcing and specialization. MNEs can capture value through creation of an architecture by which networks of suppliers can be integrated to offer value to customers, even in instances where "many value orchestrators undertake no manufacturing" and even little product design.

The Global Multi-Business Firm introduced by Tallman and Koza (2010), as a specific example of a GNO, provides a strategic model of the globally networked organization in which strategic managers assemble a loose network of units into a global value-adding network. They describe strategic assembly as the process of building the multi-business multinational firm as a network organization in a manner that explicitly considers the strategic intent of top management, chooses resources and capabilities that demonstrably support that intent from the most productive, efficient locations worldwide, and organizes governance to emphasize flexibility and innovation over static control (Koza, Tallman, & Ataay, 2011). Going beyond just recognizing the possibility of non-equity and non-hierarchical ties (Ghoshal & Bartlett, 1990), the GMBF model proposes the active, even preferential pursuit of external ties that minimize capital investments even in strategically positioned units.

Once a set of assets is assembled into a combined internal (owned and partially owned units) and external (allied and contracted units) open network, strategic direction must be provided in a way that maximizes the benefits and avoids the possible weaknesses of the organization that results from this assembly process. Multiple forms of intermediate governance (Gereffi, Humphrey, & Sturgeon, 2005) are key to organizing such a loosely coupled network of modular, but interdependent activities (Brusoni, Prencipe, & Pavitt, 2001). Finding a way to provide strategic direction to such a network of activities without the ability to enforce hierarchical rules and in the face of divergent cultures is essential to the effective functioning of a globally networked firm and is the primary purpose of this research.

THE ROLE OF STRATEGIC ANIMATION IN GUIDING THE GNO

We see strategic animation as the embodiment of the organizational management processes needed to provide direction for the global network described above. The term "animation" suggests giving life, or the power to grow, act, and evolve as a self-directing network rather than responding to bureaucratic oversight. At the same time, "strategic" suggests that these are purposeful activities engaged in by the organization as a whole rather than independent local actions. Strategic animation supports emergent processes for both exploiting existing resources and capabilities and creating (or exploring for) the new or evolving assets that are essential to establish competitive advantage within competence-creating subordinate or affiliated units (Koza & Lewin, 1998, 1999). We offer mechanisms to establish, maintain, and enable the networks that encourage and guide self-organization and the negotiation of common purpose among the many locally autonomous parts of the worldwide firm.

Strategic animation is proposed as a radical change from the principles of centralization, formalization, and enculturation proposed as management tools by Bartlett and Ghoshal (1989). For network firms, centralized command and control of the entire organization is infeasible when the loose ties across differentiated units engaged in strategic activities may not include ownership – yet, a clear strategic focus is needed to guide the overall GNO. Formal reports are essential to maintaining GVCs, but in modularized systems these can only provide oversight of technical inputs and outputs, ensuring correct interfaces and sharing technical standards, but do not offer strategic direction or incentives for within-the-module innovation. The idea of cultural controls advanced strongly by Bartlett and Ghoshal (1989) requires a common organizational heritage based on home country culture. GNOs that bring together modular (McDermott et al., 2013) or molecular (Zenger & Hesterly, 1997) units from many widely spread locations through a mix of ownership, alliance, and contract ties while avoiding internal interventions offer few opportunities to create common cultures, either geographically or organizationally. Thus, the core principles of the transnational are at odds with the demands of an open network organization.

If centralization, formalization, and enculturation, or other artifacts of hierarchical control, offer minimal possibilities for animating the GNO, what mechanisms can enable strategic animation? In many ways, the "internalized market" for knowledge and other firm-specific resources, used as a metaphor by Buckley and Casson (1976) and other internalization theorists (Rugman, 1981) to describe bringing market transactions into the firm by extending ownership and converting them to hierarchical control, becomes real. Strong-form market incentives applied to contractual, allied, and even wholly owned units replace bureaucratic controls or coercive ownership-based demands (Zenger & Hesterly, 1997). However, where Rugman and Verbeke (2001, p. 247) suggest that "bounded rationality problems ... by the parent company" in managing specialized, innovative subsidiaries might cause reversion to "simple, market-based incentives," we propose that a complex system of strategic guidelines and incentives can be applied to create an internal-external quasi-market to provide both oversight and direction to the GNO's network. Strategic animation is about bringing guidance and direction to a loosely networked global organization without command and control by a closely tied bureaucracy and without relying on non-existent common values to produce parallel strategies without active intervention.

We propose that the visible and strong hand of central headquarters control and the "invisible hand" of the market be replaced by a "virtual hand" by which the headquarters combines market-like monitoring and reward structures with benefits and incentives to encourage coordination in production and innovation. Unit-level strategic decisions ultimately are made within the unit in response to these quasi-market forces. These mechanisms provide the many parts of the organization with economic and social incentives, rather than hierarchical demands, to work with a unified purpose because working within the GNO provides greater economic rewards to unit managers than not doing so. Appropriately applied, such incentives can minimize the principal-agent problem that requires oversight and monitoring under a traditional bureaucratic governance condition (Hillman & Dalziel, 2003). They also contrast with power politics approaches in which subsidiaries with strong external networks can ignore or counter the mandates of headquarters (Andersson et al., 2007; Birkinshaw et al., 1998). As well as minimizing the bureaucratic costs of traditional hierarchy, strategic animation is intended to minimize the search, selection, and monitoring costs of true market transactional governance, but to do so without losing the strong incentives of the marketplace. Increasing experience with joint ventures and alliances, improved contracting, and vastly improved communication and monitoring make both the risk of partner opportunism and the cost of coordination much lower than in the past, even without close bureaucratic oversight (Rugman & Verbeke, 2003).

The central management challenge is to encourage and manage self-organization among subsidiaries and affiliates in ways that are consistent with the ambition of the organization as a whole, including managing the opportunities for defection that self-organization may enhance. The objective is to avoid stifling subsidiary initiative through heavy-handed intervention, while still aligning the subsidiary or affiliate unit with overall objectives — on an effectively voluntary basis. The role of the headquarters (Tallman & Koza, 2010) is one of providing incentives, guidance, common systems, monitoring, and rewards and punishment for behavior rather than "active coordination" on a regular and intrusive basis.

THE MECHANISMS OF STRATEGIC ANIMATION – STRATEGY IN THE GNO

The strategic animation concept offers a set of mechanisms to the GNO in order to motivate and guide this intentionally loose combination of internal and external networks. It maintains local market incentives, local innovation, and access to local resources and capabilities while incentivizing the disparate parts of the organization to work in concert for worldwide competitive advantage. On the local level, strategic animation's primary principle is to balance the use of strong market incentives, whether a unit is under contract, part of a formal equity alliance, or wholly owned by the global organization, with effective symbolic and motivational management. The GNO realizes the benefit of melding market and hierarchical characteristics (Zenger & Hesterly, 1997) – in effect saying that ownership in the GNO is essentially irrelevant to strategic management (while still maintaining its financial implications), and that hierarchical control is not necessarily the outcome of internalization.

The purpose of such a seemingly free-wheeling approach to oversight and control is to encourage all affiliates and subsidiaries to pursue both efficient current operations as local profitability supports global performance and effective exploration for new products, resources, and competences. Exploration/exploitation and ambidexterity models (Gibson & Birkinshaw, 2004; Tushman & O'Reilly, 1996) propose the need for companies and, at least at times, units to mix activities that emphasize current performance with those focused on innovation for the future. Most such models describe specific role assignment, separation of activities by unit or by time, or some other formalized approach by which a central authority acts as traffic cop for antagonistic (or perhaps merely orthogonal) sets of activity.

We observe, however, that local innovation often begins with a serendipitous insight derived from the practice of the local organization (Brown & Duguid, 2001; Koza & Lewin, 1999) that is effectively nurtured and adapted locally, then diffused across the organization for further application. Unlike the transnational approach (Bartlett & Ghoshal, 1989) of designating Strategic Leader subsidiaries with innovation responsibilities while other subsidiary and affiliated firms play less vital roles, or Birkinshaw et al.'s (1998) distinction between head office assignment and subsidiary choice, strategic animation proposes to extend the incentive for competence creation to all network elements that will seize it. We see this, for instance, in the case of "reverse innovation" of the portable ultrasound unit by the local Chinese subsidiary of General Electric. In this case, an incentivized and alert local management was able to combine with an aware and imaginative top management to produce remarkable insights in this relatively unlikely context (Govindarajan & Ramamurti, 2011). This was not a planned effort at global innovation, but rather a practical effort at overcoming local barriers to providing a key service by adapting established technologies. That it turned into an exploration of the possibilities for selling less capable, but more flexible, technology in developed markets was serendipity, even according to the then-CEO of the company. The GNO encourages this. Not all local businesses will be effective sources of competence creation, but local managers in a fast-changing, amorphous environment need permission, encouragement, and rewards to pursue creativity when the opportunity arises.

Five key insights on building a new concept of managerial behavior outline the framework for strategic animation and specifically address issues of competence creation. These insights must be tightly integrated in order to make animation a viable form of management, as shown in Fig. 1 and described in the following sections, a condition that has made such a government form impossible on a global scale until the development of the information-intensive environment that we face today.

Virtual Integration with Strategic Purpose

Our expected outcome in Fig. 1 is described as virtual integration with strategic purpose. Traditionally, most multi-stage value-adding chains were integrated vertically – each stage of the value-adding process tightly linked to the next, usually through a combination of ownership and hierarchical governance – when timely, quality delivery of intermediate goods to the next stage of the process was critical (Porter, 1985). In a globally dispersed value chain, this suggests close oversight, strict limitations on local degrees of freedom in activity, a large investment in logistics, and generally a costly hierarchy devoted to the smooth flow of processes in what might be considered a "firm-level command economy." The difficulty of managing such intermediate processes through pure markets drives internalization of cross-border transactions (Buckley & Casson, 1976). Headquarters gives direction and expects precise adherence to that direction to provide efficient value production (Tallman & Koza, 2010). Two difficulties remain,

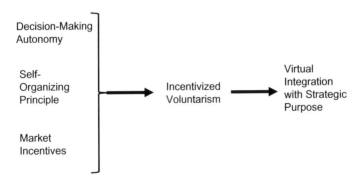

Fig. 1. The Strategic Animation System.

though: massive global bureaucracies are costly and also are inimical to the local innovation that is said to be a strength of MNEs.

Virtual Integration proposes that proper incentive structures combined with strong information and communication systems can be used to generate an "internal quasi-market" that pulls together the subsidiaries, affiliates, alliances, and contractors of the multinational firm into a vertical supply chain without the coercion and limitations of a command and control structure or the uncertainties and fear of unreliable suppliers that characterize a true market. Narula and Dunning (2010) describe the modern multinational enterprise as a global production network with a dominant lead firm, but with varied structural ties to dispersed affiliated and subsidiary firms. Structurally, a dispersed, non-hierarchical global value chain with mixed degrees of ownership is increasingly recognized as some variety of global network, but the question of how a "lead firm" can lead with limited hierarchical control of strategic activities largely remains open. This is where strategic animation becomes relevant. The benefit of disaggregating vertical bureaucracies is that the internal quasi-market "… affords an opportunity to duplicate the high-powered incentives of small firms" (Zenger & Hesterly, 1997, p. 213), and at a much lower cost than a global bureaucracy.

Under the strategic animation concept, the elements of the global value-adding chain are encouraged to focus on pursuing their own strategic interests and their own areas of expertise. They are motivated to co-specialize and cooperate with other networked units by superior incentives that offer systemic efficiency and ultimately higher returns than alternative opportunities. The key is that the GNO must offer an overall integrative architecture to strategically related, but not necessarily co-owned, modular components of the value-added chain (Brusoni et al., 2001; McDermott et al., 2013; Narula & Dunning, 2010). As Zenger and Hesterly (1997) would have it, the GNO infuses market governance elements into the hierarchy, it does not simply eliminate structure. The GNO encourages internal cooperation among vertically linked elements through such tools as investments in common IT systems, managerial rewards for coordinated actions, developing and overseeing input and output standards for modular integration, rewarding units based on customer satisfaction, exchange risk management, relationship building, engaging new members of the network and the like. The role of the HQ becomes one of reducing the transactional costs and improving the returns for the operating units in the network by taking business services and supporting activities onto itself. We see examples of such networks in the production of most electronic goods today, with branded MNEs such as Apple using networks of contractors to provide components and assembly of virtually all of their products. In a lower-technology setting, Nike has led the sport shoe industry to outsource virtually all production to foreign contract producers for years. The branded MNEs offer the rewards of product differentiation to generic manufacturers and provide integrative oversight of the network system, as well as dealing with regulatory and activist inputs, providing market intelligence, and assuming other burdens that would be expensive, if not impossible, for the specialist outsourcing suppliers to carry themselves.

The intention is that all units within the GNO's quasi-market network of value-adding subsidiaries and affiliates retain the strategic freedom to respond to incentives to pursue product and process innovations, but also are willing to commit to joint strategic goals and economic efficiencies, much as would happen in a real market. If Foxconn's factories in China fail to deliver iPhones on schedule, Apple will fail – but if Apple loses confidence in Foxconn, the latter will lose huge and lucrative contracts. On the other hand, if GE managed its Chinese subsidiary tightly for efficient production, rather than as a "local growth team" with much autonomy, the portable ultrasound machine might not exist (Govindarajan & Ramamurti, 2011). Porter (1985) describes the vital importance of linking the steps of the value chain. In the widely dispersed network of the GNO, unrestricted flows of highly accurate information about capabilities, pricing, and incentives are essential to provide the links between value-adding activities and are the responsibility of the headquarters (Tallman & Koza, 2010).

Incentivized Voluntarism

The key behavior that drives the potential for success of virtual integration as we describe it has been called "incentivized voluntarism" among the managers of the various businesses and activities tied to the GNO (Tallman & Koza, 2010). Convincing multiple loosely tied companies to participate reliably over time as strategic links in a global value-adding chain in the face of alternative market opportunities requires voluntary acceptance – avoiding the coercive aspect of hierarchical management is the entire point of the model. Voluntary decisions and actions that benefit manager, business, and global MNE are motivated by traditional incentives such as measurement and reward systems, albeit in highly innovative settings, but also by the benefits of shaping the relatively plastic preferences of organizational actors (cf., Koza & Thoenig, 2003). In a classic hierarchical multinational scheme, managers are directed to engage in activities, particularly those that work to their perceived disadvantage, creating potential agency issues within the hierarchy. Innovation among affiliated alliances is limited by contractually specified roles and by fears that core knowledge may be exposed to an unreliable alliance partner, limiting the access of the alliance to the multinational firm. In particular, relatively few incentives exist for local subsidiaries to push highly innovative activities. Tight financial controls and bureaucratic oversight suggest that the investments typically needed for competence creation will be discouraged, if not punished, for local managers, and the lack of systems to disseminate innovation throughout the firm will limit the overall value of local innovation.

Tight formal or centralized control may generate the sort of efficiencies that MNEs seek, but will not support the level of innovation that virtual integration requires. Cultural controls are touted for widely dispersed organizations, and may play some role, but as outsourcing and the integration of external with internal networks have become common practices, finding a common corporate (or home country) culture that runs throughout the network is a hopeless cause. That is not to say that some sense of direction at the center, some formalized measures to control inputs and outputs between modular activities, and some sense of common purpose do not exist and do not have value, but when applied alone with a necessarily light touch to differentiated network members, these tools are inadequate. Managers in value-generating units must willingly contribute, foregoing the opportunism that lies at the heart of transaction cost and internalization models (Teece, 1985). Strategic animation proposes that virtually integrated global value networks can use natural behavioral inclinations and appropriate incentives to develop quasi-market conditions that will keep the GNO functioning successfully.

Zenger and Hesterly (1997) characterize such processes as infusing hierarchy into markets. They find that efficient performance often requires investment in specialized physical or human assets, but that small units tend to resist such investment without safeguards. Instead of the guarantees of internalization, they propose that the use of monitoring and communication enhanced by IT allows units to observe their immediate suppliers and customers, while feedback tied to reward systems can replace direction. Cantwell (2013) suggests that the MNE offers such an institutional system to protect the IP of its networked units. Compensation schemes tied to customer (even network-wide) satisfaction can be used to incentivize individual managers to act as reliable elements of a network as effectively as ownership authority. Such mechanisms are intended to lead unit managers to commit voluntarily to working within the MNE's network rather than seeking alternative organizations or trying to compete on their own in the open market.

In the multinational model, country managers compete for the attention of the center in a zero-sum struggle for position. In the transnational model, certain subsidiaries are designated "strategic leaders" and encouraged to focus on competence creation, but other subsidiaries and affiliates are assigned roles that encourage locally exploitative, efficiency-oriented strategies (Bartlett & Ghoshal, 1989). In the multinational network, Ghoshal and Bartlett (1990) predict struggles for dominance between subsidiaries as leaders of local networks and the headquarters, with uncertain and varied outcomes. However, in the GNO, assembly of an internal/external network of affiliates and subsidiaries controlled through market-like means with strong incentives to maximize long-term returns offers a different approach to strategic management. Zenger and Hesterly (1997, p. 216) say that, "measurement advances and organizational innovations allow aggressive infusion of market control within the hierarchy." Local managers can be incentivized to pursue innovative ideas for products, resources, or capabilities – to create competences – if they perceive that doing this for the organization will also benefit them and their units. At the same time, carefully considered incentives can impose hierarchy-like limitations on local managers by rewarding them for directing their energies into activities that benefit their network partners as well. Internal quasi-markets, loose structures that offer autonomous decision authority and joint performance-oriented incentives, are intended to encourage all the multiple businesses owned by and affiliated with the GNO to work together in their own best interest – but also in the best interest of the network.

Decision-Making Autonomy and Separable Businesses

Voluntarism cannot occur without the freedom to make decisions based on an unbiased assessment of local advantage. Nor can a market function effectively if the various component members are or are perceived to be differently endowed with decision-making capacity. Therefore, to make this envisioned "internal/external quasi-market" function efficiently all subordinate units must be able to act, in so far as possible, as quasi-independent businesses. Even wholly owned subsidiaries must be provided with market or market-like incentives to coordinate and combine outputs in order to maximize their value-adding processes — the ability to act like independent small businesses. Individual activities are treated as profit centers, but, more importantly, as separable (even if not separate) businesses along both value chain and geographical location dimensions. Zenger and Hesterly (1997) maintain that infusing market incentives into ownership structures is more effective for small units, as their actions can be observed directly and incentives applied more directly, and also because they are too small to operate efficiently on their own. Our concept suggests that activities be made "separable," as if they actually were real single-business elements that engage each other on a market basis. This forces individual businesses to maintain a sharp competitive outlook, even when dealing with commonly owned units. Joint ventures and contractual alliances must be offered similar roles, possibly through the sort of board governance mechanisms suggested by Reuer, Klijn, van den Bosch, and Volberda (2011). The key to separability is allowing, even forcing, the managers of each unit to become autonomous strategic decision makers — while continuing to offer incentives to make decisions that benefit the GNO as a whole.

A major benefit of organizing the entire system as a multi-business network is that subsidiaries can be spun off into suppliers or alliance partners acquired without changing their status in the system. Investment and legal ownership change, but by retaining their separable business identities throughout the system, the strategic engagement of the units need not change. Each unit retains the right to pursue autonomous competence creation for innovative value-adding potential, but also is provided with a reduced risk of catastrophic failure by working within the virtual integration network. Thus, every unit can be offered autonomy, but with incentives to act in concert with the rest of the network. We see this sort of spinoff of value-adding activities in many industries today, from the aforementioned Apple and Nike, to the automotive industry where more and more components and subassemblies are brought together by the branded OEMs from networks of both external and commonly owned suppliers (MacDuffie, 2013), to the creation of Genpact as an independent company that still provides business process consulting to GE through long-term contracts (Chandrasekhar & Chen, 2009). We also see that Boeing, in the face of failure of its poorly organized and managed network of suppliers for the 787 Dreamliner, acquired several suppliers and took on a much more directive role in coordinating others — but did not have to eliminate or replace suppliers in the face of crises (Kotha & Srikanth, 2013).

Market Incentives for Separable Businesses

Allowing an internal quasi-market of separable businesses to function requires that single-business managers be subject to market-like incentives. Allowing component units access to external customers and suppliers (a fairly common option even in vertically integrated firms) can maintain the discipline of the larger market, as can permitting downstream units to use other suppliers when more efficient. Innovation can be encouraged in this system by offering comparable risk-reward outcomes to business managers to those offered externally to entrepreneurial owners, to include bonuses, equity grants, strategic independence, protection from short-term market challenges, and even real independence. Rather than creating multinational R&D units with governance structures, internal rules and roles, and a hierarchical management, the GNO can create market-like outcome incentives that will encourage local innovation − from all businesses, not just designated strategic leaders − and formal and informal connections across the network when business managers perceive these to be to their benefit.

At the same time, by rewarding systemically beneficial innovation more than purely local innovation the GNO can encourage sharing of concepts, resources, capabilities, and knowledge throughout the network without large investments in centralized capabilities. Markets are said to offer strong managerial incentives for pursuing sustained competitive advantage at a minimal cost. We propose that offering similar incentives, but with network support, to strategically assembled elements, whether owned, allied, or contracted, can support effective decision making for superior overall performance at a minimal bureaucratic cost within the GNO. We see international network organizations in professional services, for instance, subsidizing (and requiring) network members to move to common network software. Firms such as Apple or Nike with massive investments in design and branding offer access to lucrative product differentiation strategies to manufacturing contractors who would otherwise be forced into cutthroat cost competition. Boeing and Airbus in jet aircraft and the automotive assemblers in general offer system integration, final product design, sales and marketing skills, and branding to their suppliers that would be impossible for most of these firms to build on their own. The result is that component or production contracts can be defended through biasing market forces with incentives. If the second-best alternative for a supplier is significantly less attractive, then economic self-interest tends to ensure "trustworthy" behavior. Over time, such ties generate levels of co-specialization that make breaking contractual alliances the equivalent of selling off an internal division (Madhok & Tallman, 1998). This contrasts with the position of Andersson et al. (2007), that a more autonomous, externally embedded subsidiary, when faced with an imposed bureaucratic system, can ignore or subvert the system. Autonomy breeds initiative and creativity; our principles for strategic animation are intended to keep these aimed in the common direction – hence virtual integration *with strategic purpose.*

Zenger and Hesterly (1997) describe how innovations in measurement capabilities (innovations that have advanced considerably in subsequent years) combined with smaller, disaggregated sub-units allow firms to manage outputs in an increasingly market-like manner. Gulati and Puranam (2009) describe "compensatory fit" situations where there are large gains to ambidextrous solutions and a strong informal organizational architecture that can complement, rather than supplement, the formal architecture. Such managerial processes are particularly appropriate to geographically dispersed GNOs. The mixed internal/external network certainly offers both formal and informal architectures, and the parallel drives for efficiency and innovation that characterize the strategies of modern MNEs offer a classic setting for ambidexterity.

Instincts for Self-Organization and Emergent Processes

Self-organization refers to the natural tendency for individuals to organize collectivities to pursue common interests (cf., Bowles, 2009; Darwin, 1871). By working to reduce information asymmetries within the GNO, subsidizing process investment, supporting exchange negotiations, rewarding managers for improving efficiency, jointly offering significant rewards for successful innovation and competence creation, and organizing joint business services, top management can make the internal quasi-market more efficient than external markets, but still allow multiple businesses to come together "naturally." By providing strong incentives for innovation and efficiency in the form of profits at the unit level, and subsidizing the cost of integration within the network to make it more profitable than alternative external ties, the GNO can harness the power of self-organization to mutual benefit. Fjeldstadt, Snow, Miles, and Lettl (2012, p. 739) provide evidence that an "actor-oriented scheme" of organization will allow "[r]eliance on self-organization and local decision making in the development and delivery of complex products and services." Key to their actor orientation is extending the self-organizing aspect of internet architecture by which nodes determine the optimal routes for their own traffic to organization design.

The center focuses on matchmaking, communication, and incentives (described by Fjeldstadt et al., 2012, as protocols, processes, and infrastructures) and allows the quasi-autonomous units to sort out their exact ties. Hewlett-Packard, for instance, was actively involved in such activities to create "internal joint ventures" among its European global business units in 1996. Toyota and other automotive assemblers have complex webs of suppliers in which they control the top level or two, but accept more distant suppliers so long as quality and performance are not harmed. Put in close contact, whether geographically, organizationally, or virtually through IT systems, managers and their sub-units will tend to interact and build common interests through common practice (Brown & Duguid, 2001). The GNO sets the stage properly and provides incentives to align local and systemic needs to have the internal quasi-market network develop as an emergent outcome of this instinctual human tendency. Top management can work to maintain virtual integration with decision-making autonomy and market-like incentives to encourage efficient emergent processes, while refraining from mandating transfers or transfer prices. If the current internal market is not the efficient solution for pulling together businesses into a value-adding chain, then the headquarters must rethink its strategy, disassemble/reassemble its networks, and strengthen internal connections. Thus, creating multinational research, product development, production, or marketing networks need not require massive investments in bureaucratic control mechanisms, but only an efficient path to superior local and global performance coupled with proper incentives for desired outcomes.

The System as a Whole

Together, these five insights suggest that the GNO can be given strategic purpose and direction through animation – giving it life, then letting it run – rather than by hierarchical pressure or vague cultural and relational ties. Andersson et al. (2007) describe a "federated MNC," with loose bureaucratic controls, but a constant struggle for power between (wholly owned) subsidiaries and the headquarters. Cantwell (2013) describes an open system, but external networks are created by subsidiaries locally and interface with the MNE only through the subsidiary acting as linking pin. Properly supported and rewarded, we maintain that the businesses that are elements of the GNO will tend to organize themselves voluntarily into efficient chains of internal and external elements to keep a sharp eye for innovations in technologies, organization, products, and markets. By offering superior outcomes for coordinated activity, the firm as a whole can encourage and reward cooperative solutions rather than multiple locally efficient and competing solutions and opportunistic raids. Top management does not need to manage a highly complex system. In such networked organizations, Zenger and Hesterly (1997, p. 216) suggest, and we fully concur, that "… the formal legal distinction has become the *only* difference between market and hierarchical governance." We would go farther to suggest that neither hierarchical nor market governance as such occurs in the GNO – the hybrid system described above is an integrated approach that supplants both pure market and hierarchy.

DISCUSSION

The loosely controlled network of the GNO seems to be particularly appropriate to sectors in which innovation comes from frequent engagement experiences of individuals, country organizations, businesses, and the like more than from formal research and development. In such organizations, innovations and new competencies can arise serendipitously anywhere at any time. With a project orientation, assembling and reassembling vertical structures is essential – parts must work effectively with relatively short preparation time, but must be disassembled and applied to new projects to maintain efficient performance. At the same time, finding the proper incentives to maintain cooperation and control excessive individualism is an ongoing challenge.

Brusoni et al. (2001), focusing on technological value-adding chains, demonstrated that under conditions of unpredictable technological advances or of uncertain product interdependence, firms create loosely coupled organizations. Core firms outsource modular components of the process to specialists while maintaining "systems knowledge" about the architecture of the overall system and sufficient technical knowledge to monitor outsourcers. They suggest that a clear division of a value chain into arms-length ties occurs only in very stable systems. Systems integrators, like the GNO, delegate component level technology exploitation and exploration decisions while retaining control of the integration architecture and monitoring for new concepts leading to architectural change (Brusoni et al., 2001; Henderson & Clark, 1990). We look at similar divisions, although at a higher organizational level, as the key to managing strategic assembly in a chaotic global environment. We go further, though, in presenting a detailed system for managing a loosely coupled network – or, in Brusoni et al.'s (2001) typology, a network of mixed uncoupled, loosely coupled, and tightly coupled units – strategically as part of a coevolving and chaotic system.

We see this sort of firm emerging in various industries. Apple's global, and largely contractual, supply chain for iPads and iPhones uses many of the concepts that are incorporated into strategic animation. Li & Fung, the trading company based in Hong Kong, largely manages virtual supply chains for a variety of clients. Renault's Turkish affiliates provide an example of strategic assembly, and they are largely managed through animation principles (Koza et al., 2011). Fjeldstadt et al. (2012) provide four examples, from Accenture to Linux to Blade.org to the Network Centric Operations of NATO, of collaborative networks in increasingly network-focused businesses. However, operating such network organizations is not easy – and is particularly reliant on the selection of members and creation of the architectural rules for the network. Boeing created something very much like a GNO for production of the 787 Dreamliner (Kotha & Srikanth, 2013), providing its first tier suppliers with detailed specifications for complex assemblies, but leaving detailed design to its partners. Despite experience with outsourced component production in a more controlled architecture, Boeing proved to have inadequate organizational skills to ensure that components were on time and to specification, resulting in more than two years of delay in launching the 787. Boeing failed to ensure that all suppliers were technically capable, but also failed to create the incentives or systems for adequate coordination between suppliers who were dependent on each other. Once failure set in, Boeing had to take a more directive approach to integration, to include acquiring some of its suppliers. Giving autonomy without incentives to cooperate or systems to allow self-organization led to failure and demonstrates the need to approach strategic animation as a complete system, not a set of partial solutions that can be chosen or not at will.

CONCLUSION

We offer the vision of a new type of strategic direction – strategic animation to provide life, motivation, and direction – for a new type of firm in a new setting, that of the global information economy. Decision-making autonomy and market incentives in support of instincts for self-organization to incentivize voluntary support of virtually integrated global value networks – the five elements of strategic animation described above – constitute the morphology of strategic animation. Each element contributes to infusing and managing the life force in an organization, which in turn sustains and nurtures the GNO in a coevolving process of mutual adaptation with an evolving global business environment. The loosely structured, lightly controlled, flexible and innovative network firm, of which the GNO is an example, has many advantages in the rapidly evolving modern global business environment. However, orchestrating such an assortment of subsidiaries, affiliates, joint ventures, and alliances to compete successfully while not sacrificing the benefits of loose structure has been a matter of some concern to global strategy. Creating competence-creating subsidiaries and affiliates in a world where the source of the "next great idea," both geographically and technologically, is indeterminate even in the near future is a great challenge. Strategic animation offers a way to encourage all affiliated units of a global firm to become potential sources of new competencies and to allow market forces, both inside and outside the firm to sort the winners and losers.

We conclude with the observation that the ubiquity of self-organization and the natural tendency to organize may offer an opportunity to rethink elements of the management literature on global organizations. Rather than treating such tendencies as "the informal organization" (cf., the classic works by Mayo, 1933, 1945 or Roethlisberger & Dickson, 1939 through to the more modern variant of social network theory), which depicted such phenomena as a potential friction in effective management, or as a parallel system to be infused into a separate formal organization (Gulati & Puranam, 2009), we believe that the time is right for a new management research focus on the possibility and implications of systematic social bias, which could mirror closely the behavioral economics finding of systematic cognitive bias. Just as individuals may evidence evolutionarily produced cognitive bias in decision-making, groups may exhibit social biases in patterns of organization. Both may derive from evolutionary paths affecting the *species*. One does not need to be a student of reality television or a fan of William Golding's *Lord of the Flies* (1954) to observe that if you put a group of people on a desert island they do not go to war; first they create teams/tribes and then they go to war. How can this natural tendency to organization be harnessed for value creating activity? What special issues are raised in the highly diverse, geographically complex global organizations that we study? We believe that these processes go to the heart of the effectiveness of strategic animation as an approach to managing global organizations and their adaptation to evolving environments.

NOTE

1. We refer to our core construct as an "organization" rather than a firm, because some definitions of "the firm" require ownership as a starting assumption, and as will be seen, we see ownership, especially whole ownership, as a legal, but not strategic, construct. We also see many of the "action rules" that we propose as having a place in non-economic organizations.

REFERENCES

Andersson, U., Forsgren, M., & Holm, U. (2007). Balancing subsidiary influence in the federated MNC: A business network view. *Journal of International Business Studies*, *38*(5), 802–818.

Bartlett, C. A., & Ghoshal, S. (1989). *Managing across borders: The transnational solution.* Boston, MA: Harvard Business School Press.

Birkinshaw, J., Hood, N., & Jonsson, S. (1998). Building firm-specific advantages in multinational corporations: The role of subsidiary initiative. *Strategic Management Journal*, *19*, 221–241.

Bowles, S. (2009). Did warfare among ancestral hunter-gatherers affect the evolution of human social behavior? *Science*, *324*, 1293–1298.

Brown, J. S., & Duguid, P. (2001). Knowledge and organization : A social-practice perspective. *Organization Science*, *12*, 190–213.

Brusoni, S., Prencipe, A., & Pavitt, K. (2001). Knowledge specialization, organizational coupling, and the boundaries of the firm: Why do firms know more than they do? *Administrative Science Quarterly*, *46*(4), 597–621.

Buckley, P. J., & Casson, M. (1976). *The future of the multinational enterprise.* London: Macmillan.

Cantwell, J. (2013). Blurred boundaries between firms, and new boundaries within (large, multinational) firms: The impact of decentralized networks for innovation. *Seoul Journal of Economics*, *26*(1), 1–32.

Cantwell, J., & Mudambi, R. (2005). MNE competence-creating subsidiary mandates. *Strategic Management Journal*, *26*(12), 1109–1128.

Chandrasekhar, R., & Chen, S.-F. (2009). *Genpact Inc. – Business process outsourcing to India.* London: Richard Ivey School of Business.

Darwin, C. (1871). *The descent of man, and selection in relation to sex.* London: John Murray.

Doz, Y., Santos, J., & Williamson, P. (2001). *From global to metanational: How companies win in the knowledge economy.* Boston, MA: Harvard Business School Press.

Fjeldstadt, O. D., Snow, C. C., Miles, R. E., & Lettl, C. (2012). The architecture of collaboration. *Strategic Management Journal*, *33*, 734–750.

Gereffi, G., Humphrey, J., & Sturgeon, T. (2005). The governance of global value chains. *Review of International Political Economy*, *12*(1), 78–104.

Ghoshal, S., & Bartlett, C. A. (1990). The multinational corporation as an interorganizational network. *Academy of Management Review*, *15*(4), 603–625.

Ghoshal, S., & Nohria, N. (1989). Internal differentiation within multinational corporations. *Strategic Management Journal*, *10*, 323–337.

Gibson, C. B., & Birkinshaw, J. (2004). The antecedents, consequences, and mediating role of organizational ambidexterity. *Academy of Management Journal*, *47*(2), 209–226.

Golding, W. (1954). *The lord of the flies*. London: Faber and Faber.

Govindarajan, V. J., & Ramamurti, R. (2011). Reverse innovation, emerging markets and global strategy. *Global Strategy Journal*, *1*(3–4), 191–205.

Grandori, A. (2006). Innovation, uncertainty and relational governance. *Industry and Innovation*, *13*(2), 127–133.

Gulati, R., & Puranam, P. (2009). Renewal through reorganization: The value of inconsistencies between formal and informal organization. *Organization Science*, *20*(2), 422–440.

Hedlund, G. (1986). The hypermodern MNC – A heterarchy? *Human Resource Management*, *25*(1), 9–35.

Henderson, R. M., & Clark, K. B. (1990). Architectural innovation: The reconfiguration of existing product technologies and the failure of established firms. *Administrative Science Quarterly*, *35*, 9–30.

Hillman, A. J., & Dalziel, T. (2003). Boards of directors and firm performance: Integrating agency and resource dependency perspectives. *Academy of Management Review*, *28*(3), 383–396.

Hymer, S. H. (1976). *The international operations of foreign firms: A study of direct foreign investment*. Cambridge, MA: MIT. (Originally, Ph.D. dissertation, MIT, 1960).

Johansson, J., & Vahlne, J. E. (1977). The internationalization process of the firm: A model of knowledge development and increasing market commitments. *Journal of International Business Studies*, *8*, 23–32.

Kotha, S., & Srikanth, K. (2013). Managing a global partnership model: Lessons from the Boeing 787 'dreamliner' program. *Global Strategy Journal*, *3*, 41–66.

Koza, M. P., & Lewin, A. Y. (1998). The co-evolution of strategic alliances. *Organization Science*, *9*(3), 255–264.

Koza, M. P., & Lewin, A. Y. (1999). The co-evolution of network alliances: A longitudinal analysis of an international professional service network. *Organization Science*, *10*(5), 638–653.

Koza, M. P., Tallman, S., & Ataay, A. (2011). The strategic assembly of global firms: A micro-structural analysis of local learning and global adaptation. *Global Strategy Journal*, *1*(1), 27–46.

Koza, M. P., & Thoenig, J. C. (2003). Rethinking the firm: Organizational approaches. *Organization Studies*, *24*(8), 1219–1229.

MacDuffie, J. P. (2013). Modularity-as-property, modularization-as-process, and 'modularity'-as-frame: Lessons from the product architecture initiatives in the global automotive industry. *Global Strategy Journal*, *3*(1), 8–40.

Madhok, A., & Tallman, S. (1998). Resources, transactions, and rents: Managing value through interfirm collaborative relationships. *Organization Science*, *9*(3), 326–339.

Mayo, E. (1933). *The human problems of an industrial civilisation* (2nd ed.). Boston, MA: Harvard University Graduate School of Business Administration.

Mayo, E. (1945). *The social problems of an industrial civilization.* Boston, MA: Division of Research, Harvard University Graduate School of Business Administration.

McDermott, G., Mudambi, R., & Parente, R. (2013). Strategic modularity and the architecture of the multinational firm. *Global Strategy Journal, 3*(1), 1–7.

Narula, R., & Dunning, J. H. (2010). Multinational enterprises, development and globalization: Some clarifications and a research agenda. *Oxford Development Studies, 38*(3), 263–287.

Ouchi, W. G. (1980). Markets, bureaucracies and clans. *Administrative Science Quarterly, 25,* 129–141.

Porter, M. E. (1985). *Competitive advantage: Creating and sustaining superior performance.* New York, NY: The Free Press.

Powell, W. W. (1990). Neither market nor hierarchy: Network forms of organization. *Research in Organizational Behavior, 12,* 295–336.

Prahalad, C. K., & Doz, Y. (1987). *The multinational mission: Balancing local demands and global integration.* New York, NY: The Free Press.

Reuer, J., Klijn, E., van den Bosch, F. A. J., & Volberda, H. (2011). Bringing corporate governance to international joint ventures. *Global Strategy Journal, 1*(1), 54–66.

Roethlisberger, F. J., & Dickson, W. J. (1939). *Management and the worker: An account of a research program conducted by the Western electric company, Hawthorne works, Chicago.* Cambridge, MA: Harvard University Press.

Rugman, A. M. (1981). *Inside the multinationals: The economics of internal markets.* New York, NY: Columbia University Press. (Reissued by Palgrave Macmillan, 2006).

Rugman, A. M. (2005). *The regional multinationals.* Cambridge: Cambridge University Press.

Rugman, A. M., & Verbeke, A. (2001). Subsidiary-specific advantages in multinational enterprises. *Strategic Management Journal, 22,* 237–250.

Rugman, A. M., & Verbeke, A. (2003). Extending the theory of the multinational enterprise: Internalization and strategic management perspectives. *Journal of International Business Studies, 34*(2), 125–137.

Tallman, S., & Koza, M. P. (2010). Keeping the global in mind: The evolution of the headquarters' role in global multi-business firms. *Management International Review, 50,* 433–448.

Teece, D. J. (1985). Multinational enterprise, internal governance, and industrial organization. *American Economic Review, 75*(2), 233–238.

Tushman, M. L., & O'Reilly, C. A. (1996). The ambidextrous organization: Managing evolutionary and revolutionary change. *California Management Review, 38,* 1–23.

Westney, D. E., & Zaheer, S. (2009). The multinational enterprise as an organization. In A. M. Rugman (Ed.), *The Oxford handbook of international business* (pp. 341–366). Oxford: Oxford University Press.

Zenger, T. R., & Hesterly, W. S. (1997). The disaggregation of corporations: Selective intervention, high-powered incentives, and molecular units. *Organization Science, 8*(3), 209–222.

THE AGENCY PERSPECTIVE FOR STUDYING HEADQUARTERS-SUBSIDIARY RELATIONS: AN ASSESSMENT AND CONSIDERATIONS FOR FUTURE RESEARCH

Adrian Schulte Steinberg and Sven Kunisch

ABSTRACT

Despite the increasing use of the agency perspective in studies of head-quarters-subsidiaries relations in the multinational corporation (MNC), opponents fundamentally question its utility. In an attempt to contribute to this debate, we evaluate prior studies and develop considerations for future research. Our review of extant studies of headquarters-subsidiaries relations that make (explicit) use of the agency perspective reveals two significant shortcomings. First, we identify a need to validate the underlying assumptions when using the agency perspective in studies of head-quarters-subsidiaries relations. Second, we detect a need to better account for the complex nature of headquarters-subsidiary relations in

Perspectives on Headquarters-Subsidiary Relationships in the Contemporary MNC
Research in Global Strategic Management, Volume 17, 87–118
Copyright © 2016 by Emerald Group Publishing Limited
ISSN: 1064-4857/doi:10.1108/S1064-485720160000017004

the MNC. A focus on these two areas can improve the use of the agency perspective and, ultimately, help resolve the contentious debate over the utility of the agency perspective.

Keywords: Headquarters-subsidiary relation; agency theory; multinational corporation

INTRODUCTION

In their examinations of the relations between headquarters and subsidiaries in multinational corporations (MNCs), scholars have used a variety of theoretical lenses (see, e.g., Andersson & Holm, 2010; Kostova, Marano, & Tallman, 2016; Kunisch, Menz, & Ambos, 2015; Menz, Kunisch, & Collis, 2015). In this chapter, we focus on the use of the agency perspective for studying headquarters-subsidiaries relations – a common perspective for this context (Fama & Jensen, 1983; Jensen & Meckling, 1976; O'Donnell, 2000; Roth & O'Donnell, 1996). This perspective suggests that the headquarters is a principal that delegates tasks to its subsidiaries, which are the agents, and that headquarters and subsidiaries have different self-interests and levels of information. These "attributes of headquarters-subsidiary relations make them very similar to principal-agent relationships" (Nohria & Ghoshal, 1994, p. 492).

Despite the continuous use of the agency perspective in studies of MNC headquarters-subsidiaries relations, its utility remains subject to widespread debate. On the one hand, proponents argue that the perspective is valuable for shedding light on various aspects of headquarters-subsidiary relations, such as knowledge flows (Blomkvist, 2012), top management compensation (Fey & Furu, 2008), or subsidiary staffing (Gong, 2003). Furthermore, some scholars from this camp even claim that agency theory is underutilized in studies of headquarters-subsidiary relations and that studies could profit from more diligent exploration (Hoenen & Kostova, 2014; Kostova, Marano, & Tallman, 2016; Kostova, Nell, & Hoenen, in press).

On the other hand, critics question the fundamental utility of the agency perspective because of its strong assumptions (for a related argument, see Lane, Cannella, & Lubatkin, 1998). For example, Johnson and Medcof (2007) mention that the assumptions of agency theory might be too strict in the headquarters-subsidiary context, a view that is in line with those of other critics who highlight an undue degree of simplification (Doz &

Prahalad, 1991). Scholars in this camp also claim that overcoming this simplification by looking at individual actors adds too much complexity, as there are then many principals and many agents, and the agency relationships become blurred (O'Donnell, 2000).

In its attempt to contribute to this debate, this chapter has two goals. First, from a *descriptive* standpoint, we aim to evaluate how the agency perspective has been used in prior studies of headquarters-subsidiary relations in the MNC. Specifically, we scrutinize how prior studies have explicitly or implicitly considered the assumptions, as well as which areas of investigation have received the most attention. This first step aims to evaluate the grounds for the prevalent critiques of the agency perspective's strict assumptions and its over-simplification of reality. Second, from a *prescriptive* standpoint, we highlight two considerations that will allow for the more effective use of the agency perspective. First, we discuss the need to consider and validate the underlying assumptions when using the agency perspective in studies of headquarters-subsidiaries relations. Second, with respect to the focal phenomena, we detect a need to better account for the complex nature of headquarters-subsidiary relations in the MNC.

It is important to note that we do not discuss the general utility of the agency perspective for studying headquarters-subsidiary relations. Instead, we believe that fostering a more considerate use of the perspective in studies of headquarters-subsidiary relations will eventually resolve the debate concerning its utility in this context. Our evaluation, therefore, is intended to help researchers identify appropriate research questions and foundations that should be considered when applying an agency theory lens.

CONCEPTUAL BACKGROUND AND APPROACH

We now first review the general assumptions of agency theory, and then discuss them in the context of headquarters-subsidiary relations.

The Underlying Assumptions of the Agency Perspective

Agency theory, which is rooted financial economics research, describes the relation that stems from a principal delegating a task to an agent (Jensen & Meckling, 1976). As it targets the owner-manager context, agency theory is mainly concerned with the principal's need to ensure that the agent acts in the principal's best interests and maximizes the principal's outcomes given risk attitudes and information asymmetries (Fama & Jensen, 1983; Jensen & Meckling, 1976). This agency relation between a principal and an agent balances the risk-reward expectations of both parties (Eisenhardt, 1985, 1989; Fama & Jensen, 1983; Jensen & Meckling, 1976). The relationship is governed by controls the principal applied toward the agent. Principals control behavior when there are no information asymmetries or it is cost optimal for principals to (re-) establish perfect information. If principals face risks arising from agents' information advantages, they shift to controlling outcomes instead of behavior. The control choice is also influenced by several key tenets, such as the measurability of outcomes, outcome uncertainty, task programmability, and the length of the relationship (Eisenhardt, 1989).

In her seminal article, Eisenhardt (1989) laid out three sets of assumptions underlying principal-agent relations (for a summary, see Table 1): (1) human assumptions, (2) organizational assumptions, and (3) information assumptions. With regard to *human assumptions*, both parties have an

Table 1.   Agency Assumptions regarding Headquarters-
Subsidiary Relations.

	In Agency Theory	In Headquarters-Subsidiary Relations
Unit of analysis	Relation between principal and agent	Relation between headquarters (principal) and subsidiary (agent)
Human assumption	Self-interest	Optimization of benefits for the MNC (increase maximum rents) and the subsidiary (absorb maximum rents)
	Bounded rationality	Decision making at headquarters and subsidiaries subject to bounded rationality
	Risk attitudes	Headquarters less risk averse than subsidiaries
Organizational assumptions	(Partial) goal conflict	Fulfillment of maximum desires of both headquarters and the subsidiary is impossible in the relationship
	Efficiency-as-effectiveness criterion	Headquarters knows what maximizes MNC benefits and what the efficient achievement of those benefits looks like
	Information asymmetry	Subsidiaries have some kind of knowledge or skill advantage that is impossible or too costly for headquarters to access
Information assumption	Information as a purchasable commodity	Headquarters can invest in information gathering to reduce the knowledge or skill advantages of subsidiaries

Source: Based on Eisenhardt (1989).

interest in maximizing their welfare. Furthermore, they make decisions under conditions of bounded rationality. However, they have different attitudes toward risk. Principals can diversify their investments and are risk neutral, while managers are risk averse because they cannot easily find other employment. In terms of the relation between principal and agent, there are three *organizational assumptions*. First, principals and agents have conflicting goals. Second, principals are assumed to know which outcomes would be in their best interest, meaning that efficient implementation of the principal's best interest equals effective welfare maximization for the principal. Third, agents are assumed to have better knowledge than the principal about their own contexts or abilities, which creates information asymmetries between the principal and the agent. Moreover, agency theory encompasses an *information assumption* – the belief that the principal can invest in obtaining complete information, although doing so may not be cost optimal.

These assumptions need to be considered when headquarters-subsidiary relations are conceptualized as an agency relation. On an abstract level, the headquarters is generally viewed as the principal, while subsidiaries are viewed as the agents, and both have self-interest. Headquarters wish to maximize value for shareholders and, thereby, the MNC (i.e., create maximum rents for distribution), while subsidiaries want to maximize their rent absorption. Furthermore, decision making at headquarters and subsidiaries is subject to bounded rationality, and subsidiaries are generally risk averse, while headquarters are less risk averse or risk neutral. Fulfillment of the goals of both principals and agents is impossible in the mutual relationship, which leads to goal conflict. In the eyes of headquarters, efficient compliance maximizes principal outcomes, making efficiency the effectiveness criterion. Furthermore, subsidiaries hold some information or skill advantages that are hard for headquarters to access, which creates information asymmetries. To gather information about local contexts, headquarters may be able to invest in information systems (e.g., IT, expatriates, or local embeddedness), but doing so might not be cost optimal.

Whether or not and how these assumptions have been considered in the prior studies is crucial for assessing the utility of the agency perspective. That is, beyond *mentioning* the assumptions, details on the specific *operationalization* of such aspects as self-interests, risk attitudes, or goal conflicts are necessary if we are to truly understand how agency theory can contribute to the study of headquarters-subsidiary relations. In the following, therefore, we review the extant articles with respect to their mentioning and operationalization of agency theory assumptions in their analyses of head-quarters-subsidiary relations.

Systematic Review Approach

We followed the suggestions for conducting systematic literature reviews found in the extant research (e.g., Cropanzano, 2009; Jones & Gatrell, 2014; Short, 2009; Tranfield, Denyer, & Smart, 2003; Webster & Watson, 2002). In order to identify the relevant studies, we used Thomson Reuters Web of Science™ as of April 8, 2015. In line with the study's first purpose, we decided to focus on those studies that dominantly use the agency perspective to study headquarters-subsidiary relations in order to evaluate the utilization of this perspective. Given this approach, we expected the focal studies to explicitly use agency theory assumptions and translate them into this context. We acknowledge that this approach is rather restrictive, as it does not capture all studies that may build on or relate to agency logics. For example, studies that draw on agency logic but primarily use another perspective to explore headquarters-subsidiary relations would not be covered by the search. However, this approach fits our objective of capturing the explicit and core articles that apply agency theory to the phenomenon of interest. We ran our search by entering the combinations "agency theory" and "headquarters" as well as "agency theory" and "subsidiary" into the "topic" field. As we suspected that some of the relevant work, such as studies of specific organizational functions or specific contexts, might have been published in non-managerial or lower-ranked journals, we searched without limiting the journal titles or the timeline.

This initial search yielded 40 distinct articles, of which only those written in English and accessible through the database were selected. Subsequently, one researcher manually screened the abstracts to remove those articles that did not fit. In addition, we removed two review articles (namely Filatotchev & Wright, 2011; Hoenen & Kostova, 2014). We thus focused solely on conceptual and empirical work. At a later point in the review process, two additional articles were removed due to topic misfit. In total, therefore, we examined 25 articles in which the agency perspective was applied to the study of headquarters-subsidiary relations. All articles were systematically analyzed with respect to whether the agency perspective's assumptions were mentioned and how they were applied, as well as with respect to the findings that were generated.[1]

ASSESSMENT OF PRIOR RESEARCH

In line with the study's first purpose, we now evaluate extant studies that have applied the agency perspective to headquarters-subsidiary relations. We start by evaluating whether and how studies that explicitly use the agency perspective as a theoretical lens in examinations of headquarters-subsidiary relations have considered the aforementioned assumptions. To further prepare us for a prescription for future work, we move beyond the assumptions to review the insights provided by the extant studies. On that basis, we then develop a set of considerations for future research.

Consideration of Assumptions in Prior Research

In the following, we discuss whether and how the agency perspective's assumptions have been mentioned and translated to the headquarter-subsidiary context. Table 2 provides an overview of the assumptions across all reviewed studies.

With regard to *human assumptions* (i.e., self-interest, bounded rationality, and risk aversion), studies have looked at both headquarters and subsidiaries. These studies describe headquarters' self-interest as focused on top- or bottom-line growth, and on overall MNC performance (Fey & Furu, 2008; Mellahi & Collings, 2010; Tasoluk, Yaprak, & Calantone, 2006). As performance necessitates subsidiary inputs, subsidiaries' contributions can also be viewed as one of headquarters' key interests (Björkman, Barner-Rasmussen, & Li, 2004). Moreover, some studies equate headquarters' interests with owners' interests (Campbell, Datar, & Sandino, 2009; Chung, 2014). Subsidiary self-interests have been linked to survival in internal competition (Blomkvist, 2012) and to rent seeking (Kawai & Strange, 2014). While most studies refer to headquarters and subsidiaries as disaggregated entities, some studies look at self-interests among individuals in terms of, for example, the placement of friends or relatives in subsidiary management (Chang & Taylor, 1999; Mirchandani & Lederer, 2004), or career advancement (Connelly, Hitt, DeNisi, & Ireland, 2007). Only two studies explicitly investigate headquarters' bounded rationality (Chung, 2014; Mellahi & Collings, 2010), while four discuss risk aversion as reflected in multi-parent ownership structures and headquarters' expectations (Chang & Taylor, 1999; Tasoluk et al., 2006), or in relation to subsidiaries' entrepreneurial orientations (Campbell et al., 2009; Yu, Wong, & Chiao, 2006).

Table 2. Summary of Reviewed Articles.

Study[a]	Assumptions[b]							Translation of Agency Assumptions into Headquarters-Subsidiary Relations
	SI	BR	RA	GC	EE	IA	IP	
Roth and O'Donnell (1996)	X			O	O	O	O	*GC/IA:* Cultural distance, strategic and operational role of subsidiary, commitment or psychological alignment at individual level, decisions that are suboptimal at the subsidiary level *EE:* Perceived subsidiary effectiveness as a desired outcome *IP:* Information is costly for headquarters to acquire
Chang and Taylor (1999)	O		O	X		O		*SI:* Subsidiary staff managers' personal relationships *RA:* Multi-parent ownership structures *IA:* Culture, language, political/legal systems, geographical and cultural distance
Bjorkman and Furu (2000)				O		O	O	*GC:* Subsidiary managerial behavior in joint ventures *IA:* Specialized knowledge, autonomy, complex interactions, cultural distance, parent-company fit of managers *IP:* Difficult to obtain and interpret information
O'Donnell (2000)	X		X	X		O	O	*IA:* Subsidiary actions, subsidiary strategic role, subsidiary autonomy *IP:* Absence of proximity increases monitoring difficulties
Gong (2003)			X	X		O		*IA:* Subsidiary's unique knowledge, information about work processes and behaviors, cultural distance (differences in accounting procedures, levels of market maturation, accurate and comparable subsidiary performance), subsidiary knowledge of environment, actions and performance

	1	2	3	4	5	
Mirchandani and Lederer (2004)	O		X	X	O	*SI:* Subsidiary staff managers' personal relationships *IA:* Subsidiaries' unique knowledge about required resources and their deployment, language differences, legal/accounting systems, capital- and labor-market imperfections *IP:* Monitoring costs related to expenditures to obtain information
Björkman et al. (2004)	O		O		O	*SI:* Subsidiary contributes to MNC *GC:* Subsidiaries do not want to share best people or proprietary knowledge *IP:* Costs associated with sharing knowledge
Andersson et al. (2005)	O		X	X		*IA:* Foreign subsidiary
Tasoluk et al. (2006)	O	O	X	X	O	*SI:* Superior performance of the MNC *RA:* Headquarters' expectations of subsidiary *IA:* Subsidiary capabilities and processes, learning *IP:* Costly and cumbersome to obtain information through budgeting systems or reporting procedures
Johnson and Medcof (2007)	O		X			
Connelly et al. (2007)	O		X		O	*SI:* Advancement of expatriates' careers *IA:* Knowledge residing in expatriates not accessible to headquarters *IP:* Costs associated with knowledge sharing
Collings, Morley, and Gunnigle (2008)	O		O			*SI:* Economic interests of both headquarters and subsidiary top management *GC:* Loss of economic decisions
Fey and Furu (2008)	O	X	O		O	*SI:* MNC top-line or bottom-line growth, performance of whole corporation, performance of subsidiary in its local market

Table 2. (*Continued*)

Study[a]	Assumptions[b]							Translation of Agency Assumptions into Headquarters-Subsidiary Relations
	SI	BR	RA	GC	EE	IA	IP	
								GC: Adjustments and rationalization of products and services suboptimal for subsidiaries EE: Performance enhanced through efficient use (including sharing) of knowledge IA: Subsidiary managers' knowledge about local markets and successful operations in local markets, headquarters' knowledge about interdependencies and requirements of the whole corporation
Campbell et al. (2009)	O		O	X		O	O	SI: Headquarters self-interests represent owners' self-interests, transfer knowledge, adapt consumer tastes RA: Lack of entrepreneurial skills among store managers IA: Heterogeneous and uncertain markets, geographical dispersion IP: Increase ratification and monitoring, high costs for gathering and analyzing market-specific data
Mellahi and Collings (2010)	O	O		X	O	O	O	SI: Hold and protect local talent, pool talent, overall MNC performance BR: Uncertainty and consideration of ill-structured information EE: Effective management of talent IA: Subsidiary top managers have power and obligation to influence headquarters' decisions by controlling the flow of the information to headquarters managers, on-site information.

Study				Concepts
Benito et al. (2011)	X		O	ability to gage local talent, lack of direct communication for cultural reasons; *IP*: Headquarters lack resources and incentives to observe and gage talent at subsidiaries; O — *GC*: Subsidiary autonomy, independently acting individuals; *IA*: Cultural and geographical distance; *IP*: Knowledge becomes more complete with divisional headquarters abroad; *IA*: Local culture and knowledge
Bruning et al. (2011)	X		O	
Du et al. (2011)	X	X	O	*IA*: Environmental and strategic complexities, specialized knowledge through mandates; *IP*: Subsidiary boards can increase the information available to headquarters
Mumdziev (2011)		O	O	*EE*: Effective operation of the local outlet; *IA*: Knowledge about host market, geographical and cultural distance; *IP*: Monitoring costs increase in line with the number of partners in a foreign market and cultural differences
Xue et al. (2011)	X		O	*IA*: Local responsiveness, business unrelatedness; *IP*: Decentralization requires extra effort to monitor decision processes
Blomkvist (2012)	O	O	O	*SI*: Internal competition, survival, competitive advantage, rent seeking; *GC*: Subsidiary's willingness to transfer knowledge; *IA*: Subsidiary's unique capabilities and competencies; *EE*: Integration, adoption, and use of knowledge
Mahlendorf et al. (2012)	X	O	X	*IA*: Distant market environments; *EE*: Effectiveness of PMS

Table 2. (*Continued*)

Study[a]	Assumptions[b]							Translation of Agency Assumptions into Headquarters-Subsidiary Relations
	SI	BR	RA	GC	EE	IA	IP	
Chung (2014)	O	O				O	O	*SI:* Controlling family as principal exploits minority interests *BR:* Actors' sense-making frame as the basis for family owners' control decisions *IA:* Geographical, economic, and cultural distance *IP:* Family capital in the closed family management lowers monitoring costs
Kawai and Strange (2014)	O	X		X		O		*SI:* Subsidiary rent-seeking behavior *IA:* Firm-specific capabilities and complementary resources

Notes: [a]In chronological order.

[b]Human assumptions: *SI* = self-interest, *BR* = bounded rationality, *RA* = risk aversion; Organizational assumptions: *GC* = goal conflict, *EE* = efficiency-is-effectiveness criterion, *IA* = information asymmetry; Information assumptions: *IP* = information as a purchasable good; *X* = mentioned in headquarters-subsidiary context, *O* = operationalized in headquarters-subsidiary context.

The application of *organizational assumptions* (i.e., goal conflict, the efficiency-as-effectiveness criterion, and information asymmetry) is more versatile. Goal conflicts are traced to subsidiary autonomy and strategic roles (Benito, Lunnan, & Tomassen, 2011; Roth & O'Donnell, 1996), and to headquarters' decisions and modifications that are suboptimal in local contexts (Fey & Furu, 2008; Roth & O'Donnell, 1996). While most studies focus on aggregated goal conflicts, Roth and O'Donnell (1996) also consider top managers' willingness to embrace corporate goals and their parenting commitment. The latter exists, for example, on aggregated levels with regard to knowledge transfer or talent sharing (Björkman et al., 2004; Blomkvist, 2012). Few studies explicitly refer to efficiency as an effectiveness criterion. However, some traces of this can be found in Blomkvist (2012), who identifies the integration, adoption, and use of knowledge as effective knowledge use, and in Fey and Furu (2008), who look at the efficient use of knowledge as a way of improving performance. Other previously noted forms of effectiveness include the effective operation of local franchising outlets (Mumdziev, 2011) and overall subsidiary effectiveness (Roth & O'Donnell, 1996). Information asymmetry, which is the most frequently mentioned assumption, is typically traced back to advantages stemming from local knowledge, skills, culture, embeddedness, linkages, or local responsiveness advantages (e.g., Chang & Taylor, 1999; Fey & Furu, 2008; Mumdziev, 2011; O'Donnell, 2000; Xue, Ray, & Gu, 2011; Yu et al., 2006).

Finally, the *information assumption* (i.e., information as purchasable good) is detailed in many studies. It is typically linked to the costs associated with accessing subsidiary knowledge or frames of reference (Bjorkman & Furu, 2000; Björkman et al., 2004; Campbell et al., 2009; Du, Deloof, & Jorissen, 2011; Mirchandani & Lederer, 2004; Roth & O'Donnell, 1996).

Overall, we first find that assumptions have not been properly discussed in the extant studies. More specifically, 9 of the 25 studies do not mention even half of the assumptions, and 17 of the 25 do not operationalize more than half of the assumptions. In addition, human assumptions are generally the least considered – notably, seven studies disregard them altogether. Furthermore, the assumptions are explored to different extents. Across all studies, organizational assumptions are subject to more intense investigations, while numerous studies fail to consider human assumptions at all. Interestingly, most studies consider the headquarters and subsidiary as single entities, and few studies view individual managers or internal units as agents. This might be one point of entry into a discussion on enhancing the representation of human assumptions. Second, none of the existing studies holistically mentions all of the assumptions or operationalizes them simultaneously. Third, empirical evidence on the assumptions is largely absent. For example, few studies measure distance as an approximation of information asymmetry. Moreover, no study uses large-scale, quantitative data to measure such key elements as information asymmetry or goal conflicts involving headquarters and subsidiaries.

Assessment of the Insights of Prior Studies

We organize the insights gained by the prior studies along characteristics of principal-agent relations, governing mechanisms, and outcomes. Fig. 1 summarizes our findings.

With regard to *principal-agent relation characteristics*, the considerations and findings cover headquarters (principal) characteristics, subsidiary (agent) characteristics, and relation characteristics. First, a few studies offer information on relevant principal characteristics when looking at headquarters. For example, we know that degree of headquarters' ownership of a subsidiary influences whether that headquarters unit creates divisional headquarters or internationalizes, and which controls they choose (Benito et al., 2011; Chang & Taylor, 1999; Chung, 2014; Mumdziev, 2011). Another relevant headquarters characteristic is the strategy type in terms of whether the MNC has a global, international, transnational, or multi-domestic strategy, as the choice of strategy type affects the degree of information asymmetry and, thereby, the agency situation (Connelly et al., 2007). Extant studies also point to temporal effects and demonstrate that headquarters learn over time, which helps them reduce information asymmetries (Gong, 2003). In general, however, the principal side remains relatively unexplored.

Second, conceptualizations of subsidiaries as a whole or subsidiary managers as agents provide insights about various agent characteristics. Studies that view whole subsidiaries as agents find that their characteristics influence the agency relation and, thereby, organizational outcomes. Two common characteristics of subsidiaries in this conceptualization are embeddedness in the form of local linkages and experiences, and cultural or geographical distance, which can create information asymmetry and affect knowledge creation and sharing in the MNC, or lead to the establishment of divisional headquarters and the subsequent implementation of controls (e.g., Andersson, Bjorkman, & Forsgren, 2005; Benito et al., 2011; Blomkvist, 2012; Yu et al., 2006). The consequences of information asymmetry can be considered in terms of bargaining power, which also affects knowledge-sharing behavior (Blomkvist, 2012; Connelly et al., 2007). Another

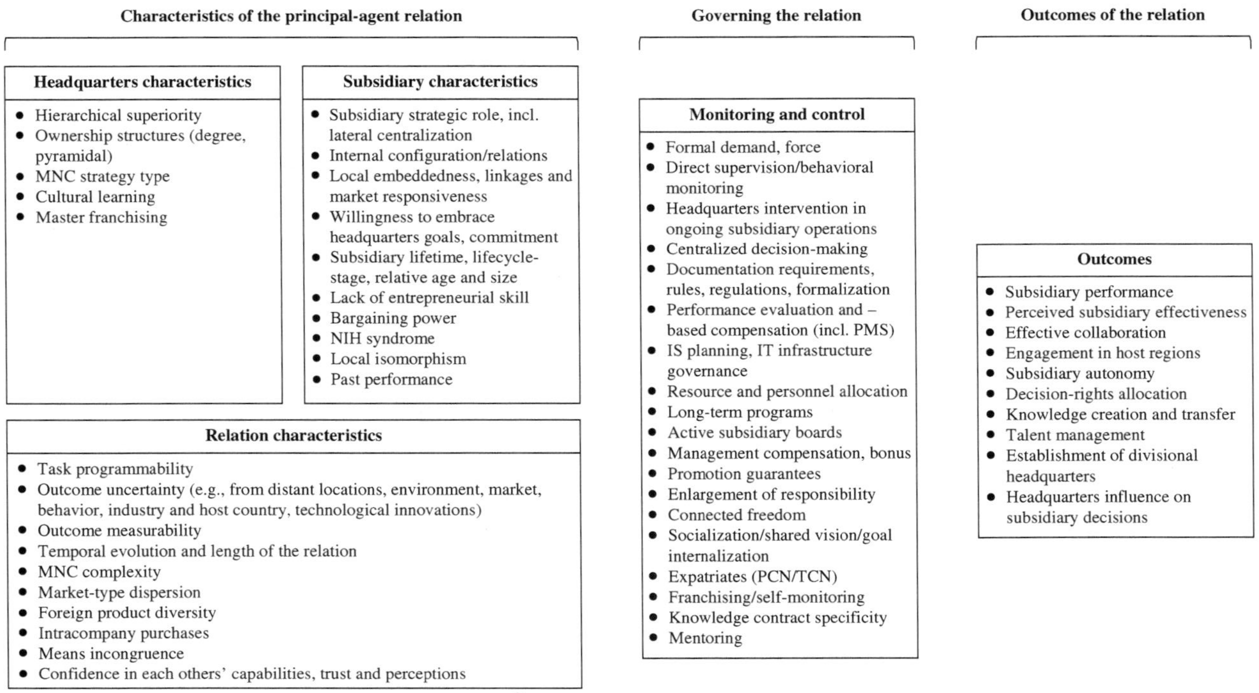

Characteristics of the principal-agent relation

Headquarters characteristics	Subsidiary characteristics
• Hierarchical superiority • Ownership structures (degree, pyramidal) • MNC strategy type • Cultural learning • Master franchising	• Subsidiary strategic role, incl. lateral centralization • Internal configuration/relations • Local embeddedness, linkages and market responsiveness • Willingness to embrace headquarters goals, commitment • Subsidiary lifetime, lifecycle-stage, relative age and size • Lack of entrepreneurial skill • Bargaining power • NIH syndrome • Local isomorphism • Past performance

Relation characteristics

• Task programmability
• Outcome uncertainty (e.g., from distant locations, environment, market, behavior, industry and host country, technological innovations)
• Outcome measurability
• Temporal evolution and length of the relation
• MNC complexity
• Market-type dispersion
• Foreign product diversity
• Intracompany purchases
• Means incongruence
• Confidence in each others' capabilities, trust and perceptions

Governing the relation

Monitoring and control

• Formal demand, force
• Direct supervision/behavioral monitoring
• Headquarters intervention in ongoing subsidiary operations
• Centralized decision-making
• Documentation requirements, rules, regulations, formalization
• Performance evaluation and – based compensation (incl. PMS)
• IS planning, IT infrastructure governance
• Resource and personnel allocation
• Long-term programs
• Active subsidiary boards
• Management compensation, bonus
• Promotion guarantees
• Enlargement of responsibility
• Connected freedom
• Socialization/shared vision/goal internalization
• Expatriates (PCN/TCN)
• Franchising/self-monitoring
• Knowledge contract specificity
• Mentoring

Outcomes of the relation

Outcomes

• Subsidiary performance
• Perceived subsidiary effectiveness
• Effective collaboration
• Engagement in host regions
• Subsidiary autonomy
• Decision-rights allocation
• Knowledge creation and transfer
• Talent management
• Establishment of divisional headquarters
• Headquarters influence on subsidiary decisions

Fig. 1. Synthesis of Insights from Reviewed Articles.

characteristic of subsidiaries is that their strategic and operational roles drive headquarters' choice of control mechanisms, such as compensation structures (Bjorkman & Furu, 2000) or boards of directors (Du et al., 2011). In addition, some common subsidiary characteristics, such as size, lifetime, life-cycle stage, or importance, can affect control and subsidiary autonomy (e.g., Chang & Taylor, 1999; Du et al., 2011; Mirchandani & Lederer, 2004). Notably, studies that examine subsidiary top managers as agents are fewer in number. They mainly find that certain aspects, such as advancements of personal wealth or career, increase or decrease the agency problem (e.g., Björkman et al., 2004; Chang & Taylor, 1999). These studies also show that parenting commitment among individuals determines headquarters' control choices (Roth & O'DOnnell, 1996).

In addition, one study considers expatriates as agents of headquarters (Connelly et al., 2007). However, this view is rare — most studies that focus on expatriates perceive them as control or monitoring mechanisms (e.g., Andersson et al., 2005; Björkman et al., 2004; Bruning, Bebenroth, & Pascha, 2011; Chang & Taylor, 1999; Gong, 2003).

Third, investigations of relation characteristics offer informative findings. Many of these studies explore the tenets described by Eisenhardt (1989). For example, some studies show that task programmability, outcome measurability, and outcome uncertainty affect headquarters' control choices (Bjorkman & Furu, 2000; O'Donnell, 2000; Roth & O'Donnell, 1996). Furthermore, several studies note that certain complexities, such as the internal, multi-layered structure or foreign product diversity, are important considerations, as these factors influence subsidiaries' planning autonomy and the establishment of divisional headquarters (Benito et al., 2011; Mirchandani & Lederer, 2004). One study, which examines more advanced conceptualizations of conflicts, finds that conflicts over means can arise despite goal congruence (Tasoluk et al., 2006).

With regard to *governing mechanisms*, studies have explored numerous factors. These studies find three types of control to be relevant: behavioral (or process) control, outcome control, and cultural (or social) control. In some studies, control is used as the dependent variable. For instance, research shows that control-related choices are affected by the subsidiary's strategic roles, ownership structures, the subsidiary's nationality, and the relative importance of the subsidiary (Bjorkman & Furu, 2000; Chang & Taylor, 1999). In studies in which control is viewed as the independent variable, effects have been shown in relation to embeddedness, knowledge creation, and knowledge sharing (Andersson et al., 2005; Björkman et al., 2004; Blomkvist, 2012). Note that control and monitoring may take different forms, such as management compensation, centralization of the IT infrastructure, expatriate involvement, bureaucratic mechanisms, performance measurement systems (PMS), subsidiary boards, socialization, and even self-monitoring (e.g., Bruning et al., 2011; Du et al., 2011; Kawai & Strange, 2014; Mahlendorf, Rehring, Schaffer, & Wyszomirski, 2012; Mumdziev, 2011; Roth & O'Donnell, 1996; Xue et al., 2011).

With regard to *outcomes*, a few studies build explicit links between subsidiary or MNC performance and expatriate staffing, subsidiary autonomy, or control (e.g., Gong, 2003; Kawai & Strange, 2014; Roth & O'Donnell, 1996). However, most studies look at more intermediary outcomes. One common area of interest is knowledge sharing, which is affected by different control choices (e.g., Andersson et al., 2005; Björkman et al., 2004; Blomkvist, 2012; Fey & Furu, 2008). Other performance intermediaries in agency situations include talent management, the establishment of divisional headquarters, and headquarters' influence on subsidiary decisions (Benito et al., 2011; Mahlendorf et al., 2012; Mellahi & Collings, 2010).

Overall, we make two key observations from our integration of these insights. First, in terms of highlighting "white spots" in the landscape of extant research, we find that principal characteristics, socialization as a control, and the direct performance outcomes of agency situations are relatively underrepresented in the extant research. Many studies have focused on different forms of control and subsidiary characteristics, while others have tested certain agency tenets, such as task programmability, outcome uncertainty, and measurability (as suggested by Eisenhardt (1989)) in headquarters-subsidiary contexts. However, few studies explore principal characteristics. This is surprising, as recent research in other streams has pointed to principal characteristics as important in agency relations with regard to conflicting interests among principals or dual roles (e.g., Arthurs, Hoskisson, Busenitz, & Johnson, 2008; Deutsch, Keil, & Laamanen, 2011; Hoenen & Kostova, 2014; Hoskisson, Hitt, Johnson, & Grossman, 2002). Moreover, socialization as a control mechanism is, in general, not explored largely beyond its effect through expatriates. However, many other paths can lead to shared visions or goal internalization, such as joint work efforts, travel, teams, or taskforces (e.g., Kirsch, 1996). In addition, direct performance outcomes are often theoretically linked with such intermediaries as knowledge creation and knowledge transfer through other theories, such as the knowledge-based view (Grant, 1996). However, their empirical explorations remain unsatisfactory.

Second, while the extant studies tend to acknowledge complex structures and their effects, they do not study them in detail. Most studies conceptualize headquarters and subsidiaries as whole entities with a single set of characteristics. This straightforward, amenable view invites several criticisms. First, this simplistic perspective fails to consider intermediary structures, such as regional headquarters (Alfoldi, Clegg, & McGaughey, 2012; Ambos & Schlegelmilch, 2010; Mahnke, Ambos, Nell, & Hobdari, 2012). Second, it ignores the possibility that different internal units and structures (Nohria & Ghoshal, 1994) might not have unified interests, rationality, risk attitudes, or information. Third, it neglects nested interdependencies among multiple actors inside headquarters and subsidiaries (Hoenen & Kostova, 2014). Finally, it does not allow for lateral hierarchies, such as a subsidiary's global mandates (Birkinshaw & Morrison, 1995; O'Donnell, 2000). While several studies allude to these points, the distinct effects are largely unexplored.

CONSIDERATIONS FOR FUTURE RESEARCH

In the previous section, we discovered that existing applications of agency theory in headquarters-subsidiary contexts lack completeness and operationalization when it comes to the discussion of agency assumptions. Moreover, we showed that there are a few white spots in the generated insights as well as a general disregard for the more complex nature of the relationship.

Based on this assessment of the extant studies, we now turn to suggestions for future research. While we see several specific research opportunities with respect to each of the elements in the agency relations between headquarters and subsidiaries (e.g., principal characteristics, direct performance outcomes, effects of socialization), we believe that two meta-level concerns must be considered in order to make better use of the agency perspective in this context: (1) the need to validate the agency relation and (2) the need to embrace the complexities in headquarters-subsidiary relations in the MNC.

(1) The Need to Validate the Agency Relation

We believe that a first necessary step is to establish the agency relation. This should be done in two steps. First, the agency assumptions need to be conceptualized for headquarters-subsidiary contexts. Second, those assumptions need to be empirically validated.

Researchers should question the extent to which human assumptions apply to aggregated units, such as headquarters or subsidiaries. If possible, the self-interests of subsidiaries as a whole and of subsidiary managers as individuals should be explicitly distinguished. For the subsidiary as a whole, self-interests may be hard to grasp. Some examples of self-interests might include subsidiary survival (Björkman et al., 2004) or talent retention (Mellahi & Collings, 2010). Future research could also consider profit maximization for subsidiaries' minority shareholders, employee satisfaction and compensation, or capital acquisition for venture projects.

With respect to bounded rationality, future studies could follow the example of Mellahi and Collings (2010) and explicitly explore related arguments. The bounded rationality of headquarters, as the principal, can be easily affected by, for example, drawing headquarters' attention to subsidiaries (Ambos & Birkinshaw, 2010). Exploration of the effects of such subsidiary-influenced bounded rationality bears potential for agency theory as a lens for studying headquarters-subsidiary relations.

Furthermore, different risk attitudes require theoretical grounding. Along these lines, researchers can ask several questions: Are subsidiaries more risk averse than headquarters? If so, why? Are an MNC's subsidiaries similar with regard to risk aversion? This assumption is particularly important for MNCs with diversified portfolios in which some subsidiaries are involved in industries that require risk-taking and others are active in sectors that are relatively conservative. Moreover, different geographical and cultural distances between subsidiaries and the MNC's headquarters will affect this assumption and, thereby, the relationship between headquarters and subsidiaries (e.g., Ambos & Ambos, 2009). In addition, the degree of risk aversion may change depending on parenting objectives e.g., synergies versus cost minimization (Collis, Young, & Goold, 2007; Goold & Campbell, 1998; Goold, Campbell, & Alexander, 1994). Finally, the risk-aversion assumption in relation to subsidiary initiatives and entrepreneurial orientation remains unclarified (see, e.g., Yu et al., 2006).

With regard to the organizational assumptions, a better understanding of goal conflicts and the efficiency-is-effectiveness assumption would be welcome. For example, in terms of goal conflicts, Mudambi and Navarra (2004) state that subsidiaries seek autonomy and headquarter centralization, but there could be other sources of conflict, such as challenges related to technology transfers (Kaufmann & Roessing, 2005). Furthermore, the least frequently mentioned assumption is the efficiency-as-effectiveness criterion. Headquarters depend on subsidiaries' local knowledge and specialized skills. How does that dependence affect whether headquarters' interests are best met when subsidiaries behave as headquarters desires? This is even more important when subsidiaries are expected to innovate proactively (Johnson & Medcof, 2007). Finally, we suggest that studies should at least mention all of the assumptions or explicitly explain why some are not considered.

We also recommend that future studies should empirically explore the assumptions using innovative study designs that involve both headquarters and subsidiaries in data collection. This is particularly important in terms of testing whether the headquarters-subsidiary relation makes a good agency theory context from an empirical point of view. Currently, agency theory's application to headquarters-subsidiary relations is somewhat limited, a state that O'Donnell (2000) traces back to conceptual issues related to complexity. However, some of the fundamental assumptions may not hold even on aggregated levels when investigated empirically. Some studies have looked at the dyad between two parties specifically. For example, the literature on perception gaps suggests that organizational tensions stem from misaligned perceptions (Asakawa, 2001; Birkinshaw, Holm, Thilenius, & Arvidsson, 2000; Chini, Ambos, & Wehle, 2005) and entail consequences for control. Similarly, the literature on procedural justice proposes that shared perceptions lead to higher performance outcomes (Luo, 2005). Research on headquarters-subsidiary relations could utilize these and other approaches to explore whether the basic agency assumptions hold and how they are affected by organizational-context variables.

(2) The Need to Embrace the Complexities in Headquarters-Subsidiary Relations

Our second consideration, which offers ample opportunities for future research, refers to the internal, multi-layered structure of headquarters-subsidiary relations in the contemporary MNC. If studies applying the agency perspective want to advance our understanding of these internal relations, they probably have to help explain these more complex relations. In other words, they need to avoid the "reductive fallacy of reducing complexity to simplicity, or diversity to uniformity" (Fisher, 1970, p. 172). This call for consideration of the heterogeneities *inside* headquarters and subsidiaries is similar to Nohria and Ghoshal's (1994) call for the study of heterogeneities *among* subsidiaries.

These criticisms can be addressed by considering the multi-layered structure of headquarters-subsidiary relations. Fig. 2 illustrates the differences

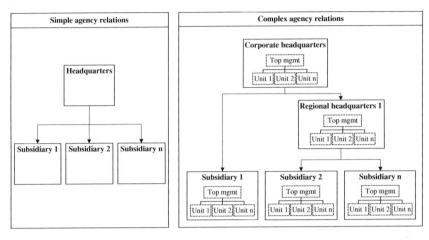

Fig. 2. Conceptualizations of Headquarters-Subsidiary Relations.

between simplified and complex views of headquarters-subsidiary relations. For example, intermediary structures, such as regional headquarters, split the "headquarters" unit into corporate headquarters, and regional or divisional headquarters (Alfoldi et al., 2012; Ambos & Schlegelmilch, 2010; Benito et al., 2011; Dellestrand, 2011; Mahnke et al., 2012; Nell, Ambos, & Schlegelmilch, 2011). Furthermore, headquarters and subsidiaries have internal, heterogeneous units. For example, MNCs may have headquarters-internal units with unique functions that require distinct consideration (Kunisch, Mueller-Stewens, & Campbell, 2014; Menz et al., 2015). Finally, all headquarters-internal and subsidiary-internal units are coordinated internally by top management teams, which implies the presence of hierarchies (Nohria & Ghoshal, 1994). Taken together, this disaggregation affects how agency theorists may think about headquarters-subsidiary relations. Based on this logic, we suggest that three elements of a complex structure warrant future exploration: (a) Relation multiplicity and internal heterogeneity, (b) multiple principals, and (c) role duality. We therefore discuss opportunities for future research for each of these elements. Table 3 illustrates these points and provides examples of research opportunities.

(a) Relation Multiplicity with Internal Heterogeneity
Relation multiplicity refers to the fact that there are many principal-agent relations between a headquarters and a single subsidiary. An examination of relations between individuals would entail insurmountable complexity,

Table 3. Exemplary Research Opportunities for Complex Headquarters-Subsidiary Relations.

	Relation Multiplicity with Internal Heterogeneity	Multiple Principals	Role Duality
Illustration			
Description	Headquarters-internal and subsidiary-internal units have direct relations with each other	Internal hierarchies and intermediaries create situations of multiple principals for ultimate agents (subsidiary-internal units)	Cascading relations; lateral centralization, hierarchies, and intermediaries create actors who are simultaneously principals and agents
Future research	• Relations of headquarters-internal and subsidiary-internal units other than marketing, R&D, and IS • Differences in relations of headquarters-internal and subsidiary-internal units with different tasks • Simultaneous control strategies • Differences in lateral control strategies depending on functional areas	• More subsidiary owners than just headquarters • Differences stemming from different owner combinations • Regional headquarters (e.g., location, goal conflicts, information asymmetry) in relation to the ultimate agent • Power of different principals • Influence of principals on agents' bargaining power • Differences between peer and headquarters principals • Interdependencies, power, and influence among principals	• Effects of subsidiary mandates on headquarters-subsidiary relations over time • Interdependencies in relations in which parties are simultaneously principal and agent

Notes: ----▶ Relation from principal to agent.

⌐ ⌐ Actors in dual roles.

but considering efforts on the subsidiary level entails too much aggregation to allow for precise predictions (Blomkvist, 2012; Hoenen & Kostova, 2014; O'Donnell, 2000). Hoenen and Kostova (2014) speak of multiple sets of principal-agent relations when calling for the inclusion of complexity in the agency view of MNCs.

Headquarters-internal and subsidiary-internal units are charged with heterogeneous tasks, and headquarters and subsidiaries are assigned distinct tasks. For headquarters, common groupings are administrative versus entrepreneurial tasks (Chandler, 1962, 1991), value-adding versus loss-preventing tasks (Campbell, Goold, & Alexander, 1995; Foss, 1997), and internal-stakeholder-facing versus external-stakeholder-facing tasks (Birkinshaw, Braunerhjelm, Holm, & Terjesen, 2006). For subsidiaries, tasks may stem from their strategic roles (Birkinshaw & Morrison, 1995). Typically, these differences are reflected in the organizational structure and often take the form of functional units, such as marketing, finance, information systems, R&D, or accounting (Campbell, Kunisch, & Muller-Stewens, 2012).

The acknowledgment of relation multiplicity with internal heterogeneity has consequences for the interpretation of existing research and for future research. First, it explains the mixed or weak findings of agency theory in studies characterized by high levels of aggregation (O'Donnell, 2000). In such cases, viewing the subsidiary as a whole only leads to significant results when the scope of all subsidiary activities is narrow. Otherwise, "when multiple units jointly contribute to a collective output, it is difficult to determine the contribution of each individual unit and therefore [...] monitoring and incentives become less effective" (Hoenen & Kostova, 2014, p. 6).

Second, this recognition allows researchers to address multiple control strategies. Agency theorists typically find it hard to accommodate multiple control strategies. They consequently tend to focus on behavioral, output, or social controls. However, studies adopting other theoretical perspectives have found the simultaneous application of multiple control strategies to be successful (Ambos & Schlegelmilch, 2007; Cardinal, Sitkin, & Long, 2003). Such studies have also suggested analyzing headquarters' control mechanisms on different levels (Andersson et al., 2005). As heterogeneous subsidiary-internal units need different control strategies, multiple simultaneous control strategies can be explained in agency theory. Future studies should, therefore, either focus on subsidiaries with a narrow set of tasks or on task-specific headquarters-subsidiary relations.

Third, future research can extend the number of functional areas under investigation to include, for example, finance, accounting, or customer-relations management. It would be particularly interesting to investigate differences among functions related to task programmability, outcome uncertainty, outcome measurability, or relationship length (Eisenhardt, 1989).

Finally, additional research is warranted if subsidiary-internal units feature lateral centralization in the form of global mandates or task responsibilities for other subsidiary-internal units (Birkinshaw & Morrison, 1995; O'Donnell, 2000). For example, a subsidiary with a global mandate plays a dual role as principal to other subsidiary-internal units and, at least to a certain extent, as agent to the headquarters-internal unit (see below for a more detailed discussion of role duality).

(b) Multiple Principals
The notion of multiple principals was acknowledged in the very early work on agency theory (Jensen & Meckling, 1976). It refers to the idea that an agent may be engaged in more than one agency relation with regard to the same or overlapping delegated tasks. As long as the principals are fully aligned in their objectives and perspectives on means, the situation does not warrant specific attention. However, when the principals have diverging interests, the complex structure of the agency situation matters (Hoskisson et al., 2002; Young, Peng, Ahlstrom, Bruton, & Jiang, 2008).

The issue of multiple principals can stem from multiple owners, internal hierarchies, and the presence of intermediaries. In terms of ownership, subsidiaries might be owned by entities other than just their MNC headquarters. For example, in joint-venture situations, control might be highly difficult owing to the existence of multiple parents (Bjorkman & Furu, 2000; Chang & Taylor, 1999). Moreover, the presence of different kinds of investors with diverging interests may lead to confusion for top managers resulting in suboptimal consequences (Hoskisson et al., 2002). Such confusion could arise, for instance, when there are both local and non-local owners (Mirchandani & Lederer, 2004).

With regard to internal hierarchies, multiple headquarters-internal and subsidiary-internal units lead to vertical principal-agent relations. Fey and Furu (2008) allude to this point, but they do not acknowledge a multiple-principal situation. Instead, they state that "the subsidiary top management team also has incentives to encourage all other people working at the subsidiary *(and who as top managers have good possibilities to induce)* [italics added] to follow ..." (Fey & Furu, 2008, p. 1307). Nohria and Ghoshal (1994) critically review their own contribution and state that they did not take into account the internal structure of subsidiaries. They also point to the existence of internal hierarchies and the resulting consequences of multiple principals. Notably, acknowledgment of internal hierarchies has two effects. First, this recognition means that subsidiary-internal units have multiple principals at headquarters and locally. Second, headquarters-internal units take on dual roles because they serve as principals to subsidiary-internal units and as agents to headquarters' top management.

With regard to internal intermediaries, regional headquarters may not be just intermediaries. They may also create a dual reporting structure as seen, for example, in matrix structures (Egelhoff, Wolf, & Adzic, 2013). Agents then simultaneously have two principals: corporate and regional.

The presence of multiple principals within the MNC offers several research opportunities. One area for future research is joint ownership by principals with diverging interests. Different kinds of investors and different combinations of investor types affect the goal conflicts between headquarters as principals and subsidiaries as agents (Bjorkman & Furu, 2000; Chang & Taylor, 1999). For example, a combination of government and public ownership differs substantially from a situation in which ownership is solely held by different governments. Another area for future research is found in the characteristics of intermediary organizational actors, such as location proximity or the embeddedness of the intermediary, as these characteristics might affect the intensity of the agency problem. Moreover, future research could look into questions related to the power held by the different principals or the bargaining power of the agent relative to one of the principals (Mudambi & Navarra, 2004). Finally, future research could examine lateral centralization, and the resulting mix of horizontal and vertical principals.

(c) Role Duality

Role duality refers to "cascading agency relations" (Hoenen & Kostova, 2014, p. 7) in which an actor simultaneously takes on roles as principal and agent (Arthurs et al., 2008; Deutsch et al., 2011). In headquarters-subsidiary contexts, three elements produce role duality: lateral centralization, internal hierarchies, and intermediaries. With respect to lateral centralization, subsidiary-internal units may have a corporate mandate (Birkinshaw & Morrison, 1995), which means that they serve as principal to their peers. However, this relation must not be considered in isolation, as a global mandate implies that the subsidiary-internal unit is charged with a mandate that was given to it by the headquarters-internal unit to which it reports. Accordingly, the subsidiary unit will also serve as an agent in this relationship.

With regard to internal hierarchies and intermediaries, headquarters-internal units play a dual role as principal to subsidiary-internal units and as agent to headquarters' top management. This view can be extended to subsidiary boards by viewing them not only as a control mechanism (Du et al., 2011) but also as an intermediary structure that reports to headquarters as owner and serves as a principal to the subsidiary. Another example would be master franchising in which master franchisors act as intermediary owners that coordinate the chain's headquarters and the individual franchise units (Mumdziev, 2011). In addition, regional headquarters play dual roles in that they are agents to corporate headquarters and principals to subsidiaries (Benito et al., 2011).

Role duality offers several avenues for future research. Given that subsidiaries' role duality is linked to questions of subsidiary mandates (Birkinshaw & Morrison, 1995), the relation between headquarters and subsidiaries may change over time, with subsidiaries' mandates being terminated or extended. This possibility affects the current agency relation between corporate headquarters and subsidiaries. Hence, it would be interesting to analyze how specific mandates affect subsidiary advantages and their longevity (Birkinshaw, Hood, & Jonsson, 1998). Moreover, it may be interesting to examine the drivers that affect whether the upward or downward relation is the greater agency problem.

CONCLUSION

Research on the MNC devotes a significant amount of attention to headquarters-subsidiary relations because those relations are fundamental to our understanding of the nature and functioning of the MNC. The agency perspective has increasingly been applied to the study of headquarters-subsidiary relations in the MNC. However, its utility in these studies remains subject to widespread debate.

With this study, we attempt to contribute to this debate. While we have not discussed the general utility of the agency perspective for studying headquarters-subsidiary relations, we have attempted to stimulate more considerate application of the theory in two respects. We first proposed that scholars should explore the underlying assumptions, including those associated with empirical testing, to support their use of the agency perspective in studies of headquarters-subsidiary relations. Second, we suggested that scholars should embrace the complex structure of headquarters-subsidiary relations in the MNC. More specifically, we discussed a need to examine relation multiplicity in the presence of internal heterogeneity, multiple principals, or role duality. It is our hope that this study contributes to the explicit and appropriate use of agency theory and, ultimately, helps to inform the debate on the validity of agency theory in studies of headquarters-subsidiary relations.

NOTE

1. Appendix provides detailed information on the search results.

ACKNOWLEDGMENTS

We thank the editors — Tina Ambos, Björn Ambos, and Julian Birkinshaw — as well as an anonymous reviewer for their guidance and helpful comments. In addition, we are grateful to Albert Cannella, Phillip Nell, and Metin Sengul for their constructive comments on an earlier version of this manuscript.

REFERENCES

Alfoldi, E. A., Clegg, L. J., & McGaughey, S. L. (2012). Coordination at the edge of the empire: The delegation of headquarters functions through regional management mandates. *Journal of International Management*, *18*(3), 276–292.

Ambos, B., & Schlegelmilch, B. B. (2007). Innovation and control in the multinational firm: A comparison of political and contingency approaches. *Strategic Management Journal*, *28*(5), 473–486.

Ambos, B., & Schlegelmilch, B. B. (2010). *The new role of regional management*. Hampshire, UK: Palgrave Macmillan.

Ambos, T. C., & Ambos, B. (2009). The impact of distance on knowledge transfer effectiveness in multinational corporations. *Journal of International Management*, *15*(1), 1–14.

Ambos, T. C., & Birkinshaw, J. (2010). Headquarters' attention and its effect on subsidiary performance. *Management International Review*, *50*(4), 449–469.

Andersson, U., Bjorkman, I., & Forsgren, M. (2005). Managing subsidiary knowledge creation: The effect of control mechanisms on subsidiary local embeddedness. *International Business Review*, *14*(5), 521–538.

Andersson, U., & Holm, U. (Eds.). (2010). *Managing the contemporary multinational: The role of headquarters*. Cheltenham: Edward Elgar Publishing Limited.

Arthurs, J. D., Hoskisson, R. E., Busenitz, L. W., & Johnson, R. A. (2008). Managerial agents watching other agents: Multiple agency conflicts regarding underpricing in IPO firms. *Academy of Management Journal, 51*(2), 277–294.

Asakawa, K. (2001). Organizational tension in international R&D management: The case of Japanese firms. *Research Policy, 30*(5), 735–757.

Benito, G. R. G., Lunnan, R., & Tomassen, S. (2011). Distant encounters of the third kind: Multinational companies locating divisional headquarters abroad. *Journal of Management Studies, 48*(2), 373–394.

Birkinshaw, J., Braunerhjelm, P., Holm, U., & Terjesen, S. (2006). Why do some multinational corporations relocate their headquarters overseas? *Strategic Management Journal, 27*(7), 681–700.

Birkinshaw, J. M., & Morrison, A. J. (1995). Configurations of strategy and structure in subsidiaries of multinational corporations. *Journal of International Business Studies, 26*(4), 729–753.

Birkinshaw, J., Holm, U., Thilenius, P., & Arvidsson, N. (2000). Consequences of perception gaps in the headquarters-subsidiary relationship. *International Business Review, 9*(3), 321.

Birkinshaw, J., Hood, N., & Jonsson, S. (1998). Building firm-specific advantages in multinational corporations: The role of subsidiary initiative. *Strategic Management Journal, 19*(3), 221.

Björkman, I., Barner-Rasmussen, W., & Li, L. (2004). Managing knowledge transfer in MNCs: The impact of headquarters control mechanisms. *Journal of International Business Studies, 35*(5), 443–455.

Bjorkman, I., & Furu, P. (2000). Determinants of variable pay for top managers of foreign subsidiaries in Finland. *International Journal of Human Resource Management, 11*(4), 698–713.

Blomkvist, K. (2012). Knowledge management in MNCs: The importance of subsidiary transfer performance. *Journal of Knowledge Management, 16*(6), 904–918.

Bruning, N. S., Bebenroth, R., & Pascha, W. (2011). Valuing Japan-based German expatriate and local manager's functions: Do subsidiary age and managerial perspectives matter? *International Journal of Human Resource Management, 22*(4), 778–806.

Campbell, A., Goold, M., & Alexander, M. (1995). The value of the parent company. *California Management Review, 38*(1), 79–97.

Campbell, A., Kunisch, S., & Muller-Stewens, G. (2012). Are CEOs getting the best from corporate functions? *MIT Sloan Management Review, 53*(3), 12–14.

Campbell, D., Datar, S. M., & Sandino, T. (2009). Organizational design and control across multiple markets: The case of franchising in the convenience store industry. *Accounting Review, 84*(6), 1749–1779.

Cardinal, L. B., Sitkin, S. B., & Long, C. P. (2003). Creating control configurations during organizational founding. *Academy of Management Best Conference Paper, 2003 (ENT: D6)*.

Chandler, A. D., Jr. (1962). *Strategy and structure: Chapters in the history of the industrial enterprise.* Oxford: MIT Press.

Chandler, A. D. (1991). The functions of the HQ unit in the multibusiness firm. *Strategic Management Journal, 12*, 31–50.

Chang, E., & Taylor, M. S. (1999). Control in Multinational Corporations (MNCs): The case of Korean manufacturing subsidiaries. *Journal of Management, 25*(4), 541–565.

Chini, T., Ambos, B., & Wehle, K. (2005). The headquarters subsidiaries trench: Tracing perception gaps within the multinational corporation. *European Management Journal*, 23(2), 145–153.

Chung, H. M. (2014). The role of family management and ownership on semi-globalization pattern of globalization: The case of family business groups. *International Business Review*, 23(1), 260–271.

Collings, D. G., Morley, M. J., & Gunnigle, P. (2008). Composing the top management team in the international subsidiary: Qualitative evidence on international staffing in US MNCs in the republic of Ireland. *Journal of World Business*, 43(2), 197–212.

Collis, D., Young, D., & Goold, M. (2007). The size, structure, and performance of corporate headquarters. *Strategic Management Journal*, 28(4), 383–405.

Connelly, B., Hitt, M. A., DeNisi, A. S., & Ireland, R. D. (2007). Expatriates and corporate-level international strategy: Governing with the knowledge contract. *Management Decision*, 45(3), 564–581.

Cropanzano, R. (2009). Writing nonempirical articles for Journal of Management: General thoughts and suggestions. *Journal of Management*, 35(6), 1304–1311.

Dellestrand, H. (2011). Subsidiary embeddedness as a determinant of divisional headquarters involvement in innovation transfer processes. *Journal of International Management*, 17(3), 229–242.

Deutsch, Y., Keil, T., & Laamanen, T. (2011). A dual agency view of board compensation: The joint effects of outside director and CEO stock options on firm risk. *Strategic Management Journal*, 32(2), 212–227.

Doz, Y. L., & Prahalad, C. K. (1991). Managing DMNCs: A search for a new paradigm. *Strategic Management Journal*, 12, 145–164.

Du, Y., Deloof, M., & Jorissen, A. (2011). Active boards of directors in foreign subsidiaries. *Corporate Governance − An International Review*, 19(2), 153–168.

Egelhoff, W. G., Wolf, J., & Adzic, M. (2013). Designing matrix structures to fit MNC strategy. *Global Strategy Journal*, 3(3), 205–226.

Eisenhardt, K. M. (1985). Control: Organizational and economic approaches. *Management Science*, 31(2), 134–149.

Eisenhardt, K. M. (1989). Agency theory: An assessment and review. *Academy of Management Review*, 14(1), 57–74.

Fama, E. F., & Jensen, M. C. (1983). Separation of ownership and control. *Journal of Law and Economics*, 26(2), 301–325.

Fey, C. F., & Furu, P. (2008). Top management incentive compensation and knowledge sharing in multinational corporations. *Strategic Management Journal*, 29(12), 1301–1323.

Filatotchev, I., & Wright, M. (2011). Agency perspectives on corporate governance of multinational enterprises. *Journal of Management Studies*, 48(2), 471–486.

Fisher, D. H. (1970). *Historian's fallacies*. New York, NY: Harper and Row.

Foss, N. J. (1997). On the rationales of corporate headquarters. *Industrial and Corporate Change*, 6(2), 313–338.

Gong, Y. P. (2003). Subsidiary staffing in multinational enterprises: Agency, resources, and performance. *Academy of Management Journal*, 46(6), 728–739.

Goold, M., & Campbell, A. (1998). Desperately seeking synergy. *Harvard Business Review*, 76(5), 131–143.

Goold, M., Campbell, A., & Alexander, M. (1994). How corporate parents add value to the stand-alone performance of their businesses. *Business Strategy Review*, 5(4), 33–55.

Grant, R. M. (1996). Toward a knowledge-based theory of the firm. *Strategic Management Journal*, *17*, 109–122.

Hoenen, A. K., & Kostova, T. (2014). Utilizing the broader agency perspective for studying headquarters-subsidiary relations in multinational companies. *Journal of International Business Studies*, *46*, 104–113.

Hoskisson, R. E., Hitt, M. A., Johnson, R. A., & Grossman, W. (2002). Conflicting voices: The effects of institutional ownership heterogeneity and internal governance on corporate innovation strategies. *Academy of Management Journal*, *45*(4), 697–716.

Jensen, M. C., & Meckling, W. H. (1976). Theory of the firm: Managerial behavior, agency costs and ownership structure. *Journal of Financial Economics*, *3*(4), 305–360.

Johnson, W. H. A., & Medcof, J. W. (2007). Motivating proactive subsidiary innovation: Agent-based theory and socialization models in global R&D. *Journal of International Management*, *13*(4), 472–487.

Jones, O., & Gatrell, C. (2014). Editorial: The future of writing and reviewing for IJMR. *International Journal of Management Reviews*, *16*(3), 249–264.

Kaufmann, L., & Roessing, S. (2005). Managing conflict of interests between headquarters and their subsidiaries regarding technology transfer to emerging markets — A framework. *Journal of World Business*, *40*(3), 235–253.

Kawai, N., & Strange, R. (2014). Subsidiary autonomy and performance in Japanese multinationals in Europe. *International Business Review*, *23*(3), 504–515.

Kirsch, L. J. (1996). The management of complex tasks in organizations: Controlling the systems development process. *Organization Science*, *7*(1), 1–21.

Kostova, T., Marano, V., & Tallman, S. (2016). Headquarters-subsidiary relationships in MNCs: Fifty years of evolving research. *Journal of World Business*, *51*(1), 176–184.

Kostova, T., Nell, P. C., & Hoenen, A. K. (in press). Understanding agency problems in headquarters-subsidiary relationships in multinational corporations: A contextualized model. *Journal of Management*. doi:10.1177/0149206316648383.

Kunisch, S., Menz, M., & Ambos, B. (2015). Changes at corporate headquarters: Review, integration and future research. *International Journal of Management Reviews*, *17*(3), 356–381.

Kunisch, S., Mueller-Stewens, G., & Campbell, A. (2014). Why corporate functions stumble. *Harvard Business Review*, *92*(10), 8.

Lane, P. J., Cannella, J. A. A., & Lubatkin, M. H. (1998). Agency problems as antecedents to unrelated mergers and diversification: Amihud and Lev reconsidered. *Strategic Management Journal*, *19*(6), 555.

Luo, Y. (2005). How important are shared perceptions of procedural justice in cooperative alliances? *Academy of Management Journal*, *48*(4), 695–709.

Mahlendorf, M. D., Rehring, J., Schaffer, U., & Wyszomirski, E. (2012). Influencing foreign subsidiary decisions through headquarter performance measurement systems. *Management Decision*, *50*(3–4), 688–717.

Mahnke, V., Ambos, B., Nell, P. C., & Hobdari, B. (2012). How do regional headquarters influence corporate decisions in networked MNCs? *Journal of International Management*, *18*(3), 293–301.

Mellahi, K., & Collings, D. G. (2010). The barriers to effective global talent management: The example of corporate élites in MNEs. *Journal of World Business*, *45*(2), 143–149.

Menz, M., Kunisch, S., & Collis, D. J. (2015). The corporate headquarters in the contemporary corporation: Advancing a multimarket firm perspective. *Academy of Management Annals*, *9*(1), 633–714.

Mirchandani, D. A., & Lederer, A. L. (2004). Is planning autonomy in US subsidiaries of multinational firms. *Information & Management, 41*(8), 1021–1036.

Mudambi, R., & Navarra, P. (2004). Is knowledge power? Knowledge flows, subsidiary power and rent-seeking within MNCs. *Journal of International Business Studies, 35*(5), 385–406.

Mumdziev, N. (2011). Allocation of decision rights in international franchise firms: The case of master and direct franchising. In M. Tuunanen, J. Windsperger, G. Cliquet, & G. Hendrikse (Eds.), *New developments in the theory of networks: Franchising, alliances and cooperatives.* New York, NY: Springer.

Nell, P. C., Ambos, B., & Schlegelmilch, B. B. (2011). The benefits of hierarchy? Exploring the effects of regional headquarters in multinational corporations. *Dynamics of Globalization: Location-Specific Advantages or Liabilities of Foreignness, 24,* 85–106.

Nohria, N., & Ghoshal, S. (1994). Differentiated fit and shared values: Alternatives for managing headquarters-subsidiary relations. *Strategic Management Journal, 15*(6), 491–502.

O'Donnell, S. W. (2000). Managing foreign subsidiaries: Agents of headquarters, or an interdependent network? *Strategic Management Journal, 21*(5), 525.

Roth, K., & O'Donnell, S. (1996). Foreign subsidiary compensation strategy: An agency theory perspective. *Academy of Management Journal, 39*(3), 678–703.

Short, J. (2009). The art of writing a review article. *Journal of Management, 35*(6), 1312–1317.

Tasoluk, B., Yaprak, A., & Calantone, R. J. (2006). Conflict and collaboration in headquarters-subsidiary relationships: An agency theory perspective on product rollouts in an emerging market. *International Journal of Conflict Management, 17*(4), 332–351.

Tranfield, D., Denyer, D., & Smart, P. (2003). Towards a methodology for developing evidence-informed management knowledge by means of systematic review. *British Journal of Management, 14*(3), 207–222.

Webster, J., & Watson, R. T. (2002). Analyzing the past to prepare for the future: Writing a literature review. *MIS Quarterly, 26,* xiii–xxiii.

Xue, L., Ray, G., & Gu, B. (2011). Environmental uncertainty and its infrastructure governance: A curvilinear relationship. *Information Systems Research, 22*(2), 389–399.

Young, M. N., Peng, M. W., Ahlstrom, D., Bruton, G. D., & Jiang, Y. (2008). Corporate governance in emerging economies: A review of the principal–principal perspective. *Journal of Management Studies, 45*(1), 196–220.

Yu, C.-M. J., Wong, H.-C., & Chiao, Y.-C. (2006). Local linkages and their effects on headquarters' use of process controls. *Journal of Business Research, 59*(12), 1239–1247.

APPENDIX

Table A1. Distribution of Articles per Journal and Year.

Journal Title	1996	1997	1998	1999	2000	2001	2002	2003	2004	2005	2006	2007	2008	2009	2010	2011	2012	2014	Total
Academy of Management Journal	1							1											2
Accounting Review														1					1
Corporate Governance-An International Review																1			1
Information & Management									1										1
Information Systems Research																1			1
International Business Review										1								2	3
International Journal of Conflict Management											1								1
International Journal of HRM					1											1			2
Journal of Business Research											1								1
Journal of International Business Studies									1										1
Journal of International Management												1							1
Journal of Knowledge Management																	1		1
Journal of Management			1																1
Journal of Management Studies																1			1
Journal of World Business													1		1				2
Management Decision												1					1		2
New Developments in Theory of Networks																1			1
Strategic Management Journal					1								1						2
Total	1			1	2			1	2	1	2	2	2	1	1	5	2	2	25

PART II
PERSPECTIVES ON TENSIONS AND CONFLICTS IN HQ-SUBSIDIARY RELATIONSHIPS

CONFLICT RESOLUTION IN HEADQUARTERS-SUBSIDIARY RELATIONSHIPS: THE ROLES OF REGULATORY FIT AND MORAL EMOTIONS

Rajesh Kumar and Jens Gammelgaard

ABSTRACT

We demonstrate the role of regulatory fit and moral emotions, that is, contempt and anger, in influencing conflict resolution between the headquarters and subsidiary boundary spanners. We develop a theoretical framework, which integrates literature on international business and headquarters-subsidiary relationships with regulatory focus, moral emotions, and conflict resolution. The chapter outlines the relationships between the regulatory focus of a headquarters' boundary spanner, and his or her manner of engagement, conflict sensitivity, violation of code, moral emotions, and the way conflicts are resolved. The theoretical framework developed here provides a starting point for future research on bargaining processes between boundary spanners of a multinational corporation (MNC). This chapter is the first one to discuss regulatory

Perspectives on Headquarters-Subsidiary Relationships in the Contemporary MNC
Research in Global Strategic Management, Volume 17, 121–140
Copyright © 2016 by Emerald Group Publishing Limited
All rights of reproduction in any form reserved
ISSN: 1064-4857/doi:10.1108/S1064-485720160000017005

focus, and moral emotions, in the contexts of a MNC headquarters-subsidiary relationship.

Keywords: Headquarters-subsidiary relationships; conflict resolution; regulatory focus; moral emotions

INTRODUCTION

The multinational enterprise (MNE) and its subsidiaries are simultaneously independent and interdependent organizational units (Otterbeck, 1981). The dynamics of the headquarters-subsidiary relationship as well as the management of that relationship have been of considerable interest to international business scholars. A major focus has been on understanding how a subsidiary derives its initial sense of mission and vision, and the degree of autonomy granted to it by corporate headquarters (Birkinshaw & Hood, 1997). A sense of mission and vision is essential for establishing the unit's identity. As Mudambi and Navarra (2004) note, subsidiary managers have their own unique identities and interests, which they would like to maintain and even strengthen as they help the MNE realize its strategic ambitions.

One potential source of conflict between the MNE and the subsidiary revolves around the degree to which the subsidiary devotes its time and resources to either profit seeking for the benefit of the MNE or individual rent seeking. The headquarters unit, while being cognizant of its subsidiary's interests, primarily focuses on ensuring that the subsidiary fulfills its mandates. Therefore, the interactions between headquarters and subsidiary management must be of a quality that allows the MNE to optimize its performance. In large part, this is dependent on managerial actions, and on the interactions between the headquarters and the subsidiary managers (Tippmann, Scott, & Mangematin, 2012).

Conflicts may arise between headquarters and subsidiaries for a number of reasons. Differences in strategic objectives (Dörrenbächer & Geppert, 2009) are most fundamental, but differences rooted in geography, language, and culture may aggravate the problem (Björkman, Barner-Rasmussen, & Li, 2004; Morris et al., 1998). Information asymmetries between the headquarters and the subsidiaries (Aghion & Tirole, 1997) can also worsen a problem. Conflict is thus an essential and defining feature of the headquarters-subsidiary relationship. It is the management and resolution of this conflict that determines whether the value-creation potential of the relationship is maximized (Blazejewski & Becker-Ritterspach, 2011; Rahim, 2002).

In this context, conflict is defined as "an interactive process manifested in incompatibility, disagreement, or dissonance, within or between social entities" (Rahim, 2002, p. 207). Consequently, conflict is an interactive process involving two or more entities with conflicting preferences or goals (Rahim, 2002). Conflicts may relate to either a task or a relationship (Jehn, 1997; Pinkley, 1990). Task conflicts are typically fact oriented, and they revolve around different viewpoints on substance and how to deal with a particular issue. Relationship conflicts tend to involve personal issues, and to be emotion based to a higher degree (Jehn & Mannix, 2001; Rahim, 2002). The two types of conflicts are interlinked; as an unresolved task, conflict may generate a relationship conflict and vice versa (Rahim, 2002). Although excessive conflict may be dysfunctional, organizational scholars agree that a moderate amount of conflict is essential for enhancing organizational performance (Rahim & Bonoma, 1979).

Conflicts between headquarters and subsidiaries can be analyzed at either the macro- or micro-levels. The macro-level perspective focuses on the distribution of power between the headquarters and the subsidiary. The conventional assumption is that the headquarters has more power. Although a macro-level perspective has its utility, it neglects the fact that individuals often take center stage in determining the actions that the headquarters and/or the subsidiary should pursue, and how those actions should be implemented. More broadly, there has been surprisingly little focus on the role of the individual in the fields of strategy and international business. As Jarzabkowski and Spee (2009, p. 69) note: "There is a curious absence of human actors and their actions in most strategy theories, even those that purport to examine the internal dynamics of the firm, such as the resource-based." This criticism has been echoed by many strategic management scholars, who note that the psychological foundations of strategic management remain underdeveloped (Hodgkinson & Healey, 2011; Powell, Lovallo, & Fox, 2011). Likewise, only a few surveys in the international business literature examine the role played by managerial cognition. Notable exceptions are the studies by Collinson and Houlden (2005), and Reid (1981), where the latter examines managers' beliefs and attitudes in relation to export behavior.

This chapter analyzes interactions between headquarters and subsidiaries from a micro-behavioral level (Das & Kumar, 2011), a perspective that places top-level decision makers at the center of the analysis. The micro-behavioral perspective views the relationships between headquarters and subsidiary management as an outcome of ongoing interactions between boundary spanners. Boundary spanners are top-level decision makers who aim to overcome the cultural and strategic differences between headquarters and subsidiaries (Yagi & Kleinberg, 2011). They work to reconcile the conflicting interests and priorities of the headquarters and the subsidiary, as well as those of the different institutional environments. Yagi and Kleinberg (2011) view boundary spanning as the interplay among these various contextual elements. This focus on boundary spanners highlights the role and the importance of individual cognitions and emotions in shaping how conflict is managed within the confines of the headquarters-subsidiary relationship. However, although Yagi and Kleinberg's (2011) work focuses on negotiations between the headquarters and the subsidiary regarding cultural identities, it overlooks issues of managerial psychology, as well as the more general theme of conflict and conflict resolution. Given the inevitability of conflict between headquarters and subsidiaries, this chapter departs from the premise that a headquarter-subsidiary relationship may experience a task and/or a relationship conflict (Rahim, 2002). In such situations, we assume that boundary spanners at headquarters and subsidiaries have the assignment of managing that task and/or relationship conflict.

To this basic analysis, we add the cognitive orientation of the boundary spanner. Based on regulatory-focus theory, we analyze interactions between boundary spanners at headquarters and subsidiaries from two archetypical cognitive profiles. More specifically, we focus on whether dominant objective is to maximize gains (promotion focus) or minimize losses (prevention focus) (Higgins, 1998). Our analysis emphasizes that different regulatory foci lead boundary spanners to pursue different conflict-resolution strategies. The strategies used to resolve conflict may maintain the status quo, or they may exacerbate or lessen the conflict. These developments lead to either a regulatory fit or nonfit situation, which relates to the manner in which boundary spanners engage in negotiations and whether they "feel right" about the situation.

Furthermore, we propose that effective conflict resolution depends not only on the boundary spanners' regulatory focus but also on the moral emotions involved in the process. Differences in regulatory focus between the headquarters and the subsidiary manager may make conflict resolution difficult, and moral emotions may further accentuate the conflict. Haidt (2003, p. 853) defines moral emotions as "those emotions that are linked to the interests or welfare either of society as a whole or at least of persons other than the judge or the agent." In this chapter, we focus on the emotions that belong to the "other-condemning" category, which are contempt and anger (Haidt, 2003). We investigate the feelings these two emotions bring about, and we analyze how they affect conflict resolution between boundary spanners.

The contribution of the chapter is threefold. First, the role of boundary spanners has only rarely been used in analyses of interactions between headquarters and subsidiaries (for an exception, see Kostova & Roth, 2003). However, such a perspective has a great utility, as strategic decisions are made by senior-level managers (boundary spanners) who often have considerable latitude in terms of their discretionary choices (Hambrick & Mason, 1984). Second, the proposed framework integrates boundary spanners' cognitions, moral emotions, and conflict-resolution strategies in determining how headquarters-subsidiary relationships evolve over time. If we are to gain a deeper insight into the ongoing management of the relationship between the headquarters and the subsidiaries, we must explore the micro-behavioral processes that underpin the interactions. The framework that we propose allows us to take this step. Finally, our micro-behavioral framework may provide an alternative view on the dynamics of headquarters-subsidiary relations, as it suggests that the complex, interacting dynamics between cognitions and emotions among boundary spanners may be at least as influential in shaping the relationship between the headquarters and the subsidiary as any power gap between them.

The chapter proceeds as follows. We begin by reviewing the construct of "regulatory focus" and the related notion of "regulatory fit." We then review the extant literature on moral emotions. Subsequently, we analyze strategic interactions between the headquarters and the subsidiary as a function of the type of conflict, the regulatory focus, and the conflict-resolution strategies enacted by the participants. Thereafter, we develop relevant propositions. The chapter concludes with a discussion of the theoretical and managerial implications of our framework.

LITERATURE REVIEW

Regulatory Focus

Regulatory-focus theory is based on the premise that individuals are motivated to seek pleasure and avoid pain (Brockner & Higgins, 2001). The mechanisms by which people either seek to maximize pleasure or minimize pain may differ as a function of their regulatory focus. In humans, regulatory focus is a product of three factors: (a) people's needs; (b) the goals they wish to realize; and (c) the psychological situations that are of the greatest importance to them (Brockner & Higgins, 2001). People's needs may be oriented either towards growth and development, or towards security. "Goal" may refer either to an individual's wishes or aspirations, or to a person's duties and responsibilities (Roney, Higgins, & Shah, 1995). Moreover, psychological situations may represent the presence or absence of positive outcomes, or the absence or presence of negative outcomes. On the basis of these dimensions, Higgins (1998) draws a distinction between a promotion-focused self-regulatory system and a prevention-focused self-regulatory system.

A promotion-focused self-regulatory system highlights the importance of gains or advancement. Therefore, individuals who are promotion focused would like to move from the current status quo (0) to an improved state (+1). Promotion-focused individuals are growth oriented, concerned about their hopes and aspirations, and highly sensitive to the presence or absence of positive outcomes. The prevention-focused self-regulatory system orients people toward the maintenance of the status quo. Those adopting a prevention focus need to avoid losses and, as such, will work to ensure that they do not slip from a satisfactory state (0) to an unsatisfactory state (−1). Prevention-focused individuals are safety oriented, concerned about their duties and obligations, and keen to avoid the presence of negative outcomes.

Individuals adopting a promotion focus differ from those adopting a prevention focus along a number of dimensions, which are outlined in Table 1. A first point of contrast is that promotion-focused individuals pursue strategies reflecting an eager approach, while prevention-focused individuals pursue strategies of vigilance (Higgins, 1998, 2000). As we explain below, this affects the way individuals perform in relation to conflict resolution. Second, in more general terms, promotion-focused individuals have more experimental and entrepreneurial mindsets, and they are more willing to initiate changes, accept failures, and entertain many hypothesis in order to reach the a better state. Consequently, they prefer to engage in exchange relationships, where they can utilize the opportunities those relationships might offer. In contrast, prevention-oriented individuals prefer to safeguard the status quo. As such, they are less likely to initiate changes that could lead to failure, and they view exchange relationships as risky because they could entail interacting with opportunistic partners.

Bingham and Eisenhardt (2008) examine these strategic logics. They find that prevention-oriented managers seek to secure the firm's competitive

Table 1. Differences between Promotion-Focused and a Prevention-Focused Self-Regulatory System.

Promotion	Prevention
Wishes and aspirations	Duties and responsibilities
Reaching a positive outcome; +1 better than 0	Avoiding a negative outcome; 0 better than −1
Eagerness	Vigilance
Errors acceptable	Errors not acceptable
Positive towards changes	Resistance to changes
Many hypotheses	Few hypotheses
Positive focus on exchange relationships	Negative focus on relationships

Sources: Based on Das and Kumar (2011), Weber and Mayer (2011), Higgins (1997, 1998, 2000), Liberman, Idson, Camacho, and Higgins (1999), and Liberman, Molden, Idson, and Higgins (2001).

position by strengthening the linkages among the company's existing resources and its activities. In contrast, promotion-oriented managers experiment and engage in spontaneous and improvisational actions. For these managers, the linkages between resources and activities are not necessarily a priority.

Regulatory Fit

According to Higgins (2009), people experience regulatory fit when the "manner" of their engagement in an activity sustains their regulatory orientation. Consequently, people will engage more in such activities, and they will "feel right" about that engagement. With regard to the manner of engagement, regulatory-focus theory states that an *eager* manner in goal pursuit fits the promotion focus, whereas a *vigilant* manner fits the prevention focus. However, a distinct feature of regulatory fit is that the value of the manner of goal pursuit is unrelated to the outcome of that goal pursuit. Therefore, regulatory fit only concerns the relation between the manner of the goal pursuit and the regulatory focus.

For example, in a situation where conflicts between a headquarters and a subsidiary boundary spanner need to be solved, the outcome (e.g., the benefit) to be derived from goal pursuit is excluded from the regulatory fit concept. Instead, if both actors feel a correspondence between the way they engage in their goal pursuit (the eagerness/vigilant framework), regulatory fit occurs. As such, the concept of regulatory fit differs from the hedonic value of feeling pleasure or pain, as it involves a sense of "feeling right." In other words, regulatory fit refers to the value of how goals are pursued rather than to feelings regarding the outcome of attempts at goal attainment. Therefore, the fact that two boundary spanners share a goal is an insufficient condition for "feeling right" about a conflict's resolution haven taken place. One example is an eager persuasion by a headquarters boundary spanner that is not accepted by the subsidiary boundary spanner, though both partners accept the outcome of the conflict resolution.

CONFLICT TYPES AND REGULATORY FIT

In this section, we establish the relationship between boundary spanners and conflict sensitivity. Moreover, we determine their regulatory focus, their typical manner of engagement, and their sensitivity to task-based and relationship-based conflict. The relationship is outlined in Table 2.

We noted at the outset that the relationship between headquarters and the subsidiary may be subject to either a task conflict or a relationship conflict. Examples of task conflicts are when headquarters and the subsidiary differ in their views on which goals to achieve, whether goals have been met (Blazejewski & Becker-Ritterspach, 2011), resource allocations (Mudambi, 2011), or the nature of the strategic challenge confronting them. Relationship conflicts may be related to differences in the psychosocial characteristics of managers (Schotter & Beamish, 2011), an unfavorable prior history, a lack of embeddedness (Granovetter, 1985), or a perceived lack of fairness (Luo, 2008).

Table 2. Relationships among Regulatory Fit, Conflict Sensitivity, Condemnatory Emotions, and Conflict-Resolution Strategy.[a]

Regulatory Focus HQ	Regulatory Fit Manner of Engagement	Conflict Sensitivity	Violation of Code	Moral Emotion	Conflict Resolution
Promotion	Eagerness	Task based	Community	Contempt	Integration/ compromise (dominance)
Prevention	Vigilance	Relationship based	Autonomy	Anger	Avoid/ oblige (dominance)

Note: [a]Under the condition that subsidiary boundary spanners have an opposite focus/fit.

We begin by recognizing that boundary spanners with a promotion-focused self-regulatory system will differ from their prevention-focused counterparts in terms of their sensitivity to task and relationship conflicts. A promotion-focused boundary spanner is concerned with realizing "growth and accomplishments." Therefore, these boundary spanners will adopt eager strategies aimed at achieving the stated ideals. The promotion-focused boundary spanner wants to move to an improved state ($+1$). A conflict regarding the likelihood of achieving that goal, as the counterpartner would have a more vigilant approach to this, will then be most prevalent for promotion-oriented boundary spanner. Consequently, the promotion-focused boundary spanner can more easily deal with relationship type of conflict, as long as the $+1$ goal can be achieved. We can also assume that the entrepreneurial type of promotion-oriented boundary spanner, while used to relational obstacles and inertia in organizations (Birkinshaw & Ridderstråle, 1999), is more focused on realizing his/her stated ideals. Relationship conflict is, therefore, not very salient unless it acts as an impediment to the achievement of the stated ideals. Prevention-focused boundary spanners will have a more vigilant manner of engagement, and they will be satisfied if they gain access to resources or negotiate a goal focused on securing the status quo. Therefore, we propose that the likelihood that task-related issues will lead to conflict is lower among prevention-focused actors than among promotion-oriented managers.

In contrast, the main objective of the prevention-focused boundary spanner relates to the preservation of the status quo. As task conflict involves a movement to a new state, which might be disruptive of the existing state, and as these boundary spanners are less eager to achieve new goals, they might resist actions aimed at this end. However, if the relationship conflict threatens the status quo, then these boundary spanners are likely to be quite concerned, as such a threat represents a deterioration of the existing state. In that context, prevention-focused boundary spanners will take steps to return to the status quo.

Based on the above analysis, we propose:

Proposition 1(a). A promotion-focused boundary spanner will be more sensitive to task conflict relative to a prevention-focused boundary spanner.

Proposition 1(b). A prevention-focused boundary spanner will be more sensitive to relationship conflict relative to a promotion-focused boundary spanner.

MORAL EMOTIONS

In this section, we outline two types of condemnatory emotions. In addition, we demonstrate that contempt is a moral emotion typical among promotion-oriented boundary spanners, while anger is linked to prevention-oriented boundary spanners.

As individuals, we can seek to understand and accept someone's wrong-doing, but we can also have a reactive attitude and moral sentiments towards the wrongdoing (Jones, 2006). For example, if the violator is oneself, one can feel guilt or shame. If the violator is someone else, one can feel contempt or anger, both of which belong to the group of "other-condemning" moral emotions (Haidt, 2003), which we refer to as "condemnatory emotions." Moral judgment and the condemnation of others are reactions to violations of the integrity of social order, or a type of "third-party morality" (Rozin, Lowery, Imada, & Haidt, 1999). We investigate the integrity and discretion of the headquarters-subsidiary relationships by analyzing condemnatory emotions, and we examine how feelings regarding the other boundary spanner affect conflict resolution. These relationships are outlined in Table 2.

Our analysis builds on the notion that "feeling right" or "feeling wrong" during conflict resolution between boundary spanners depends not only on the regulatory focus and the regulatory fit, but also on the individuals' own feelings about the situation. We define "emotions" as high-intensity affective states that are indicative of a situation that may be relevant to individuals' well-being (Kumar, 1997). They involve cognitive appraisal and arousal, and are associated with a tendency for action (Bagozzi, Gopinath, & Nyer, 1999). Emotions are triggered by interruptions. In other words, they occur in situations where an expected event fails to occur or an unexpected event happens (Mandler, 1975). Negative emotions arise when an individual is thwarted in realizing a goal and positive emotions arise when goals are realized.

Moral emotions differ from basic emotions in that they go beyond the self (Haidt, 2003) – they emerge as a reaction to social events and their main focus is the condemnation of others (Rozin et al., 1999). *Condemnatory emotions* include contempt and anger (Haidt, 2003). These moral emotions imply communication among people, and an awareness of moral transgressions at a social level. Furthermore, they tend to be negative and to lead to conflicts. Contempt involves a negative evaluation of others and their actions. Typically, it is linked to hierarchy and the indigna-tion one feels when members of another group are regarded as inferior (such as feelings regarding racism; Rozin et al., 1999). Anger reflects frustration regarding a goal blockage and a view of that blockage as a violation against others (often close to oneself). It can be a result of insults, transgressions, or rights violations (Rozin et al., 1999).

Rozin et al. (1999) suggest that condemnatory emotions, such as contempt and anger, are an outcome of the violation of Shweder's moral codes, as they are defined by Shweder, Much, Mahapatra, and Park (1997), who highlight different ethics that various cultures adopt for solving moral issues. One is "community" in which the individual belongs to a larger independent group, family, or community. Another is "autonomy," which refers to individual preference structures. Rozin et al. (1999, p. 575) define violation of the community as occurring when "a person fails to carry out his or her duties within a community, or to the social hierarchy within the community" and violation of autonomy as an action that "directly hurts another person or infringes upon his/her rights or freedoms as an individual."

Shweder et al. (1997) suggest that violation of the community gives rise to contempt because contempt is linked to hierarchical relations, while violation of autonomy leads to anger. This relationship is supported in a study by Rozin et al. (1999) of US and Japanese undergraduate students, in which the US students are assumed to focus relatively more on individual rights and Japanese students are believed to focus on community rights. Therefore, the relationships between violations and moral emotions are culturally based. These connections between community code and contempt, and autonomy and anger are also demonstrated by Laham, Chopra, Lalljee, and Parkinson (2010), who examine this question in India and the United Kingdom. Participants in both countries reported anger in relation to autonomy transgressions and contempt in response to community violations. However, Indian responders expressed more outrage in relation to community violations. In terms of the headquarters-subsidiary relationship, we assume the presence of the same relationships between hierarchy and contempt, and autonomy and anger. In the former, a promotion-focused headquarters boundary spanner will be most likely to despise or scorn a prevention-oriented subsidiary boundary spanner, as the latter's lack of eagerness to enhance the current state will be interpreted as disloyalty or disrespect for the hierarchy.

Violation of the autonomy code suggests that an individual has been harmed, and that his or her rights have not been respected. This gives rise to anger. We expect this to be naturally linked to a situation in which the subsidiary boundary spanner is promotion oriented. Such boundary spanners are likely to find that their eagerness and enterprising behavior are often rejected by prevention-oriented boundary spanners at headquarters. The subsidiary boundary spanner will therefore develop a feeling of being "disliked," which will lead to anger. This relationship is outlined in Table 2 and is explained in more detail below.

For the purposes of analyzing headquarters-subsidiary relationships, it is most relevant to investigate cases in which community codes (hierarchy) or autonomy (individual) have been violated. As boundary spanners from headquarters and subsidiaries interact, they are likely to run afoul of the norms of autonomy and community in their pursuit of optimizing their own goals. This may occur, for example, if boundary spanners at headquarters compel a subsidiary boundary spanner to undertake a particular course of action about which they are unhappy. This may violate autonomy norms. Similarly, if the subsidiary boundary spanner disobeys or disregards instructions from headquarters, he or she may be in breach of the community code. As the emotions that emerge from these conflicts are negative and result in contempt or anger, they are likely to escalate the conflict.

This line of argumentation leads to the following propositions:

Proposition 2(a). A promotion-focused headquarters boundary spanner is likely to perceive a violation of the community code and, therefore, feel contempt in cases of conflict resolution with a prevention-focused subsidiary boundary spanner.

Proposition 2(b). A promotion-focused subsidiary boundary spanner is likely to perceive a violation of the autonomy code and, therefore, feel anger in cases of conflict resolution with a prevention-focused headquarters boundary spanner.

CONFLICT RESOLUTION BETWEEN HEADQUARTERS AND THE SUBSIDIARY

Regulatory Focus and Conflict Resolution

In this section, we focus on the distinction between promotion- and prevention-focused boundary spanners with their respective regulatory fits and conflict sensitivities. Our aim is to develop an understanding of the links among these factors and the various conflict-resolution strategies.

A number of organizational scholars have developed typologies of conflict management (e.g., Pruitt, 1983; Rahim & Bonoma, 1979; Thomas, 1976). These models rely on the notion of dual concern – a concern for self and a concern for others (Ogilvie & Kidder, 2008). One of the most popular models of conflict styles is the one developed by Rahim (1983, 2002). He identifies five styles of conflict management: integrating, dominating, avoiding, compromising, and obliging. The integrating style is associated with a high concern for both oneself and others. This style is associated with problem solving and, therefore, "involves openness, exchanging information, looking for alternatives, and examination of differences to reach an effective solution acceptable to both parties" (Rahim, 2002, p. 218). The dominating style reflects a high level of concern for oneself and a low level of concern for others. This implies a win-lose orientation, and can be viewed as a forcing behavior, or as hierarchical enforcement designed for dealing with assertive subordinates. The avoiding style entails a lack of concern for oneself and for others. The dominant motif of this style is withdrawal or escape. Individuals typically make use of this style to avoid dysfunctional conflicts in which the negative outcomes of addressing the conflict would outweigh the benefits. The compromising style refers to situations in which there is give and take on both sides. Neither party gets all that they want, but they find a solution that they can both accept. In these situations, the actors are often equally powerful. Those adopting an obliging style have little concern for themselves and a great deal of concern for the interests of the others. In this scenario, the emphasis is on finding commonalities and downplaying any differences. The party that obliges hopes to gain some future benefits from the other party. An individual who uses this style views the preservation of relationships as important (Rahim, 2002).

What types of conflict resolution strategies are promotion- and prevention-focused boundary spanners likely to utilize? Promotion-focused boundary spanners have positive expectations for the relationship, and they value flexibility and cooperation (Weber & Mayer, 2011). They seek access to resources outside their own possession in order to enhance the state of the relationship. This leads us to assume that they are likely to employ an integrating strategy or, as a second-best option, a compromise strategy. If the boundary spanner is a headquarters representative, he or she might adopt "domination" in order to impose headquarters' will.

In contrast, the prevention-focused boundary spanner has expectations that are relatively more negative. More impersonal relations take the place of creativity and flexibility. This leads us to surmise that a prevention-focused boundary spanner is likely to pursue a strategy of avoidance in order to avoid dysfunctional conflicts that would lower the likelihood of reaching a status quo. Alternatively, they may prefer to oblige in order to preserve the relationship, especially given their sensitivity to relationship-based conflicts. We also associate domination with this category. Again, domination is likely to be an outcome of headquarters' power and authority (Lukes, 2005). However, in this case, the headquarters boundary spanner deals with highly entrepreneurial and eager subsidiaries that might control valuable resources and wish to challenge status quo. To protect the status quo, headquarters might decline many of the initiatives made by the subsidiaries (Birkinshaw & Ridderstråle, 1999). This leads to the following propositions:

> **Proposition 3(a).** A promotion-focused boundary spanner will utilize an integrating or compromise strategy when faced with a prevention-focused boundary spanner.

> **Proposition 3(b).** A prevention-focused boundary spanner will utilize an avoiding or obliging strategy when faced with a promotion-focused boundary spanner.

> **Proposition 3(c).** Promotion- and prevention-focused boundary spanners will utilize a domination strategy if they are representative of headquarters.

TASK CONFLICT, REGULATORY FOCUS, AND CONDEMNING EMOTIONS

Differences in regulatory foci and moral emotions shape the evolution of the task conflicts that arise between headquarters and subsidiaries. Task-related conflicts tend to emerge in situations in which the headquarters boundary spanner is promotion focused and the subsidiary boundary spanner is prevention focused. Promotion-focused boundary spanners are determined to achieve their goals. They are eager in their approach, and they will assess the vigilant attitude of the subsidiary boundary spanner as disrespectful and as making it impossible for them to fulfill their obligations. At the same time, the subsidiary's prevention-focused boundary spanners will feel a violation of moral codes at the individual level and they will stress the need for autonomy, which in turn leads to anger.

More specifically, promotion-focused boundary spanners will be focused on achieving their ideals. They value cooperative behavior and have a tendency to employ an integrative strategy. Prevention-focused boundary spanners are concerned with maintaining the status quo. As such, they may not be responsive to the pleadings of the headquarters boundary spanners. As prevention-focused boundary spanners rebuff their promotion-focused counterparts, the stage is set for the escalation of the conflict. First, the lack of responsiveness on the part of the prevention-oriented boundary spanner in the subsidiary may be construed as a moral violation by the promotion-oriented boundary spanner. This is because the subsidiary's boundary spanner is viewed as disrespecting the social hierarchy. As noted earlier, this violates the community ethic and may generate contempt among headquarters managers. If contempt arises, individuals develop more negative attitudes towards the object in question (Oatley & Johnson-Laird, 1987). This implies that headquarters boundary spanners will develop a more unfavorable view about their subsidiary counterparts, which is likely to accentuate the identity split between headquarters and the subsidiary to such an extent that eliciting cooperation from the subsidiary may prove impossible. In addition, the prevention-focused boundary spanner in the subsidiary may take offense at the promotion-focused boundary spanner's attempts to find a solution and view it as violating the spirit of autonomy. This generates anger, which often leads to aggression and an attempt to restructure the relationship (Haidt, 2003). The subsidiary boundary spanner may be restricted in his or her ability to do so given his or her standing in the social hierarchy. The needs for autonomy and affiliation are prominent for group members (Shapiro, 2010), and both are called into question as the group members act in increasingly divergent ways. The unresolved task conflict then has the potential to give rise to relationship conflict, which may put even greater pressure on the relationship. This leads to the following propositions:

Proposition 4(a). If the headquarters boundary spanner is promotion focused and the subsidiary boundary spanner is prevention focused, then the conflicting strategies pursued by the boundary spanners to resolve task conflict will impinge upon the norms of community and autonomy, and generate the condemnatory emotion of contempt in the headquarter boundary spanner and the condemnatory emotion of anger in the subsidiary boundary spanner.

Proposition 4(b). The emergence of the condemnatory emotions of contempt and anger enhances the identity split between the headquarters and the subsidiary, and gives rise to a relationship conflict.

*Relationship Conflict, Regulatory Focus, and
Condemning Emotions*

In this section, we consider an alternative scenario in which the headquarters boundary spanner is prevention focused and the subsidiary boundary spanner is promotion focused. The prevention-focused headquarters managers will vigilantly engage in negotiations, but will be challenged by entrepreneurial and eager subsidiary boundary spanners, who will use lobbying and other tactics to get their initiatives approved. The interaction will be more "personal," as subsidiary boundary spanners will try to influence decisions made by the headquarters boundary spanner by playing political games (Bouquet & Birkinshaw, 2008; Cantwell & Mudambi, 2005; Dutton, Ashford, O'Neill, & Lawrence, 2001). This leads to a violation of the autonomy code from the headquarters point of view (and contempt from the subsidiary's point of view). Therefore, the headquarters boundary spanner will feel angry about the situation. This might escalate the conflict, and could lead the headquarters boundary spanner to adopt either a dominant style aimed at avoiding further conflict and securing a status quo, or an avoidance or obligation style, especially in the face of powerful subsidiaries. This leads to the following propositions:

> **Proposition 5(a).** If the headquarters boundary spanner is prevention focused and the subsidiary boundary spanner is promotion focused, then the conflicting resolution strategies pursued by the boundary spanners to resolve relationship conflict will impinge upon the norms of autonomy, and generate the condemnatory emotion of anger in the headquarter boundary spanner and the condemnatory emotion of contempt in the subsidiary boundary spanner.

> **Proposition 5(b).** The emergence of the moral emotions of contempt and anger enhances the identity split between the headquarters and the subsidiary, and accentuates the relationship conflict.

DISCUSSION

Conflicts between headquarters and subsidiaries are endemic and have been a major theme in the international business literature. Much of the literature on potential conflicts between the headquarters and subsidiaries has taken a macro-view with an overwhelming emphasis on the power asymmetry between the actors, and the implications of that asymmetry for relations between the headquarters and subsidiaries.

We complement the extant research by approaching this issue from a more micro-level. Our analysis is based on the fact that key decisions at the subsidiary and headquarters levels are made by influential boundary spanners whose cognitive orientation plays an important role in determining how they engage with their counterparts. We posit that boundary spanners may have either a promotion or a prevention focus in their regulatory orientation, and that this focus has critical implications for how they manage their relationship with their counterpart. Promotion-focused boundary spanners are more likely to choose integration or compromise strategies, while prevention-focused boundary spanners may adopt obliging or avoiding approaches. However, in both cases, headquarters boundary spanners can opt for a dominating approach. Furthermore, our analysis draws upon the construct of moral emotions. We posit that, in interactions with their counterparts, boundary spanners at headquarters and subsidiaries may violate the norms of community and autonomy, which then gives rise to the emotions of contempt and anger. We develop propositions that integrate the construct of regulatory focus with that of moral emotions. The relationships between these different elements are outlined in Table 2.

Our approach is both novel and micro-foundational. This is one of the first attempts to explore the role of the individual when attempting to understand the dynamics of relationships between headquarters and subsidiaries. In so doing, we focus not just on the cognitive or the affective, but on both as we work to understand the dynamic. Boundary spanners may be constrained by their organizations' policies and practices, but their behavior is not rigidly determined by those elements. They have some room to maneuver, which is likely to be shaped by their own dispositions. Our approach complements the extant work because it focuses on individual predispositions to act in a certain way. It is imperative for researchers to go beyond the macro-construct of power to explore the inner black box of interactional dynamics between headquarters and subsidiary boundary spanners. We need to investigate how these relationships are managed in practice, and not simply who might win or lose based on the underlying power dynamics. Ethnographic studies coupled with survey-based investigations would be extremely helpful in deepening our understanding of the relationship between MNE headquarters and subsidiaries.

REFERENCES

Aghion, P., & Tirole, J. (1997). Formal and real authority in organizations. *Journal of Political Economy*, *105*, 1–29.

Bagozzi, R. P., Gopinath, M., & Nyer, P. U. (1999). The role of emotions in marketing. *Journal of the Academy of Marketing Science*, *27*, 184–206.

Bingham, C. B., & Eisenhardt, K. M. (2008). Position, leverage and opportunity: A typology of strategic logics linking resources with competitive advantage. *Managerial and Decision Economics*, *29*, 251–256.

Birkinshaw, J., & Hood, N. (1997). An empirical study of development processes in foreign-owned subsidiaries in Canada and Scotland. *Management International Review*, *37*(4), 339–364.

Birkinshaw, J., & Ridderstråle, J. (1999). Fighting the corporate immune system: A process study of subsidiary initiatives in multinational corporations. *International Business Review*, *8*(2), 149–180.

Björkman, I., Barner-Rasmussen, W., & Li, L. (2004). Managing knowledge transfer in MNCs: The impact of headquarters control mechanisms. *Journal of International Business Studies*, *35*, 443–455.

Blazejewski, S., & Becker-Ritterspach, F. (2011). Conflict in headquarter-subsidiary relations: A critical literature review and new directions. In M. Geppert & C. Dörrenbächer (Eds.), *Politics and power in the multinational corporation: The role of interests, identities, and institutions* (pp. 139–190). Cambridge: Cambridge University Press.

Bouquet, C., & Birkinshaw, J. (2008). Managing power in the multinational corporation: How low-power actors gain influence. *Journal of Management*, *34*, 477–508.

Brockner, J., & Higgins, E. T. (2001). Emotions and management: A regulatory focus perspective. *Organizational Behavior and Human Decision Processes*, *86*, 35–66.

Cantwell, J. A., & Mudambi, R. (2005). MNE competence-creating subsidiary mandates. *Strategic Management Journal*, *26*, 1109–1128.

Collinson, S., & Houlden, J. (2005). Decision-making and market orientation in the internationalization processes of small and medium-sized enterprises. *Management International Review*, *45*(4), 413–436.

Das, T. K., & Kumar, R. (2011). Regulatory focus and opportunism in the alliance development process. *Journal of Management*, *37*, 682–708.

Dörrenbächer, C., & Geppert, M. (2009). A micro-political perspective on subsidiary initiative taking; Evidence from German owned subsidiaries in France. *European Management Journal*, *27*, 100–112.

Dutton, J. E., Ashford, S. J., O'Neill, R. M., & Lawrence, K. A. (2001). Moves that matter: Issue selling and organizational change. *Academy of Management Journal*, *44*(4), 716–736.

Granovetter, M. (1985). Economic action and social structure: The problem of embeddedness. *American Journal of Sociology*, *91*, 481–510.

Haidt, J. (2003). The moral emotions. In R. J. Davidson, K. R. Scherer, & H. H. Goldsmith (Eds.), *Handbook of affective science* (pp. 852–870). Oxford: Oxford University Press.

Hambrick, D., & Mason, P. (1984). The organization as a reflection of its top managers. *Academy of Management Review*, *9*, 193–206.

Higgins, E. T. (1998). Promotion and prevention: Regulatory focus as a motivational principle. *Advances in Experimental Social Psychology*, *30*, 1–46.

Higgins, E. T. (2000). Making a good decision: Value from fit. *American Psychologist, 55*, 1217–1230.

Higgins, E. T. (2009). Regulatory fit in the goal-pursuit process. In G. B. Moskowitz & H. Grant (Eds.), *The psychology of goals* (pp. 505–534). New York, NY: The Guildford Press.

Hodgkinson, G. P., & Healey, M. P. (2011). Psychological foundations of dynamic capabilities: Reflexion and reflection in strategic management. *Strategic Management Journal, 13*, 1500–1516.

Jarzabkowski, P., & Spee, P. A. (2009). Strategy as practice: A review and future directions. *International Journal of Management Reviews, 11*, 69–95.

Jehn, K. A. (1997). A qualitative analysis of conflict types and dimensions in organizational groups. *Administrative Science Quarterly, 42*, 530–557.

Jehn, K. A., & Mannix, E. A. (2001). The dynamic nature of conflict: A longitudinal study of intra-group conflict and group performance. *The Academy of Management Journal, 44*(2), 238–251.

Jones, W. E. (2006). Explanation and condemnation. In P. A. Tabensky (Ed.), *Judging and understanding: Essays on free will, narrative, meaning and the ethical limits of condemnation* (pp. 43–64). Aldershot: Ashgate Publishing Limited.

Kostova, T., & Roth, K. (2003). Social capital in multinational corporations and a micro macro model of its formation. *Academy of Management Review, 28*, 297–317.

Kumar, R. (1997). The role of affect in negotiations: An integrative overview. *Journal of Applied Behavioral Science, 33*, 84–100.

Laham, S. M., Chopra, S., Lalljee, M., & Parkinson, B. (2010). Emotional and behavioural reactions to moral transgressions: Cross-cultural and individual variations in India and Britain. *International Journal of Psychology, 45*(1), 64–71.

Liberman, N., Idson, L. C., Camacho, S. J., & Higgins, E. T. (1999). Promotion and prevention choices between stability and change. *Journal of Personality and Social Psychology, 77*, 1135–1145.

Liberman, N., Molden, D. C., Idson, L. C., & Higgins, E. T. (2001). Promotion and prevention focus on alternative hypotheses: Implications for attributional functions. *Journal of Personality and Social Psychology, 80*, 5–18.

Lukes, S. (2005). *Power: A radical view*. Basingstoke: Palgrave Macmillan.

Luo, Y. (2008). Procedural justice and interfirm cooperation in strategic alliances. *Strategic Management Journal, 29*(1), 27–46.

Mandler, G. (1975). *Mind and emotion*. New York, NY: Wiley.

Morris, M. W., Williams, K. Y., Leung, K., Larrick, R., Mendoza, M. T., Bhatnagar, D., … Hu, J.-C. (1998). Conflict management style: Accounting for cross-national differences. *Journal of International Business Studies, 29*, 729–747.

Mudambi, R. (2011). Hierarchy, coordination, and innovation in the multinational enterprise. *Global Strategy Journal, 1*, 317–323.

Mudambi, R., & Navarra, P. (2004). Is knowledge power? Knowledge flows, subsidiary power and rent-seeking within MNCs. *Journal of International Business Studies, 35*, 385–406.

Oatley, K., & Johnson-Laird, P. N. (1987). Towards a cognitive theory of emotions. *Cognition and Emotion, 1*, 29–50.

Ogilvie, J. R., & Kidder, D. L. (2008). What about negotiator styles? *International Journal of Conflict Management, 19*(2), 132–147.

Otterbeck, L. (Ed.). (1981). *The management of headquarters-subsidiary relationships in multinational corporations* (pp. 25–78). Aldershot: Gower.

Pinkley, R. L. (1990). Dimensions of conflict frame: Disputant interpretations of conflict. *Journal of Applied Psychology, 75*, 117–126.

Powell, T. C., Lovallo, D., & Fox, C. R. (2011). Behavioral strategy. *Strategic Management Journal, 32*, 1369–1386.

Pruitt, D. G. (1983). Strategic choice in negotiation. *American Behavioral Scientist, 27*, 167–194.

Rahim, M. A. (1983). A measure of styles of handling interpersonal conflict. *Academy of Management Journal, 26*, 368–376.

Rahim, M. A. (2002). Towards a theory of managing organizational conflict. *International Journal of Conflict Management, 13*, 206–235.

Rahim, M. A., & Bonoma, T. V. (1979). Managing organizational conflict: A model for diagnosis and intervention. *Psychological Reports, 43*, 1323–1344.

Reid, S. D. (1981). The decision-maker and export entry and expansion. *Journal of International Business Studies, 36*(1), 2–8.

Roney, C. J. R., Higgins, E. T., & Shah, J. (1995). Goals and framing: How outcome focus influences motivation and emotion. *Personality and Social Psychology Bulletin, 21*, 1151–1160.

Rozin, P., Lowery, L., Imada, S., & Haidt, J. (1999). The CAD triad hypothesis: A mapping between three moral emotions (Contempt, Anger, Disgust) and three moral codes (Community, Autonomy, Divinity). *Journal of Personality and Social Psychology, 76*, 574–586.

Schotter, A., & Beamish, P. (2011). Performance effects of multinational-headquarters subsidiary conflict and the role of boundary spanners: The case of headquarters initiative rejection. *Journal of International Management, 17*, 243–259.

Shapiro, D. L. (2010). Relational identity theory: A systematic approach for transforming the emotional dimension of conflict. *American Psychologist, 65*, 634–645.

Shweder, R. A., Much, N. C., Mahapatra, M., & Park, L. (1997). The "Big Three" of morality (Autonomy, Community, Divinity) and the "Big Three" explanations of suffering. In P. Rozin & A. Brandt (Eds.), *Morality and health*. New York, NY: Routledge.

Thomas, K. (1976). Conflict and conflict management. In W. K. Hoy & C. G. Miskel (Eds.), *Educational administration: Theory, research, practice* (pp. 100–102). New York, NY: McGraw-Hill.

Tippmann, E., Scott, P. S., & Mangematin, V. (2012). Problem solving in MNCs: How local and global solutions are (and are not) created. *Journal of International Business Studies, 43*, 746–771.

Weber, L., & Mayer, K. (2011). Designing effective contracts: Exploring the influence of framing and expectations. *Academy of Management Review, 36*, 53–75.

Yagi, N., & Kleinberg, J. (2011). Boundary work: An interpretive ethnographic perspective on negotiating and leveraging cross-cultural identity. *Journal of International Business Studies, 42*(5), 629–653.

THE AMBIDEXTROUS SUBSIDIARY: STRATEGIES FOR ALIGNMENT, ADAPTION AND MANAGING ALLEGIANCES

Marty Reilly and Pamela Sharkey Scott

ABSTRACT

Increased global competition originating from both within the multinational corporation (MNC) and from global adversaries dictates that subsidiaries must be responsive to change, adaptable, and capable of sensing and seizing new opportunities for capability development and growth. For many subsidiaries adhering to, or being seen to adhere to, the wider organizational goals dictated by their parent represents an additional complexity. While it may be necessary to divert slack resources towards capability development, subsidiaries which do so, on their own initiative, may well run the risk of being categorized as an unruly node in the MNC's network. Further, by failing to show compliance with organizational strategy future subsidiary-driven efforts may be curbed or prohibited.

The need to demonstrate value to the MNC through developing new and novel capabilities while complying with parent-driven strategy thus represents a key subsidiary dilemma, yet remains an underexplored

Perspectives on Headquarters-Subsidiary Relationships in the Contemporary MNC
Research in Global Strategic Management, Volume 17, 141–164
Copyright © 2016 by Emerald Group Publishing Limited
ISSN: 1064-4857/doi:10.1108/S1064-485720160000017006

phenomenon in international business research. Framing this dilemma via an ambidexterity lens, our chapter explores how five subsidiary units balance and negotiate allegiances within a modern MNC context. We find that in the subsidiary context aligning and adapting may not be competing or exclusive strategies, but in effect two sides of the same coin. The structural context can shape relative levels of alignment via controlling mechanisms and monitoring of operations while the subsidiary's behavioral context, idiosyncratic to the subsidiary, can dictate its capacity to generate initiatives and to create new and novel capabilities for diffusion across the MNC network.

Keywords: Ambidexterity; MNC subsidiary; subsidiary allegiances; headquarter-subsidiary relationships; capability development

INTRODUCTION

Operating as an "insider in two systems" (Collinson & Wang, 2012, p. 1516) this chapter argues that a subsidiary must be both aligned with its parent's strategy while remaining adaptive enough to seize local opportunities and to develop new capabilities. Studies to date focus on either subsidiary alignment strategies (e.g., Reilly, Sharkey Scott, & Mangematin, 2012) or adaptive/capability building strategies (Birkinshaw & Hood, 1998; Chen, Chen, & Ku, 2012; Colakoglu, Yamao, & Lepak, 2014) largely in isolation rather than encompassing the dual systems in which the subsidiary engages. Prompted by existing research recognizing the inherent difficulties in achieving what is referred to as contextual *ambidexterity*, an approach which blends, rather than separates two seemingly conflicting goals (Gibson & Birkinshaw, 2004), we propose that being ambidextrous is not an outcome for the subsidiary but rather a critical means of survival. In accordance, we explore how subsidiaries meet the competing demands of alignment within the multinational corporation (MNC) through fulfilling their mandate as assigned by headquarters (HQs) while adapting to their local environment through developing initiatives and capabilities, which also serve to demonstrate their value to their parent.

Our in-depth study of five cases in the dynamic information and communications technology (ICT) industry investigates how some subsidiaries pursue the seemingly competing goals of balancing alignment with their

HQ while building the adaptive capacity conducive for capability development and strategic renewal at the subsidiary level. We contribute to theory on subsidiary ambidexterity by identifying how alignment and adaption strategies are operationalized in the subsidiary context whilst also providing new insight into the complexities of subsidiary allegiances, where they lie and how they are balanced against parent expectations and objectives.

LITERATURE REVIEW

The basic premise of ambidexterity, as conceived by Duncan's (1976) seminal work, is that organizations must overcome the inherent difficulties in facing two competing and seemingly contradictory tensions. An ability to adeptly manage conflicting goals can lead to greater firm performance (Gibson & Birkinshaw, 2004; Raisch & Birkinshaw, 2008), higher levels of organizational learning (March, 1991), and/or sustainability (Boumgarden, Nickerson, & Zenger, 2012; O'Reilly & Tushman, 2008). Conflicting goals examined include balancing strategies of exploitation and exploration (Gupta, Smith, & Shalley, 2006; He & Wong, 2004; O'Reilly & Tushman, 2004), responsiveness and integration (Bartlett & Ghoshal, 1989; Harzing, 2000; Taggart, 1997), flexibility and efficiency (Adler, Goldoftas, & Levine, 1999; Eisenhardt, Furr, & Bingham, 2010), or the pursuit of both alignment and adaption (Birkinshaw & Gibson, 2004; Duncan, 1976; Gibson & Birkinshaw, 2004).

A further complexity relates to whether organizations actually balance two competing goals or *vacillate* between them, alternating sequentially over time (Boumgarden et al., 2012). In this sense ambidexterity can essentially be considered as a trade-off (either/or) between two goals or as paradoxical (both/and) where both goals are managed simultaneously (Gibson & Birkinshaw, 2004). For example, in a case study on *Toyota*, Adler et al. (1999) found managers moved between flexibility and efficiency through periodic model changeovers facilitated by meta-routines, the partitioning of operations, and subsequent switching between the two. In contrast, "semi-structures" emphasize simultaneity in balancing two tasks at the same time (Bingham, Eisenhardt, & Furr, 2007; Eisenhardt et al., 2010). To achieve efficiency and flexibility via the latter method there needs to be structure to guide actions in conjunction with the latitude required to respond to actual events with flexibility. By way of illustration Birkinshaw and Gibson (2004) show how *Oracle* managed to adapt their core product offering to include services whilst simultaneously redefining what alignment meant by breaking down formal processes and making decision making more unilateral.

Despite this growing body of knowledge, there is still uncertainty as to how organizations overcome contrasting tensions: do they create a balance between two competing goals (Eisenhardt et al., 2010) or do they systematically switch between two mutually exclusive solutions? (Duncan, 1976; Lubatkin, Simsek, Ling, & Veiga, 2006). Applying this question to the example above, *Oracle* built ambidexterity through the former balancing approach, while *Toyota* followed a more systematic, segregated approach; yet both organizations are considered ambidextrous despite their very different strategies.

The vast majority of empirical studies on ambidexterity focus on organizational performance as an outcome. Measuring performance in the subsidiary context serves little purpose however unless the measure captures subsidiary performance relative to its peers. Further, current performance can underplay the importance of adaption by neglecting to take into account subsidiary specific factors which threaten to disrupt operations in the future including growing intra-MNC competition for mandates (Mudambi & Navarra, 2004) and increased outsourcing of activities (Buckley, 2009, 2011; Buckley & Ghauri, 2004). In accordance, this study moves from the organizational level to explore how ambidexterity is approached at the subsidiary level, where the need to balance alignment and adaptation is a constant demand and a critical element in shaping subsidiary strategy. In the subsequent sections we argue that ambidexterity at the subsidiary level is distinct both theoretically and in practice from that observed at an organizational level due to complexities and nuances inherent within MNC contexts including multiple embeddedness, internal competition for mandates, governance mechanisms, and the rent-seeking behaviors of subsidiaries.

Ambidexterity and the Subsidiary Context

Building upon Ghoshal and Bartlett's (1994) work on organizational context, ambidexterity at an *organizational* level relies heavily on the structural context of the organization and is shaped by both "soft elements" and "hard elements" (Gibson & Birkinshaw, 2004). These "soft" elements encompass *stretch* − or ambitious objectives, and *discipline* − which captures clear standards of performance. The "hard" elements include *support* – characterized by a supportive environment involving assistance and countenance to others, while *trust* – captures equity and fairness in decision making.

Recent research however, which captures both growing intra-MNC competition for mandates (Mudambi & Navarra, 2004), and increased outsourcing of activities (Buckley, 2009, 2011; Buckley & Ghauri, 2004), suggests that the factors highlighted above may not paint a true or accurate picture of a modern subsidiary context. For example, in terms of "soft elements" it is likely that *discipline* (or clear standards of performance) become blurred in an increasingly competitive MNC arena characterized by subsidiary managers using slack resources to develop local initiatives that support their local agenda (Delany, 2000). When we look at the "hard elements" of *support* and *trust* the applicability of existing organizational frameworks must also come under greater scrutiny in explaining the contextual factors conducive to building ambidexterity at the subsidiary level. Firstly, for *support* to positively influence developing ambidexterity we would expect business units to share access to resources and to lend assistance and countenance to others (Gibson & Birkinshaw, 2004). Evidence from recent studies however shows that knowledge sharing within the MNC (particularly subsidiary–subsidiary knowledge flows) may be curbed or thwarted as subsidiaries opt to use knowledge to exert bargaining power (Mudambi & Navarra, 2004) or to build their profile or "voice" (Bouquet & Birkinshaw, 2008a, 2008b). Ultimately, the result is that many subsidiaries are becoming more proprietorial about their knowledge in an effort to preserve its value whilst keeping peer internal competitors in check. As such, it is likely that knowledge protectionism takes precedence over collaborative efforts or knowledge sharing. Finally, in a similar vein, we highlight that *trust* – intended to capture equity and fairness in decision making – may also be less applicable in a modern MNC context which is shaped by internal lobbying, issue selling, politics, and the leveraging of key actors to influence the allocation of remits (Dörrenbächer & Gammelgaard, 2011; Dörrenbächer & Geppert, 2006; Ling, Floyd, & Baldridge, 2005). For example, Dörrenbächer and Gammelgaard (2011, p. 32) address how the subtleties of micro-political bargaining power manifests in how "subsidiaries exercise their influence on headquarters through a combination of their own initiatives, issue selling, strategic information politics and manipulative behavior." At this juncture we point out that it is not our intention to merely point out potential problems in the applicability of existing theory, rather we aim to highlight and discuss the complexities of the subsidiary context with a view to identifying new and insightful avenues for theory development.

Operationalizing Ambidexterity: Alignment and Adaption in the Subsidiary

Recognizing that the demands on an organization are always in conflict to some degree (Duncan, 1976), the concept of ambidexterity not only captures an ability to align, whilst remaining adaptive enough to "still be around tomorrow" (Gibson & Birkinshaw, 2004, p. 209), but also provides a suitable lens to explore the complexities inherent in the pursuit of two seemingly opposing or contradictory tensions (Eisenhardt et al., 2010).

Struggling to compete in an increasingly competitive global arena, many subsidiary units face the difficult task of fulfilling domestic and/or regional responsibilities whilst simultaneously developing the new and novel capabilities needed to demonstrate value to the MNC. On one hand, subsidiaries must demonstrate value by leveraging their local external knowledge base and the opportunities that it provides (Ambos, Ambos, & Schlegelmilch, 2006; Collinson & Wang, 2012; Yamin & Andersson, 2011). On the other hand however, the subsidiary must also maintain a "shared vision" (Colakoglu, 2012) through alignment with parent-driven objectives. What makes this task inherently difficult is that opportunities arising from external embeddedness are rooted in the subsidiary's local environment and likely to have a local "flavor." This suggests that it may be difficult for parents to recognize the value of a particular initiative, and that independent subsidiary initiatives which stray too far from corporate strategy, or are perceived as misaligned with existing goals, can be seen as rent-seeking behavior (Mudambi & Navarra, 2004), empire building (Bouquet & Birkinshaw, 2008a), or indicative of the agency problem (O'Donnell, 2000).

An adaptive capacity captures flexibility and facilitates greater responsiveness by allowing organizations to adjust fluidly to unanticipated change (Eisenhardt et al., 2010). At the subsidiary level an adaptive capacity not only captures an ability to respond effectively to external contingencies but also underpins capability development when the adaption and reconfiguring of the resource base is used to create value in new and novel ways (Teece, Pisano, & Shuen, 1997). This capacity allows the subsidiary to respond to local opportunities and to absorb knowledge from its local environment and from across its parent's operations, but it also implies that the subsidiary may sometimes diverge, at least to a minor extent, from the role assigned by its parent.

In contrast, alignment refers to greater coherence in the organization's pattern of activities (Gibson & Birkinshaw, 2004). It encompasses strict compliance with the parent's expectations of subsidiary operations and achieving the aims and objectives which cascade down from HQs. Alignment often calls for a more mechanistic organizational structure; characterized by greater monitoring of operations, more restrictive controlling mechanisms, and vertically integrated systems (Boumgarden et al., 2012). Perhaps most importantly, in a more structured environment there is less room for subsidiaries to utilize "slack" resources meaning that the exploitation of short-term certainties is likely to take precedence over the exploration of new opportunities. In summary, ambidexterity captures how alignment and adaption are operationalized in practice; the former via coherence and strict adherence to the subsidiary mandate as decreed by MNC strategy while adaptation encompasses the behaviors and mechanisms that lead to stepping outside of that mandate. Within any organization however, we expect managers and actors to also be bounded by biases, rationality, and allegiances. For example, at a HQ level, managers must overcome problems stemming from cultural and administrative distance; such challenges become increasing apparent when "head office managers face bounded rationality problems when trying to distinguish between valuable subsidiary initiatives and initiatives that can best be pursued outside of the company boundaries" (Verbeke & Greidanus, 2009, p. 1480). Essentially, cultural or cognitive biases may impede HQs recognition of a valuable initiative. In contrast, it is less likely that local subsidiary management (influenced by cognitive distances and their own local biases) would adopt the same rational mechanisms to guide their decision making, especially if such decisions conflicted with local interests or curbed an ability to expand, modify, or grow local operations. The subsidiary is, we suggest, likely to perceive local initiatives more positively, driven not just by self-interest but also by genuine commitment to contributing to its organization. It is in accordance with such assumptions that we now address how subsidiary allegiances not only manifest in the shaping of subsidiary strategy but also create additional complexities in the building of ambidexterity at the subsidiary level.

Subsidiary Allegiances and Scope for Theoretical Contribution

Subsidiary research has paid significant attention to how subsidiaries can become embedded in their local environments, providing access to local knowledge (Andersson, Forsgren, & Holm, 2001, 2002), which can then be diffused throughout the MNC network (Ambos et al., 2006; Tsai, 2001). Critically, embeddedness enables subsidiaries to utilize local knowledge in the pursuit of seizing of new opportunities (Figueiredo, 2011; Meyer, Mudambi, & Narula, 2010; Reilly & Sharkey Scott, 2014).

Related streams of literature suggest that when subsidiaries come across lucrative opportunities in their local environment they may quickly diverge from, or abandon entirely, the roles assigned to them by HQs in an attempt to pursue opportunities more attuned with the safeguarding of their long-term survival within the MNC (Delany, 2000; Dörrenbächer & Gammelgaard, 2011). Through various micro-political mechanisms including the leveraging of local knowledge and the exertion of "bargaining power" (Mudambi & Navarra, 2004), the relative allegiances of the subsidiary become more visible. Such approaches by subsidiary units can be met with mixed responses from the parent however, including greater monitoring of the subsidiary's subsequent operations, which in turn can decrease their autonomy (Ambos, Andersson, & Birkinshaw, 2010). Subsidiaries must therefore find a balance between exercising local allegiances or embeddedness to their local environment with expectations of alignment within their organization; it is likely that such a "sweet spot" rests somewhere along a continuum from total adaptation to total alignment. For example, Delany (2000, p. 229) identifies how initiative-taking subsidiaries, in an effort to support their local agenda, use slack resources to build and develop local capabilities without express authority from their parent; adopting the mindset that it is "usually easier to seek forgiveness than permission." It is often only after such initiatives have been tested that the parent organization is informed and subsequently lobbied for investment. The need for subsidiary managers to act as champions of local initiatives or as "national advocate" reflects just one side of their dyadic "dual organizational identification" (Vora, Kostava, & Roth, 2007, p. 596), and the often conflicting local and organizational interests facing subsidiaries.

While the value of strong regional ties has been identified in the international business domain (Arregle, Beamish, & Hébert, 2009; Rugman & Verbeke, 2004, 2005), there is a distinct lack of studies which explore how dual allegiances are managed and negotiated at the subsidiary level. Vora et al. (2007) for example, provide insights into how individual subsidiary managers are prone to develop "dual organizational identification" in terms of role fulfillment rather than on how allegiances are actually managed and balanced. While their study outlines the criticality of dual identification for the effectiveness of subsidiary managers there is also a need for greater insights into the actual mechanisms employed at the subsidiary level to balance local allegiances and self-serving initiatives with those demands that cascade down from HQs.

An unresolved dilemma thus arises: should the subsidiary's allegiance to the parent be evidenced by strict adherence to parent-driven objectives via unvarying alignment to its mandate? Arguably, such an approach comes with many caveats including the real risk of becoming a peripheral node in the MNC's network due to an inability to shape local strategy or without the capacity to adapt and evolve as a unit. Or, in contrast, should local priorities take precedence as the subsidiary strives to continuously build the new capabilities needed to stay ahead of internal competitors within the MNC? The latter approach prompts the risk of the subsidiary being categorized as rent-seeking, wasteful of MNC resources, or as an unruly node in the MNC network.

In sum, despite the recognition of the conflicting demands on subsidiary managers, a gap in our understanding remains as to how dual allegiances are balanced at the subsidiary level. We argue that the concept of ambidexterity (as operationalized by alignment and adaption strategies) within foreign-owned subsidiaries is not only theoretically distinct from that applying to large organizations but also that in this context, the capacity to be ambidextrous is not an outcome, but rather a means of balancing conflicting MNC and local demands in ensuring subsidiary survival. In order to theorize on how subsidiaries can achieve ambidexterity, particularly given allegiances to their local context, it is both necessary and imperative that we encompass the complexities of how subsidiary managers balance local priorities with those that cascade down from HQs.

METHODOLOGY

Research Design, Research Setting, and Sample

The study adopts a multiple case study design in line with recent calls for greater qualitative studies within the IB domain (Birkinshaw, Brannen, & Tung, 2011; Doz, 2011). More specifically, it can be argued that a micro-perspective is warranted in exploring how contextual factors including subsidiary embeddedness, initiative taking, and local strategy can shape the subsidiary's ability to align and adapt. Our multiple case study approach, encompassing a cross-case analysis, allowed us to better ground any emerging insights by determining if findings were idiosyncratic to each case or reflective of more general commonalities across the cases sampled. The use of multiple cases was therefore central in ensuring that findings were not only reflective of shared phenomena, behaviors, and observations but also more transferable from a theoretical perspective (Eisenhardt, 1991; Eisenhardt & Graebner, 2007; Yin, 2009).

As a research setting, Ireland has demonstrated a long-term capacity to attract high levels of foreign direct investment (FDI) from MNCs. A number of factors, including a low corporate tax regime, liberal trade policies, and membership of the European Union all contribute to fueling a FDI-intensive economy based around three distinct industries: pharmaceuticals, medical devices, and ICT (Monaghan, Gunnigle, & Lavelle, 2014). To enhance internal validity and to control for environmental effects (Welch, Piekkari, Plakoyiannaki, & Paavilainen-Mantymaki, 2011) our study focuses on the ICT industry due to its dynamic nature and the recognition that it is primed for exploring the development and adaption of capabilities (Brown & Eisenhardt, 1997; Tippmann, Mangematin, & Sharkey Scott, 2013).

From a potential population of subsidiaries within the ICT sector a representative sample was shortlisted and requested to participate in the study. In accord with our research objectives we shortlisted and chose candidates where the scope to provide fresh insight into our understanding of adaption and capability development within the MNC was greatest. Semi-structured interviews (28) were carried out in five subsidiaries over a six month period; ranging from 13 at a middle management level to 15 at the senior/executive level. The rationale for diversity in respondent levels is addressed in the subsequent section. For reasons of confidentiality and anonymity the subsidiaries sampled are referred to as *Gamma*, *Omega*, *Epsilon*, *Delta*, and *Sigma*.

Collecting and Analyzing the Data

A structured discussion was developed prior to conducting the research which was then tested and piloted among industry experts. The revised discussion guide encompassed two key domains of inquiry; the first of these was the behavioral dimension where we examined and assessed adaptive strategies in the subsidiary. The second dimension, a structural dimension, assessed how alignment and coherence was managed and negotiated within the wider MNC and directly with parent expectations.

The data collection encompassed both archival data and interviews. The archival data was initially gathered via internal and external sources. External sources included media published articles and academic papers about each organization identified using ABI Inform. Internal sources were gathered both prior to, and during, the interview program. This material was then analyzed and integrated to provide both a contextual background and to triangulate respondent data. The data collection process comprised of four phases including: (1) study of archival data, (2) interviews with middle managers, (3) interviews with senior directors/executives, and finally (4) the study of further archival materials. The rationale behind achieving diversity in respondent levels was not only based on the ability to capture a broader contextual background to the study but was also guided by the recognition that middle managers would be primed to provide insight on capability development at the operational levels and possess an ability to draw on first-hand experiences of how change and adaption is adopted and incorporated into subsidiary strategy. This is in comparison with senior level management which, given their experience, were deemed to be the most knowledgeable informants in terms of organizational strategy, structure, and performance (Hambrick, 1981). In accordance, it was expected that senior management would offer the greatest insight on how alignment is pursued and negotiated in the subsidiary context as their position would necessitate direct communication with their parent or regional HQs.

The data analysis process was iterative, running concurrent with the data collection. As interviews were transcribed the emergence of new insights helped inform subsequent interviews and allowed for the inclusion of emergent themes as well as those existing in the literature (Miles & Huberman, 1994). An initial open coding approach involved broad thematic codes including, for example, "balancing/prioritizing allegiances" and "alignment strategies" which were then reorganized, merged, and clustered. Second-order coding then allowed for the consolidation of linked themes. Nvivo9 software was used to create a database of transcripts and all internal and external archival data assisting in the management of analysis in a consistent and systematic manner.

FINDINGS

We identified a number of avenues by which subsidiary management balance dual allegiances and attempt to overcome the challenges and tensions associated with pursing strategies of both alignment and adaption. Previous research indicates that contextual ambidexterity, built at an organizational level, is dependent upon stretch, discipline, support, and trust (Gibson & Birkinshaw, 2004). It is these four interdependent dimensions which Ghoshal and Bartlett (1994) first attributed to shaping organizational context and ultimately managerial actions within the firm. Our findings highlight how the nuances of subsidiary context, characterized by increasing internal competition and an onus to balance dual allegiances create additional challenges for building contextual ambidexterity at the subsidiary level whilst also presenting some new opportunities for theory development.

We identify a number of alignment mechanisms (*demonstrating mutual benefits, identifying influencers, creating new champions/leveraging expats*) and adaptation mechanisms (*identifying new opportunities for capability development and engaging in recurrent cycles of capability development*) used by subsidiaries to balance both their relationship with their parent and their local allegiances. The following tables highlight the two aggregate dimensions of alignment and adaption including second-order constructs and supportive illustrative data. Table 1 presents alignment strategies as a function of the structural restraints of the MNC while Table 2 presents the behavioral dimension and captures how adaptive strategies are pursued at the subsidiary level.

While exploring how subsidiary management attempts to balance both local and HQ allegiances, our findings evidence efforts to sustain headcount locally, or to ensure that "*there's no lock on that gate when I finish*" *(Gamma, SM2)*. This strategy was supported by demonstrating to HQ that the activities carried out by the subsidiary were of critical importance to the MNC whilst also using and leveraging key organizational actors to influence the allocation of mandates.

In Table 2, we show how the behavioral context drives adaptive strategies and places a distinct onus on subsidiary management to engage in cycles of strategic renewal via a process of sensing new opportunities for capability development and ultimately in committing local resources and efforts into realizing those opportunities. As observed in *Delta*: "*If we deliver the results we have better conversations, and group are much more likely to give us what we're asking ... if we're telling a good story and we have the results behind it then group are much more likely to give us the budgets we need*" *(Delta, SM1)*. In this sense alignment and adaption need not be perceived as mutually exclusive, or as requiring sequential alternating (Boumgarden et al., 2012) as subsidiary management strive

Table 1. Alignment Strategies: The Structural Dimension.

Second-Order Concepts	First-Order Themes (Illustrative Data)
Demonstrating mutual benefits	*"One of the challenges we have constantly is trying to get buy-in to develop products, to be able to get the funding to actually make them happen. Ideally you would have a strong business case locally to do it and then you will simply push on, you will convince the powers that are, 'look we need the funding, this is the reason why, this is the return we're going to get etc.', and the business case accordingly. If you can demonstrate that this is something that could actually have an appeal globally then obviously that adds weight to it" (Delta, SM3)*
	"If the business doesn't support it or feels they don't need it then it won't get the funding behind it so it's up to us to make sure that they understand what this capability can do for them, what that looks like to the market ... they hold the purse strings at the end of the day" (Delta, MM1)
	"We would take the Gamma strategy and then we look at Ireland — what are our strengths?, what can we do? Where can we grow? and then we put efforts into that locally ... we wouldn't go against the corporate strategy, we would enhance it, we would take the piece out of the strategy that we want to work with" (Gamma, SM1)
	"Once you can show you could deliver on that basic mandate you could then look for more and more responsibility. The site has always been well perceived strategically within the wider organization" (Omega, MM1)
Identifying key influencers	*"A central theme of that strategy [recent mandate expansion] was to maintain and grow the headcount, no question about it and we would have been continuously coming up with ideas to do that, we would have drawn up plans, we would then draw up a communication plan where we would all have people to target in Sweden, so I would have four or five people and it was my role to get those, you know to meet them to get them to understand what we were doing, absolutely, it was forensic" (Gamma, SM2)*
	"If the CTO comes to me with it, as CTO he has access to funding or has ways of manipulating budgets etc. that if you wanted to make something happen you could potentially access it. So I think one of the key things is you need to have senior management backing and we do have that locally" (Delta, SM3)
	"We very much focus on relationship building so I would have my personnel constantly talking to the guys in the US to make sure they're building up a rapport" (Sigma, MM1)
	"It's very important for management in Ireland to keep close to the senior management team in the region to influence what remits go where" (Gamma, SM3)
	"The site here would have a good profile. Any time we have upper levels of management visiting the plant they always say they are happy with the level of achievement that comes out of here — with that comes an accountability where there's definitely more opportunities provided" (Omega, MM1)

Table 1. (*Continued*)

Second-Order Concepts	First-Order Themes (Illustrative Data)
Creating new champions/ leveraging expats	"*We would place people in Sweden. So the decision maker for certain activities would be Irish and you have to do that if you want to maintain [operations]... some countries are really blatant about it .... Presence is huge, the key influencers, the decision makers are at the center*" (*Gamma, SM1*)
	"*The headquarters for us are in America so you're going to have to spend some time in America, working it, not on a business trip for a week – you need to move to the Americas to do it ... to be a true global leader, which is what we're trying to get to here you have to spend time in other regions ... we have people in the States, we have a lot of people there now because we realize that if you want a global role or a senior role within the organization you've got to have a presence in other countries*" (*Epsilon, SM2*)
	"*You need strong people pushing that agenda at group to get things here, with real belief and concrete reasons for Ireland*" (*Delta, MM2*)
	"*We need to be providing the senior people, the consultants, the people that can go into the CTOs*" (*Gamma, SM3*)

to demonstrate coherence and alignment by delivering upon previous objectives whilst simultaneously positioning the site as a source of capability development primed for further investment. Such findings also support Gibson and Birkinshaw's (2004, p. 221) assertion that contextual ambidexterity is facilitated via a process of "aligning themselves around adaptability."

While the factors outlined above in Tables 1 and 2 capture commonalities across the subsidiaries, it was also observed that a differing emphasis, or greater prominence was placed on certain factors across the sites sampled. For example, in *Epsilon* a stronger focus was placed on demonstrating *mutual benefits* to the HQ by positioning the site as an overlay organization – uniquely positioned as a solutions-orientated subsidiary within the wider network – while in *Gamma* meticulous planning centered on leveraging influencers and trying to place new influencers in positions of power within the MNC at group level.

We found that local allegiances were evidenced by a drive to maintain headcount, secure new mandates, and protect local knowledge. To operationalize such strategies subsidiary management identified and leveraged key influencers within the MNC whilst also focusing on sensing and seizing new opportunities for growth and engaging in recurrent cycles of capability

Table 2. Adaption Strategies: The Behavioral Dimension.

Second-Order Concepts	First-Order Themes (Illustrative Data)
Identifying new opportunities for capability development	*"Cloud computing is going to be huge for Epsilon – a huge opportunity within the industry and it just so happens that we're building expertise here, we're going to have a cloud center, lots of great people with lots of knowledge internally" (Epsilon, SM1)*
	"Identifying what the technology is, when it's coming, what the dependencies are between technology components in order to realize capability and then putting down the milestones throughout long range planning" (Delta, SM3)
	"How do I use my competence to get to the next goal ... the ability to see the next thing, having the ability and agility and confidence to go after it and to gain it" (Omega, SM2)
	"People see problems and say I have an idea for improvement here, they are captured on a local project list.. the engineering team are very much focused on driving that activity but the inputs would come from the operators, technicians and the engineers themselves" (Omega, MM2)
	"We understand what the groups strategic direction is – what group wants to do in the technology space and we develop a local roadmap for Ireland that would be closely aligned" (Delta, SM2)
Engaging in recurrent cycles of capability development	*"We've driven things like IP competence, strategies where we said Ireland is primed and in a perfect position to become an IP hub for everything we want to do in the Gamma world. There would obviously be internal competition within the Gamma subsidiaries to get such a mandate so we would formulate a strategy, pitch that, secure advocates from senior stakeholders and then enlist their support in making that happen" (Gamma, SM3)*
	"If you're doing your job today and in six months' time you're still doing the exact same job you're behind the curve, you've lost it. You need to keep innovating, either bringing in new skills or new skill sets, new offerings and pushing the boundaries" (Epsilon, MM3)
	"In the background you need to be working on other specific stuff in parallel with that so that you're managing your resources on site albeit at different levels ... improving that capability, moving that capability and knowing you're going to impact your operations" (Omega, SM2)
	"You get to the point where a platform and potentially the technology has outlived its usefulness – but probably two years before that point you start planning for the next technology platform to replace that, and you start building it, and doing your last continuous improvements on the old stack" (Delta, SM2)

development. While such adaptive strategies undoubtedly protected local interests there was also a need to demonstrate bilateral benefits for the collective MNC. In balancing this tension, subsidiary management typically focused on developing capabilities which were complementary, supportive, or even preemptive of MNC general strategy. As an "insider in two systems" (Collinson & Wang, 2012, p. 1516), the need to balance such allegiances was deemed challenging yet a crucial element of driving local strategy; as one senior manager observed *"we're a global company but we've got local roots" (Delta, SM1)*. Similarly, senior management in *Gamma* discussed how interdependencies, developed over time, shape both internal relationships and the subsidiary's relative positioning within the MNC: *"We've evolved to that part where we are a trusted member of the Multinational — we're seen as a key part of what they do, we own some of the stuff that they cannot transfer anywhere else. It's too expensive to do and too hard to build the competence" (Gamma, SM1)*.

DISCUSSION

A growing body of research indicates that the capacity to pursue both alignment and adaptive strategies simultaneously is not such an insurmountable challenge as was previously assumed (Raisch & Birkinshaw, 2008). The recognition of *contextual* ambidexterity Gibson and Birkinshaw (2004), an approach which blends rather than separates two seemingly conflicting goals captures this viewpoint and builds upon Ghoshal and Bartlett (1994) to identify key contextual factors including stretch, discipline, trust and, support which facilitate building ambidexterity at an organizational level.

This chapter makes the argument that ambidexterity at the subsidiary level is distinct both theoretically and in practice from that observed at an organizational level not least due to the complexities inherent within MNC contexts including internal competition for mandates, governance mechanisms, and the rent-seeking behaviors of subsidiaries. We highlight that whilst there is a body of literature presenting a wide range of organizational solutions that mediate, moderate, or act as antecedents to building contextual ambidexterity these existing studies fail to provide adequate insight on how ambidexterity can be built at the subsidiary level.

Using the subsidiary as a unit of analysis and adopting a multiple case study research design we have examined how subsidiary units balance the goals of alignment with achieving the adaption needed for capability development and strategic renewal. Building upon the literature and insights gained from our findings we now highlight key contributions including a broader discussion of operationalizing both alignment and adaption strategies in the subsidiary (Tables 3 and 4). We also identify how the fulfillment of these objectives is apparent in the shaping of subsidiary allegiances. Finally, we suggest some avenues for future research and implications for management.

Table 3. Operationalizing Alignment Strategies in the Subsidiary.

Demonstrating mutual benefits

Captures the interdependent nature of parent subsidiary relationships and reveals how initiative taking by the subsidiary must also demonstrate immediate and reciprocal benefits for the parent. As suggested previously, is it likely that management and decision makers in the parent organization act in accordance with bounded rationality when facing decisions on subsidiary mandates and resource allocation (Verbeke & Greidanus, 2009, p. 1480). It is crucial for subsidiary management to reconcile or curb any concerns pertaining to subsidiary-driven capability development or expansion of current activities via a process of explicitly outlining their contribution to the collective organization.

Identifying key influencers

The MNC as an interorganization network (Ghoshal & Bartlett, 1990) is often characterized by an uneven distribution of power and resources. For subsidiaries without significant formal power the capacity to gain access to key influencers and to gain "centrality within strategic networks" (Bouquet & Birkinshaw, 2008b, p. 484) arguably becomes of paramount importance. The identification of key power actors and enlisting and channeling their support to pursue opportunities was a critical mechanism utilized by subsidiary managers to gain the traction necessary to pursue their objectives.

Creating new champions/leveraging expats

The development of social capital as a function of interactions in the MNC allows actors to secure resources or benefits by virtue of their membership within that network (Kostova & Roth, 2003). Our empirical results reveal that in many cases expats, while on assignment or having relocated to the parent organization or regional HQs were used expressly for this purpose. The leveraging of employees who were strategically placed in places of power within the MNC helped in creating what Kostova and Roth (2003, p. 302) referred to as "an environment conducive to valued discretionary behaviors on both sides of the relational dyad" and again contributed to gaining traction to support local objectives.

Table 4.   Operationalizing Adaption Strategies in the Subsidiary.

Identifying new opportunities for capability development
The ability to sense and seize new opportunities for growth and capability renewal mirrors the
   key tenets of the dynamic capabilities literature (Eisenhardt & Martin, 2000; Teece et al.,
   1997). To realize strategies of adaption, modification of existing resource bases or to
   develop the capabilities necessary to respond to external opportunities subsidiary units must
   identify new opportunities which offer reciprocal benefits both locally and for the collective
   organization. Our findings reveal how subsidiary units firstly screen their external
   environments to identify new opportunities for capability development before selecting
   those opportunities most closely aligned with path-dependent knowledge developed on
   site – thereby reinforcing and strengthening their ability to respond to those opportunities.

Engaging in recurrent cycles of capability development
Cognizant of the dangers of both core rigidities and redundant competencies (Leonard-
   Barton, 1992) subsidiary units made continuous efforts to engage in cycles or "rounds" of
   capability development whereby not only was the current resource base constantly modified
   but efforts were also made to develop responsive capabilities in new technological domains.
   In many cases such a strategy was made possible via technology roadmaps and formal
   capability planning whereas across other sites, similar to that observed by Delany (2000), we
   found that slack resources were sometimes used without the express permission of the
   parent to test the viability and tangibility of local capability development. While achieved
   via very different approaches, it is arguably such strategies which enabled subsidiary units to
   adjust fluidly to unanticipated changes in the external environment (Eisenhardt et al., 2010).

Managing Subsidiary Allegiances

Our chapter also contributes to our understanding of how subsidiary
management balances local priorities with those that cascade down from
HQs and ultimately how subsidiary allegiances are managed. Building
upon the findings and discussion above it is argued that the balancing of
allegiances at the subsidiary level may not be as antagonistic as expected.
Findings indicate that subsidiary units balance allegiances between local
self-preserving interests and parent expectations by creating and communicating bilateral benefits for both parties. Further, identifying key influencers within the MNC network and using these actors to channel
support allows the subsidiary to make more explicit any mutual benefits
afforded to the collective organization. Leveraging key influencers, creating new champions, and ultimately gaining their support for subsidiary-
driven capability development not only ensures that subsidiary-driven
efforts gain greater visibility and traction, but may also serve to quell
potential rent-seeking concerns coming from the parent. Arguably such
strategies help subsidiary units to pursue locally driven exploratory

trajectories whilst alleviating concerns of the parent or regional HQs. Linking such findings with theory again points to "dual organizational identification" (Vora et al., 2007) and the literature on resource dependencies within the MNC (Andersson, Forsgren, & Holm, 2007; Dörrenbächer & Gammelgaard, 2011). Just as ambidexterity in the subsidiary requires the balancing of two objectives the same can be said of how the subsidiaries sampled managed their allegiances; when capability development at the subsidiary level is complementary, supportive, or preemptive of MNC general strategy allegiances need not be mutually exclusive but rather serve to benefit both parties. Resource dependencies afford the subsidiary the capacity to maintain headcount and may also provide a potential avenue for extending current mandates – while the parents' benefits stem from the economic opportunities, expertise, or specialized knowledge generated by the subsidiary (Dörrenbächer & Gammelgaard, 2011).

Future Directions for Research

While our study examined how subsidiary units balanced allegiances, parent expectations and the pursuit of adaptive capability building strategies there is also scope to extend this avenue of inquiry to look beyond subsidiary-parent relationships and to examine how issues relating to alignment and adaptation are resolved between interdependent subsidiaries. Given the increased interdependent nature of MNC operations globally, further research into how internal conflicts are managed would provide valuable insight into the challenges stemming from balancing cooperation and coopetition (Luo, 2005) within the modern MNC.

Management Implications

While capability building, adaption of the resource base, and the pursuit of initiatives have generally been lauded as a path to survival it is just one constituent part of building ambidexterity at the subsidiary level. As such, our findings suggest that adaptive strategies should not be pursued to the extent that they conflict with expectations of alignment within the MNC. To curb or negate parent concerns over rent-seeking behavior, subsidiary managers need to explicitly demonstrate reciprocal benefits afforded to the parent and indeed to the collective organization of any initiatives pursued locally. To achieve this aim, enlisting the support of key influencers and creating new champions for local initiatives becomes critical to ensuring that opportunities identified gain the traction necessary to allow the subsidiary to engage in recurrent cycles of capability development and ultimately, to secure their position with their MNC.

CONCLUSION

In this chapter we argue that ambidexterity, at the subsidiary level, is distinct in both theory and practice from that observed at an organizational level. The nuances of the subsidiary context indicate that aligning and adapting need not be perceived as two competing or exclusive strategies, but in effect two sides of the same coin as subsidiary units strive to maintain ambidexterity. The structural context may ultimately shape relative levels of alignment via controlling mechanisms and monitoring of operations while the behavioral context, which is idiosyncratic to the subsidiary may dictate the capacity or scope to generate initiatives, to innovate and to create new and novel capabilities for diffusion across the MNC network. Building upon the ambidexterity literature and adopting the lens of subsidiary allegiances we advance some of the complexities which shape allegiances both locally and within the wider MNC.

REFERENCES

Adler, P. S., Goldoftas, B., & Levine, D. I. (1999). Flexibility versus efficiency? A case study of model changeovers in the Toyota production system. *Organization Science*, 10, 43–68.

Ambos, T. C., Ambos, B., & Schlegelmilch, B. B. (2006). Learning from foreign subsidiaries: An empirical investigation of headquarters' benefits from reverse knowledge transfers. *International Business Review*, 15, 294–312.

Ambos, T. C., Andersson, U., & Birkinshaw, J. (2010). What are the consequences of initiative-taking in multinational subsidiaries? *Journal of International Business Studies*, 42, 1099–1118.

Andersson, U., Forsgren, M., & Holm, U. (2001). Subsidiary embeddedness and competence development in MNCs – A multi-level analysis. *Organization Studies*, 22(6), 1013–1034.

Andersson, U., Forsgren, M., & Holm, U. (2002). The strategic impact of external networks: Subsidiary performance and competence development in the multinational corporation. *Strategic Management Journal*, 23, 979–996.

Andersson, U., Forsgren, M., & Holm, U. (2007). Balancing subsidiary influence in the federative MNC: A business network view. *Journal of International Business Studies*, *38*(5), 802–818.

Arregle, J., Beamish, W. E., & Hébert, L. (2009). The regional dimension of MNEs' foreign subsidiary localization. *Journal of International Business Studies*, *40*, 86–107.

Bartlett, C. A., & Ghoshal, S. (1989). *Managing across borders: The transnational solution*. Boston, MA: Harvard Business School Press.

Bingham, C. B., Eisenhardt, K. M., & Furr, N. R. (2007). What makes a process a capability? Heuristics, strategy, and effective capture of opportunities. *Strategic Entrepreneurship Journal*, *1*(1–2), 27–47.

Birkinshaw, J., Brannen, M. Y., & Tung, R. L. (2011). From a distance and generalizable to up close and grounded: Reclaiming a place for qualitative methods in international business research. *Journal of International Business Studies*, *42*, 573–581.

Birkinshaw, J., & Gibson, C. B. (2004). Building ambidexterity into the organization. *Sloan Management Review*, *45*(4), 47–55.

Birkinshaw, J., & Hood, N. (1998). Multinational subsidiary evolution: Capability and charter change in foreign-owned subsidiary companies. *The Academy of Management Review*, *23*, 773–795.

Boumgarden, P., Nickerson, J., & Zenger, T. R. (2012). Sailing into the wind: Exploring the relationships among ambidexterity, vacillation, and organizational performance. *Strategic Management Journal*, *33*, 587–610.

Bouquet, C., & Birkinshaw, J. (2008a). Weight versus voice: How foreign subsidiaries gain attention from corporate headquarters. *Academy of Management Journal*, *51*, 577–601.

Bouquet, C., & Birkinshaw, J. (2008b). Managing power in the multinational corporation: How low-power actors gain influence. *Journal of Management*, *34*(3), 477–508.

Brown, S. L., & Eisenhardt, K. M. (1997). The art of continuous change: Linking complexity theory and time-paced evolution in relentlessly shifting organizations. *Administrative Science Quarterly*, *42*, 1–34.

Buckley, P. J. (2009). Internalisation thinking: From the multinational enterprise to the global factory. *International Business Review*, *18*, 224–235.

Buckley, P. J. (2011). International integration and coordination in the global factory. *Management International Review*, *51*(2), 269–283.

Buckley, P. J., & Ghauri, P. N. (2004). Globalisation, economic geography and the strategy of multinational enterprises. *Journal of International Business Studies*, *35*, 81–98.

Chen, T., Chen, H., & Ku, Y. (2012). Resource dependency and parent-subsidiary capability transfers. *Journal of World Business*, *47*(2), 259–266.

Colakoglu, S. (2012). Shared vision in MNE subsidiaries: The role of formal, personal, and social control in its development and its impact on subsidiary learning. *Thunderbird International Business Review*, *54*, 639–652.

Colakoglu, S., Yamao, S., & Lepak, D. P. (2014). Knowledge creation capability in MNC subsidiaries: Examining the roles of global and local knowledge inflows and subsidiary knowledge stocks. *International Business Review*, *23*(1), 91–101.

Collinson, S. C., & Wang, R. (2012). The evolution of innovation capability in multinational enterprise subsidiaries: Dual network embeddedness and the divergence of subsidiary specialisation in Taiwan. *Research Policy*, *41*, 1501–1518.

Delany, E. (2000). Strategic development of the multinational subsidiary through subsidiary initiative-taking. *Long Range Planning*, *33*, 220–244.

Dörrenbächer, C., & Gammelgaard, J. (2011). Subsidiary power in multinational corporations: The subtle role of micro-political bargaining power. *Critical Perspectives on International Business, 7*(1), 30–47.

Dörrenbächer, C., & Geppert, M. (2006). Micro-politics and conflicts in multinational corporations: Current debates, re-framing, and contributions of this special issue. *Journal of International Management, 12,* 251–265.

Doz, Y. (2011). Qualitative research for international business. *Journal of International Business Studies, 42,* 582–590.

Duncan, R. (1976). The ambidextrous organization: Designing dual structures for innovation. In R. H. Killman, L. R. Pondy, & D. Sleven (Eds.), *The management of organization* (pp. 167–188). New York, NY: North Holland.

Eisenhardt, K. M. (1991). Better stories and better constructs: The case for rigor and comparative logic. *The Academy of Management Review, 16*(3), 620–627.

Eisenhardt, K. M., Furr, N., & Bingham, N. (2010). Crossroads — Microfoundations of performance: Balancing efficiency and flexibility in dynamic environments. *Organization Science, 21*(6), 1263–1273.

Eisenhardt, K. M., & Graebner, M. E. (2007). Theory building from cases: Opportunities and challenges. *Academy of Management Journal, 50*(1), 25–32.

Eisenhardt, K. M., & Martin, J. A. (2000). Dynamic capabilities: What are they? *Strategic Management Journal, 21,* 1105–1121.

Figueiredo, P. N. (2011). The role of dual embeddedness in the innovative performance of MNE subsidiaries: Evidence from Brazil. *Journal of Management Studies, 48,* 417–440.

Ghoshal, S., & Bartlett, C. A. (1990). The multinational corporation as an interorganizational network. *The Academy of Management Review, 15*(4), 603–625.

Ghoshal, S., & Bartlett, C. A. (1994). Linking organizational context and managerial action: The dimensions of quality of management. *Strategic Management Journal, 15,* 91–112.

Gibson, C. B., & Birkinshaw, J. (2004). The antecedents, consequences and mediating role of organizational ambidexterity. *Academy of Management Journal, 47,* 209–226.

Gupta, A. K., Smith, K. G., & Shalley, C. E. (2006). The interplay between exploration and exploitation. *The Academy of Management Journal, 49*(4), 693–706.

Hambrick, D. C. (1981). Environment, strategy, and power within top management teams. *Administrative Science Quarterly, 26,* 253–275.

Harzing, M.-W. (2000). An empirical analysis and extension of the Bartlett and Ghoshal typology of multinational companies. *Journal of International Business Studies, 31*(1), 101–120.

He, Z. L., & Wong, P. K. (2004). Exploration vs. exploitation: An empirical test of the ambidexterity hypothesis. *Organization Science, 15,* 481–494.

Kostova, T., & Roth, K. (2003). Social capital in multinational corporations and a micro-macro model of its formation. *Academy of Management Review, 28*(2), 297–317.

Leonard-Barton, D. (1992). Core capabilities and core rigidities: A paradox in managing new product development. *Strategic Management Journal, 13,* 111–125.

Ling, Y., Floyd, S. W., & Baldridge, D. C. (2005). Toward a model of issue-selling by subsidiary managers in multinational organizations. *Journal of International Business Studies, 36*(6), 637–654.

Lubatkin, M. H., Simsek, Z., Ling, Y., & Veiga, J. F. (2006). Ambidexterity and performance in small-to medium-sized firms: The pivotal role of top management team behavioral integration. *Journal of Management, 32*(5), 646–672.

Luo, Y. (2005). Toward coopetition within a multinational enterprise: A perspective from foreign subsidiaries. *Journal of World Business, 40*(1), 71–90.

March, J. G. (1991). Exploration and exploitation in organizational learning. *Organization Science, 2*, 71–87.

Meyer, K. E., Mudambi, R., & Narula, R. (2010). Multinational enterprises and local contexts: The opportunities and challenges of multiple embeddedness. *Journal of Management Studies, 48*, 235–252.

Miles, M. B., & Huberman, M. A. (1994). *Qualitative data analysis: An expanded sourcebook.* London: Sage.

Monaghan, S., Gunnigle, P., & Lavelle, J. (2014). Courting the multinational: Subnational institutional capacity and foreign market insidership. *Journal of International Business Studies, 45*, 131–151.

Mudambi, R., & Navarra, P. (2004). Is knowledge power? Knowledge flows, subsidiary power and rent-seeking within MNCs. *Journal of International Business Studies, 35*, 385–406.

O'Donnell, S. W. (2000). Managing foreign subsidiaries: Agents of headquarters, or an interdependent network? *Strategic Management Journal, 21*, 525–548.

O'Reilly, C. A., & Tushman, M. L. (2004). The ambidextrous organization. *Harvard Business Review, 82*, 74–81.

O'Reilly, C. A., & Tushman, M. L. (2008). Ambidexterity as a dynamic capability: Resolving the innovator's dilemma. *Research in Organizational Behaviour, 28*, 185–206.

Raisch, S., & Birkinshaw, J. (2008). Organizational ambidexterity: Antecedents, outcomes, and moderators. *Journal of Management, 34*, 375–409.

Reilly, M., & Sharkey Scott, P. (2014). Subsidiary driven innovation within shifting MNC structures: Identifying new challenges and research directions. *Technovation, 34*(3), 190–202.

Reilly, M., Sharkey Scott, P., & Mangematin, V. (2012). Alignment or independence? Multinational subsidiaries and parent relations. *Journal of Business Strategy, 33*, 4–11.

Rugman, A. M., & Verbeke, A. (2004). A perspective on regional and global strategies of multinational enterprises. *Journal of International Business Studies, 35*(1), 3–18.

Rugman, A. M., & Verbeke, A. (2005). Towards a theory of regional multinationals: A transactions cost economics approach. *Management International Review, 45*, 5–17.

Taggart, J. (1997). An evaluation of the integration-responsiveness framework: MNC manufacturing subsidiaries in the UK. *Management International Review, 37*, 295–318.

Teece, D. J., Pisano, G., & Shuen, A. (1997). Dynamic capabilities and strategic management. *Strategic Management Journal, 18*(7), 509–533.

Tippmann, E., Mangematin, V., & Sharkey Scott, P. (2013). The two faces of knowledge search: New solutions and capability development. *Organization Studies, 34*(12), 1869–1901.

Tsai, W. (2001). Knowledge transfer in intraorganizational networks: Effects of network position and absorptive capacity on business unit innovation and performance. *Academy of Management Journal, 44*, 996–1004.

Verbeke, A., & Greidanus, N. S. (2009). The end of the opportunism vs trust debate: Bounded reliability as a new envelope concept in research on MNE governance. *Journal of International Business Studies, 40*(9), 1471–1495.

Vora, D., Kostova, T., & Roth, K. (2007). Roles of subsidiary managers in multinational corporations: The effect of dual organizational identification. *Management International Review, 47*(4), 595–620.

Welch, C., Piekkari, R., Plakoyiannaki, E., & Paavilainen-Mantymaki, E. (2011). Theorising from case studies: Towards a pluralist future for international business research. *Journal of International Business Studies*, *42*(5), 740–762.

Yamin, M., & Andersson, U. (2011). Subsidiary importance in the MNC: What role does internal embeddedness play? *International Business Review*, *20*, 151–162.

Yin, R. K. (2009). *Case study research: Design and methods*. London: Sage.

EXPLORING SUBSIDIARIES' PERCEPTIONS OF CORPORATE HEADQUARTERS: SUBSIDIARY INITIATIVES AND ORGANIZING COSTS

Randi Lunnan, Sverre Tomassen and
Gabriel R. G. Benito

ABSTRACT

The chapter examines how distance, integration mechanisms, and atmosphere influence the level of organizing costs and subsidiary initiatives in headquarter—subsidiary relationships. Survey data were collected at the subsidiary level in one major Norwegian multinational company. Empirical analyses were based on regression and partial correlation analyses. Organizing costs are driven by distance to headquarters as well as the integration mechanisms and the atmosphere that exists in subsidiary—headquarter relationships. Another important insight gained by this study is that integration mechanisms influence subsidiary initiatives.

Keywords: Multinational companies; subsidiaries; organizing costs; subsidiary initiatives

Perspectives on Headquarters-Subsidiary Relationships in the Contemporary MNC
Research in Global Strategic Management, Volume 17, 165–189
Copyright © 2016 by Emerald Group Publishing Limited
All rights of reproduction in any form reserved
ISSN: 1064-4857/doi:10.1108/S1064-485720160000017007

INTRODUCTION

Multinational companies (MNCs) are complex multiunit, multilocation organizations that have attracted the attention of management and international business (IB) scholars for decades. Much of this research has taken a "view from the top" in the sense that it has focused on a range of decisions, typically of a strategic kind, made at headquarters by top-level company managers; see Menz, Kunisch, and Collis (2015) for a recent and very thorough overview of the literature on corporate headquarters.

While the "view from the top" is, of course, a fully legitimate perspective on MNCs, it does not convey the complete picture of how such large and complex companies actually work. A "bottom-up" approach, in which the corporation is looked at from the viewpoint of a given subsidiary unit — especially those located in a foreign country — has gradually become widespread amongst scholars interested in MNCs (Holm & Pedersen, 2000). Initially inspired by groundbreaking work like Hedlund's (1986) treatise on the heterarchy, and White and Poynter's (1984) study of heterogeneity among foreign-owned local subsidiaries, it has evolved into a rich stream of literature looking into a diverse range of topics. Issues like subsidiary roles and evolution (e.g., Benito, Grøgaard, & Narula, 2003; Birkinshaw & Hood, 1998; Birkinshaw & Morrison, 1995; Dörrenbacher & Gammelgaard, 2006), reverse knowledge transfer (e.g., Rabbiosi & Santangelo, 2013), local embeddedness (e.g., Andersson & Forsgren, 1996), subsidiary autonomy (e.g., Ambos, Asakawa, & Ambos, 2011), and subsidiary initiatives (e.g., Ambos, Andersson, & Birkinshaw, 2010; Strutzenberger & Ambos, 2014) rank prominently in this line of research.

The top-down and bottom-up views of the MNC have recently seemingly come together in recognizing the relationship between corporate headquarters and subsidiaries as being potentially crucial for the functioning of MNCs. However, views differ on how best to describe headquarter–subsidiary relationships and their consequences. Foss, Foss, and Nell (2012) argue that the existing literature on the MNC and its headquarters fundamentally considers them as well informed — if not omnipotent — and benign in its activities and managerial actions. In the case of MNC research, that does not go beyond the point at which major decisions are taken by companies about, say, where and how to enter a foreign country and how to organize their activities there. This is intuitive as headquarters ought to make sensible decisions, also in the long run. MNCs often expand abroad by making foreign direct investments (FDI), that is, they establish a subsidiary when they regard the commitment as justified by the need for control over activities and assets in a foreign country. Everything else constant, they choose FDI over another mode of operation due to the lower governance costs of operating through a subsidiary that they own and control (Benito & Tomassen, 2010; Hennart, 1991).[1]

However, Tomassen, Benito, and Lunnan (2012) and Richter (2014) demonstrate that operating through foreign subsidiaries is not an end-solution, especially in terms of organizing costs.[2] Making a FDI does not prevent positive organizing costs. Because MNCs are per definition multi-unit, multilocation organizations, they operate across geographical space and cultural and institutional diversity that pose challenges for how headquarters and subsidiaries relate to each other. These challenges expose themselves in terms of organizing costs: Adaptation problems, bargaining issues, resources spent on developing common norms and goals, communication distortions, etc. are all common traits, especially in IB activities.

Based on previous studies we should expect organizing costs to be widespread in MNCs. Understanding such costs, knowing more about their antecedents, and organizing and managing foreign operation in ways that minimize them could be turned into a strong competitive advantage for companies. So far, the (admittedly few) studies of organizing costs in international operations have taken the view of the parent corporation when looking at organizing costs in headquarter–subsidiary relationships. Those valuable insights notwithstanding, in this study we turn the table around and examine how subsidiaries observe organizing costs as they deal with demands from and interactions with corporate headquarters in an MNC.

While costs convey an undesirable aspect of headquarters–subsidiary relationships, initiatives taken at subsidiaries are actions that potentially increase value creation. Subsidiary initiatives – that is, entrepreneurial action at the subsidiary level (Birkinshaw, 1997) – include efforts to develop new business opportunities, creating R&D-based innovations, and organizing in novel, more effective and efficient ways. Given the value creation potential of subsidiary initiatives, one could expect that MNC headquarters would appreciate and even support such actions. However, unbounded autonomy could lead to increased complexity, pose coordination challenges, and lead to costly and unproductive experimentation excesses. Ambos et al. (2010, p. 1102) make the sharp remark that headquarters "recognize that some subsidiaries are likely to pursue initiatives, and they know some of these will be positive and successful for the whole corporation and others will not, but they do not know ex ante which are which." Empirical evidence suggest that headquarters typically control subsidiaries tightly, often to the point that they do not have degrees of freedom to identify or pursue new ideas and actions. Because subsidiary initiatives may disrupt the status quo, they trigger responses from the corporate immune system (Birkinshaw & Ridderstråle, 1999). Ambos et al. (2010) report that when headquarters become aware of subsidiaries' initiatives, they tend to increase the monitoring of subsidiaries and limit their scope for action, which subsequently stifles subsidiary initiatives.

Even though the ideal situation would conceivably be one of zero organizing costs and the highest possible return from entrepreneurial action throughout the organization, in reality, positive organizing costs prevail and many initiatives imply negative expected returns. Ultimately, organizing costs and subsidiary initiatives are about performance. MNCs need to balance carefully the returns potentially achieved by subsidiary initiatives with the costs imposed by attempts at governing them. From the viewpoint of subsidiary managers, how they perceive costs in their relations with corporate headquarters influence their willingness and ability to make initiatives and carry out strategies locally. The more time they spend on negotiations with headquarters, on securing timely and accurate information, and on developing and sustaining a common culture, the higher organizing costs, and the less time, energy, and talent can be devoted to initiatives. If the relationship with headquarters is being perceived as friction-free and less costly to maintain, the subsidiary manager could spend time more efficiently securing and increasing actions that may improve subsidiary performance.

Given the uncharted nature of our research topic, our investigation will be exploratory. Specifically, we advance three ideas that we want to examine empirically in more detail. The first is simply — but which we nevertheless regard as essential — to try out the applicability of existing measures of organizing costs in the novel context of subsidiaries' perceptions of organizing costs in subsidiary–headquarters relationships. The second is to look at to what extent organizing costs and subsidiary initiatives vary across different contexts. In this study, we examine more closely how factors such as distance, integration mechanisms, and atmosphere may influence the level of organizing costs and subsidiary initiatives in subsidiary–headquarters relationships. Finally, we seek to explore the association between organizing costs and subsidiary initiatives. Is it so, for example, that initiatives cause costs, or will a situation of low perceived organizing costs stimulate subsidiary initiatives?

THEORY AND HYPOTHESES

The economics of organization fundamentally involve making efficient alignments of transactions and activities to different governance structures conveying different levels of organizing costs. These costs can be categorized as ex ante and ex post costs (Williamson, 1985). The former are the costs of drafting, negotiating, and safeguarding an arrangement. The latter are the costs related to maladaption when transactions drift out of alignment, haggling to correct misalignment, setting up and running the contract, and bonding the parties involved in the transaction. Hence, organizing costs are costs related to the management of a relationship, be it within or across organizational boundaries, and according to transaction cost economics and internalization theory, the most efficient way to organize is the one that minimizes organizing costs in the long run (Hennart, 1982; Williamson, 1979).[3] It seems naive to presuppose that organizing costs vanish with the internalization of the transactions, and previous studies have indeed documented they occur and how they vary within MNCs (Richter, 2014; Tomassen et al., 2012). While governance structures may promote or curb certain behaviors, they do not fundamentally transform human nature or environmental contingencies. This means that one should expect organizing costs to vary even within different internal transactions depending on characteristics of the headquarters–subsidiary relation as well as on external market conditions.

Ex post organizing costs can be classified into four main types: monitoring costs, information costs, bargaining costs, and bonding costs (Benito & Tomassen, 2010; Tomassen & Benito, 2009). Monitoring costs arise when control provisions are made to reduce shirking and when resources are used to assure that agreements are fulfilled (Hennart, 1991). Monitoring costs can be significant in MNCs, but because our study focuses on the organizing cost perceptions held by subsidiary managers, and since corporate headquarters rarely are agents for principal subsidiaries, we do not look into monitoring costs in this study.

Bargaining costs are due to renegotiations and changes in the former agreements between the MNC headquarters and its various subsidiaries (Andersson, Forsgren, & Holm, 2007). Both time and resources spent on bargaining, and losses that occur because of nonefficient agreements can be classified as bargaining costs (Dahlstrom & Nygaard, 1999). Typical examples include disagreements regarding various aspects of transfer prices and the deliberate withholding of knowledge.

Communication and coordination failures between corporate headquarters and subsidiaries lead to information costs. Such costs are particularly significant if they in turn make subsidiaries less capable to react rapidly to changing conditions. Adaptation issues are especially important when the environment is diverse and volatile. Appropriate responses to environmental changes require prompt but correct information; and incomplete, inaccurate, or poorly formulated information may lead to suboptimal choices.

Bonding costs arise as a need to secure commitments made by the partners involved. In the context of an MNC headquarters–subsidiary relationship, bonding comprises a range of activities including actions like establishing personal ties between parties, developing common identities, building incentive systems, spending time together to solve third-party problems, and developing career possibilities within the MNC (Rabbiosi, 2011).

Our perspective deals with ex post organizing costs as perceived by subsidiary managers, but our study also builds on subsidiary initiative theorizing (e.g., Ambos et al., 2010), which springs out of corporate entrepreneurship (e.g., Birkinshaw, 2000). A subsidiary initiative is defined as "entrepreneurial proactive behavior in organizational subunits aiming to influence strategy-making in the organization" (Strutzenberger & Ambos, 2014, p. 314). Although, to our knowledge, no studies have measured subsidiary ex post organizing costs, the relation between subsidiary initiatives and headquarters monitoring is not novel. Ambos et al. (2010) find a positive relation between subsidiary initiatives and headquarters attention, which subsequently increase headquarters monitoring. Excess monitoring from corporate headquarters limit subsidiary autonomy, which in turn negatively affect subsidiary initiatives. Following this logic, we argue that subsidiary managers' perception of ex post organizing costs influence their ability to pursue strategies locally. The higher organizing costs vis-à-vis their global headquarters, the more time they use in bargaining agreements, securing timely and accurate information, and communicating and developing a common culture. If the relationship with corporate headquarters is perceived as being friction-free and less costly to maintain, the subsidiary manager could spend time more efficiently securing and increasing subsidiary performance.

As previously stated, the primary aim of our study is to examine what drives initiatives and organizing costs in headquarters–subsidiary relations, and, as an extension, to explore how initiatives and organizing costs relate to each other. Here, we examine three types of antecedents: distance, coordination mechanisms, and business atmosphere.

Distance, perceived organizing costs, and subsidiary initiatives: The concept of distance is central in the IB literature including a variety of measures of differences between geographical locations (e.g., Ghemawat, 2001). Distance generally limits subsidiary visibility from corporate headquarters and increases the costs of coordinating action. Bouquet and Birkinshaw (2008) find a positive relation between subsidiary initiative taking and headquarters attention as distance increases. Their argument is that subsidiaries close to home have more mechanisms for getting attention from headquarters than distant subsidiary managers, who need to put more effort into getting the attention from headquarters. Increasing distance leads to more conflict, increases misunderstandings and cost of communication. At the same time, because headquarters monitoring and control gets more difficult as distance increases, it becomes easier for subsidiaries that are a long way from headquarters to act more autonomously. We therefore expect that:

H1a. Ex post organizing costs increase with geographical distance.

H1b. Subsidiary initiatives increase with geographical distance.

Coordination mechanisms, perceived organizing costs, and subsidiary initiatives: The IB literature generally divides coordination mechanisms into formal mechanisms (i.e., formalization, centralization, standardization) and social mechanisms (i.e., committees, meetings, liaisons); see for example, Baliga and Jaeger (1984). Social mechanisms are becoming more widespread in MNCs, albeit still used more sparingly as they are typically regarded as costly (O'Donnell, 2000). Formal and social coordination mechanisms define norms and expectations, thereby clarifying behavior and performance (Roth & Schweiger, 1991), and it is reasonable to expect that organizing costs are reduced when such mechanisms are firmly in place. Additionally, because formal and social coordination mechanisms help developing a sense of order in an organization, they may promote the willingness of subsidiary managers to engage in local actions and activities that while in principle not requested from headquarters, might lead to future value creation. Overall, we expect that:

H2a. Ex post organizing costs decrease with formal and social coordination mechanisms.

H2b. Subsidiary initiatives increase with formal and social coordination mechanisms.

Business atmosphere, perceived organizing costs, and subsidiary initiatives: The IB literature has focused on the social aspect of the relation between subsidiaries and headquarters, either in the shape of general trust or shared philosophy (Roth & Schweiger, 1991) or business atmosphere. When subsidiary managers perceive the relationship to headquarters as being characterized by trust and mutual understanding, renegotiations and bonding take place in a more conducive environment, and exchange of information is more trusted. Correspondingly, when subsidiary–headquarters relationships exist within a trustful atmosphere, the involved subsidiaries could be more willing to take chances and generally act entrepreneurially since the prevalent sentiment is that actions − even if not always successful at the end − are sincerely taken with the common good in mind. Hence, we expect that:

H3a. Ex post organizing costs decrease with the perceived quality of the business atmosphere.

H3b. Subsidiary initiatives increase with the perceived quality of the business atmosphere.

Perceived organizing costs and subsidiary initiatives: As suggested above, one would expect a relationship between subsidiary initiatives and organizing costs. The ability and willingness of subsidiary managers to pursue actions and strategies that are planned locally hinges on how they perceive the costs of dealing with headquarters. However, organizing costs and subsidiary initiatives might relate to and affect each other in complicated and reciprocal ways, making predictions about their relationship ambiguous. On the one hand, the more time subsidiary managers spend in bargaining agreements, securing timely and accurate information, and communicating with headquarters, the less opportunities they have to pursue initiatives. Some subsidiary initiatives may even be heavily dependent on a low friction context − characterized by shared understanding of goals and the absence of fear of negative sanctions − to come to fruition. On the other hand, organizing costs might increase precisely because subsidiary managers have initiated unsolicited actions, which headquarters in turn respond to in the form of demands for information, meetings, negotiations, and perhaps even tightening its control over the subsidiary in question. Since we think that organizing costs can both affect and be affected by subsidiary initiatives, their interrelationship is most appropriately regarded as one of association rather than causality. Hence, we hypothesize that:

H4. There is an association between ex post organizing costs and subsidiary initiatives.

METHODS AND DATA

The data come from one Norwegian MNC (here called SIMO), which serves the worldwide oil and gas industry with consulting and certification services. SIMO has more than 100 years of international experience, and had at the time of the survey (2008) 177 wholly owned business units located in 24 different countries across the globe. Since we focus on subsidiary—headquarters relations from the perspective of subsidiary managers, the choice of a one-company context, and hence a single head-quarters, is advantageous from a research viewpoint because we eliminate variation that would emerge in a multiple MNC setting.

In close cooperation with key personnel in the company and a project committee that knew the company well, our research instrument (questionnaire) was sent to the leaders of each of the 177 units. The questionnaire had been pretested to make sure that respondents under-stood phrases, terms, questions, and language (English). We received responses from 115 of them, which gives a response rate of 65 percent. The final analyses were executed with 104 complete data sets across 17 countries.

The measures used in this study were evaluated with regard to both reliability and validity, and we also assessed their unidimensionality (Hair, Anderson, Tatham, & Black, 1998). We ran exploratory principal component analyses with oblique (promax) rotation resulting in nine distinct factors. All were in accordance with our theoretical assumptions, and all resulted in loadings well above the $\pm.50$ "significance" threshold (Hair et al., 1998). Reliability assessments were done by inspecting the Cronbach's α measures (see Appendix for details): For all variables, $\alpha \geq .70$ (Nunnally & Bernstein, 1994).

Because common method biases might occur in survey research, potential issues ought to be dealt with upfront when designing the research, and afterwards with statistical tests. We did both. First, some of the scales were reversed and questions of interest for this study were mixed with other questions that were deemed less relevant. Second, a Harman's single factor test was performed (Podsakoff, MacKenzie, Lee, & Podsakoff, 2003; Podsakoff & Organ, 1986). Nine factors with eigenvalues higher than 1.0 emerged from the factor solution and the first factor explained less than 30 percent of the variance. Hence, we believe that our results are not significantly affected by common method bias issues.

Measures

We adapted the measures of organizing costs from Benito and Tomassen (2010) and Tomassen and Benito (2009), which capture costs that occur due to frictions in the relationship between headquarters and a subsidiary. We focus on bargaining costs, bonding costs, and information costs, using seven-point multi-item reflective scales (Bollen & Lennox, 1991) to measure them (see Appendix for a more detailed overview).

Bargaining costs are perceived expenses related to negotiations between subsidiary and headquarters. Three items are used to measure this variable (Cronbach's α = .76).

Bonding costs are due to time spent on activities together with headquarters to improve their mutual relationship. Four items are used to measure this variable (Cronbach's α = .83).

Information costs are perceived communication and coordination failures related to information from headquarters to a subsidiary. Four items constitute this variable (Cronbach's α = .90).

Subsidiary initiatives denote different kinds of entrepreneurial actions that a subsidiary performs. We have divided them into three distinct categories: radical innovations, process innovations, and organizational initiatives. All subsidiary initiative scales are measured on a seven-point Likert scale inspired by Fagerberg, Mowery, and Nelson (2005) and Nijssen, Hillebrand, and Vermeulen (2005).

Radical innovation is measured by two items describing the number of new services and improvements the subsidiary has offered in the last two years (Cronbach's α = .70).

Process innovation is measured by six items, which describe minor changes in work practices and improvements in the service delivery system towards clients (Cronbach's α = .79).

Organizational initiatives are measured by five items, which measure the initiatives the subsidiary has done concerning organizational structure, management, and incentive systems (Cronbach's α = .70).

Independent Variables

Most of the independent variables are measured on a seven-point scale. The only exception is *geographical distance*, which is operationalized by a simple categorical variable indicating distance from headquarters (1 = Scandinavia, 2 = Europe, and 3 = Rest of the World).

Formal integration mechanisms, which measure to what extent the organization has systems that support seamless communication across organizational units, are measured by five items adapted from Kim, Park, and Prescott (2003) (Cronbach's $\alpha = .78$).

Social integration mechanisms, which capture the extent of social interaction across organizational units and to what extent the organization promotes informal social contact across the organization (Kim et al., 2003), are measured by three different items (Cronbach's $\alpha = .83$).

Relationship atmosphere is measured by six items, all of which were adapted from Tomassen et al. (2012), but reversed in order to provide a more meaningful understanding of the variable for our subsidiary–headquarter relationship setting. It describes whether the relationship is trustful, open, and supportive, or whether it could be characterized by deceitfulness, broken promises, and self-interest action at the sacrifices of the local unit (Cronbach's $\alpha = .91$).

Control Variables

In principle, we have a rather "clean" empirical context, since our data are all from one single corporation. Nonetheless, we included two control variables that might pick up some of the variation in organizing costs as well as in subsidiary initiatives: (1) *Utilization rate of employees* (one item) and (2) *Employee skills* (one item). With a low utilization rate, the headquarters will most likely interfere more frequently. Hence, subsidiaries might observe an increase in bonding and bargaining costs. It is also likely that both utilization rates and employee qualifications affect a subsidiary's ability to innovate since innovations are closely linked to resources within the organization.

Estimation

We tested for the assumptions of normality, linearity, and multicollinearity in our data. No problems were detected regarding normality and linearity, and since all VIF values are below 1.5, multicollinearity does not seem to be a problem.

RESULTS

Our statistical analysis and tests of the hypotheses required two different approaches. The first three hypotheses are tested by ordinary least squares

(OLS) regressions. However, due to the lack of direction in Hypothesis 4, we used a partial correlation approach when testing for the relationships between organizational costs and subsidiary initiatives.

Testing Hypotheses H1a/b−H3a/b

The results of the OLS regressions are reported in Table 1. In Models 1−3, we test the hypotheses concerning the effects of geographical distance, formal and social coordination mechanisms, and atmosphere on organizing costs (Hypotheses H1a−H3a). All three models are strongly significant with F-values ranging from 4.35 (sig. $F < .000$) for Model 2, 7.60 (sig. $F < .001$) for Model 1, and 10.7 (sig. $F < .000$) for Model 3. The results reveal that both distance and social integration mechanisms have significant positive effects on bargaining costs ($\beta_{distance\_Mod1}$ = .25, $p < .05$; β_{social_Mod1} = .33, $p < .01$). The positive effect of distance is according to our Hypothesis (H1a). Concerning social integration mechanisms (H2a), we hypothesized a negative effect, but we find the opposite effect in our data; a strong positive relationship towards bargaining costs and bonding costs (β_{social_Mod1} = .33, $p < .001$; β_{social_Mod2} = .47, $p < .001$). Conversely, formal integration mechanisms lead to lower bargaining costs (β_{formal_Mod1} = −.18, $p < .10$), and lower information costs (β_{formal_Mod3} = −.29, $p < .01$), which are all in accordance with our Hypothesis (H2a). Both distance and socialization mechanisms are non-significant versus information costs.

Concerning relationship atmosphere, both bargaining and information costs decrease significantly with the perceived quality of the atmosphere, which also is according to our Hypothesis H3a (β_{atmos_Mod1} = −.40, $p < .001$; β_{atmos_Mod3} = −.51, $p < .001$).

While we identify strong effects on organizing costs in the first three models, the regressions with respect to subsidiary initiatives (Models 4−6) provide less clear results. Model 4 in particular is rather weak (Model 4: F = 1.92, sig. $F < .10$). We also detect much smaller effects and less explained variance compare to the effects on organizing costs. In short, process innovations appear to increase with social integration mechanisms (β_{social_Mod5} = .30, $p < .01$), and formal integration mechanisms seems to enhance both radical (β_{formal_Mod4} = .24, $p < .05$) and process innovations (β_{formal_Mod5} = .20, $p < .10$), which all support Hypothesis H2b.

Table 1. OLS Regressions, Hypotheses 1–3.

Variables	Model 1 Bargaining costs	Model 2 Bonding costs	Model 3 Information costs	Model 4 Radical innovations	Model 5 Process innovations	Model 6 Organization initiatives
Constant[a]	5.73***	3.28**	8.07***	2.19	2.64**	2.34†
Control variables						
Utilization rate	.10	.15†	.07	−.06	−.14	−.10
Employee skills	−.17*	−.11	−.05	.14	.04	.21*
Independent variables						
Distance	.25**	−.09	.14†	−.12	.01	.08
Integration mechanisms						
Formal	−.18†	−.14	−.29**	.24*	.20†	.10
Social	.33***	.47***	.09	.07	.30**	.12
Relationship atmosphere	−.40***	−.13	−.51***	.01	.04	.12
Adjusted R^2/F	.28/7.60***	.16/4.35***	.36/10.7***	.05/1.92†	.18/4.74***	.07/2.21*

Notes: $N = 104$; reported values are standardized coefficients.

[a]Unstandardized coefficient.

† $p < .10$; * $p < .05$; ** $p < .01$; *** $p < .001$.

Table 2.   Partial Correlations:[a] Relationship between Organizing Costs
and Subsidiary Initiatives, Hypothesis 4.

	Bargaining Costs	Bonding Costs	Information Costs
Radical innovation	−.03	−.20*	−.14
Process innovation	.22*	.01	.12
Organizational initiatives	.28**	.26**	.09

Notes: N = 104; reported values are standardized coefficients.
[a]The following control variables were included: Utilization rate, Employee skills, Distance,
Formal and Social integration mechanisms, and Relationship atmosphere.
* $p < .05$; ** $p < .01$.

Testing Hypothesis H4

The relationships between organizing costs and subsidiary initiatives are shown in Table 2. While controlling for the same six independent variables as we included in Models 1−6, we find that there is a strong positive relationship between bargaining costs and process innovations (corr. = .22, $p < .05$), as well as between bargaining costs and organizational initiatives (corr. = .28, $p < .01$). Further, bonding costs are negatively related to radical innovations in a subsidiary (corr. = −.20, $p < .05$). Conversely, there is a positive association between bonding costs and organizational initiatives (corr. = .26, $p < .01$). However, no associations are found between information costs and subsidiary initiatives. Hence, Hypothesis H4 is partly supported.

DISCUSSION AND IMPLICATIONS

The overall ambition in this chapter has been to explore the notion of ex post organizing costs seen from the perspective of subsidiary managers. Ex post organizing costs have been studied before, but then − perhaps quite expectedly − from the perspective of corporate headquarters. We find that such costs are also relevant from the viewpoint of subsidiaries. Our analysis confirms that ex post organizing costs vary across subsidiaries. Such variance implies that relationships between headquarters and subsidiaries are neither simple nor uniform; they result in different perceptions of the costs of coordinating, bonding, and being kept informed. As a corollary, it seems highly likely that such costs influence subsidiary behavior and outcomes, and as such it is a phenomenon that deserves further scholarly attention.

We find that ex post organizing costs vary with distance, coordination mechanisms, and atmosphere, albeit in different ways. Geographical distance, in general, increases organizing costs. This finding is in line with previous literature proposing that in addition to costs of moving goods, distance incurs costs of learning as well as operating within a different culture (Ellis, 2007). Both bargaining costs (renegotiating and coordinating) and information costs increase with distance from headquarters, demonstrating that with physical distance, interactions become more complex and open up for flaws and misunderstandings.

Bonding costs do not vary with distance. This finding suggests that subsidiaries, regardless of their physical location, feel a need to build relations to headquarters. Building relations is time consuming, also when distances are short. Over longer distances, their need to build close relations may vary depending on the mandate of the subsidiary and the need for interaction between headquarters and the subsidiary. Some subsidiaries, for example, may be more independent and oriented towards their context for resources (Andersson & Forsgren, 1996).

Formal integration mechanisms lower bargaining and information costs, also in line with our predictions. Formalization implies a routinization of decision making, which decreases the power of both headquarters and subsidiaries (Ghoshal & Nohria, 1989). Regulating exchanges between headquarters and subsidiaries through clear procedures in a structured context (Burgelman, 1984) increases predictability and expectations. Implementing common rules, policies, and procedures and sharing information through common databases, intranet, etc. significantly reduce information costs, making information from headquarters more clear, complete, and understandable. Formalization, in the shape of common rules also, has a positive effect on bargaining costs. We expected formal integration mechanisms to reduce bonding costs, but that relation is not significant, indicating that clarity of rules and procedures and internal information systems do not replace the need to develop social relationships between headquarters and subsidiaries.

Several studies have argued for and found positive effects of normative integration (Ghoshal & Nohria, 1989), social control (O'Donnell, 2000), and boundary spanning interpersonal interaction (Kostova & Roth, 2003; Nohria & Eccles, 1992; Rabbiosi, 2011). The common mechanisms driving these issues are personal meetings and the facilitation of human interaction that enables two-way communication (Mäkelä & Brewster, 2009). O'Donnell (2000) found, for example, that vertical coordination mechanisms, such as formal training, visits, and meetings were more frequently used when subsidiaries were more dependent on headquarters; as a way to improve mutual understanding and develop a common culture. We find that social coordination (international transfers, meetings, committees) increase both bargaining and bonding costs, which is against our predictions. It is perhaps not surprising that bonding costs increase as opportunities to socialize broaden. What is more surprising is the positive relation between social control and bargaining costs, meaning that the more interaction the subsidiary has with headquarters, the higher the costs of coordination and bargaining. This finding contradicts previous studies (e.g., O'Donnell, 2000). Instead of building trust, our findings show that interaction through social arenas open up for possible conflicts, coordination issues, and renegotiations between subsidiaries and their headquarters.

Atmosphere relates to behavioral and motivational assets in relationships, such as trust, norms of behavior, and expectations (Kang, Morris, & Snell, 2007; Nahapiet & Ghoshal, 1998). Trust is particularly relevant in MNCs due to added complexity from distance and cultural differences (Westney, 2001). Trust denotes a willingness to be vulnerable to the actions of another party (e.g., Mayer, Davis, & Schoorman, 1995), and has been shown to be positive for collaboration and performance (e.g., Zaheer, McEvily, & Perrone, 1998). In line with our predictions, atmosphere reduces organizing costs of bargaining and information. In a trusting atmosphere, conflict levels are lower, reducing the need for coordination and renegotiations, and information is perceived to be more accurate and correct. Atmosphere does not reduce bonding costs, which suggests that the cost of building relations depends less on the relationship climate.

The MNC we study is a service company. Services typically implicate a higher level of tacit knowledge than physical products. Tacit knowledge must be communicated through personal relations, and can only very incompletely be transferred through formal systems or databases. One tentative explanation of the surprising finding of no relation between bonding costs and atmosphere is that some subsidiaries need to communicate tacit knowledge through relations (thereby incurring bonding costs) irrespective of atmosphere.

Lowering overall ex post organizing costs requires the development of a comprehensive agenda within the MNC, as well as a research agenda.

Whereas the subsidiary initiative literature has grown lately (see, e.g., Strutzenberger & Ambos, 2014), most research have so far treated initiatives as a single construct. If and to what extent initiatives are multifaceted, and which dimensions of subsidiary initiatives are the most relevant, remains rather unclear. Conceptually, it represents a "seed of change" (Birkinshaw, 2000, p. 51), but empirically it covers operationalizations such as subsidiaries climate change mitigation activities (Hamprecht & Schwarzkopf, 2014) and a scale based on acquisitions, investments, and product developments (Ambos et al., 2010). We offer a more differentiated view of subsidiary initiatives by introducing three different initiatives within the same context: a radical change initiative, an emergent process initiative, and an organization initiative covering changes in the internal structure within the subsidiary. We see the first type of initiatives as representing more dramatic, radical changes, whereas the two other initiatives cover more emergent initiatives.

It has previously been argued that factors such as geographical distance, and the structural and relational elements of the subsidiary–headquarters relationship should influence subsidiary initiatives (Ambos et al., 2010; Strutzenberger & Ambos, 2014). Our study shows positive associations between formal and social integration mechanisms and subsidiary initiatives (radical and process), but finds no associations with distance and atmosphere, contrary to the predictions set forth in Birkinshaw, Hood, and Jonsson. (1998). The existence of formal databases, communication systems, and procedures assist initiatives in the form of innovations, both radical and emergent, whereas social integration facilitates process innovations. If the formal communications with headquarters are clear, and headquarters provide social meeting places, we would expect a higher level of subsidiary initiatives. Integration mechanisms provide resources, through data/information and relations, which seem to be more useful than a general atmosphere. However, initiatives that concern internal changes within the subsidiary are not affected by subsidiary–headquarters relations, but seem to be driven by factors that are not covered in our study.

We also look at associations between organizing costs and subsidiary initiatives, and find evidence that suggests a negative relation between costs and radical initiatives and a positive relation between costs and more emergent initiatives.

Subsidiary initiatives are instigated to increase the value of the subsidiary and the MNC (Birkinshaw, 1997), and may be encouraged by the MNC to seek renewal and explore new innovations in units that are less affected by the corporate immune system. Headquarters may deliberately stay out of subsidiaries that undertake radical innovation because they are given autonomy (Ambos et al., 2010), or because the subsidiary is entering unchartered territory where headquarters have limited understanding and therefore have lower ability to control and coordinate (Hennart, 1991). A degree of autonomy that provides opportunities for radical subsidiary initiatives may also be a result of sheer ignorance from headquarters (Forsgren et al., 1995).

Emergent subsidiary innovations are different because they are more likely to fall within or not far from the current knowledge domain of the MNC. It is therefore easier for headquarters to understand such initiatives, and subsequently initiate efforts to coordinate the initiatives with those of other subsidiaries. Headquarters may also feel the need to step up on control efforts to secure that subsidiary initiatives are covered through the overall MNC control system. Such efforts, however, also increase organizing costs as perceived by the subsidiary.

This chapter is a first attempt to theorize on the relations between initiatives and costs. Given the initial results demonstrating a connection between the two, we propose this as a topic for future investigation.

CONCLUSION

The essential basis of this exploratory study of ex post organizing costs and subsidiary initiatives is that MNCs need to balance the returns potentially attained by subsidiary initiatives with the costs imposed by attempts at governing them. We began our inquiry by looking systematically into what types of costs subsidiaries experience in their dealings with corporate headquarters, and which factors might drive such costs.

One key contribution of our study is that while costs of organization and governance have been addressed previously, as far as we know this is the first study that analyzes such costs from the perspective of subsidiaries. In short, we find that organizing costs are driven by distance to headquarters as well as the integration mechanisms and the atmosphere that exist in subsidiary–headquarter relationships. Another important insight gained by this study is that integration mechanisms also influence the occurrence of subsidiary initiatives. The notion of subsidiary initiatives has remained underdeveloped despite the sizeable number of studies having looked into the phenomenon over the last two decades.

Another key contribution of our analysis is the provision of a differentiated treatment of subsidiary initiatives. Specifically, we distinguish between organizational initiatives, process innovations, and radical innovations. We find that formal integration facilitates both radical and process innovations in subsidiaries, whereas social integration is conducive to process innovations. Finally, we look into the interrelationships between organizing costs and initiatives, and uncover that whereas radical initiatives are negatively related to costs – especially bonding costs – the opposite seems to be the case for more emergent initiatives pertaining to process and organizational innovations. Being an exploratory study, we are obviously only scratching the surface of what are important, but intricate aspects of subsidiary–headquarter relationships in MNCs. We think nonetheless that our study certainly points to opportunities for further investigation of how complex organizations like MNCs are able to create value on a sustained basis.

This study examines a single MNC with many units across the world. Given the exploratory nature of our study, that choice gave the central advantage of providing a relatively clean empirical context, thereby minimizing the need to control for a large number of potentially important sources of variation. The single company design is obviously also a major limitation of our study, but one that can be remedied with further studies.

NOTES

1. It has been recognized that headquarters' actions might be suboptimal due to sheer ignorance (Forsgren, Holm, & Johanson, 1995), information overload (Egelhoff, 2010), complexity (Benito, Lunnan, & Tomassen, 2014), and pervasive uncertainty (Forsgren & Holm, 2010). More generally, it has been noted that any unit and individual will struggle with bounded rationality (Simon, 1976). The assumption that headquarters actions add to the value to the MNC is nevertheless both influential and enduring. Headquarters' actions are supposedly done to ensure that subunit activities keep on being effective and efficient (Benito et al., 2014). This assumption does not hold true, however, if the specific action leads to demotivated subsidiary management and employees, or if the typically unmeasured governance costs of the initiative outweigh the benefits.

2. Such costs are sometimes called governance costs (see Tomassen & Benito, 2009, for an analysis of governance costs in MNCs). Because our study focuses on costs that occur inside the firm and at the subsidiary level, we denote such costs as *organizing costs*.

3. In our further discussion, the main attention will be on ex post organizing costs – that is, the costs that occur after the governance structure has been chosen and is up and running.

REFERENCES

Ambos, B., Asakawa, K., & Ambos, T. C. (2011). A dynamic perspective on subsidiary auton-
    omy. *Global Strategy Journal*, *1*(3–4), 301–316.
Ambos, T. C., Andersson, U., & Birkinshaw, J. M. (2010). What are the consequences of
    initiative-taking in multinational subsidiaries? *Journal of International Business Studies*,
    41(7), 1099–1118.
Andersson, U., & Forsgren, M. (1996). Subsidiary embeddedness and control in the multina-
    tional corporation. *International Business Review*, *5*(5), 487–508.
Andersson, U., Forsgren, M., & Holm, U. (2007). Balancing subsidiary influence in the federa-
    tive MNC: A business network view. *Journal of International Business Studies*,
    38(5), 802–818.
Baliga, B. R., & Jaeger, A. M. (1984). Multinational corporations: Control systems and
    delegation issues. *Journal of International Business Studies*, *15*(2), 25–39.
Benito, G. R. G., Grøgaard, B., & Narula, R. (2003). Environmental influences on MNE sub-
    sidiary roles: Economic integration and the Nordic countries. *Journal of International
    Business Studies*, *34*(5), 443–456.
Benito, G. R. G., Lunnan, R., & Tomassen, S. (2014). The virtue of in-between
    pragmatism – A balancing act between responsiveness and integration in a multina-
    tional company. *Advances in International Management*, *27*, 75–97.
Benito, G. R. G., & Tomassen, S. (2010). Governance costs in headquarters-subsidiary rela-
    tionships. In U. Andersson & U. Holm (Eds.), *Managing the contemporary MNC: The
    role of headquarters* (pp. 138–160). Cheltenham: Edward Elgar Publishing.
Birkinshaw, J. M. (1997). Entrepreneurship in multinational corporations: The characteristics
    of subsidiary initiatives. *Strategic Management Journal*, *18*(3), 207–229.
Birkinshaw, J. M. (2000). *Entrepreneurship in the global firm*. London: Sage.
Birkinshaw, J. M., & Hood, N. (1998). Multinational subsidiary evolution: Capability and
    charter change in foreign-owned subsidiary companies. *Academy of Management
    Review*, *23*(2), 773–795.
Birkinshaw, J. M., Hood, N., & Jonsson, S. (1998). Building firm-specific advantages in multi-
    national corporations: The role of subsidiary initiative. *Strategic Management Journal*,
    19(3), 221–241.
Birkinshaw, J. M., & Morrison, A. J. (1995). Configurations of strategy and structure in subsi-
    diaries of multinational corporations. *Journal of International Business Studies*,
    26(4), 729–753.
Birkinshaw, J. M., & Ridderstråle, J. (1999). Fighting the corporate immune system: A process
    study of subsidiary initiatives in multinational corporations. *International Business
    Review*, *8*(2), 149–180.
Bollen, K. A., & Lennox, R. (1991). Conventional wisdom on measurement: A structural
    equation perspective. *Psychological Bulletin*, *110*(2), 305–314.
Bouquet, C., & Birkinshaw, J. M. (2008). Weight vs. voice: How foreign subsidiaries gain
    attention from corporate headquarters. *Academy of Management Journal*,
    51(3), 577–601.
Burgelman, R. A. (1984). Designs for corporate entrepreneurship in established firms.
    California Management Review, *16*(3), 154–166.
Dahlstrom, R., & Nygaard, A. (1999). An empirical investigation of ex post transaction costs
    in franchised distribution channels. *Journal of Marketing Research*, *36*(2), 160–170.

Dörrenbacher, C., & Gammelgaard, J. (2006). Subsidiary role development: The effect of micro-political headquarters-subsidiary negotiations on the product, market and value-added scope of foreign owned subsidiaries. *Journal of International Management, 12*(3), 266–283.

Egelhoff, W. G. (2010). How the parent HQs adds value to a MNC. *Management International Review, 50*(4), 413–431.

Ellis, P. D. (2007). Paths to foreign markets: Does distance to market affect firm internationalization? *International Business Review, 16*(5), 573–593.

Fagerberg, J., Mowery, D. C., & Nelson, R. R. (Eds.). (2005). *The Oxford handbook of innovation.* Oxford: Oxford University Press.

Forsgren, M., & Holm, U. (2010). MNC headquarters' role in subsidiaries' value-creating activities: A problem of rationality or radical uncertainty. *Scandinavian Journal of Management, 26*(4), 421–430.

Forsgren, M., Holm, U., & Johanson, J. (1995). Divisional headquarters go abroad – A step in the internationalization of the multinational corporation. *Journal of Management Studies, 32*(4), 475–491.

Foss, K., Foss, N. J., & Nell, P. C. (2012). MNC organizational form and subsidiary motivation problems: Controlling intervention hazards in the network MNC. *Journal of International Management, 18*(3), 247–259.

Ghemawat, P. (2001). Distance still matters: The hard reality of global expansion. *Harvard Business Review, 79*(8), 137–147.

Ghoshal, S., & Nohria, N. (1989). Internal differentiation within the multinational corporation. *Strategic Management Journal, 10*(4), 323–337.

Hair, J. F., Jr., Anderson, R. E., Tatham, R. L., & Black, W. C. (1998). *Multivariate data analysis* (5th ed.). Upper Saddle River, NJ: Prentice-Hall.

Hamprecht, J., & Schwarzkopf, J. (2014). Subsidiary initiatives in the institutional environment. *Management International Review, 54*(5), 757–778.

Hedlund, G. (1986). The hypermodern MNC – A heterarchy? *Human Resource Management, 25*(1), 9–35.

Hennart, J.-F. (1982). *A theory of multinational enterprise.* Ann Arbor, MI: University of Michigan Press.

Hennart, J.-F. (1991). Control in multinational firms: The role of price and hierarchy. *Management International Review, 31*(4), 71–96.

Holm, U., & Pedersen, T. (Eds.). (2000). *The emergence and impact of MNC centres of excellence: A subsidiary perspective.* London: MacMillan.

Kang, S.-H., Morris, S. S., & Snell, S. S. (2007). Relational archetypes, organizational learning, and value creation: Extending the human resource architecture. *Academy of Management Review, 32*(1), 236–256.

Kim, K., Park, J. H., & Prescott, J. E. (2003). The global integration of business functions: A study of multinational businesses in integrated global industries. *Journal of International Business Studies, 34*(4), 327–344.

Kostova, T., & Roth, K. (2003). Social capital in multinational corporations and a micro-macro model of its formation. *The Academy of Management Review, 28*(2), 297–317.

Mäkelä, K., & Brewster, C. (2009). Interunit interaction contexts, interpersonal social capital, and the differing levels of knowledge sharing. *Human Resource Management, 48*(4), 591–613.

Mayer, R. C., Davis, J. H., & Schoorman, F. D. (1995). An integrative model of organizational trust. *Academy of Management Review*, *20*(3), 709–734.

Menz, M., Kunisch, S., & Collis, D. J. (2015). The corporate headquarters in the contemporary corporation: Advancing a multimarket firm perspective. *Academy of Management Annals*, *9*, 633–714.

Nahapiet, J., & Ghoshal, S. (1998). Social capital, intellectual capital, and the organizational advantage. *Academy of Management Review*, *23*(2), 242–266.

Nijssen, E. J., Hillebrand, B., & Vermeulen, P. A. M. (2005). Unraveling willingness to cannibalize: A closer look at the barrier to radical innovation. *Technovation*, *25*(12), 1400–1409.

Nohria, N., & Eccles, R. G. (1992). Face-to-face: Making network organizations work. In N. Nohria & R. Eccles (Eds.), *Networks and organizations: Structure, form, and action* (pp. 288–308). Cambridge, MA: Harvard Business School Press.

Nunnally, J. C., & Bernstein, I. H. (1994). *Psychometric theory* (3rd ed.). New York, NY: McGraw-Hill.

O'Donnell, S. W. (2000). Managing foreign subsidiaries: Agents of headquarters, or an independent network. *Strategic Management Journal*, *21*(5), 525–548.

Podsakoff, P. M., MacKenzie, S. B., Lee, J.-Y., & Podsakoff, N. P. (2003). Common method biases in behavioral research: A critical review of the literature and recommended remedies. *Journal of Applied Psychology*, *88*(5), 879–903.

Podsakoff, P. M., & Organ, D. W. (1986). Self-reports in organizational research: Problems and prospects. *Journal of Management*, *12*(4), 531–542.

Rabbiosi, L. (2011). Subsidiary roles and reverse knowledge transfer: An investigation of the effects of coordination mechanisms. *Journal of International Management*, *17*(2), 97–113.

Rabbiosi, L., & Santangelo, G. (2013). Parent company benefits from reverse knowledge transfer: The role of the liability of newness in MNEs. *Journal of World Business*, *48*(1), 160–170.

Richter, N. (2014). Information costs in international business: Analyzing the effects of economies of scale, cultural diversity and decentralization. *Management International Review*, *54*(2), 171–193.

Roth, K., & Schweiger, D. (1991). Global strategy implementation at the business unit level: Operational capabilities and administrative mechanisms. *Journal of International Business Studies*, *22*(3), 369–402.

Simon, H. A. (1976). *Administrative behavior* (3rd ed.). New York, NY: The Free Press.

Strutzenberger, R. A., & Ambos, T. C. (2014). Unravelling the subsidiary initiative process: A multilevel approach. *International Journal of Management Reviews*, *16*(3), 314–339.

Tomassen, S., & Benito, G. R. G. (2009). The costs of governance in international companies. *International Business Review*, *18*(3), 292–304.

Tomassen, S., Benito, G. R. G., & Lunnan, R. (2012). Governance costs in foreign direct investments: A MNC headquarters challenge. *Journal of International Management*, *18*(3), 233–246.

Westney, E. (2001). Multinational enterprises and cross-border knowledge creation. In I. Nonaka & T. Nishiguchi (Eds.), *Knowledge emergence: Social, technical, and evolutionary dimensions of knowledge creation* (pp. 147–175). Oxford: Oxford University Press.

White, R. E., & Poynter, T. A. (1984). Strategies for foreign-owned subsidiaries in Canada. *Business Quarterly, 49*(4), 59–69.

Williamson, O. E. (1979). Transaction-cost economics: The governance of contractual relations. *Journal of Law and Economics, 22*(2), 233–261.

Williamson, O. E. (1985). *The economic institutions of capitalism.* New York, NY: The Free Press.

Zaheer, A., McEvily, B., & Perrone, V. (1998). Does trust matter? Exploring the effects of interorganizational and interpersonal trust on performance. *Organization Science, 9*(2), 141–159.

APPENDIX: MEASURES (R: REVERSED)

Bargaining costs (1–7)	• We spend a lot of time in renegotiating agreements made with our headquarters • We spend a lot of time in coordinating activities with our headquarters • The coordination of the relation with our headquarters is too costly compared with the outcome of these interactions	Cronbach's α: .76
Bonding costs (1–7)	• We spend a lot of time in communicating with our headquarters • We spend a lot of time in developing personal ties with the headquarters • We spend a lot of time together with people from headquarters in developing a common company culture • We spend a lot of time together with our headquarters in order to solve conflicts with third parties	Cronbach's α: .83
Information costs (1–7)	• Information from the headquarters is often incomplete and difficult to understand • Information from the headquarters is often too voluminous and therefore difficult to understand • Information from the headquarters is often poorly formulated and difficult to understand • Information from the headquarters seldom comes at the right time	Cronbach's α: .90
Relationship atmosphere (1–7)	• Sometimes headquarters hide facts that can help us in doing a good job (r) • The headquarters have not kept promises made then the relationship was established (r) • Occasionally, people at the headquarters alter information in order to carry out things their own way (r) • Sometimes people from headquarters promise to do thinks without actually doing them later (r) • Sometimes the headquarters ignore company policies that were designed to increase our ability to reach and service customers (r) • Whenever a conflict or difficulty arises, our headquarters always try to seek a solution that is in their own best interests, not considering our interests (r)	Cronbach's α: .91
Social integration (1–7)	• We have meetings where managers from different international locations meet • There is personal contact between managers from different international locations in our company • Committees meet regularly to plan and integrate activities internationally	Cronbach's α: .83

Appendix. (*Continued*)

Formal integration (1−7)	• We have databases where we share information internationally • We have worldwide electronic communications systems, like emails • We have internationally, interconnected computer systems, like server systems • We have internationally integrated software applications, like common use of applications • We have worldwide integrated information systems, like Intranet	Cronbach's α: .78
Distance	• Scandinavia (1); Europe (2); Rest of the World (3)	
Radical innovation (1−7)	• We have offered a number of new services/products the last two years • A lot of improvements have been done with our services/products the last two years	Cronbach's α: .70
Process innovation (1−7)	• We have made improvements in our work practices the last two years • We have developed the service delivery system last two years • We have revised the service delivery system last two years • We have made changes in our value chain the last two years • We have developed a new customer/client interface last two years • We have revised our customer/client interface last two years	Cronbach's α: .79
Organizational initiatives (1−7)	• We have made changes in our organizational structure during the last two years • We have introduced new management systems during the last two years • We have made changes in our reward system the last two years • New incentive systems for our employees have been introduced during the last two year • We have made changes in our management system last two year	Cronbach's α: .70
Utilization rate (1−7)	• What was your utilization rate of the employees in your organizational unit last year?	
Employee skills (1−7)	• How do you assess the quality of your unit's employees compared to your competitors?	

INFORMED HEADQUARTERS, LEGITIMIZED SUBSIDIARY, AND REDUCED LEVEL OF SUBSIDIARY CONTROL IN INTERNATIONAL R&D MANAGEMENT

Kazuhiro Asakawa and Tomomine Aoki

ABSTRACT

We investigate the extent to which headquarters' perceived knowledge about overseas R&D subsidiaries influences the level of control over them. We confirm that headquarters' knowledge about its overseas R&D subsidiaries lowers the level of control over them. Surprisingly, however, granting legitimacy to R&D subsidiaries does not necessarily lead to a reduction in headquarters' control. In addition, R&D subsidiaries' legitimacy does not influence the effect of headquarters' knowledge about them on the level of control. Although headquarters' knowledge about R&D subsidiaries tends to grant them legitimacy, the effect of that legitimacy seems rather minimal. These findings imply that headquarters are reassured when it reduces its control over the subsidiaries based on

Perspectives on Headquarters-Subsidiary Relationships in the Contemporary MNC
Research in Global Strategic Management, Volume 17, 191–213
Copyright © 2016 by Emerald Group Publishing Limited
ISSN: 1064-4857/doi:10.1108/S1064-485720160000017008

updated knowledge about their current situations rather than on an already-established positive image of those subsidiaries.

Keywords: Informed HQ; legitimized subsidiary; reduced control; international R&D

INTRODUCTION

Multinational corporations' (MNCs') control is a long-standing issue in the field of international management, but examining it continues to be relevant because multinational organizations cannot function without control, even in the age of virtual networks, in which organizational boundaries have become blurred and organizational structures have become flatter. Needless to say, the degree of subsidiary control by headquarters (HQs) varies according to several factors, including the HQs' location and the subsidiary's function, location, and strategic role.

MNC control has long been the focus of attention by scholars in the field of multinational management (Ambos & Schlegelmilch, 2007; Bartlett & Ghoshal, 1989; Doz & Prahalad, 1981; Ghoshal & Nohria, 1989; Hedlund, 1981; Jaeger & Baliga, 1985; Martinez & Jarillo, 1989; Nobel & Birkinshaw, 1998; Prahalad & Doz, 1987; Welge, 1981). No optimal level of control has been identified in the prior studies because it varies by function (Hedlund, 1981; Martinez & Jarillo, 1989; Welge, 1981). Bartlett and Ghoshal (1989) illustrate that R&D tends to be more globally integrated, whereas marketing and sales tend to be more locally responsive. Moreover, control is linked to home and host-country factors: US and Japanese firms are regarded as being more centralized than European firms. Because the literature on multinational management sheds light on the dilemma of global integration and local responsiveness (Prahalad & Doz, 1987), researchers have investigated the optimal balance between local autonomy and HQs' control. Bartlett and Ghoshal's (1989) typology clarifies that the type of control should vary according to different types of environment and strategy. Nohria and Ghoshal (1994) suggest that each subsidiary is controlled differently depending on differing types of environmental contingencies, but each subsidiary is also integrated into a multinational network.

More recently, MNC research has shifted its attention from control to coordination under the assumption that subsidiaries are not merely controlled by HQ but can contribute to MNCs' activities in much more proactive ways (Birkinshaw, 1997; Birkinshaw, Hood, & Jonsson, 1998). The more each subsidiary voluntarily contributes to an MNC's activities in a differentiated way (Nohria & Ghoshal, 1997), the more coordination among subsidiaries becomes necessary for the MNC to maintain its coherence. Moreover, MNC research has shifted away from the dyadic HQ-subsidiary perspective to the open network perspective (Ghoshal & Bartlett, 1990), in which subsidiary autonomy is determined in the context of its internal embeddedness in both its HQ and other subsidiaries, along with its external embeddedness in the local and global environments (Andersson & Forsgren, 1996, 2000; Andersson, Björkman, & Forsgren, 2005; Andersson, Forsgren, & Holm, 2001, 2007; Nell, Andersson, & Schlegelmilch, 2010). Nevertheless, the control issue in the HQ-subsidiary relationship has not been fully investigated.

Moreover, a good deal more attention must be paid to the factors influencing HQs' control over its subsidiaries. Although the literature on the HQ-subsidiary relationship has implicitly assumed that HQ intends to exercise control over its subsidiaries, whereas the subsidiaries intend to maintain their autonomy (Mudambi & Navarra, 2004; Taggard, 1997), this general pattern may vary depending on the country of origin, the host country, the configuration of the MNC (Bartlett & Ghoshal, 1989), the strategic role of the subsidiary (Ambos, 2005; Cantwell & Mudambi, 2005; Kuemmerle, 1999), and both external and internal embeddedness (Andersson & Forsgren, 1996; Asakawa, 1996), among other factors. More recently, Ambos, Asakawa, and Ambos (2011) have adopted a dynamic perspective and argue that the current level of internal embeddedness between a HQ and its subsidiary lowers the future control that the HQ will have over that subsidiary.

Parallel to the MNC literature, the autonomy and control issue has been a center of attention in the field of international R&D management (Asakawa, 2001a; Behrman & Fischer, 1980; Brockhoff & Schmaul, 1996; De Meyer & Mizushima, 1989; Pearce & Singh, 1992). Since Cheng and Bolon (1993) noted that autonomy and control were largely underexplored, the issue has been relevant and strategically important, but even today, it remains largely underexplored. R&D managers (Brockhoff & Schmaul, 1996; Cheng & Bolon, 1993; De Meyer & Mizushima, 1989) face the substantial challenge of balancing pressures for local autonomy and control by HQ (Behrman & Fischer, 1980; Pearce & Singh, 1992), because the tension between business logic and science logic (Asakawa, 1996; Mudambi & Swift, 2009) makes it difficult to identify the optimal level of local control for overseas R&D subsidiaries. The challenge of overseas R&D management lies in the subtle differences among basic research, applied research, and development in terms of the optimal balance between scientific logic and business logic. What is unique about this tension in the R&D context lies in the tendency of R&D activities, especially basic research, to require more autonomy than most other corporate functions (Behrman & Fischer, 1980) in that they tend to be more open and formally/informally linked to external communities such as universities and venture firms than other activities; thus, the extent of HQs' control over overseas R&D subsidiaries should naturally be more affected by the open nature of knowledge linkages (Asakawa, 1996; Mudambi & Swift, 2009). Furthermore, R&D is a function in which the reputation of a particular R&D subsidiary, based on its prior achievements in science and technology, plays a significant role in attracting talented researchers and enhancing a firm's overall image as an innovative company. Thus, HQ should have a good reason to diminish its control over overseas subsidiaries that have a good reputation. However, given the exploratory nature of R&D tasks, it takes longer for an overseas R&D subsidiary to gain a particular level of reputation (or recognition) by its HQ. Will HQ always tighten their control over overseas R&D subsidiaries that have no clear prior achievement? Because R&D is a function that does not provide immediate results, HQ must rely on the reputation – that is, legitimacy – of each overseas R&D subsidiary. Herein lies the challenge to a company's HQ when determining the optimal level of control over its R&D subsidiaries. We argue that HQ can assess the appropriate level of control based on the legitimacy of an overseas R&D subsidiary, along with its perceived knowledge about that subsidiary.

HQ and local R&D subsidiaries often disagree about both the existing and desired levels of control (Asakawa, 2001a; Birkinshaw, Holm, Thilenius, & Arvidsson, 2000; Chini, Ambos, & Wehle, 2005).[1] These perception gaps arise from a lack of shared understanding between a HQ and its subsidiaries. However, apart from its pioneering work, the extant literature on international and R&D management has largely ignored the impact of shared knowledge between a subsidiary and its HQ on the level of subsidiary control. Therefore, along with Birkinshaw, Bouquet, and Ambos (2006), our study contributes to the literature by investigating the determinants of weakening an HQs' control of its local R&D subsidiaries in association with the level of HQs' knowledge of local operations.

One remaining issue is whether knowledge about an overseas subsidiary will always reduce an HQs' control over its subsidiary, regardless of the subsidiary's perceived importance perceived. One might argue that local control is reduced only for those subsidiaries that HQ deem important because such recognition by HQ could grant legitimacy to local subsidiaries. Subsidiaries with a substantial contributory role tend to enjoy high levels of autonomy (Birkinshaw et al., 1998). Alternatively, we argue that local control is diminished when HQ obtains knowledge about overseas subsidiaries, regardless of whether the content of the knowledge is positive or negative. The rationale of such an argument is that learning about subsidiaries reassures their HQ (Birkinshaw et al. 2006; Bouquet & Birkinshaw, 2008; Ambos, Asakawa, & Ambos, 2011).

Thus, our research question is as follows: in what way are the legitimacy of local subsidiaries, local control, and HQs' knowledge about local subsidiaries related to one another? The extant literature does not provide sufficient answer to this question. Thus, this chapter contributes to the literature by examining those associations.

Moreover, we shed light on HQs' perspective on controlling overseas R&D subsidiaries, rather than subsidiary's perspectives on obtaining local autonomy. Although there has been abundant literature featuring subsidiary autonomy (Doz & Prahalad, 1981; Gupta & Govindarajan, 1991; Martinez & Jarillo, 1989; Nohria & Ghoshal, 1997), HQs' perspective on control deserves more attention (Ambos & Birkinshaw, 2010; Ambos & Mahnke, 2010) because there is a need for much more knowledge about the condition of diminishing control by HQ. HQ can strike an optimal balance between autonomy and control to foster overseas subsidiaries' innovative performance (Ambos & Birkinshaw, 2010).

The rest of this chapter is organized as follows. After presenting our hypotheses, our methods are presented, and the results are summarized, followed by discussions and conclusions.

HYPOTHESES

Knowledge and Control

According to the organizational information-processing perspective (Egelhoff, 1982; Galbraith, 1973, 1977), MNCs must cope with environmental uncertainty (Thompson, 1967). The need for an increased amount of information processing increases as the level of uncertainty increases (Egelhoff, 1982). Here, uncertainty is defined as the difference between the amount of information required to perform a task and the amount of information already possessed by an organization (Galbraith, 1977). The use of lateral relations enables more information processing between the HQ and local subsidiaries as uncertainly increases and the level of requirements for information processing increases (Egelhoff, 1991). Overseas subsidiaries are surrounded by both uncertainty in their technical environments that is associated with the nature of their research tasks and uncertainty in their social environments that is associated with the nature of host-country institutional norms and culture (Kostova & Roth, 2002). As for research tasks, R&D results are difficult to predict given the nature of scientific discovery. This tendency is particularly salient in the pharmaceutical industry, in which recent developments in biotechnology research result in research output that is highly dependent on serendipity (Lu, 2007; Mittra, 2008). As for social environments, although science is universal, the way that research is conducted varies across institutional systems and cultures (Westney & Sakakibara, 1985). Local subsidiaries are thus torn between two intersecting R&D social communities (Lam, 2000, 2003; Lehrer & Asakawa, 2003; Westney, 1993), which make R&D norms rather vague and their practices unpredictable.

Under such high uncertainty surrounding their overseas subsidiaries, HQ is anxious to be aware of the subsidiaries' current situations. Uncertainty declines as the gap between information sought and information provided narrows (Egelhoff, 1982; Galbraith, 1977). When HQ is informed of its subsidiaries' current situations, it perceives less uncertainty about the local operations and thus have a lower need for control over local operations. Although we are aware that uncertainty does not automatically call for an increasing amount of knowledge sharing between HQ and subsidiaries, we still see a possibility that uncertainty could trigger HQs' desire to turn its attention toward its subsidiaries' activities.

Recent literature has hinted at the importance of considering the effect of knowledge sharing between HQ and subsidiaries on the level of subsidiary autonomy (Asakawa, 2001a; Mudambi & Navarra, 2004). Sufficient knowledge about local subsidiaries, in the eyes of HQ, enables HQ to grant local autonomy. Kurokawa, Iwata, and Roberts (2007) also find that knowledge flows between a local R&D subsidiary and its HQ are not necessarily low with respect to autonomous subsidiaries, in the context of international R&D management by Japanese firms in the United States.

It is reported that autonomy is granted to overseas subsidiaries on the condition that sufficient knowledge will be shared with HQ (Asakawa, 2001a; Ambos, Asakawa, & Ambos, 2011). A subsidiary with knowledge that is both developed and widely utilized tends to gain a high level of bargaining power relative to other intra-firm units (Forsgren & Pedersen, 2000), which also implies that knowledge linkages between a subsidiary and other intra-firm units provide a basis for local subsidiaries' autonomy.

In a similar vein, insight can be gained by a related study by Birkinshaw et al. (2006), who find that subsidiaries can both attract attention from HQ and achieve local autonomy at the same time. Those scholars find it necessary for subsidiary managers to ensure that their local activities show up on their HQs' radar (i.e., that HQ have sufficient knowledge about local subsidiaries) while preserving a sufficient level of local autonomy. Their study implies that it is important for HQ to have sufficient knowledge about local operations to provide local subsidiaries with autonomy. Although attention to a subsidiary is not precisely the same as knowledge about a subsidiary, this perspective provides an insight into the association between HQs' knowledge and local control.

Consistent with these research streams, we argue that HQs' perception of their need for knowledge about local subsidiaries tightens control over local operations. A lack of knowledge about local operations in the eyes of HQ results in less security about HQs' control over local operations. When HQ does not feel that it is receiving sufficient knowledge from its local operations, it tends to increase its control. This finding is consistent with Asakawa (2001a), who finds that perception gaps between HQ and local operations are most salient in terms of the amount of information shared between HQ and subsidiaries and that HQs' perception that it lacks knowledge from its local subsidiaries increases its level of control.[2] Therefore,

H1. HQs' knowledge about its overseas subsidiaries has a negative effect on the level of control.

Legitimacy and Control

Organizational legitimacy is defined as the acceptance of an organization by its environment (Kostova & Zaheer, 1999) and is considered indispensable for an organization's survival (Dowling & Pfeffer, 1975). Kostova and Zaheer explore the effect of complexity that MNCs face related to their legitimacy. Factors that shape organizational legitimacy include an environment's institutional characteristics, organizational characteristics, and legitimization process (Hybels, 1995; Kostova & Zaheer, 1999; Maurer, 1971).

Once an R&D subsidiary has gained legitimacy, HQ finds that it is less necessary to control it. Legitimacy provides a local R&D subsidiary with its raison d'être, which permits its survival to be taken-for-granted within its firm. Once an R&D subsidiary's positive image has been established as a result of sufficient knowledge sharing with HQ, that subsidiary's tasks and functions are authorized as being both important and necessary; thus, HQ finds it less important to inspect its daily operations. Moreover, once a subsidiary's role within a firm is legitimized, that subsidiary's activities become routinized (Nelson & Winter, 1982). Normally, routines are not incessantly controlled and monitored by a subsidiary's inspecting organizations. Norms and values associated with a subsidiary's activities are symbolized and established as myths (Meyer & Rowan, 1977). Such sanctioned symbols and myths are beyond the need for control by HQ. Therefore,

H2. The legitimacy of a subsidiary, as perceived by its HQ, has a negative effect on the level of control over that subsidiary.

Relationship between Knowledge and Legitimacy

Because external environment surrounding a local subsidiary is both complex and fragmented in terms of task environments (Galbraith, 1973; Thompson, 1967) and resource holders (Pfeffer & Salancik, 1978), HQ is anxious to learn about the local situation. Because each local subsidiary is surrounded by its unique intra-firm environment within a multinational firm, which poses challenges to fulfilling legitimacy requirements (Kostova & Zaheer, 1999; Lam, 2000; Lehrer & Asakawa, 2003; Selznick, 1957), HQ becomes anxious to learn about the local situation.

Because local subsidiaries face both external and internal institutional environments, which pose different and often conflicting legitimacy requirements, conforming to external and internal institutional norms becomes necessary (Rosenzweig & Singh, 1991; Westney, 1993). HQ thus finds it reassuring to keep abreast of the current situation of subsidiaries that face such multiple environments.

Obviously, we can expect that legitimacy is more likely to be granted to a subsidiary when its HQ obtains positive knowledge about it. However, we argue that legitimacy might also be granted to a local subsidiary, even when it faces challenging conditions, because HQ may feel reassured that the local subsidiary is on its radar (Birkinshaw et al., 2006). Given the highly local-specific nature of overseas R&D activities, HQs need a certain degree of local knowledge to assess the importance of the subsidiaries. Knowledge about tacit, locally specific R&D activities cannot be easily obtained unless HQ contacts its local subsidiaries and is aware of their current activities and concerns. Because geographic and psychic distance usually make it harder to transfer tacit, contextual knowledge (Ghemawat, 2001; Hakanson & Ambos, 2010; Lam, 2001, 2003), obtaining first-hand knowledge about local R&D activities provides an excellent opportunity for HQ to understand local situations and be more confident in the value of local subsidiaries' activities.[3]

In the age of rapid technological innovation on a global scale, assessing the value of overseas R&D activities is difficult for HQ. Even if an overseas subsidiary accesses valuable knowledge and conducts research unique to its location, the value of such activities cannot be properly appreciated unless their importance is effectively conveyed to HQ. The reputation of overseas R&D activities greatly facilitates the process of having HQs recognize the importance of overseas subsidiaries upon receiving knowledge about local activities. Therefore,

H3. HQs' knowledge about their overseas subsidiaries has a positive effect on the perceived legitimacy of those subsidiaries.

Fig. 1 illustrates our hypothesized model.

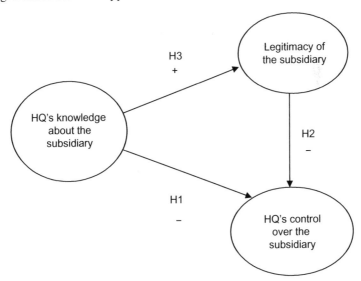

Fig. 1. The Hypothesized Model.

DATA AND METHOD

Data

A questionnaire was administered in the fall of 2006 to Japanese pharmaceutical companies that own their overseas R&D facilities. We mailed our questionnaires to 34 companies, 23 of which participated.

Questionnaires were mailed to the companies' R&D HQ to ask about their knowledge regarding overseas R&D subsidiaries, the companies' then-current level of control, and the perceived legitimacy of the local subsidiaries. Five questionnaires were mailed to each company. We asked the head of R&D HQ to forward the questionnaires to employees who had sufficient knowledge about the overseas subsidiaries − that is, those who either were in charge of controlling the subsidiaries or were directly collaborating with the subsidiaries on research or development activities. We asked each respondent to return his/her answered questionnaire directly to us. Following Dillman (1978), reminders and attached questionnaires were sent out repeatedly, up to three times, until answers were returned. In total, 74 questionnaires were returned, with an average of 3.2 questionnaires per company. The unit of analysis was the dyadic relationship between HQ and each local subsidiary. Because the number of local subsidiaries that responded to the questionnaire varied across firms, we controlled for company-specific factors. We followed a procedure adopted by prior studies (Ambos, Ambos, & Schlegelmilch, 2006; Ambos & Reitsperger, 2004; Ambos & Schlegelmilch, 2007; Asakawa, 2001a).

We requested that each respondent pick one overseas subsidiary that was the most applicable to him/her. Although this method did not allow us to control which overseas labs the respondents actually selected, it did allow us to obtain high-quality information from the people who were the most knowledgeable about particular subsidiaries. Our sample represented a wide variety of backgrounds. The respondents picked a number of tasks that had been assigned to overseas subsidiaries, including exploratory research (12%), basic research (18%), pre-clinical tasks (35%), clinical tasks (28%), and others (7%). The location of the overseas R&D subsidiaries included North America (57%), Europe (29%), Asia (11%), and other (3%). Entry modes included acquisition (17%), M&A (22%), and greenfield (61%). The portion of Japanese staff within the chosen subsidiaries ranged from 1−20% (34 subsidiaries, or 46%) to 20−40% (17 subsidiaries, or 23%). Fifty-five percent of the chosen overseas subsidiaries were headed by non-Japanese directors.

Method and Variables

We tested the hypotheses using AMOS (version 6.0) structural equation modeling software. We used three latent variables: "HQs' knowledge about overseas R&D subsidiaries" (henceforth abbreviated as "*HQ knowledge*"), "legitimacy granted to the subsidiary" (henceforth abbreviated as "*legitimacy*"), and "HQs' control over the local subsidiary" (henceforth abbreviated as "*control*"). As preparation for conducting a multiple regression, a confirmatory factor analysis was conducted for each construct, and each construct was converted into a single factor, thus confirming construct validity. The reliability for each factor was checked as below.

The latent variable "HQ knowledge" consisted of the following observable variables: $x1 = $ "HQ always keeps abreast of the subsidiary's current activities," $x2 = $ "the HQs' executive staff constantly visits the subsidiary to obtain information," and $x3 = $ "HQ is fully aware of current problems facing the local subsidiary." Cronbach's alpha was 0.782, with an average inter-item correlation of 0.544 and a cumulative explanatory rate of 55.02%.

The latent variable "legitimacy" consisted of the following observable variables: $x4 = $ "The local subsidiary is important and continues to be necessary for the firm" and $x5 = $ "The local subsidiary is so important to the firm that further investment in the subsidiary is not at all a waste." Cronbach's alpha was 0.845, with an average inter-item correlation of 0.731 and a cumulative explanatory rate of 73.07%.

The latent variable "control" consisted of the following observable variables: $x6 = $ "HQ is in charge of determining the local subsidiary's budget" and $x7 = $ "HQ evaluates the local subsidiary's researchers." Cronbach's alpha was 0.685, with an average inter-item correlation of 0.536 and a cumulative explanatory rate of 53.47%.

Respondents were asked to answer the extent to which they agreed or disagreed with each statement provided using a 5-point Likert scale ranging from 5 = totally agree to 1 = do not agree at all (Table 1).

We controlled for the following items: (1) performance of the subsidiary as perceived by HQ and (2) the directors' nationality.

(1) For the subsidiary's performance, as perceived by the respondents, 27% replied that is was "not sufficient". The subsidiary's performance was classified as follows: 1 = good enough, 0 = not good enough.

(2) Fifty-five percent of overseas R&D subsidiaries were headed by non-Japanese directors, and the directors' nationality was classified as follows: 1 = Japanese, 0 = non-Japanese.

Table 1. Measure of Constructs.

Construct	Item	Cronbach's Alpha	Average Inter-Item Correlation	Cumulative %
HQ knowledge	"The headquarters always keeps abreast of the current activities of the lab" "The headquarters' executive staff constantly visits the lab to obtain information at the lab" "The headquarters is fully aware of the current problems facing the local lab"	0.782	0.544	55.02
Legitimacy	"The local lab is important and continues to be necessary for the firm" "The local is so important to the firm that further investment in the lab is not a waste at all"	0.845	0.731	73.07
Control	"The headquarters is in charge of determining the local lab's budget" "The headquarters evaluates the researchers of the local lab"	0.685	0.536	53.47

RESULTS

Overview of the Model Fit

Table 2 reports the means, standard deviations, and correlations among all variables. The correlations provide initial evidence of good convergent and discriminant validity. Table 3 presents the results of structural equation modeling.

The model simultaneously controls for subsidiary performance and the directors' nationality. The Chi-square statistic and goodness-of-fit measures for the model indicate that the model is strong (χ^2[20df, N = 74] = 16.52, p = 0.68, AGFI = 0.90, RMSEA = 0.00, AIC = 66.52).

Results of Hypotheses Tests

H1 predicts that HQs' knowledge about an overseas subsidiary has negative and statistically significant effects on the level of control over that

Table 2. Variable Means, Standard Deviations, and Correlations.

	Mean	SD	N	1	2	3	4	5	6	7	8	9
1. Control	0.000	0.834	74									
2. Performance	0.432	0.499	74	−0.114								
3. Task	0.473	0.503	74	−0.061	0.921**							
4. Director's nationality	0.446	0.500	74	0.352**	0.095	0.130						
5. Entry mode	0.338	0.476	74	−0.412**	0.242*	0.182	−0.411**					
6. Region	0.581	0.497	74	0.081	0.078	0.091	−0.065	0.143				
7. Knowledge	0.000	0.894	74	−0.461**	−0.168	−0.108	−0.237*	0.160	−0.017			
8. Legitimacy	0.000	0.919	74	−0.423**	0.055	0.029	−0.122	0.191	−0.102	0.522**		
9. Knowledge × Legitimacy	0.423	0.741	74	−0.067	0.106	0.034	−0.227	0.323**	−0.013	0.023	−0.102	

Notes: *$p < 0.05$; **$p < 0.01$ (two-tailed test).

Table 3.   Empirical Result.

	Path	Model		
		Coefficient	s.e.	*p*
H3	HQ knowledge → legitimacy	0.7	0.16	**
H2	Legitimacy → control	−0.13	0.2	n.s.
H1	HQ knowledge → control	−0.53	0.24	*
	Control → budget	1		
	Control → research topics	0.94	0.2	**
	Legitimacy → importance	1		
	Legitimacy → further invest	0.99	0.16	**
	HQ knowledge → abreast	1		
	HQ knowledge → visit	0.92	0.17	**
	HQ knowledge → problem	1.01	0.17	**
Control variables	Performance → HQ knowledge	−0.27	0.22	n.s.
	Performance → legitimacy	0.31	0.2	n.s.
	Performance → control	−0.48	0.22	*
	Nationality → HQ knowledge	−0.47	0.22	*
	Nationality → legitimacy	0.09	0.2	n.s.
	Nationality → control	0.52	0.22	*
Goodness-of-fit	Chi-square	16.52		
	df	20		
	N	74		
	P	0.68		
	AGFI	0.9		
	RMSEA	0		
	AIC	66.52		

Notes: **$p < 0.001$, *$p < 0.05$.

subsidiary. The relationship between HQs' knowledge about an overseas subsidiary and the level of control over that subsidiary was negative and statistically significant (with the coefficient of −0.53 in Model 3a at $p < 0.05$ level). Therefore, H1 is supported.

H2 predicts that the legitimacy of a subsidiary, as perceived by HQ, has negative and statistically significant effects on the level of control over that subsidiary. The relationship between the legitimacy of a subsidiary, as perceived by HQ, and the level of control over that subsidiary was negative but statistically not significant (with a coefficient of −0.13, non-significant at the $p = 0.10$ level). Therefore, and unexpectedly, H2 is not supported.

H3 predicts that HQs' knowledge about an overseas subsidiary has positive and statistically significant effects on the legitimacy of that subsidiary, as perceived by HQ. The relationship between HQs' knowledge about an overseas subsidiary and the legitimacy of that subsidiary, as perceived by HQ, is both positive and statistically significant (with a coefficient of 0.70 at the $p < 0.001$ level). Therefore, H4 is supported.

Further Analysis on Control Variables

The analysis of the impact of control variables on each latent variable results in several interesting observations. First, it is surprising to find that HQ tends to know less about a local subsidiary when the subsidiary director is Japanese. Such a finding is counterintuitive but interesting. We argue that sufficient knowledge about a locally embedded context cannot sufficiently be obtained by an expatriate director. This argument indicates the importance of communication with local staff to obtain real, locally embedded knowledge. It also implies a caveat against staffing expatriate directors at overseas subsidiaries. Alternatively, we also argue that HQ trusts Japanese expatriate managers as a substitute for its own knowledge, so that HQ no longer needs as much information.

Second, it is equally interesting to find that HQ tends to exercise greater amount of control over a subsidiary when its director is Japanese (at the $p < 0.05$ level). This finding reminds us of an old assumption that expatriate managers are used as a tool for cultural control (Edström & Galbraith, 1977).

Third, we find that the HQ tends to execute less control over high performers (i.e., those subsidiaries that HQ perceives as high performers) at the $p < 0.05$ level. This finding implies that gaining recognition as a high performer might help a local subsidiary secure greater autonomy, to some extent.

DISCUSSION AND CONCLUSION

Interpretation of the Results

The results of H1 reconfirm the conventional wisdom gained from the prior literature. H1's result implies that HQs' knowledge about a local subsidiary lowers its level of control over that subsidiary. In contrast, H2's result is surprising. Although the direction of coefficient is negative, as expected, the result is not statistically significant, even at the $p < 0.10$ level. This result implies that the level of control over a local subsidiary does not necessarily decline, even when the subsidiary gains recognition from HQ that it is necessary for the company and, therefore, that further investment is not a waste. Once the activities at a subsidiary are known, HQ seems to be reassured and thereafter sees the subsidiary's operations as both taken-for-granted and legitimate. However, although HQs' knowledge about a local subsidiary increases its legitimacy, as confirmed by H3, such recognition does not, per se, help the local subsidiary gain greater autonomy.

It is intriguing to compare this result with the H1 result, which confirms that HQs' knowledge about a local subsidiary decreases the level of control over that subsidiary (and thus increases the level of local autonomy). If HQ is always kept abreast of a local subsidiary's current situation, if HQ staff constantly visits the local subsidiary to obtain explicit and tacit, locally specific knowledge and if HQ understands the problems facing a local subsidiary, then HQ is less inclined to exercise control. From this, we can interpret that having updated knowledge about a subsidiary's current situation is reassuring to HQ, even if that knowledge relates to that subsidiary's problems rather than an established, positive image that reflects past achievements. For HQ to grant autonomy to and decrease its control over a local subsidiary, the perception that HQ grasps the subsidiary's current situation is more important than the subsidiary's established image, no matter how good it is.

In this study, the importance of HQs' knowledge about local operations is confirmed based on how local autonomy is granted to local subsidiaries. Our results imply that knowledge about local operations can serve as perceived power for HQ and therefore serves as an underlying condition that enables local subsidiaries to obtain greater autonomy. Because knowledge is satisfying, it plays the role of pseudo-control vis-à-vis subsidiaries. Because knowing something that is a matter of concern is reassuring, keeping abreast of what is going on is a prerequisite for granting more autonomy.

This trend offers specific implications for MNC control in the R&D context. Given the longer term nature of R&D compared to other, more downstream functions, it typically takes longer for an overseas R&D subsidiary to achieve its objectives, and therefore gaining recognition takes a long time. Accordingly, HQ remains hesitant to reduce their control over R&D subsidiaries unless they are informed of the current local situation. Conversely, once a subsidiary gains legitimacy, its perceived importance renders HQ more willing to align the subsidiary's activity with corporate R&D policy to fully leverage the subsidiary's research output. Our findings are consistent with this interpretation in the context of overseas R&D management.

Contribution to the Literature

This study's contribution to the literature includes the following. First, the study demonstrates the importance of studying the level of local autonomy and control in association with the amount and nature of HQs' knowledge over local subsidiaries. The extant literature has not paid sufficient attention to this point.

Second, the study reveals that HQs' understanding of a subsidiary's current situation is a more important prerequisite for granting local autonomy than is confirming that subsidiary's established reputation. This finding implies the importance of revisiting communication issues in international R&D (DeMeyer, 1991, 1992, 1993). It also supplements the information-processing view of organizations (Egelhoff, 1982, 1991; Galbraith, 1973, 1977), in which it is argued that the need for an increased amount of information processing increases with the level of uncertainty (Egelhoff, 1982, 1991). However, this perspective does not consider the nature and content of the information to be processed. Our study thus complements this perspective by suggesting that processing updated information, whether good or bad, through incessant communication processes is more crucial than transmitting information about already-established reputations and images.

Third, our findings suggest a subtle relationship between knowledge and control, in terms of the extent of substitutability between the two. To what extent do knowledge and control substitute for one another? When HQ perceives that it has knowledge about a local subsidiary, it tends to become reassured and feels less need for control. If HQ does not perceive that it has knowledge about a local subsidiary, it feels more uneasy about the situation facing that subsidiary, thus leading to a greater amount of control. Here, knowledge is valued as a form of control.

Contribution to Practice

This study's contribution to practice is as follows. Our findings imply that HQ tends to provide local subsidiaries with more autonomy (and thus, less control) when it has sufficient knowledge and information about the situation facing those subsidiaries. Lack of knowledge about a local subsidiary, in the eyes of HQ, would raise concern and, consequently, encourage HQ to increase its control. Therefore, if overseas autonomy must be guarded, it is imperative that a certain level of communication be maintained within a firm so that HQ perceives that it is being kept abreast of the local situation on a regular basis. In sum, autonomy and knowledge sharing are not trade-offs, but they can co-exist if managed properly. However, it takes relatively sophisticated management skills and quality to maintain the subtle balance between these two forces.

Directions for Further Investigation

The limitations of this study are as follows. First, although the prior litera-ture suggests that autonomy and control issues are closely linked to the issues of external-internal collaborations and networking (Asakawa, 1996; Westney, 1990), the present study does not incorporate variables related to external collaborations with local R&D communities and internal colla-borations with intra-firm units. Second, this study does not incorporate the evolving nature of the relationship between HQ and overseas R&D subsidi-aries (Asakawa, 2001b; Birkinshaw & Hood, 1998; Ronstadt, 1977, 1978), but the relationship among knowledge, legitimacy and control should change as HQ-subsidiary relationships evolve. Further studies would bene-fit from accounting for these points, which deserve more attention. Third, we only have data from the HQ side. Although we chose to collect data from HQ to investigate the way in which HQs' control over overseas R&D subsidiaries is influenced by the degree of their knowledge about those sub-sidiaries and their legitimacy, the study could certainly be enriched by look-ing at these relationships from the local side. Future research could shed light on this issue to further validate our findings.

NOTES

1. This tension is associated with both the extent of external and internal connec-tivity (Asakawa, 1996; Westney, 1990) and the evolutionary stage of local labora-tories (Asakawa, 2001b; Birkinshaw & Hood, 1998; Ronstadt, 1977, 1978).

2. One could theoretically argue for reverse causality, i.e., that tighter control over local subsidiaries allows headquarters to obtain a larger flow of information and knowledge. We argue that this direction may evolve along the dynamic process of subsidiary autonomy. If headquarters receives less knowledge, it attempt to increase control over the local subsidiaries, which in turn would guarantee more knowledge inflow from local subsidiaries, which eventually satisfies headquarters and causes a reduction in control (Ambos, Asakawa, & Ambos, 2011). Because we limit our investigation to a cross-sectional analysis, we do not cover this dynamic aspect of local autonomy/control.

3. Alternatively, one could think of a possibility of reversed causality between the legitimacy of a subsidiary, as perceived by HQ, and headquarters' knowledge about the overseas subsidiary. Nevertheless, we maintain that a good understanding of local subsidiary's knowledge enhances its HQs' recognition of that lab for two reasons. First, the importance of a subsidiary cannot be fully understood a priori unless knowledge about local R&D activities is provided; second, tacit, locally specific knowledge pertinent to a local subsidiary can be a source of new ideas that may be relevant for other intra-firm labs. Because our main focus of inquiry centers around the effect of HQs' knowledge about local R&D subsidiaries, we maintain this causal direction.

REFERENCES

Ambos, B. (2005). Foreign direct investment in industrial research and development: A study of German MNCs. *Research Policy, 34*(4), 395–410.

Ambos, B., Asakawa, K., & Ambos, T. (2011). A dynamic perspective on subsidiary autonomy. *Global Strategy Journal, 1*(2), 301–306.

Ambos, B., & Mahnke, V. (2010). How MNC headquarters add value? *Management International Review, 50*, 403–412.

Ambos, B., & Reitsperger, W. (2004). Offshore centers of excellence: Social control and success. *Management International Review, 44*(Special Issue), 51–65.

Ambos, B., & Schlegelmilch, B. (2007). Innovation and control in the multinational firm: A comparison of political and contingency approaches. *Strategic Management Journal, 28*, 473–486.

Ambos, T., Ambos, B., & Schlegelmilch, B. (2006). Learning from foreign subsidiaries: An empirical investigation of headquarters' benefits from reverse knowledge transfers. *International Business Review, 15*, 294–312.

Ambos, T., & Birkinshaw, J. (2010). Headquarters' attention and its effects on subsidiary performance. *Management International Review, 50*(4), 449–469.

AMOS (version 6.0). SPSS Inc., Chicago, IL, AMOS Development Corporation, Spring House, PA.

Andersson, U., Björkman, I., & Forsgren, M. (2005). Managing subsidiary knowledge creation: The effect of control mechanisms on subsidiary local embeddedness. *International Business Review, 14*(5), 521–538.

Andersson, U., & Forsgren, M. (1996). Subsidiary embeddedness and control in the multinational corporation. *International Business Review, 5*(5), 487–508.

Andersson, U., & Forsgren, M. (2000). In search of centre of excellence: Network embeddedness and subsidiary roles in multinational corporations. Management *International Review, 40*(4), 329–350.

Andersson, U., Forsgren, M., & Holm, U. (2001). Subsidiary embeddedness, expected performance and competence development in MNCs – A multilevel analysis. *Organization Studies, 22*(6), 1013–1034.

Andersson, U., Forsgren, M., & Holm, U. (2007). Balancing subsidiary influence in the federative MNC: A business network view. *Journal of International Business Studies, 38*, 802–818.

Asakawa, K. (1996). External-internal linkages and overseas autonomy-control tension: The management dilemma of the Japanese R&D in Europe. *IEEE Transactions on Engineering Management, 42*(1), 24–32.

Asakawa, K. (2001a). Organizational tension in international R&D management: The case of Japanese firms. *Research Policy, 30*(5), 735–757.

Asakawa, K. (2001b). Evolving headquarters-subsidiary dynamics in international R&D: The case of Japanese multinationals. *R&D Management, 31*(1), 1–14.

Bartlett, C. A., & Ghoshal, S. (1989). *Managing across borders: The transnational solution.* Boston, MA: Harvard Business School Press.

Behrman, J. N., & Fischer, W. A. (1980). *Overseas R&D activities of transnational companies.* Cambridge, MA: Oelgeschlager, Gunn & Hain.

Birkinshaw, J. (1997). Entrepreneurship in multinational corporations: The characteristics of subsidiary initiatives. *Strategic Management Journal, 18*(3), 207–229.

Birkinshaw, J., Bouquet, C., & Ambos, T. (2006). Attention HQ. *Business Strategy Review, Autumn*, 5–9.

Birkinshaw, J., Holm, U., Thilenius, P., & Arvidsson, N. (2000). Consequence of perception gaps in the headquarters-subsidiary relationship. *International Business Review, 9*, 321–344.

Birkinshaw, J., & Hood, N. (1998). Multinational subsidiary evolution: Capability and charter change in foreign-owned subsidiary companies. *Academy of Management Review, 23*(4), 773–795.

Birkinshaw, J., Hood, N., & Jonsson, S. (1998). Building firm-specific advantages in multinational corporations: The role of subsidiary initiative. *Strategic Management Journal, 19*(3), 221–241.

Bouquet, C., & Birkinshaw, J. (2008). How foreign subsidiaries gain attention from corporate headquarters. *Academy of Management Journal, 51*(3), 577–601.

Brockhoff, K. L. K., & Schmaul, B. (1996). Organization, autonomy and success of internationally dispersed R&D facilities. *IEEE Transactions on Engineering Management, 43*(1), 33–40.

Cantwell, J., & Mudambi, R. (2005). MNE competence-creating subsidiary mandates. *Strategic Management Journal, 26*(12), 1109–1128.

Cheng, J. L. C., & Bolon, D. S. (1993). The management of multinational R&D: A neglected topic in international business research. *Journal of International Business Studies, 24*(1), 1–18.

Chini, T., Ambos, B., & Wehle, K. (2005). The headquarters-subsidiaries trench: Tracing perception gaps within the multinational corporation. *European Management Journal, 23*(2), 145–153.

De Meyer, A., & Mizushima, A. (1989). Global R&D management. *R&D Management, 19*(2), 135–146.

DeMeyer, A. (1991). Tech talk: How managers are stimulating global R&D communication. *Sloan Management Review, 49*(Spring), 49–58.

DeMeyer, A. (1992). Management of international R&D operations. In O. Granstrand, L. Hakanson, & S. Sjolanden (Ed.), *Technology management and international business.* New York, NY: Wiley.

DeMeyer, A. (1993). Management of an international network of industrial R&D laboratories. *R&D Management, 23*(2), 109–120.

Dillman, D. A. (1978). *Mail and telephone surveys: The total design method.* New York, NY: Wiley.

Dowling, J., & Pfeffer, J. (1975). Organizational legitimacy: Social values and organizational behavior. *Pacific Sociological Review, 18,* 122–136.

Doz, Y., & Prahalad, C. K. (1981). Headquarters influence and strategic control in MNCs. *Sloan Management Review, 23*(1), 15–29.

Edström, A., & Galbraith, J. (1977). Transfer of managers as a coordination and control strategy in multinational corporations. *Administrative Science Quarterly, 22,* 248–263.

Egelhoff, W. G. (1982). Strategy and structure in multinational corporations: An information processing approach. *Administrative Science Quarterly, 27*(3), 435–458.

Egelhoff, W. G. (1991). Information-processing theory and the multinational enterprise. *Journal of International Business Studies, 22*(3), 341–368.

Forsgren, M., & Pedersen, T. (2000). Subsidiary influence and corporate learning: Centres of excellence in Danish foreign-owned firms. In U. Holm & T. Pedersen (Eds.), *The emergence and impact of MNC centres of excellence* (pp. 357–388). London: Macmillan.

Galbraith, J. R. (1973). *Designing complex organizations.* Reading, MA: Addison-Wesley.

Galbraith, J. R. (1977). *Organization design.* Reading, MA: Addison-Wesley.

Ghemawat, P. (2001). Distance still matters. *Harvard Business Review, September,* 1–12, Reprint R0108K.

Ghoshal, S., & Bartlett, C. (1990). The multinational corporation as an interorganizational network. *Academy of Management Review, 15*(4), 603–625.

Ghoshal, S., & Nohria, N. (1989). Internal differentiation within multinational corporations. *Strategic Management Journal, 10,* 323–337.

Gupta, A. K., & Govindarajan, V. (1991). Knowledge flows and the structure of control within multinational corporations. *Academy of Management Review, 16*(4), 768–792.

Hakanson, L., & Ambos, B. (2010). The antecedents of psychic distance. *Journal of International Management, 16*(3), 195–210.

Hedlund, G. (1981). Autonomy of subsidiaries and formalization of headquarters-subsidiary relations in Swedish MNCs. In L. Otterbeck (Ed.), *The management of headquarters-subsidiary relations in multinational corporations* (pp. 25–78). Hampshire: Gower.

Hybels, R. C. (1995). On legitimacy, legitimation and organizations: A critical view and integrative theoretical model. *Best Paper Proceedings of the Academy of Management, 1995, 241*–245.

Jaeger, A. M., & Baliga, B. R. (1985). Control systems and strategic adaptation: Lessons from the Japanese experience. *Strategic Management Journal, 6,* 115–134.

Kostova, T., & Roth, K. (2002). Adoption of an organizational practice by subsidiaries of multinational corporations: Institutional and relational effects. *Academy of Management Journal, 45*(1), 215–233.

Kostova, T., & Zaheer, S. (1999). Organizational legitimacy under conditions of complexity: The case of the multinational enterprise. *Academy of Management Review, 24*(1), 64–81.

Kuemmerle, W. (1999). The drivers of foreign direct investment into research and development: An empirical investigation. *Journal of International Business Studies, 30,* 1–24.

Kurokawa, S., Iwata, S., & Roberts, E. B. (2007). Global R&D activities of Japanese MNCs in the US: A triangulation approach. *Research Policy, 36,* 3–36.

Lam, A. (2000). Tacit knowledge, organizational learning and societal institutions: An integrated framework. *Organization Studies, 21*(3), 487–513.

Lam, A. (2003). Organizational learning in multinationals: R&D networks of Japanese and US MNEs in the UK. *Journal of Management Studies, 40*(3), 673–703.

Lehrer, M., & Asakawa, K. (2003). Managing intersecting R&D social communities: A comparative study of European 'knowledge incubators' in Japanese and American firms. *Organization Studies, 24*(5), 771–792.

Lu, T. Y.-W. (2007). *Genomics research and cultivating serendipity in pharmaceutical drug discovery: Assessing the competitiveness of R&D serendipity between the West and Asia.* S.M. Thesis, Harvard University – MIT Division of Health Sciences and Technology.

Martinez, J. I., & Jarillo, J. C. (1989). The evolution of research on coordination mechanisms in multinational corporations. *Journal of International Business Studies, 20*(3), 489–514.

Maurer, J. G. (1971). *Readings in organization theory: Open-system approaches.* New York, NY: Random House.

Meyer, J. W., & Rowan, B. (1977). Institutionalized organizations: Formal structures as myth and ceremony. *American Journal of Sociology, 83*, 340–363.

Mittra, J. (2008). Impact of the life sciences on organization and management of R&D in large pharmaceutical firms. *International Journal of Biotechnology, 10*(5), 416–440.

Mudambi, R., & Navarra, P. (2004). Is knowledge power? Knowledge flows, subsidiary power and rent-seeking within MNCs. *Journal of International Business Studies, 35*(5), 385–406.

Mudambi, R., & Swift, T. (2009). Professional Guilds, tension and knowledge management. *Research Policy, 38*(5), 736–745.

Nell, P. C., Andersson, U., & Schlegelmilch, B. (2010). Subsidiary contribution to firm-level competitive advantage: Disentangling the effects of MNC external embeddedness. In J. Pla-Barber & J. Alegre (Eds.), *Reshaping the boundaries of the firm in an era of global interdependence (Progress In International Business Research)* (Vol. 5, pp.173–195). Bingley, UK: Emerald Group Publishing Limited.

Nelson, R. R., & Winter, S. (1982). *An evolutionary theory of economic change.* Cambridge, MA: Belknap Press.

Nobel, R., & Birkinshaw, J. (1998). Innovation in multinational corporations: Control and communication patterns in international R&D operations. *Strategic Management Journal, 19*(5), 479–496.

Nohria, N., & Ghoshal, S. (1994). Differentiated fit and shared values: Alternatives for managing headquarters-subsidiary relations. *Strategic Management Journal, 15*, 491–502.

Nohria, N., & Ghoshal, S. (1997). *The differentiated network: Organizations knowledge flows in multinational corporations.* San Francisco, CA: Jossey-Bass.

Pearce, R. D., & Singh, S. (1992). *Globalizing research and development.* London: Macmillan.

Pfeffer, J. R., & Salancik, G. R. (1978). *The external control of organizations: A resource dependency perspective.* New York, NY: Harper & Row.

Prahalad, C. K., & Doz, Y. (1987). *The multinational mission: Balancing local demands and global vision.* New York, NY: Free Press.

Ronstadt, R. C. (1977). *Research and development abroad by U.S. multinationals.* New York, NY: Praeger.

Ronstadt, R. C. (1978). International R&D: The establishment and evolution of research and development abroad by seven U.S. multinationals. *Journal of International Business Studies, 9*, 7–24.

Rosenzweig, P. M., & Singh, J. V. (1991). Organizational environments and the multinational enterprise. *Academy of Management Review, 16*(2), 340–361.

Selznick, P. (1957). *Leadership in administration.* New York, NY: Harper & Row.

Taggard, J. H. (1997). Autonomy and procedural justice: A framework for evaluation of subsidiary autonomy. *Journal of International Business Studies, 28*(1), 51–76.

Thompson, J. D. (1967). *Organizations in action.* New York, NY: McGraw Hill.

Welge, M. (1981). The effective design of headquarters-subsidiary relationships in German MNCs. In *The management of headquarters-subsidiary relationships in multinational corporations.* Hampshire: Gower.

Westney, D. E. (1990). Internal and external linkages in the MNC: The case of R&D subsidiaries in Japan. In C. Bartlett, Y. Doz, & G. Hedlund (Eds.), *Managing the global firm* (pp. 279–300). London: Routledge.

Westney, D. E. (1993). Institutionalization theory and the multinational corporation. In S. Ghoshal & D. E. Westney (Eds.), *Organization theory and the multinational corporation* (pp. 53–76). Houndmills: St. Martin's Press.

Westney, D. E., & Sakakibara, K. (1985). *Comparative study of the training, careers, and organization of engineers in the computer industry in Japan and the United States.* Cambridge, MA: MIT Japan Science and Technology Program Working Paper.

SUBSIDIARY AUTONOMY AND FACTORY PERFORMANCE IN JAPANESE MANUFACTURING SUBSIDIARIES IN THAILAND

Kiyohiro Oki

ABSTRACT

This chapter aims to investigate the relationship between levels of subsidiary autonomy and the performance of a subsidiary's subunit (factory) in Japanese manufacturing subsidiaries in Thailand. We conducted ordinary least squares regression analysis based on a questionnaire survey of 50 Japanese manufacturing subsidiaries in Thailand and multiple case studies to investigate the causal relationship between subsidiary autonomy and factory performance. We have three main findings. First, the autonomy level of Japanese manufacturing subsidiaries is linked to the subsidiaries' factories' performance compared to factories in Japan, but not in other foreign countries. Second, high levels of subsidiary autonomy are negatively associated with factory performance. Third, there are two causal relationships: high factory performance leading to low subsidiary autonomy and high/low subsidiary autonomy leading to low/high factory performance. From this, we discussed whether

Perspectives on Headquarters-Subsidiary Relationships in the Contemporary MNC
Research in Global Strategic Management, Volume 17, 215–243
ISSN: 1064-4857/doi:10.1108/S1064-485720160000017009

the degree of resource centralization in the home country influences the relationship between the level of subsidiary autonomy and a subunit's performance in the foreign subsidiary. Moreover, we discussed the possibility that the causal relationships between them are not necessarily direct causal relationships. We identified a new factor determining subsidiary autonomy and investigated the relationship between the subsidiary autonomy and performance of a subunit in the foreign subsidiary compared to the home country. Because this has not been discussed in previous studies, this chapter contributes to the study of headquarters—subsidiary relationships and gives guidelines to practitioners on managing subsidiary autonomy.

Keywords: Subsidiary autonomy; factory performance; multinational corporations; Japanese companies; Thailand

INTRODUCTION

This chapter aims to clarify the factors that influence headquarters—subsidiary relationships in contemporary multinational corporations (MNCs). This chapter focuses on subsidiary autonomy and investigates the relationship between levels of subsidiary autonomy and factory performance in Japanese manufacturing subsidiaries in Thailand.

The centralization or decentralization of decision-making in MNCs has long been an important topic in international business literature (Bartlett & Ghoshal, 1989; Gate & Egelhoff, 1986; Young & Tavares, 2004). Headquarters need to control foreign subsidiaries to align their activities with corporate strategy. However, although they are strictly controlled by headquarters initially, they tend to gain autonomy over time. As subsidiaries mature, not only do headquarters tend to grant them high levels of autonomy (Prahalad & Doz, 1981), they are able to achieve these levels through bargaining processes within MNCs (Mudambi & Navarra, 2004; Taggart & Hood, 1999; Young & Tavares, 2004).

Increasing subsidiary autonomy can improve the overall competitive advantage of both subsidiaries and MNCs. A high degree of subsidiary autonomy may foster subsidiary initiative (Birkinshaw, Hood, & Jonsson, 1998), stimulate the creation of innovation (Ghoshal & Bartlett, 1988; Venaik, Midgley, & Devinney, 2005), and encourage adaptation to the local environment (Harzing, 1999). Various recent studies have clarified the positive relationship between subsidiary performance and the level of subsidiary autonomy (Gammelgaard, McDonald, Stephan, Tuselmann, & Dorrenbacher, 2012; Gomez & Werner, 2004; Kawai & Strange, 2014;

Keupp, Palmie, & Gassmann, 2011; McDonald, Warhurst, & Allen, 2008; Newburry, Zeira, & Yeheskel, 2003; Tran, Mahnke, & Ambos, 2010; Venaik et al., 2005).

For this background, the determinants − the factors that determine the levels of subsidiary autonomy − have also been discussed (Ambos, Asakawa, & Ambos, 2011; Ambos, Andersson, & Birkinshaw, 2010; Edwards, Ahmad, & Moss, 2002; Fenton-O'Creevy, Gooderham, & Nordhaug, 2008; Jakobsen & Rusten, 2013; Johnston & Menguc, 2007; Pisoni, Fratocchi, & Onetti, 2013; Shuler-Zhou & Schuller, 2013; Taggart & Hood, 1999). These studies have identified the characteristics of MNCs or subsidiaries that serve as determinants of the level of subsidiary autonomy.

This chapter examines the determinants of the levels of subsidiary autonomy in Japanese manufacturing subsidiaries in Thailand. The decision-making authority and resources of Japanese multinationals are highly centralized in their headquarters, which exercise tight control over their subsidiaries (Bartlett & Ghoshal, 1989; Harzing, 1999). By analysing multinationals that operate under such an ethnocentric management strategy, this chapter finds that factory performance, as compared to factories in Japan, is negatively associated with high levels of subsidiary autonomy. In addition, this chapter also conducted case studies to investigate the causal relationship between levels of subsidiary autonomy and factory performance.

This chapter is structured as follows: in the next section, it discusses the theoretical background of subsidiary autonomy, the determinants of levels of subsidiary autonomy, and subsidiary autonomy in Japanese multinationals. Then it develops hypotheses about the relationship between levels of subsidiary autonomy and factory performance in Japanese manufacturing subsidiaries. The section "Research Design" describes the research design, the data collection, and the measurements. The section "Results" reveals the results of the empirical tests and case studies to supplement the results of empirical tests. In "Discussion" and "Conclusions and Limitations" section, we discuss the results and conclude our findings.

THEORETICAL BACKGROUND AND HYPOTHESIS DEVELOPMENT

Subsidiary Autonomy

Subsidiary autonomy has been an important topic in international business literature. In this chapter, we define subsidiary autonomy as 'the extent to which the subsidiary is given operational and strategic decision-making authority vis-à-vis headquarters' (Ambos & Birkinshaw, 2010, p. 459).

Although there had been few studies on the impact of levels of subsidiary autonomy on performance before 2000 (Young & Tavares, 2004), recent studies have revealed that high-autonomy levels lead to high performance levels for subsidiaries and MNCs overall (Gammelgaard et al., 2012; Gomez & Werner, 2004; Kawai & Strange, 2014; Keupp et al., 2011; McDonald et al., 2008; Newburry et al., 2003; Tran et al., 2010; Venaik et al., 2005). A high degree of subsidiary autonomy may foster subsidiary initiative (Birkinshaw et al., 1998), stimulate the creation of innovation (Ghoshal & Bartlett, 1988; Venaik et al., 2005), and encourage adaptation to the local environment (Harzing, 1999). Venaik et al. (2005) proposed that 'greater autonomy is likely to motivate the local subsidiary managers to take initiatives, which may result in marketing innovations that are either useful locally or are leveraged by the MNC on a global basis. (p. 659)'. Moreover, Hobday and Rush (2007) clarified that foreign subsidiaries that developed engineering capabilities were not controlled strictly by parent headquarters.

In addition, high autonomy also contributes to the performance of MNCs overall. Ghoshal and Bartlett (1988) revealed that subsidiaries with high autonomy had the role of creating innovation. Birkinshaw et al. (1998) showed that the high contributory role of subsidiaries in MNCs is strongly associated with the high level of subsidiary autonomy.

The Determinants of Subsidiary Autonomy

While the relationships between subsidiary autonomy and performance have been discussed, various studies also have discussed the determinants of the level of subsidiary autonomy (Ambos et al., 2010, 2011; Edwards et al., 2002; Fenton-O'Creevy et al., 2008; Gates & Egelhoff, 1986; Jakobsen & Rusten, 2013; Johnston & Menguc, 2007; Pisoni et al., 2013; Shuler-Zhou & Schuller, 2013; Taggart & Hood, 1999; Wang, Luo, Lu, Sun, & Maksimov, 2014). For example, Gates and Egelhoff (1986) clarified the company-wide and subsidiary-level conditions that influence the degree of centralization. They found some company-wide conditions (e.g. size of MNCs, complexity of business) and subsidiary-level conditions (e.g. size of subsidiaries, environmental changes that subsidiaries face).

Recent studies have focused more on the relationship between levels of subsidiary autonomy and subsidiary-level factors: the role and position of subsidiaries, subsidiary initiative, and a subsidiary's performance level in its area of activity (Ambos et al., 2010, 2011; Edwards et al., 2002;

Jakobsen & Rusten, 2013; Shuler-Zhou & Schuller, 2013; Taggart & Hood, 1999; Wang et al., 2014). These studies take the view that autonomy is not only gained by headquarters granting autonomy to subsidiaries but also gained by subsidiaries through a bargaining process within MNCs (Taggart & Hood, 1999; Mudambi & Navarra, 2004).

Taggart and Hood (1999) revealed some determinants of subsidiary autonomy related to a subsidiary's role. They identified a subsidiary's sales size, export propensity, market scope, and the complexity of R&D activity as the determinants of the level of subsidiary autonomy. Moreover, the data in Birkinshaw, Hood, and Young (2005) implied that subsidiaries, which have a wide range of value-added scope (the number of different functional activities subsidiaries were engaged in), have high levels of subsidiary autonomy. Because subsidiaries have some degree of control over their role (Birkinshaw & Hood, 1998), they can change their role in order to gain autonomy.

The position of subsidiaries inside or outside MNCs also determines the level of subsidiary autonomy. Ambos et al. (2011) examined the impacts of external/internal embeddedness on the level of subsidiary autonomy. They found that internal embeddedness increases subsidiary autonomy while external embeddedness decreases it. In addition, Jakobsen and Rusten (2013) revealed that subsidiaries with a high degree of autonomy are more involved in co-operation with other firms in the region.

Subsidiaries' initiative is also related to the level of subsidiary autonomy. Ambos et al. (2010) found that subsidiary initiative increases subsidiary autonomy and also increases headquarters monitoring, which in turn decreases subsidiary autonomy. They revealed a complicated relationship between a subsidiary's initiative and its autonomy.

Moreover, some studies revealed that the performance level of a subsidiary's activity is associated with a higher autonomy level. Ambos et al. (2011) found that the performance of R&D units is positively associated with higher levels of subsidiary autonomy. Taggart and Hood (1999) identified that high-autonomy subsidiaries have more complex R&D activity than those with low levels of autonomy. Johnston and Menguc (2007) revealed that a higher level of technology in primary operations in a subsidiary is positively associated with subsidiary autonomy. While the level of subsidiary autonomy is considered to be one of the determinants of a subsidiary's overall performance, the performance of a subunit in a subsidiary, which engages in some of the subsidiary's activities (e.g. factory, R&D unit, sales unit), is considered as one of the factors determining a subsidiary's level of autonomy.

In line with recent studies, this chapter also focuses on subsidiary-level factors, especially on the performance of a subunit in a subsidiary as a determining factor of subsidiary autonomy levels in Japanese manufacturing subsidiaries.

Autonomy in Japanese Multinationals

The determinants of subsidiary autonomy are especially important for Japanese multinationals, because they tend not to grant high levels of autonomy to their subsidiaries (Bartlett & Ghoshal, 1989; Harzing, 1999; Kopp, 1994). The decision-making authority and resources of Japanese multinationals are highly centralized in their headquarters, which exercise tight control over their subsidiaries.

This tendency has been continuously mentioned by studies of international human resource management since the 1980s. Tung (1982) found that Japanese multinationals tend to use Japanese expatriates more than European and American multinationals do. Kopp (1994) criticized Japanese ethnocentric management in which Japanese multinationals abroad used a large number of Japanese workers and did not grant autonomy to subsidiaries. Tungli and Peiperl (2009) revealed that when Japanese multinationals employ expatriate workers in their overseas operations, they use almost exclusively Japanese workers. Some studies insisted that this ethnocentric management approach had a negative impact on the performance of Japanese multinationals (Bartlett & Yoshihara, 1988; Kopp, 1994; Lam, 2003; Legewie, 2002; Wong, 2005). Because Japanese multinationals tend not to give foreign subsidiaries high levels of autonomy, which can result in a negative impact on their performance, knowing the determinants of levels of autonomy is vitally important in order to ensure foreign subsidiaries with high levels of autonomy.

The stimulus for such centralization of authority and resources emanates from their unique management strategy, which depends on utilizing the advantages of their subunits in Japan (Abo, 1994; Aoki, 2008; Brannen, Liker, & Fruin, 1999; Oki, 2015; Suh, 2015; Taylor, 1999). Centralization and formal integrative mechanisms stimulate knowledge inflows to subsidiaries from the parent corporation (Gupta & Govindarajan, 2000). To facilitate the smooth transfer of knowledge developed in Japan to foreign subsidiaries, the headquarters of Japanese multinationals exercise tight control over these subsidiaries.

In Japanese multinationals, there is particular control of foreign manufacturing subsidiaries regarding knowledge transfer. For example,

Brannen et al. (1999) examined the case of the Japanese multinational NSK. NSK's manufacturing subsidiary in the United States had been kept under strict control by the parent company while at the same time receiving considerable support from the Japanese factory; the president of the subsidiary was Japanese and investment, production equipment, and the production system were decided by the parent company. Once the U.S. subsidiary had developed their manufacturing capability, they gained some autonomy; they could make operational changes to some extent, gained R&D functions, and an American manager became the president of the U.S. subsidiary. On the other hand, Japanese R&D subsidiaries abroad tend to have high autonomy from the beginning since they tend to be more independent of knowledge developed in Japan than are manufacturing factories (Asakawa, 1996).

Under such an ethnocentric management strategy, the headquarters may increase a subsidiary's autonomy when a subunit in that subsidiary performs on par with or better than a subunit in Japan. Because they emphasize transferring knowledge developed in Japan, they may evaluate their subunits in a subsidiary by comparing them with their subunits in Japan. In the case mentioned earlier, the U.S. subsidiary gained autonomy after the U.S. factory had fully mastered Japanese factory operations and exceeded a certain level of manufacturing capability (Brannen et al., 1999). Therefore, in Japanese multinationals, the extent of subsidiary autonomy may depend on the performance of the subunits in a subsidiary, especially as compared to a Japanese subunit.

However, previous studies have not analysed the influence on a subsidiary's autonomy of the performance of a subunit of the subsidiary in the host country as compared to a subunit in the home country. Although there are some studies that discuss the relationship between a subsidiary's autonomy and its overall performance, there are only a few studies that focus on the relationship between a subsidiary's autonomy level and the performance of a subunit of the subsidiary in the host country (Ambos et al., 2011; Johnston & Menguc, 2007; Taggart & Hood, 1999), though they did not discuss the performance of a subunit as compared to one in another country.

However, the performance of a subunit as compared to a subunit in another country may be one of the determinants of subsidiary autonomy. Roth and Morrison (1992) referred that functional competence, which is defined as a subsidiary's ability to perform value activities, as compared to sister subsidiaries, could be positively associated with a subsidiary global mandate. Birkinshaw and Hood (1998) suggested that internal benchmarking in plants in various sites by headquarters influences changes in the subsidiary's charter – the business (or elements of the business) in which the subsidiary participates and for which it is recognized to have responsibility within the MNC (p. 782). Performance comparison among subunits in MNCs influences headquarters' evaluation of subsidiaries.

It is possible that the level of subsidiary autonomy is more strongly associated with relative performance than absolute performance. McDonald et al. (2008) found that high levels of strategic autonomy only had a positive relationship with subjective measures of subsidiary performance, which was based on labour productivity compared to their main competitors, and not with objective measures of subsidiary performance, which was based on sales turnover. This study clarified the possibility that the level of a subsidiary's autonomy is more related to its performance (compared to others) than its absolute performance. In case of subunits in MNCs, it is easier for headquarters to compare the performance of their subunit to other subunits in the MNCs because they cannot have specific knowledge of the performance of a competitor's subunit, even if they know the overall performance of its subsidiary. As companies rarely disclose subunit performance, headquarters cannot compare their subunit performance to those of rivals. Therefore, performance comparison among subunits in MNCs might influence the decision-making about subsidiary autonomy by headquarters.

Furthermore, in the case of foreign manufacturing subsidiaries in Japanese multinationals, which centralize resources in the home country, the performance of a subunit of the foreign subsidiary as compared to a subunit in Japan may be more important for headquarters than the performance as compared to a subunit in another country. Since they emphasize transferring knowledge developed in Japan, the headquarters may tend to evaluate subunit performance by comparing it to the subunit in Japan (Brannen et al., 1999). Therefore, this study investigates this relationship between levels of subsidiary autonomy and the performance of a subunit of the subsidiary in the host country as compared to a subunit in the home country.

Hypothesis Development

Based on the above logic, we develop a hypothesis about the relation between the level of subsidiary autonomy and the performance of a subunit of the subsidiary in the host country as compared to a subunit in the home country. First, in a Japanese manufacturing subsidiary, the performance of a subunit of the subsidiary in the host country as compared to a subunit in the home country will be related to the level of subsidiary autonomy

(Brannen et al., 1999). The results of this comparison will be far more relevant in determining levels of subsidiary autonomy than comparing the performance of a subunit of the subsidiary in the host country to a subunit in another foreign country. Our first hypothesis is thus.

H1. In a Japanese manufacturing subsidiary, a subsidiary's autonomy is more related to the performance of a subunit of that subsidiary in the host country as compared to a subunit in the home country, than the performance of a subunit of that subsidiary in the host country as compared to a subunit in another country.

Next, we develop a hypothesis about whether the relationship is positive or negative. Previous studies have found a positive relationship (Ambos et al., 2011; Johnston & Menguc, 2007; Taggart & Hood, 1999). Higher performance subunits are likely to be granted more autonomy because they are able to gain positive attention from headquarters and take a contributory role within MNCs (Birkinshaw et al., 1998; Bouquet & Birkinshaw, 2008; Roth & Morrison, 1992). Moreover, higher autonomy is likely to motivate the local subsidiary managers to take initiatives, which may result in higher subsidiary performance (Venaik et al., 2005). In the case of Japanese overseas manufacturing subsidiaries, they are strongly controlled by parent companies when their factory performance is low (Brannen et al., 1999). Therefore, this study also examines the following hypothesis:

H2. In a Japanese manufacturing subsidiary, the level of a subsidiary's autonomy is positively associated with the performance of a subunit of that subsidiary in the host country as compared to a subunit in the home country.

Our conceptual framework is summarized in Fig. 1.

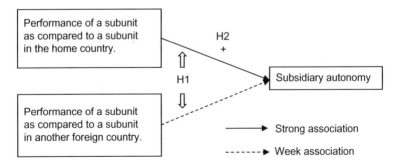

Fig. 1. The Conceptual Framework.

RESEARCH DESIGN

Sample and Data

This study employs data from a questionnaire survey of Japanese managers working in manufacturing subsidiaries in Thailand owned by Japanese multinationals. There are three reasons for focusing on Thailand. First, Thailand is strategically important for Japanese companies, because there were 1,777 Japanese subsidiaries in Thailand in 2012, ranked second after China (5,695 subsidiaries) in Asia, making Thai subsidiaries especially significant for Japanese multinationals (Toyo Keizai Inc., 2012). Second, these manufacturing subsidiaries in Thailand are less dispersed regionally than are those in China. Subnational regions in China have an impact on the influence of parent companies on subsidiaries (Ma, Tong, & Fitza, 2013). Manufacturing units in China are dispersed in various regions like Beijing, Shanghai, and Guangzhou; the distance between Beijing and Shanghai is over 1,000 km. On the other hand, the main industrial park in Thailand is within 180 km of Bangkok and within 30 km of Chiang Mai. We consider we can control the subnational region effect in advance by choosing Thailand. Third, Japanese multinationals invested in Thailand earlier than in India and Indonesia, which are countries where Japanese multinationals have recently invested. While the number of subsidiaries in Thailand that were established before 1995 is 1,258, the number of subsidiaries in India is 112, and the number in Indonesia is 648 (Toyo Keizai Inc., 2005). It is possible that Japanese subsidiaries in India and Indonesia are not granted high levels of autonomy because of having fewer years of operational experience.

This study examined manufacturing subsidiaries because foreign factories are subunits whose capability building tends to depend on knowledge transfer from Japan. Japanese foreign R&D subsidiaries tend to be more independent of knowledge developed in Japan, because their role is a knowledge creator (Asakawa, 1996). Manufacturing subsidiaries are preferable to investigate the impact on subsidiary autonomy of comparing a subunit of a foreign subsidiary to a subunit in the home country.

The Toyo Keizai Kaigai Shinshutsu Kigyo Soran (2012) [Directory of Japanese Companies Abroad 2012] was used to gather data on Japanese manufacturing subsidiaries in Thailand. This study particularly focused on subsidiaries belonging to the electronic machinery, transportation equipment, general machinery, and precision equipment industries. Subsidiaries in these industries were chosen because they are labour-intensive industries and continue to sustain manufacturing sites in Japan. Companies in labour-intensive industries need continuous knowledge transfer from a parent factory to foreign factories because not only do they need to transfer equipment, they also need to educate local employees in order to facilitate the transfer of knowledge from the parent factory. In particular, in order to transfer Kaizen (continuous improvement) activities, which are more important in labour-intensive industries, they need to give continuous support to foreign factories (Elsey & Fujiwara, 2000). The suitable samples for this research are companies that emphasize knowledge transfer from a parent factory, which means companies in labour-intensive industries. Moreover, companies that have already closed manufacturing sites in Japan are not able to compare their foreign factory to one in Japan. Therefore, we exclude chemical companies, which are capital-intensive industries, and textile companies, which tend not to maintain manufacturing sites in Japan.

In addition, this study identified and focused on subsidiaries with Japanese presidents or senior managers whose names are disclosed in the directory, because respondents would need to understand the status of factories in Japan or in another country to be able to compare them with factories in Thailand. Japanese managers can precisely compare a factory in Thailand and another factory, as they tend to have longer experience of working in factories in Japan and supporting other factories. In addition, we presume that the evaluation by Japanese managers is likely to be consistent with evaluation by headquarters that influences the level of subsidiary autonomy.

This study selected a final sample of 195 subsidiaries and distributed questionnaires to their managers in May 2013. The questionnaire items were translated from English to Japanese. The Japanese questionnaire was then checked by three scholars to ensure that the questionnaire items could be easily answered. Replies from 59 subsidiaries were received. After excluding nine subsidiaries because of incomplete answers, the final number of valid respondents was 50, comprising 18 companies in electronic machinery, 20 companies in transportation equipment, 10 companies in general machinery, and 2 companies in precision equipment industries (the effective response rate was 25%). According to Harzing (1997), this response rate can be considered acceptable. Moreover, this study conducted a *t*-test between the responding firms and the non-responding firms, to confirm that there were no non-response biases. No significant differences in the mean values were found (subsidiary employees: *t*-statistic $= -0.013$; subsidiary age: *t*-statistic $= 0.225$).

Measurements

This study conducted an ordinary least square (OLS) regression analysis. Table 1 explains how each of the variables was measured. A detailed discussion is as follows.

Table 1. Operationalization of the Variables.

Variable	Questionnaire Items
Subsidiary autonomy (based on Gupta & Govindarajan, 2000)	How would you assess the level of a subsidiary's autonomy on each of the following decisions? (1) formulation of the subsidiary's annual budget, (2) discontinuing an existing product or product line, (3) expanding existing product capacity, (4) changing a product's selling price, (5) buying from an outside vendor, (6) increasing and decreasing the subsidiaries' employee count. Ranging from 1 = 'exclusively decided by headquarters' to 5 = 'exclusively decided by the subsidiary'
Factory performance as compared to Japan/another foreign county (based on Birkinshaw et al., 2005; Hayes & Wheelwright, 1984)	Relative to a factory in Japan or in another country within your MNC, how would you rate your factory's performance on each of the following dimensions? (1) productivity, (2) production quality, (3) lead time, (4) improvement by operators. Ranging from 1 = 'very low' to 5 = 'very high'
Subsidiary size	Total number of local employees (log)
Subsidiary age	Years since establishment
Scope of activity	The number of activities the subsidiary undertakes (basic research, product development, process development, ramp up, mass production, and sales)
Percentage of sales exported	Percentage of total sales exported
Japanese customer dummy	Binary variable with a value of 1 if its main customer in Thailand is Japanese multinationals
Technology turbulence (based on Jaworski & Kohli, 1993)	How would you rate your level of agreement with each description? (1) The technology in our industry is changing rapidly, (2) Technological changes provide significant opportunities in our industry, (3) It is very difficult to forecast where the technology in our industry will be in the next 2–3 years, (4) A large number of new product ideas have been made possible through technological breakthroughs in our industry, (5) Technological developments in our industry are rather minor (negative). Ranging from 1 = 'fully disagree' to 5 = 'fully agree'

Dependent Variable
The dependent variable was the level of subsidiary autonomy. *Subsidiary autonomy* was measured using six decision items based on the decentralization measurement developed by Gupta and Govindarajan (2000). The items were: (1) formulation of the subsidiary's annual budget; (2) discontinuing an existing product or product line; (3) expanding existing product capacity; (4) changing a product's selling price; (5) buying from an outside vendor; and (6) increasing and decreasing the subsidiaries' employee count. Respondents were asked to assess the level of a subsidiary's autonomy in each decision on a scale from 1 (exclusively decided by headquarters) to 5 (exclusively decided by the subsidiary) and the scores were averaged into a composite measure. The Cronbach's alpha was 0.797.

Independent Variables
The independent variables were the performance of a factory in Thailand as compared to a factory in Japan (*factory performance as compared to Japan*) or another foreign country (*factory performance as compared to another foreign country*). A factory's performance was measured using four question items based on the measurement developed by Birkinshaw et al. (2005) and Hayes and Wheelwright (1984). The question items were: (1) productivity, (2) production quality, (3) lead time, and (4) improvement by operators. Because we asked respondents for one-year factory performance, the performance items that do not easily fluctuate in the short term are suitable for this research to eliminate a one-year effect. Because improvement in these areas normally occurs as a result of long-term capability-building (Aoki, 2008; Brannen et al., 1999; Fujimoto, 1999), we consider that they were not fluctuating in the short term, and we therefore selected them. Respondents were asked to assess the level of a factory's performance on a scale from 1 (much worse than a Japanese factory/another foreign factory) to 5 (much better than a Japanese factory/another foreign factory) and the scores were averaged into a composite measure. The Cronbach's alphas were 0.790 (Japan) and 0.867 (another foreign factory).

Control Variables
As control variables, this study used subsidiary size, subsidiary age, scope of activity, percentage of sales exported, Japanese customer dummy, and technology turbulence. Various studies considered that *subsidiary size* and *subsidiary age* have an association with levels of subsidiary autonomy (Ambos et al., 2011; Jakobsen & Rusten, 2013; Kawai & Strange, 2014; Shuler-Zhou & Schuller, 2013; Taggart & Hood, 1999). Subsidiary size was

measured as the log of the total number of local employees. Subsidiary age was measured in years since establishment. The number of different functional activities may be associated with the level of subsidiary autonomy (Birkinshaw et al., 2005). Therefore, *scope of activity* was measured by the number of activities being carried out by a subsidiary from 1 to 6 (basic research, product development, process development, ramp up, mass production, and sales). *Percentage of sales exported* is one of the determinants of subsidiary autonomy (Taggart & Hood, 1999). This was measured by the percentage of total sales that were exported. *Japanese customer dummy* was created and coded '1' for subsidiaries whose main customers in Thailand are Japanese multinationals. A subsidiary whose products are all for export is '0'. Japanese headquarters may tend to intervene when their subsidiaries mainly ship their products to Japanese customers in Thailand. Therefore, we control the nationality of the main customer in Thailand. Finally, we control *technology turbulence*. The technology environment influences subsidiary autonomy (Johnston & Menguc, 2007) and the relationship between subsidiary autonomy and subsidiary performance (Kawai & Strange, 2014). Technology turbulence was measured by five criteria developed by Jaworski and Kohli (1993) ($\alpha = 0.740$).

RESULTS

Result of OLS Regression

Table 2 presents a summary of the descriptive statics and correlations for all variables. We conducted OLS regression analysis to test the hypothesis using SPSS 20. The variance inflation factors (VIF) did not exceed the value of 2 and were well below the threshold value of 10 (Hair, Anderson, Tathem, & Black, 1998).

In addition, we checked for common method bias by Harman's single-factor test (Podsakoff & Organ, 1986) because we asked one person to answer all the questions. We included all items from the four constructs in this study in a factor analysis. As a result, the first factor accounted for only 22.4% of variance, below the generally accepted threshold of 50%. Accordingly, therefore, the extent of common method variance is significantly limited.

The results of the regression analysis are summarized in Table 3. Model 1 presents the base model, including the control variables only. Model 2

Table 2. Descriptive Statics and Correlations for all Variables.

Variables	Mean	SD	N	1	2	3	4	5	6	7	8	9
1 Subsidiary size (log)	2.710	0.513	50	1								
2 Subsidiary age	19.040	7.248	50	0.150	1							
3 Scope of activities	3.500	0.931	50	-0.025	0.221	1						
4 Percentage of sales exported	52.760	33.630	50	0.187	0.098	0.005	1					
5 Japanese customer dummy	0.740	0.443	50	-0.146	-0.486**	0.124	-0.315*	1				
6 Technology turbulence	3.336	0.661	50	0.080	-0.051	-0.099	-0.081	-0.016	1			
7 Factory performance as compared to Japan	2.560	0.662	50	0.065	0.058	-0.066	0.259	-0.068	0.074	1		
8 Factory performance as compared to another foreign country	3.401	0.732	48	-0.063	-0.064	0.260	-0.060	0.187	0.017	0.210	1	
9 Subsidiary autonomy	3.607	0.756	50	-0.306*	-0.011	0.406**	-0.477**	0.044	-0.090	-0.455**	0.068	1

Notes: $*p < 0.05$; $**p < 0.01$.

Table 3. Regression Models of Subsidiary Autonomy and Factory Performance.

	Model 1		Model 2		Model 3		Model 4	
	β	t-Value	β	t-Value	β	t-Value	β	t-Value
Subsidiary size	−0.206	−1.846†	−0.206	−2.003†	−0.188	−1.623	−0.207	−1.916†
Subsidiary age	−0.183	−1.389	−0.155	−1.269	−0.200	−1.501	−0.159	−1.265
Scope of activity	0.473	4.095***	0.446	4.172***	0.497	4.048***	0.437	3.746**
Percentage of sales exported	−0.524	−4.513***	−0.438	−3.946***	−0.524	−4.392***	−0.428	−3.652**
Japanese customer dummy	−0.300	−2.223*	−0.276	−2.212*	−0.266	−1.937†	−0.271	−2.116*
Technology turbulence	−0.083	−0.756	−0.054	−0.532	−0.060	−0.532	−0.057	−0.544
Factory performance as compared to Japan			−0.305	−2.933**			−0.302	−2.637**
Factory performance as compared to another foreign country					−0.066	−0.568	0.021	0.183
R squared	0.501		0.586		0.509		0.584	
Adjusted R squared	0.432		0.517		0.423		0.498	
F	7.199***		8.490***		5.930**		6.830***	
N	50		50		48		48	

Notes: †$p < 0.1$; *$p < 0.05$; **$p < 0.01$; ***$p < 0.001$.

adds the performance of its factory as compared to a factory in Japan to Model 1. Model 3 adds the performance of its factory as compared to a factory in another foreign country to Model 1. Model 4 includes both independent variables.

Based on the results of Models 2–4, H1 is supported. Factory (subunit) performance compared to Japan is associated with subsidiary autonomy, while factory performance compared to another country is not associated with subsidiary autonomy. Comparing factory performance in a foreign subsidiary to the performance of a Japanese factory, but not factories in another country, can have an impact on the level of subsidiary autonomy granted by headquarters.

H2, however, is rejected (Model 2, 4). Contrary to expectation, there is a negative relationship between a subsidiary's autonomy level and the performance of its factory as compared to a factory in Japan (Model 2). The reason for this negative relationship is discussed next.

Additional Analysis

An additional analysis was undertaken to investigate the negative relationship between subsidiary autonomy and factory performance. The prior regression analysis based on cross-section data did not indicate a causal relationship. In addition, without clarifying the causal relationship, the possibility of endogeneity bias remains. The qualitative data are useful for understanding the theory-underlying relationships revealed in the quantitative data (Eisenhardt, 1989). Therefore, we conducted additional multiple case studies.

The sampling frame for the research was created as follows. First, we created a 'subsidiary autonomy and factory performance matrix', as shown in Fig. 2. We focused on the 34 subsidiaries in the upper left cell (subsidiary autonomy is over three and factory performance is three or less) and 5 subsidiaries in the lower right cell (subsidiary autonomy is three or less and factory performance is over three). These companies are suitable as samples for multiple case studies to investigate the negative relationship between subsidiary autonomy and factory performance because these companies possess either low subsidiary autonomy and high performance levels or high subsidiary autonomy and low performance levels respectively. Of these 39, we chose 22 that had already expressed an interest in their questionnaire replies in participating in additional research. Of these, 18 subsidiaries

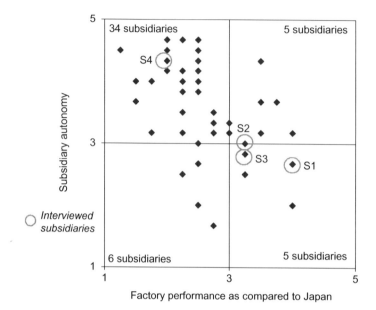

Fig. 2. Subsidiary Autonomy and Factory Performance Matrix (50 Subsidiaries).

were in the upper left cell and 4 in the lower right. We then conducted additional research with these 22 subsidiaries.

As a result of this, we were able to interview three subsidiaries in the
lower right cell (Subsidiary 1, Subsidiary 2, Subsidiary 3) and a subsidiary
in the upper left cell (Subsidiary 4). The data on these four subsidiaries
were gathered from the previous questionnaires, publications and interviews. We conducted semi-structured interviews and investigated the historical change in subsidiary autonomy and factory performance in each
subsidiary. The information on these four subsidiaries is summarized
in Table 4.

First, high performance resulted in low autonomy in S1, S2, and S3. S1
was involved in shipping products to customers that had previously been
shipped by a Japanese factory, while S2 was involved in manufacturing
products that had previously been manufactured by a Japanese factory
because their factory performance improved. S1 and S2 are considered by
their respective headquarters as being equivalent to a Japanese factory. S3
transferred their knowledge to a Japanese factory and to other foreign factories because they have developed their factory performance. Therefore,

Table 4. Information on Subsidiaries.

	Subsidiary 1 (S1)	Subsidiary 2 (S2)	Subsidiary 3 (S3)	Subsidiary 4 (S4)
Subsidiary size	570	1,800	1,900	80
Subsidiary age	25	25	19	22
Scope of activity	4	4	3	6
Percentage of sales exported	95	100	100	70
Japanese customer dummy	1	0	0	1
Technology turbulence	4	4	3.6	2.8
Subsidiary autonomy	2.67	3	2.83	4.17
Factory performance	4	3.25	3.25	2
Industry	Electronic machinery	Electronic machinery	Electronic machinery	General machinery
Interview time	3 hours	2 hours	2 hours	1.5 hours
Subsidiary autonomy at first	Lower than now	Lower than now	Lower than now	Almost the same as now
Factory performance change	Improved	Improved	Improved	Not much improved
Past support from a Japanese factory	Strong	Strong	Strong	Weak
Headquarters' Monitoring				
Benchmarking	Frequently	Very frequently	Frequently	Rarely
Request to improve factory performance	Frequently	Very frequently	Frequently	Sometimes
Role of subsidiary (product/customer/knowledge transfer)				
Manufacturing products that a Japanese factory had produced instead of the Japanese factory	Sometimes	Very frequently	Rarely	Sometimes
Dealing with customers that a Japanese factory had dealt with instead of the Japanese factory	Frequently	Rarely	Sometimes	Sometimes
Knowledge transfer from the Thai factory to the Japanese factories	Frequently	Rarely	Frequently	Rarely
Knowledge transfer from the Thai factory to other foreign factories	Sometimes	Sometimes	Frequently	Sometimes

S3's headquarters consider them to be one of the manufacturing centres of excellence (Frost, Birkinshaw, & Ensign, 2002). Because of high factory performance, the respective headquarters of S1, S2, and S3 considered these manufacturing subsidiaries as strategically important sites that headquarters need to control. Therefore, they have not granted high autonomy to their subsidiaries. In S1, S2, and S3, high factory performance increased the strategic importance of subsidiaries to headquarters, which in turn led to a suppression of the level of subsidiary autonomy granted by the headquarters.

Second, high autonomy led to a low performance level in S4. The headquarters of S4 did not control a subsidiary strongly when they made a profit. As a result, they did not focused on improving factory performance. Moreover, as the products and customers of the Thai subsidiary became different from those of a Japanese factory because S4 was able to decide its products and customers by itself to some extent, the monitoring of headquarters became even weaker. The end result was that the headquarters have not given their foreign factories continuous support in order to improve their performance. In fact, the headquarters of S4 has benchmarked their factory performance or requested an improvement in factory performance less frequently than in the cases of S1, S2, and S3. In S4, high autonomy led to weak monitoring and reduced support from the headquarters, which in turn did not encourage the improvement of factory performance.

On the other hand, low autonomy led to high performance levels in S1, S2, and S3. These three subsidiaries, which possess relatively low autonomy, were strongly controlled from the beginning. The headquarters decided product variety, production volume, product price, and the customers for their foreign factory. Since they frequently monitored product cost, quality, and lead time, they felt a strong need to improve factory performance. Therefore, the headquarters had continually supported foreign factories in order to improve their performance. In S1, S2, and S3, low autonomy led to close monitoring by the headquarters; this stimulated support from the headquarters, which in turn encouraged the improvement of factory performance.

From these case studies, we find two reasons for this negative relationship between levels of subsidiary autonomy and factory performance. First, high factory performance leads to low levels of subsidiary autonomy because high performance influences the strategic importance of a subsidiary in the eyes of its headquarters. Second, high or low subsidiary autonomy leads to low or high factory performance because the level of subsidiary autonomy influences the headquarters' monitoring, and, therefore, the level of support from headquarters. We found that the causal relationships between them are not necessarily direct causal relationships. They could be indirect causal relationships that some factors mediate.

DISCUSSION

The findings of this study are as follows. First, the autonomy of Japanese manufacturing subsidiaries in foreign countries is related to the performance of the subsidiaries' factories as compared to factories in Japan, but not as compared to another foreign country. Japanese multinationals tend to improve the performance of foreign factories by transferring the advantages of Japanese factories to them. Under this form of management, the Japanese headquarters tend to evaluate subunit performance by comparison with subunits in the home country. Japanese multinationals use the comparison between the subsidiaries' factories and factories in Japan as a determinant of the level of subsidiary autonomy that will be allowed.

The performance of subunits in a foreign subsidiary as compared to a subunit in the home country can also be a determinant of subsidiary autonomy in non-Japanese multinationals. MNCs, which tend to improve the performance of foreign subunits by transferring the advantages of subunits in the home country, can evaluate subunit performance by comparing it to a subunit in the home country. In MNCs, which centralize their resources in the home country, performance comparison between a subunit in a foreign subsidiary and a subunit in the home country can have an effect on decisions relating to levels of subsidiary autonomy.

Second, there is a negative relationship between high levels of subsidiary autonomy and factory performance. This result is contrary to the hypothesis. Therefore, additional case studies were undertaken to investigate this, revealing two reasons for this negative relationship.

First, a high factory performance level can lead to low subsidiary autonomy. When the factory of an overseas subsidiary has sufficient capability to have the role of a factory in the home country, the factory is considered by the headquarters as being equivalent to a home factory, leading to an increase in control over the subsidiary. High factory performance increases the strategic importance of subsidiaries to the headquarters, which in turn suppresses the subsidiary's autonomy.

Previous studies have considered that higher performance subunits were likely to be granted more autonomy because they are able to gain positive headquarters' attention (Bouquet & Birkinshaw, 2008). However, in the cases here, a high factory performance level led to low subsidiary autonomy. The reason for this difference may be a result of the ethnocentric approach to management of Japanese multinationals.

Japanese multinationals tend to consider Japanese factories as manufacturing centres of excellence, which create and diffuse innovation (Bartlett & Ghoshal, 1989). Therefore, when the performance of a factory in a subsidiary becomes equal to or better than that of a Japanese factory, the factory tends to be considered as a manufacturing centre of excellence, which can be considered as being equivalent to the Japanese factory. Frost et al. (2002) found that centres of excellence might be forced to give up some of their autonomy because of their strategic importance. Similarly, MNCs, which consider a subunit in the home country as a centre of excellence, can suppress the autonomy of a foreign-based subsidiary whose subunit also comes to be considered as a centre of excellence as a result of comparing its performance to the subunit in the home country.

Second, the level of subsidiary autonomy affects factory performance. Low autonomy leads to strong headquarters' monitoring, stimulating support from headquarters and encouraging the improvement of factory performance. On the other hand, high autonomy leads to weak monitoring from headquarters; this suppresses support from the headquarters and results in a lack of encouragement to improve factory performance. The level of subsidiary autonomy influences headquarters' monitoring and, therefore, the amount of support from headquarters and the degree of improvement of factory performance.

Previous studies have mentioned that a high degree of subsidiary autonomy leads to a high performance level because it stimulates innovation and adaptation to the local environment (Ghoshal & Bartlett, 1988; Harzing, 1999; Venaik et al., 2005). However, for Japanese manufacturing subsidiaries, support from headquarters, especially knowledge transfer from the parent factory, is more important to build their manufacturing capabilities (Abo, 1994; Aoki, 2008; Brannen et al., 1999; Oki, 2015; Suh, 2015; Taylor, 1999). Under this management style, high subsidiary autonomy can cause stagnation in the improvement of factory performance because, as mentioned above, it suppresses headquarters' monitoring, which in turn suppresses support from headquarters. When the ability of a subunit of a foreign-based subsidiary to develop its capability is dependent on the support from a subunit in the home country, granting a high degree of autonomy to the subsidiary can be an obstacle to this ability.

It is true that these causal relationships are only some of the existing causal relationships. We neither discuss all causal relationships, nor did we discuss to what extent these causal relationships can be applicable to other cases. However, it is an important finding that both causal relationships are related to the ethnocentric management style of Japanese multinationals as mentioned above. When multinationals have centralized their resources in the home country and consider a subunit in the home country as a centre of excellence, a high performance level by a subunit in a foreign subsidiary as compared to the subunit in the home country can increase the strategic importance of the subsidiary, leading to its autonomy being suppressed. When MNCs have centralized their resources in the home country and emphasized knowledge developed in the home country, a high degree of subsidiary autonomy can suppress knowledge transfer from headquarters, which is needed to build and improve the capabilities of subunits in overseas subsidiaries. Although previous studies have not considered the degree of centralization of resources in the home country as a contingency variable, it is possible that this degree of resource centralization influences the relationship between the level of subsidiary autonomy and the performance of a subunit in the overseas subsidiary.

In addition, it is also an important finding that the causal relationships between them are not necessarily direct causal relationships. Many previous studies assumed a direct relationship between subsidiary autonomy and a subunit or subsidiary's performance. This chapter also assumed a direct relationship in quantitative analysis. However, the case studies clarified the possibility that subunit performance can affect the level of subsidiary autonomy via its strategic importance as recognized by headquarters, and the level of subsidiary autonomy can affect subunit performance via headquarters' monitoring and support from headquarters in a Japanese manufacturing subsidiary. Although these findings did not totally deny the direct causal relationship, we clarified the possibility of there being a complicated causal relationship between them.

CONCLUSIONS AND LIMITATIONS

This study investigated the relationship between levels of subsidiary autonomy and factory performance in Japanese manufacturing subsidiaries in

Thailand. We found three things. First, we found that the autonomy level of Japanese manufacturing subsidiaries is linked to the performance of the subsidiaries' factories as compared to factories in Japan, but not as compared to those in another foreign country. Second, we found that the level of subsidiary autonomy is negatively associated with the level of factory performance. Third, by conducting multiple case studies, we found that a high level of factory performance led to low subsidiary autonomy levels and low/high levels of subsidiary autonomy led to high/low factory performance. By identifying these causal relationships, we discussed the possibility that the degree of centralization of resources in the home country influences the relationship between the level of subsidiary autonomy and the performance of a subunit in the foreign subsidiary. Furthermore, we discussed the possibility that the causal relationships between them are not necessarily direct causal relationships.

There are several academic contributions. First, we found that the performance of a subunit in the subsidiary as compared to a subunit in the home country is one of the determinants of subsidiary autonomy in Japanese manufacturing subsidiaries, an issue that has not been discussed by previous studies. In other words, we found a new determinant of subsidiary autonomy that previous studies have not mentioned. Second, we found that the performance of a subunit in the subsidiary as compared to a subunit in the home country is negatively associated with subsidiary autonomy in foreign-based Japanese manufacturing subsidiaries. While previous studies expected a positive relationship, this research found the performance of a subunit in the subsidiary is not always positively associated with high levels of subsidiary autonomy. Third, we noted the possibility that the degree of centralization of resources in the home country influences the relationship between the level of subsidiary autonomy and the performance of a subunit in the foreign subsidiary. Again, this has not been mentioned by previous studies and represents a new contingency variable that can influence this relationship. Fourth, we found the possibility that the causal relationships between them are not necessarily direct causal relationships. Although many prior studies assume a direct relationship between subsidiary autonomy and a subunit or subsidiary's performance, it is possible there could be indirect causal relationships that some factors mediate. This research suggests that future research in this area should consider the possibility of indirect causal relationships between subsidiary autonomy and a subunit's or subsidiary's performance.

This chapter has several managerial implications for practitioners in managing subsidiary autonomy. First, managers should understand that headquarters, which have centralized resources in the home country, tend to suppress the degree of autonomy of a subsidiary whose subunit's performance become equal to or better than that of a subunit in the home country. If headquarters suppress the degree of autonomy of a subsidiary more than necessary, the subunits in the subsidiary are not able to improve their performance by taking the initiative. They should ensure that these tendencies of headquarters do not lead to levels of subsidiary autonomy becoming overly suppressed.

Second, managers should understand that increasing subsidiary autonomy does not always lead to better performance of a subunit in a subsidiary. When foreign subsidiaries are still dependent on resources developed in the home country, high levels of subsidiary autonomy can cause stagnation in the improvement of factory performance as headquarters' monitoring and, consequently, support becomes reduced. In such a situation, managers should either intentionally suppress a subsidiary's degree of autonomy in order to ensure continuous support for a subunit in the subsidiary or should think of a way to continue to support the subunit.

This chapter does, however, have several limitations. First, this chapter used only the data from subsidiaries in Thailand and belonging to certain industries, which may have influenced the result. For the future, we have to retest our analysis model using subsidiaries from different countries or in different industries. Second, it is not clear whether the findings of this chapter are unique to Japanese manufacturing subsidiaries or not. We believe they can be applicable to subsidiaries of non-Japanese multinationals whose headquarters centralize resources in the home country. However, more empirical investigation is still needed using the data on the subsidiaries of MNCs of different nationalities or non-manufacturing subsidiaries.

Third, we cannot compare relative factory performance to absolute factory performance. It was difficult for us to gain data on absolute factory performance through a questionnaire because data on absolute factory performance tend to be confidential. We need to gather this information by developing favourable relationships with the respondents for future research. Fourth, although we investigated the causal relationship using case studies, we could not check the possibility of endogeneity bias statistically. For future research, an analytic model is required to check endogeneity bias. Fifth, the causal relationship was investigated by only a few exploratory case studies. We could not investigate all cases. Therefore, we need to investigate and understand the causal relationship more thoroughly by increasing the number of cases or by using longitudinal research in order to build a new theory. These remain for future research.

Although there are several limitations, this chapter has a significant contribution to make to the studies of headquarters—subsidiary relationships
by identifying and clarifying the relationship between levels of subsidiary
autonomy and factory performance in overseas Japanese manufacturing
subsidiaries.

ACKNOWLEDGMENTS

The thoughtful comments of the editors and anonymous referees are grate-
fully acknowledged. This work was supported by JSPS KAKENHI Grant
Numbers 25285116, 26780228.

REFERENCES

Abo, T. (1994). *Hybrid factory: The Japanese production system in the United States.*
    New York, NY: Oxford University Press.
Ambos, B., Asakawa, K., & Ambos, T. C. (2011). A dynamic perspective on subsidiary auton-
    omy. *Global Strategy Journal, 1*(3–4), 301–316. doi:10.1002/gsj.25
Ambos, T. C., Andersson, U., & Birkinshaw, J. (2010). What are the consequences of initia-
    tive-taking in multinational subsidiaries? *Journal of International Business Studies,
    41*(7), 1099–1118. doi:10.1057/jibs.2010.19
Ambos, T. C., & Birkinshaw, J. (2010). Headquarters' attention and its effect on subsidiary
    performance. *Management International Review, 50*(4), 449–469. doi:10.1007/s11575-
    010-0041-4
Aoki, K. (2008). Transferring Japanese kaizen activities to overseas plants in China.
    International Journal of Operations & Production Management, 28(6), 518–539.
    doi:10.1108/01443570810875340
Asakawa, K. (1996). External-internal linkages and overseas autonomy-control tension: The
    management dilemma of the Japanese R&D in Europe. *IEEE Transactions on
    Engineering Management, 43*(1), 24–32. doi:10.1109/17.491265
Bartlett, C. A., & Ghoshal, S. (1989). *Managing across borders: The transnational solution.*
    Boston, MA: Harvard Business School Press.
Bartlett, C. A., & Yoshihara, H. (1988). New challenges for Japanese multinationals: Is organi-
    zational adaptation their Achilles heel? *Human Resource Management, 27*(1), 19–43.
    doi:10.1002/hrm.3930270102
Birkinshaw, J., & Hood, N. (1998). Multinational subsidiary evolution: Capability and charter
    change in foreign-owned subsidiary companies. *Academy of Management Review, 23*(4),
    773–795. doi:10.5465/AMR.1998.1255638
Birkinshaw, J., Hood, N., & Jonsson, S. (1998). Building firm-specific advantages in multina-
    tional corporations: The role of subsidiary initiative. *Strategic Management Journal,
    19*(3), 221–241. doi:10.1002/(SICI)1097-0266(199803)19:3 < 221::AID-SMJ948 > 3.0.CO;2-P

Birkinshaw, J., Hood, N., & Young, S. (2005). Subsidiary entrepreneurship, internal and external competitive forces, and subsidiary performance. *International Business Review*, *14*(2), 227–248. doi:10.1016/j.ibusrev.2004.04.010

Bouquet, C., & Birkinshaw, J. (2008). Weight versus voice: How foreign subsidiaries gain attention from corporate headquarters. *Academy of Management Journal*, *51*(3), 577–601. doi:10.5465/AMJ.2008.32626039

Brannen, M. Y., Liker, J. K., & Fruin, W. M. (1999). Recontextualization and factory-to-factory knowledge transfer from Japan to the United States: The case of NSK. In J. K. Liker, W. M. Fruin, & P. S. Adler (Eds.), *Remade in America: Transplanting and transforming Japanese management systems* (pp. 117–153). New York, NY: Oxford University Press.

Edwards, R., Ahmad, A., & Moss, S. (2002). Subsidiary autonomy: The case of multinational subsidiaries in Malaysia. *Journal of International Business Studies*, *33*(1), 183–191. doi:10.1057/palgrave.jibs.8491011

Eisenhardt, K. M. (1989). Building theories from case-study research. *Academy of Management Review*, *14*(4), 532–550. doi:10.5465/AMR.1989.4308385

Elsey, B., & Fujiwara, A. (2000). Kaizen and technology transfer instructors as work-based learning facilitators in overseas transplants: A case study. *Journal of Workplace Learning*, *12*(8), 333–342. doi:10.1108/13665620010378831

Fenton-O'Creevy, M., Gooderham, P., & Nordhaug, O. (2008). Human resource management in US subsidiaries in Europe and Australia: Centralisation or autonomy? *Journal of International Business Studies*, *39*(1), 151–166. doi:10.1057/palgrave.jibs.8400313

Frost, T. S., Birkinshaw, J. M., & Ensign, P. C. (2002). Centers of excellence in multinational corporations. *Strategic Management Journal*, *23*(11), 997–1018. doi:10.1002/smj.273

Fujimoto, T. (1999). *Evolution of manufacturing systems at Toyota*. New York, NY: Oxford University Press.

Gammelgaard, J., McDonald, F., Stephan, A., Tuselmann, H., & Dorrenbacher, C. (2012). The impact of increases in subsidiary autonomy and network relationship on performance. *International Business Review.*, *21*(6), 1158–1172. doi:10.1016/j.ibusrev.2012.01.001

Gate, S. R., & Egelhoff, W. G. (1986). Centralization in headquarters-subsidiary relationship. *Journal of International Business Studies*, *17*(2), 71–92. doi:10.1057/palgrave.jibs.8490425

Ghoshal, S., & Bartlett, C. A. (1988). Creation, adoption and diffusion of innovations by subsidiaries of multinational corporations. *Journal of International Business Studies*, *19*(3), 365–388. doi:10.1057/palgrave.jibs.8490388

Gomez, C., & Werner, S. (2004). The effect of institutional and strategic forces on management style in subsidiaries of U.S. MNCs in Mexico. *Journal of Business Research*, *57*(10), 1135–1144. doi:10.1016/S0148-2963(03)00066-3

Gupta, A. K., & Govindarajan, V. (2000). Knowledge flows within multinational corporations. *Strategic Management Journal*, *21*(4), 473–496. doi:10.1002/(SICI)1097-0266(200004)21:4<473::AID-SMJ84>3.0.CO;2-I

Hair, J. F., Anderson, R., Tathem, R. L., & Black, W. C. (1998). *Multivariate data analysis*. London: Prentice Hall.

Harzing, A. W. K. (1997). Response rates in international mail surveys: Results of a 22-country study. *International Business Review*, *6*(6), 641–665. doi:10.1016/S0969-5931(97)00040-1

Harzing, A. W. K. (1999). *Managing the multinationals: An international study of control mechanisms*. Northampton, MA: E. Elgar.

Hayes, R. H., & Wheelwright, S. C. (1984). *Restoring our competitive edge: Competing through manufacturing*. New York, NY: Wiley.

Hobday, M., & Rush, H. (2007). Upgrading the technological capabilities of foreign transnational subsidiaries in developing countries: The case of electronics in Thailand. *Research Policy, 36*(9), 1335–1356. doi:10.1016/j.respol.2007.05.004

Jakobsen, S. E., & Rusten, G. (2013). The autonomy of foreign subsidiaries: An analysis of headquarter-subsidiary relations. *Norwegian Journal of Geography, 57*(1), 20–30. doi:10.1080/00291950310000794

Jaworski, B. J., & Kohli, A. L. (1993). Market orientation: Antecedents and consequence. *Journal of Marketing, 57*(3), 53–70. doi:10.2307/1251854

Johnston, S., & Menguc, B. (2007). Subsidiary size and the level of subsidiary autonomy in multinational corporations: A quadratic model investigation of Australian subsidiaries. *Journal of International Business Studies, 38*(5), 787–801. doi:10.1057/palgrave. jibs.8400294

Kawai, N., & Strange, R. (2014). Subsidiary autonomy and performance in Japanese multinationals in Europe. *International Business Review, 23*(3), 504–515. doi:10.1016/j. ibusrev.2013.08.012

Keupp, M. M., Palmie, M., & Gassmann, O. (2011). Achieving subsidiary integration in international innovation by managerial tools. *Management International Review, 51*(2), 213–239. doi:10.1007/s11575-011-0072-5

Kopp, R. (1994). *The rice-paper ceiling: Breaking through Japanese corporate culture*. Berkeley, CA: Stone Bridge Press.

Lam, A. (2003). Organizational learning in multinationals: R&D networks of Japanese and US MNEs in the UK. *Journal of Management Studies, 40*(3), 673–703. doi:10.1111/ 1467-6486.00356

Legewie, J. (2002). Control and co-ordination of Japanese subsidiaries in China: Problems of an expatriate-based management system. *International Journal of Human Resource Management, 13*(6), 901–919. doi:10.1080/09585190210134273

Ma, X., Tong, T. W., & Fitza, M. (2013). How much does subnational region matter to foreign subsidiary performance? Evidence from *Fortune* Global 500 Corporations' investment in China. *Journal of International Business Studies, 44*(1), 66–87. doi:10.1057/jibs.2012.32

McDonald, F., Warhurst, S., & Allen, M. (2008). Autonomy, embeddedness, and the performance of foreign owned subsidiaries. *Multinational Business Review, 16*(3), 73–92. doi:10.1108/1525383X200800014

Mudambi, R., & Navarra, P. (2004). Is knowledge power? Knowledge flows, subsidiary power and rent-seeking within MNCs. *Journal of International Business Studies, 35*(5), 385–406.doi:10.1057/palgrave.jibs.8400093

Newburry, W., Zeira, Y., & Yeheskel, O. (2003). Autonomy and effectiveness of equity International Joint Ventures (IJVs) in China. *International Business Review, 12*(4), 395–419. doi:10.1016/S0969-5931(03)00036-2

Oki, K. (2015). Managing internal competition in multinational corporations: The role of home bases. *International Journal of Productivity and Quality Management, 15*(2), 252–267. doi:10.1504/IJPQM.2015.067766

Pisoni, A., Fratocchi, L., & Onetti, A. (2013). Subsidiary autonomy in transition economies: Italian SMEs in Central and Eastern European countries. *Journal for East European Management Studies, 18*(3), 336–370.

Podsakoff, P. M., & Organ, D. W. (1986). Self-reports in organizational research: Problems and prospects. *Journal of Management, 12*(4), 531–544. doi:10.1177/014920638601200408

Prahalad, C. K., & Doz, Y. L. (1981). An approach to strategic control in MNCs. *Sloan Management Review, 22*(4), 5–13. doi:10.1002/tie.5060240102

Roth, K., & Morrison, A. J. (1992). Implementing global strategy: Characteristics of global subsidiary mandates. *Journal of International Business Studies, 23*(4), 715–735. doi:10.1057/palgrave.jibs.8490285

Shuler-Zhou, Y., & Schuller, M. (2013). An empirical study of Chinese subsidiaries' decision-making autonomy in Germany. *Asian Business & Management, 12*(3), 321–350. doi:10.1057/abm.2013.1

Suh, Y. (2015). A global knowledge transfer network: The case of Toyota's global production support system. *International Journal of Productivity and Quality Management, 15*(2), 237–251. doi:10.1504/IJPQM.2015.067765

Taggart, J., & Hood, N. (1999). Determinants of autonomy in multinational corporation subsidiaries. *European Management Journal, 17*(2), 226–236. doi:10.1016/S0263-2373(98)00081-4

Taylor, B. (1999). Japanese management style in China? Production practices in Japanese manufacturing plants. *New Technology, Work and Employment, 14*(2), 129–142. doi:10.1111/1468-005X.00058

Toyo Keizai Inc. (2005). *Kaigai Shinshutsu Kigyo Soran: Kuni Betsu Hen. [Japan Overseas Company: Country Classification].* Tokyo: Toyo Keizai Shinpousha.

Toyo Keizai Inc. (2012). *Kaigai Shinshutsu Kigyo Soran: Kuni Betsu Hen. [Japan Overseas Company: Country Classification].* Tokyo: Toyo Keizai Shinpousha.

Tran, Y., Mahnke, V., & Ambos, B. (2010). The effect of quantity, quality and timing of headquarters-initiated knowledge flows on subsidiary performance. *Management International Review, 50*(4), 493–511. doi:10.1007/s11575-010-0046-z

Tung, R. L. (1982). Selection and training procedures of United-States, European, and Japanese multinationals. *California Management Review, 25*(1), 57–71. doi:10.1002/tie.5060250204

Tungli, Z., & Peiperl, M. (2009). Expatriate practices in German, Japanese, U.K., and U.S. multinational companies: A Comparative survey of changes. *Human Resource Management, 48*(1), 153–171. doi:10.1002/hrm.20271

Venaik, S., Midgley, D. F., & Devinney, T. M. (2005). Dual paths to performance: The impact of global pressures on MNC subsidiary conduct and performance. *Journal of International Business Studies, 36*(6), 655–675. doi:10.1057/palgrave.jibs.8400164

Wang, S. L., Luo, Y., Lu, X., Sun, J., & Maksimov, V. (2014). Autonomy delegation to foreign subsidiaries: An enabling mechanism for emerging-market multinationals. *Journal of International Business Studies, 45*(2), 111–130. doi:10.1057/jibs.2013.40

Wong, M. M. L. (2005). Organizational learning via expatriate managers: Collective myopia as blocking mechanism. *Organization Studies, 26*(3), 325–350. doi:10.1177/0170840605049801

Young, S., & Tavares, A. T. (2004). Centralization and autonomy: Back to the future. *International Business Review, 13*(2), 215–237. doi:10.1016/j.ibusrev.2003.06.002

PART III
PERSPECTIVES ON KNOWLEDGE TRANSFER IN THE MNC NETWORK

COMPLEMENTARITY AND SUBSTITUTION IN THE KNOWLEDGE NETWORKS OF R&D SUBSIDIARIES

Ulf Andersson, Suma Athreye and Georgios Batsakis

ABSTRACT

We argue that a foreign-based R&D subsidiary of a multinational enterprise (MNE) can potentially source knowledge from three diverse knowledge networks, namely (i) external knowledge network of the home country, (ii) external knowledge network of the host country, and (iii) internal (MNE) knowledge network. Drawing on the relative costs and benefits associated with the process of synergistic knowledge, this study examines whether a substitutive or a complementary relationship exists when two of the aforementioned networks collaborate in order to generate new knowledge at the subsidiary level. Our study's sample is based on a survey questionnaire addressed to foreign-based R&D subsidiaries of Fortune 500 companies. We assess the existence of complementarity/ substitutability using the "production function approach." Our results indicate that a complementary relationship exists between external knowledge network of the host and the home country, as well as between

Perspectives on Headquarters-Subsidiary Relationships in the Contemporary MNC
Research in Global Strategic Management, Volume 17, 247–274
Copyright © 2016 by Emerald Group Publishing Limited
All rights of reproduction in any form reserved
ISSN: 1064-4857/doi:10.1108/S1064-485720160000017010

external knowledge network of the host country and internal knowledge network. On the other hand, external knowledge network of the home country and internal knowledge network form a substitutive relationship. Our study offers a more comprehensive view of the diverse sources/knowledge networks that R&D subsidiaries are sourcing knowledge from when compared to existing research. We also specify and account for the costs/benefits involved in knowledge sourcing and thereby detect possible substitution/complementarity between different sources of knowledge. So far, there has been limited to nonexistent research into the diversity of knowledge networks of R&D subsidiaries and the examination of potential substitutabilities and complementarities. Hence our empirical study contributes to the development of this particular research stream.

Keywords: Knowledge networks; knowledge sourcing; complementarity; substitution

INTRODUCTION

Extant research on knowledge and innovation management has shown the complementarity of different knowledge sources and how complementing the internal stock of knowledge with external (nonredundant) knowledge can increase the innovative performance, and indeed also financial performance, of the firm (Ambos, Nell, & Pedersen, 2013; Burt, 1993; Kang & Kang, 2009). The same holds for the multinational enterprise (MNE) subsidiary as well. Thus, the involvement of R&D subsidiaries in the host country network of firms, institutions, and universities has been shown to impact the subsidiary's performance (Andersson, Forsgren, & Holm, 2002; Figueiredo, 2011; Yamin & Otto, 2004), and the parent MNE's competence development (Andersson, Forsgren, & Holm, 2001; Nell, Ambos, & Schlegelmilch, 2011).

Integrating knowledge from different geographical locations and subsequently exploiting this knowledge in different markets is also the *raison d'être* of the MNE (Grant, 1996; Kogut & Zander, 1996). Research on international R&D management has increasingly focused on interfirm relationships and network participation, and more specifically on subsidiary (relational embeddedness) in the host country context as an important vehicle for realizing knowledge development and innovation (Andersson, Björkman, & Forsgren, 2005; Santangelo, 2012).

Although the majority of existing works in this area have focused exclusively on the R&D subsidiary's relationships in the host country environment, other categories of technological and knowledge flows may also be important. For example, in their recent review paper, Michailova and Mustaffa (2012) classify extant research on knowledge flows to four different categories, depending on the focus of examination. From our perspective, one research strand points out that foreign-based subsidiaries are simultaneously embedded in two distinct knowledge networks, the MNE *internal* network of parent and affiliates and the *external* network of the host country (see e.g., Almeida & Phene, 2004; Ambos, 2005; Phene & Almeida, 2008). Another strand of studies shows that subsidiaries are simultaneously embedded in the *host* and the *home* (parent) knowledge networks (see e.g., Bas & Sierra, 2002; Criscuolo, 2009). These findings are all couched in terms of dichotomies (external-internal, host-home), which of course simplify the lessons for technology and knowledge management, but also conceal important traits of the different possible networks a subsidiary can be sourcing knowledge from.

Such dichotomous relationships often obscure some element of the true picture facing the subsidiary in their operational context. In the case of the internal–external dichotomy, the relationships that the foreign subsidiary might have with universities and laboratories in the home country are assumed to be fully mediated by the parent, hence being part of the "internal" source. In the case of the home–host dichotomy, the focus is shifted to the parent and it is assumed that the host country links of parent (usually managed by the foreign subsidiary in that country) is nevertheless part of the parent's external links thus disregarding the internal link, which makes these relationships possible. Such miss-classification needs to be looked at more closely in order to detect the different sources' "true" contribution to MNE performance.

More importantly, the costs of sourcing knowledge from the different sources seem absent or understated in the prevailing dichotomized perspectives. Since both dichotomies seem to conclude a complementary relationship between the different pairs the implicit assumption seems to be that costs outweigh the benefits. Yet, maintaining links to all three sources of knowledge may not be costless for the R&D subsidiary. As well, the kind of costs that come into play might differ. Thus, maintaining links with the external environments whether in the host or home country gives rise to knowledge dissipation costs as collaborations may disclose technological information valuable to competitors (Ghemawat & Spence, 1985). On the other hand, engaging in the internal knowledge network of the MNE gives rise to coordination costs of various kinds that may take up valuable managerial time and resources. Miss-specification of the sources of knowledge which are also associated with an over- or under-estimation of the true costs of using one knowledge source or the other may not be a good basis for managerial practice. This is particularly important when the subsidiary has as its main task creating and developing technological knowledge.

In this study, we seek to remedy this lacuna in existing studies. To this end, we first develop a framework where we associate the source of knowledge to particular costs of coordination and leakage. From the point of view of the (foreign) R&D subsidiary, the knowledge for their capability development can be sourced from three different networks (and locations). These are the host country sources of technology and knowledge, the MNE internal network of parent and affiliates, and the home country networks of knowledge and technology relationships – access to which are often (but not always) controlled by the parent. Consider for example the use of expatriates in foreign R&D subsidiaries; these expatriates certainly have their own contacts with external home country actors since working at the parent company. They will therefore also use these known sources of knowledge when needed in their "new" capacity as expatriates too, without necessarily involving headquarters (HQs) as a mediating actor. Similarly, recent research also suggests that firms use "Diaspora populations" for their links to the host country (Saxenian & Hsu, 2001). It is said that the decision by Texas Instruments to set up its R&D subsidiary in Bangalore was prompted by senior management from Bangalore who understood the potential of the location for R&D development.

Next, we assume that subsidiary managers and the HQ as informed agents will seek to assess if the benefits derived from accessing two sources together will be outweighed by the costs of undertaking such collaborations. A complementary relationship between any two sources of knowledge must occur when there is a net benefit from engaging with the two sources of knowledge together. However, a substitutive relationship may develop whenever the predicted costs outweigh the benefits due to the complementarities of knowledge sources. Recent empirical research draws on similar relationships and shows that MNE subsidiaries forming a substitutive relationship are likely to adopt less knowledge than their counterparts, which are under a complementary relationship (Andersson, Gaur, Mudambi, & Persson, 2015). Hence it can be argued that there are costs and benefits that are taken into consideration under a state of collaborative knowledge generation between MNE units.

In this study, we develop a more detailed understanding of the costs of collaboration in order to assess the complementary or substitutive nature of the relationship between the different knowledge sources facing the subsidiary. Our empirical analysis reveals that knowledge from host locations and intra-MNE sources, as well as the external linkages at home and host locations do show complementarity in the sense that more of one leads to a better innovative performance due to the other. However, subsidiaries are likely to find that coordination costs outweigh the benefits of complementarity when they try to use the home country's external network together with the intra-MNE network. We conjecture that this may be because overtime the MNE internalizes the important home economy advantages into its internal network. Thus, R&D subsidiaries will probably tend to use the intra-MNE network where the costs of dissipation to third parties are lower.

Our contribution to the literature is threefold. First we offer a more comprehensive view of the different sources that R&D subsidiaries are sourcing knowledge from when compared to existing research. Second, this comprehensive specification of the knowledge sources enables us to specify and account for the costs involved in knowledge sourcing and thereby detect possible substitution between different sources of knowledge. Third, we show why internal knowledge networks are so important for the R&D subsidiary. Apart from introducing coherence, the internal network allows the R&D subsidiary to tap into those home country advantages that are most useful for the operation of the MNE. Successful internalization by the MNE ensures that overtime home country advantages are available through the internal network for the benefit of all subsidiaries.

The remainder of the chapter is organized as follows. Next section reviews the relevant literature in order to draw the hypotheses regarding the relationship between the three forms of subsidiary knowledge sourcing. The third section presents the methodology employed and data used for the assessment of potential complementarity/substitutability among the three forms of R&D subsidiary knowledge sources. Subsequently we present the findings of the econometric analysis. Thereafter we discuss the findings, their implications, limitations; propose potential areas for future research; and draw conclusions.

LITERATURE REVIEW AND HYPOTHESES DEVELOPMENT

Costs of Knowledge Sourcing in External and Internal Networks

When striving to tap into different knowledge sources for better performance of the firm, the R&D subsidiary relies on forming mutually beneficial relationships with the three sources of knowledge. These relationships also encounter different types of costs. A schematic model on where these types of costs emanates can be seen in Fig. 1. Relationships with external sources (whether in the home or in the host location) always contain the risk of leaking proprietary knowledge that might hurt the MNEs' competitive position, not only at the single subsidiary's level, but also at the level of the firm. Overtime however, the firms learn to internalize the learning from external home and host sources, and in Fig. 1 we show this in the expansion of the internal knowledge base of the firms.

Analysis of patent data strongly supports a conjecture of internalization of home country advantages. For example, Di Minin and Palmberg (2007) examine the home and foreign patenting of four multinational wireless telephony firms (Ericsson, Motorola, Nokia, and Qualcomm) and find that the essential patents held by these firms are more likely than other patents to have originated in the firm's HQ country.[1] The authors argue that such a strong home country effect in the holding of essential patents occurs both because there is inertia in the organization of a firm's R&D and also because more strategic R&D is likely to be conducted at home.

It is known that the extant knowledge sourced from other intra-MNE units can bring the subsidiary to a position where it can achieve high efficiency in a shorter time span (Hansen, 2002). Drawing on the internal network of subsidiaries however entails coordination costs. The MNE will pay attention to coordination costs originating from the duplication of activities or sourcing of the same knowledge from different sources. Such costs will appear when subsidiaries are simultaneously sourcing knowledge from

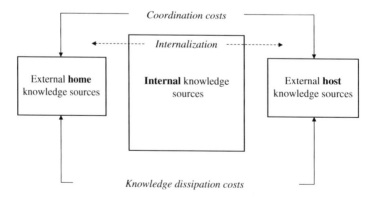

Fig. 1. Coordination and Knowledge Dissipation Costs between the Examined Forms of Knowledge Sourcing.

the two external sources. Another type of coordination cost is ensuring that the relevant market information is combined with the technological information produced in the R&D unit. Patel and Pavitt (1991) noted this as the most important coordination cost which prevented R&D from becoming more internationalized. Lastly, as pointed out by Bartlett and Ghoshal (1999), there is a need to consider the complexity of the knowledge being exchanged. Locating where the complex knowledge is can be an effective strategy if either market or technological information is complex. However, in cases where market and technological information are complex there may need to be greater rotation of people and roles. In turn, this can make the cost of coordination more complex and contingent on the willingness of key people to move.

In assessing whether to source knowledge from two networks simultaneously, firms will choose to evaluate if the benefits of pooling knowledge across two sources yield a larger benefit than the costs that such joint participation entails. When such net benefits are visible the two forms of knowledge networks (sources) are complementary. However, when such net benefits are not visible the R&D subsidiary will tend to substitute one network for the other.

The Relationship between the Two Forms of External Knowledge Sourcing

Although the innovative activities of the leading MNEs have followed a more globalized route throughout the years (Cantwell, 1995), it is also known that MNEs internationalizing their R&D activities usually locate them in technological fields where they are strong at home (Bas & Sierra, 2002; Patel & Vega, 1999). This fact underlies the common notion that innovative activities implemented in the home country confer huge competitive advantages for the MNE (Bas & Sierra, 2002). The host location where the R&D subsidiary is located can provide a network of resources and partners whose contribution (knowledge) is likely to complement the existing knowledge derived from the home location of the MNE. Empirical evidence for this proposition comes mainly from the study of patent citation data drawn from European and US MNEs (Criscuolo, Narula, & Verspagen, 2005). Likewise, Criscuolo (2009) argues that substituting home with host location's national system of innovation (NSI) carries significant negative drawback for the whole MNE (e.g., knowledge spillovers to competitors in the host location). More recently, D'Agostino and Santangelo (2012) showed that R&D subsidiaries of OECD-based firms with a pure adaptation profile tend to complement host R&D with home region knowledge creation.

We argue that foreign-based R&D subsidiaries will simultaneously rely on both forms of external knowledge (i.e., home and host). We draw on this argument for two main reasons. First, overseas subsidiaries will keep on carrying synergies from the home country's network to the host location. This is likely to happen since the parent firm has long-established partnerships with actors established in the home location, rather than in the host one. Accordingly, we argue that the subsidiary will be dictated by the HQs to retain these relationships. This will be the case even when the affiliate unit is based in a foreign, long-distanced location. Second, the overseas subsidiary will equally need to establish relationships with actors located in the host environment, either for research- or market-related reasons. As a result, we may expect that the two external networks − home and host − will have a complementary relationship and firms that are strongly embedded at home may also be strongly embedded in the host economy. Accordingly, we hypothesize that:

H1. External knowledge network of the home country and external knowledge network of the host country in which foreign R&D subsidiaries are embedded will form a complementary relationship.

The Relationship between External (Home and Host) and Internal Knowledge Sourcing

The relationship between R&D subsidiaries' internal and external knowledge networks on the other hand appears to be a bit more ambiguous. Foreign-based R&D subsidiaries are less likely to hold inimitable knowledge assets that cannot be replaced by similar amount and quality of knowledge from the rest of the MNE internal network, or from the external environment. At first glance, this argument holds even more for subsidiaries, which have limited years of operation in the host economy, and consequently it is less likely that they have already developed a high level of independence from the federated network. This kind of subsidiaries is expected to rely heavily on internal knowledge sources.

On the other hand, and based on the resource dependency point of view, as subsidiaries grow and gain more experience and power through their longtime establishment in the host environment, it is likely that they will be in position to establish stronger ties and absorb more knowledge from the external network. Hence after a certain point these R&D subsidiaries could rely more on external knowledge sources and less (or even not at all) on internal sources of knowledge. Cantwell and Mudambi (2005) argue that in the case of competence-creating subsidiaries, internal knowledge may over time show a U-shape, with internal knowledge rising again as the subsidiary grows in competence. Gammelgaard and Pedersen (2010) studying the relationship between internal and external knowledge sourcing provide support for this argument. Precisely, they research on subsidiary's sources of knowledge and find that the relationship between those two forms of knowledge (i.e., internal and external) is initially complementary, but is transformed to a substitutive one when the subsidiary's resource constraints become predictable and binding. These resource constraints in turn lead the R&D subsidiary to a more tied relationship with only one of the two networks.

Although the relationship between external (either home or host) and internal sources of knowledge is not unambiguous, there is evidence supporting a complementary relation among external and internal knowledge sources. Studies conducted from a strategic alliance perspective (Kumar & Nti, 1998; Nielsen, 2005), as well as from a technology management point of view (Audretsch, Menkveld, & Thurik, 1996; Cassiman & Veugelers, 2006; Foss & Pedersen, 2002; Veugelers, 1997) confirm the positive link between these two forms of knowledge sourcing. Recent research on the relationship between the role of R&D subsidiaries and their dual embeddedness shows that R&D subsidiaries whose role evolves to a competence-creating mandate are likely to seek for a simultaneous growth regarding their degree of embeddedness in both internal and external networks (Achcaoucaou, Miravitlles, & León-Darder, 2014). Likewise, evidence from domestic (noninternationalized) enterprises shows that internal and external resources form a complementary relationship that enhances the firm's absorptive capacity as regards the external knowledge acquisition (Hervas-Oliver & Albors-Garrigos, 2009). From a different perspective, Lee, Lee, and Pennings (2001) amalgamated two fundamental theories, the resource-based view (RBV) and social capital (SC) theory in their attempt to explain entrepreneurial wealth creation. The findings suggest that both form a complementary relationship, since the one (i.e., SC) is valuable if and only if a firm is endowed with the other (i.e., internal capabilities). Taking into consideration that firm's internal capabilities are closely related to internal knowledge sourcing, as well as that SC is associated with the external knowledge acquisition, the above findings provide useful information in our attempt to explain the relationship of the three forms of knowledge sourcing.

Our conjectures are based on the notion that external knowledge sourcing of the foreign-based R&D subsidiary is divided to two distinct environments. These are the home and the host locations. First, concerning external host and internal knowledge sourcing, we trust that R&D subsidiaries will not be able to entirely substitute the internal knowledge with an equivalent amount of knowledge that is available in the host economy, mainly because such a strategy is possibly associated with a high degree of exposure to third parties characterized by a mutual interest. Even when the subsidiary is located in a well-protected (e.g., IPR protection regime) environment, knowledge spillovers are likely to occur, mainly because of the coexistence of highly competitive firms in the same cluster. Furthermore, although knowledge may be highly internalized due to possible knowledge spillovers in weak IPR protection regimes (Zhao, 2006), the subsidiary will always need to make use of external channels and related facilities, which are vital for its day-to-day operations. Accordingly, we formulate the following hypothesis:

H2. External knowledge network of the host country and internal knowledge network in which foreign R&D subsidiaries are embedded will form a complementary relationship.

Regarding the relationship among home external and internal knowledge sourcing, we speculate that such a relationship is more likely to evolve into a substitutive one. The literature so far has shown that foreign-based R&D subsidiaries are not very likely to become highly independent of their parent and affiliate units, unless they have developed technological competences, which are inimitable and highly valuable to the rest of the MNE network (Mudambi & Pedersen, 2007). At the same time, *ceteris paribus*, the parent organization has much greater possibilities to source knowledge from external actors in the home country (due to proximity) when compared to the subsidiary. The parent might also already have the knowledge sought by the subsidiary and their ability to detect duplicate knowledge sourcing is much greater when it happens in their "backyard."

Taking into consideration that subsidiaries will always rely on the parent company (either for basic or less important needs) which is highly embedded in the home location's environment, and due to the coordination costs and inefficiency of sourcing knowledge from external home country actors when the parent country might already have "easy" access to knowledge from external counterparts located in the home country, we conjecture that there will be a substitutive relationship between the internal and external home knowledge sourcing of the subsidiary (Fig. 2). Accordingly, we formulate our hypothesis as follows:

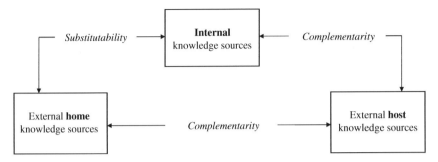

Fig. 2. Conceptual Schema: Complementarity and Substitutability between the Examined Forms of Knowledge Sourcing.

H3. External knowledge network of the home country and internal knowledge network in which foreign R&D subsidiaries are embedded will form a substitutive relationship.

METHODS AND DATA

Methodology

Carree, Lokshin, and Belderbos (2011, p. 263) note that "there are two econometric approaches used to test for complementarity, viz. the 'adoption' or 'correlation' approach and the 'production function approach'." The first, due to Arora and Gambardella (1990), is applied by testing conditional correlations of the produced residuals based on (restricted form) regressions. An important issue that undermines its validity is that the correlated residuals may be a product of various measurement errors or omitted variables. Thus, the main drawback of this method is that it only tests complementarity of practices and not substitutability. This is due to the fact that the error terms can be contaminated by other unobservable effects.

The production function approach uses exclusive combinations of practices (strategies) as independent variables and measures the impact of the former on any chosen output measure.[2] The approach is based on the common understanding of complementarities in production economics, which is that two inputs are complementary if more of one input increases the marginal productivity of the second input (Milgrom & Roberts, 1990). This technique was suggested by Athey and Stern (1998), and was refined further for use in innovation studies by Belderbos, Carree, and Lokshin (2006) and Carree et al. (2011). The methodology used in this study draws upon Carree et al. (2011).

The output of knowledge sourcing we consider is the innovative performance (i.e., innovation output) produced within the R&D subsidiary. Thus, we assume that the subsidiary maximizes its innovative performance f ($\mathbf{X}$, $\mathbf{Z}$), with respect to the vector of all possible combinations of three knowledge sourcing practices, $\mathbf{X}$ = (external home, external host, internal) and a number of control factors $\mathbf{Z}$.[3] Accordingly, the complete technology production function of our study can be written as follows:

$$\text{Ln(Patents}_i + 1) = a + \sum_{r=0}^{1}\sum_{s=0}^{1}\sum_{t=0}^{1} \beta_{rst} K_{(x_1,x_2,x_3)=(r,s,t)} + \beta Z_i + \varepsilon_i$$

where $\varepsilon \sim \left(\sigma_{\varepsilon}^2\right)$, Ln (Patents$_i$ + 1) is the subsidiary's production of innovation measured as the total number of patent counts issued to the R&D subsidiary within a 5-year window $(t + 5)$, where t is the point where the knowledge sourcing is observed. $\mathbf{Z}$ is a vector of other control factors at the subsidiary-, country- and industry-level that are expected to have an impact on subsidiary's innovative performance, and ε an error term.

The vector $\mathbf{X}$ consists of x_1, x_2 and x_3, which refers to the three unique knowledge sourcing practices (i.e., external home (x_1), external host (x_2), and internal (x_3)), and the indicator function $\mathbf{K}$ indicates all exclusive combinations of knowledge sourcing practices coefficients. The coefficients β indicate the performance impact of adopting a particular sourcing practice or a combination of the three possible sources of knowledge.

The above technology production function acts as the basic model. In order to test the hypothesized complementarity/substitutability we first need to proceed to multiple inequality restrictions based on the "supermodularity theory" (Milgrom & Roberts, 1990, 1995). In our case, and in order to test whether presence of complementarity or substitutability is observed for the exclusive combinations of knowledge sourcing practices, we need to estimate three different versions of the aforementioned model using maximum-likelihood estimation; an unconstrained model and two models with imposed inequality constraints (i.e., one with greater than or equal restrictions and another with less than or equal restrictions). Finally, in order to test for or against complementarity we proceed to a likelihood-ratio (LR) test between the unconstrained and the constrained models.

DATA

We had great problems finding data that included all three sources of knowledge and the associated measures of embeddedness. The only available data that actually ask questions about all three sources of knowledge is the University of Reading survey of the Internationalization of R&D conducted in 1989 (described in Athreye, Batsakis, & Singh, 2016; Pearce & Singh, 1992). The sampling frame of the survey consisted of the Fortune 500 list published in 1986 when only 405 of the 500 units had established R&D facilities abroad. However, this was a period when internationalization of R&D was just emerging as a growing phenomenon and this context must be borne in mind in interpreting our results. Specifically, during this period the volume of internationalized R&D was low and modern techniques involving virtual communication and teams did not exist. So our findings on host and internal interactions need to be interpreted with caution.

In the Reading survey a questionnaire was sent via post to the existing population of foreign-based R&D units,[4] where the subsidiary's CEO or R&D manager was responsible for providing answers to the survey's questions. Given that many of the returned questionnaires were suffering from missing values, only 67 of the responses could be fully utilized in the existing study. The survey targeted the MNE's largest international R&D unit[5] whose role was to support local marketing and/or engineering activities, or to be capable of advanced research by contributing in a globally integrated research program. Although this selection strategy may exclude a number of MNE's R&D units, it ensures that the examined foreign subsidiary is also a strategic subsidiary.

The survey data distribution is quite representative of what we know about global research activity of MNEs in the late 1980s. Patent data analysis for the same period, such as this conducted by Patel and Pavitt (1991), has shown that the United States accounts for almost half of the global R&D activity, with Japan and the United Kingdom following with large shares. In our survey sample, R&D subsidiaries based in the United States, the United Kingdom, and Japan account for 71.4% of the total sample. Further, about 75% of it consists of R&D subsidiaries in pharmaceuticals, electronics, and chemicals and petroleum sectors – which are among the most internationalized sectors concerning R&D activities.

Nonresponse Bias and Common Method Bias

We test for possible nonresponse bias and common method bias in our sample in several ways. First, we compare the number of respondents to that of the original population for all the examined geographical locations. Almost all the foreign locations where R&D subsidiaries operate are well represented in the returned questionnaires, except for Canada and France, which are underrepresented. Second, since some questionnaires were collected after respondents received a second notice (reminder), we test for a possible nonresponse bias that may negatively affect our sample's explanatory power. Following Armstrong and Overton, 1977, we compared subsidiaries' age and size characteristics in the responses collected under first and second attempt and found no statistically significant difference between the two groups. Finally, in order to test if a common method bias had inflated the relationships between the variables used in the analysis, we used the Harman's single-factor test on the items included in our model (Podsakoff & Organ, 1986). The factor analysis extracted four factors with eigenvalues greater than 1, while the first one explains 21.12% of the total variance (eigenvalue = 4.37). These results reject the presence of a single emerging factor, and also confirm that no factor accounts for the majority of the variance (> 50%). Thus, the survey data we use are reliable and common method bias is not a major issue.

Variables

Dependent Variables
Innovative performance: The production function approach to complementarity requires an output measure of inventiveness based on knowledge sourced internally, externally, or in combination by firms. Although innovative performance can be assessed in many ways (e.g., utilizing financial data by adopting the ratio of R&D expenditures to total return on investment or sales, or implementing survey questionnaires under which the innovativeness of the company was evaluated by the response of a general manager or CEO), patent count data are perceived as a more objective measure of true inventiveness of firms in new product and new technology

generation (Hagedoorn & Cloodt, 2003). Patent data have been used as an output proxy of subsidiary inventiveness in several studies (e.g., Almeida & Phene, 2004; Phene & Almeida, 2008; Sampson, 2007). More specifically, the measure of innovative performance we use is the total number of USPTO patents issued to the R&D subsidiary within a 5-year window from the time the Reading survey was conducted.[6] Since the survey was conducted in 1989, then the 5-year window corresponds to the period 01/01/1989–31/12/1993.

Independent Variables
The knowledge sourcing variables: We developed three measures of knowledge sourcing from the survey instrument. Two of these are measures of external knowledge sourcing and one of internal knowledge sourcing. The survey instrument asked respondents to provide information on the frequency of the subsidiary's contact with their internal and/or external knowledge sources using a 3-point Likert-scale, ranging from no contacts (1) to regular contacts (3) between the two interacted parties. In total three variables were constructed, namely *external home* ($\alpha = 0.65$), *external host* ($\alpha = 0.60$), and *internal* ($\alpha = 0.73$). The questions used for each construct are presented in Table 1. In order to adjust our data to the specific assumptions of the econometric method, we transformed the upper three scale variables to dichotomous ones.[7] Since the original scaling of these variables ranges from "1" (weak) to "3" (strong) we transformed all the variables with values lower than "2" to "0", and the variables with values equal or greater than "2" to "1". Hence, the newly constructed variables take the value "1" when a rather frequent to strong relationship with other sources of knowledge exists. On the other hand they are valued with "0" when a quite infrequent to none sort of relationship with other sources of knowledge is observed.

Control Variables
We use a number of subsidiary level controls that are indicated by literature on the subject of subsidiary innovativeness. The *mandate of the subsidiary* is clearly an important variable for the study. The questionnaire asks each R&D subsidiary to classify its activities (using again a 3-point Likert-type structure) into the following three categories: Support Laboratories (SLs), Locally Integrated Laboratories (LILs), and Internationally Integrated Laboratories (IILs). Furthermore, we construct a variable for measuring the degree of R&D subsidiary's centralization to the HQ. Following previous studies (e.g., Birkinshaw & Hood, 2000; Nell & Andersson, 2012), we use a

Table 1.   Operationalization of Variables.

Variables	Questions Used from the Questionnaire in Order to Construct Multi-Item Variables
External home	"Does any liaison exist between this R&D unit and the home country: (a) research institutions; (b) universities; and (c) R&D labs of local and/or foreign companies?" The answers to this question have a categorical-Likert operationalization, ranging from 1 (no contacts reported) to 3 (regular contacts reported).
External host	"(i) Does this R&D unit give contract jobs to the following institutions in this country: (a) independent research labs; (b) universities; (ii) Does any exchange program of scientists exist between this unit and other local research institutions/labs? (iii) Are seminars relating to ongoing research in this unit held in collaboration with other local research units/institutions? (iv) Are research findings of this unit published in journals? (v) Are local independent researchers one of the most likely sources of project ideas initiated in this unit?" The answers to all the above questions also have a categorical-Likert formation, based on the frequency of interaction, and range from 1 (never) to 3 (regularly).
Internal	"Are the parent or other sister R&D units involved in your projects in any of the following ways? (i) systematic coordination of your projects into wider programs; (ii) to bring about a major change in the direction of the project; (iii) to advise on the development of a project; (iv) technical assistance at the request of the R&D unit." The answers to all the above questions also have a categorical-Likert formation, based on the frequency of interaction, and range from 1 (never) to 3 (regularly).
Centralization	"(i) Are promising projects shifted to parent or other strategic labs of the group around the world? (ii) Does this and other R&D units of the parent company interact?" The answers to both questions range from 1 (never) to 3 (regularly). "(iii) If the unit has grown in size over time has this been (a) mostly as a result of its own success; (b) because of its own success and parent's encouragement; (c) mostly at the encouragement of the parent. (iv) How do you perceive the strategy of the parent towards its various R&D units? (a) Allowing substantial autonomy; (b) Allowing them to develop independent initiatives, but under close central scrutiny; (c) Incorporating their work into a carefully coordinated programme."
Local endowment	"Which conditions or circumstances do you consider have most influenced recent decisions with regard to the development of this unit? (i) a distinctive local scientific, educational, or technological tradition conducive to certain types of research project; (ii) presence of a helpful local scientific environment and adequate technical infrastructure; (iii) availability of research professionals; (iv) favorable wage rates for the research professionals." The answers to the above questions have a categorical-Likert formation, based on the frequency of interaction, and range from 1 (never) to 3 (regularly).

multi-item scale for this measure. The *Centralization* construct ($\alpha = 0.51$)[8] is based on four 3-point Likert-type questions. The items included decisions regarding shift of projects to parent or other strategic labs and the level of interaction with them, the general decentralization strategy of the parent towards its foreign affiliate unit, and growth dependence of the R&D lab. We also include the subsidiary's mode of entry (*Greenfield*), size (*LnSize*), and age (*LnYears*) — all obtained from the survey questionnaire.

We also incorporated several industry dummies to control for the parent firm's field of operation and included traditional aggregate measures, such as *Geographic Distance* (e.g., Monteiro, Arvidsson, & Birkinshaw, 2008) and *Cultural Distance* (Kogut & Singh, 1988) of the R&D subsidiary as factors capable of influencing the subsidiary's innovativeness. We further introduce a variable named *Local endowment* to control for the host location's endowment richness (i.e., local scientific and technological resources, scientific environment and technical infrastructure, availability of research professionals, and favorable wage rates for research professionals). This variable was also created from the survey questionnaire. Finally, we included two home country dummies for two of the most internationalized countries (in terms of R&D activities) of our sample (United States and United Kingdom). Table 2 summarizes the variables created, provides information about their source, as well as it presents basic descriptive statistics for each of the variables.

FINDINGS

Our sample seems quite representative of the R&D subsidiaries in the early 1990s. In fact, 68% of the sample consists of production subsidiaries, with support labs emerging as the most popular mandate. The average level of centralization of R&D decisions is high. The average age of an R&D subsidiary in the sample was 26.2 years and the average R&D employment size was 154.3 people. The raw scores (untransformed into dichotomized variables) suggest that the extent of home country knowledge sourcing is higher than its host country equivalent, though a slightly smaller number of firms seem to report the opposite.

Considering that survey data are prone to multicollinearity between the variables and the constructed factors we estimated the variance inflation factors (VIFs) for each coefficient in each examined model. The VIFs scores for the coefficients of the technology production function model

Table 2. Variable Operationalization, Data Sources, and Descriptive Statistics.

Variables	Number of Items Used	Cronbach's Alpha (α)	Source	Type	Mean	SD	Min	Max
Ln (Patents + 1)			USPTO	Scale	2.16	1.92	0.69	6.00
External home	3	0.65	Survey	Binomial	0.44	0.49	0	1
External host	6	0.60	Survey	Binomial	0.30	0.46	0	1
Internal	4	0.73	Survey	Binomial	0.54	0.50	0	1
SLs			Survey	Categorical	1.77	0.75	1	3
LILs			Survey	Categorical	2.05	0.74	1	3
IILs			Survey	Categorical	2.11	0.88	1	3
Centralization	4	0.51	Survey	Scale	2.34	0.33	1.5	3
Endowment	4	0.72	Survey	Scale	1.73	0.54	1	3
Greenfield			Survey	Binomial	0.68	0.46	0	1
LnYears			Survey	Scale	2.95	0.93	0.69	4.82
LnSize			Survey	Scale	4.14	1.36	1.38	7.54
LnGeographical distance			CEPII database	Scale	8.55	0.80	5.83	9.74
Cultural distance			Own calculations based on Kogut and Singh (1988)	Scale	2.14	2.51	0.09	9.70

range from 1.43 to 3.08, indicating that multicollinearity is not a problem for our model (Hair, Anderson, Tatham, & Black, 1998). Table 3 presents pairwise correlations between variables, while the last row reports the exact VIFs score for each of the variables.

Table 4 presents the estimation results of the unrestricted equation (based on technology production function). Regarding the explanatory power of the model, it seems that the incorporated variables explain a rather significant amount of variance, since the R^2 has a value of 50.9%. The regression results in Table 4 seem to explain only a fraction of relationships regarding single or even combinative knowledge sourcing practices. Actually, the only significant values are observed on the combinative practice among external home, external host, and internal knowledge sourcing ($\beta_{111} = -2.121$, $p < 5\%$). Regarding the other variables we find that innovative performance is enhanced if subsidiaries are larger R&D subsidiaries, while being a US or UK subsidiary does not seem to have a positive impact on the innovative performance of the unit. Given that the regression results in Table 4 are not directly related to our hypotheses, we do not focus on the significance of these effects on innovative performance. However, we are mostly interested in assessing the complementarity/substitutability test.

The complementarity test results (see Table 5) corresponding to the imposed inequality constraints show that these are supporting the conjecture of complementarity for two out of the three pairs of knowledge sourcing practices, while the assumption of substitutability (subadditivity) is in favor of the third pair. Specifically, the LR test turned out to confirm the argument of complementarity for the pairs of knowledge sourcing practices of (i) external home/external host and (ii) external host/internal. On the other hand, the third pair (external home/internal) of knowledge sourcing practices is indicated as substitutive one, since the relative LR test turned out to be significant between the unrestricted and restricted (assuming substitutability) models.

DISCUSSION

Extant literature has highlighted the benefits of obtaining knowledge from different sources (Cassiman & Veugelers, 2006; D'Agostino & Santangelo, 2012; Foss & Pedersen, 2002). A particular trait of these studies is the dichotomization of the possible sources at hand for an R&D unit in its sourcing efforts. We have argued that apart from limiting the amount of

Table 3. Correlation Matrix.

	1	2	3	4	5	6	7	8	9	10	11	12	13	14	15	16	17	18	19	20	21	22	23
1 Ln (Patents + 1)	1																						
2 SLs	0.21	1																					
3 LILs	-0.08	0.12	1																				
4 IILs	-0.07	-0.30	-0.57	1																			
5 Centralization	-0.02	-0.21	0.39	-0.40	1																		
6 Endowment	-0.01	-0.17	-0.23	0.33	-0.18	1																	
7 Greenfield	-0.05	-0.04	-0.16	0.27	-0.28	0.21	1																
8 ln_Size	0.04	-0.13	-0.41	0.34	-0.26	0.15	0.12	1															
9 ln_Years	-0.28	-0.10	0.23	-0.10	0.37	-0.02	0.11	0.12	1														
10 ln_Geo_Distance	-0.06	0.09	0.14	-0.11	0.03	-0.08	0.08	0.07	0.08	1													
11 Cultural distance	0.17	0.09	-0.03	0.07	-0.08	-0.10	-0.19	-0.14	-0.38	-0.02	1												
12 US	-0.18	-0.08	0.00	-0.06	0.16	-0.12	0.10	0.10	0.36	0.06	-0.16	1											
13 UK	-0.24	-0.04	0.21	0.02	0.13	-0.09	-0.04	-0.00	0.04	0.00	-0.15	-0.38	1										
14 CP	-0.01	0.23	0.03	0.04	-0.25	-0.00	0.11	0.02	-0.04	0.32	0.00	-0.14	0.20	1									
15 EC	0.13	0.01	-0.05	-0.06	-0.13	0.01	-0.01	-0.10	-0.16	-0.25	0.12	0.12	-0.19	-0.37	1								
16 PH	0.00	-0.25	-0.24	0.33	0.12	0.25	0.03	0.12	0.09	-0.08	-0.11	0.20	-0.11	-0.40	-0.22	1							
17 β_{100}	-0.00	-0.06	0.16	0.03	0.15	-0.05	-0.07	-0.08	0.12	0.13	-0.02	0.04	-0.06	-0.16	0.13	0.20	1						
18 β_{010}	-0.20	-0.13	0.09	0.04	0.05	0.00	-0.16	-0.08	0.12	-0.01	-0.01	-0.04	0.29	0.11	-0.09	0.07	-0.08	1					
19 β_{001}	0.23	0.12	0.09	0.04	-0.03	-0.05	0.12	-0.20	-0.16	0.15	0.12	-0.11	-0.03	0.21	-0.23	-0.08	-0.21	-0.11	1				
20 β_{110}	0.01	0.05	0.09	-0.27	0.11	-0.06	-0.05	-0.09	-0.08	0.03	0.04	-0.18	0.10	-0.17	-0.09	0.07	-0.08	-0.04	-0.11	1			
21 β_{101}	0.09	-0.07	-0.22	0.08	-0.10	0.15	-0.05	0.05	-0.14	0.03	0.07	0.08	-0.11	0.22	0.02	-0.13	-0.08	-0.05	-0.14	-0.05	1		
22 β_{011}	0.13	0.09	-0.05	0.07	-0.03	-0.09	0.10	-0.06	-0.08	-0.32	0.02	-0.03	0.04	-0.08	0.24	-0.10	-0.16	-0.08	-0.21	-0.08	-0.11	1	
23 β_{111}	-0.37	-0.03	-0.25	0.19	-0.30	0.31	0.06	0.36	0.11	0.05	-0.22	-0.10	0.01	0.09	-0.20	0.05	-0.18	-0.09	-0.23	-0.09	-0.12	-0.18	1
VIFs	–	1.53	2.31	3.08	2.57	1.64	1.57	1.64	1.98	1.43	1.44	1.99	1.79	2.44	2.31	2.51	2.00	1.6	2.55	1.52	1.93	1.83	2.71

Note: Coefficients with values greater than 0.14 are significant at the 10% level of significance.

Table 4. OLS Regression Estimates on Innovative Performance.

	Innovative Performance
SLs	0.405 (0.310)
LILs	−0.081 (0.395)
IILs	−0.363 (0.382)
Centralization	0.738 (0.927)
Endowment	0.025 (0.490)
Greenfield	−0.121 (0.515)
ln_Size	0.473** (0.174)
ln_Years	−0.155 (0.289)
ln_Geo_Distance	−0.130 (0.324)
Cultural distance	−0.024 (0.093)
External home (β_{100})	−0.270 (0.773)
External host (β_{010})	−1.067 (1.193)
Internal (β_{001})	0.788 (0.744)
External home, external host (β_{110})	−0.531 (1.164)
External home, internal (β_{101})	0.414 (1.005)
External host, internal (β_{011})	0.371 (0.759)
External home, external host, internal (β_{111})	−2.121* (0.835)
Industry dummies	Included
Major country dummies	Included
Constant	0.712 (3.923)
R-squared	0.509

Note: Levels of significance: **$p < 1\%$; *$p < 5\%$ (robust S.E. in parentheses).

Table 5. Tests for Complementarity/Substitutability between Different Forms of Knowledge Sourcing.

	LR Test Complementarity ($\geq$)	LR Test Substitutability ($\leq$)
External home and external host	11.99**	0
External home and internal	3.34	7.89*
External host and internal	15.95**	3.33

Note: Levels of significance: **$p < 1\%$ and *$p < 5\%$.

sources available for obtaining new knowledge the dichotomization obscures the costs involved in knowledge sourcing. In this study we set out to study the phenomenon of complementarity and substitutability of different knowledge sources. Introducing a pertinent view of the different sources available from an R&D subsidiary's point of view (internal, host external, and home external), rather than the internal–external, or home–host dichotomies prevalent in extant research makes it possible to better account for the costs involved in knowledge sourcing. We have studied the relationships in the context of foreign-based R&D subsidiaries. Firms locate R&D units in different countries to tap into local knowledge and utilize cost advantages in qualified labor (Athreye et al., 2016). Accordingly we have argued that the possible coordination costs and inefficiencies of sourcing knowledge will surface if we acknowledge all the sources from which an R&D subsidiary can obtain new knowledge.

Through utilizing a production function approach, we were able to account for the substitutability or complementarity of specific combinations of knowledge sourcing. As was indeed confirmed from our study, the dichotomization of sources obscures the true traits of the sources at hand for an R&D subsidiary obtaining knowledge.

Our findings show that sourcing knowledge from both internal (federated MNE network) and home external networks has a substitutive effect due to coordination costs and inefficiencies. The phenomenon of increased coordination costs implies that the subsidiary will have to maintain relationship with both the federated MNE and the home external knowledge networks, which are both, located in the home country. The simultaneous maintenance of ties is possibly associated to establishment of more advanced and complex coordination mechanisms, which in turn lead to increased costs for the MNE. Another possibility is that the simultaneous maintenance of ties with these two knowledge networks may produce duplicative effects, which are also detrimental for the MNE in terms of costs. As a result, after a certain point, where the coordination costs that mainly arise from the simultaneous maintenance of ties and the duplicative effects, the foreign-based R&D subsidiary opt to substitute the one form of knowledge sourcing with the other. This argument can also be framed under the over-embeddedness lenses (e.g., Hagedoorn & Frankort, 2008; Nell & Andersson, 2012; Uzzi, 1997) where at a certain point the increasing network of interfirm relationships becomes too complex and interconnected, that diminishing returns of new information gains starts to occur. This is the point where the over-embeddedness costs (which results from the simultaneous maintenance of ties between the knowledge networks of home external and internal) push the subsidiary to substitute one form of knowledge sourcing with the other.

On the contrary, sourcing externally in both the home and the host knowledge network is complementary as is internal and host external knowledge network sourcing. This result implies that for an MNE it is of utmost importance that its subunits are sourcing knowledge from sources complementary to each other so that the coordination costs do not spoil the leverage effects of knowledge combinations.

As with the majority of existing empirical studies, this study has several limitations. First, our data are in cross-sectional rather than in panel formation. Accordingly, we were not able to observe whether our findings are consistent over time. The incorporation of a longitudinal study would be an efficient way to control for evolution of knowledge sourcing practices and their relationships over time. Second, the datedness of our data may be an additional limitation for our study, since some of the relationships could have been atrophied or overtaken by technology. This holds especially for internal knowledge sourcing, where recent advances in information technology can have improved the monitoring, control, and coordination mechanisms of subsidiaries' activities. However, we already know from the literature that the degree of embeddedness and the social relationships are slowly developed and equally slowly amended. The notion of social interaction is universal across time and strengthens rather than weakens with time, as trust plays a vital role on this relationship.

The incorporation of an additional form of knowledge source can be both beneficial and inspirational for future research aiming to examine the context of the foreign-based subsidiary and its relationship with surrounding knowledge networks. We are particularly keen to see future research that complements and widens the knowledge stemming from our findings and can contribute to our understanding of this research question. Accordingly, future research studies can potentially test for complementarities between knowledge sources that arise from an even more objective measure, such as co-patenting, co-inventions, etc. Furthermore, taking into consideration that the external knowledge network of the affiliate units' country of residence has not been taken into empirical examination under this study, we assume that there might be another possibility that the forms of knowledge sourcing can be augmented even more. The same applies when we view the internal knowledge network in terms of dichotomies (i.e., knowledge network of HQ and knowledge network of affiliate units).

CONCLUSION

Overall, the general view of the foreign-based R&D subsidiary's networks of knowledge, as well as the accompanying empirical results, contribute to our understanding regarding the context under which the subsidiary seeks for combinative sources of knowledge. Furthermore, this study contributes in the extant IB literature by responding to recent calls for viewing the available knowledge networks beyond the classic single- or dual-dimensionality of embeddedness. A realistic depiction of the subsidiary's surrounding knowledge networks show that the forms of the subsidiary's knowledge sources are multiple and more complex compared to the existing dichotomization (as is also discussed in Meyer, Mudambi, & Narula, 2011). As a result, the combination of these knowledge sources is characterized by an equally complex relationship, which this study has empirically examined.

NOTES

1. Essential patents are those defined by the European Telecommunications Standards Institute as essential to a telecommunication standard and these firms held 553 out of 834 such patents.
2. Although the production function approach is a well-respected estimation method it should be noted that there are several limitations characterizing it (see Carree et al., 2011, p. 266, for more information).
3. The complementarity/substitutability test requests the cross-derivative to be nonnegative for all possible cross-term interactions of practices (Carree et al., 2011). In our data, this was the case only when we used a dichotomous transformation.
4. The first questionnaires were sent out in October 1988 and the last ones in June 1989, while the first completed questionnaire was received back in November 1988 and the last one in August 1989.
5. The identification of the largest foreign R&D subsidiary was made after consulting a number of the leading directories of R&D facilities and evaluating its size according to financial and employment characteristics.
6. Since we are interested in the patent activity of R&D units located in multiple locations, we set up the search by using the assignee name (e.g., SIEMENS), the host invention location (e.g., United States), as well as the 5-year window for which we are interested in.
7. The transformation of these variables from scale to dichotomous ones was made after having extracted the already developed three factors (i.e., *external home*, *external host*, and *internal*).
8. Although the reliability score for this construct does not reach a high level of efficiency, Nunnally, Bernstein, and Berge (1967) suggested that a score ranging between 0.50 and 0.60 is considered as acceptable reliability.

REFERENCES

Achcaoucaou, F., Miravitlles, P., & León-Darder, F. (2014). Knowledge sharing and subsidiary R&D mandate development: A matter of dual embeddedness. *International Business Review*, 23(1), 76–90.

Almeida, P., & Phene, A. (2004). Subsidiaries and knowledge creation: The influence of the MNC and host country on innovation. *Strategic Management Journal*, *25*(8–9), 847–864.

Ambos, B. (2005). Foreign direct investment in industrial research and development: A study of German MNCs. *Research Policy*, *34*(4), 395–410.

Ambos, T. C., Nell, P. C., & Pedersen, T. (2013). Combining stocks and flows of knowledge: The effects of intra-functional and cross-functional complementarity. *Global Strategy Journal*, *3*(4), 283–299.

Andersson, U., Björkman, I., & Forsgren, M. (2005). Managing subsidiary knowledge creation: The effect of control mechanisms on subsidiary local embeddedness. *International Business Review*, *14*(5), 521–538.

Andersson, U., Forsgren, M., & Holm, U. (2001). Subsidiary embeddedness and competence development in MNCs a multi-level analysis. *Organization Studies*, *22*(6), 1013–1034.

Andersson, U., Forsgren, M., & Holm, U. (2002). The strategic impact of external networks: Subsidiary performance and competence development in the multinational corporation. *Strategic Management Journal*, *23*(11), 979–996.

Andersson, U., Gaur, A., Mudambi, R., & Persson, M. (2015). Unpacking interunit knowledge transfer in multinational enterprises. *Global Strategy Journal*, *5*(3), 241–255.

Armstrong, J. U. S. T., & Overton, T. (1977). Estimating nonresponse bias in mail surveys. *Journal of Marketing Research*, *14*, 396–402.

Arora, A., & Gambardella, A. (1990). Complementarity and external linkages: The strategies of the large firms in biotechnology. *The Journal of Industrial Economics*, *38*(4), 361–379.

Athreye, S., Batsakis, G., & Singh, S. (2016). Local, global, and internal knowledge sourcing: The trilemma of foreign-based R&D subsidiaries. *Journal of Business Research* (forthcoming). doi:10.1016/j.jbusres.2016.02.043

Athey, S., & Stern, S. (1998). *An empirical framework for testing theories about complimentarity in organizational design* (No. w6600). Cambridge, MA: National Bureau of Economic Research.

Audretsch, D. B., Menkveld, A. J., & Thurik, A. R. (1996). The decision between internal and external R & D. *Journal of Institutional and Theoretical Economics (JITE)/Zeitschrift für die gesamte staatswissenschaft*, *152*(3), 519–530.

Bartlett, C. A., & Ghoshal, S. (1999). *Managing across borders: The transnational solution* (Vol. 2). Boston, MA: Harvard Business School Press.

Bas, C. L., & Sierra, C. (2002). 'Location versus home country advantages' in R&D activities: Some further results on multinationals' locational strategies. *Research Policy*, *31*(4), 589–609.

Belderbos, R., Carree, M., & Lokshin, B. (2006). Complementarity in R&D cooperation strategies. *Review of Industrial Organization*, *28*(4), 401–426.

Birkinshaw, J., & Hood, N. (2000). Characteristics of foreign subsidiaries in industry clusters. *Journal of International Business Studies*, *31*(1), 141–154.

Burt, R. S. (1993). The social structure of competition. *Explorations in Economic Sociology*, *65*, 103.

Cantwell, J. (1995). The globalisation of technology: What remains of the product cycle model? *Cambridge Journal of Economics*, *19*, 155–174.

Cantwell, J., & Mudambi, R. (2005). MNE competence-creating subsidiary mandates. *Strategic Management Journal*, *26*(12), 1109–1128.

Carree, M., Lokshin, B., & Belderbos, R. (2011). A note on testing for complementarity and substitutability in the case of multiple practices. *Journal of Productivity Analysis*, *35*(3), 263–269.

Cassiman, B., & Veugelers, R. (2006). In search of complementarity in innovation strategy: Internal R&D and external knowledge acquisition. *Management Science*, *52*(1), 68–82.

Criscuolo, P. (2009). Inter-firm reverse technology transfer: The home country effect of R&D internationalization. *Industrial and Corporate Change*, *18*(5), 869–899.

Criscuolo, P., Narula, R., & Verspagen, B. (2005). Role of home and host country innovation systems in R&D internationalisation: A patent citation analysis. *Economics of Innovation and New Technology*, *14*(5), 417–433.

D'Agostino, L. M., & Santangelo, G. D. (2012). Do overseas R&D laboratories in emerging markets contribute to home knowledge creation? *Management International Review*, *52*(2), 251–273.

Di Minin, A., & Palmberg, C. (2007). *Why is strategic R&D (still) homebound in a globalized industry? The case of leading firms in wireless telecom.* Industry Studies Working Paper No. 2007–12.

Figueiredo, P. N. (2011). The role of dual embeddedness in the innovative performance of MNE subsidiaries: Evidence from Brazil. *Journal of Management Studies*, *48*(2), 417–440.

Foss, N. J., & Pedersen, T. (2002). Transferring knowledge in MNCs: The role of sources of subsidiary knowledge and organizational context. *Journal of International Management*, *8*(1), 49–67.

Gammelgaard, J., & Pedersen, T. (2010). Internal versus external knowledge sourcing of subsidiaries and the impact of headquarters control. In U. Andersson & U. Holm (Eds.), *Managing the contemporary multinational. The role of headquarters* (pp. 211–230). Cheltenham: Edward Elgar.

Ghemawat, P., & Spence, A. M. (1985). Learning curve spillovers and market performance. *The Quarterly Journal of Economics*, *100*, 839–852.

Grant, R. M. (1996). Toward a knowledge-based theory of the firm. *Strategic Management Journal*, *17*, 109–122.

Hagedoorn, J., & Cloodt, M. (2003). Measuring innovative performance: Is there an advantage in using multiple indicators? *Research Policy*, *32*(8), 1365–1379.

Hagedoorn, J., & Frankort, H. T. (2008). The gloomy side of embeddedness: The effects of overembeddedness on inter-firm partnership formation. *Advances in Strategic Management*, *25*, 503–530.

Hair, J., Anderson, R. E., Tatham, R. L., & Black, W. (1998). *Multivariate data analysis with readings*. Englewood Cliffs, NJ: Prentice-Hall.

Hansen, M. T. (2002). Knowledge networks: Explaining effective knowledge sharing in multiunit companies. *Organization Science*, *13*(3), 232–248.

Hervas-Oliver, J. L., & Albors-Garrigos, J. (2009). The role of the firm's internal and relational capabilities in clusters: When distance and embeddedness are not enough to explain innovation. *Journal of Economic Geography*, *9*(2), 263–283.

Kang, K. H., & Kang, J. (2009). How do firms source external knowledge for innovation? Analysing effects of different knowledge sourcing methods. *International Journal of Innovation Management*, *13*(1), 1–17.

Kogut, B., & Singh, H. (1988). The effect of national culture on the choice of entry mode. *Journal of International Business Studies*, *19*(3), 411–432.

Kogut, B., & Zander, U. (1996). What firms do? Coordination, identity, and learning. *Organization Science, 7*(5), 502–518.

Kumar, R., & Nti, K. O. (1998). Differential learning and interaction in alliance dynamics: A process and outcome discrepancy model. *Organization Science, 9*(3), 356–367.

Lee, C., Lee, K., & Pennings, J. M. (2001). Internal capabilities, external networks, and performance: A study on technology-based ventures. *Strategic Management Journal, 22*(6–7), 615–640.

Meyer, K. E., Mudambi, R., & Narula, R. (2011). Multinational enterprises and local contexts: The opportunities and challenges of multiple embeddedness. *Journal of Management Studies, 48*(2), 235–252.

Michailova, S., & Mustaffa, Z. (2012). Subsidiary knowledge flows in multinational corporations: Research accomplishments, gaps, and opportunities. *Journal of World Business, 47*(3), 383–396.

Milgrom, P., & Roberts, J. (1990). The economics of modern manufacturing: Technology, strategy, and organization. *The American Economic Review, 80*(3), 511–528.

Milgrom, P., & Roberts, J. (1995). Complementarities and fit strategy, structure, and organizational change in manufacturing. *Journal of Accounting and Economics, 19*(2), 179–208.

Monteiro, L. F., Arvidsson, N., & Birkinshaw, J. (2008). Knowledge flows within multinational corporations: Explaining subsidiary isolation and its performance implications. *Organization Science, 19*(1), 90–107.

Mudambi, R., & Pedersen, T. (2007). Agency theory and resource dependency theory: Complementary explanations for subsidiary power in multinational corporations. *Bridging IB theories, constructs, and methods across cultures and social sciences.* Basingstoke: Palgrave Macmillan.

Nell, P. C., Ambos, B., & Schlegelmilch, B. B. (2011). The MNC as an externally embedded organization: An investigation of embeddedness overlap in local subsidiary networks. *Journal of World Business, 46*(4), 497–505.

Nell, P. C., & Andersson, U. (2012). The complexity of the business network context and its effect on subsidiary relational (over-)embeddedness. *International Business Review, 21*(6), 1087–1098.

Nielsen, B. B. (2005). The role of knowledge embeddedness in the creation of synergies in strategic alliances. *Journal of Business Research, 58*(9), 1194–1204.

Nunnally, J. C., Bernstein, I. H., & Berge, J. M. T. (1967). *Psychometric theory.* New York, NY: McGraw-Hill.

Patel, P., & Pavitt, K. (1991). Large firms in the production of the world's technology: An important case of "non-globalisation". *Journal of International Business Studies, 22*, 1–21.

Patel, P., & Vega, M. (1999). Patterns of internationalisation of corporate technology: Location vs. home country advantages. *Research Policy, 28*(2), 145–155.

Pearce, R. D., & Singh, S. (1992). *Globalizing research and development.* London: Macmillan.

Phene, A., & Almeida, P. (2008). Innovation in multinational subsidiaries: The role of knowledge assimilation and subsidiary capabilities. *Journal of International Business Studies, 39*(5), 901–919.

Podsakoff, P. M., & Organ, D. W. (1986). Self-reports in organizational research: Problems and prospects. *Journal of Management, 12*(4), 531–544.

Sampson, R. C. (2007). R&D alliances and firm performance: The impact of technological diversity and alliance organization on innovation. *Academy of Management Journal, 50*(2), 364–386.

Santangelo, G. D. (2012). The tension of information sharing: Effects on subsidiary embedd-edness. *International Business Review*, *21*(2), 180–195.

Saxenian, A., & Hsu, J. Y. (2001). The silicon valley–Hsinchu connection: Technical commu-nities and industrial upgrading. *Industrial and Corporate Change*, *10*(4), 893–920.

Uzzi, B. (1997). Social structure and competition in interfirm networks: The paradox of embeddedness. *Administrative Science Quarterly*, *42*, 35–67.

Veugelers, R. (1997). Internal R & D expenditures and external technology sourcing. *Research Policy*, *26*(3), 303–315.

Yamin, M., & Otto, J. (2004). Patterns of knowledge flows and MNE innovative performance. *Journal of International Management*, *10*(2), 239–258.

Zhao, M. (2006). Conducting R&D in countries with weak intellectual property rights protec-tion. *Management Science*, *52*, 1185–1199.

HOW DOES GEOGRAPHIC DISTANCE IMPACT THE RELEVANCE OF HQ KNOWLEDGE? THE MEDIATING ROLE OF SHARED CONTEXT

Phillip C. Nell, Benoit Decreton and Björn Ambos

ABSTRACT

With this chapter, we seek to shed light on the question how headquarters (HQ) can cope with geographic distance and effectively transfer relevant knowledge to their subsidiaries. By constructing a mediating model, we aim at disentangling the effects of geographic distance on the relevance of HQ knowledge to their subsidiaries, via the creation of a shared context between HQ and their subsidiaries. We tested our hypotheses using partial least squares based structural equation modelling on a sample of 124 European subsidiaries. We did not find a significant direct relationship between geographic distance and HQ knowledge relevance. Yet, we found support for our mediation hypotheses that geographic distance makes it more difficult for HQ to establish a shared normative and operational context, but that both dimensions of shared context can help

Perspectives on Headquarters-Subsidiary Relationships in the Contemporary MNC
Research in Global Strategic Management, Volume 17, 275–298
Copyright © 2016 by Emerald Group Publishing Limited
All rights of reproduction in any form reserved
ISSN: 1064-4857/doi:10.1108/S1064-485720160000017011

HQ to transfer relevant knowledge to their subsidiaries. We contribute to the research on knowledge flows in multinational corporations (MNC) by investigating knowledge relevance directly rather than knowledge flows as such. We also advance our understanding of shared context in HQ-subsidiary relationships by showing that shared context comprises an operational and a normative dimension. Moreover, we contribute to social learning theory in basing our reasoning on the idea that shared practices and social relationships help overcoming distance to manage knowledge transfer more effectively. Finally, we add to the research of distance in international business by conceptualizing space, organizational context and knowledge transfer in one comprehensive model.

Keywords: MNC knowledge transfer; geographic distance; knowledge relevance; shared context; headquarters-subsidiary relationships

INTRODUCTION

Transferring knowledge across borders has been highlighted as one of the competitive advantages of multinational corporations (MNCs) (Doz, Santos, & Williamson, 2001; Kogut & Zander, 1993). Because knowledge transfer is crucial to the success of MNCs, HQs take an active part in organizing knowledge sharing to and within their geographically dispersed units (Foss, 1997; Nell & Ambos, 2013; Poppo, 2003; Yang, Mudambi, & Meyer, 2008). However over the past decades, MNCs have become dominant players on a global scale. Thus, the question whether and how HQs cope with geographic distance to transfer knowledge that adds value to their dispersed subsidiaries is timely and relevant (Beugelsdijk, McCann, & Mudambi, 2010; Dow & Karunaratna, 2006).

While earlier research on MNCs has focused on the amount of knowledge transferred (knowledge flows), more recent work has also looked at the relevance or the benefits of transferred knowledge (Ambos & Ambos, 2009; Andersson, Gaur, Mudambi, & Persson, 2015; Schulz, 2003). In fact, the key element in knowledge transfer is not the underlying knowledge, but rather the extent to which the receiver acquires potentially useful knowledge and utilizes this knowledge in its own operations (Minbaeva, Pedersen, Björkman, Fey, & Park, 2003). In other words, pure transmission of knowledge from the source to the recipient has no useful value if the recipient does not use the new knowledge (Minbaeva et al., 2003). Hence, Schulz (2003) defines relevant knowledge as knowledge from which it is easy to derive valuable implications. Moreover, if the knowledge to be transferred is inappropriate for and cannot be adapted to the new context, negative effects on performance can also occur (e.g. Baum & Ingram, 1998). Thus, only relevant knowledge may be beneficial to the MNC and it seems reasonable to focus on the transfer of relevant knowledge, rather than knowledge flows as such.

Previous literature has found that knowledge transfers from HQ to subsidiaries can benefit from shared values or norms. When the different organizational units of the MNC share similar values, the quality of informal relationships is high and goals are aligned, both of which are necessary for valuable knowledge transfers (Björkman, Rasmussen, & Li, 2004; Nohria & Ghoshal, 1994; Schulz, 2003). However, existing research has used shared context uni-dimensionally in the sense of shared values (e.g. Björkman et al., 2004; Nohria & Ghoshal, 1994) to explain knowledge transfers, and has neglected the impact of shared task environments or shared business partners. Insights from social learning theory (Plaskoff, 2003) accentuate the importance of considering shared business partners. According to social learning theory, knowledge is socially constructed through collaborative efforts and learning occurs when individuals are jointly engaged in a shared activity (Fox, 2000). Sharing business partners implies more regular and thorough interaction between two actors, eventually increasing the propensity of one actor effectively gaining knowledge from the other. Hence, when investigating shared context and knowledge transfer, we need to integrate the dimension of shared activity to capture a more accurate picture of the role of shared context.

Furthermore, shared values have been treated somewhat differently in the international business literature. Some scholars argue that shared values are important for overcoming challenges due to geographic distance between organizational units. Shared values can for example be used to replace the formal oversight by the HQ that is less feasible due to large geographic distances (e.g. Nohria & Ghoshal, 1994). Others argue that distance impedes the creation of shared values in the first place, because trust is more difficult to establish within distant groups (e.g. Björkman, Stahl, & Vaara, 2007). Therefore, we need to take a closer look at the questions how distance makes it more difficult to establish shared values and how the creation of shared values is useful regarding knowledge transfer between HQ and subsidiaries.

We conceptualize shared context as two-dimensional and comprising of shared normative context and shared operational context. Following Kostova and Roth (2002), we consider subsidiaries as main knowledge recipient and study how HQs overcome geographic distance by creating a shared context to eventually transfer knowledge that adds value to their subsidiaries. We propose that HQs will have more difficulty to create a shared normative and a shared operational context with their subsidiaries when the geographic distance is large. However, the creation of both shared contexts will make HQs better able to transfer knowledge that will improve the subsidiaries' local operations. Our study draws on a sample of 124 HQ – subsidiary dyads that vary with regard to geographic distance and shared context. Our findings suggest that distance indeed still matters and that it is more difficult for HQ to establish a shared context with the subsidiaries that are most distant to them. Additionally, we find that the creation of a shared context helps HQs to transfer relevant knowledge to their subsidiaries.

We contribute to the literature on knowledge flows in MNCs (e.g. Gupta & Govindarajan, 2000; Minbaeva et al., 2003; Schulz, 2003) by investigating knowledge relevance directly rather than knowledge flows as such. Additionally, we also contribute to our understanding of shared context (e.g. Nell & Ambos, 2013; Nohria & Ghoshal, 1994) by showing that the two dimensions (operational and normative) play a key role in international knowledge transfers. Moreover, we contribute to social learning theory (e.g. Fox, 2000; Wenger & Snyder, 2000) in basing our reasoning on the concept of communities of practice and showing that geographic distance makes it difficult to establish the shared practices and social interactions required for successful knowledge transfer in MNCs. Finally, we add to the literature of distance in international business (e.g. Beugeulsdijk, et al., 2010; Dow & Karunaratna, 2006) by integrating spatial distance, organizational context and knowledge relevance in one model to explain how relevant knowledge is transferred from HQ to subsidiaries.

THEORETICAL BACKGROUND

Geographic Distance and Knowledge Transfer in MNCs

MNCs face a paradox regarding distance and knowledge transfer. On the one hand, the ability to integrate knowledge between dispersed units is their potential largest competitive advantage; on the other hand, the distance between the different units is what makes knowledge transfers particularly difficult (Forsgren, 1997).

Studying the impact of distance on the use of personal and technology-based coordination mechanisms, Ambos and Ambos (2009) found that geographic distance is especially harmful for knowledge transfer effectiveness when personal coordination mechanisms are high. Personal coordination mechanisms may be particularly sensitive to geographic distance, because of the costs and complexity of knowledge search and communication. Thus, in the case of tacit knowledge transfer implicating personal coordination, geographic distance may be particularly detrimental. In another study, Monteiro, Arvidsson, and Birkinshaw (2008) point out the phenomenon that some subsidiaries are isolated from the knowledge transfer activities of the MNC. They show that knowledge transfers in MNCs typically occur between highly capable members. In addition, their findings also indicate that geographically distant subsidiaries receive significantly less knowledge from the HQ than other subsidiaries do. Similarly, Nell, Beugelsdijk, and Ambos (2014) found that it is harder for HQ to add value to distant subsidiaries when these subsidiaries are strongly embedded in their local contexts. In other words, when subsidiaries are embedded in the host country, it is more difficult for HQ to understand how they can add value, and the geographic distance makes it even more complex.

Therefore, geographic distance seems to increase the difficulty for HQ to transfer knowledge to their subsidiaries. However, some argue that informal relations and familiarity can help HQ to overcome geographic distance when transferring knowledge. In fact, while Hansen and Løvås (2004) found that teams steer away from spatially distant subsidiaries, even when both have related competencies, they also show that these negative effects can be overcome by establishing informal relations. Likewise, investigating the most important barriers to knowledge seeking within MNCs, Haas and Cummings (2014) recently showed that geographic differences create great barriers to knowledge seeking within MNCs. Yet, they also found that familiarity from a previous team mitigated this negative effect.

In sum, geographic distance has been generally found as increasing the complexity of transferring (tacit) knowledge in MNCs. Furthermore, informal relations and familiarity from a previous team can help to overcome the barriers of geographic distance when transferring knowledge across borders.

Shared context between HQ and subsidiaries then appears as particularly relevant for successful conventional knowledge transfers to happen and insights from social learning theory can help us understand the mechanisms behind this process.

Social Learning Theory and Knowledge Transfer in MNCs

Most of the research on knowledge transfer in MNCs has conceptualized knowledge as an economic good (that has value by mere exchange) rather than as information good (that has value in use) (Ambos & Ambos, 2009). This was done under two assumptions that do not accurately represent the actual process of knowledge transfers in MNCs. First, research investigating knowledge flows and its performance consequences (e.g. Chang, Gong, & Peng, 2012; Fang, Jiang, Makino, & Beamish, 2010) has assumed that every knowledge transfer is valuable. Yet, the application of transferred knowledge into a new context depends on important characteristics (e.g. whether the knowledge is understood by the receiver) that make this assumption erroneous. Because not every transfer of knowledge is beneficial, we should focus on the ones that eventually add value, and how they occur.

Second, the analysis of knowledge flows between units or individuals has been done under the assumption that knowledge is physically transmitted from one to another. However, social learning theory helps us understand how this representation is flawed. In fact, knowledge is not acquired in a mechanical way as an object would be (Handley, Sturdy, Fincham, & Clark, 2006; Plaskoff, 2003). Lave and Wenger (1991) introduced the notion of communities of practice in which learning and the creation of knowledge occur. They argued that the learning process is linked to activities and practices inside communities of people through social interaction rather than by isolated individuals. Communities of practice are tightly knit groups that have been working together enough to develop into a cohesive community with relationships of mutuality and shared understandings (Lindkvist, 2005). Thus, communities of practice potentially give a set of conceptual tools which help us understand how tacit knowledge is transferred within organizations (Fox, 2000; Wenger & Snyder, 2000). With regard to the transmission of knowledge from HQ to subsidiaries, the transferred knowledge is likely to be relevant when HQ and subsidiaries are engaged in shared practices (i.e. when there is a shared operational context). Additionally, social learning theory posits that social cohesion around a relationship (i.e. when there is a shared normative context) affects the willingness and motivation of individuals to invest time, energy and effort in sharing knowledge with others (Noorderhaven & Harzing, 2009; Reagans & McEvily, 2003).

HYPOTHESES

Distance matters and geographic distance matters especially when communications are vital for the firm's activities (Ghemawat, 2001). Communications are vital for knowledge transfers and in MNCs, geographic distance can thus make it difficult for HQ and subsidiaries to work together and to share relevant knowledge across borders (e.g. Hansen & Løvås, 2004; Kogut & Singh, 1988). We argue that geographic distance can negatively impact relevant knowledge identification and transfer. First, geographic distance increases the difficulty to identify knowledge that is relevant for the subsidiaries. Indeed, geographic distance has been shown as preventing partnering among employees (cf. Allen, 1977), which is the basis of information exchange (Ambos & Ambos, 2009). In MNCs, physical remoteness makes it less feasible for HQ and subsidiaries to interact, because of high communication barriers such as long travel time, onerous meetings or time differences (cf. Krugman, 1991). As a result, significantly reduced interaction between HQ and subsidiaries makes it more difficult for HQ to understand the local operations of the subsidiaries. Moreover, little interaction also reduces subsidiaries' opportunities to communicate to HQ about their specific needs. Second, geographic distance also increases the difficulty to transfer knowledge that is relevant for the subsidiaries. Global dispersion makes coordination difficult with the different units of the MNC and thus creates more barriers to knowledge diffusion between HQ and their subsidiaries (Asmussen, Pedersen, & Dhanaraj, 2009). Indeed, even though knowledge can accurately be identified as relevant knowledge, it can easily become irrelevant to the subsidiaries once transferred, because it has been distorted during the transfer (Ambos & Ambos, 2009; Asmussen et al., 2009). In sum, geographic distance reduces the ability of HQ to both identify and transfer relevant knowledge to their subsidiaries.

Hypothesis 1. Geographic distance will negatively impact HQ knowledge relevance.

A shared normative context is developed through socialization mechanisms which help to establish shared values, objectives and practices across the MNC (Nohria & Ghoshal, 1994). These different mechanisms require frequent face-to-face communication that can for example be fostered through international trainings (Edström & Galbraith, 1977). Starting with an extremely short geographic distance, the case of collocation between parent and subunit shows that it provides more opportunities for informal relationship building (Parmigiani & Holloway, 2011). Indeed, the costs of setting up face-to-face communication are very low when HQ and subsidiary are collocated, but increase rapidly with geographic distance (Ganesan, Malter, & Rindfleisch, 2005). If establishing informal relations is more difficult because of geographic distance, then it will consequently be more difficult for HQ to create a shared normative context with their distant subsidiaries as well. Therefore, the larger the geographic distance between an HQ and its subsidiary is, the less likely there will be enough face-to-face contacts to establish a shared normative context.

Hypothesis 2a. Geographic distance will negatively impact shared *normative* context.

A strong corporate culture can minimize divergent interests and enhance the sense of mutual interdependence across the firm (Nohria & Ghoshal, 1994; Ouchi, 1980). A sense of mutual interdependence facilitates individual and group actions that can benefit the whole organization (Tsai & Ghoshal, 1998). Reiche, Harzing, and Pudelko (2015) argue that shared HQ goals and vision increase only the ability of subsidiary managers to understand HQ knowledge. We adopt a slightly different reasoning and argue that shared normative context can increase both the motivation and the ability of HQ and subsidiary in the knowledge transfer process, eventually increasing the relevance of the knowledge transferred from HQ to the subsidiaries. First, common goals are thought to bind together spatially dispersed parts of an organization and facilitate inter-unit cooperation (Orton & Weick, 1990). Additionally, strong informal relations play a key role on the motivation of the different units to facilitate knowledge sharing across the MNC (Hansen & Løvås, 2004; Schulz, 2003). Because of the increased sense of mutual identity and interdependence, both HQ and subsidiaries will be more motivated to make the efforts necessary for HQ to successfully transfer relevant knowledge to the subsidiaries (Foss, Foss, & Nell, 2012; Handley et al., 2006). Hence, shared normative context between HQ and subsidiaries can act as a bounding mechanism that encourages productive information exchanges. Second, sharing the same goals and values can also increase the ability of both HQ and subsidiaries to make the best out of knowledge exchanges. Subsidiaries and HQ that are embedded in the same social structure exhibit a higher degree of trust and a higher capacity for information sharing and mutual problem solving (Gupta & Govindarajan, 2000; Uzzi, 1997). When organization members have the same perceptions about how to interact with one another, they can avoid possible misunderstandings in their communications and have more opportunities to share ideas freely (Ghoshal, Korine, & Szulanski, 1994; Tsai & Ghoshal, 1998). Also, the strong relationships developed through a shared normative context are particularly helpful in the transfer of complex knowledge, because the people involved in the transfer process have established some heuristics for working together, reducing the time it takes to explain the knowledge and understand one another (Hansen, 1999; Uzzi, 1997). Finally, a shared normative context increases the frequency of interactions between the HQ and the subsidiaries. Since the subsidiaries may not acquire the knowledge completely during the first interaction with the HQ, but needs multiple opportunities to assimilate it (Polanyi, 1966), a shared normative context will make it more likely that the knowledge transferred from HQ to the subsidiaries is more relevant.

Hypothesis 2b. Shared *normative* context will positively impact HQ knowledge relevance.

HQ can create a shared operational context with their subsidiaries by being involved with their subsidiaries' business partners. For HQ to be embedded in the local context of their subsidiaries requires that HQ managers frequently visit their subsidiaries and spend time there to for example help them during important negotiations (Nell & Ambos, 2013; Nell, Ambos, & Schlegelmilch, 2011). We expect that geographic distance will increase the difficulty of establishing a shared operational context. Indeed, physical remoteness makes it more costly and time consuming for HQ managers to become familiar with the subsidiary's operations and local context (Nell et al., 2014). It would for example be cheaper and easier for an HQ located in Italy to build relationships with the partners of its subsidiary in France, than it would be with its subsidiary's partners in Australia.

Hypothesis 3a. Geographic distance will negatively impact shared *operational* context.

Coordination between an HQ and its subsidiary is necessary for the HQ to successfully identify and transfer relevant knowledge (Schulz, 2003; Szulanski, 1996). We argue that shared operational context between HQ and subsidiaries makes coordination easier regarding knowledge transfer. In fact, sharing the operational context of their subsidiaries shows that the

HQs are both motivated and able to identify and transfer relevant knowledge. First, HQs that are embedded in the operational context of their subsidiaries are showing that they are interested in adding value to the subsidiaries, because HQ managers already spent time building relationships with the subsidiaries' partners (Nell & Ambos, 2013). Consequently, an HQ's willingness to add value to its subsidiaries implies that HQ managers spend time and energy in identifying and transferring knowledge to their subsidiaries. Second, HQs that are embedded in the operational context of their subsidiaries are more knowledgeable about their subsidiaries' operations (Goold, Campbell, & Alexander, 1994; Hoenen, Nell, & Ambos, 2014; Nell & Ambos, 2013). Being more aware of the local requirements of the subsidiaries, HQs will be more able to identify and transfer knowledge that will help the subsidiaries in their local operations (Fox, 2000; Holm, Johanson, & Thilenius, 1995). This is in line with Schulz (2003) who argues that the more a subunit is aware of the knowledge requirements of another unit, the more relevant the knowledge transferred to this subunit will be.

Hypothesis 3b. Shared operational context will positively impact HQ knowledge relevance.

METHODS

Sample

This study involves a sample of 124 subsidiaries. All subsidiaries are located in Europe and have manufacturing operations. The data was collected using a carefully designed simple random sampling approach based on commonly used firm databases.[1] Only subunits that were owned by at least 51% by other firms located abroad were used. Key informants of the study were subsidiary top managers that have considerable influence over subunit operations such as CEOs, CFOs or general managers. They received a pre-tested questionnaire. Follow-up calls and two different ways of responding to the survey instrument (via pdf or via mail) were used to ensure a decent response rate. Throughout the whole process, confidentiality was assured to reduce the likelihood that respondents artificially inflate or disguise their responses. Total return of 124 questionnaires represented a response rate of 9.5% which is not optimal but within the scope of recent years' multi-country studies (Harzing, 1999). Non-response bias was analysed through a series of *t*-tests between the sample and the sample frame and no significant differences were found regarding number of employees as well as turnover.[2] There was also no evidence of late response bias or a bias due to the fact that two different response forms were used. To this end, there is no doubt that the analysis sample is representative of the total population of foreign-owned European manufacturing subsidiaries.

The received sample is well-spread across countries and industries. Most of the units in the sample can be allocated to four main industries: transportation equipment, industrial machinery and equipment, food products, as well as chemical products. The subunits are located in more than 20 countries with some concentration in larger economies such as Germany, Spain, Poland, France and the United Kingdom as expected (roughly half of the sample). The foreign owners of the production units were located mostly in Europe with the exception of 13% of the units which had overseas owners. The data shows also good variance across key demographic variables for the subsidiaries. Roughly one third of the subsidiaries were between 1 and 10 years old, another third between 11 and 20 years. The number of employees spread across the sample with 33% of all subunits having between 201 and 500 employees; the second biggest group (101–200 employees) represent 25% of the sample. Average sales were approximately 170 million EUR.

Measures

Relevance of HQ Knowledge

The measure of HQ knowledge relevance is newly developed for the study and based on two items measured on a five-point scale. It is directly linked to the definition of relevance: we capture implications that HQ knowledge has for the subunit (cf. Schulz, 2003). Subunit informants were asked to indicate their level of agreement with the two items 'Your parent's way of challenging your subsidiary's strategies and tactics has improved your local performance' and 'Without your parent your subsidiary would receive less information which is important to your business'. Low levels of agreement with these statements indicate that HQ knowledge is perceived by the subunit as having low relevance.

Shared Normative Context

This construct is defined as the extent to which the parent invests into creating a shared normative context and organizational culture, for example via extensive trainings and international workshops. To build common

norms and values, early research has put a strong emphasis on mechanisms
such as selection, training and rotation of managers (Edström & Galbraith,
1977). We measured it with a three-item construct on a five-point scale:
'There is a strong commitment to training and developing skilled managers'; 'Your HQ puts a lot of effort to establish a common corporate culture'; 'Your subsidiary executives participate in extensive international
trainings initiated by your HQ'.

Shared Operational Context
We used the inverse of a common multi-dimensional distance measure to
capture shared operational context. It is defined as the negative value of
the multi-dimensional Euclidean distance between the extent to which the
subunit is embedded in a specific local context and the extent to which the
HQs is embedded in exactly the same subunit context. Instead of using a
Likert scale, we used an adapted graphical scale (similar to Nell et al.,
2011) to measure the extent to which the subunit's operations were
strongly embedded to a number of partners in their environment.
Respondents were asked to estimate on a six-point scale the strength of the
subunit's relationships to different types of business partners such as local
and domestic customers and suppliers, governments and industry associations. This is a good proxy for indicating the local embeddedness of a
subunit, in other words, the extent to which the subunit is operating in a
specific local context (cf. Andersson, Forsgren, & Holm, 2002; Luo, 2001).
We then asked to rate the extent to which the HQ unit was linked to
exactly the same business partners that formed the subsidiaries' context.
Both measures were used to create the shared operational context variable.[3]
Formally put:

$$\text{Shared operational context} = (-1) \times \sqrt{\sum_{i=1}^{6} \left(\text{Subunit}_{ij} - \text{Parent}_{ij} \right)^2}$$

where Shared operational context = the inverse of the distance between
subunit's *j*'s and parent *j*'s embeddedness values (strength of relationship);
Subunit *ij* is the subunit *j*'s score on the *i*th relationship dimension (the *i*th
actor category); Parent *ij* is the parent *j*'s score on the *i*th relationship
dimension (the *i*th actor category).

This proxy is appropriate for the study since it characterizes well by
which kind of partners the subunit's daily task context is dominated and

how distant the HQ is to this context. For example if the subunit has a relationship strength of 4 and the parent of 2 with regard to one particular partner, then the distance between the two is |2|. If the subunit has a relationship strength of 2 and the parent of 2, then the distance is |0|. Hence, the shared operational context variables takes on higher values, when the HQ as well as the subunit become more similar to each other in terms of day-to-day operations with partners in the market space.

Controls

First, *subsidiary autonomy* was included to control for the effect that very autonomous subunits could perceive HQ input differently than units which are directly bound to HQs. We used a four-item scale (from 1 to 5; higher scores indicating higher autonomy). The respondents answered the question 'For the following decisions, please indicate the degree of autonomy of your subsidiary' on a five-point scale, where 1 = 'The subsidiary decides 100%' and 5 = 'The parent decides 100%'. The questions referred to investments in a major plant or equipment to expand manufacturing capacity, increase (beyond budget) of expenditures, switching to a new manufacturing process and to sub-contracting large portions of the subsidiary's activities. Second, *competition* was controlled for as it may impact the importance for HQ to transfer relevant knowledge to the subsidiary. Respondents had to answer the question 'Do you agree or disagree with the following statements characterizing the conditions of your subsidiary market'? on a five-point scale (1 = strongly disagree; 5 = strongly agree). The two items were 'Competition in your market is very fierce' and 'Heavy price competition is a characteristic of your industry'. Third, we controlled for *market interdependence* since it might impact the importance the subsidiary has to the MNC as a whole and thus affect the relevance of knowledge transferred from the HQ. Market interdependence was measured as the extent to which customers and suppliers are important beyond the local subunit environment, that is also in other markets relevant for the MNC. If the local subunit environment hosts both important customers and suppliers then multi-market interdependence is given. Two items that were originally measured on five-point Likert-type agreement scales were summed, and the subunit environments with high scores (above the median) were designated as creating international interdependencies. We included *technological turbulence* as a control, because it may be more difficult for HQ to transfer relevant knowledge to subsidiaries located in markets enduring high technological turbulence. Technological turbulence was measured with a two-item construct and the items related to the difficulty to forecast technological development in the next three years and to the number of new product ideas that have been possible through technological break-throughs. We used a five-point scale and higher scores indicating strong technological turbulence. Additionally, *length of operations* was measured as the number of years between the subunit's date of establishment and the year of data collection as it can impact the knowledge HQ has of the sub-sidiary's local context. *Size of operations* was measured as the number of employees of the subunit. Larger sizes of operations may affect the impor-tance of the subsidiary to the HQ and the relationship between the two regarding knowledge transfer. We used the logarithm of both length and size of operations. Finally, we added a dummy variable for *matrix struc-ture*, which was coded '1' when the subsidiaries indicated that they reported to more than one headquarters. Multiple levels or units might make it more difficult for HQ to transfer relevant knowledge to their subsidiaries.

ANALYSIS

We analysed the data using a partial least squares (PLS) based structural equation modelling (Wold, 1985). PLS was chosen for several reasons. First, the originality of our model and measures makes the use of PLS appropriate. Second, the restively small size of our sample (124 observa-tions) makes PLS a suitable analytical technique. Finally, PLS can be appropriately used even when the residuals of the indicators and latent variables are correlated (Falk & Miller, 1992).

We followed a two-stage sequence to analyse our results. First, we assessed the measurement model in terms of construct reliability as well as convergent and discriminant validity. Second, we evaluated the structural part of the model in terms of the significance of the construct relationships based on a bootstrapping technique, variance explained of the endogeneous constructs (R^2) and overall quality of the model (Tenenhaus, Vinzi, Chatelin, & Lauro, 2005).

Our measures have a high internal consistency in terms of construct reliability (Werts, Linn, & Jöreskog, 1974). Although the Cronbach's alpha for two of our constructs were below the 0.7 acceptance cut-off value (Table 1), we decided to keep them, because of high construct reliability and because our measures are original and in their initial stage of

Table 1. Construct Reliability and Average Variance Extracted.

Construct	Construct Reliability	Cronbach's Alpha	Convergent Validity Average Variance Extracted (AVE)
Subsidiary autonomy	0.823	0.716	0.538
Competition	0.880	0.728	0.786
HQ knowledge relevance	0.850	0.647	0.739
Shared normative context	0.887	0.810	0.723
Technological turbulence	0.684	0.398	0.564

development as scales (Chin, 1998). The amount of the constructs' variance explained by their respective measures (Table 1) exceeds the 0.5 threshold (Fornell & Larcker, 1981). Finally, the constructs differ from each other as they demonstrate discriminant validity (Table 2). All this indicates that our measurement model is based on reliable and valid measures.

Concerning the structural model, based on a 999 sub-sample bootstrap, four of the five hypothesized relationships are significant. In particular, the relationships between 'geographic distance' and 'shared operational context' ($b = -0.229$), between 'shared operational context' and 'HQ knowledge relevance' ($b = 0.253$), between 'geographic distance' and 'shared normative context' ($b = -0.167$), between 'shared normative context' and 'HQ knowledge relevance' ($b = 0.195$) are all significant (Table 3). In other words, Hypotheses 2a/b and 3a/b are supported, while Hypothesis 1 is not (Fig. 1). Additionally, the control 'technological turbulence' has a significant positive effect on 'shared operational context', the controls 'competition' and 'technological turbulence' have a significant positive effect on 'shared normative context', while 'subsidiary age' and 'market interdependence' have a significant negative effect on 'shared normative context'. Finally, the controls 'competition' and 'market interdependence' have a significant positive effect on 'HQ knowledge relevance'. Our findings are discussed in the following section.

DISCUSSION

By investigating conventional knowledge transfers in MNCs, this study addresses how HQ can cope with geographic distance and transfer relevant knowledge to their subsidiaries. The results suggest that geographic distance does not directly impact the relevance of the knowledge transferred from HQ to the subsidiaries, but that it is more difficult for HQ to establish

Table 2. Correlations and Square Root of the Average Variances Extracted (AVE).

Construct	1	2	3	4	5	6	7	8	9	10	11
1 Autonomy	**0.733**										
2 Competition	0.065	**0.887**									
3 Geographic distance	−0.012	−0.118	**1.000**								
4 Knowledge relevance	0.162	0.129	−0.087	**0.860**							
5 Market interdependence	0.177	0.004	0.083	0.184	**1.000**						
6 Shared normative context	0.073	0.131	−0.185	0.224	−0.049	**0.851**					
7 Shared operational context	−0.158	−0.101	−0.237	0.308	−0.135	0.084	**1.000**				
8 Technological turbulence	−0.117	0.197	−0.053	0.121	0.103	0.250	0.229	**0.751**			
9 Subsidiary age (logged)	0.104	0.038	−0.008	−0.188	−0.106	−0.052	−0.223	−0.027	**1.000**		
10 Matrix organization (dummy)	−0.177	0.047	0.108	−0.008	0.045	0.072	−0.054	0.011	−0.083	**1.000**	
11 Subsidiary Size (logged)	−0.043	0.098	−0.024	−0.143	−0.232	0.100	−0.067	−0.135	0.120	0.085	**1.000**

Notes: Diagonal values in bold are the square root of the variance shared between the reflective constructs and their measures. To achieve discriminant validity, the diagonal values must be greater than the off-diagonal ones in the corresponding rows and columns.

Table 3. Effects on Endogeneous Variables, *t*-Values and Total Variance Explained.

	Direct Effect	*t*-Value	Variance Explained
Effects on knowledge relevance			**0.253**
H1: Geographic distance	**0.030**	**0.333**	
H2b: Shared normative context	**0.195***	**2.013**	
H3b: Shared operational context	**0.349***	**3.563**	
Autonomy	0.161	1.554	
Competition	0.154*	1.688	
Market interdependence	0.181*	1.720	
Technological turbulence	−0.052	0.485	
Subsidiary age	−0.091	1.100	
Matrix organization	0.008	0.096	
Subsidiary size	−0.101	1.396	
Effects on shared normative context			**0.141**
H2a: Geographic distance	**−0.167***	**1.988**	
Autonomy	0.144	1.138	
Competition	0.035*	0.365	
Market interdependence	−0.074*	0.815	
Technological turbulence	0.272**	2.383	
Subsidiary age	−0.077**	0.875	
Matrix organization	0.098	1.078	
Subsidiary size	0.120	1.258	
Effects on shared operational context			**0.214**
H3a: Geographic distance	**−0.229***	**2.167**	
Autonomy	−0.081	0.793	
Competition	−0.157	1.796	
Market interdependence	−0.156	1.710	
Technological turbulence	0.244**	2.640	
Subsidiary age	−0.220	2.396	
Matrix organization	−0.047	0.464	
Subsidiary size	−0.033	0.353	

Notes: $*p < 0.05$; $**p < 0.01$; $***p < 0.001$.

a shared context with distant subsidiaries and that a shared context increases the relevance of HQ knowledge. Thus, we can better understand how HQ can cope with distance to benefit from the competitive advantage related to cross-border knowledge transfer.

Our findings make several contributions to research on HQ-subsidiary knowledge flows, shared context, social learning theory and distance in international business.

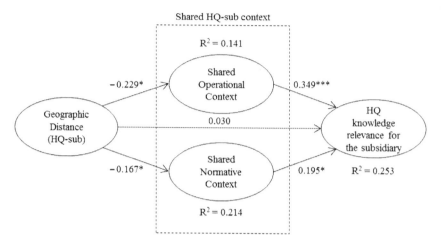

Fig. 1. Path Values and Variance Explained. $N = 124$. *$p < 0.05$; ***$p < 0.001$.

First, by focusing on the relevance of the knowledge transferred rather than knowledge flows as such, we add to the literature of knowledge transfer in MNCs (e.g. Gupta & Govindarajan, 2000; Minbaeva et al., 2003; Schulz, 2003). The relevance of knowledge has been seldom measured directly (Schulz, 2003; Yang et al., 2008). By consequence, research on the antecedents of knowledge relevance is scarce (Yang et al., 2008) and requires further investigation (Schulz, 2003). While Andersson et al. (2015) conceptualize knowledge transfer performance along the two dimensions of knowledge adoption and cost efficiency, we measure the relevance of the knowledge transferred in terms of knowledge adoption and do not consider the costs associated with the knowledge transfer itself.

Second, we also contribute to our understanding of shared context (Nell & Ambos, 2013; Nohria & Ghoshal, 1994). We are among the first to establish the distinction between shared normative and shared operational contexts, and capture shared context holistically as a way of managing HQ-subsidiary relationships. While Reiche et al. (2015) argue that shared values between the HQ and the subsidiaries only impact the ability of subsidiary managers to understand HQ knowledge, we argue that shared normative context increases both the motivation and the ability of managers in the knowledge transfer process. More specifically, we show that the two dimensions of shared context impact the motivation and ability of managers to identify and transfer relevant knowledge. In addition, while some scholars argue that normative integration and the resulting shared normative context can have negative performance effects (e.g. Ambos & Reitsperger, 2004) or run counter to the need to adapt to local circumstances (e.g. Egelhoff, 1999), we show that shared normative context relates positively to the relevance of the knowledge transferred from HQ to subsidiaries.

Third, by basing our reasoning on the concept of communities of practice (Wenger & Snyder, 2000), we contribute to social learning theory and increase our understanding of how individuals work together to enable the transfer of knowledge across dispersed organizational units. We are able to complement social learning theory and situated learning theory (Fox, 2000) in investigating key theoretical assumptions in an international context. More precisely, we demonstrate that geographic distance makes it more difficult to establish the appropriate context for successful knowledge transfer to happen, namely shared practices and social cohesion around a relationship.

Finally, we add to the literature of distance in international business (Dow & Karunaratna, 2006; Ghemawat, 2001). Beugelsdijk et al. (2010) recently asked for a better understanding of the interplay between MNCs and their spatial environments. We contribute in investigating how spatial distance, organizational context and knowledge relevance interact in MNCs. Our findings exhibit that it is more difficult for distant HQ to create an organizational context facilitating the transfer of relevant knowledge.

Managerial Implications

Our study entails several implications for managers. By conceptualizing knowledge as socially constructed, we highlight the importance of creating a shared context between HQ and subsidiaries. Specifically, we show that it is important for HQ to be involved in the subsidiaries' operations to be able to identify and transfer knowledge that will add value to the subsidiaries. Besides, it is also important for HQ managers to ensure that their subsidiaries have aligned goals and values with HQ so that transfer actors are more motivated and able to make the most out of knowledge exchanges. Additionally, while geographic distance makes it more difficult for HQ to establish a shared context, our findings show that this is in fact a good way of coping with distance and that managers should use it to manage the transfer of relevant knowledge.

Limitations and Future Research

There are, of course, a number of limitations in the study. First, this is a cross-sectional study which means that we have to take causality interpretations with caution. Second, we are not simultaneously testing for the effect that knowledge relevance has for the amount of knowledge transfers (along the lines of previous research). We argued that it is a more realistic picture to assume that managers figure out the relevance of the knowledge only after a while and that, hence, knowledge relevance assessments come after the transfer has been achieved. However, our measurement does not distinguish between the actual flows and the relevance of the knowledge. We also do not distinguish different knowledge domains such as Marketing know-how or technology know-how. To this end, our study is relatively coarse-grained. Therefore, the conclusions that can be drawn from our findings are only a first step into evaluating the alternative reasoning regarding the relevance-transfer issue and its relationship to shared context. Third, we do not control for shared language between knowledge sender (HQ) and receiver (subsidiaries), although this can be a significant factor in international knowledge transfer, both in terms of increasing the ability to create a shared normative context as well as in terms of increasing the motivation and ability of actors to make relevant knowledge transfer feasible (Reiche et al., 2015).

Consequently, future research could investigate the relationship between knowledge flows and knowledge relevance. Questions such as whether the amount of flows impacts the relevance of the knowledge transferred or whether managers can choose relevant knowledge out of the total flow without any negative consequences are still relatively unexplored. Additionally, investigating the impact of shared context on the relevance of reverse or lateral knowledge transfers appears to be a promising avenue for future research. Finally, investigating the indirect performance impact of shared context via knowledge transfer would shed light on the very established statement that MNCs' main competitive advantage lies in their ability to transfer knowledge across borders.

NOTES

1. Such as Dun & Bradstreet we used a similar database called Amadeus.
2. The estimates showed a single significant difference between the final sample and the target population in terms of age (mean of 25.5 years vs. mean of 24.6

years). To this end, there is a slight bias towards older subsidiaries in the sample. We consider this bias as being unimportant for the conclusions of the study.

3. The multiplication with (-1) merely reverses the scale so that increased values signify increased levels of shared context and not of distance.

ACKNOWLEDGEMENTS

The authors would like to thank Alison Holm for her valuable and helpful comments.

REFERENCES

Allen, T. J. (1977). *Managing the flow of technology.* Cambridge, MA: MIT Press.

Ambos, B., & Reitsperger, W. D. (2004). Offshore centers of excellence: Social control and success. *Management and International Review, 44*(2), 51–65.

Ambos, T. C., & Ambos, B. (2009). The impact of distance on knowledge transfer effectiveness in multinational corporations. *Journal of International Management, 15*(1), 1–14.

Andersson, U., Forsgren, M., & Holm, U. (2002). The strategic impact of external networks: Subsidiary performance and competence development in the multinational corporation. *Strategic Management Journal, 23*(11), 979–996.

Andersson, U., Gaur, A., Mudambi, R., & Persson, M. (2015). Unpacking interunit knowledge transfer in multinational enterprises. *Global Strategy Journal, 5*(3), 241–255.

Asmussen, C. G., Pedersen, T., & Dhanaraj, C. (2009). Host-country environment and subsidiary competence: Extending the diamond network model. *Journal of International Business Studies, 40*(1), 42–57.

Baum, J. A., & Ingram, P. (1998). Survival-enhancing learning in the Manhattan hotel industry, 1898–1980. *Management Science, 44*(7), 996–1016.

Beugelsdijk, S., McCann, P., & Mudambi, R. (2010). Introduction: Place, space and organization — Economic geography and the multinational enterprise. *Journal of Economic Geography, 10*(4), 485–493.

Björkman, I., Barner-Rasmussen, W., & Li, L. (2004). Managing knowledge transfer in MNCs: The impact of headquarters control mechanisms. *Journal of International Business Studies, 35*(5), 443–455.

Björkman, I., Stahl, G. K., & Vaara, E. (2007). Cultural differences and capability transfer in cross-border acquisitions: The mediating roles of capability complementarity, absorptive capacity, and social integration. *Journal of International Business Studies, 38*(4), 658–672.

Chang, Y. Y., Gong, Y., & Peng, M. W. (2012). Expatriate knowledge transfer, subsidiary absorptive capacity, and subsidiary performance. *Academy of Management Journal, 55*(4), 927–948.

Chin, W. W. (1998). The partial least squares approach to structural equation modeling. *Modern Methods for Business Research, 295*(2), 295–336.

Dow, D., & Karunaratna, A. (2006). Developing a multidimensional instrument to measure psychic distance stimuli. *Journal of International Business Studies*, *37*(5), 578–602.

Doz, Y. L., Santos, J., & Williamson, P. J. (2001). *From global to metanational: How companies win in the knowledge economy*. Cambridge, MA: Harvard Business Press.

Edström, A., & Galbraith, J. R. (1977). Transfer of managers as a coordination and control strategy in multinational organizations. *Administrative Science Quarterly*, *22*(2), 248–263.

Egelhoff, W. G. (1999). Organizational equilibrium and organizational change: Two different perspectives of the multinational enterprise. *Journal of International Management*, *5*(1), 15–33.

Falk, R. F., & Miller, N. B. (1992). *A primer for soft modeling*. Akron, OH: University of Akron Press.

Fang, Y., Jiang, G. L. F., Makino, S., & Beamish, P. W. (2010). Multinational firm knowledge, use of expatriates, and foreign subsidiary performance. *Journal of Management Studies*, *47*(1), 27–54.

Fornell, C., & Larcker, D. F. (1981). Evaluating structural equation models with unobservable variables and measurement error. *Journal of Marketing Research*, *18*(1), 39–50.

Forsgren, M. (1997). The advantage paradox of the multinational corporation. In I. Björkman & M. Forsgren (Eds.), *The nature of the international firm: Nordic contributions to international business research* (pp. 69–83). Copenhagen: Copenhagen Business School Press.

Foss, K., Foss, N. J., & Nell, P. C. (2012). MNC organizational form and subsidiary motivation problems: Controlling intervention hazards in the network MNC. *Journal of International Management*, *18*(3), 247–259.

Foss, N. J. (1997). *Resources, firms, and strategies: A reader in the resource-based perspective*. Oxford: Oxford University Press.

Fox, S. (2000). Communities of practice, Foucault and actor-network theory. *Journal of Management Studies*, *37*(6), 853–868.

Ganesan, S., Malter, A. J., & Rindfleisch, A. (2005). Does distance still matter? Geographic proximity and new product development. *Journal of Marketing*, *69*(4), 44–60.

Ghemawat, P. (2001). Distance still matters. *Harvard Business Review*, *79*(8), 137–147.

Ghoshal, S., Korine, H., & Szulanski, G. (1994). Interunit communication in multinational corporations. *Management Science*, *40*(1), 96–110.

Goold, M., Campbell, A., & Alexander, M. (1994). *Corporate-level strategy: Creating value in the multibusiness company*. New York, NY: Wiley.

Gupta, A. K., & Govindarajan, V. (2000). Knowledge flows within multinational corporations. *Strategic Management Journal*, *21*(4), 473–496.

Haas, M. R., & Cummings, J. N. (2014). Barriers to knowledge seeking within MNC teams: Which differences matter most? *Journal of International Business Studies*, *46*(1), 36–62.

Handley, K., Sturdy, A., Fincham, R., & Clark, T. (2006). Within and beyond communities of practice: Making sense of learning through participation, identity and practice. *Journal of Management Studies*, *43*(3), 641–653.

Hansen, M. T. (1999). The search-transfer problem: The role of weak ties in sharing knowledge across organization subunits. *Administrative Science Quarterly*, *44*(1), 82–111.

Hansen, M. T., & Løvås, B. (2004). How do multinational companies leverage technological competencies? Moving from single to interdependent explanations. *Strategic Management Journal*, *25*(8-9), 801–822.

Harzing, A. W. (1999). *Managing the multinationals: An international study of control mechanisms*. Cheltenham: Edward Elgar.

Hoenen, A. K., Nell, P. C., & Ambos, B. (2014). MNE entrepreneurial capabilities at intermediate levels: The roles of external embeddedness and heterogeneous environments. *Long Range Planning*, *47*(1), 76–86.

Holm, U., Johanson, J., & Thilenius, P. (1995). Headquarters' knowledge of subsidiary network contexts in the multinational corporation. *International Studies of Management & Organization*, *25*(1/2), 97–119.

Kogut, B., & Singh, H. (1988). The effect of national culture on the choice of entry mode. *Journal of International Business Studies*, *19*(3), 411–432.

Kogut, B., & Zander, U. (1993). Knowledge of the firm and the evolutionary theory of the multinational corporation. *Journal of International Business Studies*, *24*(4), 625–645.

Kostova, T., & Roth, K. (2002). Adoption of an organizational practice by subsidiaries of multinational corporations: Institutional and relational effects. *Academy of Management Journal*, *45*(1), 215–233.

Krugman, P. R. (1991). *Geography and trade*. Cambridge, MA: MIT Press.

Lave, J., & Wenger, E. (1991). *Situated learning: Legitimate peripheral participation*. Cambridge: Cambridge University Press.

Lindkvist, L. (2005). Knowledge communities and knowledge collectivities: A typology of knowledge work in groups. *Journal of Management Studies*, *42*(6), 1189–1210.

Luo, Y. (2001). Determinants of local responsiveness: Perspectives from foreign subsidiaries in an emerging market. *Journal of Management*, *27*(4), 451–477.

Minbaeva, D., Pedersen, T., Björkman, I., Fey, C. F., & Park, H. J. (2003). MNC knowledge transfer, subsidiary absorptive capacity, and HRM. *Journal of International Business Studies*, *34*(6), 586–599.

Monteiro, L. F., Arvidsson, N., & Birkinshaw, J. (2008). Knowledge flows within multinational corporations: Explaining subsidiary isolation and its performance implications. *Organization Science*, *19*(1), 90–107.

Nell, P. C., & Ambos, B. (2013). Parenting advantage in the MNC: An embeddedness perspective on the value added by headquarters. *Strategic Management Journal*, *34*(9), 1086–1103.

Nell, P. C., Ambos, B., & Schlegelmilch, B. B. (2011). The MNC as an externally embedded organization: An investigation of embeddedness overlap in local subsidiary networks. *Journal of World Business*, *46*(4), 497–505.

Nell, P. C., Beugelsdijk, S., Ambos, B. (2014). Contextual and geographic distance between headquarters and subsidiaries and its relationship with headquarters value added. Presented at the Strategic Management Society Annual Conference, Madrid.

Nohria, N., & Ghoshal, S. (1994). Differentiated fit and shared values: Alternatives for managing headquarters-subsidiary relations. *Strategic Management Journal*, *15*(6), 491–502.

Noorderhaven, N., & Harzing, A. W. (2009). Knowledge-sharing and social interaction within MNEs. *Journal of International Business Studies*, *40*(5), 719–741.

Orton, J. D., & Weick, K. E. (1990). Loosely coupled systems: A reconceptualization. *Academy of Management Review*, *15*(2), 203–223.

Ouchi, W. G. (1980). Markets, bureaucracies, and clans. *Administrative Science Quarterly*, *25*(1), 129–141.

Parmigiani, A., & Holloway, S. S. (2011). Actions speak louder than modes: Antecedents and implications of parent implementation capabilities on business unit performance. *Strategic Management Journal*, *32*(5), 457–485.

Plaskoff, J. (2003). Intersubjectivity and community building: Learning to learn organizationally. In *The Blackwell handbook of organizational learning and knowledge management* (pp. 161–184). New York, NY: Wiley.

Polanyi, M. (1966). The logic of tacit inference. *Philosophy, 41*(155), 1–18.

Poppo, L. (2003). The visible hands of hierarchy within the M-Form: An empirical test of corporate parenting of internal product exchanges. *Journal of Management Studies, 40*(2), 403–430.

Reagans, R., & McEvily, B. (2003). Network structure and knowledge transfer: The effects of cohesion and range. *Administrative Science Quarterly, 48*(2), 240–267.

Reiche, S., Harzing, A. W., & Pudelko, M. (2015). Why and how does shared language affect subsidiary knowledge inflows? A social identity perspective. *Journal of International Business Studies, 46*(9), 528–551.

Schulz, M. (2003). Pathways of relevance: Exploring inflows of knowledge into subunits of multinational corporations. *Organization Science, 14*(4), 440–459.

Szulanski, G. (1996). Exploring internal stickiness: Impediments to the transfer of best practice within the firm. *Strategic Management Journal, 17*(S2), 27.

Tenenhaus, M., Vinzi, V. E., Chatelin, Y. M., & Lauro, C. (2005). PLS path modeling. *Computational Statistics & Data Analysis, 48*(1), 159–205.

Tsai, W., & Ghoshal, S. (1998). Social capital and value creation: The role of intrafirm networks. *Academy of Management Journal, 41*(4), 464–476.

Uzzi, B. (1997). Social structure and competition in interfirm networks: The paradox of embeddedness. *Administrative Science Quarterly, 42*(1), 35–67.

Wenger, E. C., & Snyder, W. M. (2000). Communities of practice: The organizational frontier. *Harvard Business Review, 78*(1), 139–146.

Werts, C. E., Linn, R. L., & Jöreskog, K. G. (1974). Intraclass reliability estimates: Testing structural assumptions. *Educational and Psychological Measurement, 34*(1), 25–33.

Wold, H. (1985). Partial least squares. In *Encyclopedia of statistical sciences*. New York, NY: Wiley.

Yang, Q., Mudambi, R., & Meyer, K. E. (2008). Conventional and reverse knowledge flows in multinational corporations. *Journal of Management, 34*(5), 882–902.

TRANSFER OF SOCIAL AND ENVIRONMENTAL ACCOUNTING AND REPORTING KNOWLEDGE: SUBSIDIARY ABSORPTIVE CAPACITY AND ORGANISATIONAL MECHANISMS

Gabriela Gutierrez-Huerter O, Stefan Gold,
Jeremy Moon and Wendy Chapple

ABSTRACT

This chapter investigates the antecedents to the development of the three components of subsidiaries' absorptive capacity (ACAP): recognition, assimilation and application of transferred knowledge in the context of the vertical flow of social and environmental accounting and reporting (SEAR) knowledge from the HQ to acquired subsidiaries. Our analysis is based on an embedded multiple case study of a UK-based MNC, informed by 44 semi-structured interviews and capitalising on agency theory and socialisation theory. Prior knowledge is not a sufficient explanation to the development of ACAP but it is also dependent on

Perspectives on Headquarters-Subsidiary Relationships in the Contemporary MNC
Research in Global Strategic Management, Volume 17, 299–328
Copyright © 2016 by Emerald Group Publishing Limited
ISSN: 1064-4857/doi:10.1108/S1064-485720160000017014

organisational mechanisms that will trigger the learning processes. Depending on the nature and degree of the social, control and integration mechanisms, the effects of prior stocks of knowledge on ACAP may vary. Our propositions only hold for one direction of knowledge transfer. The study is based on an embedded multiple case study in one sector which restricts its generalisation. It excludes the specific relationships between the three ACAP learning processes and the existence of feedback loops. Our findings suggest that the HQ's mix of social, control and integration mechanisms should account for initial stocks of SEAR knowledge. The contribution lies in uncovering the interaction between heterogeneous levels of prior knowledge and organisational mechanisms deployed by the HQ fostering ACAP. We address emerging issues regarding the reification of the ACAP concept and highlight the potential of agency theory for informing studies on HQ-subsidiary relations.

Keywords: Absorptive capacity; MNC knowledge transfer; organisational mechanisms; social and environmental accounting and reporting; HQ-subsidiary relationships

INTRODUCTION

Globalisation has intensified calls for multi-national corporations (MNCs) to engage in social initiatives ranging from community outreach and environmental protection, to ethical business practices. Alongside the rise of corporate social responsibility (CSR), there has been a demand for the accountability and the transparency on CSR issues leading to the emergence of social and environmental accounting and reporting (SEAR). Ninety three per cent of the world's largest MNCs annually report information about their environmental and social impacts (KPMG, 2013) and research suggests that MNCs can benefit from reporting through improved corporate reputation and brand value, superior competitiveness, benchmarking against competitors and access to capital (Cheng, Ioannou, & Serafeim, 2014).

The ability to create and transfer knowledge internally has been considered one of the main competitive advantages of MNCs (Bartlett & Ghoshal, 1989; Hedlund, 1994). By transferring knowledge, MNCs can replicate competences originated in the home country across their subsidiaries which may recombine this transferred knowledge with related knowledge assets (Hansen & Løvås, 2004) and exploit it to prosper in local markets (Kuemmerle, 1999). The literature in knowledge transfer has extensively discussed the role of internal mechanisms inducing knowledge flows between the HQ and the subsidiary (Michailova & Mustaffa, 2012 for an extensive review). However, many of these studies assume that the benefit created from the flow is a function of how much knowledge an organisational unit receives (Ambos, Nell, & Pedersen, 2013; Andersson, Gaur, Mudambi, & Persson, 2015) but they seem to disregard that subsidiaries possess heterogeneous knowledge stocks (Ambos et al., 2013; Foss & Pedersen, 2002) and thus require tailored mechanisms to develop the capabilities to filter, assimilate and apply the transferred knowledge. While the MNC literature has acknowledged the role of absorptive capacity (ACAP) as it refers to firm's capacity to recognise, assimilate and apply external knowledge (Cohen & Levinthal, 1990), it has rarely discussed its antecedents at the subsidiary level (Song, 2014 for a recent review).

This chapter fills these research gaps by addressing the question of how prior knowledge as well as control, social and integration mechanisms influence subsidiaries' ACAP. We build on the intra-MNC knowledge literature and growing literature in ACAP with reference to agency theory and socialisation theory. Our analysis is based on an embedded multiple case study (Yin, 2009) conducted in a British MNC (FINEST)[1] with subsidiaries in France, Denmark, the Netherlands, the United States and Brazil.

The contribution lies in uncovering the interaction between heterogeneous levels of prior knowledge and organisational mechanisms deployed by the HQ fostering ACAP, as our theoretical understanding of how incoming knowledge is linked to existing knowledge stocks is, to date, scarce and fragmented (Ambos et al., 2013; Michailova & Mustaffa, 2012). We show that the effects of prior stocks of knowledge on the development of ACAP will be contingent on the nature and intensity of the organisational mechanisms supporting the argument that prior knowledge is a necessary condition rather than a sufficient condition for a subsidiary to develop ACAP. The research design addresses emerging issues regarding the reification of the ACAP concept and highlights the value of empirically studying ACAP in a non R&D context capitalising on qualitative methods. The findings have implications for the study of HQ-subsidiary relationships using agency theory.

The rest of the chapter is divided into five sections. The first part is dedicated to our theoretical framework. Following a section describing the research methods, we report the main findings by building propositions regarding the influence of prior knowledge and organisational mechanisms on the development of the three dimensions of ACAP. The discussion highlights the significance of the findings. We conclude by reviewing the implications and limitations of the chapter and by suggesting future research avenues.

THEORETICAL FRAMEWORK

Our theoretical framework defines SEAR knowledge recognising its explicit and tacit dimensions, and then critically examines current issues in the ACAP literature followed by a review of prior studies investigating antecedents of ACAP.

Social and Environmental Accounting and Reporting Knowledge

The literature suggests that an important competitive advantage of MNCs is their superior ability to transfer and combine capabilities across geographically dispersed units (Grant, 1996; Gupta & Govindarajan, 2000). HQs possess valuable intangible assets and capabilities that subsidiaries can use to develop context-specific knowledge and which they may exploit in order to address local problems and challenges (Johanson & Vahlne, 1977) and thus prosper in their local markets.

Social and environmental accounting and reporting (SEAR) refers to the practices enabling the production of an account about an organisation's social, environmental, employee, community, customer and other stakeholder interactions (Gray, 2000). To prepare these reports MNCs' subsidiaries adopt corporate policies, standardised processes and systematic methods to collect, measure, analyse and communicate the social and environmental impact of their operations. The technical knowledge surrounding the use of management information systems centralising the collection of data, as well as MNC guidelines for users across subsidiaries (e.g. calculation of KPIs), is considered explicit knowledge because it can be written down, encoded and explained (Kogut & Singh, 1988). Conversely, the knowledge related to the meaning of the data collected, the organisational implications and responses to those social and environmental issues, including solving problems such as quantification and comparability of data, is considered as tacit knowledge or 'know-how'. Nowadays,

SEAR knowledge is considered 'strategic' (Child & Rodrigues, 1996) because of its greater consequences for the operations of the whole MNC as part of reputation risk management processes and enabling access to capital (Cheng et al., 2014).

Absorptive Capacity

Absorptive capacity (ACAP) is one of the most prominent constructs in organisational research in recent decades which finds its roots with the work of Cohen and Levinthal (1990) who defined it as the firm's ability to identify, assimilate and exploit external knowledge to commercial ends. Despite the rapid expansion of the ACAP literature, recent comprehensive reviews (Lane, Koka, & Pathak, 2006; Todorova & Durisin, 2007) have identified several issues such as the omission of insights from the original conceptualisation, the lack of specification of the underlying assumptions and its portrayal as a one-dimensional construct (often assessed as a function of the unit's familiarity with the incoming knowledge or as a sum of employees' prior knowledge). Most of the empirical studies have examined ACAP in an R&D context – often with R&D intensity as a proxy and relying on quantitative research methods. This has limited the generalisability of findings to other types of business-related knowledge and restricted the possibility of building new theory regarding the processes underpinning ACAP.

Despite current attempts to refine and reconceptualise the ACAP construct, studies continue to exhibit some of the issues outlined above reinforcing its reification (Lane et al., 2006). For example, Zahra and George (2002) reconceptualise ACAP as a dynamic capability embedded in an organisation's routines through which knowledge is acquired, assimilated, transformed and exploited, and they regroup the four dimensions into two distinct factors: potential and realised. Nevertheless, their model does not build systematically enough on Cohen and Levinthal's original contribution and introduces a new component (knowledge transformation) which recent scholars (e.g. Todorova & Durisin, 2007) do not consider it the step after knowledge assimilation but an alternative process linked to assimilation.

Given the reification issues in the field and recent contributions, considering ACAP from a process perspective (Easterby-Smith, Graça, Antonacopoulou, & Ferdinand, 2008; Lane et al., 2006; Sun & Anderson, 2010; Todorova & Durisin, 2007), recognising its conceptual affinity with organisational learning, our chapter draws from the dynamic capability view linking specific learning processes (Lane et al., 2006; Sun & Anderson, 2010) to each of the three dimensions of ACAP originally proposed by Cohen and Levinthal (1990). ACAP is thus defined as the subsidiary's ability to utilise HQ's transferred knowledge through three sequential processes: (1) recognising and understanding potentially valuable new HQ knowledge through exploratory learning, (2) assimilating valuable new knowledge through transformative learning and (3) applying the assimilated knowledge to create new knowledge and commercial outputs through exploitative learning.

Antecedents of Subsidiary ACAP

The literature in knowledge transfer has extensively discussed the impact of internal mechanisms inducing knowledge flows between the HQ and the subsidiary (see Michailova & Mustaffa, 2012 for an extensive review). An often implicit assumption of these studies is that the benefit created from the flow is a function of how much knowledge an organisational unit receives (Ambos et al., 2013; Andersson et al., 2015). While the literature has focused on the occurrence of 'flows' it has paid less attention to the means of transferring knowledge which will influence the subsidiary capabilities to filter, assimilate and apply the diffused knowledge and the ways in which these mechanisms interact with heterogeneous subsidiary knowledge stocks (Ambos et al., 2013; Tsai, 2001).

In the context of acquisitions, managing the transfer of SEAR knowledge within MNCs is a challenging task especially as acquired subsidiaries may vary in their level of familiarity with the transferred knowledge. Thus, systems, structures and processes deployed by the HQ are vital for the effective assimilation and exploitation of knowledge by subsidiaries which may possess either 'limited competence' (Hoenen & Kostova, 2014) or 'too much experience'.

While the MNC literature has identified ACAP as one of the most significant determinants of internal knowledge transfer (Gupta & Govindarajan, 2000), it has rarely discussed its antecedents at the subsidiary level (see Song, 2014 for a recent review). The broader ACAP literature offers interesting theoretical and empirical insights regarding the influence of organisational mechanisms on the development of these capabilities at the intra-organisational level. Van den Bosch, Volberda, and De Boer (1999) argue that the level of ACAP is not only determined by the level of prior-related knowledge, but also by the moderating determinants of organisation forms and combinative capabilities. Zahra and George (2002) consider knowledge sources and experience as antecedents of potential ACAP and social integration mechanisms as reducing the gap between potential ACAP and realised ACAP.

The study of Jansen et al. (2005) is one of the few empirical studies of organisational antecedents to ACAP which included three types of mechanisms: coordination, systems and socialisation capabilities. They found that coordination capabilities (i.e. cross-functional interfaces, participation in decision making and job rotation) primarily enhance potential ACAP while organisational mechanisms associated with socialisation capabilities (i.e. connectedness and socialisation tactics) primarily increase realised ACAP. However, the main weakness of their study is their reliance on the ACAP construct making a neat distinction between potential and realised ACAP reinforcing the reification of the construct.

Our model illustrated in Fig. 1, builds from previous models and integrates two clusters of antecedents (1) prior-related knowledge and (2) organisational mechanisms deployed by the HQ.

Prior Knowledge
Prior-related knowledge is described as various related knowledge domains, basic skills and problem-solving methods, learning experience, learning skills and shared language (Cohen & Levinthal, 1990). One of the main assumptions of ACAP is that organisations will only be able to benefit

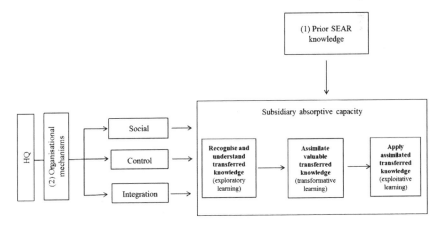

Fig. 1. Antecedents of ACAP.

from incoming knowledge if they possess a stock of knowledge in the respective field that allows them to connect the different knowledge elements (Cohen & Levinthal, 1990). Subsequent studies in the ACAP literature have argued that a unit's response to knowledge inflows is influenced by its interpretations and perceptions, which are primarily shaped by its existing knowledge stocks (Tsai, 2001; Van den Bosch et al., 1999) but are unclear about how heterogeneous repository knowledge stocks will influence those capabilities. In the MNC literature, some empirical studies equate ACAP to relevant prior knowledge (e.g. Gupta & Govindarajan, 2000) and overlook the process capability aspect initially suggested by Cohen and Levinthal (1990).

Organisational Mechanisms

To study the influence of organisational mechanisms we capitalise on agency theory and socialisation theory integrating three types of mechanisms which we broadly classify as control, social and integration.

The HQ-subsidiary relationship can be viewed as a principal-agent relationship (O'Donnell, 2000), because the HQ delegates decision-making authority to subsidiaries which may have divergent motivations and not behave in the corporate best interest. To mobilise transferred knowledge, HQ relies on various mechanisms to influence subsidiaries' ACAP to ensure that the outcomes of such transfer are aligned with the strategic goals of the HQ. Traditionally, agency researchers have proposed the use of behaviour and output control.

Behaviour Control. Direct behaviour control implies intervention by the HQ in the subsidiaries' operations, through centralised decision making and/or through direct supervision by HQ's representatives. The authority-based hierarchical mechanisms have been suggested as suitable for promoting 'obedience to authority for material and spiritual security' (Adler & Kwon, 2002, p. 18). These mechanisms stimulate interactions that are based on the latent threat that a lack of cooperation will trigger sanctions. The literature has suggested that rather than 'consummate cooperation', hierarchical control mechanisms may result in purely 'perfunctory compliance' (Ghoshal & Moran, 1996, p. 25). Examples of these mechanisms are close personal surveillance and budget controls.

Output Control. Output control implies evaluation of the subsidiary's performance through use of evaluation criteria such as financial performance, market share, productivity or knowledge development. From an equity theory perspective, employees expect that they receive the rewards they are entitled to, based on their contribution to the organisation (Minbaeva, Pedersen, Björkman, Fey, & Park, 2003). MNC's HQ may put in place financial compensation systems that encourage the subsidiary capabilities to assimilate and use the transferred knowledge. Examples of output mechanisms are financial incentives and specification of performance evaluation.

Social Mechanisms. In the knowledge transfer literature, the concept of social relations has received substantial attention (Bresman, Birkinshaw, & Nobel, 2010; Gupta & Govindarajan, 2000). Management can positively influence knowledge transfer by deploying non-market, intrinsic incentives (Osterloh & Frey, 2000, p. 541) that 'allow for establishing psychological contracts based on emotional loyalties'. While the literature has indeed found positive effects of social mechanisms on the transfer of knowledge, particularly of tacit nature (Szulanski, 1996), our review reveals rather opposite conclusions on their impact on any of the three dimensions of ACAP (Jansen et al., 2005; Zahra & George, 2002).

Integration Mechanisms. Operational integration through team structures and liaison mechanisms may facilitate the transfer and assimilation of more tacit knowledge, as processes and practices will have to be articulated and possibly codified. Jansen et al. (2005) found that cross-functional interfaces not only enhance the knowledge acquisition and assimilation of new external knowledge but also enable employees to combine sets of existing knowledge and newly acquired knowledge thus increasing the transformation and exploitation of new knowledge (thus affecting the three dimensions) and that formalisation contributes to a unit's realised ACAP.

METHODOLOGY

Research Design

We adopted an embedded multiple case study design of a British MNC in the information systems' industry (FINEST). FINEST provides information, analytical tools and marketing services to organisations and assists individuals managing their credit relationships and minimising risks of identity theft. We selected FINEST's French, Danish, Dutch, American

and Brazilian acquired subsidiaries based on a theoretical sample approach
(Eisenhardt, 1991) assuming different levels of SEAR prior knowledge in
comparison to the HQ's transferred knowledge. The French and Dutch
acquisitions were of software companies with products that filled the gaps
in FINEST's existing portfolio. The Danish acquisition was the first part of
the expansion in the Nordic region. The 1980 US acquisition enabled
FINEST to enter its largest and most mature market, and the acquisition
of the largest credit bureau in Brazil provided access to the Latin American
market. The HQ has transferred SEAR knowledge to the five subsidiaries
since 2008.

Data Sources and Interview Structure

The data are qualitative, mainly derived from interviews and complemented
with internal documents, website information, annual and CSR reports,
and brochures. Given that the focus of this study is on the vertical inflows
of SEAR knowledge from the HQ to subsidiaries, we conducted interviews
with managers and employees involved in the transfer of SEAR knowledge
in FINEST's HQ and its five subsidiaries (Table 1). Forty-four semi-
structured interviews in total were conducted between November 2013 and
December 2014 (24 in the first round, 20 in the second round) by one of the
authors. Interviewees were selected through purposeful sampling (Patton,

Table 1. Conducted Interviews.

At HQ	Ex-Global Head of CSR (*P1*), Global Head of CSR (*P2*), CSR Reporting Manager (*P3*), Corporate Responsibility Advisor (*P4*), Managing Director UK (*P5*), Global Head of Communications (*P6*)
In French subsidiary	Financial Responsible and Coordinator of Reporting (*P7*), HR Manager (*P8*), Sales Effectiveness Director (*P9*)
In Danish subsidiary	CSR and Marketing Manager (*P10*), Finance Assistant (*P11*), Head of Data Service (*P12*)
In Dutch subsidiary	HR Manager (*P13*), Marketing & Communication Executive (*P14*), Sales Support Manager (*P15*)
In Brazilian subsidiary	Sustainability Manager (*P16*), Corporate Citizenship Manager (*P17*), former CSR Coordinator (*P18*), Financial Education Ambassador (*P19*), Employee Ambassador (*P20*)
In American subsidiary	Community Relations Manager (*P21*), Director of Public Education (*P22*), Consultancy Business Analyst (*P23*), Vice-president of Corporate Marketing (*P24*)

2002) following a key informant approach. Each interview lasted between 45 and 60 minutes. Our interview guide was developed to elicit detailed descriptions of participants' perceptions of their experiences regarding the HQ's knowledge transfer. Respondents were asked to outline the forms of engagement that the HQ generally used in promoting and diffusing SEAR knowledge in the subsidiaries, the specific SEAR related activities in which they participated and the processes that unfolded since the transfer of knowledge. Finally, we asked about the challenges and benefits they perceived in these mechanisms used by the HQ. All interviews were taped and transcribed. After completing the first analysis, the same interviewees were interviewed again to clarify issues not initially made clear, expand on interesting topics and confirm emerging insights. The transcripts, reports and organisational documents were entered as project documents into the N-Vivo computerised data management programme.

Data Analysis

The overall method of analysis is a hybrid approach of qualitative methods of thematic analysis, as it incorporated both the data-driven inductive approach of Boyatzis (1998) and the deductive a priori template of codes approach outlined by Crabtree and Miller (1999). Previous studies were integral to the process of deductive thematic analysis while allowing for themes to emerge directly from the data using inductive coding. Our research is explanatory in essence and thus, our analysis consisted of different analytic stages described below.

First, we used a template approach in the form of codes to be applied as a means of organising text for subsequent interpretation. One of the researchers defined the template a priori based on our literature review of the antecedents of ACAP. The codes developed for the manual were entered as nodes in N-Vivo and one of the authors coded the text by matching the codes with segments of data selected as representative of the code. Based on our literature review, we organised the codes in three clusters: control, social and integration. The segments of text were then sorted, and a process of data retrieval organised the clustered codes for each project document across all the six sets of data (HQ and the French, Danish, Dutch, American and Brazilian subsidiaries).

Rather than using a proxy to assess ACAP (as most of prior studies), codes were inductively developed from the data in order to capture each of its dimensions in a manner appropriate for the context (Fig. 2). A data

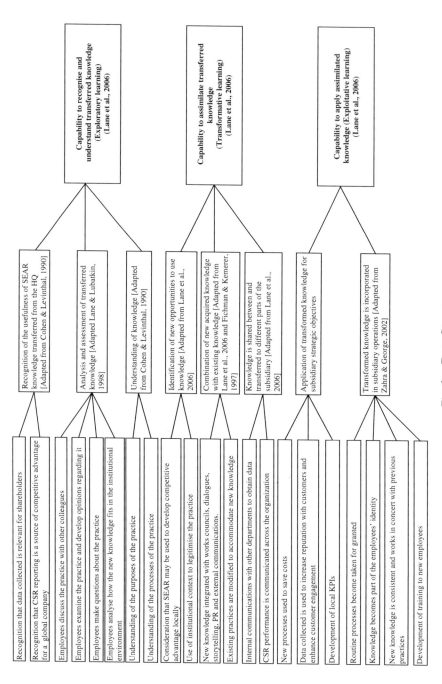

Fig. 2. Data Structure.

structure was developed consisting of first, second and third-order concepts. The data structure was developed through a process of constant comparison (Glaser & Strauss, 1967) between theory and data. We derived labels from the literature to capture the second-order constructs by using items used by previous studies from broader measures of ACAP as recommended by Lane et al. (2006) and tailored to the specific context of SEAR. Our data structure was consistent with the three dimensional conceptualisation of ACAP proposed by Cohen and Levinthal (1990). Evidence to support the first-order constructs is provided throughout the text.

In order to develop our propositions, we proceeded with the strategy of 'stacking comparable cases' as suggested by Miles, Huberman, and Saldana (2014). Once each case was well understood, we 'stacked' the case-level in a meta-matrix condensing the findings from the associated antecedents (prior knowledge and the three types of organisational mechanisms) and level of development of ACAP. It was possible to detect ranges based on the patterns and directions of answers obtained and thus, allocate the precise assessment (Low, Moderate and High); the presence or absence of a particular mechanism was also noted. This systematic comparison allowed us to establish patterns in the data (Crabtree & Miller, 1999) by identifying the corresponding mechanisms influencing the three components of ACAP (Table 2).

Reliability was ensured by following the pre-designed interview protocol and organising a case-data base for each subsidiary. To dynamically construct a valid-theory-creating process (Pauwels & Matthyssens, 2004) three strategies were adopted. To build a coherent justification of the themes, the information gathered from the interviews was triangulated using the evidence from the other secondary sources and from converging perspectives of our interviewees. We used 'member checking' procedures (Lincoln & Guba, 1985) taking specific descriptions or themes back to participants to ascertain whether they considered them accurate during our second round of interviews. Finally, our iteration between case selection, data collection, data analysis and comparison with extant theories and emergent theory allowed us to critically assess the possible impact of sources of misfit or invalidity.

FINDINGS AND PROPOSITIONS

We present our findings in light of our theoretical framework by analysing separately each of the antecedents and offering a related proposition regarding the antecedents of the three ACAP dimensions.

Table 2.   Predictor-Outcome Matrix.

Antecedents			French Subsidiary	Danish Subsidiary	Dutch Subsidiary	American Subsidiary	Brazilian Subsidiary
	Prior knowledge[a]		Very Low	Moderate	Low	Moderate	Very High
Control	Output	Specification of performance evaluation	Unknown	Known	Unknown	Known	Known
		Financial incentive systems	Absent	Absent	Absent	Absent	Absent
	Behaviour	SEAR budget control from HQ	High	Absent	Moderate	Absent	Absent
Social mechanisms		Intensity of communications	Low	Moderate	High	High	High
		Corporate socialisation	Low	High	Moderate	High	High
		Visits from the HQ to the subsidiary	Present[b]	Present[b]	Present[b]	Present[b]	Present[b]
Integration		Liaison mechanisms	Existent	Existent	Existent	Absent	Absent
		Structure of local teams	Temporary and voluntary	Temporary and voluntary	Temporary and voluntary	Permanent	Permanent
ACAP		Capability to recognise new external knowledge	Low	High	Moderate	High	High
		Capability to assimilate valuable external knowledge	Low	High	High	Moderate	Low
		Capability to apply assimilated external knowledge	Low	High	Moderate	High	Low

Notes: [a]Relative to knowledge transferred by the HQ.
[b]Present at the start of the transfer.

Prior Knowledge

We found that the levels of SEAR prior knowledge varied across the subsidiaries and this was generally explained by the differences of SEAR practices developed historically in the host country and particularly regarding the employees' awareness of SEAR laws and regulation, competitors' behaviour and national social and environmental agendas.

In the European subsidiaries, on average only one out of three employees interviewed had experience with SEAR, and this only between one and two years. Differences across the European subsidiaries emerged when we enquired about SEAR practices of the competitors, current regulation and national SEAR. French employees had a low awareness of these topics followed by the Dutch employees who possessed moderate levels of prior knowledge. Danish employees were highly cognizant of the SEAR topics, claiming that SEAR is a 'big thing' (P8) and that 'going green' (P10) is a characteristic of the Nordic countries.

The Brazilian subsidiary had the highest level of SEAR prior knowledge. Since 1960 it had developed a strong commitment to SEAR and was the only subsidiary of FINEST that produced a CSR report following the Global Reporting Initiative (GRI) B + standard. The local SEAR team was integrated by highly experienced employees (both in terms of working with SEAR as part of FINEST and previous professional experience in other companies and CSR-related institutions). The American subsidiary was also characterised by a high level of SEAR previous knowledge; employees had also been involved in SEAR related jobs and identified current trends, behaviours of competitors and were aware of the pressures for SEAR in the American context.

The cross-case analysis (Table 2) shows that subsidiaries with moderate to higher levels of prior knowledge (American and Danish subsidiaries) with exception of the Brazilian subsidiary were generally better at coping with the processes of recognising, understanding, assimilating and applying the transferred SEAR knowledge than the French and Dutch whose employees were introduced to that knowledge by FINEST's HQ. Thus we can propose that:

Proposition 1. Prior knowledge eases the ability of subsidiaries to utilise transferred knowledge through the three sequential processes of ACAP.

Control (Output) Mechanisms

Specification of Performance Evaluation

From the entire interviewee sample, we found that only three managers in the Danish, Dutch and Brazilian subsidiaries were aware of the existence of performance evaluation criteria related to SEAR. The interviews with employees implementing SEAR processes revealed uncertainty about the inclusion of SEAR as part of the evaluation criteria particularly in the French subsidiary where employees considered that SEAR was nor relevant, nor 'strategic' for FINEST and only committed themselves to implement routinely the new processes (application of the knowledge at the very low level) but did not dedicate additional efforts in analysing and understanding the purposes of the transferred knowledge nor incorporating the knowledge to address local organisational objectives. Thus we can propose that:

Proposition 2. The absence of SEAR specification of performance evaluation for employees is likely to limit the subsidiary's processes of recognition, understanding and assimilation of transferred knowledge.

Financial Incentive Systems
We found a general lack of market incentives across all the subsidiaries, including those subsidiaries with permanent CSR or SEAR related positions. The message sent by the lack of financial incentive systems was similar to what we observed with the performance evaluation criteria. Although from a HQ perspective SEAR was considered as a source of competitive advantage and thus SEAR knowledge was seen as 'strategic', the French, Danish and Dutch subsidiaries that relied on non-permanent voluntary positions did not share this perception and did not view SEAR as a 'business priority' and thus they 'shouldn't' dedicate more effort and time to it. While the Danish subsidiary managed to quantify the monetary impact of the exploitation of SEAR knowledge which represented a measure of subsidiary performance and thus, could use this evidence to obtain rewards from the HQ, the other European subsidiaries lacked these performance measures. So, other than the indirect financial incentive through subsidiary performance, our interviewees did not mention any rewards, promotions and/or increments which for many employees underscored their doubts about the strategic nature of the SEAR knowledge.

Employees occupying permanent positions (i.e. Brazilian and American subsidiaries) had as part of their job descriptions the identification, application and use of SEAR knowledge so the need for compensation as a salient issue did not emerge during our interviews. In contrast, employees performing voluntarily SEAR roles (e.g. French, Dutch and Danish subsidiaries) limited their engagement to the lowest level of application of knowledge and committed their efforts to the implementation of repetitive routines of the processes but did not display extensive exploratory nor transformative learning. We can thus propose that:

Proposition 3. The absence of financial incentives is likely to limit the subsidiary's processes of recognition, understanding and assimilation of transferred knowledge.

Control (Behaviour) Mechanisms

SEAR Budget Control

We identified that SEAR budgetary control over the CSR function varied across the subsidiaries and was related to the subsidiary's respective strategic significance within the MNC. For instance the Brazilian, American and Dutch offices had a budget allocated by the local management while for the Dutch and French subsidiaries this budget was allocated by the HQ. We found that this form of control inhibited the way subsidiaries applied SEAR knowledge as subsidiaries were dependent on resources from the HQ. Our data suggest that those subsidiaries with a relatively higher autonomy to allocate their budget, as in Brazil, the US and Denmark, had leveraged the knowledge to develop specific projects and tasks without the constant need to justify the purposes to the HQ. For example, in the American subsidiary this money was used to develop tailored training and buy a complementary management system. In the Danish subsidiary, the employees could access this budget to propose new projects incorporating the knowledge. For the French and Dutch subsidiaries, it was felt that the resources allocated by the HQ were insufficient to apply the knowledge transferred. Thus, we can propose that:

Proposition 4. The greater the subsidiary autonomy of SEAR budget, the more likely the subsidiary will engage in processes of application of the transferred knowledge.

Social Mechanisms

Intensity of Communications

We found differences in the intensity of the communications across the five subsidiaries. In France, employees receiving and implementing SEAR knowledge participated in one conference call each year to give feedback on the results of reporting to the HQ. The quarterly email conversations between the CSR corporate team and the local managers were overall perceived as 'very poor' (P7, P8) and more of a 'control' mechanism (P7) rather than a two-way communication between the HQ and the subsidiary:

> They (HQ) look for people that are interested in projects and when they find them, they ask them what is happening in their country and what have they done, and in fact it works more in that way than a real communication system. (P7)

A lack of communication also created uncertainty and anxiety among Dutch employees who considered they were missing some information from the HQ:

> Well, what I found coincidentally last year is that we have also been audited on the details we submit in the system. What happened in the past is that every month I would enter all the details and then forget about the background and not collect all the supporting details in a certain way. I did not expect being audited ... that was something that we were a little bit surprised about and found out a little bit late. (P13)

The Brazilian and American subsidiary CSR managers had direct contact with the corporate CSR team and reported a greater intensity of communications than did the European subsidiaries for whom SEAR knowledge was filtered through the local managers or liaison personnel.

Interestingly, those subsidiaries with greater intensity of communications between HQ and subsidiary were able to obtain key information from the HQ regarding the value of the knowledge which allowed employees to process and understand the tacit knowledge. Not surprisingly, the French and Dutch subsidiaries were those offices in which the tacit knowledge was the most difficult to understand. Thus the evidence suggests that:

Proposition 5. The greater the intensity of communications between the HQ and the subsidiary, the greater is the opportunity for the subsidiary to engage in the processes of recognition and assimilation of the new knowledge.

Corporate Socialisation

In 2012, FINEST hosted its first CSR conference in Mumbai, India with 150 delegates to enable the HQ to sensitise employees about the importance of SEAR for the MNC as suggested by the former Head of Global CSR (P1):

> They didn't understand SEAR and the business benefits weren't clear enough. It was not becoming central enough, so we took the opportunity of encouraging our management team to understand it, we went to Mumbai ... it was not a normal conference it

was something that I deliberately did ... I used that opportunity to get my message across.

CSR managers in the Danish, American and Brazilian subsidiaries attended the conference and assessed the outcome of such conference as 'very positive'. They considered this event as a 'turning point' which helped them to see the 'bigger picture' about the importance of SEAR knowledge. These managers developed a shared mission and a unitary corporate culture around SEAR, demonstrated the capability to recognise the value of SEAR for FINEST and the impact that it had for its shareholders and the reputation for the global company. Upon their return, these individuals also diffused these values to other local employees involved in SEAR who increasingly appreciated internal knowledge.

Another corporate socialisation mechanism was the employee programme driven by HR which served as the 'social responsible arm' (P20) that linked the employees with their community and SEAR activities and was rebranded as the 'FINEST' employee corporate social responsibility programme in 2013, according to the 2014 FINEST CSR report.

As illustrated by P14, socialisation through interaction with the employee programme, allowed employees to share experience, discuss and gain 'common knowledge' about SEAR and learn each other's experiences

I mean everybody is working in their own specialism, but the employee culture program gives the opportunity for people from different professions to work together and engage more than in the past, communicating about these things. (P14)

Based on these two illustrations of corporate socialisation one can propose that:

Proposition 6. Corporate socialisation mechanisms will enhance the processes of recognition, understanding and assimilation of the transferred knowledge.

Visits from the HQ to the Subsidiary
Visits to the acquired subsidiaries took place at the beginning of the knowledge transfer, at which time the Global Head of CSR visited numerous subsidiaries (including those in our sample) to introduce SEAR and find the ways in which the subsidiaries could leverage their own capabilities:

We really didn't have our arms around a CSR reporting strategy ... the Global head of CSR took a pragmatic approach saying: Ok what do we already have in the country that we can build on? (P10)

Our interviews highlight that between 2008 and 2010, these visits encouraged employees to embrace the new processes and establish a dialogue with the corporate managers regarding the HQ expectations. The knowledge that was diffused through these visits was mostly articulated, explicit knowledge about management systems but it also gave a framework for employees to develop an initial sense of the reasons for this transfer of knowledge. Nevertheless, the visits subsequently stopped when the HQ considered that most subsidiaries had attained an 'integration' level in which the transferred knowledge was becoming routinised.

Our interviewees in the Brazilian subsidiary described that the way in which the HQ determined SEAR targets were considered very 'top-down' and 'distant' (P18) and that visits could help to solve these issues:

> It would be very good if the CSR manager could visit our country again, see our reality, our way to work at least once per year to structure our future aligned with the global targets and guidelines

We learnt from our interviews that following the acquisition of the Brazilian subsidiary, the transfer of SEAR was not smooth because of the long-standing SEAR engagements that the previous company had had since the 1960s. Thus, our findings support the argument that visits to the country in the early stages of the transfer are positively related to the development of the capacity to analyse, process and interpret new knowledge but may be also crucial for acquisitions after the ramp-up process where the subsidiary will go through a restructuring process and will need support in understanding how to best apply the knowledge based on the local conditions as illustrated in the Brazilian case. Thus, we can propose that:

Proposition 7. HQ visits to the country during the integration process will positively influence the processes of recognition and assimilation of the transferred knowledge. After the ramp-up process, HQ visits may enhance the application of the transferred knowledge.

Integration Mechanisms

Temporary and Voluntary Structures versus Permanent Structures

Our findings suggest that the incorporation of formal SEAR teams into the subsidiary structure had a more positive influence on subsidiary's assimilation and application of knowledge than the voluntary structures. Permanent teams were only found in Brazil and in the United States with five permanent positions in each country dedicated to coordinate the SEAR and related programmes. Meanwhile, in all the European subsidiaries the structures were both temporary and voluntary. HR, marketing and sales managers had adopted SEAR roles as part of their core roles and were supported by a local network of temporary 'ambassadors' who were either nominated by the HQ and the local management or voluntarily self-nominated as 'data providers'. The informal nature of the ambassadors' role in supporting the SEAR activities meant that there was a lack of continuity in the role (turnover rate of ambassadors was very high). As noted above, the ambassadors adopted this role driven by their personal beliefs but this commitment was bounded to their core role responsibilities. This issue was particularly pronounced in the European subsidiaries which relied on these ambassadors to receive and apply the knowledge. This was acknowledged in the HQ as illustrated in the following quote:

> I think having people where SEAR is not part of their core role it's difficult. People will sometimes come and go, will leave the business which means that there is another challenge of how do you ensure that there is some continuity and learning that they will pass to the next person. (P13)

In contrast, the permanent teams in the United States and Brazil managed to leverage the knowledge by building on experiences over time, accumulated in individuals, team processes, procedures and routines (Persson, 2006). Thus, formalisation and permanency of their teams allowed employees to devote their resources not only to assimilate the new processes and routines but to go further and apply the knowledge in the development of strategies to create impact for the whole subsidiary. Continuity was ensured and previous knowledge was not lost but rather transferred to whoever adopted the new position. We find an example of the development of this capacity in the American subsidiary where the permanent positions engaged in SEAR skill development tailoring an intensive training programme across the 39 offices trying to emphasise the importance of SEAR and all the activities carried out throughout the country.

Overall, with the exception of the Brazilian subsidiary, our data show that rigidity and formal team composition was more favourable to the assimilation and exploitation of SEAR knowledge than the more flexible structures. Thus, we can propose that:

Proposition 8. Permanent positions will have a greater positive influence on the processes of assimilation and application of the transferred knowledge than temporary positions.

Liaison Mechanisms

The 'liaison mechanism' existed in Europe but neither in Brazil nor the United States, and we found that this was a decision that came from the HQ to compensate for the absence of SEAR:

> So when I started this role, the CSR teams were developed in completely different ways, so North America and Latin America were fantastic, they had great processes, they had projects, they were very strong at reporting but in Europe there wasn't that CSR leader .... (P6)

In 2008, the HQ indicated that one of the HR or Marketing managers in Europe would act as coordinators of SEAR knowledge across the European subsidiaries on an annual rotation basis. Some of our interviewees highlighted many benefits of this liaison role such as deeper personal relationships to others involved in SEAR. A liaison role holder reported that:

> What we also did was not only the calls, I had bi-weekly meetings so if I felt that if a certain country was a little bit silent, I used to phone the ambassadors directly, on a personal level and have some chat with them to find out if there was anything that I could help with. (P14)

Given the lack of communications highlighted before between the HQ and the European subsidiaries, the liaison personnel served as a bridge between these two as suggested by the CSR manager in the HQ:

> She was taking responsibility for the European group and she would organise quarterly if not more frequent conference calls ... we provided a lot of information about what standards they were reporting to, what type of information we needed ....

This manager was actively engaged in communications with the region, where she would address some of the difficulties transferring SEAR knowledge and particularly those related to its *tacit* nature:

> We had a monthly conference call and on each conference we would go through what is in the pipeline for the next quarter ... What other data we need to collect ... if it was electricity data for instance you have differences in how the data is collected in France and Denmark ... so we cannot adopt the same approach. (P10)

At the country level, employees testified the benefits of the liaison personnel who gave clear direction to the team. Moreover, as part of this role, the manager earned a significant level of discretion from the HQ to develop tailored tasks in the subsidiaries such as local training.

In contrast to the low intensity of the communications between the HQ and the European managers, the liaison coordinator organised between one and two video conferences per month with all the European subsidiaries and every two weeks only with the local team. Not only did liaison personnel adopt a translator role, helping employees to recognise the value and interpret the knowledge, but they also invested time in grounding and applying the knowledge to the local conditions of the subsidiary. For instance, the liaison mechanism identified that a 'saving costs' strategy could be developed in Denmark applying the knowledge transferred by the HQ. Thus, we suggest that liaison mechanisms have a positive impact in the three processes of ACAP.

Proposition 9. Liaison mechanisms will positively influence the subsidiary's processes of recognition, assimilation and application of the transferred knowledge.

DISCUSSION

Our work has offered a set of propositions regarding the relationship between prior knowledge, social, control and integration mechanisms and the three components of ACAP by specifying their respective independent influence. The comparative perspective yields a number of insights regarding their interaction that require further consideration.

Among the Dutch and French subsidiaries (those with the lowest levels of prior knowledge) the moderate level of control and extensive social mechanisms helped to foster the three ACAP dimensions in the former subsidiary (Table 2). Intense control and weak social mechanisms exacerbated the effects of a lack of prior knowledge in the French subsidiary leaving the three ACAP dimensions underdeveloped. An interesting outcome is that those subsidiaries with moderate levels of prior knowledge (Danish and American) developed the three capabilities with particular unfolding of the exploitative learning capabilities (e.g. embedded the new knowledge in the subsidiary operations and reflected on how to continuously improve those learning processes). Trade-offs between integration mechanisms can be identified in these two cases. Despite having temporary and voluntary team structures, the liaison mechanisms helped the Danish subsidiary to enhance its learning capabilities. Conversely, American subsidiaries lacked liaison mechanisms but benefited from the permanent structures.

The Brazilian subsidiary illustrates the negative effects of high initial stocks of knowledge. Despite its high level of expertise, the control and social mechanisms limited its learning capabilities. This finding supports the argument that different types of mechanisms need to be deployed in subsidiaries with high levels of experience in SEAR knowledge to avoid damaging their learning processes and instead, ensure that their capabilities are of potential use and diffused in the wider MNC context (Yang, Mudambi, & Meyer, 2008).

Contrary to Jansen et al. (2005) in which socialisation mechanisms were found to increase both the transformation and exploitation capabilities, we found that the social mechanisms influenced only the processes of recognition and assimilation of knowledge. This might be explained by the fact that Jansen et al. (2005) adopted a broad definition of knowledge and conceptualised ACAP into the ambiguous potential and realised subsets.

The literature has recognised that tacit knowledge is difficult to codify and thus its transfer requires intense communications (Szulanski, 1996), personal presence and face-to-face interactions in order to enable the development of a single social community suitable for the transmission of 'rich' information. Our findings confirm that most of the social mechanisms such as communications, visits and corporate socialisation practices are significant predictors of the capability to assimilate 'know-how'; we expand those findings by highlighting that in the absence of face-to-face interaction and expatriate managers, experienced liaison personnel may enable the development of tacit knowledge stocks. The fact that the liaison personnel were local managers — speaking several languages and adopting translating roles not only in the literal sense but also interpreting the meaning of SEAR — enhanced the credibility of the transfer and the potential to apply this knowledge. Our study also suggests that HQ visits to the country of acquisitions during the ramp-up process enhance recognition and assimilation of the transferred knowledge, but they may be also crucial during the integration process where knowledge application processes may start to unfold.

Formal team structures have a positive impact on the development of the three dimensions permitting continuous exploitation and refinement of acquired knowledge (Sun & Anderson, 2010) in contrast to the argument in the literature that formal structures damage the integration of knowledge in an organisation (Grant, 1996). Our finding is thus related to some extent to the results of Jansen et al. (2005) where formalisation procedures such as documenting rules, procedures, processes and systems positively influenced the capability of exploitation.

Although our findings could not be conclusive about the impact of control (output) mechanisms we found an effect of their absence limiting the three processes of ACAP. This finding is in line with the literature in social capital which has suggested that a consistent use of mechanisms such as rewards sends 'a signal to organizational members about the kinds of activities and habits that are valued by the organization' (Leana & Van Buren, 1999, p. 545). In our cases, the absence of financial incentives was perceived by employees as a signal that SEAR was neither a 'business priority' nor 'strategic', contrary to the HQ's intention to make SEAR a competitive advantage. A similar perception was also identified with the lack of specification of performance criteria which raises questions on the choice of mechanisms by the HQ matching its strategic objectives.

Our findings suggest that the control behaviour mechanism exerted by the HQ in the form of budget control was detrimental to the application of SEAR knowledge. Thus, in the context of transfer of vertical inflows of SEAR knowledge from the HQ to acquired subsidiaries, control (output) mechanisms may be more beneficial than behaviour mechanisms. An interesting finding is that integration mechanisms and visits from the HQ (contingent on the time of the visit) can trigger the three dimensions of ACAP and thus are crucial for HQs to include in the transfer given their cost-effectiveness.

CONCLUSIONS

This study builds and contributes to our theoretical as well as empirical understanding of the antecedents of subsidiaries' ACAP in the context of intra-MNC knowledge transfer and contributes to the ACAP and MNC transfer of knowledge literatures in several ways.

The main contribution of this research lies in considering the interaction between heterogeneous levels of prior knowledge and organisational mechanisms fostering ACAP, as the theoretical understanding of how incoming knowledge is linked to existing knowledge stocks is, to date, scarce (Ambos et al., 2013; Michailova & Mustaffa, 2012). Our findings demonstrate that prior knowledge is not a sufficient explanation to the development of the capability to recognise, assimilate and apply external knowledge (Cohen & Levinthal, 1990) but is also dependent on organisational mechanisms that will trigger those learning processes. Depending on the nature and degree of organisational mechanisms, the effects of previous stocks of knowledge on the development of ACAP may vary from positive to negative. In other words, prior levels of knowledge can be an asset or an obstacle for subsidiaries to trigger learning processes. Our findings thus suggest that HQs aiming at increasing the learning processes of subsidiaries need to manage their foreign subsidiaries so as to stimulate the development of capabilities of recognition, assimilation and application through a mix of control, social and integration mechanisms that complement their repository stocks of knowledge. These finding thus, echo the argument by agency theorists that a variety of mechanisms to control and coordinate their foreign subsidiaries is necessary as the different mechanisms are predominantly complementary rather than substitutes of one another (Tosi, Katz, & Gomez-Mejia, 1997).

Our chapter highlights the potential of agency theory informing studies of HQ-subsidiary relations (Hoenen & Kostova, 2014). The fact that some subsidiaries did not develop the processes of recognition, assimilation and application of the transferred knowledge highlights that the problem in essence was not the incompatibility of goals between the principal (HQ) and the agent (subsidiary) but rather a combination of very low or very high levels of prior knowledge and control, social and integration mechanisms that did not compensate for those levels of knowledge. If SEAR is considered strategic to the MNC and key to the development of local competitive advantages to solve social and environmental dilemmas, the HQ must consider the different existing stocks of knowledge and capabilities of the subsidiaries when designing the organisational mechanisms underpinning the transfer of knowledge. Our research highlights the need for agency theory to consider more than the usual control mechanisms and consider their combination with the other types such as social and integration mechanisms.

Based on our findings, our work engages with recent critiques questioning the overemphasis in the literature on the occurrence of 'flows' and the underlying assumption that the benefit created from these knowledge flows is a function of how much an organisational unit receives knowledge (e.g. Ambos et al., 2013; Andersson et al., 2015), our findings in the Brazilian case provide evidence to break this misconception by revealing that the transfer disrupted and ultimately damaged the learning capabilities of the subsidiary, shedding light on a 'darker side' of knowledge transfers (Reus, Lamont, & Ellis, 2015).

Following the calls in the field to address the reification of the construct of ACAP (Lane et al., 2006), our work builds from a rather novel perspective linking ACAP and OL and drawing from the dynamic capability view linking specific learning processes (Lane et al., 2006; Sun & Anderson, 2010) to each of the three dimensions of ACAP originally proposed by Cohen and Levinthal (1990). We believe that the use of a qualitative study has helped to inductively examine the processes of ACAP specific to the SEAR context and determine the mechanisms that trigger the three processes of ACAP, contributing to clarify how the construct operates in a non R&D context.

This chapter has managerial implications. Based on the available resources, HQ managers may consider liaison mechanisms, which less costly than permanent positions can act as substitutes of direct communication with the HQ in small size subsidiaries and have the advantage to enhance the three processes of ACAP. Based on our finding that integration mechanisms can be mutually compensated, managers could also choose one that suits the MNC structure (e.g. liaison mechanisms instead of permanent positions or the opposite).

Our study has some limitations. It is limited in explaining the relationships between the three processes and accounting for the existence of feedback loops (Song, 2014). Future work could examine these phenomena through the lens of system dynamics so as to uncover the complexity of the capabilities and time-dependent contingencies involved.

This chapter is based on an embedded multiple case study in one sector and has some limitations in terms of generalisation to MNCs operating in other sectors. Nevertheless, the conceptual framework developed in this research has generated contingent generalisations which should assist in further comparisons. For instance, the findings are probably relevant in other settings such as the transfer of other business-types of knowledge (non R&D) – for example regarding diversity management or quality management – to MNC-acquired subsidiaries with heterogeneous stocks of knowledge. In our study, SEAR knowledge was transferred arbitrarily by the HQ to subsidiaries. In this sense, the arguments of this study should be limited to knowledge transfers in which receivers have low discretion.

Our propositions only hold for one direction of knowledge transfer although subsidiaries also engage in knowledge flows in other directions. Future work could consider the processes of reverse diffusion of SEAR knowledge from subsidiaries with higher levels of repository knowledge that contribute to build the HQ's ACAP. While we have considered the local stocks of knowledge, we have not considered the influence of different kinds of distance between the HQ and the subsidiary that may interact with organisational mechanisms enhancing or deterring processes of ACAP. Further studies could investigate the impact of cultural, institutional and linguistic distance on the development of subsidiaries' ACAP.

326

NOTE

1. For confidentiality, the name of the MNC has been changed to the pseudonym 'FINEST'.

REFERENCES

Adler, P. S., & Kwon, S.-W. (2002). Social capital: Prospects for a new concept. *Academy of Management Review*, 27(1), 17–40.

Ambos, T. C., Nell, P. C., & Pedersen, T. (2013). Combining stocks and flows of knowledge: The effects of intra-functional and cross-functional complementarity. *Global Strategy Journal*, 3(4), 283–299.

Andersson, U., Gaur, A., Mudambi, R., & Persson, M. (2015). Unpacking interunit knowledge transfer in multinational enterprises. *Global Strategy Journal*, 5(3), 241–255.

Bartlett, C., & Ghoshal, S. (1989). *Managing across borders: The transnational solution*. Boston, MA: HBS Press.

Boyatzis, R. E. (1998). *Transforming qualitative information: Thematic analysis and code development*. London: Sage.

Bresman, H., Birkinshaw, J., & Nobel, R. (2010). Knowledge transfer in international acquisitions. *Journal of International Business Studies*, 41(1), 5–20.

Cheng, B., Ioannou, I., & Serafeim, G. (2014). Corporate social responsibility and access to finance. *Strategic Management Journal*, 35(1), 1–23.

Child, J., & Rodrigues, S. (1996). The role of social identity in the international transfer of knowledge through joint ventures. In S. R. Clegg & G. Palmer (Eds.), *The politics of management knowledge* (pp. 46–68). Thousand Oaks, CA: Sage.

Cohen, W. M., & Levinthal, D. A. (1990). Absorptive capacity: A new perspective on learning and innovation. *Administrative Science Quarterly*, 35, 128–152.

Crabtree, B. F., & Miller, W. L. (1999). Using codes and code manuals: A template organizing style of interpretation. In B. F. Crabtree & W. L. Miller (Eds.), *Doing qualitative research* (Vol. 2, pp. 163–177). Thousand Oaks, CA: Sage.

Easterby-Smith, M., Graça, M., Antonacopoulou, E., & Ferdinand, J. (2008). Absorptive capacity: A process perspective. *Management Learning*, 39(5), 483–501.

Eisenhardt, K. M. (1991). Better stories and better constructs: The case for rigor and comparative logic. *Academy of Management Review*, 16(3), 620–627.

Foss, N. J., & Pedersen, T. (2002). Transferring knowledge in MNCs: The role of sources of subsidiary knowledge and organizational context. *Journal of International Management*, 8, 49–67.

Ghoshal, S., & Moran, P. (1996). Bad for practice: A critique of the transaction cost theory. *Academy of Management Review*, 21(1), 13–47.

Glaser, B., & Strauss, A. (1967). *The discovery of grounded theory*. London: Weidenfeld & Nicolson.

Grant, R. M. (1996). Prospering in dynamically-competitive environments: Organizational capability as knowledge integration. *Organization Science*, 7(4), 375–387.

Gray, R. (2000). Current developments and trends in social and environmental auditing, reporting and attestation: A review and comment. *International Journal of Auditing, 4*(3), 247–268.

Gupta, A. K., & Govindarajan, V. (2000). Knowledge flows within multinational corporations. *Strategic Management Journal, 21*(4), 473–496.

Hansen, M. T., & Løvås, B. (2004). How do multinational companies leverage technological competencies? Moving from single to interdependent explanations. *Strategic Management Journal, 25*(8–9), 801–822.

Hedlund, G. (1994). A model of knowledge management and the n-form corporation. *Strategic Management Journal, 15*(S2), 73–90.

Hoenen, A. K., & Kostova, T. (2014). Utilizing the broader agency perspective for studying headquarters-subsidiary relations in multinational companies. *Journal of International Business Studies, 46*(1), 104–113.

Jansen, J. J. P., Van den Bosch, F. A. J., & Volberda, H. W. (2005). Managing potential and realized absorptive capacity: How do organizational antecedents matter? *Academy of Management Journal, 48*(6), 999–1015.

Johanson, J., & Vahlne, J.-E. (1977). The internationalization process of the firm-a model of knowledge development and increasing foreign market commitments. *Journal of International Business Studies, 8*(1), 23–32.

Kogut, B., & Singh, H. (1988). The effect of national culture on the choice of entry mode. *Journal of International Business Studies, 19*(3), 411–432.

KPMG. (2013). The KPMG survey of corporate responsibility reporting 2013. KPMG International, the Netherlands.

Kuemmerle, W. (1999). The drivers of foreign direct investment into research and development: An empirical investigation. *Journal of International Business Studies, 30*, 1–24.

Lane, P. J., Koka, B. R., & Pathak, S. (2006). The reification of absorptive capacity: A critical review and rejuvenation of the construct. *Academy of Management Review, 31*(4), 833–863.

Leana, C. R., & Van Buren, H. J. (1999). Organizational social capital and employment practices. *Academy of Management Review, 24*(3), 538–555.

Lincoln, Y. S., & Guba, E. G. (1985). *Naturalist inquiry.* Beverly Hills, CA: Sage.

Michailova, S., & Mustaffa, Z. (2012). Subsidiary knowledge flows in multinational corporations: Research accomplishments, gaps, and opportunities. *Journal of World Business, 47*(3), 383–396.

Miles, M. B., Huberman, A. M., & Saldana, J. (2014). *Qualitative data analysis: A methods sourcebook* (3rd ed.). London: Sage.

Minbaeva, D., Pedersen, T., Björkman, I., Fey, C. F., & Park, H. J. (2003). MNC knowledge transfer, subsidiary absorptive capacity, and HRM. *Journal of International Business Studies, 34*(6), 586–599.

O'Donnell, S. W. (2000). Managing foreign subsidiaries: Agents of headquarters, or an interdependent network? *Strategic Management Journal, 21*(5), 525–548.

Osterloh, M., & Frey, B. S. (2000). Motivation, knowledge transfer, and organizational forms. *Organization Science, 11*(5), 538–550.

Patton, M. Q. (2002). *Qualitative research and evaluation methods* (3rd ed.). Thousand Okas, CA: Sage.

Pauwels, P., & Matthyssens, P. (2004). The architecture of multiple case study research in international business. In *Handbook of qualitative research methods for international business* (pp. 125–143). Cheltenham: Edward Elgar.

Persson, M. (2006). The impact of operational structure, lateral integrative mechanisms and control mechanisms on intra-MNE knowledge transfer. *International Business Review, 15*(5), 547–569.

Reus, T. H., Lamont, B. T., & Ellis, K. M. (2015). A darker side of knowledge transfer following international acquisitions. *Strategic Management Journal, 37*(5), 932–944.

Song, J. (2014). Subsidiary absorptive capacity and knowledge transfer within multinational corporations. *Journal of International Business Studies, 45*(1), 73–84.

Sun, P. Y., & Anderson, M. H. (2010). An examination of the relationship between absorptive capacity and organizational learning, and a proposed integration. *International Journal of Management Reviews, 12*(2), 130–150.

Szulanski, G. (1996). Exploring internal stickiness: Impediments to the transfer of best practice within the firm. *Strategic Management Journal, 17*(S2), 27–43.

Todorova, G., & Durisin, B. (2007). Absorptive capacity: Valuing a reconceptualization. *Academy of Management Review, 32*(3), 774–786.

Tosi, H. L., Katz, J. P., & Gomez-Mejia, L. R. (1997). Disaggregating the agency contract: The effects of monitoring, incentive alignment, and term in office on agent decision making. *Academy of Management Journal, 40*(3), 584–602.

Tsai, W. (2001). Knowledge transfer in intraorganizational networks: Effects of network position and absorptive capacity on business unit innovation and performance. *Academy of Management Journal, 44*(5), 996–1004.

Van den Bosch, F. A. J., Volberda, H. W., & De Boer, M. (1999). Coevolution of firm absorptive capacity and knowledge environment: Organizational forms and combinative capabilities. *Organization Science, 10*(5), 551–568.

Yang, Q., Mudambi, R., & Meyer, K. E. (2008). Conventional and reverse knowledge flows in multinational corporations. *Journal of Management, 34*(5), 882–902.

Yin, R. K. (2009). *Case study research: Design and methods* (4th ed.). Thousand Oaks, CA: Sage.

Zahra, S. A., & George, G. (2002). Absorptive capacity: A review, reconceptualization, and extension. *Academy of Management Review, 27*(2), 185–203.

PART IV
ADDITIONAL CONTRIBUTIONS BY
AIB FELLOWS (EDITED BY
JEAN BODDEWYN)

HISTORY OF THE AIB FELLOWS: THE DEANSHIP OF ALAN RUGMAN (2011–2014)

Jean Boddewyn

ABSTRACT

This chapter complements the one that appeared as "History of the AIB Fellows: 1975–2008" in Volume 14 of this series (International Business Scholarship: AIB Fellows on the First 50 Years and Beyond, Jean J. Boddewyn, Editor). It traces what happened under the deanship of Alan Rugman (2011–2014) who took many initiatives reported here while his death in July 2014 generated trenchant, funny, and loving comments from more than half of the AIB Fellows. The lives and contributions of many other major international business scholars who passed away from 2008 to 2014 are also evoked here: Endel Kolde, Lee Nehrt, Howard Perlmutter, Stefan Robock, John Ryans, Vern Terpstra, and Daniel Van Den Bulcke.

Keywords: Academy of International Business; AIB Fellows; history; Alan Rugman

Perspectives on Headquarters-Subsidiary Relationships in the Contemporary MNC
Research in Global Strategic Management, Volume 17, 331–368
Copyright © 2016 by Emerald Group Publishing Limited
All rights of reproduction in any form reserved
ISSN: 1064-4857/doi:10.1108/S1064-485720160000017028

As Stefanie Lenway, former AIB President, wrote in the Preface of Volume 14 of this Series: "The Fellows of the Academy of International Business provide the institutional memory for the Academy of International Business (Lenway, 2008, pp. xi–xiv)," since among its members, it counts the founders of this field as well as its subsequent senior scholars, educators, and administrators. The AIB Fellows, through their awards, have recognized executives who have made outstanding contributions to the practice of international business, eminent scholars who have produced pioneering studies that provided new research perspectives, and educators as well as administrators who have built outstanding academic courses and programs in international business, and have thereby helped legitimize the IB field. Many of these developments surface in this chapter which evokes the key issues that preoccupied the AIB Fellows who have kept functioning as the *avant-garde* of the Academy of International Business (AIB) during the deanship of an outstanding AIB Fellow – namely, Alan M. Rugman.

ALAN RUGMAN'S DEANSHIP (2011–2014)

Alan was warmly applauded as our new Dean in Nagoya, Japan (June 24–28, 2011) where the AIB held its annual conference, and he appointed Alain Verbeke as our new Secretary-Treasurer after thanking Ravi Ramamurti for his excellent services in the role. Alan succeeded Dean Eleanor Westney (2008–2011) whose achievements are recounted in the complete History of the AIB Fellows to be found at <Fellows@aib.msu.edu>. During her tenure, seven important Fellows passed away: Robert Hawkins, John Dunning, Hans Thorelli and Richard Robinson in 2009, C.K. Prahalad in 2010 as well as Susan Douglas and John Stopford in 2011.

New Committees

Our new dean resurrected the practice of appointing separate committees for our Honorary Fellows. *Arie Lewin* headed the one for the International Executive of the Year who chose James Whitehurst, CEO of Red Hat, the open-source software company. It turned out to be a very difficult task because several potential candidates (e.g., IBM's Samuel Palmisiano) were not available or had never heard of the AIB and its Fellows! *Sid Gray's* International Educator of the Year Committee found it easier to select, at the suggestion of Rob Grosse, Jorge Talavera, President of Esan University in Peru and former Executive Director of CLADEA, the Latin American Council of Management Schools. Finally, *Don Lessard* and *Tarun Khanna* recommended our new Eminent Scholar who was unanimously elected by the Fellows – namely, *Ikujiro Nonaka* (Hitotsubashi University, Japan) who had been identified by checking the authors most cited in JIBS articles and using various other criteria. Professor Nonaka is best known for his work on knowledge management – especially, the interaction between explicit and tacit knowledge.

Another committee chaired by *Rosalie Tung* proposed various amendments to our Constitution, which were approved by the Fellows. While many of the changes were cosmetic, we decided that an elected Fellow becomes an "Active Fellow" immediately after payment of his lifetime dues while "Participating" Fellows are now simply "Active Fellows." However, a proposal to reduce the percentage of votes needed to elect an Eminent Scholar from 75 percent to 60 percent was not approved.

Two Fellows Gone

Many messages from the Fellows followed the announcement of *John Stopford's* death on August 13, 2011 – in particular from Lorraine Eden, who sent pictures of John, and Dong-Sung Cho, who co-chaired our 1995 Seoul meeting with John and lauded his subtle but effective leadership. Dean Alan Rugman recounted that John had the remarkable ability to be simultaneously a first-rate academic, an expert teacher especially of MBAs and executives and a guru able to connect with top-management practitioners. John will also be remembered for his pioneering articles and book (with Lou Wells) on the strategy and structure of MNEs and for his ability to combine economic and political analysis in his work on government policy toward foreign direct investment (FDI).

Steve Kobrin thought of John Stopford as someone with whom you could have a serious intellectual discussion and then have a great time with afterwards – or simultaneously! José de la Torre, whose friendship with John went back to 1966, visited John in the hospital earlier this summer and found him unwilling to give up as he continued his professional activities until the very end. His wit and humor and the pleasure he derived from all of his activities will not be forgotten either, nor his contributions to the development of the AIB, EIBA, and the IB field in general. Our Dean, Alan Rugman, attended the Memorial Service in John Stopford's honor in October 2011 in London, and delivered a message on behalf of the Fellows.

Howard Perlmutter passed away on November 8, 2011. As Steven Kobrin put it: "He was one of the elders in our field and one of the more original and creative thinkers in international business. He was the founder with Russ Root of the Multinational Enterprise Unit at Wharton where he was Professor of Social Architecture but I suspect that only he knew what that meant. He had an amazing mind and an ability to focus on big issues, and he really wanted to make the world a better place. I was always amazed at his ability to connect with the students and shape discussion so that it was always productive. His article on "ethno-poly-geo-centrism" has long since passed into the vernacular."

Fellows' Honors

Peter Buckley was much complimented by the Fellows when the news broke out in early January 2012 about his Order of the British Empire award "for services to higher education, international business and research." However, Peter was seen at our Washington conference *not* wearing the OBE's gold badge suspended on a rose-pink ribbon with pearl-grey edges and bearing the fierce motto "For God and Empire" – probably because it was too hot, what with temperatures reaching 103–104 degrees Fahrenheit! Peter was also nominated "Professor of the *Week*" by the *Financial Times* – which goes to show how quickly "Sic transit gloria mundi!"

Meanwhile, *Geert Hofstede* had been appointed in 2011 as a Knight of the Order of the Dutch Lion, the highest civil honor granted by the Queen of the Netherlands. *Jean-François Hennart* received the 2012 Booz & Co./ Strategy + Business Eminent Scholar in International Management Award. This reward was long overdue on account of his sustained and excellent work on transaction-cost economics. This prestigious award has been given to other Fellows in the past: John Dunning, Alan Rugman, Peter Buckley, John Child, Chris Bartlett, Sumantra Ghoshal, Yves Doz, C.K. Prahalad, and Steven Kobrin last year. We practically own it!

Fellows on the Move

Robert Grosse keeps pursuing his migrations and permutations after leaving his deanship at the business school (EGADE) of the Monterrey Technological University of Mexico to become Director of the Center for

Global Business Innovation and Transformation at George Mason University. Before Mexico, Rob was in South Africa with the Standard Bank as head of its leadership program. He has also just been elected President of the AIB for 2012–2014, continuing the record series of Fellows becoming AIB Presidents (Mary Ann Von Glinow, Yves Doz, Stefanie Lenway, Alan Rugman, Peter Buckley, Steve Kobrin, José de la Torre, and so on – all the way back to Bob Hawkins in 1983–1984).

Fellow Authors

Karl Sauvant keeps writing, publishing, and editing handbooks and reports (*Columbia FDI Perspectives*) which cover many topics ranging from the geographical ("FDI Outward and Inward Investments in China") to the institutional (e.g., "Towards the Successful Implementation of the Updated OECD Guidelines for Multinational Enterprises"). *Steve Kobrin* is now the publisher of the Wharton Digital Press which has already issued several e-books.

Pankaj Ghemawat and *Oded Shenkar* received much attention in *The Economist* in 2012 for their respective books on global prosperity and copy-cat firms. Pankaj also contributed to the new AACSB curriculum requirements regarding the globalization of business enterprises by providing a course outline and support materials. This "course on a disk" is a follow-up on the AACSB report of February 2011 on this topic.

Fellows in the News

Sri Zaheer was appointed Dean of the Carlson School of Management earlier this year. The press highlighted that: "Dean-designate Zaheer is a rare combination of someone who is renowned for her insights on international business, highly regarded for her understanding of the global and local businesses that drive the Minnesota economy, and acutely aware of the needs of the Carlson School as it continues to educate the world's current and future business leaders."

George Yip left his deanship at Rotterdam for a professorship at the renowned China Europe International Business School while *Jean Boddewyn* was ranked as the 202,306th scholar on the "Author Statistics" of the Social Science Research Network but his paper on "The Provisioning of Collective Goods by MNEs in Emerging Markets" won both the 2012 Temple/AIB Best Paper Award and the AOM/IMD Skolkovo (Moscow School of Management) Best Paper Award! The *Academy of Management Perspectives* of May 2012 (26/2) listed the "scholarly impact" of hundreds of researchers. Among them, Bruce Kogut, C.K. Prahalad, Sumantra Ghoshal, Ikujiro Nonaka, Geert Hofstede, Mike Peng, Tomás Hult, Udo Zander, Julian Birkinshaw, and Srilata Zaheer were cited.

Timothy Devinney and *Torben Pedersen* (plus Laszlo Tihanyi) pursued the publication of *Advances in International Management* series whose volumes have been quite successful. Timothy also became in 2012 the Co-Editor of *Academy of Management Perspectives* which now ranks highly as a business and management journal. His book, *The Myth of the Ethical Consumer*, won the Best-Book Award of the Social Issues in Management Division of the Academy of Management. Many Fellows have posted a short CV with a picture at the Fellows' section of the AIB Website <http://aib.msu.edu/community/memberdir.asp>.

2012 AIB Conference in Washington, DC

A session chaired by Alan Rugman was devoted to the work of *John Stopford*, where Lou Wells, Don Lessard, Eleanor Westney, Julian Birkinshaw, and José de la Torre recounted John's exemplary contributions to IB scholarship. Also honored were our new Eminent Scholar, *Ikujiro Nonaka* of Hitotsubashi University and *Jean Boddewyn* who made a presentation based on his contributions to the fields of MNE political-action theory, international business-government relations, and the management and organization of the International Public-Affairs function. Our Dinner at the National Press Club inspired our Dean Alan Rugman to comment that "we should celebrate every single day the freedom of thought and expression we all enjoy as scholars."

A Wonderful Eulogy to a Departed Fellow

It is a bit late to report that *Endel Kolde* died at the age of 92 on September 20, 2009. He was one of the first ten elected AIB Fellows in 1978 on account of his sustained scholarly work in international trade, foreign-area analysis, and MNE environments. His obituary in *The Seattle Times* recounted his dramatic underground work in Estonia during the brutal

Soviet and German occupations of his country which he left in 1944 before its annexation by the Soviet Union.

Fred Truitt first observed that "the essence of an authentic Estonian is a deep-seated longing to be left alone and independent from foreign domination *and* from each other — preferably in the middle of some forest!" Fred then recounted that he first met Endel Kolde in 1968 at a conference on the future of international business at Indiana University:

> I was a graduate student at IU and was assigned to go to the Indianapolis airport to fetch Endel and his new wife Helga and bring them to Bloomington. While driving them, I tried a simple greeting and conversation in the very limited kitchen Estonian learned from my wife's grandmother. He let me speak a bit and then interrupted and told me: "I must say that your parents are probably not well educated and have failed miserably to teach you decent Estonian!" I responded that my parents were from South Philadelphia and what little Estonian I knew I picked up from my wife's grandmother. He then said: "Well, in that case, you must be a very intelligent and capable boy ... really remarkable ... I never met an American who could even pronounce two words of Estonian! Call me when you want a job."

A few years later, about two weeks after starting at the University of Washington with visions of collaboration and collegial conversation about international business, Fred Truitt approached Endel and asked if they might go out to lunch together. His reply was: "No, not today ... and ... not ever. On Wednesdays, I go to lunch at the Swedish Club (in downtown Seattle) and the other days I run ten to twenty kilometers at lunchtime." This seemed to fit his independent and loner mentality very well. Dick Moxon added:

> Endel was a very productive scholar/teacher but he liked to work by himself. If there was a big project that we were all going to work on, he would carve out his piece and go off by himself to work on it. Before the rest of us were halfway along, he would appear with his part already done, usually in the form of a stand-alone book or monograph. Frustrating for those of us who wanted to collaborate and coordinate efforts but pretty productive!

The Passing Away of Lee Nehrt

Our first Dean (1978–1981) died at age 87 on March 13, 2013, in Bloomington. Immediate condolences and remembrances were expressed by Noritake Kobayashi who spoke fondly of Lee's integrity, helpfulness, and hospitality, and by Raj Aggarwal who always enjoyed his interactions with Lee who had led multiple lives as Coast Guard officer, Administrator of the World Trade Institute at the World Trade Center in New York, leader of various development projects in underdeveloped countries, and − of course − as President of the AIB, educator, and researcher at several places. He finally retired from Ohio State in 1986.

John Daniels delivered one of the best eulogies of a deceased Fellow, and he will always remember Lee as living every day to the fullest, with a reverence for the past and precise plans for the future. Lee could "change hats" quickly, driving a tractor to plant trees one minute and then racing in one of his two Porsche sports cars along Indiana's back roads. He could also communicate easily and convincingly with everyone. For example, John told the story of how Lee Nehrt advised a student to major in accounting and to take his IB course. "He completely changed my life. I was hooked." So spoke *Lee Radebaugh* who later had Lee Nehrt as his dissertation Chair at Indiana.

Together with four other now deceased AIB Fellows − Stephen Robock, Richard Farmer, Hans Thorelli, and William Hoskins − plus living Ken Simmonds, Lee Nehrt pioneered international business education and research at Indiana University. With Lee's passing away, seven of the AIB Fellows' past Deans are now dead, including the first six. "All of them have inspired us to push the IB field forward." After this stimulating remark, John Daniels proposed a toast in memory of our past leader. Attila Yaprak, who served as AIB Executive Secretary, added that "Lee Nehrt was the person who inspired me to pursue international business as a field of study and to become an IB professor. I also feel fortunate that I was inspired by a 'gentleman,' a warm and caring person who was like a father to me."

Lee Nehrt was the first Dean of the AIB Fellows (1978−1981), having been appointed by then AIB President *Richard Farmer* and his Executive Committee after the first Constitution of the AIB Fellows had been drawn up in 1977. As past AIB President (1973−1974), he was one of the 16 *de jure* "Founding Members" of the AIB Fellows, who were soon joined by the first ten "elected" members in 1978. Lee should be forever remembered for getting our Group going as an effective organization and for his very active role with Paul Garner in getting the AACSB to include an "international" component in business curricula. Besides, the width and depth of Lee Nehrt's consultancy are remarkable. He was Ford Foundation Advisor to the Minister of Economics and Planning in Tunisia (1965−1967), Chief of Party of a Ford Foundation project to develop the Institute of Business Administration at Dacca University in East Pakistan (1969−1971), and World Bank Advisor to the Ministry of Planning in Jakarta, Indonesia

(1986—1989). He was also a frequent consultant to the United Nations and the World Bank, and was Chief of Mission of 23 consultancies to various countries in Africa, the Middle East, and South Asia.

Lee Nehrt's wife Ardith recollected many unique events in his and their lives. He was the first U.S. person to get a Ph.D. in International Business — which he did at Columbia University in 1962 — and his multiple careers took him or them to some 100 domestic and foreign locations. Ardith Nehrt recounted that she had set up household on 32 occasions and that, during what she "mistakenly thought would be his retirement," he built a home for them near Bloomington and Indiana University, established a library in his hometown, created a blacksmith museum, developed some 173 acres into multiple lots — with the main road named the "Nehrt Road" and others for their granddaughters and grandsons — and purchased 400 more acres for a tree farm where more than 250,000 seedlings were planted with the help of children and grandchildren to provide hardwood some 30 years later to pay for the education of the great-grandchildren and "to hold the extended family together in a common cause." As Ardith said at the "Celebration of the Life of Lee Nehrt," family, friends, and opportunities were his main concerns. Their eldest son, Chad Nehrt — also an educator — recounted seeing a tee-shirt marked "Live your life so the preacher won't have to lie at your funeral," and he thought his dad had lived that way! Truly, there is much to remember and celebrate of the man we always met neatly dressed with a blazer and a bow tie!

William (Bill) Hoskins Passes Away

One of the founders of the AIB and a faithful Secretary-Treasurer to John Fayerweather when the latter served as the first AIB President (1959—1961) and as Dean of the AIB Fellows (1984—1987), Bill died at the age of 88 on April 30, 2013, in Austin, TX. Both John and Bill had served on the steering committee that brought the AIB into being in 1958 at the urging of, and with the help of, the National Foreign Trade Association's Education Committee and with the support of several businessmen who remained active in the AIB for a dozen years or so. As one of the founders, Bill became in 1978 one of the 16 original AIB Fellows who then proceeded to elect ten new Fellows for the first time.

The section on John Fayerweather's deanship is one of the largest ones in the History of the AIB Fellows because John and Bill Hoskins worked very closely together since Bill had served in the same capacity when John

became the first President of the AIB in 1959–1961. They took many initiatives that have rarely been matched ever since – for example, many
detailed surveys to gauge the AIB Fellows' readiness to alter our
Constitution and to engage in new initiatives before a final voting took
place – besides publishing 14 long newsletters.

Jim Goodnow – the longest serving Secretary-Treasurer of the Fellows
from 1987 to 1993 – recounted that he met Bill Hoskins in 1963 at Indiana
where the latter taught international business before moving to Bowling
Green University in Ohio until his first retirement, following which he
moved to Thunderbird to teach some more in the mid-1980s and to develop
a business-simulation game similar to the famous one of Hans Thorelli. Bill
and his wife Ruth then took a second and final leave from academia and
the AIB in Texas until his death there.

Fellows as Leaders

The current AIB leadership remains peopled with AIB Fellows – what
with *Robert Grosse* serving as 2012–2014 President and to be succeeded by
Nakiye Boyacigiller while *Klaus Meyer* will be VP Program in Vancouver,
BC (2014) with *Ram Mudambi* following him in 2015 in Bangalore, India.
Meanwhile, *John Cantwell* keeps serving as JIBS Editor-in-Chief and
Tomás Hult perseveres as AIB Executive Director.

Fellows' Publications

Don Lessard is contributing a chapter on "The Evolution of EMNCs and
EMNC Thinking: A Capabilities Perspectives" to a book edited by
A. Cuervo-Cazurra and *Ravi Ramamurti* on *Understanding Multinationals
from Emerging Markets* (Cambridge University Press, 2014). *Sam Park*
published *Rough Diamonds: The Four Traits of Successful Enterprises in
BRIC Countries* (Jossey-Bass/Wiley, 2013) while *Tomás Hult* (MSU) and
George Yip wrote a textbook on *Total Global Strategy* (Pearson Prentice
Hall, 2012) which highlights five "global strategic levers" (e.g., the location
of value-adding global activities). Tomás (with William Motz) has measured the degree to which community colleges emphasize IB education in
their curricula – 85 percent of them offered a basic IB course in 2012
versus 51 percent in 2008 – but other measures (e.g., funding) are also used
by them to ascertain these colleges' commitment to the IB field. Meanwhile,

MSU's International Business Center, under Tomás' leadership, continues to produce the Market Potential Index for emerging markets.

George Yip (CEIBS in Beijing) co-authored *Strategic Transformation: Changing While Winning* (Palgrave Macmillan, 2012) which received a very favorable review in the *Financial Times* of January 24, 2013. It commented that "*Strategic Transformation* is the chief executive's in-depth guide to how to sustain and refresh strategy over time." This book is based on the colorful travails of Tesco, Cadbury Schweppes, and Smith & Nephew from Great Britain.

John Daniels was recently working on the 15th edition of his *International Business* textbook co-authored with *Lee Radebaugh* and *Daniel Sullivan*. He said that it will be his last textbook revision although his co-authors may go on, and he commented that:

> I was lucky to hit the market at a time of growth and feel lucky to be divesting at the right time [before textbooks may disappear and be replaced with something else] ... When I first started, textbook-writing was looked upon very favorably by deans and promotion-and-tenure committees. Now, one almost has to hide that one is a textbook author! I greatly regret this change. Similarly, almost no one is writing cases anymore for the same reason although we certainly need good cases in the classroom.

Bruce Kogut's 2012 edited book on *The Small Worlds of Corporate Governance* (MIT Press) maps the influence of economic and social networks – communities of people or firms and the ties among them – on corporate behavior and governance, and it stresses the surprising heterogeneity of network structures, which contradicts the common belief in a single Anglo-Saxon model. "What matters to Americans in terms of social, economic and political values?" *Timothy Devinney* is the first author of this 2012 "Anatomy of Civil Societies Research Project" which reports on religious activity, political orientation and affiliation, donating and volunteering behavior, and personality measures as an alternative to standard Likert-based polling. Timothy is also one of the two editors of the *Academy of Management Perspectives* whose Editorial Board includes *Paul Beamish, Nakiye Boyacigiller, Ram Mudambi, Michael Peng,* and *Rosalie Tung*.

Mira Wilkins, while on sabbatical at Florida International University, is working on the third volume of her history of foreign investment in the United States, which will cover the period 1945–2012. *Peter Buckley, Lorraine Eden,* and *Ram Mudambi* assisted in various capacities the preparation of UNCTAD's *World Investment Report 2013* on *Global Value Chains: Investment and Trade for Development.* This report highlighted the fact that, for the first time, developing economies surpassed developed ones as recipients of FDI (52.0% vs. 41.5%).

Karl Sauvant keeps writing, editing, and co-authoring *Columbia FDI Perspectives* which discusses topical FDI issues. Thus, Report 101 of August 2013 addressed "The Need for an International Investment Consensus-Building Process" in terms of achieving an appropriate balance between strong investor protection and the right of governments to pursue legitimate public-policy objectives in bilateral and multilateral FDI regimes. A previous issue (No. 98) dealt with the important topic of "Do Host Countries Really Benefit from Inward Foreign Direct Investment?" while "Towards the Successful Implementation of the Updated *OECD Guidelines for Multinational Enterprises*" by Tadahiro Asami highlighted the major changes in this very important document which is the most comprehensive government-endorsed code of responsible business practice, including the area of human rights. Karl also edited the *Yearbook on International Investment Law & Policy 2011–2012* (Oxford) which analyzes the magnitude and salient features of FDI flows, home-country policies, international law and arbitration, and trends in international investment agreements. Karl co-edited the second edition of *FDI Perspectives: Issues in International Investment*, which is available free of charge for download from <www.vcc.columbia.edu>. It contains a chapter by *Mira Wilkins* on indirect foreign investment.

Fellows in the News

Torben Pedersen (Copenhagen Business School) was quoted in a special report of *The Economist* (February 2–8, 2013) on "The Nordic Countries," which stated that: "The Vikings' modern descendants believe they can turn globalization to their advantage." Torben pointed out that "Nordic countries are past masters at adjusting to rules dictated by big countries such as Germany or America. Surely, they can cope with China and India?" Also quoted in *The Economist* (December 22, 2012) was *Pankaj Ghemawat* (IESE) in a piece titled "Globalization: Going Backwards — The World is Less Connected Than It Was in 2007." It borrowed from the latest DHL Global Connectedness Index which is overseen by Pankaj who concluded that the economic crisis of 2008 made connections both shallower and narrower, with people — particularly, company bosses — underestimating the gains that could be made by further globalization. Pankaj will spend the academic year 2013–2014 at NYU's Business School.

Fellows' Honors

Stefanie Lenway, recently appointed Dean of Michigan State's Business School, was elected for a 3-year term (2012–2015) to the Board of Directors of the renamed AACSB (Association to Advance Collegiate Schools of Business "International"). Stefanie had already participated in a discussion of the future of undergraduate business education as member of the AACSB Task Force which produced a report to which *Pankaj Ghemawat* also contributed: *The Globalization of Management Education: Changing International Structures, Adaptive Strategies and the Impact of Institutions* (2011). In this context, Pankaj has prepared a very useful GLOBE disk containing basic materials for an introductory course on the "Globalization of Business Enterprise."

Eleanor Westney was the 2013 recipient of "The Booz & Co./ Strategy + Business Eminent Scholar in International Management Award" at the 2013 AOM Annual Meeting in Orlando, FL. She joins a distinguished list of AIB Fellows who have received this prestigious honor year after year! At the same meeting, *Bernard Yeung* received the AOM's Business Policy & Strategy (BPS) "Outstanding Educator Award." Bernie is the Dean and Distinguished Professor of Finance & Strategic Management at the National University of Singapore's Business School after teaching at NYU and Michigan. *José de la Torre* received the same award from the International Management Division of the AOM.

Torben Pedersen (Copenhagen Business School) was the co-author of the JIBS article "MNC Knowledge Transfer, Subsidiary Absorptive Capacity, and HRM" that won the 2013 JIBS Decade Award. To be considered for this award, an article must be one of the five most cited JIBS publication for the year being considered – 2003 in Torben's case. The International Section of the American Accounting Association announced in 2012 the creation of the "*Lee H. Radebaugh* Notable Contribution to International Research Decade Award." Meanwhile, *Marjorie Lyles* has been elected President of the Strategic Management Society.

Fellows at the 2013 AIB Conference in Istanbul

Nakiye Boyacigiller was our superb Local Hosting Chair who organized a great venue for our meeting and was in charge of selecting the new International Awardees of the Year. *Bernard Ramanantsoa* (Dean, HEC Paris) was our International Educator of the Year and *Muhtar Kent*,

Chairman and CEO of the Coca-Cola Company (which provided us with free soft drinks!) our International Executive of the Year.

There was an AIB Fellows' Eminent Scholar Award Session honoring *David Teece* (Professor of Global Business, University of California at Berkeley) who almost singlehandedly invented the "dynamic-capabilities" approach in strategic management, which is also used extensively by international business scholars. The main focus of his work is value creation and capture through innovation, taking into account that protecting the fruits of innovation requires a threshold level of "inimitability" by competitors as well as "complementary assets."

An AIB Fellows Plenary dealt with "How Much Does Distance Still Matter in International Business?" while an AIB Fellows Special Panel celebrated "25 Years of J.-F. Hennart's 'A Transaction-Costs Theory of Equity Joint Ventures'." Another one on "Celebrating 25 Years of Kogut and Singh's 'The Effect of National Culture on the Choice of Entry Mode' " included Bruce's challenging speech on the role of genetics in culture. *George Yip* organized another "guru" Senior Executive Seminar on the topic of "The Integration of Emerging Markets in the Global Economy: Insights for Turkish Firms."

The AIB Fellows' Dinner in Istanbul took place aboard the Gümüş Damla Yacht which took us through the tumultuous waters of the Bosphorus Strait, with magnificent views of the city, its shores, and islands while the AIB Conference was held at the sumptuous Hilton Istanbul. It is close to Gezi Park and Taksim Square which have been the sites for many stone-throwing protests – including one during our Closing Reception!

Speaking of throwing stones, Prakash Sethi of Baruch College (CUNY) took to task AIB Fellows and key AIB members who attended the 2013 AIB Conference for devoting over 90 percent of the papers and sessions to "the pursuit of making corporations more efficient and profitable" in lieu of discussing MNEs' externalities and the world's problems – labor exploitation, environmental degradation, bribery, corruption, and income inequality.

Fellows' Thoughts

Ken Simmonds, the last of the "Gang of Six" at Indiana (see above), recently found an old paper he wrote for the group of four that started its International Business Department in 1963, with Steve Robock as Chair, Dick Farmer as Associate Professor, and Lee Nehrt and Ken as Assistant

Professors — Indiana being the first place where one could major in IB. To survive the wrath of other departments, they deliberately avoided adding the tag "International" to courses in Economics, Marketing, Accounting, and Management because that would have invited quick recapture by the other departments but they invented other names for their new courses. This was good advice because: "Years later, Columbia's faculty did to Steve Robock's exactly what we had feared. The battle still rages. I refused to set up an IB department at the London Business School unless it properly funded it and gave IB courses a proper place in the School's MBA. The Dean would not do so. Under some pressure, John Stopford took [this project] over by renaming it 'Policy, Strategy & International Business.' Nevertheless, he and I continued to teach IB courses outside the department structure." How many times has this battle been fought? Alan Rugman, in his 2003 edited book *Leadership in International Business Education and Research*, included several chapters about the development of IB education at Indiana, including one about the history of the IB group at that school.

Jack Behrman remains concerned that "so little attention has been given to the work of Sen, Stiglitz, Nussbaum, and other eminent scholars on tracking progress rather than the growth of mere numbers of transactions (e.g., the GDP), with no attention given to content or distribution. He commented: "That GDP has not been abandoned despite having been shown irrelevant, is testimony to the crazy adherence to quantification in economics in an effort to become 'scientific' — which it cannot! I have tried long enough to offer some sense to economists but with little success. I can only say 'I tried' and, in some cases, my efforts were approved long after they were relevant." What a sincere and humble scholarly confession!

New Fellows

Keith Brouthers, Andrew Delios, Klaus Meyer, and *Sam (Seung Ho) Park* joined our august ranks in 2013 — four out of nine candidates. It is not quite a record but better than the two new Fellows elected in 2012. Our Dean, *Alan Rugman,* reminded us that we are still short of about 20 Fellows below the age of 66 to fill our ranks which have been depleted by the death of 35 Fellows so far. The use of ratings and citation numbers has increased in nomination and seconding letters although their meanings and implications are not always clear to the voters.

Odds and Ends

Chris Bartlett reported that his postacademic life has been very full and enjoyable as he works with several nonprofit organizations in Australia, the United States, and Cambodia, which leaves him with little time for teaching and writing. Eleven recent (2008−2012) Fellows are presently writing a chapter for the second AIB Fellows' Book (Volume 16) to succeed the one published in 2008 in our Dean *Alan Rugman*'s series of *Research in Global Strategic Management* (Emerald Press), and to come out in 2014. Twice as many Fellows are helping review their drafts for this book edited by *Jean Boddewyn.*

Fellow Publisher

Our Dean, *Alan Rugman*, published a well-documented history of the AIB Doctoral Dissertation Award in *AIB Insights* (Vol. 13, No. 3, 2013). This award was first named in 1987 after Richard N. Farmer − a prior Chair of the Indiana IB Department, a past President of the AIB (1977−1978), and a pioneer with Barry Richman of IB research − passed away. Thanks to Alan, Indiana University took over the sponsorship of the award from the AIB for a number of years until he left for Reading University which, together with the University of Leeds, is now providing the funding for the newly named *Peter J. Buckley and Mark Casson Doctoral Dissertation Award* in 2013 to honor these two eminent IB scholars.

Fellows in the News

Raj Aggarwal and his co-authors were quoted in the *Washington Post* of August 29, 2013, for their study that examined the association of GMAT scores with cultural characteristics borrowed from Geert Hofstede. They found that people with high GMAT scores are less able to deal with an organization's hierarchy, those who do well in business schools are less likely to take the risks to become entrepreneurs, and candidates from nations with the highest levels of ethics have the lowest GMAT scores. Perhaps business schools should start recruiting students with the lowest GMAT scores!

Fellows on the Move

Timothy Devinney left Australia for the University Leadership Chair and Professorship in International Business at Leeds University's Business School where he joins *Peter Buckley*. Timothy will be the Founding Editor of the new journal *Foundations and Trends in International Business and Management*.

Our 2014 Eminent Scholar and Other Fellows Awards

The committee appointed by Dean Rugman to nominate the 2014 Eminent Scholar selected *Richard P. Rumelt* (UCLA, Anderson) – the well-known godfather of the modern theory of corporate diversification and of the resource-based view in strategy that emphasizes firm-specific advantages – and the Fellows voted him in. *Dominic Barton*, Global Managing Director of McKinsey&Co., was selected as our 2014 International Executive of the Year. Barton has extensively written on the future of capitalism, long-term value creation and business leadership in society. The International Educator of the Year Committee chose *Daniel Shapiro*, Dean of the Beedie School of Business at Simon Fraser University.

Death's Toll

Three Fellows died in less than four months! Besides *John Ryans* who passed away on September 14, 2013, from a fall at home, *Vern Terpstra*, a former AIB President and early IB scholar, left us on November 6, 2013, while beloved *Daniël Van Den Bulcke* died on January 8, 2014.

John Ryans did much to develop the field of international marketing at Kent State during 34 years of service there. Some of you may recall his often cited 1964 article "Is It Too Soon to Put a Tiger in Your Tank?" in the *Columbia Journal of World Business*, where he warned against too much standardization in advertising. *Vern Terpstra* got his BBA, MBA, and Ph.D. from the University of Michigan where he taught from 1968 to 1992 after a short stint at Wharton. Before his academic career, Vern had been a missionary with his wife Bonnie in the former Belgian Congo where they helped build a school. He authored 12 books, including his doctoral dissertation on *American Marketing in the European Common Market*, which came out in book form in 1967 and made quite a splash then − plus several short volumes later on in international marketing, the cultural environment of international business, and related topics.

What an explosion of love for *Danny Van Den Bulcke* who died so unexpectedly on January 8, 2014, at age 74! "Come on, Danny, tell us it is not true! Join us one more time to talk to us, laugh with us, advise us, inspire us, photograph us!" Alas, that will not happen. Professor Filip De Beule, his former Ph.D. student and now Professor at the Catholic University of Leuven (Belgium), confirmed that Danny had died of esophageal cancer that had spread to his liver and lungs after being transferred to palliative care. What a calm ending for this good man who did so much so well so far and so long, and who deeply touched the lives of many of us! *José de la Torre* reminded us of the book of wonderful and whimsical memories of, and tributes to Danny, gathered in 2009 on the occasion of his 70th birthday by Filip De Beule (www.ua.ac.be/download.aspx?c = *CIMDA&n = 4548&ct = 001876&e = 208033).

Fellow on the Move

Robert Grosse is moving again! After landing a couple of years ago at George Mason University as Director of its Center for Global Business Innovation and Transformation, following his deanship of EGADE in Monterrey, Mexico, Rob has accepted to be Dean again − this time of the business school at the American University of Sharjah in Dubai, starting in early 2014. Besides, he is finishing a book on *Emerging Markets: Where the Action Is*, and completing with his wife Chris a project to have banks in Honduras lend more to small and medium firms. He also recently spent a week climbing Mount Kilimanjaro in Tanzania with his daughter. You just cannot pin this man down, who is also AIB President until Summer 2014.

Honors

Tamer Cavusgil was co-author with Gary Knight of the article that won the 2014 JIBS Decade Award: "Innovation, Organizational Capabilities, and the Born-Global Firm" published in 2004. *Ivo Zander* chaired the Selection Committee and will be one of the discussants at a special session of the AIB Conference in Vancouver, BC, in June 2014.

More Publications

The Fellows remain steady contributors to *Transnational Corporations* whose April 2011 (20/1) issue had articles by *Karl Sauvant* on "FDI, the Global Crisis and Sustainable Development," *Ravi Ramamurti* on "The Impact of the Crisis on FDI Players," and *Alan Rugman* on "The International Financial Crisis and Transnational Corporation Strategy." In a preceding issue of August 2010 (19/2), *Peter Buckley* wrote a very perceptive article on "Twenty Years of the WIR: Retrospect and Prospect."

Anil Gupta contributed "The Relational Perspective and East Meets West" in *AOM Perspectives* (9/11, 2011) where he provided an in-depth analysis of the relational and transactional perspectives, pointing out that they both suffer from serious limitations although they complement each other. *Kwok Leung* published in 2011 a very interesting piece in the Asia-based *Management and Organization Review* on "Presenting *post-hoc* Hypotheses as *a priori*: Ethical and Theoretical Issues." He criticizes authors who develop hypotheses *after* collecting their empirical findings as if these hypotheses had been developed a priori and tested thereafter.

Jean Boddewyn published in 2011 "The Control of 'Sex in Advertising' in France" in the *Journal of Public Policy & Marketing* (with Esther Loubradou), "The Evolving Discipline of Public Affairs" in the *Journal of Public Affairs*," "Global Strategy and the Collaboration of MNEs, NGOs, and Governments for the Provisioning of Collective Goods in Emerging Markets" in the *Global Strategy Journal* (with Jonathan Doh), and, in 2012, "Using Organization Structure to Buffer Political Ties in Emerging Markets: A Case Study" (with Marleen Dieleman as first author) in *Organization Studies*.

Fellows in the News

Pankaj Ghemawat's 2011 book *World 3.0: Global Prosperity and How to Achieve it* was highlighted in *The Economist* (April 20, 2011) as "The Case Against Globaloney – At last, Some Sense on Globalization." In it, Pankaj calls for a new worldview where both regulation and cross-border integration coexist and complement each other. He shows that increased globalization can actually alleviate problems of job losses, environmental degradation, macroeconomic volatility as well as trade and capital imbalances – no less! Pankaj also contributed to the development of the DHL Global Connectedness Index which ranks 125 countries accounting for 98 percent of the world's GDP and 92 percent of its population. It reveals that 12 policy and structural variables can explain nearly 80 percent of the variation in countries' depth of connectedness with each other. *The Economist* must have a soft spot for the Fellows because it cited at great length on May 12, 2012, the recent book by *Oded Shenkar: Copycats: How Smart Companies Use Imitation to Gain a Strategic Edge.*

Sri Zaheer was appointed Dean of the Carlson School of Management in early 2012. The press highlighted that: "Dean-designate Zaheer is a rare combination of someone who is renowned for her insights on international business, highly regarded for her understanding of the global and local businesses that drive the Minnesota economy, and acutely aware of the needs of the Carlson School as it continues to educate the world's current and future business leaders." Quite a compliment but Sri replied that "reading emails at 2:15 AM" was a little too much!

Fellows' Correspondence

We had two "Letters from One Fellow to the Others." *Yair Aharoni* commented on the need to complement secondary-research with primary interviews of practitioners and case studies because one can always generate spurious statistical correlations which do not reflect reality. He recounted his original research which found that it takes a powerful initiating force to make a firm look abroad. He concluded that strategy is not about gaining competitive advantage in an industry but about creating a monopoly in a newly-defined niche. *Noritake Kobayashi* followed with a summary of his book on *Japanese Multinational Enterprises: Internationalization and Performance.* He classified 66 firms into 28 that maintained their status as international champions in 2005–2009 but the number of troubled enterprises had increased from three to eight. "Very large" and "large" enterprises had more difficulty than smaller ones in maintaining their performance. Focusing on the recession period of 2008–2009, the number of industrial sectors belonging to the "international champion" category decreased from 10 to 2. Besides, profitability was rather poor as far as the super-large Japanese MNEs were concerned. Thank you Noritake for giving us this surprising picture of Japanese multinationals!

Good Business

In February 2012, we ran our election of new AIB Fellows. There were three candidates — Mike Peng, Ram Mudambi, and Rajneesh

Narula — but only the first two candidates got at least 55 percent of positive votes. *Mike Peng* and *Ram Mudambi* were introduced as New Fellows at our Dinner in Washington, DC, together with *Anil Gupta* who was elected two years ago.

More Eulogies

Two Fellows passed away this year. *Steve Robock* was the oldest one among us at age 97. He died of natural causes on August 1, 2012, in South Carolina. If you read his obituary, you found out that he got all the military, administrative, and economic experiences necessary to become one of the pioneers in international business and management after 1960 at Indiana University and then at Columbia's Graduate School of Business where an endowed Chair in Finance and Economics honors him. Many of us benefitted from his IB textbook which went through several editions. *Noritake Kobayashi* recounted that Steve had offered him his first experience teaching IB outside Japan at Indiana while *Dong-Sung Cho* remembered sending a poem to Steve who kept it on his refrigerator to remind himself to "die young at one hundred!" He almost made it!

The Accounting, Finance, and Taxation fraternity was particularly effusive at mourning the death of *Frederick Choi* on October 2, 2012. He served not only as Chairman of the Accounting, Taxation, and Business Law Department at New York University but also as Dean of NYU's Undergraduate College, and he was the founding editor of *The Journal of International Financial Management and Accounting*. Everybody thought of him as a friendly, kind, helpful, and humble person, and *Lee Radebaugh* lauded him as "one of the good guys" who did a lot but never bragged about it.

In his eulogy in Istanbul in 2013, Sid Gray recounted that Fred was a prolific and widely respected scholar. He authored numerous books including his award-winning *International Accounting* (with Gary Meek, now in its seventh edition). He published more than 50 academic articles in many leading journals, including the *Journal of Accounting Research* and the *Journal of International Business Studies*, along with dozens of book chapters, essays, and reviews. Fred was a recipient of the Citibank "Excellence in Teaching Award" and of the American Accounting Association's "Outstanding International Accounting Educator Award."

Odds and Ends

Rob Grosse is now the 2012–2014 AIB President while *Klaus Meyer* will be AIB Vice-President Program in 2014 and a future AIB President. *Ingo Walter* is alive and well as Vice Dean of the Faculty at NYU's Stern School of Business and traveling a lot to the Middle East and Asia for NYU's programs in Abu Dhabi and Shanghai. Did you know that the UK chapter of the AIB honors our past and beloved *Michael Z. Brooke* with a prize for the best paper by a doctoral student?

I got reprimanded by our leaders for providing the names of those AIB members nominated but never elected since 2000! At the risk of another spanking, I will reveal that presently there are 80 alive Fellows of which only 40 are below the age of 66. The youngest Fellows are *Mike Peng* and *Tomás Hult* while *Jack Behrman* is in his 90s. After three serious illnesses, he is hitting the golf ball again while planning to write one more article on the silliness of relying on GNP/GDP data for policy purposes.

I have checked Google and obituaries for the fate of some of the early AIB Fellows and found that *Joseph M. Bertotti*, one of the AIB founders, passed away on May 7, 2002. He was Manager of Education Relations at General Electric and served as international educator for the U.S. State Department. He was one of the businessmen who urged the founding of an IB education association which became the AIB born "Association for Education in International Business" (AEIB) in 1958.

Our Next Dean (2014–2017)

Paul Beamish was selected by our previous three deans' Nominating Committee of Donald Lessard, Jean Boddewyn, and Eleanor Westney. Paul will be our second Canadian leader but his merits as a scholar outshine that of his citizenship as he has significantly developed the study of FDI and of international joint ventures over many years through numerous articles and cases.

Histories

Shige Makino has just written a case on the 2011 Nagoya AIB Conference for our forthcoming Dean *Paul Beamish*'s ample series of Ivey cases (9B12M071). It deals with the impact of the March 11, 2011, catastrophic

Japanese tsunami and earthquake (9.0 magnitude) on the planning of the AIB Conference, following the U.S. State Department's travel alert urging U.S. citizens to avoid nonessential travel to Japan, followed by a number of universities around the globe banning staff and students from traveling to Japan.

Shige was our AIB Vice-President Program in 2011 for the Nagoya conference which he ran from Hong Kong where he teaches but he was born in this Japanese town which means a lot to him. From his well-documented and gripping analysis – "Should the AIB Leaders Cancel the Conference?" – you can learn several interesting things about the AIB and its meetings:

- Nagoya elicited a record number of submissions (1,536) from 53 countries but also of cancellations.
- The AIB Secretariat usually estimates attendance at conferences at 1.2 times the number of submissions.
- Many local firms in Nagoya originally declined to sponsor the AIB conference out of a cultural sentiment of *jishuku* (= self-discipline) which justifies the scaling down of festivals, ceremonies, events, and parties following a disaster or misfortune, as a way of expressing solidarity in times of crisis.
- The Nagoya conference was estimated to cost $400,000.
- AIB conferences generate more than $300,000 of conference revenues (mostly our rich registration fees), host schools contribute some $200,000, and conference expenses add up to $360,000 – all numbers based on our 2010 meeting in Rio.
- Cancellation was considered but Shige Makino and the AIB leadership had a Plan B ready for holding the AIB Conference in Hong Kong, which was kept secret. Instead, on March 30, the AIB Executive Board under AIB President *Mary Ann Von Glinow* and AIB Foundation President *Tomás Hult* confirmed the AIB's commitment to meet in safe Nagoya as scheduled.

Speaking of histories, you can read an account of "The Birth of the AEIB[AIB]" in 1958 by John Fayerweather in JIBS, [5(2) 1974: 69–80]. Our association sprang out of the interest of several people in "U.S. companies abroad" – compared to what had been until then the main academic focus on export-import activities by economists and practitioners. As AIB co-founder and first AIB President, John Fayerweather recounts that these teachers and business people "were quite 'charged up' with a sense that we were pioneers at the early stage of something very big and important" and they were "an excited group with a missionary urge looking for an organized outlet." Without them (15 professors and 4 businessmen), there would not be the AIB we know and the Fellows we are even though we lost the voice of businessmen over time since no new ones were elected after 1980. We replaced them by our "International Executive of the Year Award" in 1982.

How Many Fellows?

A quick count reveals 83 Active Fellows of whom only 38 are below the age of 66 so that we could elect 22 new Fellows before reaching our upper limit of 60 Fellows born after 1948. Yet, *we elected only one new Fellow this 2014 year – Witold Henisz – out of six candidates –* as happened also in 1986, 1987, 1990, 2000, and 2003 (and no new Fellow at all in 1988 out of 11 candidates!). Seldom, over 35 years of history, have we elected our maximum of five new Fellows a year (1979, 1980, 1994, 2007, 2008, 2009, and 2010) although we also did well in 2011 and 2013 when four new Fellows made it. Are we running out of new stars or do they not get nominated? Are some very good candidates never to be recognized?

Fellows Keep Publishing

The April 2014 issue of JIBS had no less than three articles co-authored by *Jan-Erik Vahlne, Torben Pedersen*, and *Mike Peng* while the preceding issue involved *Yadong Luo, Tatiana Kostova,* and *Kendall Roth. Oded Shenkar* was another JIBS author with Simcha Ronen who expanded in 2013 on their well-known 1985 "clustering of countries" based on cultural attitudes. In another vein, Wikipedia now includes an essay on internalization theory by *Alan Rugman* and one on nonmarket forces by *Jean Boddewyn.*

Yair Aharoni provided "a few lessons from my long experience in IB research" in *AIB Insights* (13/4, 2013). He started by arguing for the importance of "talking to practitioners" in order to get a real grab of a problem or practice. He recounted how such a habit prevented him from conducting a questionnaire study that would have erroneously proved that tax holidays are desirable to spur FDI in Israel because respondents would probably have answered "Yes." *Geoffrey Jones* has published *Entrepreneurship and Multinationals* (Edward Elgar, 2013) which demonstrates how MNEs have driven globalization through the transfer of innovation and cultural values while *Karl Sauvant* co-edited *Inward and Outward FDI Country Profiles* (Vale Columbia Center, 2013) which offers 77 standardized profiles dealing with the FDI experience of these countries.

George Yip co-authored "Innovation in Emerging Markets – The Case of China" and *Seung Ho (Sam) Park* did the same for "How Much We Can Trust the Financial Report" in the *International Journal of Emerging Markets* (2014, 9/1). *Lou Wells* contributed to *Columbia FDI Perspectives* a piece on "Government-held Equity in Foreign Investment Projects: Good For Host Countries?" His answer was mainly negative because government equity is often not needed since taxes and royalties are more reliable sources of revenue than dividend returns on capital invested.

2014 AIB Conference in Vancouver, BC

AIB members were welcomed by AIB President *Robert Grosse* and Program Chair *Klaus Meyer*. We had again *Café* sessions, thanks to *Eleanor Westney's* resurrection of this popular set of early-morning discussion meetings of Fellows with Conference attendants on a variety of topics (e.g., "What is the role of culture in Finance?"). This conference had the AIB Fellows: (1) present their Educator of the Year Award to Dean *Daniel Shapiro* of the local host business school at Simon Fraser University; (2) man a panel on "Context in International Business;" (3) grant their Eminent Scholar Award to *Richard Rumelt* whose magnum opus was discussed by several Fellows, and (4) celebrate the recipient of our International Executive of the Year, *Dominic Barton*, CEO of McKinsey, as well as *Daniel Shapiro* as our International Educator of the Year. In 2015, we will meet in Bangalore, India, where *Ram Mudambi* will be the Program Chair while another Fellow, *Rosalie Tung*, will be the AIB President in 2015–2016 under the new one-year rotating system for AIB leaders.

There were many discussions of UNCTAD's *World Investment Report 2014* which presented "An Action Plan for Investment in Sustainable Development." It revealed that: (1) Global FDI returned to growth, with inflows rising nine percent in 2013; (2) FDI outflows from developing and transition countries reached a new record level and represented 30 percent of Global FDI outflows; (3) "Developing Asia" is the largest FDI recipient – much more so than the European Union and North America; (4) the share of regulatory or restrictive national investment policies increased to 27 percent although the majority of measures remains geared toward promotion and liberalization, and (5) faced with common global economic, social, and environmental challenges, the international community is defining an ambitious set of "Sustainable Developing Goals" for the period 2015–2030.

At the Fellows' Dinner at the Terminal City Club, eulogies helped us remember *Vern Terpstra* (by Jim Goodnow) and *Danny Van Den Bulcke* (by Alain Verbeke) while, at our Business Meeting, final reports were made by our departing Dean *Alan Rugman* and Secretary-Treasurer *Alain Verbeke* who were warmly thanked and applauded. Positive financial accounts were approved, and a hot discussion accompanied a proposal by *José de la Torre* to modify the way we calculate the newly available "Abstain" votes when we elect new Fellows. This hot ball was lobbed to our new Dean, Paul Beamish, who can now wield the steel hockey stick that serves as his commanding baton − a gift fashioned by Alan Rugman.

We Miss Alan Rugman

A bare 12 days after our Vancouver, BC, conference, Alan Rugman passed away. Some 44 Fellows − more than half of the 83 active ones − expressed their surprise, debt, and loss after they learned that our most recent Dean had passed away on July 8, 2014, from a kidney cancer − less than a fortnight after many of us met and heard him at the AIB Conference, and at his last presiding of the AIB Fellows' Dinner and Business Meeting. Their thoughts and feelings sent to Helen, his wife, did manifest our joy and gratitude of having known him, learned from him, and enjoyed the best of his personality. Here is what some of us said:

Paul Beamish:	Like everyone else, I am saddened by Alan's death from cancer. I knew him for over 30 years. As we all acknowledge, he contributed a great deal to the international business domain for a long time but what a personality! I will remember him most for his character, the kindness he would show to Ph.D. students and junior professors.
Alain Verbeke:	Alan was a man of extraordinary honesty and intelligence, who devoted his entire professional life to the study of the multinational enterprise and its impacts

on society. Most of what I know about what constitutes good IB research, I learned from Alan. He was one of the founding fathers of our field.

Peter Buckley:

Alan was fiercely honest, forthright, and utterly dedicated to academic values. What you saw was what you got, and there was no duplicity in his nature. I will miss his combative frankness.

Timothy Devinney:

Like many of us, I was the recipient of Alan's guidance, cajoling – some of which was more like shoving – and, on more than one occasion, his "correction" of my misguided ideas. I loved what I like to call "Alan being Alan." When he stood up in a meeting, I could watch the audience prepare itself for what was no doubt going to be a bit of a show. I will miss these shows! With Alan's passing – along with those of Danny Van Den Bulcke, the two Johns' (Stopford and Dunning), plus a host of others in the last few years (Lee Nehrt, Vern Terpstra, John Ryans, etc.) – I see the passing away of a generation in our field that will be very hard to replace intellectually and impossible to replace as human beings.

Tatiana Kostova:

I hope he knew how much he was respected and loved by his colleagues and friends.

José de la Torre:

He was always willing to go anywhere and anytime to foster the mission of international business scholarship and education. I would often challenge him on some of my ideas, and he would typically reply: "José, go read my book!" I will miss his lightning-fast intellect, his sharp sense of humor, and our friendly bantering. His bigger-than-life persona will endure as will his impact on several generations of IB scholars throughout the world.

Lorraine Eden:

When Alan was sitting in the audience, we all knew that, at some point after the presentations, he would get up to ask a question – as he always did. Whatever the question, we expected more and got more from Alan's questions than from anybody else in the audience. He was a born entertainer as well as an academic and scholar.

Sri Zaheer:	Alan was always there in the audience at many regular paper sessions at every conference – paying attention, asking probing questions, talking to junior presenters afterwards. It has become so rare for senior academics to attend regular sessions any more … *mea culpa!*
Mike Peng:	Like everyone else, I was shocked by this tremendous loss. I truly regret not going to Vancouver to be with Alan one last time. I am probably one of the few who co-taught with him because he used to visit us every year in Dallas to teach in our Global Leadership EMBA program. Alan's one-day class on regional multinationals was always a provocative one that opened our students' eyes!
Yadong Luo:	Alan was very solicitous and supportive of scholars from emerging countries. To memorialize him, we could create the "Alan Rugman Emerging Scholar Award."
Lee Radebaugh:	I want to remember Alan as the consummate probing professional with a wry sense of humor.
Ram Mudambi:	I always viewed him as a founding member of the Reading School of Business. It is fitting that he ended his career at the helm of International Business & Strategy at that very institution. If he upset some people, it was usually because he was right. With Alan, there was no subterfuge. He wore his heart on his sleeve and, if he disagreed with you, he told you bluntly, directly and to your face.
Geoffrey Jones:	His remarkable productivity, energy, and intellectual honesty are things to which we all aspire but few of us deliver as Alan did.
James Goodnow:	When I eulogized the late Vern Terpstra at the AIB Fellows' Dinner in Vancouver, his kind remarks about my early contributions to the AIB as its Executive Secretary were totally unexpected and reminded me of what a wonderful person he was.
John Daniels:	Alan championed the controversy on whether IB is regional or global but we can all agree that his death is a loss *pour tout le monde* in the IB field.

Farok
Contractor: Helping the underdog, an intense focus on a quest or
                       idea, and being able to separate the wheat from the chaff
                       in academic as well as human affairs — these were some
                       of his wonderful qualities.

Arie Lewin: He was a mentor to me, he became a strong supporter
                       and he embraced the new JIBS when I became its
                       Editor-in-Chief.

Lou Wells: Alan was always ready to argue against any point
                       someone made but these arguments were intended to
                       generate improvements in ideas, not to destroy them. In
                       this, he had the proper "doubting" attitude that is
                       essential to a good academic.

Johny
Johansson: Alan had already accomplished more than we others can
                       hope to achieve but he still had many years left to
                       contribute. He will be greatly missed.

Donald
Lessard: At the last Fellows' Dinner in Vancouver, he was
                       gracious and clearly was enjoying his Dean's role as he
                       passed the hockey stick to Paul Beamish.

Karl Sauvant: I can't believe it after having discussed the future with
                       Alan in Vancouver! What a loss of a friend and a
                       dear colleague!

Raj Aggarwal suggested: "How about a special session on, and a
prize for, the best paper presented at the AIB conferences, that raises
the most important new questions and challenges for IB?" In the same
vein, AIB Vice-President Ram Mudambi plans to bring up the issue of
a suitable memorial for Alan to the AIB Executive Board at its
next meeting.

What "a tremendous outpouring of love, appreciation and respect," as
Duane Kujawa and his wife Sharon put it! "Apparently, Alan meant many
things to many people — all of them good, constructive and heart-touching.
Each of us is clearly thankful that Alan was part of our lives. He was a
blessing! We are thankful too to you Helen [Alan's wife] for providing the
loving, supportive home environment and companionship that allowed
Alan to bloom as beautifully as he did."

My wife Marilyn and I entertained him at our home in New York the year
he was visiting at Columbia University and, the next day, we went shopping
together for a smart double-breasted suit for Alan. I became an ardent fan of
his and nominated him for AIB Fellowship but succeeded only on the fourth

try in 1991 because some older Fellows thought him too young and brash until they relented in view of his obvious brilliance. I knew he would make an excellent Dean of the Fellows, and I promoted his candidacy to the prior deans who, with me, selected him in 2011. In return, I am grateful to him for encouraging and assisting me in writing the history of the AIB Fellows to this day. He was a very dear, prickly friend and a bright light all along.

Peter Buckley represented the AIB Fellows at Alan's funeral in Reading and *Rob Grosse* was the AIB's delegate. Subsequently, *Alain Verbeke* became the Inaugural Alan Rugman Memorial Fellow at the Henley Business School, University of Reading (UK).

Leadership

AIB Fellows have now cornered four ongoing AIB presidencies: *Mary Ann Von Glinow*, Outgoing Past President (2010–2012), *Rob Grosse*, ongoing President (2012–2014), *Nakiye Boyacigiller*, Incoming President (2014–2015), and *Rosalie Tung*, Incoming President-Elect (2015–2016). Notice that AIB has now switched to one-year presidencies and a five-year ladder of elected positions, with *Klaus Meyer* (2014 Vancouver Program Chair) and *Ram Mudambi* (2015 Bangalore Program Chair) in the wings. This perfect score has been complemented by *John Cantwell* as JIBS Editor-in-Chief and *Tomás Hult* as AIB Executive Director.

Recent Publications

Our new Fellow *Witold Henisz* (2014) published *Corporate Diplomacy: Building Reputations and Relationships with External Stakeholders* (Greenleaf Publishing, 2014) which advises senior managers to build the capacity to strategically develop these most important traits. Vit Henisz was interviewed about his new book by *Steve Kobrin* and, in their lively exchange, the author stressed that "nobody makes a political or social judgment based on the facts. They do it based on emotion, based on gut."

Anil Gupta, with co-authors G. Pande and H. Wang, published *The Silk Road Rediscovered: How Indians and Chinese Companies Are Becoming Globally Stronger by Winning in Each Other's Markets* (Jossey-Bass/Wiley, 2014). *Karl Sauvant* and Federico Ortino published the freely downloadable booklet "Improving the International Investment Law and Policy Regime: Options for the Future" that was commissioned by the Finish Ministry of Foreign Affairs. Edited by *Jean Boddewyn*, the second AIB Fellows' Book offers ten chapters written by eleven recently (2008–2012) elected Fellows in *Multidisciplinary Insights From New AIB Fellows* (Emerald Press, June 2014).

That's Interesting

John Daniels reported that he and *José de la Torre* spent some time researching past AIB dissertation award winners. "We hit three surprises. First, the majority of past winners, even recent ones, are no longer AIB members. Second, very few have become AIB Fellows – that is, four out of the first 27 winners. Third, of those that have become Fellows, it has taken them a minimum of 15 years after winning the AIB Best Dissertation Award."

Did you read "The Changing Business of Business Schools" by Johan Roos, Dean of the Jonköping International Business School in Sweden? It was posted by the AIB in April 2014 with the subtitle: "The critics have a valid question: Why aren't business schools changing *faster* to keep up with changes in the business world?" In the same vein, *The Economist* of June 18–July 4, 2014, carried a title page and an inside article marked "Creative Destruction: Reinventing the University" which claims that: "A cost crisis, changing labour markets and new technology will turn an old institution on its head." If business schools must and will change, how will this development affect IB education? What can Fellows do about it, and should they?

Honors

In recognition of his "seminal research and groundbreaking contributions to the fields of international-marketing and international business performance," *Tamer Cavusgil* was honored as Doctor Honoris Causa by the Belgian University of Hasselt in May 2014. Earlier on, he and Gary Knight – a former doctoral student of his – received the 2014 JIBS Decade Award for their 2004 article on "Innovation, Organizational Capabilities and the Born-Global Firm," which has generated more than 1,000 citations since then.

This chapter on Alan Rugman's deanship (2011–2014) ends the *History of the AIB Fellows* who have served the IB community since the start of their operations in 1978. The full text of this history can be found at <Fellows@aib.msu.edu>.

REFERENCE

Lenway, S. (2008). Preface. In J. Boddewyn (Ed.), *International business scholarship: AIB fellows on the first 50 years and beyond* (pp. xi–xiv). Bingley, UK: Emerald Publishing Group Limited.

APPENDIX

Table A1. Active Fellows and Their Status as of June 2015.

Active Fellows	Year Elected/Inducted
Adler, Nancy	1992
Aggarwal, Rag	1994
Aharoni, Yair	1990
Asakawa, Kaz	2015
Bartlett, Christopher	1994
Beamish, Paul	1997
Behrman, Jack	F (1978 – Inducted)
Benito, Gabriel	2015
Birkinshaw, Julian	2008
Boddewyn, Jean	1980
Boyacigiller, Nakiye A.	2007
Brouthers, Keith	2013
Buckley, Peter	1985
Cantwell, John	2005
Casson, Mark	1993
Cavusgil, Tamer	1998
Chi, Tailan	2015
Child, John	2009
Cho, Dong-Sung	2002
Contractor, Farok	1995
Daniels, John	1985
de la Torre, José	1991
Delios, Andrew	2013
Devinney, Timothy	2008
Doh, Jonathan	2015
Doz, Yves	1994
Eden, Lorraine	2004
Ghauri, Pervez	2015
Ghemawat, Pankaj	2007
Gray, Sidney	2009
Goodnow, Jim	FES (1978 – Inducted)
Green, Robert	1994
Grosse, Robert	2001
Gupta, Anil	2010
Henisz, Witold J.	2014
Hennart, Jean-François	1999
Hult, Tomás	2010
Johansson, Jan	2010
Johansson, Johny	2011
Jones, Geoffrey	2010
Khanna, Tarun	2009
Kobayashi, Noritake	1979
Kobrin, Stephen	1989
Kogut, Bruce	1996

Table A1.   (*Continued*)

Active Fellows	Year Elected/Inducted
Kostova, Tatiana	2011
Kotabe, Masaaki	1998
Kujawa, Duane	1983
Lenway, Stefanie	2002
Lessard, Donald	1989
Lewin, Arie	2009
Luo, Yadong	2008
Lyles, Marjorie	2005
Macharzina, Klaus	1998
Makino, Shige	2009
McDougall-Covin, Patricia	2015
Meyer, Klaus	2013
Mudambi, Ram	2012
Park, Sam (Seung Ho)	2013
Pausenberger, Ehrenfried	1980
Pedersen, Torben	2011
Peng, Mike	2012
Radebaugh, Lee	1995
Ralston, David	2015
Ramamurti, Ravi	2008
Ricks, David	1992
Roth, Kendall	2008
Sauvant, Karl	2011
Shenkar, Oded	2004
Simmonds, Kenneth	1979
Stobaugh, Robert	P (1981 − Inducted)
Stonehill, Arthur	1984
Tallman, Stephen	2008
Toyne, Brian	2000
Tung, Rosalie	2003
Vahlne, Jan-Erik	2010
Verbeke, Alain	2007
Vernon, Ivan	ES (1984 − Inducted)
Von Glinow, Mary Ann	2007
Walter, Ingo	1987
Wells, Louis T., Jr.	1983
Westney, Eleanor	1997
Wilkins, Mira	1996
Wills, James R.	2006
Yeung, Bernard	2005
Yip, George	1999
Zaheer, Srilata	2007
Zander, Udo	2006

FES − Inducted as past AIB Executive Secretary at the time of the founding of the Fellows in 1978.
P − Inducted as past AIB president after 1978.
ES − Inducted as past AIB Executive Secretary after 1978.
F − AIB Founder.

Table A2. Inactive Fellows.

Inactive Fellows	Year Elected/Inducted
Cateora, Philip R.	1979
Mandell, Stuart	F (1978 – Inducted)
Mueller, Gerhard G.	1980

F – AIB Founder.

Table A3. Deceased Fellows as of June 2015.

	Year Elected/Inducted	Date of Death
Arpan, Jeffrey	1993	May 28, 2005
Bednarik, Mojmir	F (1978 – Inducted)	February 28, 1983
Benoit, Emile	F (1978 – Inducted)	May 4, 1978
Bertotti, Joseph M.	F (1978 – Inducted)	May 7, 2002
Blough, Roy	F (1978 – Inducted)	February 25, 2000
Brooke, Michael Z.	1982	April 1, 2003
Domke, Martin	F (1978 – Inducted)	
Douglas, Susan	1991	January 3, 2011
Dowd, Lawrence	F (1978 – Inducted)	April 24, 1980
Dunning, John	1979	January 29, 2009
Dymsza, William A.	1981	June 20, 2007
Farmer, Richard	P (1979 – Inducted)	February 28, 1987
Fayerweather, John	F (1978 – Inducted)	February 3, 2005
Garner, Paul	1979	1997
Ghoshal, Sumantra	1999	March 3, 2004
Grub, Phillip	FP (1978 – Inducted)	April 14, 2008
Hart, James A.	F (1978 – Inducted)	
Hattery, Lowell	F (1978 – Inducted)	July 28, 1989
Hawkins, Robert	1981	August 22, 2008
Haynes, Elliott	1979	
Hoskins, William	F (1978 – Inducted)	April 30, 2013
Keegan, Warren	1984	December 31, 2014
Kellar, Harold	F (1978 – Inducted)	March 20, 1980
Kolde, Endel	F (1978 – Inducted)	September 20, 2009
Kramer, Roland	F (1978 – Inducted)	
Leung, Kwok	2008	May 25, 2015
Mason, R. Hal	1986	September 3, 2005
Mikesell, Raymond	1981	September 12, 2006
Nehrt, Lee C.	F (1978 – Inducted)	March 13, 2013
Ogram, Jr., Ernest W.	1980	1999
Pélissier, Ray	F (1978 – Inducted)	
Perlmutter, Howard	1991	November 8, 2011
Prahalad, C.K.	2002	April 17, 2010
Reef, Arthur	F (1978 – Inducted)	

Table A3.   (*Continued*)

	Year Elected/Inducted	Date of Death
Robinson, Richard	FP (1978 — Inducted)	September 5, 2009
Robock, Stefan	1979	August 1, 2012
Root, Franklin	P (1983 — Inducted)	August 4, 2005
Rugman, Alan	1991	July 8, 2014
Ryans, John	1994	September 14, 2013
Stopford, John	1993	August 13, 2011
Terpstra, Vern	FP (1978 — Inducted)	November 6, 2013
Thorelli, Hans	1981	August 18, 2009
Van Den Bulcke, Daniël	1992	January 8, 2014
Vernon, Raymond	1979	August 26, 1999
Wade, Robert H.B.	1980	January 26, 2015

F — AIB Founder.
FP — Inducted as past AIB President at the time of the founding of the Fellows in 1978.
P — Inducted as past AIB president after 1978.

Honorary Fellows as of June 2015

John Fayerweather Eminent Scholars

Kindleberger, Charles (MIT) 1987 (deceased)
Penrose, Edith (INSEAD and University of London) 1994 (deceased)
Hofstede, Geert (Tilburg University) 1998
Caves, Richard (Harvard University) 1999
Chandler, Alfred (Harvard Business School) 2000 (deceased)
Williamson, Oliver (University of California, Berkeley) 2003
North, Douglass (Washington University in St. Louis) 2007
Dore, Ronald P. (London School of Economics) 2008
Nelson, Richard (Columbia University) 2011
Nonaka, Ikujiro (Hitotsubashi University) 2012
Teece, David (University of California, Berkeley) 2013
Rumelt, Richard (University of California, Los Angeles) 2014

International Educators of the Year (formerly International Deans of the Year)

Bess, David (University of Hawaii at Manoa) 1988
Easton, Susanna (U.S. Department of Education) 2009
Elam, Joyce (Florida International University) 2007
Gomez, Jaime A. (Tecnologico de Monterrey) 2005

Hawkins, Robert (Georgia Institute of Technology) 1998
Horváth, Dezsö (York University) 2004
Kane, James (University of South Carolina) 1996
Loeser, Norma (George Washington University) 1984
Patten, Ronald (DePaul University) 1987
Porat, Moshe (Temple University) 2001
Purg, Danica (IEDC Bled School of Management, Slovenia) 2010
Ramanantsoa, Bernard (HEC, Paris) 2013
Rameau, Claude (INSEAD) 1994
Rose, John (University of Melbourne) 2000
Shapiro, Daniel (Simon Fraser University) 2014
Stetting, Lauge (Copenhagen Business School) 1995
Talavera, Jorge Travesto (Esan University, Peru) 2012
Wyman, Harold (Florida International University) 1997
Zang, Guohua (China Europe International Business School) 2006

International Executives of the Year (originally Business Leader of
the Year*)*
Agnelli, Giovanni, CEO of FIAT, 1986
Barnevik, Percy, CEO of ASEA Brown, Boveri, 1992
Barton, Dominic, Global Managing Director, McKinsey & Co, 2014
Chey, Jong-Huyon, CEO of Sunkyong (SK) Group, 1995
Cho, Fujio, Chairman of Toyota Motor Company, 2011
Chow, Sir C.K., CEO of Brambles Industries, Ltd., 2001
Culver, David, CEO of ALCAN, 1990
Desmarais, Jr., Paul, Chairman of Power Corporation of Canada, 2005
Felsinger, Donald E., CEO and Chairman of Sempra Energy, 2009
Hammer, Armand, Chairman of Occidental Petroleum Company, 1987
Kent, Muhtar, Chairman and CEO of Coca-Cola Company, 2013
Liu, Chuanzhi, Chairman of the Legend Holdings Group/Lenovo/
IBM, 2006
Maisonrouge, Jacques, Executive VP of IBM World Trade, Air
Liquide, 1982
Monty, Jean, CEO of Northern Telecom Corporation, 1996
Morita, Akio, CEO of SONY Corporation, 1983
Murthy, N. R., CEO of Narayana Corporation, Infosys Technologies
Ltd., 2003
Sada, Federico, CEO of Grupo Vitro, 2002
Shih, Stan, CEO of ACER Group, 1999
Silva, Ozires, former Chairman and CEO of Embraer and Petrobras, 2010

Solso, Theodore, Chairman and CEO of Cummins Inc., 2007
Sutherland, Peter, CEO of Goldman Sachs International Group, 1998
Whitehurst, James, CEO of Red Hat, 2012
Wriston, Walter, CEO of Citicorp, 1985
Yamamoto, Takuma, CEO of Fujitsu Corporation, 1993
Zambrano, Lorenzo, CEO of CEMEX, 1997

AIB 50th Anniversary Award for the Support of International Business Education and Research

Jagdish Sheth (Emory University) 2010

HOW DOES THE CONTEXT OF LANGUAGE USE AFFECT THE PERCEPTION OF LANGUAGE BARRIERS?

Àngels Dasí and Torben Pedersen

ABSTRACT

Language commonality and barriers are often taken as exogenous given variable and independent of the context; however in this chapter we investigate the factors determining perception of language barriers. As such we are responding to the question of when do managers perceive language barriers and which business contexts foster the perception of language barriers and which do not? Language serves different purposes and entails different communicative requirements depending on the context in which it is used. In addition, language has multiple dimensions and we argue that the different dimensions of language vary in their importance depending on the specific context, where the contextual variation in this case is related to the operation mode chosen in the foreign market. More specifically, we argue that language distance (relatedness in language) matters when the firms conduct business abroad through their own employees, while language incidence (accuracy in language) is

Perspectives on Headquarters-Subsidiary Relationships in the Contemporary MNC
Research in Global Strategic Management, Volume 17, 369–400
ISSN: 1064-4857/doi:10.1108/S1064-485720160000017012

critical when operating through a local agent. The different use of language implies a need for different language skills. The combination of the operation mode and the availability of people with the needed language skills will affect managers' perception of language barriers. The hypotheses are tested on a large data set encompassing 390 multinational corporations headquartered in Finland, South Korea, New Zealand, and Sweden that have undertaken a business operation in a foreign country.

Keywords: Communicative requirements; language barrier; language distance; language incidence; operation mode

The importance of language differences has attracted much attention in international business (IB) and several studies have advanced our understanding of the significance of language commonality and barriers for conducting international activities. However, while many studies have focused on the impact of language on IB activities, the issue on what actually determines the perception of language barriers has largely been ignored. In other words, language commonality and barriers have been heavily studied as an independent variable affecting IB activities but very few studies have looked at what determines the perception of language in terms of commonality as well as barriers. When do managers perceive language barriers? Which business contexts foster the perception of language barriers and which do not? In this chapter, we claim that the variation in the perception of language barriers is an outcome of the use of language and the international context in which it is used. More specifically, we study how the different contexts of operations modes (home-based sales force, local agent, or own subsidiary) comprise different use and requirements of language and thus affect the perception of language as a barrier differently. As such, we are not taking the perception of language barriers as an exogenous given variable but are explaining how it emerges.

Some studies highlight the importance of language within multinational corporations (MNCs) in terms of their effect on organizational dynamics (Björkman & Piekkari, 2009; Luo & Shenkar, 2006; Marschan-Piekkari, Welch, & Welch, 1999; Peltokorpi & Vaara, 2012; Tenzer, Pudelko, & Harzing, 2014). Other studies propose language differences as a predictor of entry mode (Demirbag, Glaister, & Tatoglu, 2007; Dow & Ferencikova, 2010; Dow & Larimo, 2011; López-Duarte & Vidal-Suárez, 2012; Slangen, 2011) or as an impediment to knowledge-transfer processes within MNCs (Ambos & Ambos, 2009; Brannen, 2004; Dellestrand & Kappen, 2012;

Harzing & Feely, 2008; Mäkelä, Andersson, & Seppälä, 2012; Schomaker & Zaheer, 2014; Welch & Welch, 2008).

These studies emphasize the disruptive effects that language differences have for IB as they create noticeable barriers that impede different processes that firms undertake when going abroad. Language barriers are "obstacles to effective communication, which arise if interlocutors speak different mother tongues and lack a shared language in which they all have native proficiency" (Tenzer et al., 2014, p. 2). Most of the cited studies operationalize language barriers through two indicators. The first one is "linguistic distance" (or the opposite of linguistic relatedness) which recognizes that some languages are closer between them than others due to the similarity of such structural elements as sound, writing systems, and grammatical rules (Dow & Karunaratna, 2006; Schomaker & Zaheer, 2014). The second indicator is "language incidence" that measures the proportion of the population in one country who are able to speak the major language of another country (Dow & Karunaratna, 2006). Both indicators reflect different dimensions of language differences and help to understand why the perception of language barriers depends on the languages involved.

However, in most cases, the above cited studies make the tacit assumption that language differences work similarly to other cultural distance indicators – that is, in a linear and scalable way – without theoretically explaining the mechanisms that underpin the barrier's perception (Demirbag et al., 2007; Dow & Ferencikova, 2010; Dow & Larimo, 2011; López-Duarte & Vidal-Suárez, 2010, 2012; Slangen, 2011). Additionally, the language construct has been used in a fairly superficial way, without much attention to the context where language is used and how the context poses different requirements to language, that subsequently affect the perception of language barriers (Zaheer, Schomaker, & Nachum, 2012). This leads to the following questions: *Is language used in the same way across context or is the use of language more context-specific? What dimensions of language differences affect the perception of a language barrier? What are the exact mechanisms at work for the link between language and context?*

We claim that language is a multidimensional concept where the use of language and the perception of language barriers do, in fact, vary with the context. Language serves different purposes depending on the international activity in question and, as such, the importance of the dimensions of language varies with the international activity (Luo & Shenkar, 2006). Only by deconstructing the concept of language and by considering the interaction with the specific context will we be able to understand the mechanisms at play (Zaheer et al., 2012). We build on contextual heterogeneity for explaining when, how, and why the two constructs used for measuring language differences — language distance and language incidence — are more or less appropriate for capturing the manager's perception of language barrier.

In this chapter, we study the *use of language* in the context of firm's different operation modes. More specifically, we focus on how different contextual uses of language affect the perception of language as a barrier when firms serve the foreign market via home-based sales force, local agent, or own subsidiary, respectively. We analyze how these operation modes allow firms to organize their relationships with the foreign market under the lens of the theory of the firm (Powell, 1990; Ring & van de Ven, 1992). These modes are related to two archetypical forms of economic organization: markets and networks that, as we claim, require specific and different uses of language that eventually affect the perception of language barriers.

In the following sections, we outline the theoretical logic and tease out the different dimensions that language carries and how these are connected to the use of language in the foreign operation modes. This results in the formulation of theoretically grounded hypotheses for how language differences affect the perception of language as a barrier. We build on the measure of language differences developed by Dow and Karunaratna (2006) in that we propose different effects of their language indicators — language distance and language incidence — depending on the foreign operation mode. The proposed hypotheses are tested on a unique data set encompassing 390 MNCs from Finland, New Zealand, South Korea, and Sweden. The results show that the language dimensions that are most important for the perception of language barriers vary with the use of language that goes together with the operation mode. As such, we begin to deconstruct the concept of language differences and develop an understanding of the mechanisms through which the deconstructed dimensions of language affect IB activities.

THEORETICAL FRAMEWORK

Language Differences and the Perception of Language as a Barrier for IB Activities

The development of measures of language differences (Dow & Karunaratna, 2006; West & Graham, 2004) has allowed IB researchers to include the language barrier as one of the psychic factors affecting different decisions on IB activities (Child, Rodrigues, & Frynas, 2009; Håkanson & Ambos, 2010). This has been beneficial in that it has improved our understanding of decisions (e.g., on entry mode choices and MNC's knowledge-transfer processes). Unfortunately, much of the research that introduces language is assuming that the applied secondary and objective measures reflect uniformly manager's perception of language barrier without taking into account the context in which the language is used. As such, language-differences measures are suffering from similar problems as other psychic-distance measures (Håkanson & Ambos, 2010; Nebus & Chai, 2014; Shenkar, 2001; Zaheer et al., 2012). Luo and Shenkar (2006) suggested that language is not just a linear and scalable variable since the perception of language differences between the home and the host country are dependent on the specific context. While some studies (Demirbag et al., 2007; Dow & Ferencikova, 2010; Dow & Karunaratna, 2006; Dow & Larimo, 2011; López-Duarte & Vidal-Suárez, 2012) treat language just as a cost component of doing business abroad without paying much attention to the context, Luo and Shenkar (2006) highlighted that the cost is determined, at least in part, by the nature of the transaction and the partners involved.

We argue along the same line that language barriers are not perceived uniformly across the potential operation modes in a foreign market. In fact, the different operation modes form different contexts that affect the perception of language barriers differently. Language interferes in the various information-related processes that a firm must conduct when engaging in foreign operations (Petersen, Pedersen, & Lyles, 2008). However, the importance of this interference varies depending on the specific operation mode. Based on this reasoning, we analyze the different uses of language depending on whether the contact with the external counterpart in the foreign market is directly organized through one's own employees that typically communicate with many customers on an ongoing basis (e.g., home-based sales force or local subsidiary) or indirectly through a local agent that acts on behalf of the firm and where communication is typically more discrete. The theoretical model of this chapter is illustrated in Fig. 1.

The Contextual Nature of the Perception of Language Barrier

The operation mode is the main platform into the foreign market and as such determines how the firms approach, relate, bond, interact, and

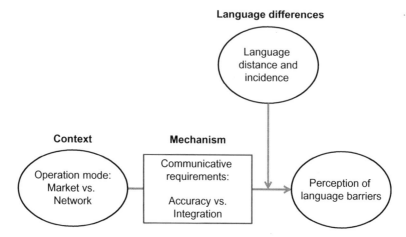

Fig. 1. Illustration of the Theoretical Model.

communicate with counterparts in the foreign market (Benito, Petersen, & Welch, 2009). We focus on the operation mode as a way of capturing contextual differences in the uses of language due to specific communicative requirements.

The operation modes are different ways of organizing activities in the foreign market that are basically variations of the more general forms of economic organization that are examined in the theory of the firm. The theory of the firm identifies three archetypical forms of economic organization: market, hierarchy, and network (e.g., see Powell, 1990; Ring & van de Ven, 1992 for comprehensive overviews). For the purposes of this chapter, we will focus on the organizational forms of market and network,[1] that is, whether the firm chooses to approach the foreign market via a local agent (the market form) or to build up local relationships through its own employees (the network form).

A brief review of the characteristics of the organizational forms of market and network is instructive as it provides the starting point for understanding how the uses of language interact with the operation modes. In Table 1, some of the key features — in particular the communication related features — of the two economic forms of market and network are outlined.

The market form is designed to facilitate an economically efficient transfer of property rights between highly autonomous sellers and buyers and, as such, market transactions mainly consist of discrete and relatively

Table 1. Some Key Characteristics of Market and Network as Different Forms of Economic Organization.

	Market	Network
	Forms of Economic Organization	
Nature of communication	Discrete	On-going
Means of communication	Prices	Relational
Terms of communication	Clear-cut, complete, and monetized agreement	Open and incomplete
Climate of communication	Precision and/or suspicion	Open-ended
Logic of communication	Persuasion	Trust, shared values
Needs of communication	Negotiation, coordination, and monitoring	Knowledge exchange and socialization
Main threat	Exit	Voice
	Context of Operation Modes	
	Local agent serving the foreign market	Own employees (subsidiary or home-based sales force) serving the foreign market
Main relation to foreign market	Firm → local agent (acts on firm's behalf)	Firm (own employees) → local counterparts
Commitment	Short-term	Long-term
Language barriers	Uncertainty and information asymmetry	Local embeddedness

Sources: Based on Powell (1990) and Ring and van de Ven (1992).

short-term contracts. Ring and van de Ven (1992, p. 485) highlight that the conditions for market transactions "are 'sharp-in,' that is, they are accompanied by a clear-cut, complete, and monetized agreement. They are also 'sharp-out,' that is, the seller's debt of performance and the buyer's debt of payment are unambiguous." In a stylized perfect market, information is freely available, alternative buyers and sellers are easy to come by, and there are no carry-over effects from one transaction to another. The market is open to all comers but, while it brings people together for efficient exchange, it does not establish strong bonds and relationships. As such, markets are a form of noncoercive organization that has coordinating, but not integrative, effects. The participants in a market transaction are free of any future commitments (Powell, 1990; Ring & van de Ven, 1992).

In contrast, network forms of organization carry more open-ended and relational features where trust and shared values are the basis for building stronger network relationships (Powell, 1990). In network forms of resource allocation, the interacting participants exist not by themselves but in relation to other participants. These relationships take considerable effort to establish and sustain. Therefore, there are obvious carry-over effects from one transaction to the other and, as networks evolve, it becomes more economically sensible to exercise voice rather than exit (Powell, 1990).

In the context of foreign operation modes, the economic organizations of market or network can be translated into having a contract-based relation with a local agent or having own employees to serve the foreign market, respectively. The local agent is an independent firm from the host country that takes care of the business and acts on behalf of the entrant firm in the foreign market. When the firm has its own employees to serve the foreign market, these employees can be based in the home country (i.e., home-based sales force) or in a subsidiary in the foreign market.

These operation modes imply different levels of commitment, direct control of foreign activities (Brouthers & Hennart, 2007; Zhao, Luo, & Suh, 2004) as well as different needs and levels of integration in the host environment — that is, the degree of local embeddedness (Forsgren, Holm, & Johanson, 2005) that will be discussed in the section where we scrutinize how exactly the operation modes are related to the use of language and the perception of language barriers. Therefore, the operation modes serve as a context for analyzing the mechanisms that affect the perception of language barrier.

Different Dimensions of Language Differences

Since West and Graham (2004) and Dow and Karunaratna (2006), an increasing number of studies have relied on the concept of *language distance* when analyzing differences between two languages. These studies use a genealogical or genetic[2] method to capture the degree of similarity. By using secondary data, Dow and Karunaratna (2006) develop an elaborate measure that aims to capture the nuances of language differences. Their measure is composed of three indicators that reflect two dimensions of language differences: (1) the degree of relatedness between two languages (language distance), and (2) the degree of knowledge or incidence of one country's major language in another country (language incidence). This operationalization recognizes that there are some dimensions of language differences that alleviate the language barrier perception and overcome the simplicity of previous dummy measurements.

The first indicator, *language distance* (L_1), departs from the genealogical method of categorizing major languages of any two countries in that it calculates the differences between their languages, taking into account to what extent languages are part of a family tree (Dow & Karunaratna, 2006, p. 585). L_1 acknowledges that some languages are structurally more related than others – for example, their sounds, vocabulary, and grammar rules – and that, in such cases, their speakers might perceive a lower language barrier. Relatedness among a pair of languages facilitates their speakers' ability to learn the other language and raises the likelihood that individuals share the same sets of linguistic resources used for communication (Schomaker & Zaheer, 2014). Both mechanisms ease communication and, therefore, might affect the individuals' perception of language barriers.

The second and third indicators (L_2 and L_3) are new in the analysis of language differences and of their effect on IB decisions. Both measures consider the "reported incidence of one country's major language within the other's countries" (Dow & Karunaratna, 2006, p. 585). More specifically, as we are taking home and host countries into account, L_2 captures the proportion of the host-country population that can speak the home-country's main language. L_3 reflects the proportion of the population in the home country that is able to speak the main language of the host country. These two indicators, denoted as *language incidence*, are related to the availability of language-skilled people of the other language in the home and host countries. As such, the higher the language incidence, the easier it is to recruit people with high proficiency in the other language. We argue that language incidence mitigates language barrier perception by different mechanisms than language distance. As language incidence reports the availability of language-skilled people, it affects both the MNCs' language policies and practices (Luo & Shenkar, 2006; Peltokorpi & Vaara, 2012, 2014) and the probability of power/authority distortion when dealing with the external counterparts (Harzing & Pudelko, 2013).

However, most researchers ignore this important distinction between the different dimensions of language (Ambos & Ambos, 2009; Dellestrand & Kappen, 2012; Demirbag et al., 2007; López-Duarte & Vidal-Suárez, 2012; Slangen, Beugelsdijk, & Hennart, 2011). In addition, the extant studies on the effect of language differences do not pay attention to whether the objective (macro) measures of language differences are actually reflecting the managers' perception of language barriers (micro-measures). Along the same line, with the exception of Slangen (2011), there has to our knowledge not been any attempt to delve into the actual mechanism of how exactly language barriers are related to operation modes. Furthermore, many studies include a language variable as a proxy for cultural and other differences but few of them are really outlining the theoretical mechanism of how language barriers are affecting strategic choices.

HYPOTHESES DEVELOPMENT

Network Organization of Foreign Operations

Firms can directly manage overseas operations either through own home-based sales force (e.g., via direct exports) or through their own subsidiaries. Both cases imply establishing relationships with local counterparts and having some commonalities in that they raise several challenges for managers even though we recognize that the differences in commitment and control between these operation modes might have an effect on the ensuing arguments.

When the firm manages directly foreign operations, its managers have to analyze the local environment with the purpose of exploring and exploiting potential sources of competitive advantage. Likewise, they have to establish competitive and cooperative relationships with local partners in a way that not only fits the firm's current needs but also takes the future development of these relationships into account. In this regard, the adoption of a network perspective (Forsgren et al., 2005; Powell, 1990) is useful because it allows us to consider the network members' need for information exchange, coordination, and adaptation if they are to access embedded knowledge. Network relationships take time and effort to establish and evolve, imply carry-over effects, and need complementarity and accommodation among members for achieving one of their important advantages over markets – namely, the access to reliable information (Powell, 1990).

The concept of embeddedness highlights the social element of the economic exchange, and it recognizes the temporal and structural dimensions of networks (Forsgren et al., 2005). However, embeddedness implies social relations and requires relation-specific investments (Forsgren et al., 2005; Uzzi, 1996). In this sense, the establishment of embedded relationships carries specific requirements for communication between the firm and the local network which underpin the social, temporal, and structural dimensions of exchanges. Generating trust and shared values are pivotal for maintaining an open-ended climate in communication (Powell, 1990).

Obviously, language differences are a barrier to communication and a source of misunderstanding that can affect the level of trust in a relationship because they increase uncertainty and suspicion, and reduce credibility (Harzing & Feely, 2008; Henderson, 2005; Schweiger, Atamer, & Calori, 2003). However, not all language dimensions have the same effect irrespective of the context. We argue that language relatedness — or low language distance (L_1 in Dow & Karunaratna, 2006) — can reduce the perception of language as a barrier through two main mechanisms: (1) the relationship between language relatedness and management thinking, and (2) the impact of language distance on informal organization or "shadow structures."

West and Graham (2004) demonstrated the relationship between the language spoken and management thinking. They explained differences in managerial values across countries in terms of differences in the languages spoken. Thus, language relatedness facilitates cultural similarity, and makes it easier to build common shared values and trust between parties. As Schomaker and Zaheer (2014, p. 60) pointed out, linguistic relatedness raises the likelihood that both parties in a communication process have recourse to the same resources (similar words or grammatical constructions) thereby making it less necessary to turn to compensatory strategies — for example, code switching — which slow down communication and reduce trust (Tenzer et al., 2014). On the other hand, linguistic relatedness might have a beneficial effect by improving the self-confidence in the ability to communicate (Schomaker & Zaheer, 2014; Tenzer et al., 2014).

Furthermore, language similarity has an effect on group formation and group identity (Harzing & Feely, 2008; Marschan-Piekkari et al., 1999). As Marschan-Piekkari et al. (1999) showed, when the proximity of the languages spoken by individuals increases, the tendency to engage in informal or shadow relationships also rises. Although their study focused on the context of the relationships within the MNC, the same mechanisms might be expected to lower the perception of language as a barrier in cases of low language distance between the host and home countries. In this sense, similarity among languages can improve the acceptance by local business partners because the foreign managers' ability to understand basic information allows them to follow informal conversations and to interact with local business partners in an informal way, thereby generating some opportunities for engaging in local networks and improving their local embeddedness.

However, we have to distinguish somewhat between the mechanisms applying to one's home-based sales force and to one's own subsidiary. Those firms that attend the host market through a home-based sales force are more compelled to establish their own direct contacts and to learn about business practices and customer preferences as they have to manage operation in the foreign market at a distance. Those firms need to cope with the local differences in a way that generates learning (Puthusserry, Child, & Rodrigues, 2014) and, as such, they rely on network relationships for acquiring local information. If language distance between the home and the host country is low, it can facilitate the communication process and informal engagement. On the basis of this reasoning, we hypothesize:

H1. When firms operate in the foreign market through a home-based sales force, the perception of language as a barrier is lower when language distance is low.

For those firms that establish their own subsidiaries in the host market, the relevance of local embeddedness is substantial and firms develop more committed coping strategies for bridging the differences between markets (Puthusserry et al., 2014). On top of the effect that a low language distance can have on the establishment of network relationships, subsidiaries might be more prone to implement language-sensitive recruitment policies — for example, hiring language-skilled employees or implementing language-training programs for expatriates — that reduce language barriers (Peltokorpi & Vaara, 2012, 2014). As Schomaker and Zaheer (2014) pointed out, the linguistic relatedness between two languages facilitates the learning of the other language because of the overlapping between their syntactic structures and similarity in words, easing the implementation of such policies. Thus, we hypothesize:

H2. When firms operate in the foreign market through own subsidiaries, the perception of language as a barrier is lower when language distance is low.

Market Organization of Foreign Operation

Organizing the foreign operations through markets (e.g., via a local agent) calls for less integrative efforts and more attention to contract negotiation, coordination, and monitoring. Contracts and prizes define market relationships and temporal commitments are clearly identified (Powell, 1990; Ring & van de Ven, 1992). For these reasons, clarity and accuracy in contracts is needed. Under such requirements, the need of precision and the fear of opportunism guide the use of language and the climate of communication.

These main communicative requirements are linked to the necessity of fluent communication with the local agent, which involves the need to conceptualize the terms of the contract, the necessity of being sharp and accurate, and the need to demonstrate argumentative skills when interacting with the local agent. It is known from the literature that managers' lack of rhetorical skills can be a source of uncertainty and information asymmetry that affects their perception about host countries and strategic options (Kang & Kim, 2010; López-Duarte & Vidal-Suárez, 2010).

Given this use of language when dealing with a local agent, we suggest that the perception of language as a barrier depends on the availability of people skilled in the foreign language — the language incidence in Dow and Karunaratna's (2006) measure of language differences. A high incidence of the host-country language in the home country (or the opposite) increases the possibility of hiring people with the necessary language competence as well as finding local counterparts proficient in the home-country language. Several studies demonstrate the empowering and disempowering effects of language skills in MNCs (Brannen, 2004; Harzing, Köster, & Magner, 2011; Henderson, 2005; Peltokorpi & Clausen, 2011; Vaara, Tienari, Piekkari, & Säntti, 2005). On the one hand, language skills are a source of power because people competent in language are in a favorable position. At times, they are even more powerful and dominant than their formal positions imply. This effect is more evident when the organization does not have enough available people with foreign-language skills (Andersen & Rasmussen, 2004). In any case, a low availability of people with foreign-language skills makes language-competent managers a kind of "gate keeper" as they can retain, select, and make decisions about the information they want to transfer (Marschan-Piekkari et al., 1999; Vaara et al., 2005). On the other hand, a lack of skills in the foreign language can be disempowering and can generate power-authority distortion in negotiations (Harzing & Feely, 2008; Vaara et al., 2005). The need to avoid a loss of face or the fact that less-competent managers might lose track of the conversation can create an imbalance in a negotiation or when a firm is monitoring the activities of the local agent.

Both effects — a higher dependence on some intermediaries and a loss of power — are relevant, given that language differences are a source of information asymmetry and external uncertainty (Brouthers & Hennart, 2007; Kang & Kim, 2010). Therefore, we propose that a greater incidence of one country's main language in the other country will reduce the perception of language as an obstacle because the availability of language-competent people enables the firm to be in a more balanced position when negotiating with and monitoring the local firm. Similarly, the prevalence of the foreign language allows the company to be less dependent on specific people who could control the flow of information between the firm and the local agent. Therefore, we hypothesize:

H3. When the firm operates in the foreign market through a local agent, the perception of language as a barrier is lower when there is a greater incidence of one country's main language (home or host country) in the other country (home or host country).

The empirical model that is tested here is illustrated in Fig. 2. The model basically tests how the interaction effects between the operation modes (market or network based) and the dimensions of language differences (language distance and incidence) affect the perception of language barriers. As illustrated in the figure, confirming H1 and H2 implies that the interaction

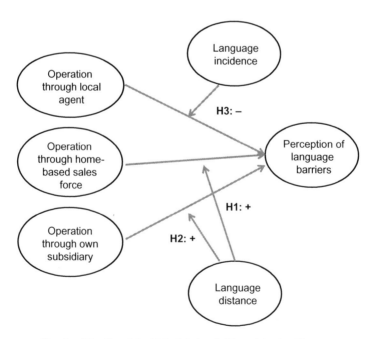

Fig. 2. The Empirical Model that is Tested in the Chapter.

effect between operating through own employees – home-based sales force or own subsidiary – in the foreign market and language distance is positively affecting the perception of language barriers while H3 proposes a negative interaction effect on the perception of language barriers of language incidence and operating through a local agent in the foreign market.

DATA AND METHOD

Data

The data for this study were gathered using a mailed survey that was part of a large international research project "Learning in the Internationalization Process." This project covered Finland, New Zealand, South Korea, and Sweden. The purposes of the survey were to gather data on individual business operations in foreign markets and to identify the learning processes connected with internationalization. These data are particularly suitable for our study because language barriers are one of the key factors investigated when studying the internationalization process. The data are unique in the sense that they capture managers' perception of language barriers related to a specific foreign operation rather than language barriers in general such as barriers related to total activities and general behavior in a country. In addition, the four countries included in the study are suitable from a genealogical perspective. For example, English and Swedish are part of the same family of Germanic languages, but the physical distance between New Zealand and Sweden is significant. Finnish and Korean are relatively isolated languages, even when compared to their neighboring countries. Sweden and Finland are neighboring countries but they are very far from each other in terms of language distance. Taken together, the four countries and their international activities represent substantial variation on the studied language dimensions.

A pilot study was conducted in which 10 managers were asked to respond to a questionnaire in an interview situation. Subsequently, the final, standardized questionnaire was sent out in all four countries to firms that were involved in international operations (i.e., firms with exports or subsidiaries abroad). The firms were identified through the business directories for each country (such as *Dun & Bradstreet* and *Kompass*) that listed the international operations of firms. All firms in which exports represented more than 10 percent of total sales, and that had between 50 and 200 employees were selected. This population was chosen because the foreign operation was of significance to the firm (the size criterion) and due to their active involvement in foreign markets, which exposed them to the "liability of foreignness" and potential language barriers (substantial sales abroad). The questionnaire was addressed to the person in charge of the firm's IB operations as this manager was deemed to be a key person in the firm's internationalization process. Executives actually engaged in the foreign operations of the firm, typically CEOs or COOs, supplied the information. A reminder and a new copy of the questionnaire were sent three weeks after the initial mailing.

Useable responses were received from 390 firms, with 94, 123, 88, and 85 responses from Finland, Sweden, South Korea, and New Zealand, respectively. The net response rate ranged from 32 percent for Sweden to 14 percent for South Korea. The local agent was chosen as the operation mode in the foreign market in 149 cases (38%), while home-based sales force was preferred in 131 cases (34%), and a subsidiary in 110 cases (28%).

A test was conducted to check the sample for possible nonresponse bias. In terms of size, exports, and industry (data obtainable from the business directories for the whole population), no statistically significant differences were found between respondents and nonrespondents, which suggests that our data is not affected by a significant nonresponse bias.

At the beginning of the questionnaire, respondents were asked to select one recent business operation in a foreign market (e.g., entering a new market, signing a new contract with an agent, or undertaking a considerable expansion of an existing business in a foreign market). The operation was to be important to the firm and its international expansion. Most of the subsequent questions in the questionnaire were related to this particular self-selected foreign operation. Each firm provided a response for only one (self-selected) foreign-market business operation. Thus, the home country referred to the firm's origin country while the host country referred to the location of the selected foreign operation.

Dependent Variable

The *language barriers* variable captures the managers' perception of language as an impediment to IB activities. More specifically, respondents were asked to indicate whether a "lack of knowledge of the host country's language is an obstacle when making and executing the chosen assignment abroad" on seven-point Likert scale (1 = fully disagree and 7 = fully agree). This implies that the extent of language as a barrier is indicated for the specific foreign operation of interest but and not for other activities conducted in the foreign country.

Independent Variables

We apply two language variables to reflect different dimensions of language differences: language distance and language incidence. The *language distance* variable is taken from Dow and Karunaratna (2006), who operationalize it as a five-point measure that focuses on the distance between the major languages of any two countries. The classification is based on Grimes and Grimes (1996), who classify 6,809 languages into families, branches, and sub-branches. The language distance between isolated languages, such as Finnish and Korean, is greater (value of 5 on the language-distance scale) than for languages such as English and Swedish (value of 3 on the language-distance scale), which belong to the same (Germanic) branch of languages.

The *language incidence* measure acknowledges the heterogeneity of languages within countries. Language distance might not be the best reflection of communication barriers if there is a large group of people in one country that speak the language of the other country. Finland and Sweden serve to illustrate this point – although the language distance between Finnish and Swedish is huge, there is a significant proportion of people in Finland who speak Swedish. As a result, the language distance between the Swedish-speaking people in Finland and Sweden is minimal. The language incidence variable is also taken from Dow and Karunaratna (2006) and it is measured as the proportion of the population in one country who are able to speak the main language of another country (on a scale from 1 to 5). In this case, we use the average of the incidences of country i's main language(s) in country j and country j's main language(s) in country I (the average of L_2 and L_3 in Dow & Karunaratna, 2006).

As shown in the correlation matrix (Table 3), although the two dimensions of language difference are distinguishable, they are also highly correlated with a correlation coefficient of 0.55. In addition, the means of the two language variables are shown for the four countries in Table 2. Here, the variation in the two language dimensions is obvious among the four countries. The means for both language variables are significantly different across the four countries at the 0.1 percent level of significance.

Table 2. Means and Analysis of Variance in the Language Variables for the Four Home Countries[a].

	Finland	New Zealand	South Korea	Sweden	*F-Value*
Language distance	4.89 (A)	2.58 (C)	5.00 (A)	3.51 (B)	153.34***
Language incidence	1.52 (B)	3.37 (A)	1.00 (B)	1.15 (B)	173.00***

Notes: [a]The letters are Duncan groupings in the analysis of variance. The letter "A" indicates the highest value, "B" is significantly (10%) lower than A, and so forth.
***indicates significance at the 0.1% level.

The language distance is much higher for Korean and Finnish, which are rather isolated languages while language distance for English (New Zealand) is clearly the lowest and Swedish lies in the middle. On the language-incidence dimension, Korean and Swedish are lowest since no other languages are regularly spoken in South Korea and Sweden. Finland's score is slightly higher, as Swedish is a minority language in Finland, and New Zealand is significantly higher since English is spoken by more people.

Controls

We added a number of variables to control for other factors that might influence the perception of language barriers. First we included whether *English* is the main language of the host country as a binary variable (No = 0, Yes = 1). As English has become a global business language and as people with sufficient English language skills are available in almost every country, we encounter a special case when the main language of the host country is English. The availability of managers with fluent knowledge of English is usually high due to the fact that knowledge of English is often part of managers' career-development paths — master courses and training programs are taught in English, and English proficiency is often a requirement for becoming an international manager. As Steyaert, Ostendorp, and Gaibrois (2011) highlighted, a simplified version of English is often used for global communication in non-English-speaking firms.

We also included variables that had been related to the host-country barriers perception such as the firm's previous experience in the country or the duration of the operation (Petersen et al., 2008). We expected both controls to be negatively related to perceived language barriers since they allow for manager's learning and the development of "bridging strategies" (Child et al., 2009). These two control variables were operationalized in the following way: the *duration* of the focal operation (as a logarithm of the number of years) and whether the firm has conducted *prior operation in the same market* (dummy, Yes = 1).

An additional variable controlled for the firm's general *international experience*. This multi-item measure covers items such as international experience in management, product adaptations, and collaboration with other firms (6 items measured on a seven-point Likert scale where 1 = low experience and 7 = high experience). We expected a negative relationship with language barriers due to the learning effect.

Two other control variables were related to the relationship between the firm and the customers: prior knowledge of customer and the customer adaptation. The firm's *prior knowledge of the customer(s)* can have a negative impact on the language barrier as it implies an established relationship with the customer that can mitigate misunderstandings. Regarding the extent to which the firm needs to *adapt its offering* to its customer(s), we expect a positive relationship with language barriers since it asks for more accuracy in the communication process. Both variables are measured on a seven-point Likert scale (1 = no prior knowledge/no adaptation and 7 = substantial prior knowledge/substantial adaptation).

Three additional control variables were included to capture decision-makers' perceptions of cultural distance related to the foreign market: a lack of *knowledge about business practices, business laws*, and *business culture* (all measured on seven-point Likert scales where 1 = lack of knowledge was not an obstacle and 7 = lack of knowledge was a very important obstacle). As shown in Table 3, these three cultural distance variables are highly correlated, with binary correlation coefficients of 0.48–0.59. The cultural distance variables should be positively related to the perceived language distance because the perception of cultural distance should go hand-in-hand with the perception of language as an obstacle (Harzing & Maznevski, 2002; West & Graham, 2004). This measure of cultural distance is favorable to many other potential measures like (macro) cultural distance indices as it captures the actual managers' perception (the micro-level measure) of the business relevant cultural distance (i.e., the lack of knowledge of business practice, laws, and culture).

Finally, we included two control variables for variation in the institutional environment in the host countries. These control variables were based on secondary data as we apply two World Bank Governance Indicators (Kaufmann, Kraay, & Mastruzzi, 2005) on regulatory quality and the control of corruption. The argument for including these control variables is that the perception of language barriers might also be affected

Table 3. Correlation Matrix ($N = 390$)[a].

	1	2	3	4	5	6	7	8	9	10	11	12	13	14
1) Language barriers	1.00													
2) Language distance	0.12	1.00												
3) Language incidence	-0.03	0.55	1.00											
4) English	-0.11	-0.47	-0.43	1.00										
5) Duration of operation (logarithm)	-0.04	0.34	0.21	-0.01	1.00									
6) Previous operations	-0.01	-0.03	-0.01	0.05	0.02	1.00								
7) Prior knowledge of customer	-0.09	0.05	-0.04	0.12	0.34	0.18	1.00							
8) Customer adaptation	-0.01	0.07	0.13	-0.10	0.02	0.02	0.03	1.00						
9) International experience of the firm	-0.05	-0.01	0.01	0.06	0.02	0.06	0.03	-0.05	1.00					
10) Lack of knowledge of business practice	0.45	0.06	-0.12	0.03	0.09	-0.01	0.08	0.05	0.03	1.00				
11) Lack of knowledge of business laws	0.51	0.13	-0.04	0.01	0.02	0.08	0.13	0.05	-0.01	0.52	1.00			
12) Lack of knowledge of business culture	0.46	0.05	-0.09	0.01	0.07	0.03	0.10	0.04	-0.01	0.59	0.48	1.00		
13) Regulatory quality	-0.20	-0.34	0.27	0.35	-0.25	0.03	0.07	-0.01	0.01	0.11	0.22	0.08	1.00	
14) Control of corruption	-0.19	-0.38	0.27	0.42	-0.22	0.06	0.09	0.04	0.01	0.15	0.25	0.12	0.59	1.00
Mean	3.84	3.80	4.61	0.34	1.54	0.63	3.73	4.03	4.61	3.99	4.04	3.95	0.76	0.97
Standard deviation	1.71	1.42	1.01	0.48	1.53	0.48	2.16	1.86	1.03	1.80	1.68	1.77	0.85	1.09
Min. values	1	1	1.5	0	-2.3	0	1	1	1	1	1	1	-2.2	-1.2
Max. values	7	5	5	1	4.6	1	7	7	7	7	7	7	2.2	2.3

Notes: [a]All values above 0.10 are significant at the 5% level.

by the quality and effectiveness of institutions in the country — and we expect these variables to be negatively related to perception of language barriers.

Common method bias is an obvious limitation of survey-based data such as the ones used here. However, we did combine the primary data with secondary data (as suggested by Chang, van Witteloostuijn, & Eden, 2010) since our independent variables of language distance and language incidence as well as the English dummy and our two institutional control variables are based on secondary data. In order to further address this issue, the questionnaire included different scales, some of which were reversed, which diminishes the risk of biases. In addition, we performed a number of statistical analyses to assess the severity of common method bias. This included a Harman's one-factor test that indicated that common methods bias was not an issue since multiple factors were detected and the variance did not stem merely from a single factor (Podsakoff & Organ, 1986). In fact, the 17 variables included in the analyses form five factors with an eigenvalue > 1, and the first two factors only capture 23 and 19 percent of the total variance, respectively. We also applied a confirmatory factor analysis to test whether a single factor accounted for all of the variance in the data, as suggested by Podsakoff, MacKenzie, Lee, and Podsakoff (2003). The goodness-of-fit of the single-factor model (GFI = 0.58, NNFI = 0.03, and RMSEA = 0.22), including all normally distributed items in the model, shows that the single-factor model offers a poor representation of the data, which indicates that a common variance factor does not explain a sizeable portion of the variation in our data.

RESULTS

Correlations

The descriptive data (means, standard deviations, and minimum and maximum values) and the correlation matrix (including binary correlation coefficients) for all of the variables are provided in Table 3. As expected, the two language dimensions are highly correlated, as are the three cultural distance variables and the two institutional variables. All other variables are correlated to a minor or moderate extent (i.e., coefficients below 0.5), which indicates that the data do not suffer from major multicollinearity issues.

Ordinary Least-Square Models

Our dependent variable (measured on a seven-point Likert scale) is suitable for a parametric statistical analysis, such as ordinary least square (OLS). Since our models include a number of interaction effects that are correlated (by design), we ran different alternative versions of the model in order to tease out the effect of adding each of the interaction effects. More specifically, we estimated four OLS models to test our hypotheses and theoretical framework. The first model (Model 0) only includes the 11 control variables and, among these, only two − lack of knowledge of business practice and lack of knowledge of business laws − come out significant. The next three models (Model 1−3) include separately for each of the three operation modes the interaction effect between the operation mode and the two language variables. Model 1 includes the interaction effects with home-based sales force (with the two other operation modes excluded as the base line), Model 2 with local agent, and Model 3 with own subsidiary. These models provide information on how the operation modes interact with the two language dimensions in affecting the perceived language barrier for each operation mode. Model 4 which contains the ultimate test of our hypotheses since it includes the interaction terms both with home-based sales force and with own subsidiary, and with the local agent that is left out as the base case (implying that results should be interpreted in comparison with this base line).

Below there are shown the equations for the four models, where LB = language barriers, LD = language distance, LI = language incidence, hb = home-based sales force, la = local agent, and os = own subsidiary:

Model 1: $LB = a_0 + (a_1*LD) + (a_2*LI) + (a_3*LD*hb) + (a_4*LI*hb) + (a_5*hb) + controls$

Model 2: $LB = b_0 + (b_1*LD) + (b_2*LI) + (b_3*LD*la) + (b_4*LI*la) + (b_5*la) + controls$

Model 3: $LB = c_0 + (c_1*LD) + (c_2*LI) + (c_3*LD*os) + (c_4*LI*os) + (c_5*os) + controls$

Model 4: $LB = d_0 + (d_1*LD) + (d_2*LI) + (d_3*LD*hb) + (d_4*LI*hb) + (d_5*LD*os) + (d_6*LI*os) + (d_7*hb) + (d_8*os) + controls$

Our expectations are that b_4 (Model 2) turns negative, signifying that language incidence interacts with the operation mode of the local agent in affecting perception of language barriers (H3), and that a_3 and c_3 are

Table 4. Results of OLS Models (Standard Errors in Parentheses)[a].

	Model 0	Model 1	Model 2	Model 3	Model 4
Language distance (a_1, b_1, c_1, and d_1)		0.21* (0.10)	0.06 (0.12)	0.20 (0.11)	0.38** (0.13)
Language incidence (a_2, b_2, c_2, and d_2)		−0.28* (0.14)	−0.02 (0.16)	−0.23 (0.14)	−0.43** (0.17)
Home-based sales force (a_5 and d_7)		0.82 (0.76)			0.85 (0.79)
Local agent (b_5)			−0.41 (0.68)		
Own subsidiary (c_5 and d_8)				−0.60 (0.91)	−0.32 (0.94)
Language distance × Home-based sales force (a_3 and d_3)		0.52** (0.17)			0.50** (0.18)
Language incidence × Home-based sales force (a_4 and d_4)		−0.32 (0.20)			−0.57* (0.25)
Language distance × Local agent (b_3)			0.35* (0.15)		
Language incidence × Local agent (b_4)			−0.46** (0.21)		
Language distance × Own subsidiary (c_3 and d_5)				0.47** (0.16)	0.43** (0.18)
Language incidence × Own subsidiary (c_4 and d_6)				−0.09 (0.25)	0.30 (0.27)
Control variables					
English	0.28 (0.16)	0.29 (0.19)	0.33 (0.19)	0.35 (0.19)	0.32 (0.19)
Duration of operation	0.01 (0.05)	0.03 (0.06)	0.02 (0.06)	0.03 (0.06)	0.02 (0.07)
Previous operations	−0.10 (0.15)	−0.12 (0.15)	−0.13 (0.15)	−0.12 (0.15)	−0.13 (0.15)
Prior knowledge of customer	0.01 (0.03)	0.01 (0.04)	−0.01 (0.03)	−0.01 (0.03)	0.01 (0.04)
Customer adaptation	−0.01 (0.04)	−0.02 (0.04)	−0.02 (0.03)	−0.01 (0.04)	−0.02 (0.04)
International experience of the firm	0.06 (0.07)	0.06 (0.07)	0.05 (0.07)	0.08 (0.07)	0.07 (0.07)
Lack of knowledge of business practice	0.35*** (0.06)	0.33*** (0.06)	0.34*** (0.06)	0.33*** (0.06)	0.34*** (0.06)
Lack of knowledge of business laws	0.43*** (0.06)	0.42*** (0.06)	0.43*** (0.06)	0.42*** (0.06)	0.43*** (0.06)
Lack of knowledge of business culture	0.08 (0.08)	0.07 (0.08)	0.08 (0.07)	0.07 (0.08)	0.08 (0.07)
Regulatory quality	−0.29 (0.18)	−0.34 (0.18)	−0.33 (0.18)	−0.32 (0.18)	−0.33 (0.18)

Table 4.   (*Continued*)

	Model 0	Model 1	Model 2	Model 3	Model 4
Control of corruption	−0.18	−0.23	−0.24	−0.24	−0.23
	(0.14)	(0.15)	(0.15)	(0.15)	(0.15)
Intercept	0.66	0.25	0.60	0.33	0.12
	(0.41)	(0.67)	(0.70)	(0.56)	(0.60)
N	390	390	390	390	390
F-value	18.37***	16.58***	17.06***	16.42***	14.43***
R-square	0.37	0.42	0.42	0.41	0.43

Notes: [a] *, **, and *** indicate significance at the 5%, 1%, and 0.1% levels, respectively.

positive, indicating that language distance interacts with the operation modes of home-based sales force (H1) and own subsidiary (H2). In Model 4, the confirmation of H1 and H2 would require that d_3 and d_5 are significantly positive. Table 4 shows the results of the OLS models.

We further tested for multicollinearity by including the variance inflation factor (VIF) in the models. The values for the VIF are all within the typical threshold, (i.e., less than 6) (Hair, Anderson, Tatham, & Black, 1995) since the highest VIF value is 3.98. In addition, we ran the models while excluding the variables with the highest VIF values, and obtained qualitatively similar results. This provides further evidence that multicollinearity is not a major problem.

When looking across the four models (in Table 4), the main effect of language distance (a_1, b_1, c_1, and d_1) is generally positively related (β vary between 0.06 and 0.38) while the main effect of language incidence (a_2, b_2, c_2, and d_2) is negatively related to the perception of language barriers (β vary between −0.43 and −0.02) as expected. However, it is also clear that the main effect of the two language dimensions show noteworthy variation across the four models, which provide some support to the argument that the importance of the two dimensions varies with the context of the operation mode.

The interaction effects between the operation modes and language distance (a_3, b_3, and c_3) are significant and positive for all three operation modes (and not just for home-based sales force and own subsidiary). However, the coefficients are larger and more significant for home-based sales force (β = 0.52, $p < 0.01$) and for own subsidiary (β = 0.47, $p < 0.01$) than for local agent (β = 0.35, $p < 0.05$).

On the contrary, for the interaction effects between the operation modes and language incidence (a_4, b_4, and c_4), the coefficient is highly significant and negative (as expected) for the local agent ($\beta = -0.46$, $p < 0.01$), while it is insignificant for both home-based sales force ($\beta = -0.32$, $p = 0.08$), and own subsidiary ($\beta = -0.09$, $p = 0.73$). This result confirms our Hypothesis 3 that serving a foreign market through a local agent will require access to language-skilled people and that the availability of these people that master the foreign language with high accuracy will affect the managers' perception of language barriers.

Our first and second hypothesis are tested in Model 4 and, as expected, the interaction effects between language distance and the two operation modes of home-based sales force and own subsidiary (d_3 and d_5) are positive and highly significant with $\beta = 0.50$ ($p < 0.01$) for home-based sales force and $\beta = 0.43$ ($p < 0.01$) for own subsidiary. Since the local agent is the excluded base line in Model 4, the results imply that language distance is much more important in determining the perception of language barriers in the case of using one's own employees rather than a local agent − which is basically confirming our Hypotheses 1 and 2. More specifically, language distance or language relatedness is the key for understanding the perception of language barrier when the foreign operation relies on a home-based sales force or own subsidiary. In such cases, similarity between speakers' native languages can help in reducing the perception of language barrier.

It is also noteworthy that, by themselves, the operation modes (the main effects of operation modes − a_5, b_5, c_5, d_7, and d_8) are not significantly affecting the perception of language barriers. It is only when the language needs that come with the operation modes are combined with the availability of people with the right language skills that they influence the perceived language barriers.

Of the control variables, the most significant are those related to lack of knowledge of business practices and business laws. As expected, these two variables are positively and significantly related to the perceived language barriers. This increases our confidence that we are actually measuring the perception of language barriers rather than general perceptions of the liability of foreignness in the foreign market, as we effectively control for the latter through these perceptual variables. This is further reinforced by two other control variables "Regulatory quality" and "English" (spoken in the host country) that are both negatively related to the perceived language barriers (and marginally significant at the 10% level), which indicate that managers perceive fewer language barriers in countries with high regulatory quality and where English is widely spoken.

The R-square for the four models are in the range of $0.41-0.43$, indicating that more than two fifth of the variation in the perceived language barriers is explained by our model. These figures are highly satisfactory. In addition, we conducted a number of robustness checks. First, we ran the models individually for each of the four home countries. The results were qualitatively the same, albeit with less significant coefficients due to the lower number of observations in each of these analyses. Second, we ran a multinomial logit model, given the character of our dependent variable. The results were also the same in qualitative terms.

DISCUSSION AND CONCLUSION

Much of the extant literature highlights language as a source of psychic distance and as a barrier to IB. This literature takes language barriers as an exogenous given variable that is formed independently of the IB context. However, as shown in this chapter, the perception of language barriers is not independent of, but rather affected by, the IB context. Here, we have shown how the contexts of operation modes together with aspects of language differences form the perception of language barriers. Our models explain no less than 40 percent of the variation in manager's perception of language barriers.

In addition, the literature tends to analyze language on an aggregated level and it often proposes a simple linear relationship in which increasing language differences impose barriers, result in greater risk, and higher costs of conducting business abroad (Demirbag et al., 2007; Dow & Larimo, 2011; López-Duarte & Vidal-Suárez, 2010, 2012; Slangen, 2011). In our view, these studies suffer from a linearity illusion as established by Shenkar (2001) for cultural-distance measures. In comparison, few studies focus on the disaggregation of language differences and the individual dimensions of such differences. As a consequence, the exact mechanisms through which language diversity affects IB have remained undefined.

Most empirical studies that analyze the role of language as a barrier view "language differences" as a homogeneous barrier with scalable effects. Such studies fail to consider the various nuances or shades of the concept, and how those nuances can play different roles in the perception of language as a barrier. By adopting the more nuanced measure of language differences (Dow & Karunaratna, 2006), we show that language differences are not just a matter of extent, but also a matter of type and context.

Language is multifaceted and its use serves different purposes, including communication of exact information and the facilitation of common understanding and trust. Language is not used in the same way in all contexts since the relevant dimension of language differences varies by context. In this study, we show that different language dimensions affect the perception of language barriers to varying degrees depending on the context in which language is being used.

Our analysis of markets and networks as main forms of organizing the firm's relationships with host-country environment has allowed us to establish the communicative requirements that the mode of market and network entail and to link them with the use of language and the perception of language barriers. In this regard, we theoretically deconstruct the concept of language differences and contribute to a better understanding of the mechanisms through which language dimensions matter (Zaheer et al., 2012).

We argue that the distinctive characteristics of markets and networks affect differently the way language is used. Organizing foreign operations through a local agent (i.e., the market form) places different communicative demands on the firm than operating abroad through one's own employees (subsidiaries or home-based sales force). A local agent reduces the need to deal directly with the local environment but entails a risk of dependence on that agent because of information asymmetry (e.g., specific knowledge of the focal market's development) and the distribution of power. In such a case, being sharp and accurate in language during the process of negotiation and monitoring of the contract, having rhetorical skills and persuasion ability, and reducing the dependence of gate-keepers and information nodes are prevalent requirements. In the case of using one's own employees to communicate directly with counterparts in the foreign market, the challenge is to establish on-going relationships where trust and shared values are facilitating the on-going communications.

Basically, the differences in communicative requirements or use of language for the local agent versus one's own employees imply a need for different language skills. The availability of people with the needed language skills is affecting managers' perception of language barriers. In brief, one can say that the needed language skills when operating through a local agent are related to the full professional proficiency in the foreign language (high language incidence) while it is more about similarity in language (low language distance) when own employees communicate directly with counterparts in the foreign market.

This is manifested in the significance of the interaction effect between the operation mode of local agent and language incidence (availability of people native in the foreign language) and the interaction effect between using one's own employees and language distance (similarity in language between home and host country).

From a methodological perspective, this is the first study we know that analyzes how secondary data on language differences impact primary and perceptual measures of language as a barrier. Studies that rely on measures for language differences based on secondary data can suffer from inadequacy problems similar to those seen with other measures – such as Hofstede's index for cultural distance (Shenkar, 2001, 2012; Shenkar, Luo, & Yeheskel, 2008; Zhao et al., 2004), which could lead to a failure to consider the subtleties of the language-barrier perception. This is one problem detected by Dow and Karunaratna (2006), who stated that "an important starting point would be to confirm the relationship between the various psychic distance stimuli and people's perceptions of psychic distance" (Dow & Karunaratna, 2006, p. 595). In our study, we provide some insight into this question by scrutinizing one of the least-analyzed psychic distance factors – namely, language. We show that the relationship between secondary measures of differences in languages and the perception of language as an obstacle is significant and has the expected sign. The R-square for the applied models allows us to explain more than two fifth of the variation in the perceived language barriers, which is highly satisfactory. In addition, one of the unique features of our data is that they cover the managers' perceptions of language barriers as related to a specific foreign operation. In this regard, we go beyond the studies that use general macro-level data on language barriers.

Studies such as this one suffer from a number of limitations that hint at possible avenues for further research. First, this study only begins to open the black box of micro-level studies on language differences. Future research should expand this line of research by including additional contexts (e.g., more operation modes) and by delving deeper into the understanding of the various communicative requirements. Second, our work deals with Luo and Shenkar's (2006) suggestion that context-specificity of language is included in studies of IB but it does not allow us to analyze content-specific aspects of the operation mode. Thus, the type of activity (e.g., manufacturing, R&D, or sales), its level of codification, and the necessity of local adaptation emerge as content characteristics that could moderate the communicative requirements associated with different operation modes.

NOTES

1. The hierarchical form where host environment relations are internalized and governed through administrative procedures and work rules is really not an option

to be considered in this case — as the focus is on the language barriers that the firms face when communicating with external counterparts and no firm can internalize all their counterparts in foreign markets.

2. Genealogical or genetic classification groups and classifies languages depending on the degree of similarity based in the existence or inference of common linguistic ancestors. So, languages belonging to the same group have genealogical affinity, implying grammatical, and lexical similarity (Chen, Sokal, & Ruhlen, 1995; West & Graham, 2004).

ACKNOWLEDGMENT

We appreciate the support from research projects ECO2013 — 43196 — R (Spanish Ministry of Science and technology) and Center for Research in Innovation, Organization and Strategy (CRIOS), Bocconi University.

REFERENCES

Ambos, T. C., & Ambos, B. (2009). The impact of distance on knowledge transfer effectiveness in multinational corporations. *Journal of International Management, 15*, 1–14.

Andersen, H., & Rasmussen, E. (2004). The role of language skills in corporate communication. *Corporate Communications: An International Journal, 19*(3), 231–242.

Benito, G., Petersen, B., & Welch, L. S. (2009). Towards more realistic conceptualisations of foreign operation modes. *Journal of International Business Studies, 40*, 1455–1470.

Björkman, A., & Piekkari, R. (2009). Language and foreign subsidiary control: An empirical test. *Journal of International Management, 15*, 105–117.

Brannen, M. Y. (2004). When Mickey loses face: Recontextualization, semantic fit, and the semiotics of foreignness. *Academy of Management Review, 29*(4), 593–616.

Brouthers, K. D., & Hennart, J.-F. (2007). Boundaries of the firm: Insights from international entry mode research. *Journal of Management, 33*(3), 395–425.

Chang, S.-J., van Witteloostuijn, A., & Eden, L. (2010). From the editors: Common method variance in international business research. *Journal of International Business Studies, 41*(2), 178–184.

Chen, J., Sokal, R. R., & Ruhlen, M. (1995). Worldwide analysis of genetic and linguistic relationships of human populations. *Human Biology, 67*(4), 595–612.

Child, J., Rodrigues, S. B., & Frynas, J. G. (2009). Psychic distance, its impact and coping modes. Interpretations of SME decision makers. *Management International Review, 49*, 199–224.

Dellestrand, H., & Kappen, P. (2012). The effects of spatial and contextual factors of headquarters resource allocation to MNE subsidiaries. *Journal of International Business Studies, 43*, 219–243.

Demirbag, M., Glaister, K. W., & Tatoglu, E. (2007). Institutional and transaction cost influences on MNEs' ownership strategies of their affiliates: Evidence from an emerging market. *Journal of World Business, 42*, 418–434.

Dow, D., & Ferencikova, S. (2010). More than just national cultural distance: Testing new distance scales on FDI in Slovakia. *International Business Review, 19*, 46–58.

Dow, D., & Karunaratna, A. (2006). Developing a multidimensional instrument to measure psychic distance stimuli. *Journal of International Business Studies, 37*, 278–602.

Dow, D., & Larimo, J. (2011). Disentangling the roles of international experience and distance in establishment mode choice. *Management International Review, 51*, 321–355.

Forsgren, M., Holm, U., & Johanson, J. (2005). *Managing the embedded multinational. A business network view*. Northampton: Edward Elgar.

Grimes, J. E., & Grimes, B. F. (Eds.). (1996). *Ethnologue: Language family index*. Dallas, TX: Summer Institute of Linguistics.

Hair, J. F., Anderson, R. E., Tatham, R. L., & Black, W. C. (1995). *Multivariate data analysis with readings*. Englewood Cliffs, NJ: Prentice-Hall.

Håkanson, L., & Ambos, B. (2010). The antecedents of psychic distance. *Journal of International Management, 16*, 195–210.

Harzing, A.-W., & Feely, A. (2008). The language barrier and its implications for HQ-subsidiary relationships. *Cross Cultural Management: An International Journal, 15*(1), 49–61.

Harzing, A.-W., Köster, K., & Magner, V. (2011). Babel in business: The language barrier and its solutions in the HQ-subsidiary relationship. *Journal of World Business, 46*(3), 279–287.

Harzing, A.-W., & Maznevski, M. (2002). The interaction between language and culture: A test of the cultural accommodation hypothesis in seven countries. *Language and Intercultural Communication, 2*(2), 120–139.

Harzing, A.-W., & Pudelko, M. (2013). Language competencies, policies and practices in multinational corporations: A comprehensive review and comparison of Anglophone, Asian, Continental European and Nordic MNCs. *Journal of World Business, 48*(1), 87–97.

Henderson, J. K. (2005). Language diversity in international management teams. *International Studies of Organization & Management, 35*(2), 66–82.

Kang, J.-K., & Kim, J.-M. (2010). Do foreign investors exhibit a corporate governance disadvantage? An information asymmetry perspective. *Journal of International Business Studies, 41*, 1415–1438.

Kaufmann, D., Kraay, A., & Mastruzzi, M. (2005). *Governance matters IV: Governance indicators for 1996–2004*. World Bank Policy Research Working Paper, 3630.

López-Duarte, C., & Vidal-Suárez, M. M. (2010). External uncertainty and entry mode choice: Cultural distance, political risk and language diversity. *International Business Review, 19*(6), 575–588.

López-Duarte, C., & Vidal-Suárez, M. M. (2012). Cultural distance and the choice between wholly owned subsidiaries and joint ventures. *Journal of Business Research, 11*, 2252–2261.

Luo, Y., & Shenkar, O. (2006). The multinational corporation as a multilingual community: Language and organization in a global context. *Journal of International Business Studies, 37*, 321–339.

Mäkelä, K., Andersson, U., & Seppälä, T. (2012). Interpersonal similarity and knowledge sharing within multinational organizations. *International Business Review, 21*, 439–451.

Marschan-Piekkari, R., Welch, D., & Welch, L. (1999). In the shadow: The impact of language on structure, power and communication in the multinational. *International Business Review, 8*, 421–440.

Nebus, J., & Chai, K. H. (2014). Putting the "psychic" back in psychic distance: Awareness, perceptions, and understanding as dimensions of psychic distance. *Journal of International Management, 20*, 8—24.

Peltokorpi, V., & Clausen, L. (2011). Linguistic and cultural barriers to intercultural communication in foreign subsidiaries. *Asian Business & Management, 10*(4), 509—528.

Peltokorpi, V., & Vaara, E. (2012). Language policies and practices in wholly owned foreign subsidiaries: A recontextualization perspective. *Journal of International Business Studies, 43*(9), 808—833.

Peltokorpi, V., & Vaara, E. (2014). Knowledge transfer in multinational corporations: Productive and counterproductive effects of language-sensitive recruitment. *Journal of International Business Studies, 45*(5), 600—623.

Petersen, B., Pedersen, T., & Lyles, M. (2008). Closing knowledge gaps in foreign markets. *Journal of International Business Studies, 39*, 1097—1113.

Podsakoff, P. M., MacKenzie, S. B., Lee, J.-Y., & Podsakoff, N. P. (2003). Common method biases in behavioral research: A critical review of the literature and recommended remedies. *Journal of Applied Psychology, 88*(5), 879—903.

Podsakoff, P. M., & Organ, D. W. (1986). Self-reports in organizational research: Problems and prospects. *Journal of Management, 12*, 531—544.

Powell, W. P. (1990). Neither market nor hierarchy: Network forms of organization. *Research in Organizational Behavior, 12*, 295—336.

Puthusserry, N. P., Child, J., & Rodrigues, S. B. (2014). Psychic distance, its business impact and modes of coping: A study of British and Indian partner SMEs. *Management International Review, 54*, 1—29.

Ring, P. S., & van de Ven, A. H. (1992). Structuring cooperative relationships between organizations. *Strategic Management Journal, 13*, 483—498.

Schomaker, M., & Zaheer, S. (2014). The role of language in knowledge transfer to geographically dispersed manufacturing operations. *Journal of International Management, 20*, 55—72.

Schweiger, D. M., Atamer, T., & Calori, R. (2003). Transnational project teams and networks: Making the multinational organization more effective. *Journal of World Business, 38*(2), 127—140.

Shenkar, O. (2001). Cultural distance revisited: Towards a more rigorous conceptualization and measurement of cultural differences. *Journal of International Business Studies, 32*, 519—536.

Shenkar, O. (2012). Beyond cultural distance: Switching to a friction lens in the study of cultural differences. *Journal of International Business Studies, 43*, 12—17.

Shenkar, O., Luo, Y., & Yeheskel, O. (2008). Form distance to friction: Substituting metaphors and redirecting intercultural research. *Academy of Management Review, 33*(4), 905—923.

Slangen, A. H. L. (2011). A communication-based theory of the choice between greenfield and acquisition entry. *Journal of Management Studies, 48*(8), 1699—1726.

Slangen, A. H. L., Beugelsdijk, S., & Hennart, J. F. (2011). The impact of cultural distance on bilateral arm's length exports. *Management International Review, 51*, 875—896.

Steyaert, C., Ostendorp, A., & Gaibrois, C. (2011). Multinational organizations as 'linguascapes': Negotiating the position of English through discursive practices. *Journal of World Business, 46*, 270—278.

Tenzer, H., Pudelko, M., & Harzing, A. W. (2014). The impact of language barriers on trust formation in multinational teams. *Journal of International Business Studies*, *45*(5), 508–536.

Uzzi, B. (1996). The sources and consequences of embeddedness for the economic performance of organizations: The network effect. *American Sociological Review*, *61*(4), 674–698.

Vaara, E., Tienari, J., Piekkari, R., & Säntti, R. (2005). Language and the circuits of power in a merging multinational corporation. *Journal of Management Studies*, *42*(3), 595–623.

Welch, D. E., & Welch, L. S. (2008). The importance of language in international knowledge transfer. *Management International Review*, *48*(3), 339–360.

West, J., & Graham, J. L. (2004). A linguistic-based measure of cultural distance and its relationship to managerial values. *Management International Review*, *44*(3), 239–260.

Zaheer, A., Schomaker, M. S., & Nachum, L. (2012). Distance without direction: Restoring credibility to a much-loved construct. *Journal of International Business Studies*, *43*, 18–27.

Zhao, H., Luo, Y., & Suh, T. (2004). Transaction cost determinants and ownership-based entry mode choice: A meta-analytical review. *Journal of International Business Studies*, *35*(6), 524–544.

THE NEXT STEP IN GOVERNANCE: THE NEED FOR GLOBAL MICRO-REGULATORY FRAMEWORKS IN THE CONTEXT OF EXPANDING INTERNATIONAL PRODUCTION

Karl P. Sauvant

ABSTRACT

Explicit barriers to international trade, investment, technology, and financial flows have been reduced considerably. As a result, "macro-liberalization" of international economic transactions has largely run its course. Now, attention needs to shift from international rules for governments to international rules dealing with the various aspects of the international operations of firms — what are called "micro-issues" in this chapter; these include, by way of example, cross-border mergers and acquisitions and international bankruptcies. Such international rules for the principal actors in international production and markets would complement (or replace) the unilateral rules that exist at the national

Perspectives on Headquarters-Subsidiary Relationships in the Contemporary MNC
Research in Global Strategic Management, Volume 17, 401–440
Copyright © 2016 by Emerald Group Publishing Limited
ISSN: 1064-4857/doi:10.1108/S1064-485720160000017013

level. International rules would set the direct parameters for certain aspects of the international activities of firms and hence provide the global governance for operating in the global production and trading spaces. This chapter exemplifies for a number of areas the state of rule-making for some micro-issues, analyzes the nature of this rule-making, and suggests a way forward. Developing international micro-regulatory frameworks of rules of the road for the various aspects of the international operations of firms in the globalizing world economy should be the new frontier of international commercial diplomacy.

Keywords: Globalization; multinational enterprises; global governance; firm-level regulation

Explicit barriers to international trade, investment, technology, and financial flows have been reduced considerably. As a result, "macro-liberalization" of, and rule-making for, international economic transactions have largely run their course. Attention is shifting toward behind-the-border issues.[1] But attention also needs to shift from international rules for governments to international rules dealing with the various aspects of the international operations of firms — what are called "micro-issues" in this chapter, including, by way of example, cross-border mergers and acquisitions (M&As) and international bankruptcies. Such international rules agreed upon by governments for the principal actors in international production and markets would complement (or replace) the unilateral rules that exist at the national level. Such international rules would set the direct parameters for certain aspects of the cross-border activities of firms and hence provide the global governance for operating in the global production and trading spaces. Developing international micro-regulatory frameworks of rules of the road for the various aspects of the international operations of firms in the globalizing world economy should be the new frontier of international commercial diplomacy.

Few such international micro-regulatory governance frameworks exist today *below* the macro-regulatory framework and *for* the global space the latter creates. Instead, firms are typically subject to myriad unilateral national rules. In the past, this was relatively unproblematic, as issues that concerned *directly* specific aspects of the operations of firms could be addressed effectively at the national level. Today, this situation makes it challenging for managers of multinational enterprises (MNEs) to navigate the regulatory frameworks of the countries in which their firms operate. It also creates governance gaps, that is, discontinuities between the needs of global markets and an integrated international production system and the global value chains that are part of it, on the one hand, and the reach of (different) national regulatory frameworks dealing with internationally operating firms, on the other. Thus, for instance, when firms headquartered in one country engage in cross-border M&As, go bankrupt, engage in lending, establish closed user-group networks (such as airline reservation systems), report on their financial performance, offer insurance services, rate the credit-worthiness of other firms or governments, produce inferior goods that endanger consumers, or engage in transactions with entities in sanctioned countries, firms and consumers from many countries, as well as various governments, may well be affected.[2] In 2014, the recognition of such a governance gap in one particular area led the G-20 to deal as a group with tax avoidance by MNEs.[3]

While this chapter suggests that international micro-regulation is necessary, and that governments and other players have to attend to this need, *more* regulation − and that of a multilateral kind − is understandably controversial. The discussion below recognizes that sentiment, as shown in the section that sets out the advantages of the current ad hoc approach. The objective is to raise an issue − more through examples than anything else − rather than to offer full-fledged solutions or conclusions. Indeed, one of the points that require attention is precisely the trade-offs relating to the advantages and disadvantages of a government-led systematic approach leading to mandatory international instruments, on the one hand, and a market-driven ad hoc approach leading to voluntary international arrangements, on the other.[4] In either case, though, the challenge is to adapt to the realities of a globalizing world economy and the integrated international production system that is at its core.[5]

MACRO-LIBERALIZATION HAS LARGELY RUN ITS COURSE

Consider the following developments:

- Bound tariffs of developed countries on trade in industrial products were reduced by about 75 percent between 1967 and 2000,[6] and they were further reduced in subsequent years on particular products. Disciplines are being put in place to dismantle nontariff barriers. Trade in services is being progressively liberalized, though mostly on a noncommitted, that is, reversible, basis. The world trading system has been strengthened with the establishment of the World Trade Organization (WTO) and its dispute-settlement mechanism.

- Financial liberalization has proceeded even faster than the liberalization of trade, perhaps too fast for some countries. A global financial architecture is emerging (even if it needs adaptation), overseen by the International Monetary Fund (IMF).
- Many obstacles to the flow of foreign direct investment (FDI) have been removed, with the great majority of policy changes at the national level going in the direction of making the investment climate more welcoming for foreign investors (although increasingly so in a more nuanced manner). At the same time, standards for the protection and treatment of international investors have been strengthened through over 3,000 international investment agreements.[7] In addition, some two-thirds of world FDI flows are covered by the WTO's General Agreement on Trade in Services, with the bulk of the rest covered by regional or bilateral agreements (which, although typically called "free trade" agreements, are increasingly becoming "free investment" agreements as well).
- The defensive national transfer-of-technology regimes of the 1960s and 1970s have given way to a strong multilateral system for the protection of intellectual property rights, embodied in the WTO's Agreement on Trade-Related Intellectual Property Rights (TRIPS) (UNCTAD-ICTSD, 2005). This regime is further expanded by regional and bilateral agreements. The international technology market has never been more favorable for the owners of intellectual property.

To be sure, things are far from perfect, setbacks take place and a number of issues remain outstanding. For example, protectionism remains an ever-present danger, both in the trade and international investment areas.[8] The Eurozone is under strain. Some key sectors of particular interest to developing countries (notably agriculture and textiles) are still not significantly liberalized. The movement of labor has barely received attention, and a multilateral framework for investment is still lacking. But, otherwise, the outstanding trade issues are either clear cut (e.g., to reduce tariff peaks and tariff escalation), or they are shifting more and more toward fairly technical questions of implementation (e.g., special and differential treatment for developing countries) or to trade-related issues (e.g., environment, competition). Similarly, managing the formidable global financial market, reducing its instability, and strengthening the global financial architecture remain a challenge. Tackling these outstanding issues is difficult. They are part of the (unfinished) old agenda, and they need continued attention.

Overall, however, the basic rules are largely in place. They constitute an open global macro-regulatory framework for international trade in goods and services, financial transactions, investment, and the movement of technology between and among countries, with the WTO and the IMF at its heart. This framework is far from perfect, and it has one glaring omission: it does not address restrictions to labor mobility to any significant degree.[9] It is also difficult to manage. It is challenged by bilateral and regional deals. Its coherence is imperfect. But it *is* in place and, on the whole, it is fairly robust.

GLOBAL SPACES, GLOBAL ACTORS

The most important characteristic of the global framework mentioned above is that it opens global spaces for firms to pursue their activities internationally. Information, communication, and transportation technologies have made it possible for firms to operate globally in real time. Competition among firms makes it likely that, what is possible is being exploited by firms, in pursuit of their own international competitiveness and profitability.

The extent to which this has already happened is reflected in the fact that, between 1990 and 2014, world exports of goods and services rose from US$4 trillion to US$23 trillion; world royalties and licensee fee receipts grew from US$29 billion to US$310 billion; and world FDI outflows increased from US$241 billion to US$1,200 billion (UNCTAD, 2015, p. 18). The volume of cross-border capital flows grew to nearly US$12 trillion in 2007, before collapsing (due to the financial crisis that began in 2008) to close to US$5 trillion in 2012 − still, an enormous amount of funds, testifying to the openness of the international financial system (Lund et al., 2013, p. 4).

Among firms, MNEs are particularly important actors. The number of MNEs headquartered in 15 Organisation for Economic Co-operation and Development (OECD) countries rose from 7,300 at the end of the 1960s (with some 27,000 foreign affiliates) (United Nations, 1973, pp. 135, 147) to, worldwide, 65,000 around the turn of the century (with around 850,000 foreign affiliates) (UNCTAD, 2002, p. 270) to, again worldwide, at least 100,000 at the end of 2010, controlling a minimum number of 900,000 foreign affiliates (UNCTAD, 2012, web table 34). (The actual number of MNEs and their foreign affiliates is likely to be considerably higher, as their coverage across countries is very uneven.) Moreover, the universe of international investors is diversifying, as private equity firms, hedge funds, more state-owned enterprises, sovereign wealth funds, and born-global entrepreneurial firms engage in international production. Moreover, firms from developing countries and economies in transition are also increasingly becoming multinational,[10] with FDI outflows in 2014 from these countries (US\$530 billion) being roughly eleven times higher than *world* FDI flows during the first half of the 1980s. Especially in developed countries, the expansion of MNEs takes place mainly through M&As,[11] fueling a global market for firms.

Given the largely open macro-framework, MNEs consider the world as one production space. Accordingly, they organize their production internationally by locating their affiliates wherever in the world particular parts of the value chain (be it in goods or services) can be produced best from their point of view, creating an international intrafirm division of labor.[12] Moreover, firms that are not tied to particular parent firms through ownership arrangements are increasingly becoming part of these production networks through nonequity arrangements. International intrafirm trade, technology, and knowledge flows tie the various units of individual corporate networks together, which remain under the common governance of their headquarters.[13] While parent firms remain the ultimate decision-makers, the role of headquarters increasingly becomes that of deciding where various production activities take place, organizing highly complex networks, providing key tangible and intangible assets (e.g., finance, brand names, research, and development), and orchestrating information and knowledge flows within the networks.[14] The results are corporate integrated international production systems (UNCTAD, 1993) and the global value chains that define them (UNCTAD, 2013, 2015).[15] In aggregation, these add up to the expanding integrated international production system that is the productive core of the globalizing world economy.

This process is reflected in the fact that roughly one-third of world trade consists of intrafirm trade, and an even higher percentage is associated with global value chains (UNCTAD, 2013, 2015), internalizing in this manner certain types of international transactions. International production – production by foreign affiliates (US\$36 trillion, compared with world exports of US\$23 trillion, both in 2014; UNCTAD, 2015, p. 18) – has become more important than exports in delivering goods and services to foreign markets. The combined domestic and foreign output of MNEs suggest that as much as one-quarter of world output – if not more – is under the common governance of MNEs, with a percentage that is considerably higher in a number of industries (UNCTAD, 1999).

In sum, technological innovations in communications and transportation have combined with government policies to shrink the distances that once separated the economies of this world. Competition among firms has ensured that the new opportunities are being utilized, as reflected in the expansion of international economic transactions undertaken by them. The production and market spaces in which many firms operate are no longer national. Rather, an integrated international production system, centered on developed countries but becoming wider, is emerging, complementing the global markets for goods, services, intellectual property, and capital, and driven by global actors.

THE NEED FOR INTERNATIONAL
MICRO-REGULATORY FRAMEWORKS

With an open macro-framework largely in place, the spotlight falls on firms, the principal actors in the international production process and in international markets. They – whether large or small, from developed or developing countries – drive the globalization process through trade, finance, technology transfer, and FDI.

To deal with firms at the international level, however, requires a paradigm shift in international commercial policy making: rules should no longer only govern the action of *governments* at the *national* level but also the operations of *firms* at the *international* level.[16] With more and more firms operating globally and in an integrated manner, more and more corporate issues acquire an international dimension as well. Even firms in big countries, be they developed or developing, are virtually compelled to orient their activities beyond their domestic markets.[17] They have become (or are becoming) part of the world economy – via exports and imports, inward and outward investment, alliances, licensing and franchising arrangements, and other business transactions. Rules need to adapt to the reality of the globalizing and integrating world economy: national regulation alone of the operations of firms is no longer sufficient, in fact, effective, in a globalizing world economy. Stable, predictable, and transparent global governance rules dealing with the operations of firms are needed.

To put it differently, the logic of the globalization process and, in particular, the emergence of an integrated international production system and
the global value chains that are part and parcel of it require that the
national rules governing corporate operations most affected by the globalization and integration process be complemented, if not supplanted, by global micro-regulatory frameworks. It is a process that involves the
internationalization of some aspects of the domestic policy agenda relating
to firms (Ostry, 1992). Only when an open macro-framework is complemented by appropriate micro-frameworks governing the various types of
operations of firms – animal spirits aside – can firms prosper, and public
and private interests be properly balanced.[18] The creation of such frameworks requires deliberate attention and action.

The *nature* of such frameworks for the various types of operations of
firms, the contents of its rules, and how the frameworks and rules are formulated and enforced (and hence which interests they reflect) are of critical
importance for all firms, as they influence who benefits from the way in
which corporate activities are carried out. This is true for firms from both
developing and developed countries: in a world in which production systems and markets are global and profit preserves are disappearing under
the onslaught of liberalized trade, technology, investment, and financial
flows, competition is everywhere. There is a particular need to see to it that
firms in developing countries are not disadvantaged in this competition, as
competitive firms are the bedrock of growth and development. Micro-rules
set the parameters for the international competitiveness of firms and hence
influence the extent to which the development prospects of the countries in
which they are located can be advanced. It is a challenge to make sure that
firms based in developing countries are not disadvantaged, as most of the
governments of these countries, as well as the business associations in these
countries, typically have only limited capacity to deal with such matters.

The establishment of micro-rules for the operations of firms in the globalizing and integrating world economy should be the new frontier for
international commercial diplomacy. It is in fact the rise of an integrated
international production system and the global value chains that are part
and parcel of it that render this challenge more urgent than before. The
question therefore arises: how are these rules to be created and by whom?
Indeed, governments have begun to recognize the importance of, and need
for, micro-rules in the context of bilateral and regional trade agreements.[19]
However, in the absence of a multilateral dialogue on these issues, this risks
creating mutually inconsistent regulatory regimes, partly overlapping,
which, in turn, would impose high administrative burdens on MNEs and

could distort their locational decisions and it would not necessarily reflect an appropriate balance between public and private interests.

CURRENT MICRO-REGULATORY FRAMEWORKS

So far, little systematic attention has been given to the issues that global micro-regulatory frameworks need to address, the substantive content of such frameworks, and the modalities of creating them.[20] Rather, to the extent that global micro-rules have emerged, they have typically done so reactively (e.g., in reaction to specific problems as they arise), and they have often been created by a limited number of business actors, typically from developed countries. This haphazard, market-driven process is in danger of not taking the interests of other actors — especially firms from developing countries and various stakeholders — fully into account.

What is the nature of current micro-regulatory frameworks? Consider the following examples:

- *Mergers and acquisitions.* If two large MNEs merge, the competition authorities in the countries in which the two have affiliates (not to count the countries that may be affected by such transactions via trade) may need to authorize the transaction for it to go ahead since, frequently, antitrust issues have to be considered.[21] (Table 1 gives an indication of the minimum number of countries that would be affected if one of the large financial MNEs should be acquired by, or merged with, another large financial firm.) Each country has its own review processes, procedures, criteria, priorities, and time frames for M&As. This can cause delays, uncertainty, costs and, in some cases, the abandonment of a merger plan.[22] Moreover, smaller countries (and especially developing countries) typically do not have the resources and expertise to examine the effects that large-scale M&As of this sort may have on them.

  If anything, this issue is becoming more urgent, as reflected in the growth of international M&As: the value of cross-border M&As rose from US\$100 billion in 1990 to a peak of US\$1 trillion in 2000, fluctuating thereafter between US\$167 billion and US\$1 trillion until 2014.[23] The number of such deals rose from 862 in 1987 to 7,800 in 2000 (UNCTAD, 2000, p. 232, 2002, p. 11), to reach 8,624 in 2013.[24]

  An international market for firms needs international rules for cross-border M&As. In the absence of such rules, enforcement remains a domestic responsibility and intergovernmental cooperation is ad hoc,

Table 1. The International Presence of Large Financial MNEs, Majority-
Owned Foreign Affiliates, 2012.

Name	Home Economy	Number of Countries in which MNE is Established
Citigroup Inc	United States	74
BNP Paribas	France	69
Allianz SE	Germany	65
HSBC Holdings PLC	United Kingdom	65
Societe Generale	France	61
Deutsche Bank AG	Germany	56
Munich Reinsurance Company	Germany	54
Assicurazioni Generali SpA	Italy	53
UBS AG	Switzerland	50
Berkshire Hathaway Inc	United States	48
Barclays PLC	United Kingdom	46
Standard Chartered PLC	United Kingdom	45

Source: UNCTAD (2013, 2015).

pretty much restricted to the U.S. and European Union competition authorities.[25] This is even more a challenge as the number of competition authorities has risen considerably in recent years (see Fig. 1). While this is a positive development, it multiplies complexities and creates uncertainties for firms.

- *Bankruptcy.* If a large MNE goes bankrupt today, not only its home country but also the many host countries in which it has affiliates are directly affected (Table 1). A high-profile early example was the 1991 collapse of the Bank of Credit and Commerce International (BCCI), which at that time operated 380 offices in nearly 70 countries — the largest international banking failure at that time. Another example was the demise of Polly Peck International, a smaller United Kingdom–based conglomerate; differences between legal systems and insolvency laws held up the settlement of this case for several years.[26] More recently, the collapse of Lehman Brothers led to a bankruptcy that spanned nine jurisdictions. This time, however, interested parties organized the proceedings under a private protocol, allowing jurisdictions to intervene in each other's proceedings.

However, most global bankruptcies still operate on a territorial basis, with separate filings in each different country (Altman, 2010–2011, pp. 469–470). In the absence of an international approach to

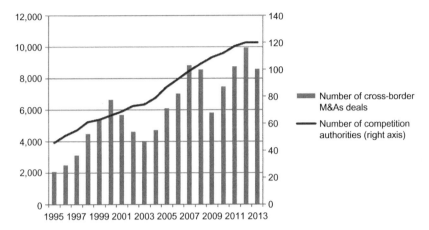

Fig. 1. More Competition Authorities Dealing With More Cross-Border M&As, 1995–2013. *Source*: OECD (2014).

bankruptcies, each country seeks to "ring-fence" the assets located on its territory, with little regard to the possible rescue of the enterprise as a whole: this is a problem because, to the extent that individual foreign affiliates are fully integrated into their corporate networks, they are typically not viable on their own, so that, in the end, both the host and home countries involved are negatively affected. With more than 100,000 MNEs (a number that is increasing), more and more of them having a rising number of affiliates in a growing number of countries, and more and more being fully integrated into the international production networks of their parent firms, more and more complicated bankruptcy cases are likely to occur. No international rules for corporate bankruptcies exist, although the United Nations Commission on International Trade Law (UNCITRAL) has developed a Model Law on Cross-border Insolvency.[27]

- *Minimum capital reserve requirements for banks, as part of the regulation of financial institutions.* The financial sector is one of the most important sectors in any economy, and it is generally very internationalized. Minimum capital reserve requirements for banks are key to the stability of this sector; national banking supervision authorities set those requirements. Work on harmonized standards for banking supervision has been on the agenda of the Basel Committee on Banking Supervision for some time. More specifically, the Committee's mandate is "to strengthen the regulation, supervision and practices of banks worldwide with the purpose of enhancing financial stability."[28] The Committee's decisions do not have legal force, but, de facto, represent governance in this particular area of activity. Rather, the Committee "expects full implementation of its standards" by its members (representing 27 jurisdictions[29]) "and their internationally active banks."[30] In practice, many nonmembers adopt the Committee's rules as well, owing to the lack of widely accepted alternatives and the standing of the Committee's rules in international financial markets for institutions that depend on such markets. For example, by July 2014, all Committee members had implemented, or were in the process of implementing, Basel III (a comprehensive set of reform measures developed by the Basel Committee), in addition to 89 non-Basel Committee member jurisdictions.[31]

• *Airline computer reservation systems (CRSs).* Airline CRSs gather all flight-related information on single platforms. Being listed on such a platform, and the precise place where the listing appears (especially on the first screen), can be crucial for airlines to attract customers. Travel agents use CRSs regularly to find flights corresponding to their clients' demands, and individuals increasingly do the same. During the mid-1970s, a few major airlines first developed CRSs that were used by the majority of airlines and travel agents. The CRS-developing airlines were soon accused of using CRSs to privilege their own flights. In the 1980s, national and regional authorities started regulating the use of CRSs, for antitrust purposes. In 1984 and 1992, for example, the U.S. Department of Transportation adopted CRS regulations prohibiting display bias and forcing airlines that used one CRS to list their flights on other CRSs as well (Caliskan & Cochran, 2003, pp. 1–3).[32] The European Community took similar steps in 1989[33] (Milde, 2008, p. 115). On the whole, CRSs and air traffic worldwide came to be regulated by a web of bilateral treaties in the absence of multilateral solutions[34] (Abeyratne, 2005–2006, p. 39). To complicate matters further, U.S. and European Union competition laws often provided for their application beyond their own borders (as shown by the U.S. regulation of CRSs), leading to conflicts of laws (Abeyratne, 2005–2006, p. 61). In 1986, the International Civil Aviation Organization (ICAO) established itself as the main body within the United Nations to regulate international air transport (Abeyratne, 2005–2006, p. 47). The ICAO issues model codes and nonbinding guidelines[35] to harmonize airline competition laws throughout the world (Abeyratne, 2005–2006, p. 43).

• *Accounting and reporting standards.* At present, MNEs in developed countries keep at least two sets of accounts: consolidated (group) accounts[36] according to the reporting requirements of their home countries, and accounts of individual foreign affiliates according to national accounting standards of the countries in which each affiliate is registered. Group accounts in most cases are prepared in accordance with one of two major accounting systems: the International Financial Reporting Standards (IFRSs) developed by the International Accounting Standards Board,[37] or the U.S. Generally Accepted Accounting Principles, established by the U.S. Financial Accounting Standards Board.[38] Firms from developing countries and from economies in transition in most cases have to use one of the two systems or variations of them for the purpose of helping them obtain access to international capital markets. Many economies in transition and a number of developing countries are in the process of reforming their national accounting systems by either adopting the IFRSs in full, or developing new national regulations on the basis of this standard. As of April 8, 2015, 114 jurisdictions required the application of IFRSs for most or all domestically listed companies, while 128 (out of 138) jurisdictions had publicly committed to the convergence of accounting standards.[39] When weaknesses in the U.S. Generally Accepted Accounting Principles were revealed by the collapse of Enron and by subsequent corporate scandals, the U.S. Congress approved the Sarbanes–Oxley Act in July 2002 to improve corporate governance (Box 1). This legislation applies to all companies listed on U.S. stock exchanges, regardless of whether they are headquartered in the United States or not;[40] it also applies to foreign affiliates of U.S. MNEs.

Today, the IFRSs are the world's most widely adopted standards. The International Accounting Standards Board and the U.S. Financial Accounting Standards Board have engaged in efforts to bring about a convergence of the two accounting standards, and both are now quite similar. The U.S. Financial Accounting Standards Board, however, has not agreed to adopt the IFRSs as the U.S. standard.[41]

- *Insurance regulation.* Insurance, too, is a sector of critical importance to any economy. The International Association of Insurance Supervisors was established in 1994, with a permanent secretariat in Basel.[42] Representing insurance regulators and supervisors in nearly 140 countries, the association agrees on "core principles" for the supervision of insurance operations, and all its members adopt these. The IMF uses its guidelines and standards when vetting the reinsurance frameworks of developing countries. The association's "Emerging Markets Committee" deals with issues of special concern to developing countries.

Box 1. The Sarbanes–Oxley Act: A Study in Global Standard Setting by One Country.

The Sarbanes–Oxley Act is a case study of a reactive approach to rule-making. It is also a case study of how, under the pressure of time to respond to an acute crisis, rule-making may not always be undertaken carefully; what technical micro-rules are like; and how in the absence of an international approach, action by one government can have implications for other governments and their regulatory regimes.

When Enron went bankrupt on December 2, 2001, Senator Paul Sarbanes and Congressperson Michael Oxley introduced, on January 23, 2002, corporate reform legislation that gained momentum as additional scandals broke. It was approved by both Houses of the U.S. Congress in July 2002, and signed into law by President George W. Bush on July 30, 2002. According to the *CPA Letter*,[a] it is "the most significant legislation affecting the accounting profession since 1933." The *Financial Times* added:[b] "most of those affected now admit that it was hastily drawn up."

While the Act deals with corporate reform in the United States, its implications reach beyond that country as it applies to all companies listed on U.S. stock exchanges as well as to the foreign affiliates of U.S. firms. At the same time, a number of its provisions were in conflict with approaches taken outside the United States. For example, the Act required that all members of a company's audit committee be independent; this conflicted with the German law that all firms with more than 2,000 employees fill half of their supervisory board seats with elected work-force representatives, with some of them also being members of the audit committee. Another example was the requirement that the chief executive and financial officers needed to certify their firms' financial statements and, hence, become personally responsible for misstatements; in Germany, on the other hand, these matters were the collective responsibilities of the management board. The Act (Sec. 106) also allowed U.S. authorities to raid the offices of European accounting firms in case of controversy between such firms and the U.S. Public Oversight Board. In fact, virtually all non-U.S. firms are subject to the Board's inspections. While most jurisdictions do not object, a few jurisdictions (like China and Hong Kong (China)) are reluctant to grant access to the Board. In many cases, the Board conducts investigations in collaboration with national oversight authorities.[c] The implication is that firms can either de-list themselves from U.S. stock markets, thereby losing direct access to the world's most important capital market, or they can seek exemptions from certain provisions (which, e.g., the European Commission was doing); the granting of exemptions might reflect, of course, the importance of the requestors and the strength of their own corporate governance standards. Companies could, of course, comply by changing their own practices if their national laws permit it.

In sum (to quote the CPA Letter again[d]): "High-profile business failures ... called into question the effectiveness of the profession's self-regulatory process ...." The resulting legislative remedy, in the words of a commercial law expert in Tokyo, amounted to: "Global standards are beginning to mean US standards imposed elsewhere."[e]

[a] CPA Letter, Vol. 82, September 2002, p. 1.
[b] December 30, 2002, p. 9. The newspaper quoted Oxley as saying that the bill was "passed in almost a panic sort of situation" (*ibid.*).
[c] "Non-US firms inspections," PCAOB's website. Retrieved from http://pcaobus.org/International/Inspections/Pages/default.aspx. Accessed on April 8, 2014.
[d] CPA Letter, Vol. 82, September 2002, p. 1.
[e] *Financial Times*, December 30, 2002, p. 9.

- *Credit rating.* Standard & Poor's, Moody's, and Fitch (all three headquartered in New York) dominate the market for the credit rating of companies and governments. When any of them reduces the creditworthiness of a government or a company, there can be immediate implications for its access to capital markets and especially the costs at which it can borrow money. In a sense, this makes these three firms quasi-official regulators of public and private debt markets.
- *Business-to-consumer commerce.* Cross-border commerce has long been largely limited to business-to-business transactions, regulated by international uniform substantive law such as the International Convention on

the Sales of Goods.[43] Recently, however, the use of the Internet has led
to unprecedented cross-border transactions directly between businesses
and consumers. These transactions, however, are yet to be regulated by
uniform international rules. As of 2014, online dispute resolution generally was the only way to resolve cross-border business-to-consumer disputes (Johnson, 2013, p. 582). Various attempts to apply national laws
have failed.[44] Treaty negotiations between the U.S. and European Union
authorities have also proved unfruitful so far.[45] This results in considerable legal uncertainty likely to deter both consumers and businesses from
engaging in cross-border transactions. It also reduces consumers' influence on the legal landscape of consumer protection. Consumer groups
advocate legislative change in their respective countries, only to see
national law supplanted by ad hoc cross-border dispute resolution processes that rely on fair principles of international law (Stewart &
Matthews, 2002, p. 1136).

- *Corporate transactions with countries on which sanctions have been
  imposed.* As the 2014 example of BNP Paribas's $8.9 billion settle-
  ment[46] illustrates, corporate entities often must comply with foreign
  sanctions laws; in this case, BNP pleaded guilty to having processed
  billions of dollars of transactions through the U.S. financial system on
  behalf of Cuban, Iranian, and Sudanese entities subject to U.S. economic sanctions (Zagaris, 2014). Some U.S. sanctions laws, for example, apply to foreign-owned subsidiaries of U.S. parent companies,
  foreign companies re-exporting U.S. goods to sanctioned entities and
  foreign companies conducting transactions through the United States'
  financial system (Rathbone, Jeydel, & Lentz, 2013, pp. 1107–1119).
  This extraterritorial application of U.S. law has resulted in conflicts of
  laws. For instance, foreign companies were threatened with U.S. sanctions for selling Cuban products or providing services to Cuban officials; on the other hand, national laws prohibited them from
  discriminating against Cuban products or officials.[47] More generally,
  foreign sanctions laws expose MNEs to compliance obligations arising
  from foreign jurisdictions that can conflict with the laws of their home
  jurisdictions. In many cases, conflicts of laws have been avoided thanks
  to international consensus on sanctions: for example, after the U.S.
  Congress passed a new sanctions law prohibiting foreign financial and
  oil companies from certain transactions with Iran, the European Union
  enacted similar provisions so as to manifest its agreement with the
  sanctions and eliminate conflict-of-law issues (Rathbone et al., 2013,
  pp. 1122–1123). However, unilateral sanctions with extraterritorial

application remain to be harmonized in a systematic way, which would arguably prompt issues of political governance.[48]

As these examples illustrate, the regulation of global corporate operations – its governance – can take various forms and have different strength (mandatory, voluntary). It also has many sources (ranging from strictly national to international approaches), originates from the private sector or individual governments, and it can be entirely absent. For example:

- *Absence of global rules.* Such is the case, for example, in matters of bankruptcy, business-to-consumer transactions, and transactions with politically sanctioned entities. In bankruptcy matters, the case of Lehman Brothers shows that national legal systems are still entirely independent in this particular area. When an MNE faces bankruptcy in multiple jurisdictions, it has no international rules to fall back on in order to restructure itself and become viable again. In the absence of global rules, voluntary and ad hoc cooperation among jurisdictions has been the only approach to deal with such situations.
- *Corporate actions with a global governance impact.* Some corporate pronouncements have such an impact throughout the world that they amount to sector-specific "governance." In the credit-rating area, for example, private companies based in the United States (such as Moody's, Standards & Poor's, Fitch) can impact companies and governments' borrowing abilities, whether in the United States or elsewhere. They have assumed a sort of de facto international quasi-regulatory role (but are themselves not regulated by anyone). They are actors that have emerged to fill a need.
- *Mandatory national regulations that, de facto, become international regulations.* For example, the United States' Sarbanes–Oxley Act is a national regulation with an international impact: it became, de facto, an international regulation as it applied to all companies – even foreign ones – registered with the U.S. Securities and Exchange Commission, as well as to the foreign affiliates of U.S. MNEs. Similarly, the regulation of airline CRSs by the U.S. Department of Transportation not only protected every airline to a certain extent (regardless of nationality) from display bias, but also prohibited[49] them from using such bias in their own CRSs. Finally, U.S. sanctions laws apply not only to U.S. companies, but also to foreign-owned subsidiaries of U.S. companies and foreign companies that use the United States' financial system or re-export U.S. goods.

○ Model arrangements that can serve as templates for the cooperation of
countries in specific areas. The above-mentioned UNCITRAL bankruptcy Model Law is an example. The Model Law does not aim at uni-
fying different national laws, but provides cooperation provisions for
incorporation in existing laws. National laws based on the Model Law
empower courts of different countries to communicate and cooperate
in making decisions. For instance, national laws based on the Model
Law would facilitate the recognition of orders issued by foreign courts.
It also gives foreign creditors and court officials a right of access to the
courts of an enacting state. By early 2015, 21 countries had adopted
legislation based on UNCITRAL's Model Law.[50] In particular, the
U.S. Congress updated the country's Bankruptcy code in 2005 with a
new chapter (chapter 15) providing a window for cooperation
with foreign courts and foreign parties.[51] Chapter 15 is now used
in bankruptcies of multinational entities. In 2009, for example, the
Southern District of New York agreed to recognize foreign bankruptcy
proceedings regarding a Switzerland-incorporated subsidiary of
Lehman Brothers (United States Government Accountability Office
[USGAO], 2011).

- *International private regulation.* In matters of accounting and insurance,
the International Accounting Standards Board and the International
Association of Insurance Supervisors harmonize corporate practices on a
global basis. Neither of the two are governmental bodies. Rather,
they are both not-for-profit organizations, with ties to national
supervisory and regulatory entities. The International Accounting and
Standards Board is accountable to the IFRSs Foundation, which is
accountable (through its Board of Trustees) to the Monitoring Board, a
"body of publically accountable market authorities" (among which are
the SEC and the European Commission).[52] The International Association
of Insurance Supervisors relies on voluntary membership of supervisors
and regulators (public and private) from nearly 140 countries. It counts
the European Commission and the U.S. Federal Insurance Office among
its members.[53]

- *International government regulation.* In some areas, the international regulation of certain activities involves virtually all countries. An example is
the International Labour Organization (ILO) under which agreements
are forged whose main aims are "to promote rights at work, encourage
decent employment opportunities, enhance social protection and
strengthen dialogue on work-related issues."[54] But there are also certain
activities for which a limited number of public authorities make de facto

rules accepted by many (if not most) countries. In the financial area, the Basel Committee brings together 27 jurisdictions, but its decisions are accepted by more than 100 jurisdictions. However, decisions are largely made by the G-10 developed countries, although the Committee expanded in 2009 to include such emerging markets as Brazil, China, India, and Russia. Still, developing countries in general seem to have little influence on the Committee's rule-making.[55] While the Committee's regulations are voluntary (i.e., have no legal force), they reach virtually all internationally active banks.

Overall, what characterizes most of the micro-regulatory efforts undertaken so far is that:

- They are partial in the sense that they address only some areas relevant to the range of corporate operations. Presumably, these are areas that, at a certain point, were particularly pressing in a globalizing environment and/or had drivers behind them that were strong enough to promote international approaches.
- They are sometimes geographically quite restricted. In fact, it may be only one country, or a small group of countries, that makes rules that become de facto global standards.
- They are elaborated by a variety of entities, sometimes in combination with each other: sometimes by governments (or specific governmental institutions), sometimes by the legislative authorities of a few or even of a single country, sometimes by the business community, sometimes by professional associations, and sometimes by one or a few dominant companies.[56]
- Governments, business associations, or firms from developing countries are often not involved in the rule-making although the rules may apply de facto equally to all firms wishing to participate in the integrated international production system or the global trading system. Even when the bodies involved pay attention to developing countries, development issues are not vital to them.

There is also the question of global rules concerning the responsibilities of market actors, and especially MNEs. An early effort to formulate a set of such rules was made in the late 1970s and 1980s, when the United Nations sought to negotiate a comprehensive set of rules dealing, among other things, with the responsibilities of MNEs, an effort that came to naught (Sauvant, 2015). However, such rules, albeit voluntary ones, were adopted by the OECD,[57] and they exist in a number of sectors[58] (most recently related to human rights[59]). This issue remains on the international agenda, including in the context of improving the international investment law and policy regime, and, sooner or later, is likely to be addressed.

As this discussion indicates, there are many efforts to build international micro-regulatory frameworks, involving a wide range of private and public institutions. It is a patchwork of efforts, with uneven geographical coverage and a variety of drivers, and it does not cover important operations of firms in a satisfactory manner. In a by-and-large reactive market-driven process, global production and market rules tend to evolve ad hoc to satisfy primarily the operational requirements of firms from developed countries, and they are voluntary. They are often informed by and/or agreed upon in "webs of influence" (Braithwaite & Drahos, 2000) by a relatively small group of large firms from developed countries (or semiprivate professional associations, typically dominated by representatives from developed countries). At times, they have acquired official status, especially through action by the competent regulatory agencies of developed countries. Governments too may take the initiative and introduce mandatory rules. Rules are often updated in light of the experiences of the principal firms affected by them and of the changing conditions in (primarily) developed countries. Most countries, and especially developing countries, tend to be rule-takers, not rule-makers. The conditions and interests of firms from these countries are therefore not a prime concern influencing the setting, implementation, and revision of the rules. As a result, firms from countries for which these rules may not be adequate may be at a disadvantage. They may even constitute barriers to their participation in the integrated international production system and global markets. Yet, the emerging micro-regulatory frameworks increasingly determine the competitive position of firms across the world and, by extension, the benefits countries derive from them.[60]

THE NEW AGENDA

Is this reactive process of global rule-making satisfactory and sustainable, or even desirable? In particular, is it satisfactory and sustainable in a globalizing world economy:

- That crises are needed, or that a situation becomes obviously unacceptable,[61] to set a rule-making process in motion?

- That issues that need an international approach continue to be left to a few (often competing) national jurisdictions, with a potential for inefficiencies and even conflict?
- That the global operations of firms might be disrupted because of some rules' limited geographical application? Or, alternatively, that certain geographical areas are left out from the rule-making or are rule-takers with little influence on the emerging global micro-regulatory frameworks?
- That one group of governments (or individual parts of one or several governments) can make rules for the rest of the world?
- That global rules are defined, at least de facto, by parts of the business community or individual firms, reflecting private (but not necessarily public) interests (including the possibility of hidden protectionism)?
- That, in each case, perhaps only the (limited) interest of the rule-makers determine the content of the rules?

These questions are particularly relevant considering that the multinationalization of firms is most likely to continue unabated and, with it, the expansion of the integrated international production system. This is not only reflected in the figures mentioned earlier regarding the growth of the number of firms that have become MNEs and the rise of FDI flows. It is also reflected in the extent to which firms that are already MNEs have become more multinational: thus, the degree of multinationalization of the world's 100 largest nonfinancial MNEs,[62] as measured by a composite transnationality index that captures the proportion of foreign assets, employment, and sales in their respective totals, grew from 47 in 1993 (UNCTAD, 2007, p. 15) to 56 in 2003 (UNCTAD, 2007, p. 15) and to 67 in 2013 (UNCTAD, 2014, web table 28). While the foreign assets of the top 100 MNEs amounted to US\$1.3 trillion in 1993 (UNCTAD, 2007, p. 7), they had risen to US\$4 trillion in 2003 (UNCTAD, 2005, table I.4, p. 17), and to US\$8 trillion in 2013, accounting that year for 59 percent of the firms' total assets.[63] What is important to note in this context is also that firms from emerging markets[64] have become important players in the world FDI market: of the 100,000 plus MNEs, some 30,000 are headquartered in emerging markets (UNCTAD, 2012, web table 34).

There are, of course, strong arguments in favor of the current process of global micro-rule-making:

- Rules are established only if and when there is a clearly defined need, often in response to specific occurrences or in response to a series of crises. Hence, the partial nature of the emerging frameworks reflects real priorities. To put it differently: if the need for international rules in a particular subject area is strong enough, rules will emerge, and they will be implemented and adapted. It is essentially a market- and demand-driven process based on trial and error, involving also a certain amount of regulatory competition. Moreover, the making of rules on a particular issue can begin at the national level and then be expanded to a region (including through mutual recognition and open codes) and eventually be multilateralized. This, for example, happened in the area of corruption.[65]

- The same arguments apply to the uneven geographical coverage of rules. There may be no urgent need to cover all countries if they play only a marginal role in a given area or if some countries want to pursue different approaches. In any event, consensus on truly multilateral rules is difficult to obtain in a world of some 200 jurisdictions.

- In line with the argument that rules ought to be established only if and when they are clearly needed, rules should also only be established by those who need them most (with others free to join in). This is also in line with the subsidiarity principle (i.e., decisions should be made at the most local level practicable). It moreover ensures that rules are adopted relatively quickly when needed (as contrasted with the typically cumbersome multilateral process), and they can be adapted relatively quickly. (The Uruguay Round of Multilateral Trade Negotiations took some eight years to complete; during that time, computer chips roughly doubled their capacity every 18 months, and the Internet was born. WTO's Doha Round, launched in 2001, was still ongoing in 2015.)

- And, of course, the current process of rule-making reflects the reality of power, as rules are often also a tool for exercising power and obtaining advantages. To put it differently, why should the countries and governments that benefit most from the current approach agree to a different approach? To give an example, why would the United States agree to restrict the global influence of "its" rating agencies in favor of a multilateral approach? Or, if, say, the accounting standards of one country or one group of countries become the global rules, the accounting firms grounded in the respective rules obtain a competitive advantage.

These considerations are important. They reflect the reality − and rationale − of the global micro-regulatory frameworks that are actually emerging. These frameworks react to perceived needs, are market-driven, and are largely voluntary in nature. And they reflect the reality that economic and business globalization has out-paced the political and social organization of states and societies.

However, there is an alternative approach – a more systematic one that deliberately seeks to identify emerging needs and addresses them before major costs have been incurred. (Braithwaite and Drahos capture the two approaches, in their ideal form, instructively in Fig. 2, under the headings "top-down" and "bottom up.") It is a systematic, government-driven, regulatory approach, an approach that was pursued when the international trade regime was created.[66] After all, it should not be necessary for a series of spectacular corporate governance failures to occur before corrective actions are taken – perhaps in the heat of the moment, but with worldwide implications. Similarly, it should not be necessary, for example, for a series of spectacular bankruptcies of large MNEs to take place before a multilateral approach to this issue is agreed upon. In the context of growing interdependence, the costs of any crisis or major event are increasingly no longer confined to the countries engulfed in a particular crisis or in which a major event has taken place; rather, the costs are likely to spread to others, with, at times, potentially systemic implications.

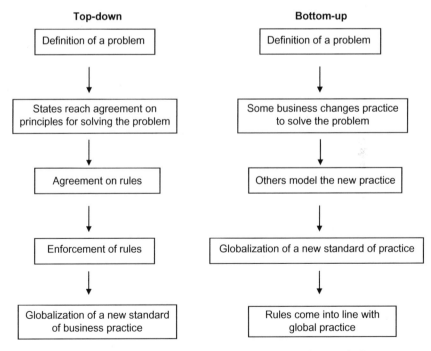

Fig. 2. Top-Down and Bottom-Up Globalization of Regulation. *Source*: Braithwaite and Drahos (2000, p. 554).

A more systematic process can move at deliberate speed and explicitly encompass both the public and private sectors (and, for that matter, other stakeholders that are affected by a particular issues) in order to ensure that a proper balance between public and private interests is found. This consideration also suggests the desirability of broad participation by representatives of governments and businesses (and other groups) from developed and developing countries. Such a process would furthermore enhance the legitimacy of the rules being established and hence contribute to their overall acceptance — and the legitimacy of any framework depends, in the long run, on its capacity to reflect broad acceptance by those that are affected by it.[67]

A good part of the emerging micro-regulatory frameworks is indeed open to criticism when it comes to the question of who formulated the rules and what is the proper balance of public versus private interest. This, in turn, is likely to raise, sooner or later, questions about their legitimacy — a challenge that can only intensify as the importance of micro-rules, their nature, their contents, and the costs of their absence become more apparent, and the weight of countries that were not involved in their formulation increases. This is not the fault of those engaged in the construction of the micro-regulatory frameworks so far: typically, they are the ones who have felt the most pressing need and have responded to it to the best of their ability. Besides, what has been achieved in this manner is noteworthy and important, and it facilitates the functioning of global markets and the integrated international production system. It is the natural response to the emergence of something new, the shape, magnitude, and characteristics of which are still vague and evolving, and which takes place at a time when governments still focus on macro-liberalization.

However, by now the reality of an integrated international production system and global markets is upon us, and more attention needs to be given to the micro-regulatory infrastructure of the globalizing world economy. The logic of globalization suggests that governments now need to give more attention to a systematic process of identifying and addressing new needs, as opposed to dealing with such needs only after they have manifested themselves (repeatedly, and negatively). This would amount to an extension of the systematic process that, over the past 60 years, has characterized macro-rule-making, to the micro-issues. The issue is not to replace macro- with micro-rule-making; rather the issue is to shift the balance more to the latter. In the end, the key challenges are efficiency, the proper balance between private and public interests, and, ultimately, legitimacy.[68]

HOW TO SET THE NEW AGENDA?

With micro-regulatory issues coming to the forefront, the nature of the current process of global micro-rule-making needs to be reviewed, at least as far as three dimensions are concerned:

- *What* are the micro-issues that require international attention? Which among them are particularly urgent? Which have interested constituencies that could move an issue forward? Which issues are most likely to be ripe for consensus, at least about basic principles? And, from a development perspective, which are particularly important for developing countries and their firms? Equally important, there are such questions as: how does trade and investment deregulation mesh with increasing micro-regulation? When are global rules important? When do voluntary arrangements work? When do they fail and why? How do we determine which global rules have persisted and which have languished? When are global rules impossible to enforce, because of the lack of global enforcement mechanisms? Do global rules have to be accepted within nation states to become effective, implying that the last word remains with individual governments? What is the best way to involve various stakeholder groups? The establishment of such a list of issues and questions is, in many ways, a very technical task. It would involve a systematic examination of a broad range of issues that, due to the emergence of global markets and an integrated international production system, are increasingly difficult to address effectively in a purely domestic context. Some of these issues may well overlap and/or may interact and/or may involve a sequencing in terms of action that needs to be taken. It would be a stock-taking exercise which, at a minimum, could serve as an early warning system to draw attention to issues that require an international approach.[69]
- *How* should priority issues be addressed in terms of form and content? Presumably, when the priority issues requiring an international approach are identified, the grounds for priorities would be explained as well. It would also be logical to suggest, at the same time, options for how these issues should be addressed internationally, including how any rules could be implemented and enforced. As to form, the earlier discussion has shown that there are many ways in which issues can be addressed internationally, ranging from business or industry arrangements to mixed business-government actions to regional agreements among governments to international codes, and to multilateral treaties negotiated in the appropriate fora.[70]

- *Who* should identify the priority issues and suggest options as to how they could be addressed? Obvious candidates to take the lead are think tanks or research institutions, a blue-ribbon commission, or an international organization.

When it comes to actual rule-making, the WTO may be a strong candidate. The WTO and, in particular, its predecessor, the GATT, have shown that substantial achievements are possible at the multilateral level. Moreover, the WTO has a broad remit, and it has already made some timid and tentative steps in the direction of dealing with micro-issues. Thus, the outcome of the Uruguay Round included a Ministerial Decision on Professional Services that provided: "As a matter of priority, the Working Party [on Professional Services] shall make recommendations for the elaboration of multilateral disciplines in the accountancy sector ...."[71] On conclusion of the negotiations on the accountancy disciplines in December 1998 (WTO, 1998), the WTO's Services Council established a Working Party on Domestic Regulation, whose mandate included to "develop disciplines as appropriate for individual sectors or groups thereof."[72] Moreover, the WTO's work in the area of telecommunications, through the formulation of its "Telecommunication Reference Paper,"[73] is relevant here. This document, drafted on an informal basis by a group of like-minded WTO members and finalized in 1997, contains a set of regulatory principles/standards for the regulation of telecommunication service providers. WTO members individually agreed upon it as containing binding commitments, and these were subsequently incorporated in the schedules of new accession countries as additional commitments. This may be one approach to move the micro-regulatory agenda forward. Indeed, this is the approach taken regarding some of the new issues that are being discussed in the new generation of services-trade agreements, for instance, on the governance of the Internet (data flows, privacy, data confidentiality, etc.).

UNCTAD could also be a candidate, especially if the idea is to pay special attention to the needs of developing countries. UNCTAD, too, has ventured — at least to a certain extent — into the area of micro-issues, for example, through its Intergovernmental Working Group of Experts on International Standards of Accounting and Reporting, established in 1982.[74] For, as observed earlier, developing countries and their firms (including state-owned enterprises) tend to be rule-takers and not rule-makers in the area of micro-regulation, and the interests of their firms thus need special attention.

Finally, there are many specialized fora dealing with specific aspects of the international operations of firms, some of them mentioned earlier in this chapter. Depending on their interests, they might be able to advance the discussion in specific fields. Special attention would need to be given to the ability of an organization to be able to react swiftly to changing circumstances, as there is the danger that, in a world of rapid innovations and changes, rules formulated by governments could be out of date by the time they are adopted.[75]

Regardless of who takes the lead, it is clear that the effort needs to involve all major stakeholders, particularly representatives from governments and businesses from developed and developing countries, but also from other parts of civil society, including trade unions, consumer organizations, and other nongovernmental organizations (NGOs).[76] The reason for government representatives is clear: after all, a good part of the emerging global micro-regulatory frameworks will (eventually) consist of governmental arrangements; even more importantly, governments represent the public interest. Representatives of the business community are crucial because, after all, they are best placed to know what the key issues are and how they could be addressed. The involvement of all major stakeholders would also lead to a situation in which the process of creating micro-regulatory frameworks would not be either government-led and systematic, leading to mandatory instruments, or market-driven and ad hoc, leading to voluntary instruments, but rather result in a mixed approach that combines the interests and expertise of all major stakeholders.

But the question of the participation of businesses, trade unions, consumer organizations, and other NGOs is broader than the expertise and interests specific groups might represent and bring to the table. Input by various stakeholders into international rule-making is a logical consequence of the globalization process and the strengthening of global institutions: in the same manner in which businesses, trade unions, consumer organizations, and other NGOs seek to influence rule-making at the *national* level, they will more and more seek to influence rule-making at the *international* level as well; and, the more important these rules are, the more they will seek to do so. If this cannot be done in a transparent institutional context, it will be done through the back door or in the streets. The only way to avoid increased interest by these groups in global rule-making is to reduce the relevance of such rule-making and of the institutions in which it takes place — which is precisely the opposite of what global markets and an integrated international production system need. To be sure, this makes global rule-making even more complicated — but it also opens new opportunities for alliances, open or tacit ones.[77]

Still, greater participation by businesses, trade unions, consumer groups, and other NGOs is easier said than done, and it will require institutional innovations to increase transparency and establish appropriate mechanisms. In any event, and independently of the mechanisms eventually established, nothing prevents whoever takes the lead in this matter from ensuring that all major stakeholders can provide their inputs on priority issues for the global agenda for micro-regulatory issues.

In conclusion, the advanced state of macro-liberalization and rule-making for international economic transactions at the level of *countries* shifts the focus to a new frontier: the need to establish micro-regulatory frameworks — and hence the regulatory infrastructure and rules of the road — for the various operations of *firms* in the globalizing world economy. These rules would constitute the governance of the international operations of firms in the globalizing world economy. The current ad hoc and market-driven process can be made more efficient, more likely to achieve a better balance between public and private interests, and ultimately more legitimate. Such a process could involve, in the first instance, the systematic identification of issues requiring an international approach, as well as the identification of options for how to address them, in a process that involves all major stakeholders. Such a process, ambitious as it would be, would amount to setting an agenda for the development of global micro-regulatory frameworks for various aspects of the international operations of firms in the globalizing world economy and, hence, its global governance as far as the operations of firms are concerned. It would be the agenda for the next generation of global commercial rule-making. Pursuing such a process would involve going forward pragmatically, beginning with issues on which consensus might be easiest to achieve, in a piece-meal approach, focusing on subjects for which constituencies can be mobilized to advance the process, in whatever organizational framework is most appropriate.[78]

While the process that is being suggested here seeks to be a rational one, it is unavoidably also a profoundly political one, in at least two senses: it involves the old question of how best to balance the role of the state and the market; and it sets the stage for determining, in Lasswell's (1936) classic definition of politics: "who gets what, when, how" in the globalizing world economy.

NOTES

1. This is exemplified by the negotiations of the Transatlantic Trade and Investment Partnership, in which regulatory harmonization is a key challenge. Behind-the-border issues are particularly important in the services sector where regulation often restricts market access. For a discussion, see Lim and De Meester (2014).

2. This list can easily be expanded, for example, by adding such issues as data flows, privacy, data confidentiality, carbon emission trading, dumping of harmful waste, minimum product quality standards, liability issues, enforcement of all sorts of contracts, and money laundering.

3. See the G-20 "Communiqué", Meeting of Finance Ministers and Central Bank Governors, February 22–23, 2014, para. 9. Retrieved from https://www.g20.org/sites/default/files/g20_resources/library/Communique%20Meeting%20of%20G20%20Finance%20Ministers%20and%20Central%20Bank%20Governors%20Sydney%2022-23%20February%202014_0.pdf. Accessed on April 8, 2015.

4. In some respects, the discussion here is akin to Lorraine Eden's analysis of regulatory changes as a result of the formation of the North American Free Trade Agreement: "A shift in the overall regulatory environment is occurring in North America, away from unilateral rules to bilateral and trilateral policy making. This shift can be seen in two ways: as a move away from weak/soft international regulation (nonbinding commitments at the regional level) towards strong/hard international regulation (binding, formal rules and procedures); as a widening of the geographic scope of the regulatory environment from the national to the regional level." See Eden (1996, p. 62).

5. This chapter does not deal with products and processes, another important area in which global standards are increasingly becoming important. The International Organization for Standardization (ISO) is a leader in setting international standards; as of early 2015, it had a portfolio of 19,500 standards (see http://www.iso.org/iso/home/standards.htm. Accessed on April 8, 2015). Even though ISO standards are voluntary, regulatory bodies have adopted a number of them, or they have become de facto standards. For a discussion, see Kearney (2012) and FIPRA (2010).

6. Information provided by Michael Finger. Tariff reductions were agreed upon in rounds of trade negotiations. During the Uruguay Round (1986–1994), most-favored-nations tariff reductions of developed countries for industrial products (excluding petroleum) amounted to 38 percent; in the preceding Tokyo Round (1973–1979), they amounted to 33 percent. See World Trade Organization (WTO) (2007, p. 207). The WTO concluded: "Industrial countries have substantially reduced their tariffs since 1947. Only in a few categories can they still be considered a significant trade barrier" (*ibid.*, p. 210).

7. To illustrate: between 1991 and 2001, some 95 percent of the policy changes in national regulatory regimes for FDI were in the direction of creating a more favorable environment for investment by MNEs (UNCTAD, 2002, p. 7) although that percentage had declined to 70 percent by 2013 (UNCTAD, 2014, p. 106), the bulk of policy changes still goes in the direction of making the investment climate more favorable for international investors.

The convergence toward similar (liberal) FDI regimes was aided by an explosion of bilateral investment treaties that strengthened the protection of foreign investment and facilitated access to markets; the number of bilateral investment treaties alone rose from 385 at the end of the 1980s (UNCTAD, 2000, p. 1) to 2,902 at the end of 2013 (UNCTAD, 2014, p. 114); to that, other international treaties covering international investment, numbering 334 by the end of the same year, need to be added. In fact, international investment agreements have become so widespread and strong, especially regarding the treatment of investors in the postestablishment phase of a project, that even a multilateral framework — if and when one should be negotiated — may do little more, at least initially, than lock in the autonomous and bilateral liberalization measures taken by many countries, which would increase predictability, stability, and transparency.

8. See, for example, the various editions of OECD, WTO, and UNCTAD, "Reports on G-20 Trade and Investment Measures" available on the websites of these institutions.

9. In principle, mode four of GATS covers labor mobility to a limited extent, as do various international investment agreements, but little has been achieved in practice.

10. For a listing of the largest 100 MNEs from developing and transition economies, ranked by foreign assets in 2012, see UNCTAD (2014), annex table 29. Retrieved from http://unctad.org/en/pages/DIAE/World%20Investment%20Report/Annex-Tables.aspx. Accessed on April 8, 2015.

11. See the annual editions of the *World Investment Report* prepared by UNCTAD.

12. In fact, a portfolio of locational assets is now an important source of corporate competitiveness in all sectors (Dunning, 1996; UNCTAD, 1995).

13. The possibility of splitting up the production of services extends also to the various functions that are traditionally performed by corporate headquarters, ranging from communications to finance. They too can be located wherever it is best from the perspective of firms as a whole, disassembling what once were unified headquarters.

14. The emergence of such complex networks makes it difficult at times to identify the boundaries of a particular firm or, for that matter, to determine its nationality and any liabilities in case of, for instance, gross negligence.

15. These developments also create challenges for international investment and trade statistics. These have always been difficult to interpret, given that countries do not necessarily follow the reporting guidelines provided by the IMF, UNCTAD, and the OECD. More recently, moreover, the rise of special-purpose entities has become a major issue, as these entities serve primarily the purpose of managing the liquid assets of MNEs by channeling investment flows from one country to another; in other words, these flows do not reflect productive investment in the reporting host countries. Such entities can be located in any country. Moreover, firms from a number of countries (including Brazil, China, and Russia) channel a substantial share of their FDI flows through tax havens or financial centers. Finally, round-tripping continues to present a statistical problem. Fortunately, UNCTAD and the OECD have begun to receive data from countries that host special-purpose entities (e.g., Luxembourg, Hungary, and the Netherlands) and to correct the data

accordingly, also for tax havens (especially in the Caribbean). However, this correction does not yet cover all countries and distortions. They have therefore recommended that all countries report data with and without special-purpose-entity transactions (For a discussion, see Organisation for Economic Co-operation and Development [OECD], 2015). Note, however, that these corrections would lead to more accurate FDI statistics on the basis of the traditional balance-of-payments approach to such statistics. These corrections would not capture, for example, FDI made on the basis of MNEs raising funds in the financial markets of host countries or in international financial markets outside their home countries. Moreover, these corrections would also not capture nonequity forms of control utilized by firms in regard to enterprises located abroad. Hence, FDI data substantially underestimate the share of production under the common governance of MNEs.

16. Traditionally, international rules are made by governments for other governments; in a sense, this process involves rules about rules. International rules that apply directly to firms (while not unheard of) have not been the domain of traditional trade policy. Moving in that direction requires a paradigm change in international law.

17. This is not a new phenomenon. U.S. firms started to move abroad from the mid-nineteenth century onwards; by 1914, practically all innovative and important firms had global operations, typically operating on a stand-alone basis. See Wilkins (1970).

18. The focus of this chapter is on the activities of firms, regardless of industry, although some of the examples below are industry specific. The same argument can be made for labor-related, environmental, consumer, and other matters. In fact, when it comes to the social dimension of globalization, it could be argued that, just as *economic* growth in many developed countries was facilitated by (and indeed may have required) a national *social* consensus, world economic growth would benefit from a *world* social consensus as well — precisely the idea underlying the Global Compact (Kell & Ruggie, 1999).

19. See, for example, the Transatlantic Trade and Investment Partnership, in which regulatory harmonization is one objective. See also the nascent efforts in the WTO discussed briefly below.

20. But see, for example, Braithwaite and Drahos (2000). The focus is here on corporate activity. There have, of course, been various (successful) efforts to establish global standards in such areas as defining time zones, the measurement of lengths and distances, etc. These types of arrangements are not considered here.

21. In a number of countries, furthermore, incoming M&As may be reviewed on the basis of national security considerations.

22. In 2001, GE abandoned its plan to acquire Honeywell. Although U.S. regulators had approved the deal, the European Commission objected and the deal did not take place.

23. Annex to UNCTAD (2015), web table 9.

24. *Ibid.*, web table 11.

25. "Perhaps the most effective model of international cooperation in merger control *currently* is the EU's 'one-stop shop,' which allows parties to avoid multiple filings in the EU by submitting a single notification to the European Commission. Even this system, for all its merits, is far from flawless: many hundreds of

transactions are still notified in more than one EU country each year." See Squire Sanders (2012).

26. For example, U.S. law traditionally defers to foreign home jurisdictions in bankruptcy matters. As a consequence, U.S. victims of Polly Peck's securities fraud could not seek recovery in the United States (Boshkoff, 1994, pp. 935–936).

27. UNCITRAL's Model Law on Cross-Border Insolvency, which seeks to encourage international cooperation, was adopted in 1997. See, UNCITRAL, retrieved from http://www.uncitral.org/uncitral/en/uncitral_texts/insolvency/1997Model.html. Accessed on April 8, 2015.

28. Basel Committee on Banking Supervision (2015).

29. The Basel Committee consists of representatives from central banks and/or supervisory authorities from 27 jurisdictions: Argentina, Australia, Belgium, Brazil, Canada, China, France, Germany, Hong Kong SAR, India, Indonesia, Italy, Japan, Korea (Republic of), Luxembourg, Mexico, the Netherlands, Russia, Saudi Arabia, Singapore, South Africa, Spain, Sweden, Switzerland, Turkey, the United Kingdom, and the United States plus the European Central Bank. See Basel Committee, retrieved from http://www.bis.org/bcbs/. Accessed on April 8, 2015.

30. Basel Committee on Banking Supervision (BCBS) Charter, *op. cit.*, section V (12).

31. It needs to be recognized, however, that compliance with Basel III (and, for that matter, Basel II) is not uniform, as "internationally active" is not a well-defined term. The incorporation of Basel II and Basel III in national rules typically covers different sets of banks differently. Moreover, Basel II and Basel III do not consist of uniform sets of rules, but include options, typically for banks with different business models and at different levels of technical sophistication.

32. Caliskan and Cochran (2003, pp. 1–3).

33. "The European Union addressed the issue of CRS well before ICAO. The Council of the European Communities issued, on 24 July 1989, Council Regulation (EEC) No. 2299/89 on a code of conduct for computerized reservation systems. The regulation applies with the force of law to computerized reservation systems for air transport products, when offered for use and/or used in the territory of the Community, and their essence is to provide equal access and non-discrimination. A revised version of the Regulation is contained in Regulation (ERC) No. 323/1999 that entered into force on 15 March 1999" (Milde, 2008, p. 115). See Council Regulation (EEC) No. 2299/89. Retrieved from http://eur-lex.europa.eu/legal-content/EN/TXT/?uri = CELEX:31989R2299. Accessed on April 8, 2015.

34. This absence of a multilateral solution is due in part to the strategic importance of national airlines in many countries, and to their double nature as both commercial service providers and public utilities (Abeyratne, 2005–2006, p. 50).

35. Regarding CRS regulation for example, the ICAO issued a Code of Conduct on the Regulation and Operation of Computer Reservation Systems (CRS) and developed a model CRS clause to be used in bilateral and multilateral agreements. See ICAO. Retrieved from http://www.icao.int/sustainability/pages/eap_ep_crs. aspx. Accessed on April 8, 2015 ("the ICAO Council completed its review of the Code and adopted a revised version on June 25, 1996, with model clauses to encourage its use. As of September 1, 1998, twenty-nine ICAO Member States either followed the ICAO Code or had CRS regulations which are consistent or compatible with it").

36. Consolidated accounts are an aggregation of financial statements of individual companies constituting a group. These companies keep a single set of accounts. In a consolidation, the lines from the statements of the individual companies are put together, making adjustments for double-counting, etc., and then amending them to the extent that local principles are not in accordance with the international rules. Part of the appeal of International Financial Reporting Standards (IFRS) is that, when MNEs can use IFRS in the books of their foreign affiliates, there are no adjustments necessary during consolidation.

37. The Board has 14 members with accounting or finance background.

38. The U.S. Financial Accounting Standards Board has seven members with expertise in accounting, finance and business. It is controlled by the Financial Accounting Foundation and advised by the Financial Accounting Standards Advisory Council with 34 members who are broadly representative of preparers, auditors and users of financial information. Members of the U.S. Financial Accounting Standards Board and the Financial Accounting Standards Advisory Council are nominated by the Board of Trustees made up of 16 members representing constituent organizations having interest in financial reporting; see FASB (2015) and FAF (2015).

39. IFRS Foundation (2015a). It should be noted, however, that not all countries adopt all the standards, and not all public companies in these countries have to use these standards. On the other hand, this is not uncommon, even within countries; for example, the U.S. Generally Accepted Accounting Principles are not applied uniformly across the United States. Both sets of standards allow for choices in some cases.

40. There were 940 non-U.S. companies registered and reporting to the U.S. Securities and Exchange Commission (SEC) as of December 31, 2014; see SEC. Retrieved from http://www.sec.gov/divisions/corpfin/internatl/companies.shtml. Accessed on April 8, 2015.

41. *The Economist* (May 9, 2012). Though the IFRSs are largely based on the U.S. standards, the SEC does not allow U.S. companies to use only the international standards. The sector's regulatory segmentation coincides with high access barriers to the profession in many countries.

42. The members of the Association account for 97% of the world's insurance premiums. See the Association's website. Retrieved from http://www.iaisweb.org. Accessed on April 8, 2015.

43. As far as trade in food products is concerned, the Codex Alimentarius seeks "to ensure safe, good food for everyone, everywhere" through international food standards, guidelines and codes of practice; See http://www.codexalimentarius.org/codex-home/en/. Accessed on April 8, 2015.

44. For example, a French court failed to prohibit Delaware-based Yahoo! from selling Nazi memorabilia to French consumers online. A U.S. District Court in California issued a declaratory judgment that ruled that the French order could not be enforced in the United States (Stewart & Matthews, 2002, pp. 1116−1118).

45. In particular, U.S. authorities have disagreed with the European Union's approach that enables consumers to sue in their country of habitual residence (Stewart & Matthews, 2002, pp. 1119−1120).

46. On July 1, 2014, the French bank BNP Paribas (BNPP) pleaded guilty to processing billions of dollars of transactions through the U.S. financial system on

behalf of sanctioned entities. BNP hence acknowledged that it processed disguised transactions for Cuban, Iranian, and Sudanese entities in violation of the International Emergency Economic Powers Act and the Trading with the Enemy Act (Zagaris, 2014).

47. In 2007, for example, Cuban officials were denied a room in a Norwegian hotel of the United States-based Hilton hotel chain. Hilton did not want to take the chance of violating the Trading with the Enemy Act. On the other hand, the Norwegian hotel faced a legal complaint in Norway for discriminating on the basis of citizenship. Similarly, in 1997, a Canadian subsidiary of Wal-Mart stopped selling Cuban pajamas when faced with potential sanctions under the U.S. Trading with the Enemy Act. Canadian authorities, however, ordered the product back on its shelves in the name of the country's Foreign Extraterritorial Measures Act, a national law barring enforcement of non-Canadian trade laws incompatible with Canada's trade interests (Rathbone et al., 2013, pp. 1072, 1120–1122).

48. Of course, this is an extremely sensitive issue, as also reflected in the leeway provided under GATT Art. XXI and GATS Art. XIV*bis*.

49. The rules apply to domestic or foreign airline-affiliated computer reservation systems "used by travel agencies in the U.S." (Leaming, 1993, p. 495).

50. UNCITRAL (2015).

51. See, 11 U.S.C. § 1501. See also United States Courts (2015).

52. See IFRS Foundation (2015b).

53. See http://iaisweb.org/index.cfm?event = getPage&nodeId = 25181. Accessed on April 8, 2015.

54. ILO (2015). Note, however, that ILO conventions commit only the countries that have actually ratified them, but they cannot be enforced.

55. Komori and Wellens (2013). Partly this is the case because the Committee's agenda deals primarily with longstanding problems that have become apparent in the Committee's more developed members or that have arisen in the context of the recent financial crisis (which involved primarily developed countries).

56. In some of these instances, rule-making may take place through a "club approach", as developed by Eden and Hampson for the cooperation of states to capture benefits of cooperation, whereby clubs "should be viewed as dynamic institutions whose membership may well change over time". See Eden and Hampson (1997, p. 380).

57. OECD (2011). As of early 2015, all 34 OECD member countries and 12 non-OECD members had adhered to the guidelines.

58. See, for example, ILO (1977) and UNCTAD (1980).

59. See the Guiding Principles on Business and Human Rights (2011).

60. To the extent that these frameworks are beginning to be formulated in the context of bilateral or regional trade agreements, it may well be that a few dominant players effectively preempt any future multilateral initiatives.

61. See, for example, the response of the G20 to the question of tax avoidance by MNEs, G20 (2014, p. 2).

62. In terms of the absolute value of their assets abroad.

63. UNCTAD (2014, p. 32). In 2013, 57 percent of employment of the top 100 was located abroad.

64. Basically all non-OECD countries.

65. In reaction to a series of scandals, the United States adopted the Foreign Corrupt Practices Act in 1977. As this Act was seen to put U.S. firms at a disadvantage vis-à-vis firms headquartered in other countries when engaging in business abroad, the country's government sought to multilateralize its approach to illicit payments. Accordingly, it succeeded in launching negotiations in the United Nations on an international agreement on illicit payments. However, when the Draft International Agreement on Illicit Payments (Retrieved from unctad.org/Sections/dite_tobedeleted/iia/docs/compendium/en/9%20volume%201.pdf. Accessed on April 8, 2015) was put before the General Assembly in 1979, that body took no action since neither the developing countries, nor other developed countries were supportive of such an instrument. However, the issue was later addressed in the OECD and led to the adoption of the "Convention on Combating Bribery of Foreign Public Officials in International Business Transactions," which entered into force on February 15, 1999 (Retrieved from http://www.oecd.org/daf/anti-bribery/ConvCombatBribery_ENG.pdf. Accessed on April 8, 2015). The issue returned to the United Nations, where the United Nations Convention against Corruption was eventually adopted by the General Assembly on October 31, 2003; it entered into force on December 14, 2005 (Retrieved from http://www.unodc.org/documents/treaties/UNCAC/Publications/Convention/08-50026_E.pdf. Accessed on April 8, 2015).

66. One difference might be that, when the trade regime was created, there was broad agreement on the principles governing trade, an agreement that is still largely absent regarding the micro-regulatory issues discussed here. At the same time, though, the need to close the governance gap is recognized from time to time, for example, when governments took action on corruption and tax avoidance.

67. There is of course the challenge that many countries – but by far not all – have limited capacity to participate in such rule-making processes. And there are of course other challenges. For example, who would decide on who is entitled to represent legitimate (social, environmental, commercial, prudential, etc.) interests? Would these interests first be balanced in a national context or could they be pursued immediately at the international level? How could the more economically powerful states/unions/business associations/NGOs be prevented from setting the agenda? What would be the appropriate forum?

68. There are some indications that a more systematic approach is already being adopted, especially in the social and environmental areas. Social and environmental issues have moved far in terms of a systematic process, partly because of support from strong constituencies (labor unions and environmental groups), partly because of their inherently global nature and partly because the need for a systematic process was recognized.

69. Although the focus of this chapter has been on business issues, such an exercise could also include related matters, such as environmental and social issues, as these are closely linked to, if not an inextricable part of, the economic globalization process.

70. It needs to be recognized that the negotiation of global micro-rules would place a great burden on developing countries, many of which are still seeking to implement the agreements negotiated in the context of macro-liberalization. But the alternative – to leave the determination of such rules to others – carries the risk

that the interests of the developing countries (or, more precisely, of their firms) would be ignored; this, in turn, would eventually raise legitimacy concerns.

71. Final Act of the Uruguay Round of Multilateral Trade Negotiations (April 1994), "Decision on Professional Services," para. 2. Retrieved from http://www.wto.org/english/docs_e/legal_e/51-dsprf_e.htm (Accessed on January 12, 2015). The job description of one of the 18 new posts that were created at that time referred to expertise in accounting — a far cry from what most people think the WTO is all about, but perhaps indicative of what that organization may increasingly be about in the years to come.

72. WTO (1999), para. 3. It should be noted, however, that the WTO domestic regulation negotiations do not seek to define the micro-regulatory framework for the globalizing world economy but rather aim at curbing protectionist and anticompetitive behavior, by establishing rules to ensure that regulations do not constitute unnecessary barriers to trade in services. In other words, the rules sought by the WTO are not prescriptive for the content of regulations nor do they seek to harmonize regulations or set standards, leaving that to regulators/governments. (See Lim and De Meester, op. cit.)

73. The Telecommunication Reference Paper was never formally adopted. But many of the WTO's new members, as well as those that negotiated it initially, incorporated it into their commitments. See, for example, WTO (2013).

74. See http://unctad.org/en/Pages/DIAE/ISAR/ISAR-Corporate-Transparency-Accounting.aspx. Accessed on December 17, 2014. For a review of the work of this Working Group, see Ruffing (2015).

75. See, for example, the situation concerning commercial drones where innovation appears to be far ahead of even national rules governing their utilization.

76. Reference was made earlier to the Codex Alimentarius. By way of example, the Codex Alimentarius Commission had, as of March 2015, 186 members and 229 observers, including a number of business organizations, consumer groups, and other NGOs; furthermore, the Codex meetings are public. See http://www.codexalimentarius.org/members-observers/en/. Accessed on April 3, 2015.

77. An example of a tacit alliance between a number of governments and NGOs was the effort on access to medicines that led to the adoption, during the 2001 Doha WTO ministerial meeting, of a resolution concerning the interpretation of the TRIPS Agreement.

78. In some ways, such a process is reminiscent of the approach taken to advance European integration; see Haas (1964).

ACKNOWLEDGMENT

The author thanks Mira Wilkins and two anonymous peer reviewers for their very helpful feedback, as well as Rudolf Adlung, Maria Cattaui, Andrew Cornford, Persa Economou, Michael Finger, Torbjorn Fredriksson, Masataka Fujita, Vishwas Govitrikar, John Kline, Aik Hoe Lim, Padma Mallampally, Herbert Oberhaensli, Pedro Roffe, Lorraine

Ruffing, Peter Walton, and Lou Wells for very helpful comments on earlier versions of this chapter, and Matthieu Wharmby, Valantina Amalraj, and Vetan Kapoor for their research assistance. All errors are of course those of the author's.

REFERENCES

Abeyratne, R. (2005–2006). Competition in air transport: The need for a shift in focus. *Transportation Law Journal, 33*, 29–110.

Altman, J. (2010–2011). A test case in international bankruptcy protocols: The Lehman brothers insolvency. *San Diego International Law Journal, 12*, 463–496.

Basel Committee on Banking Supervision. (2015). About the Basel committee. Retrieved from http://www.bis.org/bcbs/about.htm. Accessed on April 8, 2015.

Boshkoff, D. (1994). Some gloomy thoughts concerning cross-border insolvencies. *Washington University Law Quarterly, 72*, 931–942.

Braithwaite, J., & Drahos, P. (2000). *Global business regulation.* Cambridge: Cambridge University Press.

Caliskan, A., & Cochran III, J. (2003). *Mercatus center's regulatory program: Public interest comment on computer reservation systems* (pp. 1–3). Washington, DC: George Mason University. March.

Dunning, J. H. (1996). The geographical sources of the competitiveness of firms: Some results of a new survey. *Transnational Corporations, 5*, 1–30.

Eden, L. (1996). The emerging North American investment regime. *Transnational Corporations, 5*, 62.

Eden, L., & Hampson, F. O. (1997). Clubs are trump: The formation of international regimes in the absence of a hegemon. In J. R. Hollingsworth & R. Boyer (Eds.), *Contemporary capitalism: The embeddedness of institutions* (p. 380). Cambridge: Cambridge University Press.

FAF. (2015). FAF trustees and committees. Retrieved from http://www.accountingfoundation.org/jsp/Foundation/Page/FAFLandingPage&cid = 1176164681018. Accessed on April 8, 2015.

FASB. (2015). Board members. Retrieved from http://www.fasb.org/jsp/FASB/Page/SectionPage&cid = 1218220131802. Accessed on April 8, 2015.

FIPRA. (2010). Standard setting in a changing global landscape. Report to the European round table of industrialists, October. Retrieved from http://www.ert.eu/sites/default/files/Standard%20setting%20in%20a%20changing%20global%20landscape%20Final%20Report_0.pdf. Accessed on April 8, 2015.

G20. (2014). Communiqué, meeting of G20 finance ministers and central bank governors (2014). p. 2, para. 8. Cairns, September 20–21 para. 8.

Guiding principles on business and human rights: Implementing the United Nations. (2011). *Protect, respect and remedy framework.* Geneva: United Nations Human Rights Office of the High Commissioner.

Haas, E. B. (1964). *Beyond the nation-state: Functionalism and international organization.* Stanford, CA: Stanford University Press.

IFRS Foundation. (2015a). AnalysisAQ: In the reference list, two references of "IFRS Foundation (2015)" have been changed as "IFRS Foundation (2015a)" and "IFRS

Foundation (2015b)" and the text citations are also updated accordingly. Please confirm. of the IFRS jurisdictional profiles. Retrieved from http://www.ifrs.org/Use-around-the-world/Pages/Analysis-of-the-IFRS-jurisdictional-profiles.aspx. Accessed on April 8, 2015.

IFRS Foundation. (2015b). About us. Retrieved from http://www.ifrs.org/About-us/Pages/Monitoring-Board.aspx. Accessed on April 8, 2015.

ILO. (2015). Mission and objectives. Retrieved from http://www.ilo.org/global/about-the-ilo/lang-en/index.htm. Accessed on April 8, 2015.

International Labour Organization. (1977). Tripartite declaration of principles concerning multinational enterprises and social policy. Adopted by the Governing Body of the ILO on November 16, 1977. Retrieved from http://www.ilo.org/public/english/employment/multi/download/english.pdf. Accessed on April 8, 2015.

Johnson, P. (2013). Enforcing online arbitration agreements for cross-border consumer small claims in china and the United States. *Hastings International and Comparative Law Review, 36*, 577–602.

Kearney, A. T. (2012). Business implications of standard setting: Document prepared for the European Round table of industrialist, April.

Kell, G., & Ruggie, G. (1999). Global markets and social legitimacy: The case of the "Global Compact". *Transnational Corporations, 8*, December, 101–120.

Komori, T., & Wellens, K. (2013). *Public interest rules of international law: Towards effective implementation.* Farnham: Ashgate Publishing.

Lasswell, H. D. (1936). *Politics: Who gets what, when, how.* New York, NY: Peter Smith.

Leaming, M. P. (1993). Enlightened regulation of computerized reservations systems requires a conscious balance between consumer protection and profitable airline marketing. *University of Denver Transportation Law Journal, 21*, 469–518.

Lim, A. H., & De Meester, B. (Eds.). (2014). *WTO Domestic regulation and services trade: Putting principles into practice.* Geneva: World Trade Organization.

Lund, S., Daruvala, T., Dobbs, R., Häerle, P., Kwek, J. H., & Ricardo, F. (2013). *Financial globalization: Retreat or reset?* New York, NY: McKinsey Global Institute.

Milde, M. (2008). *International air law and ICAO.* The Hague: Eleven International Publishing.

OECD. (2011). *International investment and multinational enterprises.* Paris: OECD. Retrieved from http://www.oecd.org/daf/inv/investment-policy/oecddeclarationoninternationalinvestmentandmultinationalenterprises.htm. Accessed on April 8, 2015.

OECD. (2014). *Challenges of international co-operation in competition law enforcement* (pp. 24–27). Paris: OECD. Retrieved from www.oecd.org/daf/competition/challenges-international-coop-competition-2014.htm

Organisation for Economic Co-operation and Development. (2015). Implementing the latest international standards for compiling foreign direct investment statistics: FDI statistics by the ultimate investing country. Retrieved from http://www.oecd.org/daf/inv/FDI-statistics-by-ultimate-investing-country.pdf

Ostry, S. (1992). The domestic domain: The new international policy arena. *Transnational Corporations, 1*(February), 7–26.

Rathbone, M., Jeydel, P., & Lentz, A. (2013). Sanctions, sanctions everywhere: Forging a path through complex transnational laws. *Georgetown Journal of International Law, 44*, 1055–1126.

Ruffing, L. (2015). Transparency and disclosure: Lifting the veil from corporate reporting. In K. Hamdani & L. Ruffing (Eds.), *United Nations centre on transnational corporations: Corporate conduct and the public interest.* London: Routledge.

Sauvant, K. P. (2015). The negotiations of the United Nations code of conduct on transnational corporations: Experience and lessons learned. *Journal of World Investment and Trade, 16*, 11−87.

Squire Sanders. (2012). Spotlight on global merger control. Retrieved from http://www.squiresanders.com/files/Publication/24845123-1e98-4f89-892a.-f842dca3f85f/Presentation/Publication Attachment/b34e1ca8-8488-4475-96b9-f99c9945e123/spotlight-on-global-merger-control.pdf

Stewart, K., & Matthews, J. (2002). Online arbitration of cross-border, business to consumer disputes. *University of Miami Law Review, 56*, 1111−1146.

The Economist. (2012). Accounting standards: Eternal convergence, May 9.

UNCITRAL. (2015). Model law on cross border insolvency, status. Retrieved from http://www.uncitral.org/uncitral/en/uncitral_texts/insolvency/1997Model_status.html. Accessed on April 8, 2015.

UNCTAD. (1980). The set of multilaterally agreed equitable principles and rules for the control of restrictive business practices (adopted through the United Nations' General Assembly Resolution 35/63 on December 5).

UNCTAD. (1993). World investment report 1993: Transnational corporations and integrated international production. Geneva: United Nations.

UNCTAD. (1995). World investment report 1995: Transnational corporations and competitiveness. Geneva: United Nations.

UNCTAD. (1999). *World investment report 1999: Foreign direct investment and the challenge of development.* Geneva: United Nations.

UNCTAD. (2000). *World investment report 2000: Cross-border mergers and acquisitions and development.* Geneva: UNCTAD.

UNCTAD. (2002). *World investment report 2002: Transnational corporations and export competitiveness.* Geneva: United Nations.

UNCTAD. (2005). *World investment report 2005: Transnational corporations and the internationalization of R&D.* Geneva: UNCTAD.

UNCTAD. (2007). *World investment report 2007: Transnational corporations, extractive industries and development.* Geneva: UNCTAD.

UNCTAD. (2012). *World investment report 2012: Towards a new generation of investment policies.* Geneva: UNCTAD.

UNCTAD. (2013). *World investment report 2013: Global value chains. Investment and trade for development.* Geneva: United Nations.

UNCTAD. (2014). *World investment report 2014. Investing in the SDGs: An action plan.* United Nations, Geneva.

UNCTAD. (2015). *World investment report 2015: Reforming international investment governance.* Geneva: United Nations.

UNCTAD-ICTSD. (2005). *Resource book on TRIPS and development.* Cambridge: Cambridge University Press.

United Nations. (1973). *Multinational corporations in world development.* New York, NY: United Nations.

United States Courts. (2015). Chapter 15: Ancillary and other cross-border cases. Retrieved from http://www.uscourts.gov/FederalCourts/Bankruptcy/BankruptcyBasics/Chapter15. aspx. Accessed on April 8, 2015.

United States Government Accountability Office. (2011). Bankruptcies: Complex financial institutions and international coordination pose challenges. In *Report to congressional committees* (pp. 53−56). Washington, DC: U.S. Government Accountability Office, July.

Wilkins, M. (1970). *The emergence of multinational enterprise: American business abroad from the colonial era to* (p. 1914). Cambridge, MA: Harvard University Press.

World Trade Organization. (1998). Disciplines on domestic regulation in the accountancy sector, adopted by the Council for Trade in Services on December 14 (1998), document S/L/64.

World Trade Organization. (1999). Decision on domestic regulation, adopted by the Council for Trade in Services on 26 April, document S/L/70 of April 28, 1999.

World Trade Organization. (2007). *World trade report 20* (p. 07). Geneva: WTO.

World Trade Organization. (2013). Report of the working party on the accession of Yemen to the World Trade Organization. Schedule of specific commitments on services list of Article II Exemptions. Addendum, WT/ACC/YEMEN/42/Add.2 of October 4.

Zagaris, B. (2014). BNP Paribas pleads guilty and will pay $8.9 billion for economic sanctions violations. *International Enforcement Law Reporter, 30*(October), 381–384.

ABOUT THE AUTHORS

Björn Ambos is Chaired Professor of Strategic Management and managing director at the Institute of Management, University of St. Gallen. He previously held positions at the University of Edinburgh, the University of Hamburg and WU Vienna, as well as several visiting teaching positions in Europe and Asia. He also gained industry experience as a product manager for a German tour-operator in Vietnam, Italy, Paris and New York and consulted or participated in corporate trainings for major multinational firms. Professor Ambos' research interests revolve around strategy, organization and innovation in the multinational firm. He currently is a senior editor of the *Journal of Business* and Senior Word Consulting Editor of *Global Strategy Journal*. His research has been published in journals such as *Strategic Management Journal, Journal of World Business, Organization Science, and Research Policy*.

Tina C. Ambos is Professor of International Management and the Director of the Institute of Management at the University of Geneva. Before joining the University of Geneva she was a Full Professor at the University of Sussex, UK, where she also served as the Director of Research and Knowledge Exchange for the Business and Management Department. Earlier she held the Chair of the Department of International Management at Johannes Kepler University Linz (JKU), Austria as well as positions at Vienna University of Economics and Business (WU Vienna), the University of Edinburgh and London Business School. She received a Venia Docendi (Habilitation), a PhD WU Vienna. Tina's research and teaching interests include knowledge management, innovation and strategic management. She is Associate Editor for Long Range Planning and serves on the Editorial Boards of several academic journals.

Ulf Andersson is Professor of Business Studies at Mälardalen University, Sweden and Adjunct Professor at BI Norwegian Business School. He has been a Professor of International Business at Uppsala University, where he also earned his doctoral degree and Professor of Strategy and International Management at Copenhagen Business School. His research focuses on subsidiary development, knowledge governance and transfer, network theory,

441

strategy and management of the MNE. He has published more than 60 journal articles, books and book sections on these topics and his work is published in *Strategic Management Journal, Journal of International Business Studies, Organization Studies, Journal of World Business, Global Strategy Journal, International Business Review, Journal of International Marketing, Management International Review* and other leading journals.

Tomomine Aoki is Manager at Corporate Planning Department, Kowa Company Ltd., Japan. He received his MBA from Keio Business School, Japan, in March 2007, and his Bachelor of Arts in Environmental Information from Keio University in March 1995.

Kazuhiro Asakawa is Mitsubishi Chaired Professor of Management at Graduate School of Business Administration, Keio University, Japan, where he teaches international management and global innovation. Kaz received his PhD and MSc from INSEAD, France, his MBA from Harvard Business School, and his BA summa cum laude in Political Economy from Waseda University, Japan. His research interest lies in the areas of global innovation and global R&D management of multinational corporations, cross-border knowledge sourcing and leveraging, subsidiary evolution, and autonomy-control dynamics. He is best known for his work on global R&D management of Japanese MNCs. He was elected to the AIB Fellows in 2015 by the Academy of International Business (AIB). Kaz has served as an Associate Editor of *Global Strategy Journal* and a Senior Editor of *Asia Pacific Journal of Management*. He currently serves as the President of the Japan Academy of Multinational Enterprises (AMNE).

Suma Athreye is Professor in International Strategy at Brunel Business School and is a member of the Strategy, Entrepreneurship and International Business Group. She is also a Research Associate at UNU-MERIT (Maastricht), Centre for Innovation and Management Research (Birkbeck College, London) and the Enterprise Research Centre (University of Warwick, UK). Suma's main research interests lie in the fields of International Economics and the Economics of Innovation and she has won several research grants for work in these areas. She has published over 50 papers on these subjects and serves on the Editorial Board of Research Policy, *Journal of International Business Studies* and *Industrial and Corporate Change*. She has consulted to policy organisations such as the World Intellectual Property Organisation and the UK Intellectual Property Office and was Rapporteur of the European Research Area (2008) report Opening to the world: International cooperation in Science and Technology.

Georgios Batsakis is Lecturer in International Business at Brunel Business School and a member of the Strategy, Entrepreneurship and International Business Group. He has previously held academic and/or research positions at the University of Kent, the University of Greenwich, ALBA Graduate Business School and Athens University of Economics and Business. His research interests lie in the fields of internationalisation strategy of MNEs and technology management of MNEs' R&D affiliate units. His research work has been published in the *International Marketing Review, Journal of Business Research, and International Journal of Innovation Management* among others.

Gabriel R. G. Benito (PhD, Norwegian School of Economics) is Professor of Strategy at BI Norwegian Business School. He is a Consulting Editor of *Journal of International Business Studies* and member of the Editorial Boards of *Academy of Management Perspectives, Global Strategy Journal, International Business Review, Management International Review, Management and Organization Review, and Multinational Business Review*. His research agenda currently focuses on corporate governance, strategy, and organization in multinational enterprises. His research has appeared in many books and journals, including *Journal of International Business Studies, Journal of Management Studies, Journal of Economic Geography, Applied Economics, Managerial and Decision Economics, Management International Review, Journal of Business Research, and International Business Review*.

Julian Birkinshaw is Professor of Strategy and Entrepreneurship and Director of the Deloitte Institute at the London Business School. He is a Fellow of the British Academy, a Fellow of the Advanced Institute of Management Research (UK), and a Fellow of the Academy of International Business. His research focuses on issues of strategy, innovation and organisation in large multinational corporations, and his work has been published in such journals as *Strategic Management Journal, Academy of Management Journal, Organization Science, Journal of International Business Studies and Harvard Business Review*. He is the author of 12 books, including Becoming a Better Boss (2013), Reinventing Management (2010), Giant Steps in Management (2007), Inventuring: Why Big Companies Must Think Small (2003), and Entrepreneurship in the Global Firm (2001).

Jean Boddewyn is Emeritus Professor of International Business in the Zicklin School of Business of Baruch College, City University of New York, where he taught from 1973 to 2006 after teaching at New York University (1964–1973) and the University of Portland, OR (1957–1964). He holds a

PhD in Business Administration from the University of Washington. His research interests center on reciprocity as a mode of market entry, international business political behavior, public affairs, the regulation and self-regulation of advertising around the world, and MNE theory. He was recipient of a Fulbright Award (1951–1952) and received the 2002 Academy of Management's (AOM) Distinguished Service Award for serving as Founding Editor of *International Studies of Management & Organization* (1971–2006), his pioneering research on comparative management, foreign divestment and international business-government relations, and his leadership roles as an early Chair (1975) of the AOM's International Management Division and as President (1992–1994) of the Academy of International Business. He is a Fellow of the Academy of International Business, the Academy of Management and the International Academy of Management, and he served as Dean of the AIB Fellows (2005–2008). He was very ably aided in his writing and editing by Paul James Leung, his Research Assistant.

Wendy Chapple is Associate Professor in Industrial Economics at Nottingham University Business School where she is Deputy Director of the International Centre for Corporate Responsibility (ICCSR). Dr. Chapple's research background is in environmental and industrial economics and she has published in economics, management and mainstream CSR journals. Since her PhD in environmental productivity and eco-efficiency measurement, she has expanded her research portfolio to include comparative analysis of CSR in the international context with studies focusing on Asian and OECD countries. Within this research Dr. Chapple understands the influence of institutions and national business systems in understanding both the nature and form of CSR within countries and between countries. Dr. Chapple also researches corporate social performance across countries, performance measurement, socially responsible investment and corporate governance and CSR. Dr. Chapple won the Aspen Institute's Faculty Pioneer Award (Rising Star) in 2008.

Àngels Dasí is Associate Professor of International Business Strategy at the University of Valencia (Spain) where she received her PhD in strategic management. Her current research interests include knowledge management in multinational corporations, headquarters-subsidiaries relationships, and cross-cultural management in multinationals. Her work has been published in several books, the *Journal of World Business* and *International Business Review*, among others.

Benoit Decreton is a PhD student at the Vienna University of Economics and Business. He is a CEMS alumnus and received an MSc in International Marketing and Management from Copenhagen Business School in Denmark and a BSc in Business Administration from IESEG School of Management in France. His research interests concern the micro-foundations of global strategy and the organization and strategy of multinational corporations.

Frank Elter holds a doctorate in strategy and organisation from BI Norwegian Business School. He has held several positions in strategy and organisational change in Telenor since he joined the company in 1995. He is currently Vice President in Telenor Research where he heads Telenor's research strategy and is part of the research management team. He is an active researcher with special interest in strategy, organisation, and international business. Based on his research-based knowledge he regularly advises executives in Telenor.

Jörg Freiling is Full Professor and Head of Chair in Small Business and Entrepreneurship at University of Bremen, Germany. His research focuses governance issues of transnational companies, internationalization processes of small businesses particularly in the service sector, international new ventures, business model innovations and the role of entrepreneurship and dynamic capabilities in organizations. The academic work rests on organization and management theory and aims at understanding the nature and development of firms in globalized business settings. Among others, his articles are published in journals like *Organization Studies, International Small Business Journal, Service Industries Journal* or *International Journal of Technology Intelligence and Planning.* He is editor of the *Journal of Competence-Based Strategic Management* and member of editorial (advisory) boards of international journals.

Jens Gammelgaard is Professor with specific responsibilities within the field of headquarters-subsidiary relationship at the Copenhagen Business School. He is further acting as Head of Department at the Department of International Economics and Management. He is further doing research in the fields of strategic alliances, and M&A, and within the brewery sector. His work has appeared journals like *British Journal of Management, International Business Review, Journal of World Business, and Journal of International Management.* He has further co-edited a book on the Global Brewery Industry.

Stefan Gold is Assistant Professor in Sustainability Management, Systems and Reporting at the International Centre for Corporate Social Responsibility (ICCSR) of Nottingham University Business School, UK. He received his doctoral degree from the Faculty of Business and Economics of the University of Kassel, Germany in 2011. His research interests comprise supply chain and operations management, strategic management, and sustainability management.

Paul N. Gooderham is Professor of International Management and Head of the Department of Strategy & Management at NHH: Norwegian School of Economics, Bergen. Among his books are a co-authored text book, 'International Management: Theory and Practice' (Edward Elgar) published in 2013. His research interests are concentrated on international and comparative management. Since 1994 he has been a member of Cranet the largest comparative HRM research network in the world. He has published numerous articles in journals such as *Journal of Management, Journal of Management Studies, Journal of International Business Studies, Strategic Management Journal, Human Relations, Management International Review, European Journal of Industrial Relations, and Administrative Science Quarterly.*

Gabriela Gutierrez Huerter O is Teaching Fellow in Management at King's College London, UK. At present she is finishing her PhD from the International Centre for Corporate Social Responsibility (ICCSR) at the University of Nottingham, UK. Her research interests center on the cross-national transfer of CSR practices within MNCs and the determinants of subsidiary adaptation in the context of international acquisitions. Additionally, she has a keen interest in comparative CSR particularly in the study of the influence of national institutions on CSR practices.

Perttu Kähäri has 20 years of managerial experience in multinational companies in service businesses. He has held roles at corporate headquarters, regional headquarters and country subsidiary management. He defended his doctoral thesis Why do regional headquarters live and die? in 2014, and his work has been nominated for various international and national awards. While currently pursuing a new business venture, Kähäri remains affiliated with Aalto University School of Business. His current research focuses on MNC organizational design, headquarters and their dynamic nature, and international entrepreneurship.

Mitchell P. Koza is Distinguished Professor of Global Strategy at Rutgers Business School, Newark and New Brunswick. He served as Vice Dean of RBS and as Dean of the Rutgers Business School – Camden, and

Chaired several reaccreditation committees for the AACSB. He was elected to the Quality of Markets Committee of the Philadelphia Stock Exchange and presented business reports for National Public Radio. Koza is Founding Co-Chair of the SMS Global Strategy Interest Group, and served as member of the Board of Directors of the European Group for Organizational Studies (EGOS). Prior to joining Rutgers, Koza spent 18 years as an expatriate. Most recently, he was Professor of International Strategy and Director General (CEO) of INSEAD-Cedep, in Fontainebleau, France. He spent 4 years at Cranfield School of Management where he held the Chair in International Strategy, and a previous 11 years at INSEAD as a faculty member. Prior to moving to Europe, he held appointments at UCLA, Yale, and Chicago. Koza's award winning research explores issues of producing cooperation in international firms, has been published in major academic and practitioner outlets, and has been translated into eight languages.

Rajesh Kumar is Professor of International Management at Menlo College, California. Originally from India, Dr. Kumar has lived and worked in the United States, United Kingdom, France, Finland, Netherlands and Denmark. Dr. Kumar's expertise lies in International Management and within this domain his work has focused on the management of alliances, international negotiations, and managing in emerging markets with a particular focus on India. Dr. Kumar has a PhD degree in International Business from New York University, an MBA from Rutgers University, a MA degree in Economics from the Delhi School of Economics, and a BA in Economics from Stephen's College, University of Delhi in India. Dr. Kumar has published extensively and continues to maintain an active research agenda. His work has appeared in prominent journals such as the *Journal of Management, Organization Science, California Management Review, and the Journal of Management Studies* among others.

Sven Kunisch is Researcher and Lecturer with the University of St. Gallen (Switzerland) where he also serves as the executive director of the master's program in Business Management. Previously, he was a visiting research fellow at Harvard University. His research focuses on various corporate and international strategy topics, such as the corporate headquarters, headquarter-subsidiary relations, corporate programs, strategic change, and CEO successions. His work has been published or accepted for publication in leading academic and practitioner-oriented outlets, such as the *Academy of Management Annals, International Journal of Management Reviews, Harvard Business Review, Long Range Planning, MIT Sloan Management*

Review, McKinsey Quarterly. He is a co-editor of the book 'Managing the Demographic Change Successfully'. Sven received a PhD in Business Administration (summa cum laude) from the University of St. Gallen. Before starting his academic career, he had gained professional experience in the consulting and automotive industries.

Randi Lunnan (PhD, Norwegian School of Economics) is Department Chair and Professor at the Department of Strategy, BI Norwegian Business School. Her research interests include strategic alliances as well as the structuring of multinational enterprises. She is on the editorial board of *Global Strategy Journal.* Her research has appeared in many books and journals, including *Strategic Management Journal, Journal of Management, Journal of Management Studies, Journal of World Business, Journal of International Management, Scandinavian Journal of Management, Asia Pacific Journal of Management,* and *Academy of Management Executive.*

Jeremy Moon is Velux Professor of Corporate Sustainability at the Copenhagen Business School. He was previously founding Director of the International Centre for Corporate Social Responsibility, University of Nottingham. He is co-author of Corporations and Citizenship (Cambridge University Press, 2008) and author of the Very Short Introduction to Corporate Social Responsibility (Oxford University Press, 2014). Recent publications include: L. Vigneau, M. Humphreys and J. Moon (2015) 'How do firms comply with international sustainability standards'. *Journal Business Ethics*; J. S. Knudsen, J. Moon and R. Slager (2015) 'Government policies for corporate social responsibility in Europe'. *Policy and Politics*; C. H. Kim and J. Moon (2015) 'Dynamics of corporate social responsibility in Asia: Knowledge and norms'. *Asian Business & Management.*

Phillip C. Nell holds a European Master of Business Sciences (EMBSc) degree and a Diplom-Kaufmann from University of Bamberg. He received his doctorate from WU Wien (Vienna University of Economics and Business) and joined Copenhagen Business School subsequently. Before joining academia, Prof. Nell gained considerable industry experience as a consultant with Roland Berger Strategy Consultants and conducted projects in Germany, the United States, and in France in several industries such as construction, white goods, glass products, non-profit, and hospitals.

His research interests are centered on the organization of the multinational corporation, the management of subsidiaries, and the role headquarters play in large and complex organizations. His research has been accepted for publication in *Strategic Management Journal, Journal of International Management, Journal of World Business, Management International Review, International Business Review, and Research Policy.*

Kiyohiro Oki is Assistant Professor of faculty of economics at The University of Tokyo. He graduated the University of Tokyo, and took master's and doctor's degree at same university. He is interested in the capability building of foreign subsidiaries, international configuration of activities in multinational corporations, and human resource management of expatriates.

Torben Pedersen is Professor at the Bocconi University in Milan, Italy. His main research interest lies in the interface between strategy and international management, and he has published over 100 articles and books concerning the managerial and strategic aspects of globalization. His research has appeared in such prominent journals as *Academy of Management Journal, Strategic Management Journal, Journal of Management, Journal of International Business Studies, Journal of Management Studies* and *Organization Science.* In addition, he has written more than 25 teaching cases published at the Ivey Case Clearing House or in teaching-oriented books. He is co-editor of the *Global Strategy Journal* and of *Advances in International Management* besides serving on numerous editorial boards. He was AIB Vice-President (2008–2010) and Program Chair in 2009 for the Academy of International Business Conference in San Diego, and he also served as Vice Chairman of the European International Business Academy from 2007 to 2010.

Rebecca Piekkari is Professor of International Business at Aalto University, School of Business (formerly known as Helsinki School of Economics). Much of her research focuses on the challenges associated with managing foreign subsidiary operations that are embedded in diverse local environments. She has contributed to the discussion on organizational design and architecture of multinational corporations. Moreover, she has a special interest in the changing role and mobility of divisional and regional headquarters. Together with Catherine Welch and colleagues, she has paid attention to the use of qualitative methods, particularly the case study in international business research. Her work has been published in journals such as the *Academy of Management Review, Journal of Management Studies,* and *Journal of International Business Studies* as well as in several handbooks in the area.

Marty Reilly is Lecturer of Strategy and International Business at Dublin City University, Ireland. Marty's main research interests revolve around capability development, subsidiary driven innovation and paradoxes of strategy within MNCs. A focal point of his research to date has been on examining the capacity and scope of subsidiaries to pursue newly conceived explorative trajectories whilst simultaneously remaining aligned with their mandated role. He gained his PhD from Dublin Institute of Technology in 2013 before joining DCU Business School in 2014.

Karl P. Sauvant is Resident Senior Fellow at the Columbia Center on Sustainable Investment (CCSI) – a joint center of Columbia Law School and the Earth Institute at Columbia University. He also serves as Lecturer-in-Law and Senior Research Scholar at Columbia Law School, Guest Professor at Nankai University (China) and Theme Leader of the International Centre for Trade and Sustainable Development/World Economic Forum Task Force on Investment Policy. Until February 2012, Dr. Sauvant was the Founding Executive Director of the Vale Columbia Center on Sustainable International Investment, the predecessor of CCSI, and he *was Director of the UNCTAD's Investment Division until July 2005. While at the United Nations, he created the very valuable annual World Investment Report of which he was the lead author until 2004.* He authored a substantial number of publications on issues related to economic development, foreign direct investment and services (http://www.works.bepress. com/karl_sauvant/). He was elected Fellow of the Academy of International Business and Honorary Fellow of the European International Business Academy. His 1975 PhD is from the University of Pennsylvania's Wharton School.

Fabian Schmutz is Managing Director of a medium-sized, family-owned engineering company, located in the south-west of Germany. He is employed as a part-time lecturer at the University of Applied Sciences Konstanz with main focus on supply management, process management and quality management. Moreover, he is a doctoral candidate at the University of Bremen (Chair in Small Business and Entrepreneurship). In his research, he focuses on coordination of knowledge transfer in service networks of multinational, medium-sized capital goods producer.

Adrian Schulte Steinberg is Consultant with The Boston Consulting Group (BCG) in Munich (Germany). During an educational leave, he received his PhD from the University of St. Gallen (Switzerland), and was a visiting researcher at the University of Oxford. His research focuses on the relation between headquarters and subsidiaries of multinational corporations, with particular attention to the role of organizational practices, corporate controls, and the role of individual managers. At BCG, Adrian works with globally leading steel, mining and natural resource companies on projects related to the design of corporate center structures, definition of operating models, design and optimization of large capital expenditure project organizations as well as asset optimization programs.

Pamela Sharkey Scott is Professor of International Management at National University of Ireland, Maynooth. Pamela's main research interests are on strategy development and capability building within MNCs. Her research has been published in leading international journals, including *Journal of International Business Studies, Organization Studies, Technovation and Long Range Planning*.

Stephen Tallman is E. Claiborne Robins Distinguished Professor of Business at the University of Richmond's Robins School of Business. He graduated from the US Military Academy and holds a PhD in international business and strategic management from UCLA. He has been on the faculty of the University of Hawaii (1988–1990) and the University of Utah (1990–2005) and taught at the Cranfield School of Management, INSEAD, Warwick Business School, HKUST, and Thunderbird. His research interests include global strategic management, geographic clusters, organizational knowledge and learning, communities of practice, alliance strategies, and network organizations. He chaired the International Management Division of the Academy of Management (1998–1999) and co-founded and chaired the Global Strategy Interest Group of the Strategic Management Society (2001–2005). He is the founding and current Co-Editor of *Global Strategy Journal* and has been Associate Editor for *Strategic Management Journal*, and Consulting Editor for *Journal of International Business Studies*. He is a Fellow of both the Academy of International Business and the Strategic Management Society.

Sverre Tomassen (PhD, BI Norwegian Business School) is Associate Professor in international strategy at BI Norwegian Business School. His current research interests include international management, and strategies and structures of multinational enterprises. He serves on the editorial board of Management and Organization Review. His research has appeared in several books and journals, including *Journal of Management Studies, Journal of International Management, Scandinavian Journal of Management, and International Business Review*.

Svein Ulset was Professor of international strategy at NHH: Norwegian School of Economics, Bergen. For more than 20 years, one of his major

research interests centered on the area of mobile telephony network operators. During this period, a number of these operators began to operate
beyond their domestic markets. Hence, he developed a strong interest for
the field of international strategy. His research was published in journals
such as *Journal of Economic Behavior & Organization, International Journal
of the Economics of Business and Telecommunications Policy*. He passed
away on November 30, 2015, age 63.